W9-CIN-040

THE
EUROPEAN UNION
AND THE
MEMBER STATES

THE

EUROPEAN UNION

AND THE

MEMBER STATES

SECOND EDITION

EDITED BY
ELEANOR E. ZEFF
ELLEN B. PIRRO

LYNNE
RIENNER
PUBLISHERS

BOULDER
LONDON

Published in the United States of America in 2006 by
Lynne Rienner Publishers, Inc.
1800 30th Street, Boulder, Colorado 80301
www.rienner.com

and in the United Kingdom by
Lynne Rienner Publishers, Inc.
3 Henrietta Street, Covent Garden, London WC2E 8LU

© 2006 by Lynne Rienner Publishers, Inc. All rights reserved

Library of Congress Cataloging-in-Publication Data
The European Union and the member states/ edited by
Eleanor E. Zeff and Ellen B. Pirro.—2nd ed.
    Includes bibliographical references and index.
    ISBN-13: 978-1-58826-454-1 (hardcover: alk. paper)
    ISBN-10: 1-58826-454-8 (hardcover: alk. paper)
    ISBN-13: 978-1-58826-479-4 (pbk.: alk. paper)
    ISBN-10: 1-58826-479-3 (pbk.: alk. paper)
    1. Political planning—European Union countries. 2. European Union. I. Zeff, Eleanor E.,
1943– II. Pirro, Ellen B. III. Title.
JN32.E932 2006
341.242'2—dc22

                                                                              2006010342

British Cataloguing in Publication Data
A Cataloguing in Publication record for this book
is available from the British Library.

Printed and bound in the United States of America

♾   The paper used in this publication meets the requirements
    of the American National Standard for Permanence of
    Paper for Printed Library Materials Z39.48-1992.

5   4   3   2   1

*We dedicate this book to two of our former professors,
whose inspiration motivated not only our academic
careers, but also this European Union project:*

*William G. Andrews
Hans Heilbronner*

And to the memory of Leslie Eliason

Contents

Part 3 The 1980s

Part 4 The 1990s

Part 5 The 2004 Round

Part 6 Conclusion

Preface

WHEN THE FIRST EDITION of this book was conceived, after a discussion at the 1997 European Union Studies Association (EUSA) conference, researchers had just begun to look closely at policymaking in the European Union from the point of view of the nation-state. Earlier EU studies had concentrated on examining relations between EU institutions and the member states from the top down. The 2001 edition of *The European Union and the Member States* contributed to the initial wave of Europeanization studies that explored the effects of the EU on the individual member state in terms of the changes in policymaking occurring (or not occurring) at the state level. While the first edition did not assess the theoretical aspects of Europeanization, it did bring together, for one of the first times in one volume, discussions about the styles of policymaking and the rates of EU policy adaptation in each of the then 15 member states.

With the addition of 10 new EU member states in 2004, as well as the development of Europeanization and policymaking studies, we realized that it was time for a reexamination of the interactions of the EU with its member states. The result, this new edition, combines chapters written by both familiar and new authors. The book is also an example of transatlantic cooperation, as the authors come from several European countries and the United States.

Each chapter of the book now follows a similar format. The authors consider: How and in what areas does EU policy influence, and how is it influenced by, the member states? What mechanisms do the member states use to implement EU policies? What is each state's compliance record? Most of the chapters also include a brief introductory section, discussing how the country entered the EU and has interacted with it, as well as a concluding section dealing with future prospects. Our general introduction sets the book's agenda for the reader, and our concluding chapter offers some discussion of future trends and further Europeanization. One of our main purposes throughout is to provide more insight on the continuing development of the European Union, facilitating comparisons among the member states and demonstrating the important role of the states in the movement toward a united Europe. We also hope that the book will provoke interesting theoretical discussions in future studies.

* * *

We would like to thank some special people who have helped immensely with the preparation of this second edition. First, we would like to thank Clayton Cleveland for his work on the bibliography and the index, and Dale Zieske for his invaluable work in putting the final version of the manuscript together. There are many other people who also helped with the book, including our editor and publisher, Lynne Rienner, who provided valuable advice and insight; Lynne's assistant, Lisa Tulchin, who was always helpful; and various students, especially Amiyna Farouque, who read early versions of the chapters and made helpful comments. We would also like to thank our families, who have supported us throughout the two years of production. To all of these people, we say "Thank you."

—Eleanor E. Zeff and Ellen B. Pirro

THE
EUROPEAN UNION
AND THE
MEMBER STATES

1

Introduction

Eleanor E. Zeff and Ellen B. Pirro

how widely has this been seen
→ as a soul

THE EUROPEAN UNION (EU) progresses at an uneven rate. On one hand, the great expansion worked wonderfully in May 2004 when 10 new members joined the group (see Table 1.1). On the other hand, the dream of a "United States of Europe" hit a roadblock in the summer of 2005 when France and the Netherlands voted down the proposed constitution for the European Union. Of course, it doesn't end there. To successfully grow and develop, the expanded European Union faces abundant challenges—both major and minor. Three areas illustrate the complexity and significance of the decisions that must be made in the near future.

First, there are a number of membership issues. The full integration of the 10 new members still needs to be accomplished. In addition, Bulgaria and Romania are on the threshold of membership, and Turkey and Croatia are at the beginning of the accession process with much to be accomplished before they join. Equally important will be confronting a European Union with member states vastly different in economic and social development and trying to integrate each one at the same level. Already there has been talk of a "two-tier membership."

A second set of challenges concerns security and immigration issues. In 2005, several EU members experienced racially based incidents targeting immigrants and naturalized citizens, and illustrating the dilemmas of EU immigration and nationality. France faced several days of rioting and car burnings over conditions in its immigrant communities. It has also become steadily apparent that the borders of the EU are

Table 1.1   The Ever Wider Union

Original Member States (1958)	First Enlargement (1973)	Second Enlargement (1981)	Third Enlargement (1986)	Fourth Enlargement (1995)	Fifth Enlargement (2004)
Belgium	Britain	Greece	Spain	Austria	Czech Republic
France	Denmark		Portugal	Finland	Cyprus
Germany	Ireland			Sweden	Hungary
Italy					Estonia
Luxembourg					Latvia
Netherlands					Lithuania
					Malta
					Poland
					Slovakia
					Slovenia

not secure, and the resulting issues include criminality, human trafficking, smuggling, and even terrorism. The EU has only just begun to consider foreign policy for the whole EU. The establishment of common security and asylum policies for EU citizens are major components of this emerging area.

The economic arena also continues to pose challenges to the EU. The rigidity of the economic and welfare systems in many of the member states, and continuing high levels of unemployment, are only two of many areas needing continuing attention. While there is widespread agreement on protection of the environment, case after case continues to emerge pitting environmental concerns against economic development. On the international level, continuing EU objections to removal of agricultural subsidies have thwarted the World Trade Organization (WTO) free-trade agreement at the Doha Round and no comprehensive compromise has developed either within the EU or between the EU and the WTO nations, despite recent budget compromises. Within the EU, ongoing disregard of stringent deficit requirements by some of the main powers threatens the continued financial stability of the whole organization. Despite these obstacles, the European Union's development into a new kind of supranational organization continues to be a path-breaking adventure of ongoing interest to researchers and politicians alike.

As was suggested in the first edition of this book, the "we feeling"[1] described by Karl W. Deutsch remains a major objective, but has proven to be more elusive than previously expected. The goal of Europeanization is now considered widely in the literature, but has proven harder to achieve in fact. The addition of 10 new members in 2004 has added an even greater variety of people and ideas to the mix. This second edition of *The European Union and the Member States* assesses the new, enlarged Europe of 25 countries (soon to include 27 member states), in order to shed some light on the direction of its policies and the progress it has made toward Europeanization.[2]

Despite the new additions and the accompanying problems of adding members with backgrounds of widely varying economic and political systems, great progress has occurred. The successful introduction of the euro and the meshing of the single monetary system has been a notable achievement. The European court system has also added a layer of European policymaking that one could hardly have imagined even 20 years ago, and there are now steps being taken toward a joint foreign policy including both defense and peacekeeping elements.

The country chapters that follow analyze and discuss many of these important concerns. The reader will find all kinds of data and information about the contemporary EU pulled together and organized for comprehension. The book also illuminates what is actually happening in the EU through concrete illustrations and case histories. Each of the country chapters discusses some specific events and their influence, on either the EU or the member states, to help the reader get beyond dry theories to a real sense of how the EU operates throughout contemporary Europe.

■ Approaches to Studying Policy in the EU and the Member States

There are always questions about the best approach to studying the significant issues of the European Union. While the individual country chapters that follow incorporate several of the various theoretical approaches developed to understand the policy process in the EU, no single theoretical approach is imposed on the data gathered here. Instead the reader finds a basic framework and abundant information within that framework. The scholar can utilize this database with different theoretical models as desired.

This edition takes a "bottom-up" approach to studying the institutions and policies of the European Union in the early twenty-first century. A number of contemporary scholars have cited the importance of bottom-up research. Yet much recently published work still primarily utilizes the "top-down" approach, focusing on EU institutions and policymaking.[3] However, as do other authors,[4] we maintain that member states matter, and that not only do the EU and its institutions affect them, but also the member states play an important role in shaping the EU itself—what it stands for, what it does, and how it operates. Often, the policy feedback loop is completed as the member states seek to influence EU policy in areas critical to their national futures. Both national institutions and the member states are important actors in making and implementing the policies designed by the EU institutions and the directives imposed on the states.[5] It is noteworthy that this process is often problematic, both at the EU level and within the member states. There are instances of failed and outdated strategies; slow, imperfect, or even failed implementation; and unforeseen results.

In the succeeding chapters, each of the 25 member states receives coverage. Each chapter focuses on a set of questions concerning the relationship between a particular member state and the EU institutions. While we ask the same questions for each country, the authors discuss the policy or policies that they feel best represent the problems faced or solved by each member state or that best reflect the views and policy trends in that state.

The Questions Asked

1. What is the background of each member state's interaction with the EU? How did the member state arrive at its current situation? What historical "givens" shape the ongoing interaction? What are the legacies of the secession process? What were the key events along the way?

2. How and in what ways and areas does the EU influence the member states? It is apparent that the impact on policy and national institutional development is profound for each and every member state. But, for each member state, some policies and directives have been easier to adapt and/or incorporate into national laws while implementation of other directives poses considerable difficulties. To consider this dilemma, most country authors chose to discuss only a few or, in a couple of cases, only one area of great significance for that member state.

3. How and in what areas do the member states influence EU policies and implementation? In what policy areas are the member states making their views best known? For the newest members, the acceding 10, this is a developing area and there are less data available. For the other member states, it is very instructive to observe how and where states have sought to apply their influence, and where they have had difficulty in exerting it.

4. How does the member state implement and comply with EU policies and directives? It is noteworthy that for the pre-enlargement members, the process is key. Most chapters detail what each member nation has developed in terms of agencies and institutions that activate EU policies—and revolve around the hows and whys of implementation. For the 10 accession states, the substance is more crucial. The process is still quite new and not always certain. Many of the new members are still developing their infrastructures to deal with EU matters. Their concern is how to operate within these new circumstances. So, for each country additional questions apply. What institutions perform the compliance? Is it easy or difficult? Does it require a long or short time span? How has compliance impacted the political life of the nation? Have compliance issues become political issues?

5. Where does each member state fit with respect to the proposed constitution and its apparent failure, following the "No" votes by France and the Netherlands in summer 2005?

6. What are the trends and prospects for each member state in terms of EU membership? Does it have goals and objectives vis-à-vis the EU for the next several years? How likely is the road ahead to be either bumpy or smooth?

Format of the Book

Following this introductory chapter, which establishes the framework for the book, John McCormick, in Chapter 2, provides an excellent overview of the European Union and its institutions with regard to policymaking and implementation. The subsequent chapters are grouped according to the time that each country joined the Union. The first grouping consists of the six original members—Germany, France, Luxembourg, Belgium, the Netherlands, and Italy—that signed the Treaty of Rome, which went into effect in 1958. The next members to join were the United Kingdom, Ireland, and Denmark in 1973, and then Greece in 1981, followed by Spain and Portugal in 1986, after a long accession wait. Finally, in a 10-year period, the EU witnessed 13 new countries enter the EU: first Austria, Sweden, and Finland in 1995 and then, in May 2004, Poland, Hungary, the Czech Republic, Slovenia, Slovakia, Lithuania, Latvia, Estonia, Malta, and Cyprus. While there are many options about how to group the countries, we feel that the chronological order in which the states joined the Union provides a valuable historical view.

The country chapters are, as McCormick states in Chapter 2, "an attempt to pin down the nature of the EU policy process, and of the policy relationship between the EU institutions and the member states of the European Union." The authors each build on past research while contributing new data in their attempts to shed more light on the ongoing policy process in the EU. McCormick argues in his chapter, and many of the authors demonstrate, that the EU policy process is very diverse and "changeable" because each member state has its own agenda and its own special relationship with the EU. The same policy is, therefore, often implemented differently in each member state, depending on a number of variables such as different political ideologies and the competence of the member state's infrastructure. Finding theories to help understand this policy process has resulted in even more questions.[6] Each chapter illustrates, through case studies, how the individual member states respond to various EU policies and also clarifies, with concrete examples, some of the dilemmas resulting from the relationship between the EU institutions and the member states and from the implementation of policy at the nation-state level. The chapters demonstrate the diversity of the member states and the difficulty of the process of Europeanization under these challenging conditions. They are a good indicator of the several problems facing the EU as it attempts further integration.

Policy Issues Considered

The country chapters of this book reflect the challenges cited earlier. All of the chapters on the newest member states consider the membership challenge. They range from the Czech Republic's reluctant incorporation of EU directives to Poland's enthusiastic participation in EU activities. As Sharon Fisher in Chapter 17 notes, the Czech Republic was not very well prepared to take on the pressures of EU accession, and it remains a somewhat reluctant member, even today. There are some noteworthy considerations of how accession activities have had a lasting impact on some states, such as Malta's and Cyprus's need to create a whole group of new governmental bureaucracies in order to facilitate compliance with EU requirements. In some cases, such as the Baltic States, accession caused actual hardship and a rethinking of national identity and citizenship issues.

Security and foreign policy have become other important considerations for many EU members, with immigration and border issues becoming major concerns. Chapter 13 praises Sweden's efforts to help immigrants in Sweden and also discusses the country's open approach to the Baltic countries and to their imports. Slovakia and Slovenia are working on immigration and asylum policies, as detailed in Chapter 18.

Neutrality has essentially disappeared for many of Europe's formerly neutral countries: Sweden, Austria, and Ireland. Not all EU members agree on issues of foreign policy, an ongoing problem in creating consensus across the EU. Greece, Spain, Portugal, and the UK all sent troops to join the US forces in Iraq, whereas other EU members opposed that war. Both Germany and France maintain high-level foreign policies, which add to their sovereignty and prestige, and they strongly protested EU involvement in the Iraq war. Some EU member states are reaching out to Third World countries, but these efforts need to be synchronized with EU objectives. Although a new member, Poland took a leading role in foreign and security policy by spearheading EU efforts in the recent (2004) Ukrainian revolution. Many of the chapters discuss foreign policy and the slow process of attaining greater European consensus.

Economic concerns continue to dominate the EU discourse. Many of the newer members, as discussed in both the Slovenia and Slovakia and Malta and Cyprus chapters (18 and 19), are working hard to meet the requirements of the euro, and countries such as Italy have already taken tough measures to comply with European Monetary Policies, as Giuliani and Piattoni remark in Chapter 5. Of particular interest to many of the authors is the delicate balance between supporting environmental concerns while allowing economic development to proceed. Chapter 16, for example, uses environmental issues to demonstrate and explain the relationship of Hungary with the EU, as well as to clarify the complex nature of this relationship. Chapter 4 uses the reduction of greenhouse gases as a case study to illustrate how, and how well, France implements certain kinds of policies and complies with EU directives. The French chapter also discusses in some detail how its government and bureaucracy implement EU policies. Chapter 14 illustrates that even a very pro-EU member such as Finland has to establish new interministerial coordinating structures to implement EU policies, and that even Finland has had difficulty implementing EU regulations such as the Habitats Directive and protecting its flying squirrels.

Other chapters, such as Chapter 3 on Germany, give an excellent overview of how the EU operates in the economic sphere. Germany and France are of particular interest because of their recent disregard of EU deficit regulations. In contrast, Chapter 6 details how the smaller Benelux countries have managed to adhere to the EU's stringent requirements. Ireland's economic miracle in the 1990s and its attempts to cope with the changed circumstances of the new millennium (Chapter 8) form an interesting case in economic development within the EU context.

Rather than discuss a particular policy area, some of the chapters focus on how well, or badly, the member states have implemented EU policy. Both the UK and the Czech Republic have often dragged their feet when it comes to implementing EU directives. Chapter 7 describes Britain as "an awkward partner," but also has a lot of theoretical discussion. It is one of the chapters that uses theories to better understand the EU. The chapter explains the "bottom-up" and "top-down" dimensions of member state–EU relations.[7] In practice there is of course considerable overlap between these two dimensions. For example, states have a strong incentive to "upload" as many of their preferences as possible to the EU level so as to minimize the costs of "downloading."[8] Notwithstanding this overlapping and intermeshing, however, the distinction between bottom-up and top-down is a useful organizational device, to which Nugent and Mather refer when describing British policy inclinations. Sweden and Poland are other reluctant but functioning members, again demonstrating that a member state does not have to be enthusiastic to be a good member. Poland has earned the reputation of being a "difficult" or "obstinate" member, and Einhorn and Erfer describe Denmark as a "pragmatic skeptic" and the EU as a "work in progress."

The Italian and French chapters also focus on implementation and compliance procedures, and present good case studies demonstrating the ongoing nature of policy adaptation, as well as the changes that EU membership has made to national institutions in the longer-term members. Other members, such as Finland and Greece, have been more enthusiastic members, as have been some of the new members of 2004. Strong "Yes" votes in the 2005 referendums, or rapid approvals in the new members' legislatures, in Hungary and other central European countries demonstrate this enthusiasm, despite often difficult adaptations during the accession process. Nikolaos Zahariadis (Chapter 10) cites Greece as being both "enthusiastic and reluctant," a fitting description for many of the member states depending on the issue, domestic concerns, and the time lines involved.

There are several sources of funding in the EU that provide a good illustration of EU operations within member states. Many of them, including Ireland and parts of the UK (Scotland), Portugal, Greece, and Spain, have received substantial funds from the EU. The chapters on Spain, Portugal, Greece, and Ireland, in particular, acknowledge the economic benefits and political changes that EU membership has influenced. These members have made great progress, at least partly attributable to EU Cohesion and Structural Funds. Now, however, they are worried because the 10 new members are all, except Slovenia,[9] going to be net benefactors of EU funding, whereas, unless new funding becomes available, the earlier members will lose substantial funds. Each chapter highlights some of these stories, as well as some successes and losses involving the EU's interaction with its member states.

Now it is time to turn to the chapters themselves.

■ Notes

1. Deutsch, *Political Community and the North Atlantic Area.*
2. Europeanization is also understood as an "incremental process reorienting the direction and shape of politics to the degree that EU political and economic dynamics become part of the organizational logic of national politics and policy-making" (Ladrech, "Europeanization of Domestic Politics and Institutions," p. 84). For a review of the relevant literature on Europeanization see Pirro and Zeff, "Europeanization, European Integration and Globalization," pp. 209–217.
3. Bulmer and Lequesne, *The Member States of the European Union*, discuss Europeanization and policy in the EU; Börzel, "Pace-Setting, Foot-Dragging, and Fence-Sitting," pp. 193–214, discusses three categories of member-state responses to policy implementation; the chapter on Finland (14) uses this source to discuss how member states implement EU directives. Gerda Faulkner's recent work (as discussed in the chapter on Austria) differentiates three different *worlds of compliance* within the EU-15: a *world of law observance*, a *world of domestic politics*, and a *world of neglect*. Cowles, Caporaso, and Risse, in their book *Transforming Europe*, discuss "goodness of fit" when talking about policy implementation in the EU. The investigation is structured around what are often referred to as the "bottom-up" and "top-down" dimensions of member state–EU relations. The former refers to the inputs that member states make into EU processes in terms of their policy preferences and their ways of acting. The latter refers to the things member states have to do, and the adaptations they have to make, to be compliant with EU requirements and decisional outcomes. In practice there is, of course, considerable overlap and intermeshing between these two dimensions. For example, states have a strong incentive to "upload" as many of their preferences as possible to the EU level so as to minimize the costs of "downloading." Notwithstanding this overlapping and intermeshing, however, the distinction between bottom-up and top-down is a useful organizational device. Schmidt also discusses policy implementation in several of her articles/books, such as *The Futures of European Capitalism*. These are just a few of the many ways authors have used to explain and categorize Europeanization and policy adaptation in the EU.
4. Wessels, Maurer, and Mittag, *Fifteen into One;* Bulmer and Lequesne, *The Member States of the European Union.*
5. Directives are a form of European Union legislation for the member states. The results to be achieved are binding, but each member state may choose its own methods of implementation. Individual member states' records of compliance on directives are used to judge how well a state is adapting to EU membership or how much/well it is Europeanizing.

6. Wallace and Wallace, *Policy-Making in the EU*; Wessels, Mauer, and Mittag, *Fifteen into One*; Peterson and Bomberg, *Decision Making in the European Union*; Schmidt, *The Futures of European Capitalism,* for just some examples of this.

7. Nugent and Mather, Chapter 7 of this volume; and see also Börzel, "Pace-Setting, Foot-Dragging, and Fence-Sitting." The "bottom-up" approach refers to the inputs, from the member states, into EU policy and to their ways of acting. The "top-down" approach refers to the things that member states have to do, and the adaptations they have to make, in order to comply with the EU's requirements.

8. On this, see, for example, Börzel, "Pace-Setting, Foot-Dragging, and Fence-Sitting."

9. Malta and Cyprus are also doing relatively well economically, and, thus, their status of net beneficiaries could change.

2

Policymaking in the European Union

John McCormick

PUBLIC POLICY IS A complex issue. Even in democracies—where systems of government are institutionalized, stable, and generally predictable—it is not always clear how agendas are developed, who makes policy, why some options are adopted and others ignored, and whether the policies pursued have worked or not. With the European Union, the public policy process moves to a new and unique level of complexity, in which the interests of local, national, regional, European, and international policies meet and interact. Consider the following list of problems:

- The European policy menu is long, constantly changing, and more varied than at the national level.[1]
- Decisions are rarely the result of action on the part of a single actor or institution, and policymaking procedures are lengthy and complex, varying from one institution to another.[2]
- Not only are the policy structures and principles of the EU quite different from those found in conventional state systems, but also the EU presents a moving target. The membership of the EU and the balance of power among EU institutions and member states is constantly changing, as are the functions, powers, rules, and goals of EU institutions and of European integration more generally. Olsen notes the fluidity, ambiguity, and hybrid nature of the EU, and argues that it is always in the process of becoming something else, and may never actually reach a stable equilibrium.[3]

• No one has agreed on just what kind of polity the EU is now or what it will eventually become. It is regularly described as more than an international organization but less than a state, or else simply as *sui generis* (unique). The conventional vocabulary of political science—tied as it is to the state and to interstate systems—seems unable to capture the personality of the EU.[4]

The challenge of understanding the EU is reflected in studies of EU policymaking, which are peppered with such adjectives as *arcane, complex, cumbersome, distinctive, dynamic, fragmented, inefficient, uneven, unique, unpredictable,* and *unstable*. Vincent Wright describes Brussels as a "decisional maze" and an "over-crowded policy arena."[5] Helen Wallace writes of the "intellectual maze" that faces the student of EU policymaking.[6] Stubb, Wallace, and Peterson note that "there is no single catch-all way of capturing the essence of EU policy making, except to say that the central aim is almost always consensus"; they also note the experimental nature of the EU policy system, which has meant that institutions and policymakers have operated in different ways from one policy to another, and even from one issue to another, changing their approaches over time.[7] Jeremy Richardson concludes that the complexity of the EU policy process demands the use of multiple concepts from multiple models.[8]

Understanding the EU policy process might be easier if the EU had a formal constitution: a single, permanent, codified document that could function as a blueprint for understanding the powers and responsibilities of the "government" of the EU. But with the apparent death in 2005 of attempts to adopt a European constitution, at least for now, the EU has had to fall back on a convoluted set of treaties whose details have been regularly amended and whose meaning is constantly fine-tuned as a result of debates among the governments of the member states, struggles for influence among the major EU institutions, new laws adopted by the EU, decisions reached by the European Court of Justice, and the political and economic pressures of the international system. The treaties provide us with a series of policy principles, and with a list of the policy areas in which the EU is active, but they tell us little about the balance of policy responsibility between EU institutions and the member states (which anyway varies from one policy area to another).

To further complicate matters, while policy studies at the national or subnational level have the advantage of being able to focus on the formal structures of government and the pressures to which those structures are subject, in the case of the EU there is no European government as such. Hix argues that it is a political system but not a state because it does not have a monopoly on the legitimate use of coercion.[9] Seeking another channel of explanation, the term *governance* is often used in connection with the system of authority in the EU.[10] This describes an arrangement in which laws and policies are made and implemented without the existence of a formally acknowledged set of governing institutions, but instead as a result of interactions involving a complex variety of actors. The European institutions are not so much governing bodies as they are administrative bodies, and understanding them means trying to understand the interplay between the institutions themselves, the governments of the member states, interest groups, and many other sources of influence.

Undeterred by the challenges involved, this chapter will attempt to set the scene for the country case studies that follow by reviewing the nature of the European policy process, and assessing the policy relationship between the EU and the member states. It begins with a review of the EU policy cycle, outlining the major forces at work in the different stages of that cycle. It then reviews the principal features of the EU policymaking process, and tries to pin down the division of policy responsibilities between the EU and the member states. It concludes that there is no consensus on how much power the EU and the member states have relative to each other, nor on the most effective division of policy tasks.

■ The European Union Policy Cycle

Public policy consists of the deliberate actions or inactions of government. When officials are elected into power, or appointed into the bureaucracy, they (hopefully) have a sense of the problems faced by a society, and of what they consider to be the most effective responses to those problems. Many factors drive the opinions and analyses of policymakers, including their ideological bias, their economic and social status, their educational background, their world view, their personal ambitions, and even their different levels of competence and motivation. The actions they pursue—or choose to avoid—constitute their policies. When policies impact large and generalized segments of society, they become public. Ideally, there should be some logic to the manner in which policies are made and implemented, and some consistency to the values and priorities that generate policy. But the policy process is rarely so neatly structured, and most studies of public policy emphasize the opportunistic nature of policy, and the extent to which policymaking and implementation is—in the view of Charles Lindblom—simply a question of muddling through.[11]

A common approach to the study of public policy—designed to impose some order on what is ultimately a relatively disordered system—is to describe it in terms of a cycle. Reduced to its key elements, the EU policy cycle—and the key players in that cycle—runs as follows:

- The European Council sets the broad policy agenda
- The European Commission fills in many of the details of that agenda by developing proposals for new laws and policies
- The European Parliament and the Council of Ministers discuss and amend Commission proposals and make the final decisions on which laws to adopt and which policies to pursue
- The Commission oversees implementation through the member states
- The European Court of Justice interprets and adjudicates

As with all systems of administration, however, nothing is ever so simple, and this summary overlooks the many nuances, details, political realities, inconsistencies, and informalities that often color the manner in which the EU functions. We need, then, to go into more depth on the stages in the process and the key pressures that come to bear.

Problem Recognition and Agenda Setting

All governments are faced with problems that demand resolution. Before a policy choice can be made, there must be political agreement on the definition of a "problem," and a decision must be made to add that problem to the list of policy concerns that are considered part of the remit of government. In a democracy, the development of the policy agenda is normally driven by a combination of the individual preferences and priorities of elected officials and their advisers, the struggles for power among political institutions (mainly the executive and the legislature), and the combined pressures of public opinion and media attention.

To the extent that there is a European agenda,[12] it is formed and driven mainly by the European Council, which outlines broad policy goals and often sparks new policy initiatives. It was the Council, for example, that decided to draft and agree to the Single European Act and the Maastricht, Amsterdam, and Nice Treaties; that has issued major declarations on international crises; that has reached key decisions on EU institutional changes; and that has given new momentum to EU foreign policy. But it must be remembered that the 25 prime ministers, chancellors, and presidents who meet as the Council are ultimately national political leaders, and that they are torn between protecting national interests and pursuing the European interest. The pressures and influences to which they are subject come from many different sources: public opinion, treaty obligations, recommendations from consultative committees, the personal initiatives of individual leaders, tension among member states, the need to harmonize laws, international treaty requirements, discussion papers, specialist reports, and changes in the outside world. There are at least three important differences between agenda setting at the national and at the European level:

• Elected leaders at the national level often add issues to the policy agenda in response to public and media opinion, or—more cynically—in order to win legislative votes or build support for the next national election. At the EU level, however, there is no European "public" in the sense that there is a large body of citizens demanding change at the European level. Furthermore, there is no elected European government that is constantly looking to its standing in the polls or to the outcome of an election. Thus policy is heavily driven by pressures internal to the process of European integration, and by leaders rather than by citizens. This leads to the common—and reasonable—accusation that the EU policy process is elitist.

• The EU agenda is pulled in different directions by the often competing motives and interests of the major institutions. While the Commission and the Court of Justice take a supranational approach to agenda setting, for example, Parliament's choices are often driven by a desire to exert itself and to develop an identity. Meanwhile, the European Council and the Council of Ministers represent the interests of the governments of the member states.

• The complexity and variety of the needs and priorities of the member states make it more difficult to identify pan-European problems and to tease out the common causes of such problems, to build political support for a unified response, or to anticipate the potential effects of policy alternatives. This is particularly true in regard to policy issues on which there is less of a European consensus, such as foreign policy, where the member states bring different values and priorities to bear.

It is also important to appreciate that while we may talk of the "European agenda," it is little more than the accumulation of narrower agendas being pursued by all the actors with an interest in the European policy process. For example, there are the institutional agendas of the Commission, Parliament, and the Council of Ministers, as well as the subinstitutional agendas of directorates-general (DGs) within the Commission. There are the national agendas of individual member states, as well as regional agendas pursued by groups of member states (poorer states will have different needs from richer states, agricultural states will have different needs from industrial states, and so on). Finally, there are cross-national agendas pursued by like-minded groups in multiple states, such as the environmental lobby, farmers, multinational corporations, and workers and labor unions. Each of these in their own way will limit, redirect, or broaden the cumulative policy interests of the European Union.

Policy Formulation

Once a problem or a need has been recognized, a response must be formulated. In the case of the EU, this usually involves publishing discussion papers, drafting work programs or action programs, making public announcements, or developing proposals for new laws and new budgetary allocations. Whichever response is chosen, it might be reasonable to expect that some kind of methodical and rational policy analysis would be conducted in which the causes and dimensions of a problem are studied and all the options and their relative costs and benefits are considered before taking action. However, this rarely happens in practice, because the number of dependent and independent variables involved causes most EU policy to be designed and applied incrementally, intuitively, or in response to emergencies or changes in public opinion.

In national systems of government, the executive, the legislature, or government departments usually formulate policy. In the case of the EU, the major focus of policy formulation is the Commission, which not only has a monopoly on the drafting of new laws and policies, but also has a pivotal position as a broker of interests and a forum for the exchange of policy ideas.[13] The Commission does not function in a policy vacuum, however, and its proposals are routinely amended as a result of lobbying by interest groups or national governments, as a response to internal and external emergencies and crises, and as they are discussed by consultative committees, the Council of Ministers, and the European Parliament. According to the Commission's own calculations, about 30 percent of its proposals come in response to the international obligations of the EU, about 20–25 percent come as a follow-up to resolutions or initiatives from the other European institutions, about 20 percent involve the updating of existing EU laws, and 10–15 percent arise out of obligations under the treaties or secondary legislation.[14]

Legitimization

Policies cannot work in a democracy unless there is a belief by the citizens affected by these policies that they have been developed by officials and institutions with a legitimate claim to being able to make authoritative decisions for society. In political systems founded on the rule of law, there are usually few questions about the authority of government to make and implement policies. However, the reach of the authority of EU institutions has long been a subject of debate, mainly because public enthusiasm for European integration is still so heavily qualified. Eurobarometer polls have found that support peaked in 1990 at 71 percent, but then fell in the wake of the controversy over Maastricht, and in the period 2000–2004 languished at just 48–50 percent.[15] The number of Europeans who think that their country has benefited from EU membership fell from 58 percent in 1990 to 47 percent in 2004. Meanwhile, public opinion in the incoming eastern European states in 2003–2004 was mixed, with just 52 percent of respondents believing that their country would benefit from membership.

Since the member states have signed treaties of membership, and have committed themselves to meeting the terms and requirements of being part of the European Union, the de jure standing of the European Union is rarely questioned. However, given the lingering doubts about the wisdom of integration, question marks continue to hang over the de facto standing of the EU. The French and Dutch rejections of the European Constitutional Treaty in May and June 2005 emphasized the gap between the desires of European leaders and those of the European public. While the existence and the powers of the European Union are both a matter of law, and thus the decisions taken under the rubric of European integration are legitimate, this does not necessarily mean that all Europeans feel instinctively that European integration is a worthy process.

Adoption

Once the European Commission has proposed a new law or policy, it must formally be adopted before it goes into effect. The final say over adoption comes out of a complex interplay involving Parliament, the Committee of Permanent Representatives (COREPER), the Council of Ministers, the Commission, and the member states, with the Court of Justice providing legal interpretation when necessary. Changes introduced by the Single European Act and by the Maastricht, Amsterdam, and Nice Treaties have provided new powers to Parliament, which—in most areas—has now become a "co-legislature" with the Council of Ministers.

COREPER is often left out of discussions about the policymaking process of the EU, yet it is arguably the most important link in the chain. Consisting of groups of specialists from the permanent representations in Brussels of the member states, it vets all proposals from the Commission, and tends to make most of the changes and reach most of the agreements that are finally adopted in the name of the Council of Ministers. Except on the most controversial or complex issues, it is usually left to the ministers to confirm the agreements already made by COREPER.

Implementation

Arguably the most important step in the policy cycle is implementation, the point at which the goals and objectives of government result—or fail to result—in real change for the governed. Unfortunately, implementation has so far proved a relatively weak part of the EU policy process, and several structural problems have made it difficult always to be sure about the extent to which EU laws and policies are actually implemented in the manner in which they were intended by their authors, or really make a difference in the lives of Europeans.

The varied levels of implementation and enforcement of EU law have been a matter of growing concern for EU institutions, within which there has been an expanding debate on how to improve application. The Commission itself blames nonconformity between national and EU law on the existence of two or more legal systems in several member states (notably those with a federal structure), and the difficulties that arise in amending national laws because of the effect they have on provisions in a variety of other areas, such as agriculture, transport, and industry.[16]

In their study of environmental policy, Collins and Earnshaw note a related set of problems.[17] First, the range and complexity of existing national laws can make it difficult to adapt them to the requirements of EU law. Second, concepts contained in many directives may be defined differently in different member states. Third, national and subnational administrative systems vary by member state. For example, Germany is a federation where the national and Länder governments must cooperate on transposition and implementation, while regional governments have more autonomy in Italy, Belgium, and Spain than they do in Britain or France. Fourth, differences in "legislative culture" will mean some member states take longer than others to agree to new national laws. Finally, member states may occasionally decide that it is politically expedient for some reason to drag their feet on implementation.

The implementation of public policies is normally left to bureaucracies; the fundamental job of a bureaucrat, after all, is to ensure that laws and regulations are executed. However, the bureaucracy of the EU—the Commission—is small and has no powers directly to enforce European law, and so must work instead to ensure implementation through the bureaucracies of the member states. The Commission occasionally convenes meetings of national representatives and experts to monitor progress, and also carries out its own investigations using its contacts in national government agencies. Most of the time, however, the Commission must rely on other sources, including the governments of member states (who will occasionally report on other governments that are not being as aggressive as themselves in implementing law); whistle-blowing by interest groups, the media, and private citizens; the European Parliament (which since 1983 has required that the Commission submit annual reports on the failure of member states fully to implement Community legislation); and the European ombudsman (who has the power to conduct inquiries into charges of bad administration against Community institutions, except the Court of Justice and Court of First Instance).

Useful though they may be as a means of drawing attention to problems that the Commission might otherwise have missed, complaints are not an entirely reliable measure, and the system suffers at least four drawbacks. First, it is ad hoc and unstructured. Second, many of the problems drawn to the attention of the Commission are found not to be infringements because there is no relevant legal base.[18] Third, the number of complaints is influenced by the political culture of different member states, and by their varied relationships with the EU. The fact that a large number of complaints are registered in a particular member state may reflect less a problem with implementation than a high level of interest in the effects of EU law. Finally, complaints are difficult to prioritize—they may not necessarily be made about the most serious or the most urgent cases.

Evaluation

The final stage in the policy cycle is to determine whether or not a law or policy has worked. This is difficult unless specific goals were set and unless national bureaucrats can be trusted to report accurately to the Commission on the results of policies. In many cases it is almost impossible to know which actions resulted in which consequences or whether the results are being accurately reported. This is particularly true in the case of the EU, where it is always difficult to distinguish the effects of national and local government actions from those of EU law. Nonetheless, evaluation in the EU is conducted by a combination of the Commission, the Council of Ministers, the European Council, the European Parliament, and reports from member states, interest groups, and individuals.

■ The Character of European Policymaking

The complexity of the European policy process has resulted in little agreement on either its character or on how best to approach an understanding of the key steps and pressures in that process. The following models provide an illustration of the variety of approaches to understanding policymaking in the EU:

• The Community method[19] envisioned by Jean Monnet was the earliest, simplest, and perhaps purest of the different models of European policymaking, in the sense that it was simply directed at replacing national policies with common European policies. Early strides were made in the fields of agriculture, competition, fisheries, and more recently the focus of attention has shifted to foreign and security policy, immigration, and justice and home affairs.

• The coordination method relies on a comparison of national policies with each other, in order to identify those that have worked best.[20] Networks of national experts review, compare, and exchange ideas on policies, with the result that the EU has sometimes moved into new areas of activity. This happened, for example, with environmental policy, where the ideas and approaches of progressive states were copied or adapted by states with less well-developed environmental policies and laws. More recently it has led to the development of processes and strategies designed to achieve policy goals without using new laws (such as the Cardiff Process on product and capital markets, and the Lisbon Strategy on economic, social, and environmental renewal).

• Multilevel governance has emerged since the mid-1990s as a popular model, describing the manner in which power in the EU is shared between autonomous agencies working at the subnational, national, and supranational levels, and how policy is made as a result of the interaction and coordination among these levels.[21] Responsibility is shared at each stage of the decisionmaking process, with an emphasis on partnership and negotiation, rather than hierarchy.[22]

In its earliest years, the process of European integration was driven mainly by the member states. It was bottom-up in the sense that it was an accumulation of the decisions taken by the national governments of the member states: national interests were to the fore, decisionmaking was decentralized, member states were the source of most law and policy, and the European institutions had little independence. The pressures of the postwar economic and political environment cannot be ignored, but integration was ultimately an intergovernmental endeavor.

As integration evolved, however, the balance changed: European interests became more important, decisionmaking became more centralized, more laws and policies were developed by the European institutions, member states became the target as well as the source of law and policy, and European institutions developed greater independence. The European Union became increasingly institutionalized and formalized, and in order to understand the processes and pressures of public policy in western Europe it became increasingly important to study and appreciate policy at both the national and the European levels.

Put another way, policy has been Europeanized. Only studied in any methodical fashion since the mid-1990s, and exploited far more often than it has been explained,[23] Europeanization can be defined as the process by which national policies and government structures have been changed and brought into alignment by European laws and policies. It is both vertical, in the sense that it impacts the way policies are developed, and horizontal, in that it may have "a homogenizing impact" on institutions and practices across a wide range of state activities.[24] It may also have a harmonizing effect by bringing laws and practices into conjunction across different member states. In other words, policy in the member states now develops in response to developments at the European level as well as in response to independent national decisions and judgments. The administrations of the member states have changed in response to the pressures of integration: by becoming responsible for implementing European rules, by changing or abandoning existing policies, structures, and procedures, and by becoming involved in the work of European institutions.[25]

Just how far the impact of Europeanization has spread is difficult to measure; several studies have questioned the extent of the process,[26] while another study concludes that there has been neither wholesale convergence nor continuing divergence of national policy structures, but rather that there has been "domestic adaptation with national colors"—in other words, a mixture of European and national pressures and features.[27] While it is true that there is no longer a clear separation of the European and the national,[28] neither are the two levels fully integrated, nor is there a clear differentiation of power and responsibility between the two levels.

It has also been difficult to ascertain the extent to which the pressures that have led to changes at the national level have been uniquely or demonstrably "European." Clearly we can identify the impact of EU regulations that must be carried out on the ground in the member states, or the impact of EU directives that must be translated into national laws, but there are many other pressures at work in Europe that lead to policy outcomes; these include the pressures of globalization, the pressures of the international trading regime, and the requirements of international law. Isolating and distinguishing the effects of these pressures from the effects of Europeanization is no simple matter.

All policy systems have characteristics that are unique to their political, economic, and social circumstances—the same is true of the EU, where any discussion about the nature of policymaking will typically include most or all of the following concepts.

Games and Competition

Politics everywhere is driven by struggles for power and influence, but such struggles are magnified in the EU by the extent to which member states and EU institutions compete with each other. Peters describes three sets of interconnected "games" being played out in the EU: a national game among member states, which are trying to extract as much as possible from the EU while giving up as little as possible; a game played out among EU institutions, which are trying to win more power relative to each other; and a bureaucratic game in which the directorates-general in the Commission are developing their own organizational cultures and competing for policy space.[29] The institutions and the member states have different definitions of the European interest, and they often sacrifice that interest on the altar of their own more narrow political and economic goals.

Spillover

Lindberg described this as a process by which "a given action, related to a specific goal, creates a situation in which the original goal can be assured only by taking further actions, which in turn create a further condition and a need for more action."[30] In other words, as the European institutions have become active in one area of policy, so they have found that political, economic, and/or social forces have compelled them to become involved in additional areas of policy. This was particularly true of the Single Market program, where efforts to bring down barriers to trade found EU institutions making policy in areas that were not antici-pated by the authors of the Treaty of Rome, such as consumer protection and the environment. Critics of the EU (like critics of the US federal government) charge that it has tried to become involved in too many policy areas; however, it has often had little choice—the creation of new programs has revealed or created new problems, which in turn have led to demands for supporting programs in related policy areas.

Institutional Fragmentation

Power in the United States is shared between multiple different institu-tions, but the links among them are firm and stable, and each represents a relatively clear constituency, whether it is local districts (the House of Representatives), the states (the Senate and state governments), or the federal government (the president), and at the national level there is a relatively clear distinction between executive, legislative, and judicial responsibilities. In the European case, by contrast, legislative power is shared between the Commission, the Council of Ministers, the European Parliament, and national legislatures, and executive power is shared between the Commission and the member states. Kassim argues that "each institution is internally differentiated, and has its own methods, procedures, and culture, exercises varying degrees of power, and com-mands different resources."[31]

Subsidiarity

While this concept is at the core of the character of the EU, its precise meaning and implications are open to debate. An attempt was made in the Maastricht Treaty by insisting that the EU should act only if "the objectives of the proposed action cannot be sufficiently achieved by the Member States and can therefore, by reason of the scale or effects of proposed action, be better achieved by the Community" (Article 5). In other words, let the EU do what it does best, and let the member states do what they do best. While it is not always possible to agree on what kinds of actions are more effectively or efficiently undertaken at one level or the other, negotiations and political pressures over the years have led to an expansion of the body of policy areas that are considered part of the "competence" (authority) of the EU. However, levels of authority vary from one policy area to another, and have typically changed over time, not always as a result of deliberate policy decisions or changes to the treaties.

Intergovernmentalism and Supranationalism

Academic opinion is divided on whether or not the EU is ultimately a supranational organization that functions above the level of the member states and has its own internal logic and motivating energy, or whether it is an intergovernmental entity that is still driven by the decisions of the governments of the member states, pursuing national interests.[32] To complicate matters, the EU has a split personality in the sense that some of its institutions (notably the Council of Ministers) are mainly intergovernmental—because they are the meeting place for the interests of the member states—while others (notably the Commission) are driven more by the supranational concerns of the EU as a whole. This tension pulls the EU in two different directions, undermining attempts to provide it with consistency, and to provide its policies with the same underlying objectives and principles.

Informal Politics

Studies of politics and policy usually concentrate on the formal aspects of administration, and yet much of what is done by government falls into the sphere of the informal, a sphere that Middlemas argues is as critical to an understanding of how decisions are reached as the formal.[33] Just as an understanding of policymaking in the United States cannot be achieved without looking at the role of legislative assistants, presidential advisers, interest groups, and the media, so it is important to appreciate that—in the EU case—the Commission will often liaise with interest groups, experts, representatives of industry, and representatives of national government ministries and local government. Each of the Commission directorates-general has become used to working with external actors—people and organizations—that can provide it with the information most relevant to its work, and that are most likely to be involved in the implementation of EU law. There is nothing in the treaties to say that the process should be so; these informal processes have evolved out of need and circumstances.

Multi-Speed Integration

An ongoing feature of policymaking in the EU has been the extent to which different member states have opted in or out of selected policy areas, or have moved at different speeds to achieve the goals of integration. This is otherwise described as multi-speed integration or variable geometry. So, for example, only 12 member states have so far adopted the euro; Britain and Ireland have not yet signed the open-borders Schengen Agreement; and while several countries (notably Britain and France) have moved ahead relatively vigorously on security issues, others have been less enthusiastic, and several (including Austria, Finland, and Ireland) have worked hard to maintain their neutrality. Alongside these headline-making macro-level examples of disagreement on progress, it must not be forgotten that the member states are also moving at different speeds on the micro-level implementation of European laws. Each year, the Commission routinely has to take countries to task for infringements.

The Democratic Deficit

Most liberal democracies have high levels of public accountability, and public opinion plays a vital role in policymaking; leaders will not always proceed unless they can be sure that public opinion is on their side. The same is not true of the EU, however, where secrecy surrounds much of the work of the Commission and the Council of Ministers, where few policymakers are directly or even indirectly accountable to voters, and where the policy world is replete with examples of leaders proceeding even in the face of hostile or indifferent public opinion; examples include the adoption of the euro in several countries where public opinion was opposed, and EU leaders moving to ratify the draft EU constitution even when it was clear that "No" votes were inevitable. While public opinion has played an increasingly important role in EU policymaking with regard to the growth of lobbying, direct elections to Parliament, the creation of the European ombudsman, and the Commission's efforts to promote transparency, the links between policymakers and citizens are still poorly developed. The result is that policymaking in the EU remains largely an elitist, top-down phenomenon.

Incrementalism

Because of concerns over the loss of national sovereignty, the absence of a consensus about the priorities of European integration, and the need for constant compromise, EU policymaking tends to be slow, cautious, and incremental. The process sometimes slows to the point where the critics of integration complain about Euro-sclerosis, but this is probably unfair. While the Community had many problems in the 1970s, and there have been many teething troubles in the process of integration, breakthroughs have often been made in that process, such as progress on the euro, convergence on foreign policy, and agreement on the need for enlargement. All these initiatives emerged incrementally from a combination of opportunity and need.

■ The Balance of EU Policy Responsibilities

Where does this discussion about principles, variants, and characteristics leave the EU in terms of its policy responsibilities relative to those of the member states? In unitary systems of government such as those in Japan and most European states, the question of the balance of policy powers rarely arises—the national government dominates, while local government tends to play a supporting role in such areas as education, health care, and public safety. In federal systems of government, such as the United States, Germany, Russia, or India, the picture becomes more complicated because powers and responsibilities are divided among national and local units of administration. In the United States, for example, the federal government has primary responsibility for defense and foreign policy, monetary policy, interstate commerce, international trade, and social security. State and local governments for their part have the majority of responsibility for education, highways, and law enforcement, while the three levels of government share responsibility on issues such as welfare, health, and transportation. No level has exclusive powers in most areas; instead, there are overlapping circles of responsibility, with cooperation being greater in some areas than in others.

While the division of powers in the United States has reached a strong state of equilibrium, the division of powers in the EU changes constantly as the process of integration sees responsibilities shifting away from the member states and toward the EU institutions. This makes it difficult always to be sure about the balance of policy responsibilities. So when Richardson concludes that "it is beyond dispute" that as much as 60 percent of "what used to be regarded as purely domestic policy-making" takes place at the EU level,[34] or when Hix suggests that more than 80 percent of rules governing the exchange of goods, services, and capital in the markets of the member states are set by the EU,[35] these are no more than educated guesses. Clues to the relative responsibilities of the EU and the member states can be found in four main places.

The first clue comes from the treaties, revisions to which have given more clarity to the boundaries of the "competence" (responsibility) of the EU; this now extends over economic policy, agriculture, the move-

Table 2.1   Balance of Policy Interests Between the EU and the Member States

European Union	*Shared*	*Member States*
Areas in which the balance lies with the EU:	Areas in which authority is shared:	Areas in which the balance lies with the member states:
Agriculture	Culture	Broadcasting
Competition	Employment	Citizenship
Consumer protection	Energy	Criminal justice
Cross-border banking	Export promotion	Defense policy
Cross-border crime	Foreign relations	Education
Customs	Information networks	Elections
Environment	Overseas aid	Health care
EU transport networks	Regional development	Land use
Fisheries	Small and medium	Local transport
Immigration	enterprises	Policing
Monetary policy (euro zone)	Social issues	Postal services
Trade	Vocational training	Tax policy
Working conditions		

ment of workers, transport, commercial policy, culture, public health, consumer protection, research, the environment, and development cooperation. However, it is unclear from the treaties just how those responsibilities are shared with the governments of the member states. On environmental policy, for example, the relevant sections of the treaties provide more of an outline of the underlying goals and principles of EU policy than an exposition of the division of tasks. As it happens, the EU has been most active in dealing with such issues as air and water quality, waste management, and the control of chemicals, but none of these are specifically mentioned in the treaties.[36]

The second clue comes from the budget of the EU, although care must always be taken over how figures are interpreted, for two main reasons. First, the amount spent may be more reflective of the outcome of political struggles than of real need. Thus the EU famously spends more on agricultural price supports than on any other area of activity, in large part because France was able to win agreement on this at the time of the drafting of the Treaty of Rome, and has since stubbornly refused to make significant concessions. Second, there is no direct link between spending and the amount of time and effort expended by government and policymakers. Environmental management may be a major priority of a government, for example, but most of the costs of, for example, reducing emissions from vehicles and factories will be borne by manufacturers, industry, and the taxpayer. Immigration is a hot-button issue in the EU today, but it does not demand the spending of significant funds, if only because dealing with immigration is as much as anything a bureaucratic issue.

Nonetheless, an analysis of the EU budget shows clearly that agriculture has been a major priority of the process of integration (in 2004, about 45 percent of the EU budget went to the Common Agricultural Policy), while spending on the Structural Funds comes second (31 percent of spending in 2004), reflecting the extent to which the EU has placed a priority on reducing economic disparities. Barely 7 percent went to remaining internal policies, and just 5 percent to external policies. When it comes to spending, at least, the vast majority of the EU's attention appears to be focused on just two issues.

The third indicator of policy priorities comes from a subject analysis of European law: superficially, this shows that the EU has been most active in the kinds of areas listed in the treaties as being priorities of European integration, including the Single Market, agriculture, fisheries, transport, energy, economic and monetary policy, and regional matters. However, a more thorough study reveals that the EU has only been involved in very specific elements of each of these policy areas, and has rarely developed broad-ranging policies. Generally, most laws have so far been prompted by the harmonization of member-state laws arising out of the need to develop the Single Market. In that sense, they have been aimed mainly at removing the physical, fiscal, and technical barriers to free trade in support of the broad goals of integration.

The fourth indicator of policy priorities can be found in the portfolios of European commissioners and in the size and reach of the directorates-general of the Commission. Reflecting Commission priorities, the senior portfolios are those relating to trade policy, economic and monetary affairs, external relations, competition, and agriculture, while the junior portfolios include those dealing with development aid, science and research, consumer protection, and energy. The power of the portfolios—and the reach of the EU over policy—is reflected in the DGs, where some (notably those dealing with external relations, economic and financial affairs, competition, and agriculture) are well established and powerful enough to override the wishes and objections of other DGs during the development of proposals.[37]

The ongoing tensions between supranational and intergovernmental pressures have ensured that no policy areas have yet become the exclusive domain of the EU. Similarly, the contradictory attitudes of member states to the process of integration have meant that different states have retained different levels of authority over different policy areas. Thus all we can say with any certainty is that the process of integration has brought the EU to a point today where responsibilities are shared, but the focus of responsibility for some policy issues lies with the EU, while the focus for others rests mainly with the member states, but to differing degrees.

Generally speaking, the focus of policy responsibility lies with the EU on economic issues, and it is now fair to say that economic policy in the EU is driven or influenced more by the work of the EU institutions than by the initiatives of the governments of the member states. "Economic policy" means more than the Single Market, and consists of a variety of issues that are central to the Single Market, related to the need to ensure free trade among the member states, and related to the need for the member states to work in tandem in their dealings with external trading partners. The combination of the customs union and the Single Market has led to increased EU responsibility for issues such as environmental protection, consumer safety, the development of European transport and energy networks, labor issues, competition, financial services and banking, and telecommunications.

■ Conclusions

This chapter has been an attempt to pin down the nature of the EU policy process, and of the policy relationship between the EU institutions and the member states of the European Union. I have argued that the relative input of the two sides into the policy process is complex, changeable, and often ambiguous, and that the division of policy responsibilities between the EU and the member states remains unclear. While the balance of power seems to lie with the EU in some policy areas and with the member states in others, there are significant differences in the balance of responsibilities on different issues within these areas. Furthermore, there are few—if any—formal rules regarding how these responsibilities should be divided.

It was once argued that there were only three possible outcomes to the process of European integration[38]: a federal Europe, a Europe of states in which the member states play the main role, and a multi-speed Europe in which levels of integration vary from one issue to another, and from one member state to another. There is little agreement to be found anywhere (among politicians, the public, or academics) about which of these three applies to the EU today. However, the chapters that follow will examine the relationship between the EU and each of the member states, and cast more light on the nature of that relationship, and on the balance of power between the two sides.

■ Notes

1. Peters, "Agenda Setting in the European Union," pp. 9–26.
2. Kassim, "The European Administration."
3. Olsen, "European Challenges to the Nation State." See also discussion in Mazey, "European Integration."
4. See discussion in Schmitter, "Some Alternative Futures for the European Polity and Their Implications for European Public Policy."
5. Wright, "The National Co-Ordination of European Policy-Making," pp. 151–152.
6. Wallace, "Politics and Policy in the EU," p. 11.
7. Stubb, Wallace, and Peterson, "The Policy-Making Process."
8. Richardson, "Policy-Making in the EU," p. 23.
9. Hix, *The Political System of the European Union,* pp. 2–5.
10. See Cram, "Integration Theory and the Study of the European Policy Process," pp. 65–66.
11. Lindblom, "The Science of 'Muddling Through'," pp. 79–88.
12. For further discussion, see Peters, "Agenda Setting in the European Union."
13. Mazey and Richardson, "The Commission and the Lobby."
14. Commission of the European Communities, "Interim Report from the Commission to the Stockholm European Council," p. 6.
15. Eurobarometer 54, April 2001; Eurobarometer 61, July 2004.
16. European Commission, *Annual Report on Monitoring the Application of Community Law,* various years.
17. Collins and Earnshaw, "The Implementation and Enforcement of European Community Environmental Legislation," p. 217.
18. European Commission, "Fifteenth Annual Report on Monitoring the Application of Community Law–1997," p. 49.
19. See Lindberg and Scheingold, *Europe's Would-Be Polity.*
20. See Stubb, Wallace, and Peterson, "The Policy-Making Process," and Wallace, *Policy-Making in the European Union.*
21. See Hooghe and Marks, *Multi-Level Governance and European Integration.*
22. Commission of the European Communities, *First Report on Economic and Social Cohesion–1996,* p. 143.
23. Goetz has described the concept as "a cause in search of an effect." See Goetz, "European Integration and National Executives," pp. 211–231.
24. Page, "Europeanization and the Persistence of Administrative Systems."
25. Kassim, "The European Administration."
26. For a brief review, see Page, "Europeanization and the Persistence of Administrative Systems."

27. Cowles, Caporaso, and Risse, *Transforming Europe,* p. 1.

28. Bulmer and Wessels, *The European Council,* p. 10.

29. Peters, "Bureaucratic Politics and the Institutions of the European Community," pp. 106–107.

30. Lindberg, *The Political Dynamics of European Economic Integration,* p. 10.

31. Kassim, "The European Administration."

32. For an exposition on liberal intergovernmentalism, see Moravcsik, *The Choice for Europe.*

33. Middlemas, *Orchestrating Europe.* See also Andersen and Eliassen, "Informal Processes."

34. Richardson, *European Union,* p. 3.

35. Hix, *The Political System of the European Union,* p. 3.

36. For more details, see McCormick, *Environmental Policy in the European Union,* chapter 1.

37. Spence, "Structure, Functions and Procedures in the Commission," p. 97.

38. Andersen and Eliassen, "The EC as a New Political System," p. 7.

PART 1

EARLY UNION MEMBERS

3

Germany: Transforming Its Role

Carl Lankowski

GERMANY IS NOT JUST another EU member state. As the single largest country in economic size and population, how Germany performs economically, the way it is organized politically and bureaucratically, its pattern of state-society relations, and how it defines its aspirations all affect the functioning and the trajectory of EU integration fundamentally. With this as a point of departure, for both practical and theoretical reasons, the September 2005 German national elections constitute a major audit point for the country's relationship with the European Union. Practically, Germany changed course as a consequence of the elections: it has become less "green," more conservative. This change is being registered across the policy spectrum, both in policy formulation as well as in policy implementation. In a theoretical vein, the consequences flowing from the elections point to the complexity of a country's multifaceted connection to Brussels. One way to evaluate this connection—always a work in progress—is to address the question: What difference does a change in national government make in an EU member state? Given Germany's size, its status as a founding EU member, and an understanding by its political class of its role in the integration project, examining Germany's EU connection amounts to a critical case study of the exercise of state power in Europe today.

By the mid-1970s, the West German state achieved respectability at home and abroad: it had become prosperous economically and stable politically—a long way from the Weimar Republic, Germany's first experiment with democracy, which submitted to the solvent of Nazi totalitarian aspirations in 1933. Three general factors stand out in contributing to this happy result: the liberal democratic regime's incubation in Cold War structures, featuring a powerful US presence; a political structure engineered to avoid the pitfalls of Weimar; and economic institutions that were broadly integrative of the social forces populating postwar German society.

For many years the Federal Republic's political economy and its *Westbindung* via the institutions of European integration seemed like perfect complements. Its political economy facilitated social peace, the other peace in Europe. But in the 1990s, the formula was challenged, and halfway through the first decade of the new century, it appears that the two dimensions are distinctly out of synch, if not in contradiction to one another. Indeed, Germany's situation in the EU in the latter phase of the "red-green" government had become dramatic.[1] Efforts to sustain its "social market economy" have created unprecedented conflict with Germany's EU partners. Beginning in 2002, the country reported an excessive deficit under the rules of the EU's Stability and Growth Pact—rules on which German negotiators in particular had insisted. By repeating these deficits in every year since then, the federal government has invited advice and monitoring from Brussels. Rather than reduce the deficit, the government decided to attack the rules, a stratagem that provoked official alarm in a sizable number of EU national capitals, and a showdown orchestrated jointly by the EU Commission and the Council in March 2005, resulting in a substantial loosening of the pact's fiscal criteria and more conflict programmed for the future.

The Economic and Monetary Union (EMU) episode is not an isolated incident. That same weekend in March 2005, German trade unions encouraged members to participate in a huge demonstration against the Commission proposal to open up the internal market in services—a key element of the EU's overall economic strategy agreed at the Lisbon European Council in March 2000. Germany's Weimar experience caused its constitutional convention to keep referenda out of national politics. But, when French trade unionists and those with a left-of-center political preference made the services directive a key plank in the French referendum on the EU Constitutional Treaty, German chancellor Gerhard Schröder (a Social Democrat) appeared alongside French president Jacques Chirac (a Gaullist conservative) to recommend scrapping the initiative because of its "unsocial" features.

The denouement in March 2005 is but a milestone in a period of EU policy defensiveness that became visible over Germany's unification policies of the 1990s and was practically raised to a point of principle by

Chancellor Schröder in the opening phase of the governing coalition of Social Democrats (the SPD) and Greens in 1998. There followed a German campaign to stymie the nearly successful reform of EU company law via the take-over directive, a proviso to stop workers from the new EU member states in search of jobs from doing so in Germany for a "transitional period" of up to seven years, and an initiative to reduce the overall level of transfers through the EU budget from about 1.20 percent to 1.0 percent of the EU gross domestic product (GDP). Moreover, in 2004, the immediate prospect of new, poor, but economically dynamic EU members from the east led Schröder to make common cause with other euro-zone countries with large social budgets in calling for tax harmonization in order to reduce the newcomers' appeal to diverting capital away from firms operating in Germany. The impression grew that Germany's government was calling into question the fundamental calculus of participation in the project of regional integration: that market integration provides win-win policy solutions—a posture Germany had traditionally championed—and that under the guise of shaking off a penitent past, Germany now embraced a "normalcy" that aggressively defended what the government identified as national interests.

Against this background, in addition to surveying the various factors at work in defining Germany's ligature with the European Union, this chapter probes the special question of how great an impact a change in government can have in altering the elements of that ligature.

■ How and in What Ways Does the EU Affect Germany?

Economic Performance

Arguably, the launching of the Common Market on the basis of the 1957 Rome Treaty establishing the European Economic Community (EEC) already implied the basic decision to reframe German economic activity in a European rather than a national context. This reframing has proceeded in two steps: first as a process of re-regulation, then second, as a liberalizing enhancement of market-oriented reforms.

Starting with management of macroeconomic aggregates, the EMU and its precursors closed off some economic strategy options and compelled the government to develop strategies consonant with European rules. From the late 1970s, the European Monetary System (EMS), a project organized under Franco-German leadership and a precursor of the EMU, fundamentally oriented German policymakers to creating a single economic space in a Europe based on mutually contingent, parallel macroeconomic management or concertation. This project had already constituted a major departure from policies based on the notion that they might exercise a large measure of control over economic development in splendid isolation from their European neighbors.[2] German negotiators insisted upon an EMU architecture that insulated the European Central Bank (ECB) from national interference and gave it a narrow mandate to produce monetary stability in the euro zone and forbade the ECB from pursuing a monetary policy that would bail out governments that ran large debts. In 1997, again with the Germans playing the leading role, the Stability and Growth Pact (SGP) constrained the government's spending and taxing decisions by imposing limits on current account deficits (3 percent of GDP). In the 1990s, the German economy entered a period of increasing and intractable unemployment and slow aggregate growth, where it has been stuck ever since. Germany's commitment to abide by the regime it played a leading role in creating meant that governments were compelled to pay ever greater attention to policies geared to promoting increased investment in emerging sectors and requiring the introduction of appropriate regulatory institutions.

Though the open method of coordination (OMC) has been criticized for lack of any real control over policy development in the member states, the Lisbon exercise, which relies heavily on the OMC, did, in fact, provide broad authority for the Commission to pursue a market-liberalizing strategy in sectors beyond those targeted in the 1992 internal market program. This authority proved to be an ongoing irritant to the German government, especially but not exclusively after the slowing of economic growth in 2001. This irritation is likely to continue and even increase after the new Commission leadership in the summer of 2004—confirmed in the spring of 2005 after a five-year progress review—made relaunching the Lisbon strategy, in a pared-down format with fewer references to the social and environmental dimensions, the centerpiece of the EU's economic strategy.

Following are some recent examples of the constraining effects of Brussels's internal market and competition authorities:

• The Commission's Directorates-General Competition continues to challenge state aid to firms induced to operate in Germany's eastern provinces (the Länder).

• As the site of Europe's largest chemicals industry, Germany is centrally affected by the Registration, Evaluation and Authorisation of Chemicals (REACH) legislation and both the red-green and grand coalition governments have fought to remove increased controls.

• In 2001 the German government effectively eviscerated planned EU company-law legislation by leaving intact the German practice of privileging certain classes of shareholders, thus empowering the managements of German firms to fend off unwanted corporate takeovers. In October 2005, EU commissioner Charlie McCreevy relaunched the campaign to end discrimination between shareholders according to the principle of "one share, one vote." He singled out Germany's public-sector banks and the recent deal between car makers Porsche and Volkswagen for criticism.[3]

• In autumn 2005, the EU's Single Market commissioner announced the intention to shepherd a tightening of the EU banking directive to encourage cross-border mergers. This move came after Germany's *Landesbanken* were required in 2004, after years of litigation initiated by the Commission, to repay 4.3 billion of state aid.

Overall, the story of the EU impact on Germany in the economic- and social-policy areas can be summed up as cumulative pressure on its "social model" (Modell Deutschland).[4] Aside from the institutional features of Modell Deutschland, social-policy positions have been significantly constrained by the EU, as is clear from data collected on European Court of Justice (ECJ) cases in the social-policy area that reveal Germany scores significantly above average in ECJ referrals in the critical areas of free movement of workers, social security of EU migrant workers, social security of third-country migrant workers, and worker's protection and equal treatment.[5]

◼ How Does Germany Affect EU Policies and Processes?

Organizing for Influence
The fundamental channel for projection of a government's preferences in the EU arena is the distribution of competences for monitoring the EU and formulating EU policy within the machinery of government. In Germany's case, this has been subject to modification on the basis of changing government coalitions. In the aftermath of the global economic slowdown in 2001–2002, application of already extant EU rules in the areas of the internal market and competition policy provoked SPD chancellor Schröder to go public with criticism of the Commission in advance of the 2002 German federal election, accusing it of having an

anti-industrial bias against Germany.[6] Another reaction consisted of a top-level review of the organization of Germany's EU policymaking machinery, carried out by the chancellery with the objective of increasing the effectiveness of representation of German interests.

Traditionally, the economics ministry has dominated Germany's connection to the institutions of regional integration in Europe through its department for European policy (*Abteilung E*). The debate over the establishment of a ministry for European affairs was resolved by the creation of a policy unit within the Office of the Federal Chancellor after the September 2002 election. As the Foreign Office itself suggests, Chancellor Schröder became increasingly involved in EU policies and politics during his tenure in office.[7] Chancellor Merkel will continue to locate such a unit in the chancellery.

The importance of the nexus between partisan politics and governmental organization in regulating Germany's relation to the EU is further exemplified by personnel decisions within the chancellor's own family of parties during the formation of the Christian Democrat (CDU)–Bavarian Christian Democrats (CSU)–SPD grand coalition in autumn 2005. Edmund Stoiber's decision to remain in Munich as governor of Bavaria, despite national popularity, confirms the increasingly important role of the federal chancellery in the interagency process and implied a more liberal approach to market forces in the Merkel government, but it also points to the power of the Länder in regulating EU affairs in Germany. The Länder are constitutionally endowed with reserved and concurrent power in many policy areas in which the EU is active—for example, economic and regional development, environmental regulation, aspects of asylum policy, educational credentialing, and many more. Infringement of their prerogatives during the EC Internal Market program in the late 1980s and early 1990s caused the Länder to make common cause against the federal government, compelling the latter to accept their integral role in formulating and scrutinizing EU legislation wherever their competences are addressed.

Several noteworthy results affecting the structure of EU decision-making in Germany and in Brussels flowed from this bipartisan campaign. First, the Länder compelled the federal government to consult them systematically. Second, they won the right to represent Germany in the Council of Ministers whenever policies were to be decided that were predominantly in their domain of responsibility. Third, a new Article 23 was inserted into Germany's Basic Law, which enshrined the role of the federal council (*Bundesrat*) in EU policy and constitutional development. Finally, the German federal government carried the campaign into the Maastricht Treaty negotiations, securing the establishment of the EU Committee of Regions, a modification of the EU institutional architecture that transformed EU-Europe's multilevel character into a constitutional principle.

From the foregoing, it is clear that the national government is but one facet of the German EU governance structure; that it is by no means internally unified, as it is divided politically and by intramural bureaucratic interests; and that the federal states also play a role. Moreover, successive EC-EU treaties have assigned power in the EU decisionmaking process to sectoral entities, in particular the peak organizations of trade unions and employers and trade associations. Indeed, for a state such as Germany, deliberately redesigned after World War II to decentralize power, it would be a mistake to ascribe to Germany a unified subject in dealing with the EU.

Environment Policy

An application of this insight is found in the export of policy disputes between "domestic" social sectors to Brussels for resolution. Environmental regulation is a field in which a "race-to-the-top" logic is most pronounced in Germany. The country is home to Europe's greatest concentration of industrial activity; it is also home to its widest social movement sector and a very successful Green Party. The political contests between them have been played out through EU institutions since the early 1980s. Air pollution abatement policies—for example, the introduction of unleaded gas and catalytic converters—were fiercely resisted by Germany's big automakers on competitiveness grounds back then, but politicians could no longer ignore the rising electoral strength of the Greens. The solution was to export more stringent controls to Europe, compelling all European car producers to internalize the externalized costs of pollution. The selfsame logic is at work in the REACH chemical regulation legislation, which had its first reading in the European Parliament in November 2005. Both the Greens and the German chemical industry, Europe's largest, fought the issue, seeking allies throughout the EU system. Here, there were no "German" interests, *strictu sensu*, let alone a unified national German interest, but rather industrial versus environmental interests clashing locally and in a broader European framework.

Food Safety

Another application, which also demonstrates the pertinence of partisan politics, comes from reactions in Germany to food safety scares from the mid-1990s onward. With hormone-treated beef, mad-cow disease, a hoof-and-mouth disease outbreak, ongoing debates about genetically modified crops, and a scandal involving pig manure as background, the discovery of infected cows in Germany led to a cabinet shake-up and the naming of a prominent Green Party politician to the newly created cabinet post of minister of consumer affairs and agriculture in 2001. This personnel change gave immediate transnational voice to the postindustrial concerns of the new generation and made the dominance of the traditional farming lobby, which had preoccupied itself with production and price issues, more relative.

Foreign Policy

The leitmotiv of this chapter is that party politics and corresponding shifts in the composition of the national and regional governments are an important regulator of Germany's EU relationship. The Schröder government's dramatic disagreement with the United States over armed intervention in Iraq in 2002 was but one episode in a broader pattern, marking a new national, if not nationalistic, tone in German foreign and European policy.[8] In a move eliciting consternation in Brussels and EU national capitals, the Schröder government's contribution to the opening of a United Nations reform agenda was the announcement of its campaign to claim for itself a permanent seat on the Security Council. By the same token, until the Iraq war, and with the encouragement of the United States, Germany under the red-green coalition deployed more troops abroad than any country except the United States, supporting the US-led effort in Kosovo (1999) and Afghanistan (2001), with the chancellor even risking a vote of no-confidence in the process. Later, the government reinforced Germany's international profile by sending emergency relief personnel and aid to Indonesia after the December 2004 tsunami and to Louisiana after Hurricane Katrina in September 2005. Still, in the Iraq episode, Schröder was willing to split the EU while aligning with Russia under the cover of France.

On relations with Russia. Schröder evoked dark passages of national history when he proved tone-deaf to concerns voiced by Poland and the Baltic countries about reaching a deal with the Kremlin on the construction of a natural gas pipeline connecting Germany and Russia that circumvented these countries completely, thereby creating uncertainty about the fate of pipelines from Russia that run through Poland. Indeed, his revealing response to the outcry was: "German energy policy is made in Berlin." In the case of EU-China relations, the Schröder government, in keeping with its drive to cash in on the Asian market, underscored by no less than six official visits by the chancellor, had advocated abandonment of the arms embargo imposed after the 1989 Tiananmen massacre for the gross abuse of human rights that action represented. Where the EU offered support for Schröder's independent line, he embraced it, arguing for a reform of NATO in acknowledgment of the EU's collective weight in it. Germany was also content to join with the UK and France as the "EU-3" in regulating relations with Iran. Finally, Schröder's government heavily engaged itself in the Balkans. The stability pact for southeast Europe, designed to develop a perspective for eventual EU membership, was a red-green initiative launched by Foreign Minister Fischer. The government also embraced Turkish EU membership.

The Merkel government. In contrast, the Merkel government began with an entirely different accent, reflexively returning to a policy that is both Atlanticist and European, with national aspirations that are perhaps less global:

• CDU chancellor Angela Dorothea Merkel signaled her government's intention to return to a more cooperative EU foreign policy by recruiting Christoph Heusgen, one of the EU's Common Foreign and Security Policy High Representative Javier Solana's top policy advisers, as her foreign-policy adviser. The move revealed Merkel's abandonment of Schröder's quest for a permanent UN Security Council seat for Germany and was cited as an indication of her understanding of the centrality of the EU for success of any German national government and her intention to concentrate control over EU policy in the chancellery.[9]

• In order to emphasize the government's fundamental interest in intra-EU comity, Merkel's first official visits as chancellor were to France and the UK, and she had stated a desire to visit Poland early on as well.

• On the eve of Chinese president Hu Jintao's November 2005 tour of several EU capitals, the incoming Merkel government took the arms embargo off the agenda, thus bringing Germany's policy back into alignment with that of the United States.

• Though her election campaign statements attacked EU membership for Turkey, the new government's position, designed to put aside conflict between the parties to the coalition, pragmatically accepted the conduct of ongoing negotiations for membership, already opened on October 3, 2005, but expected to last for at least a decade. For Merkel and her advisers, the concern about Turkish membership is mainly about the internal cohesion of the EU.

Council presidencies provide member states an occasional opportunity to exercise leadership. In 1988 Chancellor Kohl pushed the EMU agenda, and in 1994 his conservative government advanced social Europe. Chancellor Schröder helped prepare enlargement in the Agenda 2000 budget negotiation, and two months later Foreign Minister Fischer led in opening a long-term perspective for eventual Balkan EU membership in the aftermath of the Kosovo war, launching a kind of "Marshall Plan" for the region in the form of the Stability Pact for Southeast Europe. The Merkel government announced that it intended to bring the stalled European Constitutional Treaty back from the abyss during its presidency in 2007.

Market Regulatory Elements

Perhaps the most studied and celebrated example of Germany's EU prowess as an architect and model is the European Central Bank, modeled more or less explicitly on the Bundesbank. A keystone of the Maastricht Treaty edifice, and like Chancellor Kohl's prior decision to go for a quick monetary union with East Germany, the decision to press forward with Economic and Monetary Union was quintessentially political. Done to deepen integration in pursuit of Kohl's dream of anchoring Germany firmly and together with France in an indissoluble union, he left the technical details concerning institutional structure to the *Finanzpolitiker.* Exploiting the leverage gained from Germany's willingness to give up the deutschemark (DM), symbol of postwar German economic success that other EU member states desired to harness in the interest of creating a favorable macroeconomic environment in their own countries, German negotiators created a European simulacrum of the original.

The ECB was created with more autonomy than the Bundesbank and with an even narrower mission to stabilize the new euro currency. Of note is the persistence of the competitive federalism template in this innovation. Monetary policy was to be centralized in this plan, but fiscal policy—taxing and spending—was to be left to the member states. Five years later in 1997, some 18 months in advance of the launch of the euro currency, German negotiators insisted on a code of conduct to which euro-zone aspirants were to pledge allegiance. The resulting Stability and Growth Pact had as its central requirement running a medium-term balance in the current account. Moreover, euro-zone members were not to run an excessive deficit—defined as a current account deficit greater than 3 percent of the member state's GDP—at any time. The resulting system was "more German than Germany" and was destined to come back to haunt the Federal Republic as the petard with which it was hoisted under the red-green government beginning in 2002.

Budget, Structural Funds

In keeping with the tight rein over supranational finances that was always part of Germany's basic EU vision, and reflecting the unforgiving fiscal environment of the 1990s, Germany's position on the EU budget changed fundamentally. Earlier, Germany had been EU *Zahlmeister* and could pursue checkbook diplomacy to fund new EU programs and expanding expenditure in order to facilitate political cohesion. The costs of German unification drove leaders to campaign successfully for classifying all the eastern Länder as "objective 1" regions, thus qualifying them for funding from EU Structural Funds. During their 1999 EU presidency German negotiators succeeded in the Agenda 2000 framework in providing for the first stage of eastern enlargement, from the projected 2004 accession date. At the same time, when Germany began exceeding the SGP 3 percent deficit threshold in 2002, negotiators argued that the country should reduce its net contribution and in 2004, during the opening round of consultations over the 2007–2013 financial perspective, Germany joined other net contributors in adopting the hard-line position advocating a 1 percent of EU GDP ceiling on the budget. With a cluster of poor new members, the implication of this position is that new member states will receive less funding than had poorer EU member states from the west. This logic was already implicit in the December 2002 budget deal worked out in a Franco-German bilateral meeting that capped the budget for agricultural support payments over the same six-year period and provided a graduated payout to farmers from the new, poor central and eastern European member states starting at 25 percent of the support level given to western EU farmers and rising to parity in the context of a stagnant overall farm budget. In a mercantilist turn, the Germans got even tougher in 2004–2005 when they proposed lowering the level of support to regions in the new member states from EU Structural Funds, if they lowered taxes—like the Irish "Celtic tiger"—to attract investment. Again in contrast to the Schröder government, Chancellor Merkel's EU debut at the December 2005 European Council was a policy and public relations triumph, based on her brokering a budget plan that reconciled the antagonistic positions of France and Britain, and cemented a new relationship with Poland by raising the overall level of spending and reassigning about 100 million euros of Structural Funds from the eastern German Länder to that country.

Justice and Home Affairs

This policy area grows out of the fundamental right of labor to move around in the Common Market in search of work. Prior to the fall of the Berlin Wall, the Balkan wars of the 1990s, and the emergence of "globalization III,"[10] Germany's leadership associated free movement with a welcome aspiration to identify with "Europe." The Kohl government invested heavily in the notion of a citizens' Europe in the 1980s, in 1984 co-initiating with the French government a scheme outside the EC treaty framework—very much along the lines of the Franco-German EMS initiative on monetary policy—advocating elimination of checks at borders between participating states. The resulting Schengen Agreement was supplemented by a common EU passport and, through the Maastricht Treaty, extension of the franchise to EU nationals living in other member states in local and European parliamentary elections.

Christian and Social Democratic alike—beset with "unfunded mandates" passed down from Brussels—used their newfound powers to turn Germany from a vanguard to a laggard in asylum and immigration issues.[11] Germany's prosperity made it a magnet for refugees and economic migrants. The liberal and generous asylum provision in the German Basic Law combined with the country's exposed geographic position to prompt an unprecedented escalation of asylum-seekers from 1989 to 1994 of from about 55,000 to 455,000 per year,[12] and this escalation was the occasion for mobilization of the Länder as a factor in limiting Germany's integrationist stance.

The high political salience of counterterrorism efforts in the wake of the attacks on New York and Washington in September 2001 presented Germany with the need to develop another dimension of Justice and Home Affairs. German policy in dealing with such terrorism rested on two pillars formed from two lessons of the interwar period, in tension with one another, that strongly conditioned Germany's response to "9/11": radicalism must not be allowed to threaten democratic institutions and "the moral foundation of its polity requires a secure system of norms that are legally guaranteed and firmly anchored in a human rights tradition."[13] In practice, this has led to strict limits on intelligence gathering and fragmentation of intelligence organizations along federal lines. As part of its decentralizing template, Germany had long been an advocate of European police cooperation and was a major advocate of the European Law Enforcement Organisation (EUROPOL), whose competences were expanded under the 1994 German EU presidency.

German society spent the 1990s, spurred on politically especially by the Greens, learning to acknowledge that it is a multicultural society. In the face of the facts—a higher portion of foreigners in the population than most European countries, the third-largest Turkish population in the world—some party leaders persisted in proclaiming the myth that Germany is not a land of immigration. The discovery that Al-Qaeda cells in Hamburg had supplied the hijacker-pilots who flew into the World Trade Center and Pentagon produced a corrective shock that both alerted the political class and public to the social reality and also altered the balance between liberty and security in Germany. Legislation adopted in 2002 made it possible to ban religious groups that advocate terrorism, criminalize advocacy of terrorist acts in other countries, and strengthen the ability of the state to act preemptively against terrorism. It also increased Germany's willingness to Europeanize the counterterrorism effort through acquiescence in, if not enthusiasm for, the EU arrest warrant. In parallel, were successful German initiatives to include a catalogue of basic rights accorded to EU citizens as a protocol to the 2000 Treaty of Nice and later to ensure its inclusion in legally compelling form in the 2004 EU Constitutional Treaty.

■ How Does Germany Comply with or Implement EU Policies?

Recent implementation procedures from the area of Justice and Home Affairs provide insight into the persistence of the two principles mentioned above, which continue to define the two poles of German thinking. In July 2005, Germany's federal constitutional court ordered the release of a man held on suspicion of being an accessory to financing a terrorist organization (Al-Qaeda) who was to be remanded to Spain, which had requested him in that connection under the recently adopted European arrest warrant. At issue is the proper transposition of the EU directive in Germany, not its underlying validity.

Germany is a system of administrative federalism in which the Länder play the leading role in implementing almost all law: the EU and the German federal government make some policy but (unlike the US federal system) neither possess field services to implement it. Therefore, implementation of most EU legislation and policy in Germany is twice-removed from its source. It comes as no surprise that this situation increases the likelihood of delay and inaccurate implementation. Many ECJ referrals from Germany concern just this congenital issue.

At bottom, in most cases EU law and policy are implemented because someone has an interest that they are and the resources to pursue their implementation. When national governments are the central players in implementation, policy can be contested and modified. Such is the case in the functioning of the euro zone, the subject of the following case study, chosen for its intrinsic importance in delivering highly prized public goods and because it exemplifies the evolving character of German attitudes toward the EU and the centrality of politics in defining them.

Case Study: Macroeconomic Management
Under the Stability and Growth Pact

Since about 2000, compliance with EU policy in Germany has become generally politicized. This has most often taken the form of declarations of the government of the day under the banner of defending German interests vis-à-vis the Commission and/or Council. Though certainly marking a change in the style and rhetoric of EU policy in Germany associated with the installation of the "red-green" national government of Social Democrats and Greens led by Chancellor Gerhard Schröder, it also points to the advent of an enduring phase of structural friction with Brussels. Arguably, at least since the implementation of the "EC-92" internal market program (1987–1992), Europe had entered into a new relationship between the country's political class and the population. As EC/EU policy increasingly affected ever broader domains of Germans' daily experience and as the less deferential postwar generation formed the basis of a new, often critical popular media interest in "Brussels," the environment of permissive consensus in which elites had labored heretofore gave way to the emergence of European domestic politics, or "inter-mestic" politics in Germany.

For most of the 1990s this was masked by the CDU–Liberal (FDP) national government led by Chancellor Helmut Kohl, who was committed to the EMU project on geostrategic grounds and successfully subordinated every complicating factor to its realization by the end of his 16-year term in October 1998, just two months shy of the launching of the euro currency. Kohl was never seriously challenged, though the boulevard press railed against the "Esperanto money," attacked as a sell-out of the main symbol of West Germany's postwar economic success and a project lacking technical merits to boot. The government's response to such criticism took the form of guaranteeing the stability of the new currency by insisting on a German-type institutional architecture and German policy preferences inscribed into the ECB statute. At the Dublin European Council, the Germans went further by insisting on a regime to govern the operation of the euro zone after the currency was launched. The resulting Stability and Growth Pact imposed fiscal rules on euro-zone members, in particular establishing a 3 percent current account budget deficit threshold whose crossing in any year would trigger policy advice, admonition, and ultimately fines from Brussels.

Of critical importance at that stage was the dynamic of partisan opposition, which worked in Kohl's favor. In particular, the increasingly successful Greens became the most enthusiastic supporters of European integration in the German political party spectrum over the course of the 1990s. Thus outflanked, the much larger party of opposition, the Social Democrats, was not in a position to take on Kohl. What ultimately led to the defeat of Kohl's Conservative-Liberal (CDU-FDP) government was the electoral defection of citizens of Germany's eastern Länder.

Unification and German EU Policy

German unification was carried out as a wholesale transfer of West German institutions to the reconstituted eastern Länder of the German Democratic Republic (GDR), which from February 1990 at the latest, was on the auction block of history. The one book-length work relating unification to EU policy and politics concludes that "the supreme confidence and faith placed by German elites in the German model in Europe, and the vigor with which they carried out institutional transfer, attests to [enormous resistance to change in the model's constituent ideas and institutions]."[14] On July 2, 1990, three months in advance of the treaty that would absorb the territory of East Germany into the West German state, the treaty between West and East Germany establishing German Economic, Monetary, and Social Union came into force, in effect making the GDR a member of the European Union in fact as well as in theory.

Against the advice of the Bundesbank and most economists, Chancellor Kohl insisted on imposing an exchange rate of 1:1 for the currencies of the two states. Given the approximately 3:1 productivity advantage of the western Länder, few eastern firms could compete with western ones without undergoing drastic wage reductions. But this option was foreclosed by the unions, which insisted instead on wage convergence upward to West German levels. Mass layoffs and firm restructurings were the result. In the interest of preventing what was perceived to be a destabilizing wave of migration to the western Länder, the national government developed policies to hold the population in place—paying out pensions, subsidizing job creation, and investing in infrastructure. These policies—aimed essentially at assimilating the new Länder and their populations into the old—far from involving a radical change of policy for united Germany as a whole, sought instead simply to extend western institutions and policies *tout court*. In a sense, the crisis of the eastern Länder was approached with the policy template worked out in dealing with social crises associated with declining industries (shipbuilding, coal, iron, and steel) in the west. After all, at least from the point of view of population size, the new Länder are equivalent to North Rhine–Westphalia, the locus of several such large social programs.

Quite aside from the political psychology of this move, which must in the interest of space go entirely unexamined here, the financial outlay required quickly topped DM130 billion per year (about US$85 billion or about 100 billion at the time of this writing)—over 5 percent of German GDP—with no end in sight.[15] From a macroeconomic perspective this magnitude of increased public spending simply undid the government's avowed aim of reducing the portion of GDP taxed off and redistributed by the government. It also raised questions about how Germany would stay within the euro-zone budgetary rules it had insisted be adopted before the currency launch on New Year's Day, 1999.

In this context it is not surprising that the Kohl government moved to recoup some of its unification costs through the EU budget via the structural funds—assistance to regions and sectors based on technical criteria applied across the EU space. In the negotiations over the 1994–2000 EU financial perspective it did precisely that, qualifying all five eastern Länder for money at the highest level of the EU scale. This caused a conflict between eastern and western Länder as federal policy was to maintain budget discipline in Brussels, resisting all efforts to raise the percentage of EU GDP going to the EU budget. This implied either less money for West German sectors and regions in decline, or rising debt, or some combination of these.

Bonn also notified Brussels about aid schemes for settlement of branch plants (e.g., of Volkswagen) and infusions of cash to aid the privatization and restructuring process in the east. In the energy sector, revolving around German coal subsidies especially popular with SPD constituencies, unification once again disrupted established policy networks, pitting east against west and both against the Commission and other electricity producers located in other EU member states. Meanwhile, the privatization agency (Treuhand Anstalt) set up in March

1990 to deal with GDR state enterprises. Bonn was required to notify and win Brussels's approval for all schemes of state aid, a prospect it initially welcomed, as its policy, representing the economics ministry's traditional orientation, was to use the Brussels competition authorities as an instrument to minimize market distortions in the EU economic space. But as the exigencies of unification arose, Bonn's enthusiasm for unqualified application of treaty articles diminished, and this under a Conservative government.[16]

Through the 1990s, Germany's EU posture became more contentious. Still, despite the new challenges of unification, "Germany's general approach to integration remains consistent with its pre-unification past," though the author of this line goes on to emphasize that Germany's interest constellation vis-à-vis the EU changed because of unification nonetheless.[17] That is to say, continuity of approach led to a new and in some cases conflicting set of demands on the EU. This is incontestable in my view, but it is also true that in a larger sense, unification reinforced an underlying trend, compelling the political leadership to take action sooner than may have otherwise been the case.

In spite of the disruption associated with unification, it is likely that that process occluded as much as it revealed about the evolving character of Germany's relationship with the EU. It was to require a government of a new political stripe to begin revising the conventional wisdom and working with institutional change that is occurring in any event. Developments during the six and a half years traversed by two red-green governments confirm that Modell Deutschland is fraying, but leaves open whether a policy paradigm based on a new matrix of social forces, ideas, and institutions suited to the new transnational European arena has broken through.

Red-Green: 1998–2005

Kohl's luck ran out in the 1998 election. With persistent unemployment running at least twice as high in the eastern than in the western Länder, resentment at being left behind was probably the most potent factor in the massive swing vote abandoning the CDU in favor of the SPD. On the basis of the transformed parliamentary arithmetic a "red-green" government of Social Democrats and Greens was formed and it was reelected in 2002. That said, while easterners may have been fed up with Kohl, the new government inherited all the problems his government could not solve. The difference was that the Social Democrats had always been particularly wary of the overarching liberalizing thrust of regional integration in the EU. Therefore, it comes as no surprise that in the Social

Democrat–led government, EU policy implementation—particularly the logic of the Internal Market and the constraining effects of the ECB's monetary policy—received fulsome critical review and sharper official rhetoric as Berlin pushed back against Brussels.

Economic and social policy was dominated by the Social Democrats in the red-green coalition and Chancellor Schröder staked the survival of his government on finding a workable balance between them. In particular, Schröder made progress in reducing unemployment the central challenge of his administration, explicitly inviting the German electorate to evaluate his government primarily on the basis of reducing unemployment. In the end, imperatives of the euro zone undermined his ability to achieve this central aim of red-green government from 1998 to 2005 and ultimately led to the plummeting poll figures for the SPD and Schröder's decision to force an early election in autumn 2005, which he lost.

The global market correction that brought an end to the "dot.com" boom created a much tougher environment for reform from early 2001 onward. Unemployment figures crept up again, heading toward the psychologically significant threshold of 4 million. A paradox framed further developments: while German companies prospered as never before and German exports soared—indeed, while Germany reclaimed the title as world export champion—unemployment moved up inexorably. These developments affected the government's reactions to EU policy development along a broad front. Already contending with the unprecedented fiscal challenge associated with German unification,[18] part of which was financed with new debt, rising unemployment generated increased costs to the state in the form of unemployment insurance claims, pensions associated with early retirement, and the like.

Complicating this picture further was the fact that it fell to the federal Länder to pick up costs associated with programs developed under their constitutional prerogatives. In short, solutions to Germany's budgetary problem involved intergovernmental relations within federal Germany, whose Länder were governed by a variety of political constellations and could not be controlled by the red-green national governing coalition. In the German system, Länder are empowered to run current account deficits. Under stagnant or worsening economic conditions, they collectively added to the federal deficit and could not be controlled directly by the federal government, which is held responsible by the EU for Germany's fiscal situation under the SGP. As a result, from fiscal year 2002 onward, Germany's fiscal position exceeded the SGP current account deficit threshold of 3 percent of GDP, a situation that automatically remanded Germany to review and advice by the Commission, the euro-zone group, and the EcoFin Council of Ministers.

The point is not that there is a universal prescription for economic success,[19] but rather that EMU rules impose severe constraints on macroeconomic policy in Germany. After it became obvious that Germany would breach the 3 percent threshold a third year, unwilling to make painful fiscal adjustments, it became German policy to change the rules of the euro zone. Together with the Italian and French governments, which were also plagued with low aggregate growth and high unemployment, Germany cobbled together a coalition in the Council of Ministers that reinterpreted the accounting rules attached to the SGP, such that certain categories of expenditure (investments) would not be charged as expenditures at all. At first, the Commission, playing its role as enforcer of the founding treaties, resisted to the point of filing an action against the Council in the ECJ. In this opposition, the Commission was supported by a countercoalition of mainly smaller countries, led by the government of the Netherlands, that perceived the application of an intolerable double standard according to which only smaller member states would be held to account. But when the Court, in a Solomon-like judgment that both recognized the validity of the SGP and the authority of the Council to interpret the rules flexibly, failed to grant the plaintiffs a clear victory, the coalition of the virtuous was compelled to acknowledge the loosening of the stability pact corset. By summer 2005, the compromise reached was that Germany's obligation to return to fiscal balance would be extended by two years.[20]

Germany launched a counteroffensive whose main aim was to reframe the deficit in a wider context, connecting that question to the unique challenge of German reunification. Viewed thus, as an amalgam of an original EU member state and a new one (the territory of the former German Democratic Republic), Germany's status as the biggest netpayer into the EU budget no longer made sense. If the EU expected Germany to come into fiscal balance, then it should not expect Germany to pay so much into the EU budget.

Policy preferences of the new EU member states—the "class of 2004"—were also targeted by the German government. They should not be allowed to follow the "Celtic tiger" example of Ireland by lowering taxes to attract foreign capital and draw structural funds as net recipients of EU aid at the same time. To Germany, especially to the Social Democrats, this had the appearance of "social dumping," a self-defeating, neo-mercantilist strategy presaging a "race to the bottom" that could only impoverish EU member states such as Germany. EU enlargement negotiations were also affected by the defensiveness that emanated from Germany's subpar growth and employment performance. Fearing labor market pressure from the supply side, Germany insisted on a seven-year transition period for the free movement of labor from Poland.

More broadly, in the post-bubble environment, Germany's government was quite neuralgic to any intervention by the Commission that had perceived adverse effects on employment. So, despite the government's public embrace of the March 2000 Lisbon Strategy to transform the EU into the most dynamic and information-based economy in the world by 2010, Germany resisted virtually every implementing measure proposed by the Commission. Working with European parliamentary members, the government quashed EU legislation that would have made it more difficult to prevent take-over bids aimed at German firms. It fought to retain subsidies to German banks in the mortgage business. And most famously, in spring 2005, it vocally supported a campaign aimed against opening the huge EU market for services. Moreover, with the installation of the new Commission in summer 2004, working with the German commissioner for growth and innovation, together with the French, the German government began attacking the liberalizing spirit of the Lisbon Strategy with support for "National Champions."

The partisan-political underpinning of this development is clear enough. Ahead of the Hartz-IV labor market reforms due to come into force in early 2005, street demonstrations mostly in eastern German cities, taking their inspiration from the so-called *Montagsdemonstrationen* against the Communist East German regime in 1989, challenged Schröder's modernization program. Politically, this was of great concern, since the eastern German Länder had provided the SPD's margin of victory in 1998 and 2002. Social Democratic support plummeted, leading the chancellor to take aim at market-liberalizing reforms. By late 2004, the rhetoric had become quite harsh, with the SPD party leader, Münterfering, likening hedge fund activities to a swarm of locusts descending on the German economy. This sort of language probably only further encouraged populist Euro-skepticism that gathered force to challenge the SPD from the left. In this context, the May 2005 election in the federal state of North Rhine–Westphalia produced a devastating defeat and a change of government there.

Under these circumstances, Schröder surprised Germany with his move to seek an early national election, one year ahead of schedule. A snap election campaign would reimpose party discipline and catch the surging opposition Christian Democrats off-guard. In so doing, he had successfully maneuvered the Christian Democrats into nominating their party chair, Angela Merkel, as chancellor-candidate. Now Schröder and the SPD could appeal for support for a traditional "social market economy" approach, charging the Merkel-led CDU with radical market-liberalizing experimentation, since Merkel's positions were closer to the Liberals (FDP) than to large parts of her own party. But Schröder had not counted on the reappearance of former SPD chairman, Oskar Lafontaine, who joined up with PDS *eminence grise*, Gregor Gysi, to form a national party to the left of the SPD.

Nevertheless, Schröder's strategy came within a whisker of complete political victory. The Christian Democrats, who started the campaign some 20 points ahead of the SPD, finished with less than a 1 percent advantage, just edging out the SPD 35.2 percent to 34.2 percent. Though Schröder was forced to relinquish the chancellorship in favor of Christian Democrat Angela Merkel, Germany's first female chancellor and first chancellor from eastern Germany, the Social Democrats continued in government as an almost equal partner, after consultations led by the CDU with the FDP and the Greens generated no traction. The three parties sharing the other third of the electorate more or less equally between them—Socialist Left (PDS-Linke), Greens (Bündnis 90–Die Grünen), and Liberals (FDP)—formed the national parliamentary opposition.

The consequences for the EU flowing from the shift of political direction associated with the change from "red-green" to the "grand coalition" on November 22, 2005, are significant, even in the short term. German governments organize their work according to a joint platform hammered out between the coalition parties in the run-up to the election of the chancellor. In contrast to Schröder, who rung down the curtain on his chancellorship with a broadside against EU interference in member-state affairs,[21] the Merkel team focused on Germany's agenda in EU-Europe. The November 11, 2005, coalition agreement[22] between the Christian Democrats (CDU), their Bavarian sister-party (CSU), and the Social Democrats (SPD) runs to nearly two hundred pages and is organized in nine substantive sections. It is clear from the document that the EU plays a significant role in the government's plans. The EU gets explicit mention in five of the nine substantive headlines introducing major policy fields. Under the first headline, "Innovation and Work," the EU is explicitly referenced in the first section on "competitiveness" and "fair competition"; the second section on the labor market regarding the EU posted labor directive, implementation of work-time directive, and "European social policy"; and in the eighth and final section on agricultural policy. Under the second headline on state finances "tax policy in Europe" receives explicit treatment. Headline three on constructing eastern Germany includes a reference to "securing support through the EU." The eighth headline on internal security calls for "European cooperation." In the ninth, on "Germany as a responsible partner in Europe and the world," the document gives first priority to the EU, devoting three subdivisions to "Europe of the citizens," "financial parameters," and "enlargement," respectively. The document is a manifesto of Germany's thorough policy integration in the EU.

Leitmotiv and highest priority for Germany's new government was defined during the coalition negotiations as fiscal consolidation to bring Germany back into compliance with the SGP, a path dictated as much by the logic of EU political cohesion as by purely German preferences. This required unpopular measures, normally far from the preferences of either of the two coalition parties, such as a three-point increase in the regressive VAT (value-added tax) turnover tax and reductions in federal spending. To increase control over public expenditure the coalition agreement calls for a reform of the financing of Germany's federal system as part of a wider federalism reform.[23]

To protect "German jobs" the coalition parties also agreed to carry over Schröder's resistance to the Commission's services directive proposal, and extend Germany's posted-workers legislation to cover sectors beyond the construction industry to compel non-German providers of services to pay German wages.[24] It also plans to work toward mechanisms to diminish the effect of investment incentives in the new member states.[25] Under the heading of "European social policy," the parties agreed to maintain Germany's denial of the EU's fundamental right of free movement of labor vis-à-vis the states that joined the EU in 2004 for a period of seven years.[26] On the other hand, the agreement states the government's intent to bring Germany's regulation giving younger individuals preference in hiring decisions into conformity with EU antidiscrimination legal norms.[27]

■ Germany's Record of Compliance/Implementation of EU Policy Directives

By and large, the question of compliance with EU policy and law is not a matter of "the nation," but of specific state agents operating in a complex matrix of intergovernmental relations. In Germany this is largely due to the fact that there has been a broad consensus in the political class supporting regional integration. Chancellor Kohl went so far as to state that integration comprised part of Germany's raison d'être. By way of contrast, Chancellor Schröder has emphasized Germany's "normality," a feature of which consists of robust defense of German interests in Brussels. But these views are not contradictory and are certainly not mutually exclusive—nor are they seen as such in Germany. Some landmark cases concerned German disputes. A case in point is the 1979 *casis* case, involving the German importer, RWE, which took the federal German regulator for spirituous beverages to court for denying an import license for the French libation. RWE won, establishing the mutual recognition of product standards regime that has governed the circulation of commodities in EU-Europe ever since. The case also established the prerogative of the ECJ to determine where to draw the line between consumer protections and free-market principles, removing that prerogative from the member states.

The situation is complicated by Germany's federal system. The German Basic Law assigns competences in certain policy areas to the Länder. When a directive is adopted that impinges on Länder competences, compliance is usually drawn out, since this requires intergovernmental negotiations in which the federal government cannot simply dictate the outcome. The situation is often complicated by the not infrequent pattern of contrary political constellations in control on the federal and the Länder levels. To take one example, in 1997 the Commission came close to imposing heavy fines on Germany for being out of compliance with several environmental directives. In this case, the threat of fines was sufficient to get German federal and Länder authorities to strike a deal.

■ Future Trends and Prospects

This chapter has demonstrated that Germany's role in Europe has undergone a significant transformation from a facilitator-in-principle of further integration—as architect, model, and bridge to the east—to a contentious partner in the integration process. As we have seen, associated with this change is the emergence of a partisan politics mediating Germany's relationship with the EU. This pattern accords well with the literature demonstrating the decline of the "permissive consensus" as the scope and salience of integration increased step-wise in the 1990s. Accordingly, we expect that the stability of Germany's national governing coalition will serve as a good barometer of developments in

German-EU affairs, at least with respect to the central strands of economic policy that form the most visible regulator of the German-EU relationship. It may be a sign of things to come that the SPD and CDU have indicated policy initiatives beyond the coalition agreement before the ink was dry on that document. Depending on macroeconomic developments, a CDU-led reform initiative based on further market liberalization could provoke a rupture and send Germans back to the polls, where a decision on consolidating or retrenching in a different governing constellation could result. There is no doubt that a European domestic politics is well established in the EU's biggest member state. The character of that species of politics needs be of enormous interest across the region, as political developments in Germany will continue to generate consequences with which the rest of Europe will have to live.

■ Notes

This contribution was written in the author's personal capacity and does not necessarily reflect the thinking of the US Department of State or the US government.

1. It is common to describe coalition governments in Germany by the colors associated with their constituent political parties. Red refers to the parties of the left—Social Democrats (SPD), Party of Democratic Socialism (PDS), and Left Party (Die Linke). Green referes to the Green Party (Bündnis 90–Die Grünen). Black refers to the Christian Democrats (CDU and CSU) and yellow to the Liberals (FDP).

2. There had been a lively, partisan, policy debate in the 1970s about the feasibility of assigning authority to state institutions to channel investment. More generally, building on the concept of *Sozialpartnerschaft* (social partnership), itself deriving from the political consensus supporting the *Sozialmarktwirtschaft* (social market economy), parts of the Social Democratic Party (SPD), supported by some of Germany's largest and most powerful trade unions, pressed for greater worker control in business enterprises.

3. Buck, "EU Seeks to End Bias Among Investors."

4. See Lankowski, "Fraying at the Edge."

5. Leibfried, Der Einfluss *Eruopas*, p. 81.

6. Schröder intervened on more than one occasion to help the Volkswagen company in what can only be described as a lobbyist-in-chief role for a perceived national champion. Early in his chancellorship, he overrode his own environment minister in the decisive Council of Ministers meeting to force modification of a recycling scheme. Later, he worked to kill EU legislation that would have subjected VW to take-over bids by removing privileged shareholders—among them, the federal state of Lower Saxony, a state where Schröder formerly served as governor with an ex officio seat on VW's board of directors. Continued German industrial defensiveness is recently visible in a retrograde

scheme to reestablish cross-shareholdings among German car manufacturers, for example, an increase of Porsche's stake in VW announced in September 2005.

7. Foreign Office interview, March 2005.

8. Lippert, *European Politics of the Red-Green Government*.

9. Beunderman, "Berlin Signals End to Support for Lifting China Arms Ban."

10. Friedman, *The World Is Flat*.

11. Hellermann et al., "De-Europeanization by Default?" pp. 143–164.

12. The frontiers with Poland and the Czech Republic are a shallow stream and unfenced meadowland, respectively, and thus notoriously porous.

13. Katzenstein, "Sonderbare Sonderwege."

14. Anderson, *German Unification and the Union of Europe*, p. 204.

15. See Heilemann and Rappen, *The Seven-Year Itch?*

16. Anderson, *German Unification and the Union of Europe*, chapter 5, passim.

17. Ibid., p. 206.

18. Ibid.

19. Posen, "Overview: The Euro's Success Within Limits," p. 17.

20. At the time of this writing (November 2005), the Commission promised to hold Germany to account in the modified SGP regime.

21. "Schröder warnt vor 'Überdehnung der europäischen Kompetenzen.'"

22. "Coalition Agreement Between the CDU/CSU and the SPD."

23. Ibid., p. 94.

24. Ibid., pp. 20, 30.

25. Ibid., p. 21.

26. Ibid., p. 32.

27. Ibid., p. 24.

4

France: Contradictions and Imbalances

Christian Deubner

WHILE MANY DIFFERENT ELEMENTS have helped shape the complex relationship between France and the European Union, three stand out as worthy of deeper consideration: the integrationist trend; the relationship with Germany, and the idea of French "grandeur."

Although France was one of the original signers of the Treaty of Rome in 1957, it has always had reservations about giving up its sovereignty to any international body. Some of its past actions in the EU clearly indicate the imbalances of its European positions. For example, France prevented adoption of the European Defense Community (to which a political community was to be attached in 1954). It broke the supranational orientation of the early European Economic Community's integration trajectory by the "empty chair" of 1965–1966. It almost scuttled the Treaty of Maastricht in a referendum very narrowly won. And it torpedoed the Constitutional Treaty project of 2004 in the clearly lost referendum of May 29, 2005.

The geopolitical reality of France's neighborhood with Germany has been one of the first-order determinants for French European policy. Since the beginning of the Cold War period, when the United States began to pressure for inclusion of West Germany into an anti-Soviet alliance in Europe, French postwar balance-of-power politics against a potentially stronger Germany became untenable. France's overwhelming impulse for protection against its neighbor found expression in a new strategy of binding West Germany to France through European integration.[1] If one looks closely, it is not difficult to see that, at the same time that West German power increased after 1949, French willingness to deepen European integration also increased. This series began with the French initiative for the Coal and Steel Community in 1950, and ended with French agreement to the principle of a constitutional convention in 2000.[2] To this already developing bond of integration, de Gaulle added, in 1963, the idea of a privileged bilateral cooperation with Germany, and he attempted to give flesh to the intergovernmental concept between the two most powerful member states of the Union. This special cooperation survived de Gaulle, and has come to play an essential role for France's (and for Germany's) preparation of new European policy concepts and of introducing them in the EU Councils.[3] For example, in October 2002, during the EU's discussions to reform the Common Agricultural Policy (CAP), France and Germany joined together to negotiate a compromise to maintain the prevailing support levels until after 2006.[4]

Most recently, the ongoing relationship has found expression in mutual opposition to US entry into the Iraq war and cooperative ventures into European Defense Policy, while at the same time condemning German budget deficits. There are two views of today's Germany: one as a menacing rival for France, domesticated by European integration; and the other as a privileged ally for propagating French ideas in EU Councils. Also, the bilateral closing of ranks over Iraq has certainly been interpreted as the defining event for coming years. Yet it seems less than probable that Germany will ally with France in the latter's efforts to adapt European social and economic policies to the positions of the French "*Non*" voters.

The idea of French uniqueness and "grandeur" reached a modern peak under the guidance of de Gaulle. France has been—together with the United Kingdom—the most important postwar exponent of intergovernmental tendencies. These traditions remain a significant factor today, fueling France's insistence on great-power status in any deliberations of European nations, and in discussions about participation in the creation of the new defense forces. Upheld against all tangible evidence, the idea of French uniqueness has remained to impede full acceptance of further progress toward European integration. In France, there is almost no political force remaining, in the whole spectrum, that would accept federalism as a legitimate perspective of European integration. As for the Union itself, Gaullism bequeathed it, even before Mrs. Thatcher did, a strong element of intergovernmentalism remaining even today.

■ How and in What Areas Does the EU Influence France?

The EU today influences almost every aspect of French life—ranging from the halls of government to the rural homesteads. EU membership has given France opportunities to participate in established regional cooperation with an institutional framework within which France could most effectively face, and finally take part in, a broader, more globalized world. France today is more open to free international and European trade and currency convertibility because of European integration and despite a strong protectionist tradition and strong remaining economic ties to its former colonies. There is no doubt that France, economically, is better off than it would have been "going it alone." Debatably, France might have been less open and liberal, with deeper sociopolitical cleavages internally, and perhaps more authoritarian in government with greater militarism internationally, if it were not for the EU and its institutions.

While it is recognized that there are broader geopolitical and globalizing influences affecting the country as well as the rest of Europe, there are significant areas that can be highlighted. Two of these major changes have been: the change of French industrial policy from state-supported national champions to the open, freer trade position of today, and an agricultural policy now under the EU's CAP.

There has always been a major role for the French government in industrial policy. However, the growth of the EU and its open markets and free trade has gradually restricted the governmental role more and more. Today there is no role for the "National Champion" program in the post–Single European Act organization. Today, the French market is more open and competitive than it ever has been before. French protectionism has evaporated. This has meant the demise of the Concorde—the fastest transatlantic travel ever seen. The government no longer subsidizes such industrial giants as Renault and Air France.[5]

France faces increasing opposition from environmentally conscious groups throughout Europe for its continued utilization of nuclear power generation. Germany and Sweden are phasing out their plants and there is pressure on the French to do the same. France agreed to the Kyoto Accords and has condemned the United States for its failure to sign. However, it has been slow to implement measures to reach the designated targets for fear of increasing unemployment or otherwise hurting domestic industry, with consequences for the elections of 2006–2007.

Agriculture remains the one area where France has been able to hold fast to its protectionist position. The CAP has very probably contributed to the survival of flourishing agricultural regions in many parts of France. The French countryside and small towns, "la France profonde," might well look drabber and more depopulated, Paris and Marseille slum *banlieues* might count more white French inhabitants, if there were not a protected European market in which French farmers continued—up to eastern enlargement—to be at once the most competitive producers and the first to cash in on the CAP's price guarantees and other aid schemes.

■ How and in What Areas Has France Influenced the EU and EU Policies?

France has influenced EU structures and policies in important ways. It was, for all of its postwar difficulties, the dominant power present at the creation and in the formative period. At this time, the UK was still absent (until 1973), West Germany's emerging voice still fundamentally compromised by its recent Nazi past and the half-way status of its state, and Italy was glad to be in, but without substantial conceptual weight. However, it is with the referendum on the proposed European constitution of May 2005 that France has had the most profound recent effect—changing the nature of the integration enterprise's forward movement.

The Failed Referendum of May 29, 2005
Many might be tempted to be extremely pessimistic about France's future in the EU. Did not France give a clear sign of refusal to deepen integration, as well as to continue with EU enlargement, when it voted against the Constitutional Treaty? The answer is not easy to find, even if one can argue that, in fact, France's reaction did not diverge so dramatically from either its own behavior in the past, or from that of a number of its neighbors. The preceding sections have already shown that France has from the beginning had a tumultuous relationship with European integration, with the majority for more integration having always been rather slim, and French politicians and electorates not hesitating to take dramatic decisions, or votes for that matter, against further progress in European integration. In spite of this type of behavior, France has, most of the time, been able to play a highly constructive and even crucially positive role for European integration.

So why attach so much attention to the vote of May 29, 2005? Is the popular "*Non*" majority not highly volatile? And does the political establishment not solidly and massively support further European integration via the constitution?[6] Interpreting the 29th of May 2005 in this vein should not hide the generally positive attitude that continues to underpin further integration in the EU. As for its neighbors, France's vote is not so different or radical from attitudes elsewhere, for instance in the Netherlands.

This explanation also fits with the thinking that the ideas expressed on May 29 were primarily the eternal French *esprit de barricade* turned against a political establishment considered increasingly incapable and untrustworthy. But interestingly, these sentiments for the "No" vote operated without any particular prejudice against the further progress of integration. The EU prospective constitution became the innocent victim of this antigovernment spirit, but the volatility of this spirit also indicates that if new and more convincing political leadership came to power, this negative spirit might not persist.

An additional argument adding force to this interpretation might be found in the role of socialist dignitary Laurent Fabius, former finance minister and prime minister of France and respected as one of the most serious and capable politicians of the Socialist Party (PS). It was his unexpected turn toward the "*Non*" side in the run-up to ratification, in late summer 2004, that gave a seriousness and credibility to this option within the PS and probably also for centrist-oriented parts of the population, which it would not have had without him. One might thus maintain that it was the appearance of Monsieur Fabius that permitted the "*Non*" side to collect the decisive additional 6 percent that it lacked 13 years earlier in the battle against the Treaty of Maastricht. But in fact, the volatility hypothesis is not convincing, given the following historical trends:

• Too many tendencies have run in the same direction for too long: the trust in politicians and political concepts has continuously declined during both the socialist and the conservative periods of the last two decades.
• Since Maastricht, the "*Non*" has gained ground among those voters who had either voted "*Oui*" or abstained: the middle classes, the employees, the urban dwellers, and the youth (between 18 and 34). Also, the Maastricht-"*Nons*," largely from rural regions and also workers and employees in small enterprises, did not change their vote.
• Worst of all, the main factors explaining the increase of the "*Non*" in the popular vote, unemployment and future uncertainty, have been rising for over twenty years.

None of the political strategies have accomplished anything against these problems, in spite of various gains, such as shortening the working week to 35 hours.

The evolution of the *"Non"* side has had such a significant structural logic that an uncomplicated swing-back on the next vote seems unlikely, unless circumstances change appreciably. Furthermore, in France, the slim advance for the *"Oui,"* for more integration, is now disappearing, and consequently the political support for constructive or daring steps in further European integration is losing ground.

New Actors

The European Constitutional Treaty, the referendum for its ratification, and the consequences of its failure, highlighted, in 2005, the arrival of three new actors in French-European policymaking: French national and European parliamentarians, the French electorate, and the renaissance of an interministerial committee for Europe. The parliamentarians entered negotiations during the European Convention. These actors, first used ad hoc for drafting the European Charter of fundamental rights,[7] were brought together again, in identical manner, in December 2001, to draft a constitutional text during 2002 and 2003. For the first time, this procedure allowed French parliamentarians from the National Assembly and the Senate, and from the European Parliament, to participate directly in the formulation of European treaty law.

The voice of the *electorate* takes on importance when the president submits major decisions about European integration to a referendum: The French electorate became the determining French actor when, after barely accepting the Treaty of Maastricht in 1992, it prevented the ratification of the Constitutional Treaty on May 29, 2005. But the electorate does not have the monopoly on deciding these constitutional questions. Treaty changes that result in changes to the French constitutional setup might also be ratified by a constitutional amendment procedure involving the National Assembly and the Senate in common session.

What specific problems do French voters want to sanction? The *"Non"* vote is an important indicator of some of them.[8] Most important was the fear that acceptance of the constitution would further increase unemployment in France (TNS-Sofres, 46 percent of answers). The second indicator (with 40 percent agreement) showed people's weariness with a political establishment that has proved unable, for 20 years, to correct the problem of unemployment. French voters found the EU much too liberal (34 percent) and hoped to be able to change this orientation by rejecting the nationalist, Euro-skeptic considerations of the right wing of the political spectrum, and by socialist orientations with demands for more protectionism and high social norms for the EU, on the left wing.

The emergence of this new popular actor, the *voter*, who could overturn the project of deepening integration proposed by the political elites, has consequences for the EU's integrationist elites and for their strategies. Certain groups even demanded the abdication of the ruling elites who had defended the Constitutional Treaty. At least the French government wanted to block all decisions in the European "pipeline" and to ask for renegotiation of the treaty. President Chirac refused to resign but conceded after the vote that he and his government would have to heed the results of the referendum. The post–May 29th government of Dominique de Villepin has meanwhile already shown signs of a repositioning. The reinstallation of an interministerial committee for Europe was one indication, together with the explicit aim of increasing "political" control and coordination of European policymaking, of better identifying points of "national interest" in European politics, and of better defending them, as well as French citizens, against the challenges of the modern world.[9]

The French are again demanding more economic policy coordination between the European Central Bank and the Eurogroup. French discourse on the CAP has become more affirmative without yet showing clear policy aims. As for industry, the government is demanding more French "economic patriotism" with more self-assured support and greater defense of French enterprises in international competition. Here again, the coming months should show how much to expect from this change in discourse. French opposition against the "Bolkestein" directive draft is considered to have been successful for the moment, the "country-of-origin" principle having been eliminated from the text that the Commission has transmitted to the European Parliament, and which the latter accepted with certain modifications on February 16, 2006. The second reading procedure of the Commission's amended proposal of April 4, 2006 (COM/2006/160/final), will probably confirm this line. Again, for the social agenda, the government promises to pass tougher laws on immigration, with stricter application of the "French nationals first" for jobs, more rapid expulsion for illegals, and the introduction of immigration quotas for certain qualifications.[10] On the Turkish candidacy to the EU, France has explicitly toughened the conditions, seizing on the recent Turkish refusal to recognize the Republic of Cyprus.[11] Finally, has the government given any indication of changes to the constitutional text it wants to introduce? Thus far, nothing of the kind has developed.

It would appear that changes in policies, or at least in their appearance, is the first concern of the new government.

The opposition leaders in the Socialist Party, the majority of whose members rejected the constitution, were not able to replace the pro-constitution leaders in the National Congress of Novermber 2005. The party has now asked for a new constitutional draft; the EU is to better protect European industry, and market liberalization is to be slowed.[12]

Can we expect the Union's competencies and policies to change, and if so, will these changes satisfy the *"Non"* voters in France, and will they encourage the EU to conduct more effective economic and social policies in order to reduce the pressure of commercial competition on France, and increase employment and social welfare? There is nothing that would permit expectations of that kind. The increasing heterogeneity of a Union enlarging to include central and eastern-southeastern Europe and eventually Turkey decreases opportunities for cooperation. This does not bode well for development of a consensual future growth strategy.

■ How Does France Implement and Comply with EU Policies?

French Coordination of EU Legislation and Decisionmaking into National Laws

How does France integrate European policy into its national laws? French decisionmaking on European politics is divided into different layers. Schematizing somewhat for the sake of simplicity, they can be presented as follows:

- On the one hand there is the day-to-day participation in the established polities of the Union, of legislating, of implementation. In terms of volume of activity this level is the dominant one.
- On the other hand, there is the layer of "strategic" decisions: giving new directions to the integration process, creating new common policies, changing institutions or procedures.
- And in a more general way there are the grand domains of executive action, especially in foreign and security policy and in defense.

All three kinds of policy issues come together in the European Councils, or in the bilateral Franco-German summit meetings.

Day-to-Day Decisionmaking and Implementation of EU Policies in France

French participation in most established EU policymaking is no longer considered to be "foreign policy." It is domestic politics and its coordination and decisionmaking competency is largely in the hands of the government and organized by the prime minister's office. However, the French president often directs the government in these areas. The role of the French parliament (Assemblée Nationale and Sénat) is limited to transmitting to the government its opinions and preferences concerning ongoing European legislation projects. Legally, the government is in no way bound to follow such parliamentary positions. But depending on the majority with which they are voted and on the parties that support them, they may have a certain political weight in influencing the government line.[13] These two government institutions coordinate the French positions with executive and legislative acts of the European institutions. Most acts passed fall into the domain of the Internal Market and its many related policies. These policies follow a standard procedure within which the European Commission has a monopoly on translating the aspirations of the member states and the treaty stipulations into initiatives and then presenting them to the Council, engaging national administrations and experts in countless committee sessions and exchanges of papers, a process wherein France tries hard to introduce its own preferences, and then sending out proposals for national governmental comment within a limited time.

Frequently, the permanent representatives negotiate and vote on issues of minor-to-medium importance in the Committee of Permanent Representatives (COREPER) or at least decide the less contentious parts of such issues before handing the rest over to their ministers in the respective councils. The French permanent representative, as well as his counterparts from other member states, is often the last member in the decisionmaking chain at the national level of European coordination. On the other hand, at the EU level he is part of a well-regulated European decisionmaking apparatus into which national decisions feed. As for the French government, more often than not the proposals from the Commission will concern the competencies of more than one ministry, necessitating interministerial coordination from the French government to reach a timely, coherent, and consensual reaction.

France is well equipped for this task.[14] First, it has a special agency for this coordination/implementation, the SGAE (Secrétariat Général aux Affaires Européennes). Second, since July 2005 a new interministerial committee for Europe sits once a month, at ministerial level, to assure "political" coordination, as compared to the "administrative" cooperation carried out by the Secrétariat Général du Comité Interministeriel (SGCI).[15] The SGAE assembles two hundred functionaries from all concerned ministries. It receives all proposals from the Commission in Brussels, and it hands them on to the competent ministries. It organizes the appropriate meetings between them, more than 1,700 per year, and takes care to distill their decisions in due time to be delivered to the permanent representative in Brussels, to the ministers defending French positions in the Council, and to MEPs favorable to French positions in the European Parliament.

Second, the general secretary serves as principal European policy adviser to the prime minister, to whose office the SGAE is directly attached. By virtue of this centralization, it will not just coordinate; it will also integrate decisions within a national policy line for the EU. In cases where the SGAE fails because of interministerial conflict, the PM's cabinet[16] will take over the case and attempt to arbitrate. In difficult cases the PM himself will arbitrate. On issues concerning the European Foreign and Security Policy, or EU institutional change, the Quai d'Orsay prepares the policies.

In France, the president of the Republic nominates and deposes the prime minister. Consequently, the prime minister's autonomy in European policymaking in France is limited despite formal competency. It is only during periods of cohabitation (a president and prime minister of different political parties), that the PM can fully exploit the government's constitutional competencies in European politics, even if he/she opposes the political orientations of the president.[17]

Strategic Decisions

The French president also has the decisive voice in making strategic and grand executive policies. Thus it is not the SGAE process alone that leads to the decision stage. The president and his office usually lead political planning and negotiation activities. However, sometimes the Elysée (the presidential staff) enters into day-to-day negotiations with the Matignon (the PM's office), and they decide together on the issue, especially during times when the French hold the Council presidency. In a Union in which the role of the European Council continues to become more important, the president's role grows and is bound to grow further.

Intergovernmental conferences for treaty changes will involve the president in strategic decisions, and in the question of whether the interests of France are duly accounted for by the negotiations. The government will negotiate and make its choices clear in the different policy areas of its responsibility.

Negotiating Brussels's proposals, the Conseil d'Etat (Supreme Court) plays an important role as principal legal counsel to the French government, and its help determines the compatibility of EU law proposals with internal French legislation.[18]

Normal European Union legislation is negotiated and adopted in the European institutions. Once approved in this manner, EU law takes precedence over national law. The French constitutional court (Conseil Constitutionnel) or the Conseil d'Etat decides contentious issues between the national and supranational institutions. How does France transpose and implement EU laws and decisions? Since regulations and decisions are directly applicable under the EU Treaty, and transposition is not required, and since recommendations and opinions are not binding, the most interesting questions about compliance arise around EU directives.

The French Implementation Process

The EU is an entity created and preserved by the unity of its laws and procedures, and France complies in the same principal manner as other member states. There are, however, some important differences in how France deals with EU directives,[19] an important variant of EU legislation, which are binding as to results in certain policy fields and very often with respect to policy minimums. Deadlines are fixed for the directives' transposition and member states must respect the legal quality of the norms intended by the directives. But the actual implementation of the procedures and the attainment of results are left to national institutions and processes.

Since 1986, the (SGCI and now the) SGAE and the government's general secretariat (SGG) have become responsible for transposition of EU laws into national policy in France. This process now looks like a mirror image of the coordination procedures described earlier.[20] From the moment of learning about the draft directive, the lead ministry for a given new norm begins to develop a legal-implications study to prepare national legislative steps to be taken once the directive is actually adopted. The Conseil d'Etat will again be consulted and the Assemblée Nationale given a chance to express its opinion, before the instrument of transposition can be published in the official journal and notification sent to the EU Commission.

Compliance control of an administrative and judicial kind takes place at both the European and national levels. National institutions will either react to national stimuli, for instance to complaints or lawsuits coming from civil society or administrations, or they will react to cues from EU institutions, especially the Commission, the "guardian of the treaties." If the latter perceives a case of noncompliance, it will send informal or formal notices, according to the procedure, or file a lawsuit under the Treaty on the European Community (TEC) Article 226. The second important actor is the European Court of Justice, which can act indirectly via national courts by using the preliminary ruling procedure of TEC Article 234, or it can decide directly against cases of noncompliance, again under TEC Article 226.

Judicial level. Measured by the number of these procedures at the administrative level, France's record of compliance is not first-rate. The ECJ follows the noncompliance procedure of TEC Article 226, which offers the option "formal notice" as a preliminary low-level conflict settlement leading to complaint withdrawal by the Commission.[21] France is not only the member state accumulating the largest number of such formal notices (far ahead of the UK, or even of Federal Germany), but also the second-worst in persisting in controversies.[22] It provokes some of the highest numbers of noncompliance suits filed against any member state (the second-highest in 2004; only Italy was worse and Spain and even Federal Germany did better). This record does not, however, mean a general unwillingness or inability to comply with the treaties, but it certainly signifies an exaggerated stubbornness by the French to defend their own treaty interpretations. On the other hand, it appears that French interest groups react in more activist and violent ways than elsewhere in the EU when they consider their specific interests threatened. French politicians and administrations appear to have fewer inhibitions in slowing down implementation.[23] At the judicial level, however, the highest French courts—the Conseil d'Etat for administrative, and the Cour de Cassation for civil and criminal law—are both on record for their consistent efforts to impose the primacy of EU law over French law. As for the Conseil d'Etat, its instruments are "to annul (or interpret)" nonconforming French rules "and award compensation." It stops short of giving itself "direct effect" to the articles of the directive concerned. "Bringing national law into conformity with EU law is a matter for the administrative authorities."[24] The Cour de Cassation, which frequently decides cases between individuals, considers itself bound by the ECJ position, according to which the provisions of a directive cannot by themselves "create obligations as between individuals."[25] As a rule, it will apply French law, even where France is already in default for not having adapted it to EU law in due time.[26] But for the rest, "the Cour de Cassation has constantly reaffirmed the principle of the primacy of EU law over national law, even with retrospective effect."[27] This holds true not only for the letter but also for the general principles of EU law, to be respected in implementing EU directives. The Cour de Cassation has also affirmed the direct applicability of EU regulations, ruling that they displace earlier national regulations "without any need to confirm this by means of a text in national law."[28] Finally the Cour de Cassation has consistently favored wide and unhindered utilization of the preliminary ruling procedure, to be made by French courts.[29]

European Environment Policy and France[30]

French implementation of European law can be demonstrated by looking at the manner in which a crucially important directive of European environment policy was transferred and applied. It concerns the framework directive on Environmental Impact Assessment (EIA), 85/337/CEE, amended by the framework directive 97/11/CE. It imposes on member states European emission norms for water, air, noise, landscape, and natural habitats, as a precondition for authorizing the construction or modification of certain kinds of technical installations.

France has been one of the most efficacious member states in applying this directive as is illustrated in a provisional comparison with other member states. The Commission established procedures to handle complaints against French practice brought to its attention, and to apply the noncompliance procedure of Article 226. Here, France has a better record than the average member state and much better than the "worst pupils," Spain and Ireland. There is also a clear willingness of French administrators and lawmakers to stay close to future European policy orientations in this field.

But, concerning the procedures of French implementation of environmental policy, certain difficulties remain for French implementation. Two sensitive points concern the "complex" character of EU assessment, and the participation of the public.

As to the complexity of the assessment, the directive, especially in Article 3, explicitly demands it. A new dedicated institution was to take charge of this task. But France organizes its EIA as it did before the new directives, that is, via its prefects (department administrators) who take care of "*les installations classes*" on behalf of the Ministry of Industry. It is quite evident that France is not yet able to assure "complexity" partly due to this institutional deficiency and partly because it does not have enough competent staff in the field. One of the results has been that France was extremely slow in requiring its prefectures (departmental administrations) to formulate abstract standards as to the "scope" of the EIA, which they would carry through and which applicant investors would have to anticipate. But here France is no exception. Many member states have the same kind of problem and one might ask whether the EU is being overly ambitious in this particular area.

Concerning the public's participation, the new EU directive demands and envisages an improvement over what was already practiced in France. French administrations previously informed the public and gave citizens the chance to make their opinions known, before administrators authorized investors. Normally, administrations only did the necessary minimum to satisfy French law, and they did it as late as possible in the authorization procedure so as to confront and discourage any opposition with a fait accompli. The new directive intends to involve the public at an early stage, before the start of eventual EIAs, but it does not make this a legal obligation for member states. Thus, France does not feel obligated to change its current practices even though they are contrary to the intentions of the directive. These points can also be seen in a case study of the reduction of greenhouse gases.

The reduction of greenhouse gases: A case study. As for reducing the emission of greenhouse gases, French implementation has been ambivalent. This policy is interesting to examine because it combines three commitments for the same topic: one commitment concerns the French state (and the other member states) vis-à-vis the United Nations; another concerns the French state vis-à-vis the European Union; and the third commitment considers the European Union vis-à-vis its international partners and the United Nations.[31] In the name of its member states, the EU signed the December 1997 Kyoto Protocol, stipulating that each member state, from 2008 to 2012, reduce greenhouse gases by 8 percent below the 1990 level, with 2010 as a target date. The member states[32] agreed to different national contributions for this global objective, and France was allowed to retain its 1990 emissions level during the allotted time span (whereas Germany had to accept a reduction of 21 percent).

Until spring 2004, the EU Commission's official position was that the required reduction of greenhouse-gas emissions should be achieved throughout the entire EU. The French government, in its turn, maintained its willingness to comply with its commitments. The most important additional European instrument introduced that year was a system of trading greenhouse-gas emission permits between EU member states.[33] Trading permits lowered the cost of additional emissions' reductions for the member states. In France, transpositions of these EU objectives into national legislation took place in 2004, with the expectation of a fully operational system by January 2005.

France claimed a crucial part in the initiative for that internationally progressive engagement.[34] Paris had coorganized the first big international conference on climate change at The Hague in 1989, and then contributed a number of programmatic documents to the EU in 1993, where it pledged to reduce its greenhouse-gas emissions to the 1990 level, and to the new levels set by the UN Framework Convention on Climate Change, adopted in 1992 in Rio de Janiero,[35] and reaffirmed in 1995 and in 1997. These pledges were further sharpened in France's contributions to the EU's position at the UN climate conference of Kyoto in December 1997.

The commitments resulting from this conference, for both the EU and its member states, constitute the legal framework that now guides the French government. To implement them at the national level, France drafted a more ambitious national program in January 2000 called the "Fight Against Climatic Change" or PNLCC.[36] The next government followed this up with a strong engagement of its own,[37] intending to replace and strengthen that national program by a so-called Plan Climat 2003. It organized a big national debate on energy, a *"livre blanc sur les energies"* and a *"loi d'orientation sur l'énergie,"* in November 2003. Nominal compliance with the EU's directives, which make up the European Climate Change Program (ECCP), appears exemplary. Nevertheless, French performance in this field appears marked by an increasing contradiction between its formal European commitments and its concrete efforts.

In fact, of the 16 fields affected by the ECCP, France had by 2005 already incorporated 10 of them into national policies, and only a certain number had to be reinforced. Four were EU-compatible without changes. Other EU member states (the EU-15), on average, were only covering eight fields and only 2.5 that were EU-compatible.[38] This confirms the original assessment that France had an especially early and above-average orientation on the issue of greenhouse-gas emissions, in the direction later taken by the EU, and remains in full legal compliance.

In the 1990s, French results were still excellent. Its implementation record, along with five other member states out of the 15, was fully respected.[39] But by the beginning of the next decade, its record had become highly doubtful. The 2005 report of the European Environmental Agency concedes an unconditional "on track" for 2010 only to the UK, Sweden, and Luxembourg. Even though it also credits France with being able to comply with its Kyoto obligations, this is only on the assumption of currently planned additional policies and measures being implemented—the same as for Germany and Greece.[40] All other member states are considered to be even further away from their 2010 target. But in comparing France within this group of three, a look at the EEA's projections shows Germany only 1.2 percent from target in 2010[41] in applying existing policy, whereas France still has to make good on a prospective shortfall of 9 percent, achievable only on condition of successful implementation of announced new measures.

A more detailed examination would seem to confirm this general impression. A number of examples can show that the further implementation of the greenhouse-gas policy, and of laws to comply with the EU's objectives, were increasingly behind, and less forward-looking and ambitious.[42] One good example is the fate of the "Plan Climat 2003," changed to "Plan Climat 2004." This plan could only be adopted in July 2004, eight months later than intended. Compared to the PNLCC, it proposes fewer constraining rules and relies more on voluntary commitments by the business sector and other important actors. Just three examples of the lowering of requirements include:

- The general taxation of greenhouse-gas emissions disappeared.
- Similarly, the national allocation plan for emission allowances was adopted after a delay, in October 2004, only to be rejected by the European Commission because it preserved too many national margins of maneuver. The final version, in a February 2005 *décret*, only came a few months before the end of the allocation process in June.
- For the first period of the EU emissions trading scheme (2005–2007), the total number of allowances, agreed by the European Commission for its now 25 member states, is as a yearly average 3.5 percent above the emissions of the trading sector in 2003. France overshoots this benchmark by 12.2 percent, the highest margin among the 15 member states before 2004, giving considerable margins of emission growth, under this regime, to a number of French industries.[43]

Specific material conditions made progress relatively easy for France in the first decade, conditions that remain pertinent but are not likely to play the same role in the future. The most important of them is the large part of nuclear and of hydraulic energy in electricity generation, which permitted this sector to generate much fewer emissions in France than is the case for its neighbors: only around 5 percent of total French CO_2 emissions.[44] By comparison, 26 percent of these emissions are generated by road transport, 25 percent by heating of residential and tertiary buildings, and finally 22 percent by manufacturing industry.[45] All in all, the growth of French energy production in the last decade could thus take place with less generation of emissions than in neighboring countries. But further energy consumption, growth in road transport and (nonindustrial) buildings, and the ensuing growth in emissions, will simply be too large to be compensated for in this way. Already in the 1990s those two sectors were the principal sources of further increasing CO_2 emissions (plus 19.3 and 9.6 percent, compared to an overall average reduction in all other sectors, including industry and energy transformation, of 7 percent). If France does not succeed in reducing emissions in the EU, it will not succeed in respecting its Kyoto obligations.

These sectors should therefore be the priority for French greenhouse-gas control policies. Changing the situation in these fields would require either substantial negative or positive incentives for users, owners, and construction companies for taxing of fossil-fuel consumption in these fields, or subsidizing the development and utilization of fossil-fuel economizing or replacement technologies. Or it would require simple constraint by law, forbidding the utilization or construction of motor vehicles and buildings that did not comply with certain new standards and norms on isolation and fuel efficiency. European regulations are supposed to motivate relevant actors in member states in these directions, but because they are transposed into French law in a very differentiated manner, their effective implementation in the French context is questionable.

The current strategy for automobiles is clearly to preserve the car industry and the role of the car in individual transport, but to reduce their emission potential by aiding the production of bio-gasoline, to be produced by French agriculture, which could in this manner also compensate farmers for the expected further reduction of public aids for classic agricultural production. France has therefore recently transposed the European directive on bio-fuels in a very positive manner.[46]

The European directives on buildings and construction are also, by and large, transposed in satisfactory ways. Even so, environmental interest groups deplore the insufficiency of these measures, and the transposition "à minima," as they say. In building construction, there is insufficient compliance by homeowners with the strict official rules for heat isolation. Environmentalists want higher fiscal incentives set for the installation of heat-conserving equipment in buildings. Here the new government's 2005 plan brings no improvements.

These examples show that, indeed, the government cannot be accused of either formal or positive nonrespect for European regulations. But environmental groups fear a substantial nonrespect that may well only become manifest in 2010, when the quantitative objectives of emissions reduction set for France may not be reached, due to the specific manner in which France has transposed the EU rules. In fact, the comparative data provided by the European Environment Agency appear to point toward the same possibility.

■ Trends and Future Prospects

The Contradiction Between the Objectives and the Stakes

France is today paying a price for its contradictory stance in European integration. It persisted too long in limiting EU competencies, and full application of EU integration, to certain aspects of economic, financial, and monetary policy. The end results can be seen in the slow movement toward further integration, and especially in the defeat of the EU constitution. France is especially responsible for this state of affairs, having been—together with the UK—the most reticent member state for "Europeanization" of core sovereignty competencies, and for keeping the autonomous legitimacy-base of the EU as narrow as possible. It accepted the contradictions inherent in this posture, and now is suffering the consequences.

EU competencies have been extended beyond this narrow field by the pressures of the organization. France has been moving through Maastricht and implemented the single currency (euro). France has implemented directives and is not outstandingly delinquent. However, France continues to insist on the rights of national sovereignty and is reluctant to yield further in this area. What happened in May 2005 can and will happen again.

The most problematic area of upcoming contention is the security area, where both national and international security issues are being discussed at various levels in the EU. The most tangible of these contradictions was and is the inadequacy of French concessions made on behalf of "Europe puissance," Europe as a powerful actor (including military power) on the world stage, able to speak eye-to-eye with its US partner. Charles de Gaulle and the Fouchet plans of the 1960s previously promoted this same objective. Gaullist-, centrist-, and socialist-dominated governments have long demanded a stronger orientation of integration toward "Europe puissance." But they have never wanted—in this field—to concede important transfers of sovereignty and the strong federal policymaking structure to the EU, which a dependable and effective European foreign, security, and defense policy would necessitate. Nor have they been willing to trust a defense guarantee against foreign aggression to member states that would not be as credible as the defense assurances given under NATO. France has always insisted on preserving its liberty of action over the engagement of its armed forces and refused their integration in constraining European structures of deployment or armament. No wonder then that none of the member states would exchange a proven alliance in NATO, and the remaining autonomy of disposition over its national defense force, for a "Europe puissance" of highly uncertain dependability and effectiveness.

The Constitutional Treaty was the first EU document in which a mutual defense assurance for member states was specified. The EU Defense Agency holds out the perspective of more cost-efficient armaments development and procurement, and a more cost-efficient and rational distribution of roles in a European defense system. The institutions for deciding and directing European defense action have existed since the treaty amendments of Amsterdam and Nice—but have not yet been developed.

Can these achievements be preserved and further developed even without a European constitution? In part the answer is positive: the Defense Agency already exists and is becoming operational. A kind of foreign minister with a foreign service is evolving out of the Special Representative of the EU. The EU governments could decide to advance further in that direction, and France could play a leading role in such an initiative. In the next international crisis such an investment might pay off. The same kind of advance might be possible in police cooperation. The recent examples of rioting throughout France, and of the "outing" of racial tensions, highlight France's continuing issues in these areas. In judicial cooperation, France wants to proceed further toward a European prosecutor, but because judicial systems vary widely in the member states, advances in this field might be very difficult indeed.

The decisive steps ahead would, nevertheless, have to come at a higher level of engagement. The French government and political forces would have to declare themselves willing to enter into more binding security arrangements with their EU partners than they have hitherto been willing to do. Any advance in this direction, even with only a subset of partner countries, might be an important stepping stone to get out of the conceptual and political morass of the post-*"Non"* period, and the imbalance of the French European vision.

France seems destined to continue its contradictory stance toward further European integration, especially when elections are looming. However, when France needs to come to the forefront, such as to counter potential German domination of an area, France yields and complies. But in each and every instance, French sovereignty is proclaimed and will continue to be a major factor in both promoting and preventing further European integration.

■ Notes

The author is very grateful to Eleanor Zeff and Ellen Pirro for the substantial editorial assistance that they provided in preparing this chapter for publication.
    1. A relatively extreme formulation of this argument is proposed by Eilstrup-Santiovanni and Verdier, "European Integration as a Solution to War."
    2. See also Müller-Brandeck-Bocquet, *Frankreichs Europapolitik,* for an argument in that sense.
    3. See Bocquet, *La France et l'Allemagne;* Deubner, *The Future of the Franco-German Relationship*; Deubner, "Food for Thought in 'Leftovers.'"
    4. Zeff, "The Budget and the Spending Policies," p. 180.
    5. Zeff and Pirro, *The European Union and the Member States,* 1st ed.
    6. Has not a massive majority of French parliament and Senate voted for the *"Oui"* when the referendum was decided on, together with the government, and the leaderships of the largest political parties of the country?
    7. The EU Charter of Fundamental Rights, http://europa.eu.int/comm/justice_home/unit/charte/index_en.html.
    8. The following information is mainly drawn from the public opinion poll, by TNS-Sofres and Unilog, for *Le Monde*, RTL, and TF1, carried out by telephone, with a representative sample of the population, published in *Le Monde*, no. 18770, May 31, 2005.
    9. Available at: http://premier-ministre.gouv.fr/acteurs/interventions_premier_minister_9/dans_les_medias_497/interview_premier_minister_sur_53718.html, with the text of a radio interview of the prime minister on August 2, 2005.
    10. Villepin in France 2 Television on June 9, 2005: available at http://premier-ministre.gouv.fr/ acteurs/ interventions_premier_minister_9/dans_les_medias_497/entretien_dominique_villepin_journal_53234.html.
    11. Cf. http://premier-ministre.gouv.fr/acteurs/interventions_premier_ministre_9/dans_les_medias_497/interview_premier_ministre_sur_53718.html with the text of a radio interview of the prime minister on August 2, 2005.
    12. See the concluding statement of the National Congress, available at http://congres2005.parti-socialiste.fr/article.php3?id_article=407). All this is very similar to the government's official line.

13. The original name was "Secrétariat général du comité interministeriel pour les questions de coopération économique européenne." One of the first measures of the new Villepin government was to reinstate this old interministerial committee, of which only the general secretariat had survived, and to change the name of the first into interministerial committee for Europe and that of the latter as indicated above (see the announcements made by the new prime minister on July 20, 2005, after the new interministerial committee's first session; available at http://premier-ministre.gouv.fr/acteurs/interventions_premier_minister_9/discours_498/Europe_premier_minister_se_53614.html).

14. Most of the following information comes out of the excellent report of the Commissariat général du Plan, *Organiser la politique européenne et internationale de la France*, on organizing French European policymaking. The authors, Lanxade and Tenzer, have conducted interviews of their own on this question, in the French administration, in 2002–2003.

15. See Note 13 above.

16. The group of counselors working directly with the PM, not to be confounded with the Council of Ministers.

17. Today, the system is still considered efficacious, but in France and elsewhere, informed people see a number of weaknesses, which ought to be overcome. Especially important in this view: the need for a more clearly established strategic French vision for the future European Union, and for its main axes. And a more clearly established leading player at government level. This could give French representatives a frame of reference within which they could negotiate more flexibly than today. The upcoming reforms of the Union's political system promise to strengthen its intergovernmental pillar, for instance at the level of the European Council, and in foreign and security policy—a Union of the states and of the peoples, as Jacques Delors said. If the French "state" wants fully to play its part, then these reforms of its coordination appear certainly necessary.

18. Sauron, *L'administration française et l'Union européenne*, p. 110.

19. TEC Article 249.

20. Sauron, *L'administration française et l'Union européenne,* p. 133: "In France, each ministry was responsible for transposition of legislation under its competency until the adoption of the Single Market White Paper. Inter-ministerial in-fighting rendered this method increasingly too cumbersome."

21. The coordination is again in the hands of the SGCI (with the PM's cabinet prepared to intervene).

22. Sauron, *L'administration française et l'Union européenne,* for 1997–1998 data.

23. The cases of noncompliance would merit a sifting as to their objects.

24. Sauron, *L'administration française et l'Union européenne*, p. 152.

25. Ibid., p. 153.

26. But Sauron, *L'administration française et l'Union européenne*, p. 155, also notes the acknowledgment of the Cour de Cassation "that directives can sometimes have direct effect" (insofar as the case does not concern litigation between individuals).

27. Ibid., p. 154.

28. Ibid.

29. Ibid., p. 155.

30. The following information is based on an internal study by the author

of spring 2004, for the Commissariat Général du Plan, based on interviews in the administration and on evaluation of documents. One of the most interesting of these last is the "Rapport de la Commission 2002."

31. "In deciding to fulfil their commitments jointly in accordance with article 4 of the Kyoto Protocol, the Community and the member states are *jointly responsible*, under paragraph 6 of that article and in accordance with article 24(2) of the Protocol, for the fulfilment by the Community of its quantified emission reduction commitment under Article 3(1) of the Protocol. Consequently, and in accordance with Article 10 of the Treaty establishing the European Community, member states individually and collectively have the obligation to take all appropriate measures, whether general or particular, to ensure fulfilment of the obligations resulting from action taken by the institutions of the Community, including the Community's quantified emission reduction commitment under the Protocol, to facilitate the achievement of this commitment and to abstain from any measure that could jeopardise the attainment of this commitment. Member states shall endeavour to take the necessary steps with a view to depositing their instruments of ratification or approval simultaneously with those of the European Community and the other member states and as far as possible not later than 1 June 2002." See Council Decision of April 25, 2002, concerning the approval, on behalf of the European Community, of the Kyoto Protocol to the United Nations Framework Convention on Climate Change and the joint fulfilment of commitments hereunder (2002/358/CE), OJ L 130, 15.5.2002.

32. Doc. 9702/98 of June 19, 1998, of the Council of the European Union reflecting the outcome of proceedings of the Environment Council of June 16–17, 1998, Annex I.

33. See directive 2003/87/CE. At the end of 2003, a new directive was proposed as to the energy efficiency in end-user and in energy services ("relative à l'efficacité énergétique dans les utilisations finales et aux services énergétiques").

34. See the foreword by Prime Minister Lionel Jospin, to the National Program of the Fight Against Climate Change (Programme national de lutte contre le changement climatique PNLCC) of 2000.

35. Signed by 176 states, among them all European states, and the European Community.

36. Programme National de Lutte contre le Changement Climatique (PNLCC), January 17, 2000; available at http://www.effet-de-serre.gouv.fr/fr/actions/PNLCC.pdf.

37. http://www.effet-de-serre.gouv.fr/fr/actualite/Discours.doc.

38. Author's calculation based on the list given in European Environmental Agency, "Greenhouse Gas Emissions Trends," p. 32.

39. For the newest data, see European Environmental Agency, "Greenhouse Gas Emissions Trends"; for the progress achieved in the 1990s, see also the EEA 2003 report.

40. European Environmental Agency, "Greenhouse Gas Emissions Trends," p. 7.

41. Ibid., Figure 4.3, p. 18.

42. See the overview given in France RAC, "Etat d'avancement du Plan Climat: Analyse du Réseau Action Climat," Paris, November 2005: infos@rac-f.org/http://www.rac-f.org.

43. European Environmental Agency, "Greenhouse Gas Emissions Trends," p. 29; France RAC, "Etat d'avancement du Plan Climat," p. 10.

44. Emissions per unit of the bip in 2000: 0.26 France, 0.38 EU average, 0.44 Germany (tons of CO_2 per dollar of bip PIB in buying power equivalents, based on 1995 prices). *Source:* Agence internationale de l'énergie, "Dealing with Climate Change," 2002.

45. In 2003, according to Serge Poignant, dép., "Energies renouvelables: changeons d'échelle pour lutter contre le changement climatique, rapport d'information no. 1153," Commission des affaires économiques. He cites data of Le CITEPA (Centre interprofessionnel technique d'études de la pollution atmosphérique) from 2001.

46. France RAC, "Etat d'avancement du Plan Climat," p. 7.

5

Italy: Back to the Future or Steps Toward Normality?

Marco Giuliani and Simona Piattoni

ITALY IS ONE OF the six founding members of the European Communities. To be more precise, it is one of the three "big" nations that, on the ruins of World War II, promoted the most interesting case of regional economic and political integration of modern times. This basic fact, for good and for worse, should always be kept in mind when trying to analyze the way in which Italy participates in EU politics.

More than half a century has already passed since this unique enterprise started—a time frame that, especially if one bears in mind the organizational and policy "stagnancy" of its first three decades, favored the consolidation of behaviors, practices, and styles of the Italian strategies toward the EU. Tradition, if not "path-dependency," should be carefully considered, especially in explaining some of the failures experienced by the Italian political system in reforming its European policy. After all, 50 years of "selfless" contribution to the progress of European integration cannot be easily dismissed and, quantitatively, represent a time period that is at least three times the extent of the democratic experience of many newcomers of the enlarged Union.

Nonetheless, the common stereotype for explaining the Italian participation in the EU is an odd mix of ritualistic elements, lack of initiative, Euro-enthusiasm, and extremely problematic compliance problems. At this point, the real "unidentified political object" in the EU is not the Union in itself, but Italy: often treated as an outlier in qualitative studies and in need of ad hoc dummy variables in quantitative ones. As for the stereotype, there are certainly relevant elements of truth, and we will briefly refer to or analyze them throughout this chapter. At the same time, stereotypes are simplifying mental grids that reinterpret new or discordant events in the light of long-established interpretative frameworks. Our work will try to answer the standard questions of this book, following the thin line that runs between refocusing consolidated images and identifying potential new dynamics.

■ How and in What Areas Does the EU Influence Italian Politics and Policies?

The term *vincolo esterno*—external constraint—has been specifically introduced by Dyson and Featherstone[1] in order to account for the mechanism through which the EU has affected the Italian political system during the last decade. The concept is certainly not new, having to do with the more general dynamics of two-level games,[2] but has the undeniable advantage of underlying the growing importance played by the Union in domestic policymaking.

In the turmoil of the political "transition" that has characterized Italy during the 1990s—institutional and electoral reforms, complete restructuring of the format and dynamics of the party system, high turnout of the political class, scandals involving prominent economic and political individuals, temporary technical executives governing crucial passages (e.g., the beginning of the path toward financial adjustments under Ciampi, and the opening of the 1996 presidency of the EU under Dini)—the external constraint had the double function of empowering a modernizing elite, and of supplying a public justification for the economic and structural reforms adopted.[3]

In the beginning, expectations were that the ideas channeled through this newly empowered epistemic community and the additional strength of the executive vis-à-vis the parliament could have sufficient leverage for introducing a new course between Italy and the EU. More than 10 years later, with a growingly Euro-skeptic citizenry and recurrent macroeconomic problems, those expectations appear, if not misleading, at least exceedingly confident.

Joining the European Monetary Union (EMU)—which entailed both the Italian contribution to its definition and the fulfillment of the requirements of the euro zone with the first group of participants—has been welcomed as a major success in this direction.[4] The same mechanism could have worked, through spillovers and emulation, in other policy areas in need for reform, particularly in high-spending sectors such as the welfare state, contributing to the hope that Italy could be "rescued" (from itself) by means of a proactive use of external constraints and benchmarks.[5]

Yet, despite some hard-to-deny progress, the overall picture of Italy's Europeanization is still mixed.[6] The optimistic prospect that Italy, in the new millennium, could be "bound to succeed"[7] immediately ran against the freedom (and capacity) of the domestic political system to harm itself by slowing down, limiting if not reversing the direction of the already ongoing progress.[8]

The main risk is some sort of "back-to-the-future" syndrome, with Italy playing a more traditional, acquiescent role with respect to EU policies, while its loyal commitment to the direction and pace of integration may be put into question. This "fatal attraction" toward some kind of retrenchment[9] has, among its natural causes, well-consolidated traditions. In the imprinting phases of the Communities, Italy often lacked the power and the internal cohesion for taking the lead in the integration process, besides being bound by its strong Atlantic commitment and Mediterranean interests in foreign policy.[10] While the French-German axis traditionally represented the "engine" as well as the "wheel" of the newly established "machine," and subsequently the United Kingdom somehow assumed the function of the "brakes," Italy often was (perceived and required as) the "fixer." This meant that, at least until the 1980s, Italian representatives had to play the role of loyal brokers between other delegations, not defending any particular domestic winset[11] but smoothing the process in order to prevent it from stopping.[12] This also meant that the role of "policy entrepreneurs" was usually delegated to others, as is testified by the low level of consciousness and involvement in EU affairs shown by Italian high civil servants at the eve of the 1990s, and considering how the impact itself of EU policies was systematically underestimated by the members of the Italian parliament.[13]

In its turn, particularly after the "conversion" of the Italian Communist Party in favor of the European project, a bipartisan *entente* prevented any serious questioning of the role of Europe in domestic policy. With the exception of the debates surrounding the Common Agricultural Policy, at least until the launch of the Internal Market, the intellectual and political debate around the "costs and benefits" of European integration in Italy lay well below the standards of other member states.[14]

When it came to the implementation of the Internal Market project, and then to the introduction of the euro, most policy-takers—lay people as well as interest groups—were still unprepared for the new competitive environment created by Italy's participation in EU affairs. European integration was still "a good thing," as testified by the Eurobarometer surveys, and by the consultative referendum held (only) in Italy together with the third election of the European Parliament precisely regarding its power. In sum, "permissive consensus" in Italy loomed larger and longer than anywhere else in the Community.

The internal transition to the so-called Italian second Republic inserted an element of discontinuity in this portrait, forcing domestic policymakers to recognize that even at the EU level, the basic principle of participation had changed. "The corner had been turned," to use Desmond Dinan's expression, and the rules of the game were pragmatically different.

In the second half of the 1990s, the permissive consensus guaranteed by the confidence of Italians in the European Union permitted some virtuous cycle of reform, blaming onto the "external constraint" the origin of costly (but necessary) "subtractive" policies. In terms of public attitudes, this caused a relative erosion of the trust toward the Union, especially when some components of the new center-right government began to be more explicitly Euro-skeptical.[15]

A "back-to-the-future" scenario appears to us extremely risky. First, playing the role of brokers in an enlarged Union has become far more difficult. Second, this attitude may be exceedingly costly in the new political environment: the challenges of the Single Market, the Monetary Union, and the Lisbon Process require a different political approach. Third, part of the loyalty toward the EU project secured by Italy and Italians throughout the years has been eroded in the last decade by an excess of blame-avoidance and shame-attribution strategies. For these reasons, a simple reversal to already trodden paths and rehearsed roles is impossible.

■ How and in What Ways Does Italy Influence the EU and Its Policies?

In the past, Italy managed to influence EU politics and policies by playing the role of "broker" or "fixer of the game."[16] In reality, Italian representatives, though probably in a disorganized way, did not restrain from manifesting their "voice" in the Council of the European Union, at least in the final stages of negotiations. In the last decade, the percentage of regulations, directives, and decisions in which Italy abstained or voted against, is equal to 2.6 percent[17]: a rather high level of dissent for a traditionally unanimous arena like the Council, ranking fourth, after Germany, Sweden, and the United Kingdom in the EU-15.

According to a relevant observer-participant of EU affairs, the major contribution of Italy to EU politics should be evaluated differently.[18] First of all, on several occasions Italy had a leading role in fighting the paralyzing effects of unanimity in EU affairs.[19] Second, Italy always argued in favor of the reduction of the "democratic deficit," particularly in what concerned the power of the European Parliament.[20] Third, Italy contested the principle of the *juste retour*, practiced and/or defended by all the major member states, as being intrinsically counter to the concept itself of Union. And finally, Italy always had a positive attitude toward enlargement, whose technicalities may be defined from case to case, but whose long-term aims should never be underestimated.

While these actions represent Italy's major political contributions to the integration process, things change completely if one observes its day-to-day participation in the complex games of EU policymaking. Granted, European policymaking may be thought of as a "garbage can" in which problems and solutions are randomly coupled.[21] Italy's lack of institutional coordination might thus weigh particularly heavily in a context in which rapidity of response is what allows member states to take advantage of eventual "windows of opportunity" that might suddenly open. On occasion, though, when circumstances require careful mediation among distant positions, the particular skills of Italian diplomats may become particularly useful. Italy's intermediate position—both in terms of international prestige and of substantive views—allows it at times to play a crucial (and much appreciated) mediating role. While unable to directly shape the final outcome in any predetermined direction, Italy is thus capable of carving its own unique role within EU policymaking by exploiting its capacity to mediate.[22]

◼ Italy and the Implementation of EU Policies

That Italy had, from the very beginning, problems in coping with its EC obligations is certainly not new, but this fact was initially not so relevant for several reasons. First, the common-pooled sovereignty was initially limited. Second, implementation failures in one country did not necessarily result in costs for other member states. Third, the basic "name and shame" strategy, in the hands of the European Court of Justice, was initially ineffective. Fourth, the Commission did not consider solving "the implementation problem" a priority until the Single European Act and the project for establishing the Internal Market.

Starting from the mid-1980s, things changed radically. The heterogeneous implementation of EU directives, especially those regarding the completion of the Internal Market, implied a distortion in the underlying principle of competition and represented a substantial possibility of opting for free-rider behaviors. The drive for cross-national policy convergence[23] became thus a major issue in EU politics. The Commission itself established detailed procedures for monitoring the implementation of EU policies, which successively allowed the elaboration of more specific strategies and targets.

Lack of implementation of EU policies and, in particular, failure to transpose EU directives in a timely fashion, thus became a problem also in Rome, especially because the annual report of the Commission invariably referred to Italy's sluggishness in transposing EU directives and implementing regulations, even after first and second rulings of the European Court of Justice had been issued.[24]

The Institutional Framework

The political answer appeared fairly radical, although not necessarily effective. A series of domestic institutional innovations were introduced during the 1980s in order to tackle the problem, mainly regarding the so-called descending phase of the process: from Brussels to Rome. Already in 1980 a "minister without portfolio" (the Italian expression for a junior minister) was established, who would be dedicated to EU affairs and would work closely with the presidency of the Council of Ministers. Its uncertain status and competencies, the strong competition played by the more powerful and strongly institutionalized foreign minister, and the lack of any specialized administrative structure supporting its work, together with the underestimation of coordination problems, unquestionably weakened the new minister in its first years of establishment.[25] These weaknesses also conditioned its development, as can be easily deduced by the fact that the position of minister for European affairs had probably the highest turnout rate of all the cabinet positions of the 1980s.

The Department for the Coordination of EU Policies was created in 1987 in order to support the work of the minister, but it actually started to function only in 1990. Despite its name, its main duties (revised several times) related to the implementation phase and not to the coordination of the domestic strategy in the European arena: something that was never given up by the economic directorate of the foreign minister, although formally assigned to an already existing Interministerial Committee for Economic Programming.[26] In fact, the foreign ministry resisted in many ways losing only a tiny part of its prerogatives, thus perfectly representing the traits of a Niskanian's organization.[27] Not only could it rely on the expertise built in the first decades of European integration, but the Italian Permanent Representation in Brussels, directly under its command, was mainly staffed by its diplomats.[28] Reforms introduced at the executive level, thus, had to come to terms with past legacies.

Also in the parliament things were gradually changing, although slowly. A special committee for EU policies was established in the Chamber of Deputies in 1990, mainly in order to process the Annual Community Law, whereas another ad hoc commission (*giunta*) already worked in the Senate since 1968. Although they both managed to "upgrade" themselves to the standard of "permanent committees"[29]— and were even given the power of formal review over EU compatibility with the entire Italian legislation—the (democratic) involvement of the Italian parliament in EU affairs remained comparatively limited.[30]

The same could be said for the regions, whose relevance and responsibilities came more and more to the forefront with the increasingly deeper process of devolution that had started anew in the 1990s, pushed forward through the constitutional reform of 2001, and further developed by the new reforms of the present government. Italian regions are now more directly involved in the transposition and implementation of EU policies but, although they slowly freed themselves of the previous national constraints in establishing their own offices of representation in Brussels,[31] they are still insufficiently involved in the ascending phase of the process. Since the beginning of the 1990s, regional governments had to be consulted by the executive twice a year in a special European session of the *Conferenza Stato-Regioni*—the periodic meetings of the regional presidents with the minister of the interior and of the sector-specific regional ministers with their national counterparts. Unfortunately, the European meetings seldom followed the planned calendar: there have been years without any session and, in the last decade (thus both with center-left and center-right executives), they met less than half of the expected times, ending up only with some ritualistic commitments.[32]

But the most important innovation approved in the late 1980s—first with the "Legge Fabbri" in 1987, and then with the "Legge La Pergola" in 1989—was the introduction of the "Annual Community Law." This "instrument," specifically designed in order to tackle the problems of delayed transposition of EU measures, should have taken advantage of the already described reformed institutional architecture. It established that the executive should present each year a special package-bill in order to transpose all the awaiting directives, using a vast array of legislative instruments, most of them actually delegating the real implementation to further regulations. The minister for EU policies had to take care of the timely elaboration of such a bill and follow it up until its approval; EU parliamentary committees[33] acted as reference committees during the parliamentary stage; and regions had to express their opinions on the content of the bill.

As may have been predicted from the design of the reform, the Annual Community Law partially betrayed the expectations it elicited.[34] The timetable, restricted to its presentation and not to its approval (as instead with budgetary laws), has not always been respected, sometimes due to the executive's ineffectiveness, sometimes to political crises or anticipated elections. The parliamentary process, already crowded by more or less important matters, and in spite of the bipartisan consensus normally exhibited on the bill, always needed several months before its completion. The idea itself of a package-bill revealed itself as a sort of boomerang, because less controversial directives had to proceed at the same pace of more politically sensible ones. The EU "produces" policies at a constant rate, and there is little sense in isolating this continuous flux in a single comprehensive project. Finally, the Annual Law quickly became a "big" delegating law, with the executive hardly being able to adopt the necessary delegated decrees in a timely fashion.[35] In order to speed up the process, the executive usually had to cut or shrink the "democratic controls" assured by the close parliamentary scrutiny or by the consultation of subnational levels of government, limiting at the same time the contribution of technical competencies and expertise ensured by these institutions.[36]

The Italian record in the first five years of the new millennium was not as bad as 20 years earlier, but both "hard data" and the comments of several policymakers—members of the executive, leaders of the parliamentary committees specialized in EU affairs, governors of the regions, interest groups' representatives—reveal that the situation was all but under control. Already in 2002, three different proposals for restructuring the "La Pergola" reform were presented. Following the comments of several observers, and the suggestions coming from two parliamentary inquiries, the new projects kept the overall structure for dealing with the descending phase—especially the Annual Law, although it was clarified that, in urgent cases, directives can be transposed even outside that comprehensive bill—but tried to improve *ex ante* coordination of the ascending phase, that is, how the Italian position and winset is defined prior to EU bargaining.

The redoing of the reform took almost three years to be approved (which it eventually was, almost unanimously), and the new law has completely replaced the preceding La Pergola law. It is still too early to evaluate its effects, but we can nonetheless illustrate two of its major lines of innovation.

A new ad hoc interministerial committee for EU affairs (CIACE, or *Comitato interministeriale per gli affari comunitari*), supported by a technical committee within the department for the coordination of EU policies, directed by the EU minister and composed of top officials of each governmental ministry, was created to address the problems of coordination previously experienced.[37] This new structure, roughly emulating the best experiences of other countries, is supposed to avoid the conflicts, incongruities, and reciprocal indifference and ignorance that often characterized the work of the Italian delegation in the drafting phase of EU policymaking and provide a single well-defined line of bargaining coming from Rome. Clearly not all problems have been resolved, if the present (2005–2006) minister for EU affairs—La Malfa—calls for immediately implementing the yet to be approved "Bolkenstein directive," whereas the minister of the economy—Tremonti—publicly declares that, as it is, the liberalization of services envisaged by that same directive would be unacceptable for Italy.

The second line of reform, still having to do with the *ex ante* preparation of the Italian position, regards the reduction of the so-called internal democratic deficit on EU affairs. We have already recognized that both the parliament and the local governments—especially the now powerful and accountable regions—felt kept out of the preparatory stages (which actually occurred in a rather hectic way). The problem is less one of democratic deficit as one of effectiveness, because by excluding from the preparatory phases those institutional actors, which eventually have to transpose and implement EU policies, the "goodness of fit" between domestic and European practices is correspondingly reduced.[38]

The new law has explicitly introduced a so-called reserve for parliamentary scrutiny, an instrument already present in several other countries, especially in the new entries.[39] Although it does not attribute to parliament all the constraining powers it has in the Danish case, this provision entails the possibility that the Italian delegation may ask the relevant EU institution—a working group, the Committee of Permanent Representatives (COREPER) or the Council—a 20-day break in order to let the parliament express itself, with a motion or resolution, on the project under examination. A similar mechanism is available also to regions through the already mentioned State-Region Conference and, in softer ways, to other subnational levels of government or functional representation institutions.[40]

It is too soon to assess the effectiveness of this new instrument, but hopes are not too high. On one side, it is less stringent than in other countries as it relies on the goodwill of the executive in activating the procedure and in considering the suggestions received. On the other, its effectiveness will almost certainly depend on its shaping the policymakers' expectations, who could still prefer to use their informal channels instead of activating a yet-to-be-tested formal procedure. Still, even after the reform, the executive failed to implement the provisions regarding the scope and correctness of the information to be given to the parliament, so that a real change of heart on the part of the government is not really detectable.

EU Policies: The Domestic Dimension

The institutional difficulties that have been highlighted in the preceding subsection explain why Italy is sometimes unable to use the windows of opportunity that suddenly open and then press forward its interests, even when the constellation in Brussels is not particularly hostile to them. By the same token, it explains some of the problems of poor compliance, which have been documented in Chapter 2. Here we would like to focus on a policy area where some progress toward the articulation of a truly shared national position and the pursuit of a national interest has indeed been made, yet in ways that still reveal the general difficulties of the Italian political system as a whole. As in Zeff and Pirro,[41] we selected cohesion policy (or regional development policy, as we prefer to call it) as the case study for testing the soundness of the arguments discussed above.

Italy presents a good case study of the difficulties that some states have in implementing EU policies. In accordance with the general picture sketched above, until the late 1980s Italian actors had been scarcely present in the negotiations over the Structural Funds' regulations and, therefore, had failed to make an impact on the criteria regulating the allocation of funds and the procedures for their utilization.[42] The feeble presence of Italian actors during the preliminary phases of the negotiations caused serious implementation problems, which had been due to insufficient organizational capacity of domestic institutions, insufficient technical comprehension of the issues at stake, and a sheer lack of attention to the issue.[43] Since the late 1980s, regional development policy has been characterized by marked improvements in the general coordination among domestic institutions and between these and the EU institutional level, both in the ascending phase of the policy (the reform of the regulations) and in the descending phase (the implementation of the Community Support Frameworks and Regional Operational Programs). But it was the 1999 reform process, in particular, that marked a clear break with past experience.

The first factor, insufficient organizational capacity of the relevant institutions, leads back to the lack of coordination among domestic institutions that deal with the European Union in general, and those that deal with structural policy, in particular. Coordination among institutions in charge of community policies in Rome was also faulty. It was only at the end of the 1980s that a Department for European Affairs was created within the prime minister's cabinet and that a Committee for European Affairs was created within the parliament. Regions, moreover, were still left out of all European-level policymaking. European matters fell, by law, under the rubric of foreign relations, hence under the purview of the central government. The requirement placed on the government to inform them of all proposals of community directives and regulations, which had been sanctioned by Article 9 of the "Legge Fabbri" law (see above), had only served to flood regional offices with information that the regions could not process in time. The situation was compounded by weak coordination among institutions dealing with domestic structural policy, and between these and the institutions that dealt with European structural policy.

This situation was made all the worse by the dispersion of technical expertise on structural policy, following the dismemberment of the institutions for "extraordinary intervention"—the name with which Italian regional development policy during the postwar period was known.[44] Central and regional ministerial offices simply lacked the technical preparation to draft, implement, monitor, and evaluate European regional development policy. The personnel of the Ministry for Foreign Affairs, which followed EU structural policy, had generic diplomatic training and lacked the technical preparation needed to follow European policies such as structural policy. Thus one of the principal sources (in some cases the only source) of funds for regional structural policy was blunted by insufficient coordination among the relevant institutions.[45]

The technical expertise that was missing at the center and the periphery was, unfortunately, also unavailable in Brussels. It was only in the mid-1990s that the Italian Permanent Representation in Brussels (ITALRAP) was endowed with technical support that subsequently allowed it to participate actively in the negotiations for the Structural Funds' regulations. Because structural policy was discussed at the General Affairs section of the Council of the EU, career diplomats had followed the negotiations for the programming periods 1989–1993 and 1994–1999 from the Foreign Ministry. It was not until 1996 that the Regional Policy area within ITALRAP was created, and it is only since 1997 that a treasury functionary resides permanently in Brussels to follow European structural policy and "translate" national needs into technically plausible numbers and Euro-comprehensible jargon during Council negotiations.

The confusion that followed the quasi-simultaneous termination of domestic structural policy (a process that dragged on from 1986 to 1992) and the reform of European structural policy (particularly during the years 1988–1993) took several years to overcome. It was not until 1996, and perhaps even 1998, that the relevant capacities were rebuilt. As a consequence, from 1996 it was really the treasury that followed all European economic matters, and the Department for Structural Policy within it, which was in charge of European structural policy.[46] Used to paying attention solely to the formal accordance of administrative acts to state law, the Italian bureaucracy gave little weight to the actual attainment of expenditure targets and to the active involvement of relevant public and private actors in the decisionmaking process, thus ignoring both the procedural and the substantial goals set by the Commission.

Creating new institutional structures does not amount to expressing new national preferences: structures must be put to use and applied to politically set goals. The third explanatory factor, then, is the lack of political will on the part of both central and regional authorities with regard to Structural Funds. Used to the simpler (and more flexible) procedures of the extraordinary intervention, central and regional authorities initially showed little interest in learning the complex and rigid procedures through which European Structural Funds could be obtained. Indeed, as Paolo Graziano has noted,[47] not a single organizational principle of European regional policy was present in the extraordinary intervention. In this case, the existence of policy legacies was a hindrance to the acquisition of new policy styles.

The Italian interest in cohesion policy surfaced only in 1993–1994, because of the demise of the extraordinary intervention: Italian interest in cohesion policy had therefore been, for a long time, only marginal, in the sense that Italy looked at it only as a source of money to be poured into the mold of the extraordinary intervention. This preoccupation had driven the action of the Italian actors until the mid-1990s, thus delaying the learning process that the European regional policy clearly implied and causing a much lower resource intake than might have been otherwise the case.[48] Moreover, the convergence criteria set by the Maastricht Treaty and the impending monetary tightness convinced governmental actors at the central and regional levels that the Structural Funds could not be lightly disregarded, as they would soon represent the only source of money available for sustaining structural adjustment. The joint push from the new fiscal and monetary tightness imposed by Maastricht following the decision to enter the EMU and the pull of the Structural Funds in the absence of easier sources of money for structural intervention largely explain the determination with which new institutional solutions were sought for the problem of coordination between domestic and European governmental actors in the second half of the 1990s.

After briefly experimenting with other coordination solutions,[49] at the end of the 1990s the Department for Development and Cohesion Policy (*Dipartimento per le Politiche di Sviluppo e di Coesione* [DPS]) was created within the treasury.[50] The DPS was entrusted with the coordination of all domestic and European development policy and acknowledged as the direct interlocutor with the Commission during all phases of the policymaking process. During the first two years of its existence, the DPS had to operate on two fronts. On the domestic front, it helped the regions use up the funds still available from the 1994–1999 programming cycle while training the technical personnel who would enable the regions to avoid such delays in the future. On the EU front, it managed the concertation process, which allowed Italy to express a truly shared national position at the negotiation table for the first time since the inception of the Structural Funds. The shared conviction that the forthcoming 2000–2006 programming cycle would probably be the last in which relatively underdeveloped Italian regions would manage to get any significant amount of funding from the EU made active participation in the 1999 regulation reform negotiations all the more urgent.[51]

This new concertative strategy involved two steps. The first was to create, in February 1998, a strong link with the Ministry of Foreign Affairs, which would sit at the bargaining table at the upcoming Berlin Council. With the help of external technical support, the treasury formulated a number of alternative scenarios; each derived from a different set of possible allocation criteria, and defined an Italian position for each of them. While constituting an improvement with respect to the past, two omissions are, nevertheless, apparent. First, no lobbying action had been undertaken at the EU level, thus forgoing the possibility of "suggesting" preferred options to the Commission that could have been incorporated in the draft proposal. Second, the regions were kept out of this preliminary stage, thus depriving the central structures of potentially valuable ideas and information and losing the opportunity for the regions to carry out autonomous lobbying activity.

The second step consisted of the creation of a domestic interinstitutional bargaining structure within which the DPS now wanted to involve the regions. It also created, in June 1998, a narrower "contact group" composed of a few high-level DPS functionaries, technical experts from the Bank of Italy and the National Statistics Institute, regional representatives, and external academic experts. The Commission did not adopt one of the proposals elaborated by this narrower group of experts—to entrust the management of the Structural Funds to socioeconomic entities rather than to administrative entities—and, in the meantime, it had already drafted its own reform proposal.

What distinguished the 1999 negotiations from the previous two, then, apart from revealing the partial resolution of the problems highlighted in the previous subsection, was the decision of the Italian central government authorities involved in the EU decisionmaking process to ask for input from the regional actors (both from regional institutions and from regional civil society) and to promote a unified position in Brussels. The adaptation to EU procedures allowing Italian authorities to use up the 1994–1999 Structural Funds was the result of the restructuring of domestic and EU-level decisionmaking protocols, which in turn allowed Italian institutional actors to take an active part in the 1999 regulation reform negotiation. The greater effectiveness with which Italian central authorities managed the 1999 negotiation process clearly reveals the awareness that, if Italy wanted to make maximum use of regional policy resources, it had to shape the regulations that governed their allocation and utilization activity.

◾ Italian Compliance Problems

In 1986, Italy was transposing less than half of the required directives. That amount corresponded to a difference of 23 percent from the EC-12 average, and to a gap of 37 percent with respect to the leader of that particular ranking. At the end of 2005, Italy was transposing 97.7 percent of the directives, only about one point below the EU-25 average, and two points below the member states at the top of the ranking.[52]

Although Italy is still the third to last member state in that ranking, given the clustering of countries around 98.7 percent of transposition, the very concept of leader and laggard should be entirely reconsidered particularly if we think that, even in the worst case, more than 2,500 acts have been incorporated into the domestic policy, and only around 50 remained to be fully enacted. From this perspective, it is really difficult to argue in favor of the existence of an implementation deficit, or of some member states performing better than others. Nonetheless, the compliance literature grows because those statistics do not tell the whole truth.[53]

It is impossible to dispute that the quoted Annual Community Law had the effect of reducing both the amount of Italian nontransposed directives and their average delay, but unfortunately it produced a series of less positive side effects. First of all, as a package bill, it tends to isolate how Italian policymakers process EU policies. Second, for that same reason, the quality of the process itself seems more and more inappropriate, as verified by the growing amount of infringement proceedings opened by the Commission for inadequate or incorrect implementation.[54] The diffused style of simply "copying" the original directive in order to respect the EU deadline, coupled with the fact that the Annual Law does not directly transpose, but delegates that power to the executive, makes things worse.

Actually, in spite of what the reports of the Commission say on the basis of long-term statistics, it is quite rare for Italy to transpose something on time (between one-fourth and one-third of the time, from our estimates). Annual Community Laws have reduced long-term delays, but they have also contributed to "routinizing" them, while at the same time aggravating problems with the Commission.[55] For example, an Internal Market directive regarding the harmonization of the market of electricity—directive 2003/54/CE, that was supposed to be transposed before July 2004—was included in the Italian 2004 Annual Community Law. That same law was approved in April 2005, but delegates the executive to adopt the necessary decrees in another 18 months (that is, before September 2006). Normally, unless it fails to comply with the delegation, the executive takes the entire period, so that this directive and others are, on average, approved two years after the EU deadline. In the meantime, the Commission usually opens infringement proceedings against Italy.

Things sometimes move faster but, given the lack of professionalism in the public administration—which was incidentally admitted even by the former minister for European affairs—things may even get worse. Problems often occur either because there is a bad fit between EU policies or because of the vast amount of laws and normative acts already present in the Italian system.

It is up to the Italian delegations in the drafting and formulating phases of the process to smooth out these kinds of problems and improve the "goodness of fit." Unfortunately, until now, the lack of coordination among ministers, and between Rome and Italy's Permanent Representation in Brussels, has not helped. The newly envisioned inter-ministerial committee and permanent technical committee should tackle this problem but, since they are still not at work, it is to soon to evaluate their actual functioning.

Generally speaking, the relationship between the Italian domestic and the European arenas is insufficiently institutionalized. Specific institutions have been set up to address the problem, but their actual autonomy is still questionable. The feeling is that European policies still count less than domestic policies: the centrality of European laws is not yet evident even to the most important institutional actors.

■ Trends and Future Prospects

As we have seen, Italy's participation in EU policymaking still presents a mixed picture. Yet several factors induce us to think that the structural and organizational reform drive must continue if it is to have any impact on EU-related domestic policymaking.

First, as the sheer number of national actors in the EU game has increased, Italy's position as a founding member is bound to lose significance or, at least, to require a redefinition of the ways in which it tries to count. Whether the creation of a series of concentric circles—where the older and larger member states occupy the inner core and the newer and smaller ones the more peripheral circles—will be the actual result of the process of enlargement or rather the official discourse of "equality in diversity" will be upheld cannot be known. What is certain is that the sheer complexity of the interactions has increased, and that this complexity will require different or additional skills. Identifying a "focal point"—and making sure that it satisfies national preferences—may be an expedient way of steering complex decisions in the "right" direction. Being able to articulate a truly shared national position in a timely fashion will probably be an essential skill in the new game. A different, more benign reading[56] suggests that, in an ever more complex environment, Italian representatives' well-known diplomatic skills may prove crucial and that Italy's role will mainly be that of mediator among different positions rather than carrier of yet another clear, but dissonant, voice.

Second, converging toward a national position may be important also for internal reasons. Although Italian governments now live longer, they are still fractured by internal dissent among the members of the governmental coalitions. Governing parties often disagree on fairly fundamental issues, many of which have a European dimension. We have argued that EU decisionmaking rewards the timely players, those who manage to define the issue early in the game. Under these circumstances, Italy's belated and contradictory positions may jeopardize the attainment of whatever national objectives Italian actors might eventually decide to promote and further fan internal disagreement among governing partners (and between government and opposition, of course). In other words, European issues run the risk of widening the already large areas of disagreement between government and opposition as well as within both government and opposition, and thus may add to Italy's problems of governability. This "boomerang effect" may in turn fan the smoldering fire of Italian Euro-skepticism, a new but by now established development among Italian elites and masses.[57] Whether it is due to the "unblocking" of the Italian political system, which induced people to see Europe as the motor of difficult but necessary domestic reforms, or to more specific European decisions that may have hurt Italian interests and sensitivities (from the reform of the Structural Funds to the secular and nonconfessional tone of the proposed constitution), Italians are now less enthusiastic about Europe than they once were—and this is true of the masses as well as the elites.

Third, the stalled constitutional ratification process is bound to have an effect also in Italy. Despite initial statements that Italy would be the first country to hold a constitutional referendum, Italy ratified the Constitutional Treaty after Lithuania and Hungary and through a parliamentary vote.[58] The "constitutional debate" never really took place in Italy, at least not at the popular level. Yet, echoes of the failed ratifications in France and the Netherlands reached the Italian public as well, and people have started to wonder why two of the founding member states refused to ratify the European constitution. As a country in which the constitution enshrined the conquest of political, social, and economic rights on the part of a population for long centuries subject to foreign and/or autocratic rule, the constitution still has a particular prestige. Although Italians have recently started to change their republican constitution, after many decades of single-minded preservation of its original text, it is virtually impossible to see how an EU constitution might not but be beneficial. Moreover, Italian representatives had played quite an active role within the Constitutional Convention, displaying there the best of those diplomatic skills for which they are renowned.[59] The sense of Euro-fatigue that spread as a consequence of the failed ratification is bound to hit Italians, too, though it may not be directly linked to the constitution per se—very few Italians have read it or know what it contains—but to the process of European integration more generally.

Other issues (whether really relevant or only perceived as such due to partisan propaganda)—such as the cut in living standards induced by the introduction of the euro or the cost of the most recent enlargement or again the entrance of Turkey into the Union—may be more present in Italian minds. Whatever its causes, a certain sense of disillusionment with the European project is spreading also among Italians. Under these circumstances, Italians may start to ask for "more bang for their euro" and switch to an unconventionally more pragmatic and down-to-earth approach to the EU. In other words, the "permissive consensus" is shrinking rapidly in Italy as well. A more precise and transparent articulation of what Italy gets from the EU and how its contribution to it is important to reaching desired results may be the new way of arguing and communicating the Italian position in the EU. Yet this new communicative mode is highly unlikely if the reasons for Italy's participation in the EU are unclear to (or not shared by) the Italian government and its representatives in Brussels.

To conclude, structural and organizational problems still seem to haunt Italy, yet there are areas of steady improvement. Structural adjustment seldom flows efficiently from functional needs, but when the functional pressure is strong enough, rules and behaviors may start to change accordingly. What lies ahead is a period of adjustment for all member states, Italy included. There are reasons to believe that Italy will perform this adjustment, but probably in its own way.

■ Notes

Marco Giuliani would like to acknowledge the support of the "Research Unit on European Governance" (URGE) (Foundation Collegio Carlo Alberto, Moncalieri, Torino). Simona Piattoni would like to acknowledge the support of the MIUR (Ministero per l'Istruzione Universitaria e la Ricerca Scientifica) and Marco Brunazzo's collaboration within that research project.

1. Dyson and Featherstone, "'Vincolo Esterno': Empowering the Technocrats."

2. Putnam, "Diplomacy and Domestic Politics."

3. Dyson and Featherstone, "'Vincolo Esterno': Empowering the Technocrats."

4. Sbragia, "Italy Pays for Europe"; Radaelli, "The Italian State and Europe"; Cavatoro, "Attuare Maastricht e la politica delle 'rigidità flessibili'."

5. Ferrera and Gualmini, *Rescued by Europe?*

6. Fabbrini, *L'europeizzazione dell'Italia.*

7. DiPalma, Fabbrini, and Freddi, *Condannata al successo?*

8. Padoa-Schioppa, "Italy and Europe: A Fruiful Interaction"; Falkner et al., *Complying with Europe.*

9. Börzel, "Pace-Setting, Foot-Dragging, and Fence-Sitting," and "How the European Union Interacts with Its Member States"; Börzel and Risse, "Conceptualizing the Domestic Impact of Europe."

10. Ferrera, "Italia: aspirazioni e vincoli del 'quarto grande'."

11. Putnam, "Diplomacy and Domestic Politics"; Tsebelis, *Veto Players.* The term *winset* refers to the range or subset of winning/acceptable outcomes at the national level in the multilevel game that characterizes EU policymaking.

12. Cotta, "Élite, politiche nazionali e costruzione della polity europea"; Dinan, *Ever Closer Union*; Fabbrini and Piattoni, "Introduction: Italy in the EU—Pigmy or Giant?"

13. Censis, *Le pubbliche amministrazioni negli anni '90*; Radaelli, "Europeismo tricolore."

14. Amato and Salvadori, *Europa conviene?*; Francioni, *Italy and EC Membership Evaluated.*

15. In spite of the public support for the ongoing integration process, almost in each component of the coalition ruling since 2001 there have been critics toward Brussels strategically used in order to preserve their public consent: the major targets of these attacks were the euro (fostering inflation), immigration policy (too loose), agricultural subsidies (unevenly distributed), judicial policy (exploiting domestic prerogatives), and the stability pact (too rigid). See several chapters in Cotta, Isernia, and Verzichelli, *L'Europa in Italia,* for an in-depth analysis of the attitude of laypersons, political elites, and parties toward the EU.

16. Bardach, *The Implementation Game.*

17. Data have been calculated on all legislative acts from 1995 to April 2004, at the eve of enlargement, updating Mattila and Lane, "Why Unanimity in the Council?" Obviously, one potential explanation of this rather high level of dissent in the last stage is that Italy had been unable to influence all the formal and informal stages before the last one, but this goes well beyond the aims of this chapter.

18. See Padoa-Schioppa, "Italy and Europe: A Fruiful Interaction." Padoa-Schioppa, an economist, was director-general for economic and financial affairs in the EC Commission (1979–1983), deputy director-general of the Italian Central Bank, and (former) member of the Executive Committee of the European Central Bank. He was directly put in charge by Delors of the group that wrote the so-called Padoa-Schioppa Report, which constituted the basis for

the "Delors Report" and was one of the "gang of three" coordinating the Italian strategy on EMU (Dyson and Featherstone, *The Road to Maastricht*).

19. Consider the following examples: in 1977, under the pressure of the Italian prime minister Aldo Moro, it was decided that no single national veto could prevent the first general election of the European Parliament; in 1985, at the Milan European Council, Bettino Craxi and Giulio Andreotti unexpectedly obtained a qualified majority vote to set up an Intergovernmental Conference (the one that eventually produced the SEA); in 1990, at the Rome European Council, Giulio Andreotti and Gianni De Michelis succeeded in including the essential elements of the "Delors Report" in the conclusion of the Council, against British opposition.

20. From the so-called Spinelli Report (an Italian MEP), to the ratification of the SEA after its approval by the European Parliament, to the already quoted consultative referendum in 1989, to the recent debate regarding the ratification of the treaty for an European constitution.

21. Richardson, "Policy-Making in the EU."

22. Fabbrini and Piattoni, "Introduction: Italy in the EU—Pigmy or Giant?"

23. Holzinger and Knill, "Causes and Conditions of Cross-national Policy Convergence."

24. To testify to the growing salience of the problem, it would be possible to quote the increasing number of newspaper articles devoted to this issue, and the establishment in 1991 of the first official inquiry by the Senate on the formulation and implementation of EU norms. The Low Chamber effected similar official inquiries again in the years 1999 and 2003.

25. Della Cananea, "Italy," 2001.

26. Bindi and Cisci, "Italy and Spain," p. 1005.

27. Niskanen, *Bureaucracy—Servant or Master?*

28. Della Cananea, "Italy," 2001.

29. In 1996 at the lower chamber and only in 2004 in the upper one.

30. European Centre for Parliamentarian Research and Documentation (ECPRD), *European Affairs Committees*; COSAC, "Third Bi-Annual Report."

31. Fargion, Morlino, and Profeti, *Europeizzazione e rappresentanza territoriale*.

32. See http://www.regioni.it.

33. Actually, this happened only at the Chamber of Deputies, whereas at the Senate, the Committee for Institutional Affairs was in charge until 2004.

34. We can't enter here into details, but see Giuliani, *La politica europea*, for more information and analyses.

35. Where "timely" here refers only to the delegation given by the Parliament, and not to the original deadline of the directive, which, in most cases, was already elapsed.

36. Even the annual report of the executive to the parliament has been criticized for the lack of information regarding future strategies, and for being swiftly and superficially discussed together with the Annual Community Law in what has been called a "community session" (taking the name from the "budgetary session" but with completely different characteristics).

37. It took the executive more than one year to adopt the necessary decrees

for the actual establishment of these two important institutions and thus, even after the April 2006 general elections, it will only be possible to begin to evaluate their influence after the second half of 2006.

38. Cowles-Green, Caporaso, Risse-Kappen, *Transforming Europe.*

39. COSAC, "Third Bi-Annual Report."

40. Through the State-Municipalities Conference, or through the National Chamber for the Economy and Work (CNEL).

41. Zeff and Pirro, *The European Union and Member States,* 1st ed.

42. Gualini, *Multi-Level Governance and Institutional Change.*

43. Giuliani and Piattoni, "Italy: Both Leader and Laggard."

44. Gualini, *Multi-Level Governance and Institutional Change.*

45. Graziano, "La nuova politica regionale italiana," and Graziano, *Europeizzazione e politiche pubbliche italiane.*

46. Della Cananea, "Italy," 2000.

47. Graziano, "La nuova politica regionale italiana."

48. Giuliani and Piattoni, "Italy: Both Leader and Laggard."

49. Graziano, "La nuova politica regionale italiana"; Piattoni, "Regioni a statuto speciale e politica di coesione."

50. The DPS coordinates four different treasury directions charged with different tasks connected with local development: the Direction for Community Funds, the Direction for Programming Contracts and Territorial Pacts, the Direction for Institutional Agreements, and the Direction for Sectoral Programmes. The DPS supplies public and private institutions with the information they need to plan their investments. The Evaluations and Inspection Technical Group (*Nucleo tecnico di valutazione e verifica*) is responsible for the technical functions. The four above-cited directions interact respectively with the European Commission, the central administrations, the regional governments, and the local governments. The creation of the DPS is commonly, and rightly, attributed to the vision of the then–prime minister Ciampi and the entrepreneurial drive of its first director, Fabrizio Barca (see Graziano, "La nuova politica regionale italiana"), who contributed not only to creating new institutional structures but also to shaping a new policy style at the treasury and at the regional level (Barca, "Il ruolo del Dipartimento per le Politiche di Sviluppo e Coesione").

51. Brunazzo and Piattoni, "Negotiating the Regulation of the Structural Funds."

52. The comparison is somehow flawed by the sedimentation through time, that is, by the delayed transposition of directives dating back to the 1960s, 1970s, and so on, but is still striking.

53. Börzel, "Non-Compliance in the European Union"; Mastenbroek, "EU Compliance: Still a 'Black Hole'?"

54. If in 1991 the General Secretariat of the Commission noted that most of the unobserved rulings of the ECJ against Italy were for "nontransposition," in 2003 the Italian Permanent Representative observed that infringements now stem from defective implementation and not for noncommunication of transposition measures. (Both comments are taken from interviews given in occasion of the quoted parliamentary inquiries.)

55. For each type of origin (noncommunication, nonconformity, incorrect

implementation, and infringements to treaties, regulations, and decisions), the Italian percentage of infringement proceedings in the decade 1994–2003 grows together with the severity of the stage (from letters of formal notice, to reasoned opinions, to recourses at the Court of Justice). As has been said in the parliamentary discussion regarding the Annual Law for 2005, "when the job of the executive will be finished [due to the delegated powers it will receive], we will complete the transposition of the directives for 2003."

56. Fabbrini and Piattoni, "Introduction: Italy in the EU—Pigmy or Giant?"

57. Cotta, Isernia, and Verzichelli, *L'Europa in Italia.*

58. In reality, a parliamentary vote is the standard procedure for the ratification of international treaties, such as the Constitutional Treaty really is. However, the Berlusconi government had promised that the Constitutional Treaty would be subjected to a popular referendum like real constitutions normally are (and have been also in Italy). By reverting to the conventional procedure for international treaties, the government exposed once more the ineffectiveness of the Italian governmental machine when it comes to European matters.

59. Fabbrini, *L'europeizzazione dell'Italia.*

6

Belgium, the Netherlands, and Luxembourg: Increasingly Cautious Europeans

Karen Anderson and Michael Kaeding

BELGIUM, THE NETHERLANDS, AND Luxembourg (Benelux) are founding EU members, and EU membership continues to be a cornerstone of domestic and foreign policy. All three countries enthusiastically supported the introduction of the euro, and have been among the most pro-integrationist EU members. Support for European Union membership and further integration is high among political elites and the public, although support has waned somewhat in the last decade.

Belgium continues to be one of the most pro-integration member states, and the location of the central European Union institutions in Brussels brings significant economic benefits to Belgium. Belgian EU membership must also be viewed in the context of the country's slow transformation from a unitary into a federal state. Belgium's 10 million inhabitants include three ethnic groups: French-speaking Walloons, Dutch-speaking Flemish, and a small German-speaking minority. The three regions (Flanders, Wallonia, and Brussels) each have their own government and legislature and govern policy areas such as housing, employment, energy, infrastructure, environment, spatial planning, and transport. Federalism complicates Belgium's relationship with the EU level because the regions participate in many aspects of EU policymaking and implementation.

In the Netherlands, EU membership remains an article of faith, but public skepticism to further integration has increased. The Dutch rejection of the Constitutional Treaty on June 1, 2005, is the most spectacular example of this, but it would be a mistake to conclude that the Dutch no longer support EU membership. Indeed, public support for Dutch EU membership remains high, but EU membership has become more politicized in the last decade, and the Dutch increasingly view the workings of European Union institutions with suspicion.

Luxembourg is one of the two smallest member states with 470,000 inhabitants.[1] Like Belgium, Luxembourg benefits from the location of important administrative functions in the country: the European Court of Justice (ECJ) is located in Luxembourg. As an extremely small state, Luxembourg has historically sought means of cooperating with neighboring states for economic purposes, most notably in its currency and customs union with Belgium in 1922 and its membership in the Benelux Customs Union established in 1948. EU membership and Luxembourg's pro-integration stance are logical extensions of this long-standing orientation.

■ How and in What Areas Does the EU Influence the Benelux Countries?

From the outset, the Benelux countries' participation in the European integration process has been shaped by their status as small, open economies located between two much more powerful states, Germany and France. The importance of market access for the Benelux countries can hardly be exaggerated: according to World Trade Organization statistics, the Netherlands is the sixth-largest exporter in the world.[2] Belgium is ranked tenth. All three have vigorously supported European integration as a means of guaranteeing access to European markets, and of constraining the power of more powerful states.

A closer look at the budgetary implications of EU membership is one way of approaching the issue of how the EU influences each country. All three countries are net contributors to the EU, if administrative expenditure is excluded. The Netherlands' net contribution in 2004 was 0.44 percent of gross national income (GNI), while the Belgian and Luxembourg net contributions were 0.19 percent and 0.41 percent of GNI, respectively. However, if administrative spending is included, this picture changes dramatically. In 2003, Luxembourg received EU funding equal to about 4.2 percent of its GNI, and Belgium received 0.3 percent of its GNI, with the Netherlands paying 0.6 percent of its GNI.[3] Until 1990, the Netherlands was a net beneficiary of EU funding, and the country's recent status as the EU's largest net payer has had a significant impact on Dutch voters' more skeptical attitude toward EU policies and the functioning of EU institutions. In 2003 the Dutch per capita net contribution to the EU was €180, and this figure was widely cited in the public debate about the Constitutional Treaty in 2005.[4]

The Benelux countries are net contributors to the EU budget largely because they receive little funding from the Common Agricultural Policy (CAP) and Structural Funding, the two largest EU budget items. Belgium and the Netherlands each received 1.0 percent of Structural Funding in 2004 and Luxembourg 0.1 percent.[5] Agricultural support played a larger role until the 1980s, but today the Benelux countries are among the EU members that receive the smallest amount of CAP funding.[6] Belgium received 2.5 percent of the CAP budget, the Netherlands 3.1 percent, and Luxembourg 0.1 percent.[7]

If the CAP and Structural Funds are relatively insignificant for the Benelux countries, which policies are significant? This section discusses the domestic impact of European Monetary Union (EMU) for Belgium, as well as the adjustment of Dutch and Belgian social security legislation to European law concerning gender equality in the 1980s and 1990s. Both are examples of how policies adopted at the EU level have had important implications for the structure of domestic social and economic programs.

Belgium: Adjusting to the Constraints of EMU

Qualifying for the final stage of EMU prompted substantial welfare state reforms in several member states.[8] In the run-up to EMU, the member states had to meet the Maastricht convergence criteria in order to qualify for participation in the euro zone, and the 3 percent budget deficit limit was a key constraint. Member states were free to take whatever measures they deemed necessary to achieve the target; they could choose any combination of spending cuts and tax increases, as long as the targets were met by the 1998 deadline. Belgium was one of the countries (with Greece and Italy) that faced the greatest uphill battle in qualifying for EMU. In the 1990s, Belgium had one of the largest budget deficits and public-sector debt ratios in the EU, so meeting the convergence criteria was no easy task.

Qualifying for EMU was defined as a national project requiring extraordinary policymaking, and it dominated Belgian politics in the mid-1990s.[9] The center-left government even scheduled early elections in May 1995 with the intention of increasing public support for the kinds of tough economic policies required to bring the deficit down. In 1993, the budget deficit hovered around 7 percent, while the debt ratio reached its highest level ever, at 137.9 percent of GDP.

The run-up to EMU provided the government with the political capital necessary to secure approval for several of its social security reform goals, including a major pension reform in 1995–1996 aimed at reducing long-term public pension spending. The cabinet used "special powers" legislation to pass its reform program. This involved passing "framework laws" that contained the broad outlines of policy, with the details specified in royal decrees. The legislation gave the government permission to take all necessary measures needed in order to reduce the deficit to 3 percent (an explicit reference to the EMU requirements) and to guarantee the financial balance of the social security system, including pensions.

The framework laws also allowed the government to pass legislation on the 1997 budget, employment policy, and social security reform, with only post hoc parliamentary control. The most important legislation related to EMU was the "EMU Law" that gave the government until August 31, 1997, the authority to take a wide range of measures necessary to enable Belgium to join EMU. This included both taxing and spending measures.

The role of EMU membership was a crucial factor allowing the government to gain passage of social insurance and pension reform. As the governor of the Central Bank, Fons Verplaetse, put it: "If Belgium misses the train for the European common currency, the unity of the country is endangered."

The impact of the EMU budget constraint on Belgian public finances has been substantial. Between 1995 and 1998, Belgium reduced its budget deficit from 3.9 percent to 1.6 percent of GDP. In the same period, the public debt to GDP ratio fell from 131 percent of GDP to 117 percent of GDP, a reduction of 16 percent.[10] By the end of 2004, the public debt to GDP ratio had decreased by 40 percent, and in 2003 gross debt fell below 100 percent of GDP (down from 137 percent of GDP in 1993).[11] In 2004 and 2005, the government budget was roughly in balance, in sharp contrast to the early 1990s when deficits of 7 percent were not uncommon.

The constraints of EMU have had a profound impact on Belgian fiscal policy. Until the late 1990s, Belgium was a case of increasing deficits and public debt. Indeed, federalism and the challenges associated with governance in a multiethnic polity created incentives for politicians to prioritize public-sector expansion over fiscal discipline. For Belgium, qualifying for EMU was a high-stakes political project. The welfare state is very popular, so cutting benefits is politically risky.[12] On the other hand, qualifying for EMU was a national priority of such extreme importance that failure was impossible for political elites to contemplate. The overriding importance of participating in such a significant European project enabled political actors who under other circumstances might have opposed budget consolidation measures to agree to painful cuts. What is more, Belgium has stayed on the track of budget discipline. The ultimate irony is that Belgian public finances were balanced in 2005 while Germany, the country that advocated a tough policy on budget deficits in the 1990s, struggled with budget deficits that violated the Maastricht targets.

Adapting the Welfare State to EU Law in Belgium

EU law requiring the equal treatment of men and women in social security schemes and occupational pension schemes is our second example of how EU membership has prompted substantial changes in public policies in the Benelux countries. The EU has only minimal competences in the area of social security, but an EC directive adopted in 1978 prompted significant changes in both Belgian and Dutch social security schemes, particularly pensions. Second, the ECJ's 1990 *Barber* decision set in motion the individualization of occupational pension schemes that discriminated against women. The 1978 directive required the member states to remove all provisions in statutory social security schemes that violated the principle of equal treatment between men and women, including discrimination in terms of access, the calculation and payment of contributions, and the calculation of benefits. The directive created substantial adaptational pressure for member states with "breadwinner"-based social security schemes that excluded married women (because a breadwinner benefit was available only to the husband) or unmarried women (because the assumption was that they would get married at some later point and benefit from their husbands' benefits). The deadline for transposition was December 19, 1985. In both Belgium and the Netherlands, adjusting to European law has involved far-reaching implications for the structure of welfare state programs because compliance with EU law usually requires the individualization of benefit entitlement.

Belgium was slow to transpose EU Directive 79/7/EEC. Even after the 1985 transposition deadline had passed, Belgium still had legislation in place that included different pension benefit formulas for men and women, and different retirement ages. For example, there were different contribution bases for men and women (40 for women, 45 for men), and different retirement ages. It was only a matter of time before the European Commission sued Belgium in the ECJ concerning these provisions.

Belgium failed to transpose on time, and the ECJ found Belgium in violation of EC law in 1986. The Christian-Democratic/liberal government responded by trying to harmonize retirement ages for men and women. Discussion focused on whether to increase women's retirement age to 65 or lower men's to 60. The social partners, especially the unions, fiercely opposed a higher retirement age, preferring instead to harmonize the retirement age downward. Unions organized protests, the government responded with modifications, but unions were still not satisfied. Another round of negotiation led to more adjustments (such as postponing the decision on statutory retirement age) but there was still no consensus. The unions abandoned their strikes in the summer, and on July 16, 1986, the government enacted the changes. The question of the equalization of retirement ages was not solved, however, and it would remain on the decision agenda for the next 10 years.

The issue lay dormant until 1990, when the introduction of unisex rules for a flexible retirement age in 1990 was intended to head off another challenge by the ECJ to Belgian pension law. In 1990, the government introduced a flexible retirement age that was de facto equal for men and women. However, the benefit formula was still different for men and women (40 years of contributions for women and 45 years for men), and this was considered discriminatory. The government wanted to keep the lower number of contribution years for women, but financial concerns meant that Belgium could not afford to apply this rule to men. The minister of pensions insisted publicly that the 1990 legislation solved the problem, but there was much speculation in the press that Belgian pension law still violated the directive. In July 1993 the ECJ ruled that Belgian pension rules violated the principle of equal treatment in social security and instructed Belgium to change its law and practice.[13] Legislation in 1996 introduced a temporary solution to the equal-treatment issue in anticipation of a more permanent reform. The government agreed to gradually raise women's retirement age to 65 starting in 1997 so that by 2009 the retirement age would be uniformly 65.

To summarize, Belgian adaptation to Directive 79/7/EEC was slow, incorrect, and incomplete. Only after the ECJ found Belgium in violation of EC law twice, was the government able to introduce the necessary changes. Belgian federalism and the requirements of consensual policymaking made it very difficult for the government to introduce unpopular changes in social security pensions, even in the presence of strong pressure from the EU.

Adjusting the Welfare State
to European Law: The Netherlands

The Netherlands' transposition of the 1979 directive on equal treatment was also difficult. The structure of the Dutch public pension scheme, the AOW pension, conflicted with the provisions of Directive 79/7/EEC because it was based on the breadwinner principle. Married women did not receive their own, individual benefit; instead, the husband received a benefit intended for both spouses. Unmarried women (and men) over 65 did receive an individual benefit. Similarly, the structure of AOW financing was based on the single-breadwinner principle: only the main breadwinner paid contributions, even if the spouse was employed. These provisions directly conflicted with European law concerning equal treatment. Starting in 1979, all Dutch social security schemes were adjusted to the EC equal-treatment directive. For the AOW system, this required the modification of existing rules excluding married women from eligibility.

Before the EU directive, there was little political pressure to modify the AOW system in order to provide married women with individual benefits. Because the AOW system provided married men a benefit that "included" a benefit for the wife, the system was not perceived by most to be unfair. However, when the EU issued its directive, Dutch policymakers changed the existing rules without protest, but the process took five years, and the government nearly missed the transposition deadline. Unlike other parts of the social insurance system that violated EU equality law (such as unemployment insurance), modifications to the AOW system to conform to EU rules did not require much additional AOW pension spending and did not result in *direct* benefit cuts. However, some pensioners experienced a decline in income because of the indirect effects of the changes. The basic solution that the center-right settled on was to simply divide the AOW benefit for two spouses in half and pay an individual benefit to both the husband and the wife. For married couples over the age of 65, there was no financial change in the level of benefits, and the state was not required to spend additional money on pension benefits. However, the issue of how to treat couples in which one spouse received an AOW benefit and the other was younger than 65 raised several difficulties. Conflict about how to resolve this issue resulted in late transposition, and the indirectly elected Senate nearly derailed the compromise worked out in the lower chamber of parliament (the Tweede Kamer).

The EC gave member states until December 17, 1984, to comply with the directive. After several years of consultation and preparation, the cabinet introduced its draft legislation in late 1984.[14] There was substantial agreement on the main provisions of the legislation (dividing the AOW benefit in two for couples, etc.) but the issue of AOW pensioners with a spouse younger than 65 led to difficult negotiations in parliament. After tough negotiations, parliament finally adopted the legislation in the first half of 1985.

EU legislation in the field of equal treatment also had substantial influence on the structure of occupational pensions. Until the early 1990s, many occupational pension schemes excluded married women from participation. Again, this was a legacy of the "male breadwinner" principles on which the Dutch pension systems were constructed. As a result, occupational pension schemes have had to modify their eligibility rules to comply with recent interpretations of EU law.

Until the 1980s/1990s, discrimination against women was prevalent in second-tier pension schemes. The most common types of discrimination were different participation ages for men and women, the exclusion of married women, and the exclusion of part-time workers. The *Barber*[15] decision by the ECJ in 1990 would have cost occupational pension schemes in the Netherlands an estimated NLG400 billion if pension rights were to be made retroactive for women who had previously been excluded from occupational pension schemes.[16] Because of the substantial costs involved, the Dutch government (pushed by the pension funds and employers) lobbied successfully in Brussels (along with the UK) for a protocol to the Treaty of Amsterdam that would limit the retroactivity of the *Barber* decision. In other words, the new interpretation of EU law would only take effect in 1990.

Margriet Kraamwinkel argues that these changes in the Dutch pension system were driven largely by legal actors, especially the ECJ. Domestic actors had little to do with pushing these changes, although they did exert substantial impact on the way that the rulings were implemented. There has been some reparation of pension rights for previously excluded women, but as Kraamwinkel notes, because supplementary pensions are built up over 40 years, it will take until at least 2035 before the first Dutch woman is entitled to a full pension.[17]

Today the social security and occupational pension schemes in the Benelux countries are based on individual entitlement, and men and women must be treated equally in terms of benefits and coverage. It is worth remembering that until recently, most Dutch welfare state programs and occupational pension schemes explicitly excluded married women from coverage. In Belgium, gender discrimination took another form: women had access to more favorable benefit rules than men, such as an earlier retirement age. EU legislation concerning equal treatment in social security schemes and the ECJ's *Barber* decision prompted substantial changes in public and private social policies that the Dutch and Belgian governments would not necessarily have adopted without a push from the EU.[18]

■ How and in What Areas Do the Benelux Countries Influence the EU?

Belgium, the Netherlands, and Luxembourg are small countries, so they cannot hope to shape the EU agenda like the larger countries do. However, EU decisionmaking institutions amplify the influence of small member states, and the Benelux countries have used this to their advantage. First, political elites from the Benelux countries have long occupied prominent positions in European institutions. Paul Henri Spaak, a former Belgian prime minister, was one of the architects of European integration in the 1950s and 1960s; the former Dutch finance minister Wim Duisenburg was the first president of the European Central Bank; Luxembourg's Jacques Santer was president of the Commission from 1995 to 1999; and Luxembourg's prime minister Jean-Claude Juncker was openly courted to be the president of the European Commission in 2004.

Aside from this more individualized path of influence, there are two central avenues for EU members to try to influence EU policymaking: agenda setting during the rotating presidencies and voting and coalition building in the European Council and Council of Ministers.[19] The rotating presidency is especially important for small states such as the Benelux countries, and they have exploited this to push their own policy agenda at the EU level. Indeed, two notably pro-integration treaties were signed during Dutch presidencies: the Treaty of Maastricht (1992) and the Treaty of Amsterdam (1997). In December 2001, Belgium occupied the presidency when the Laeken Declaration convened the European Convention on the draft Constitutional Treaty.

The Benelux countries have historically used the presidency to advance their pro-integrationist agenda. This is still largely true of Belgium and Luxembourg, but the Netherlands pursued a decidedly less integrationist program when it held the presidency in the second half of 2004. Although the main priorities of the Dutch presidency were enlargement, economic growth, increased security, budget reform, and a more effective role for the EU in the world, Labohm argues that the Dutch presidency was rather uneventful: "It laboured under an interruption of continuity caused by the start-up of a new European Parliament, the accession of new members, which still have to settle down, the resignation of the old Commission and the delays in connection with the acceptance by Parliament of new commissioners."[20] Nevertheless, the Dutch presidency completed accession negotiations with Romania and Bulgaria; the heads of government reached agreement to start accession negotiations with Turkey on October 3, 2005; and the European Council adopted an action plan to improve measures to combat terrorism. Member states also decided to strengthen the EU's military and civilian capabilities so that it can engage in crisis management outside its borders in accordance with its security strategy.

Luxembourg took over the presidency in the first half of 2005. The presidency started optimistically, but ended in crisis. The French and Dutch rejections of the Constitutional Treaty, as well as the failed attempt to reach a compromise on the EU budget, overshadowed the other modest accomplishments of the presidency. During the presidency, the EU reformed the Stability and Growth Pact, and set new objectives in terms of public development aid at the European Union level. On the international agenda, the Luxembourg presidency improved EU-transatlantic relations culminating in the meeting of February 22, 2005, in Brussels with President Bush and a follow-up EU-US summit thereafter.

It is instructive to compare the budget deal brokered under the British presidency with the proposal made by Luxembourg during its presidency. Prime Minister Juncker advocated a larger budget than Tony Blair proposed during the British presidency in December 2005, clearly reflecting Luxembourg's pro-integrationist agenda. Juncker's proposal was €871 billion for the 2007–2013 budget period, while Blair's initial proposal was €850 billion.[21] Luxembourg's budget proposal not only included more money, but it would also have frozen and eventually phased out the British rebate. Moreover, the Luxembourg proposal left the CAP more or less intact.

The Belgian position was very close to Luxembourg's, while the Netherlands joined the British in pushing for a smaller EU budget and fundamental CAP reform.

The Dutch in particular have adopted a hard-line position on EU budget issues, particularly their own budget contribution and the implementation of the Stability and Growth Pact (SGP). With the UK, Austria, and Sweden, the Netherlands is part of the "Gang of Four" pushing for budgetary reform. Finance Minister Zalm has openly criticized the lax implementation of the SGP and voted for tighter implementation in the Council of Ministers. Belgium and Luxembourg have not pursued a similar policy stance; both countries prefer to increase the EU's financial resources.

National Positions in the Council of Ministers

The Benelux countries are pro-integration,[22] but each tends to prioritize a different set of issues in intergovernmental bargaining, and each country relies on a different set of procedures in formulating its bargaining stances.

Erik Jones argues that the consensual nature of domestic policymaking in the Benelux countries produces a complicated relationship between national and EU-level politics.[23] In all three countries, political institutions are designed to facilitate consensual decisionmaking, and this means that multiple actors are incorporated into the decisionmaking process via bipartite or tripartite organizations such as the Social Economic Council in the Netherlands. Belgium is an extreme case in this respect because federalism complicates the formulation of a coherent Belgian position in the Council of Ministers. The constitutional reform of 1970 introduced the first elements of a federal structure, and this process was completed in 1993.[24]

At the administrative level, the Benelux countries differ in the ways they coordinate EU policymaking. Whereas the responsibility for preparing, deciding, and implementing EU dossiers in Luxembourg rests with only a few people, the Netherlands and especially Belgium are characterized by a complex system of coordination. In Luxembourg, coordination is officially the responsibility of the Ministry of Foreign Affairs. However, as Bossaert notes, "usually, the officials who are in charge of a certain EU dossier have a large degree of independence in their field and, when working within their ministry, they will generally co-operate with their minister, with whom they have direct contact in person or by telephone."[25] Because the country is so small, civil servants in the Luxembourg administration dealing with EU policy often know each other personally, and this means that the Ministry of Foreign Affairs organizes only a few regular coordination meetings.

In the Netherlands, the requirements of coalition government prevent the formulation of a strong central political direction. Instead, ministers normally have a large degree of autonomy. A characteristic of the decisionmaking in Dutch cabinets is that all members are collectively bound by the final outcome. When negotiations are conducted within the Council of Ministers, the Dutch position must be formulated by the

Dutch cabinet. The formulation of this view, to be discussed in meetings of the cabinet, is prepared by interdepartmental coordination committees, the so-called departmental *proches*. The most important departmental committee with a formal status with regard to European affairs is the Coordination Committee for EU and Association Problems (CoCo). The chairman of the committee is the minister for foreign affairs; the vice-chairman is the minister for economic affairs. The other members of CoCo are high-ranking departmental officials. However, subcouncils of the cabinet deal with important problems with the preparation and implementation of Community policies that are part of the overall policy of the government. An important subcouncil in this respect is the Council for European Affairs, presided over by the prime minister. The other members include ministers, state secretaries, and the permanent representative in Brussels. Conclusions of the CoCo, as well as those of the Council for European Affairs, are discussed in meetings of the cabinet.[26]

Due to its federal and constitutional entities Belgian ministerial departments at the federal level have their own European coordination structures. In addition, there are several interdepartmental coordination bodies. At the political level, the minister for foreign affairs is responsible for Belgium's EU policy. At the administrative level, the Ministry of Foreign Affairs and Ministry of Economic Affairs are the coordinating ministries. In the Ministry of Economic Affairs coordination takes place in an interdepartmental committee known as the Interministerial Economic Committee (IEC). Next to representatives from several ministries there are representatives of both the communities and the regions. Whereas the IEC deals with technical issues, the European coordination meetings in the Ministry of Foreign Affairs deal with the political dimensions of issues.[27]

■ How Do the Benelux Countries Implement and Comply with EU Policies?

Timely and correct transposition of Internal Market legislation into national law is a legal obligation of all member states under the EC Treaty. Whereas the Commission's data show that over the last years some member states have followed the Commission's recommendation on the "transposition into national law of directives affecting the Internal Market" of July 12, 2004, to improve their national transposition procedures, others have failed. Although Belgium dramatically improved its transposition score between 1997 and 2005, the Benelux countries did achieve the objective of reducing the transposition deficit to 1.5 percent. Whereas 11 out of the 25 member states have succeeded, the Netherlands (1.6 percent), Belgium (2.4 percent), and Luxembourg (4.0 percent) have not met the objective that was set by the EU heads of state and government in Stockholm in 2001 and later reiterated in Barcelona (2002) and Brussels (2003, 2004). Luxembourg in particular has done little to improve its poor performance. Table 6.1 shows that in 2004 and 2005 Luxembourg even managed to increase its backlog. In contrast, Belgium and the Netherlands have managed to reduce the number of outstanding directives considerably.

How Belgium, the Netherlands, and Luxembourg Implement EU Policies

On the administrative level, the Benelux transposition models are very different from each other. After the adoption of a directive by the Council and the European Parliament (if co-decision is required) and publication in the Official Journal of the EC, the Permanent Representation begins the transposition process. In Belgium the responsibility lies with the Federal Public Service (the national level) and/or the federated (regional) entity responsible for the policy covered by the directive. The regional authorities are involved in the network of European coordinators at the administrative level: they participate in the coordination meetings at the national/regional level, provide the network with information on transposition, and have access to the central database of the Federal Public Service of Foreign Affairs. On the political level, reports on transposition are made to the Interministerial Committee for Foreign Policy and the Concertation Committee.

Implementation is more straightforward in Luxembourg because it is a unitary state. Community directives are transposed exclusively at

Table 6.1   Transposition of EU Directives in the Benelux Countries, 2002–2005

	2002	2003	2004	2005
Belgium	95.4	97.6	97.2	97.6
Luxembourg	95.9	97.2	96.5	96.0
The Netherlands	96.3	97.8	97.0	98.4
EU Average	*96.2*	*98.0*	*97.5*	*98.9*

Source: European Commission.

the central level by means of legislative and regulatory procedures. There are no administrative or political guidelines, and ministerial departments are individually responsible for transposing a directive whose subject matter falls within their area of responsibility, which also holds true for the Netherlands. Here, all types of legal instruments are used (statutory law, a royal decree, a ministerial decree, and an act of another administrative authority). Especially when "formal law" has to be changed, it is a long procedure, including the advice procedure at the Council of State and consideration in both chambers of the Dutch parliament. This procedure normally takes two years or more. If "lower" rules have to be changed, the procedure is much shorter. Therefore, there have been discussions with the national parliament about a proposal to shorten the procedure for transposition of European law. Since there is too much opposition for this proposal, it has not yet been accepted. Moreover, the Ministry of Economic Affairs is currently working on a pilot plan for a faster transposition of a number of specific EU directives that it is responsible for.

With regard to the role of the national parliament, generally speaking, Belgium, the Netherlands, and Luxembourg do not have systematic consultation mechanisms prior to the adoption of a directive. In Luxembourg, for example, all draft directives are sent by the minister of foreign affairs for information purposes to the president of the Chamber of Deputies, who forwards them to the appropriate committees. But discussions between government officials and members of parliament take place within this framework only when the issue is placed on the agenda by a committee. In Belgium, after adoption there is a consultative committee within the federal parliament, from which the members automatically receive a copy of the reports to the government on transposition and they get a regular debriefing by the minister in charge. The federal parliament also has access to the central database of the Federal Public Service of Foreign Affairs. Some of the directives require the consultation of advisory bodies. Some consultations are obligatory by special laws, which stipulate that the omission of consulting the advisory bodies can lead to the annulment of the transposition by the Council of State.

The responsibility for monitoring transposition is complex. In Belgium it is the Federal Public Service for Foreign Affairs that is in charge of coordinating the transposition of EU directives. The administrative level of the Federal Public Service for Foreign Affairs reports to the state secretary for European and foreign affairs and to his/her cabinet. The director-general for juridical affairs heads a network of European coordinators. For every Federal Public Service and for every regional entity, a European coordinator is appointed who is charged with the overall transposition of directives. When different entities are concerned with the transposition of a directive, the most relevant entity is designated to the pilot department and is responsible for the coordination between the concerned entities in order to transpose a specific directive. It is then the state secretary for European and foreign affairs, deputy to the minister of foreign affairs, who is responsible for monitoring transposition as a whole. She (or he) delivers monthly reports to the Council of Ministers indicating the problem areas and solutions. Between the meetings of the Council of Ministers at the federal level, work continues between the competent entities both at the political and the administrative levels in order to execute the decisions of the Council for Ministers, the Concertation Committee, and the Interministerial Committee for Foreign Policy.

In Luxembourg, there is no government agency whose remit includes the monitoring of procedures for transposing directives, nor are there any administrative regulations or guidelines governing such monitoring. There are therefore neither requirements nor powers to provide such monitoring. Although not responsible for monitoring, the Ministry of Foreign Affairs keeps a national scoreboard. This scoreboard is regularly circulated among members of the government, accompanied by a statement of Luxembourg's ranking in the Commission's scoreboard.

In the Netherlands, there is a monitoring group under shared responsibility of the Ministry of Justice and the Ministry of Foreign Affairs. This working group meets once a month to look at the progress in transposition and reports to the Council of Ministers. At the political level, it is the secretary for European affairs who is charged with the monitoring of transposition as a whole. Whereas in the Council of Ministers the subject is brought up every three months, before and during the Dutch EU presidency it was brought up every month.

Issues of Compliance in the Benelux Countries

The problems associated with timely transposition differ in the Netherlands, Belgium, and Luxembourg. In Belgium, transposition is complex because of the multiplicity of actors involved. Transposition may also involve consultation with interest groups, for instance trade and professional unions, as well as the social partners. Luxembourg often experiences problems in the transposition process simply because it lacks the personnel to deal with the technical complexity of certain issues requiring external expertise. Although the national scoreboards have brought about an improvement in the national score, given human resource constraints, these efforts have been partly cancelled out by the substantial rise in the number of directives over the years. In the Netherlands, transposition is least problematic, but personnel reductions as well as the increasing volume of EU legislation have led to delays and incorrect transposition.

■ Future Trends and Prospects

Ratifying the Constitutional Treaty

Ratification of the Constitutional Treaty is a good example of how the Benelux counties' approaches to European integration have diverged in recent years. The ratification process in Belgium and Luxembourg has been relatively trouble-free,[28] with comfortable majorities in both countries voting "Yes" either in parliament or in a national referendum. These outcomes reflect both countries' continued support for deepening European integration. In contrast, the Dutch voters' resounding "No" to the constitution on June 1, 2005, demonstrates the Netherlands' deep ambivalence about the future direction of European integration.

The structure of Belgian federalism means that seven legislative assemblies must ratify the constitution. Both houses of the Belgian parliament ratified the constitution in April 2005 by wide majorities, and four of the five regional assemblies have also approved the constitution.[29] Belgians have very positive attitudes toward European integration, and support for the constitution is high. In January 2005, 70 percent of Belgians said they favored the constitution, and even after the French and Dutch "No" votes, support climbed to 77 percent in autumn 2005, the highest in the EU.[30] Belgians continue to view the EU favorably. In July 2005, 56 percent of Belgians polled said they had a positive view of the EU. Even higher numbers support the euro (84 percent), a common security and defense policy (89 percent), and a common foreign policy (75 percent). These are among the highest levels of public support in the EU. Belgians enthusiastically supported eastern enlargement, but show mixed feelings about further enlargement. Sixty-one percent oppose Turkish membership and 47 percent oppose future enlargement. In sum, Belgians remain firmly committed to deepening European integration. Indeed, the Belgian prime minister, Guy Verhofstadt, published a book in December 2005 titled *The United States of Europe*. The book sets out a federal vision in which the 12 countries in the euro zone form the core of a two-speed European Union.[31] It is hard to imagine the prime minister of most other member states vigorously advocating such a pro-integration position.

Until recently, the Netherlands was one of the most reliably pro-integration EU members. As recently as 1991 the Netherlands pushed the idea of "European Political Union" during its EU presidency, but the proposal was quickly dismissed by other EU members.[32] The 1990s and 2000s have been marked by an ambivalent attitude among elites and the public toward the EU. The EU and Dutch membership became politicized, and parts of the political establishment began to criticize the direction of European integration and the Netherlands' pro-integration stance. The rise of the populist politician Pim Fortuyn in 1992 accelerated this trend. Fortuyn capitalized on voter disenchantment by questioning some of the unwritten rules of Dutch politics, including multiculturalism, consensus politics, and European integration. Fortuyn was assassinated shortly before the May 2002 election, but his party did well in the election. Fortuyn's party has since disintegrated, but Fortuyn's legacy is that voters and politicians are much more likely to voice their skepticism about issues such as immigration and institutions such as the European Union.

Dutch voters' rejection of the Constitutional Treaty must be viewed against the background of the Fortuyn revolution and the Netherlands' evolution from net beneficiary of EU funding to the largest per capita contributor in 2003. Nevertheless, the Dutch result was devastating: 61.5 percent of the electorate voted "No." The Dutch "No" was different from the French "No," however. Whereas the French electorate voted against the modernization of the Common Agricultural Policy and the subsidies for French farmers, Dutch voters felt insecure. French voters expressed their reluctance toward the discipline of the free market, against the services directive, whereas Dutch citizens voted against the way Europe works and how Europe is administered. In 2005, every Dutch citizen paid €180 to Brussels, whereas a German citizen transferred only €80. Furthermore, the referendum campaigns in the Netherlands and France were led by rather unpopular leaders: Dutch prime minister Balkenende and French president Chirac.

A central irony of the referendum is that a large number of voters (49 percent) favor a European constitution, but many still voted "No."[33] According to the most recent polls, the most important reason for voting "No" was lack of information. Thirty-two percent of respondents said they did not have enough information to vote "Yes." Lack of information also kept many citizens from voting.[34] According to the same Eurobarometer poll, the second most important reason for voting "No" was potential loss of national sovereignty. Voters' view of the European Union also heavily influenced the vote. Regardless of how someone voted, his/her view of the European Union was the most important factor affecting his/her vote: 31 percent said that this was the key element influencing their vote.[35] Indeed, the referendum result closely resembles Dutch attitudes toward the EU. Only 38 percent of the Dutch have a positive image of the EU (compared to an EU average of 47 percent), and this is about the same number that voted "Yes" to the proposed constitution.

It would be a mistake to conclude that the Dutch are joining the ranks of Euro-skeptics like the United Kingdom and Sweden. Seventy-seven percent of the Dutch think EU membership is a good thing, and this number is much higher than the EU average of 54 percent. Instead, the Dutch "No" is more an expression of disapproval of the way that European institutions function. For example, there is widespread concern in the Netherlands about corruption in Brussels. In the 2004 European Parliament elections, an anticorruption party won two seats in the Netherlands. A second prominent example is the Dutch view of the Stability and Growth Pact. The Netherlands (and Austria) has been one of the strongest supporters of a strict interpretation of the SGP. When the euro-zone members agreed in March 2005 on a more flexible interpretation of the pact that would allow temporary deficits or deficits related to special circumstances such as German unification, the Dutch finance minister barely concealed his disapproval.[36]

After the French "*Non*" and the Dutch "*Nee*," Luxembourg's prime minister, Jean-Claude Juncker, and president of the EU in the first half of 2005, said that the ratification process should continue throughout the EU. Juncker is a very popular politician and he staked his political future on the outcome of the referendum. After the "No" votes in France and the Netherlands, however, polls predicted a close outcome. On July 10, 2005, however, 56.5 percent of voters approved the constitution.

Like Belgium, Luxembourg remains staunchly pro-integrationist and shows few of the signs of skepticism present in the Netherlands. Eighty-two percent think EU membership is a good thing (the highest in the EU), and 57 percent of Luxembourgers have a positive view of the EU.[37] Seventy-five percent think that Luxembourg benefits from EU membership (the second-highest score after Ireland). Like Belgium, however, Luxembourgers are skeptical about Turkish EU membership—only 22 percent favor it.

EU membership remains an article of faith in the Netherlands, Belgium, and Luxembourg. However, the Netherlands' increasing skepticism about the functioning of European institutions, especially the

Stability and Growth Pact and the budget, means that the Benelux countries are no longer as close to each other on European issues as they once were. Belgium and Luxembourg remain staunchly pro-integration, but the recent Dutch ambivalence resembles the Danish situation more than that of the strong Euro-skeptics Sweden, Austria, and the United Kingdom. As in Denmark, Dutch support for EU membership is high, but the comparison probably ends here. Unlike the Danes, the Dutch have nothing against deeper integration, as their enthusiastic adoption of the euro shows. The Dutch would probably regain their pro-integration attitude if the Netherlands were not the largest net contributor and if EU policies were more closely in line with Dutch priorities.

▉ Notes

1. The smallest member state is now Malta, with 400,000 inhabitants.
2. This figure is in absolute terms. The Dutch trading position is magnified by the fact that the port of Rotterdam is the point of entry/exit for much of the EU's trade. See: http://www.wto.org/english/res_e/statis_e/its2005_e/section1_e/i05.xls. Accessed January 1, 2006.
3. Staat van de Europese Unie, *Brief van de Minister van Buitenlandse Zaken*, p. 33.
4. Ibid., p. 34.
5. European Commission, "Allocation of EU Expenditure by Member State 2004." Spain was the largest recipient with 28.2 percent of funding, followed by Germany (13.6 percent), Italy (13.2 percent), and Portugal (10.2 percent). The numbers are much different if calculated as percent of GDP.
6. Ibid. Dutch farmers benefited from the CAP in the first three decades after the EC was established. Even though the Dutch agricultural sector remains substantial, Dutch farmers receive comparatively little CAP aid.
7. France is the largest recipient, with 21.6 percent, followed by Spain (14.6 percent) and Germany (13.9 percent).
8. There is no necessary connection between EMU and the welfare state, but because welfare state programs typically account for the majority of public spending, they are natural targets for expenditure cuts when budget consolidation is on the agenda.
9. This section draws on Anderson, "Pension Politics in Belgium."
10. Belgian Minister of Finance, "The Stability Programme of Belgium 1999–2002."
11. Belgian Minister of Finance, "The Belgian Stability Programme 2005–2008."
12. Pierson, *Dismantling the Welfare State?*
13. *Le Soir*, January 6, 1995.
14. Parliamentary Papers, Second Chamber, 1984–1985, dossier 18515.
15. The *Barber* decision extended the meaning of Article 119 to include

age requirements in occupational pension schemes. This includes both the age of entrance into a scheme and the age of retirement.

16. Kraamwinkel, *Pensioen, emancipatie en gelijke behandeling.*

17. Ibid.

18. It is fair to say that the breadwinner entitlement structure of Dutch social security and occupational pension schemes would have changed sooner or later. The essential point here is that the EU law put the individualization of benefits on the agenda much sooner than would otherwise have been the case.

19. Here our focus is on member-state governments, so we do not discuss lobbying by national interest groups in Brussels.

20. Labohm, *Evaluation of the Netherlands EU Presidency,* p. 1.

21. The final compromise agreed in December 2005 was €862 billion.

22. As noted, the Netherlands has recently backed away from this stance.

23. Jones, "The Benelux Countries."

24. In contrast to many other federal states, Belgium became a federal state because of centrifugal tendencies: a unitary state separated into parts rather than the more common pattern of autonomous regions uniting into a federation. See, for example, Hooghe, "Belgium. Hollowing the Center."

25. Bossaert, "Luxembourg: Flexible and Pragmatic Adaptation," p. 303.

26. Pappas, *National Administrative Procedures.*

27. Franck, Leclercq, and Vandevievere, "Belgium: Europeanisation and Belgian Federalism."

28. The Belgian ratification process is not yet complete. The Flemish regional parliament still has to vote. The largest party in parliament, the right-wing nationalist Flemish Interest, opposes the constitution, but this is not likely to prevent ratification.

29. The Brussels regional parliament voted "Yes" on June 17, 2005; the German community parliament voted "Yes" on June 20, 2005; the Walloon regional parliament voted "Yes" on June 29, 2005; and the French community parliament voted "Yes" on July 19, 2005.

30. Eurobarometer 64 (2005).

31. *NRC Handelsblad,* December 16, 2005.

32. The Dutch refer to this embarrassing episode as "Black Monday."

33. All opinion data are from Eurobarometer 63.4 (spring 2005), "Public Opinion in the European Union: Netherlands."

34. Flash Eurobarometer, *The European Constitution: Post-Referendum Survey in the Netherlands.*

35. Ibid.

36. *NRC Handelsblad,* March 7, 2005.

37. Seventy percent of the Irish have a positive view of the EU. The EU average is 44 percent. Eurobarometer 64, "Public Opinion in the European Union."

PART 2

—

THE SECOND WAVE

7

The United Kingdom: Critical Friend and Awkward Partner?

Neill Nugent and Janet Mather

GIVEN THAT THE UNITED Kingdom is the EU's original "awkward partner," an observer from outside could be forgiven for assuming that it has stuck sturdily to its own ways of doing things over the three-plus decades of its membership. Since a fixation on the preservation of "sovereignty" has featured prominently in UK discourse, one would expect the UK's decisionmakers to resist anything more than the most formal of relationships with their counterparts on the continental mainland. One would also expect to see that the UK's policymakers and institutions have not so much become Europeanized but rather have been dragged, protesting all the way, toward complying with the letter of those EU directives and regulations they could not avoid, while ignoring their spirit with true British unconcern. But neither of these assumptions is, in fact, correct. When analyzing the UK's membership of the EU it is always necessary to separate tradition from pragmatism and rhetoric from realism.

The investigation herein is structured around what are often referred to as the "bottom-up" and "top-down" dimensions of member state–EU relations. The former refers to the inputs that member states make into EU processes in terms of their policy preferences and their ways of acting. The latter refers to the things member states have to do, and the adaptations they have to make, to be compliant with EU requirements and decisional outcomes. In practice there is, of course, considerable overlap and intermeshing between these two dimensions. For example, states have a strong incentive to "upload" as many of their preferences as possible to the EU level so as to minimize the costs of "downloading."[1] Notwithstanding this overlapping and intermeshing, however, the distinction between bottom-up and top-down is a useful organizational device. Broadly speaking, the first two sections of this chapter focus on top-down and downloading processes and influences, with particular attention given to how EU membership has produced significant institutional adaptations in UK governance and how the EU deals with the implementation of EU policies and laws. The third section focuses on the bottom-up and uploading side of the equation.

■ How and in What Ways Does the EU Influence the UK?

The Core Executive

The UK executive is widely recognized as having among the best, possibly *the* best, political and administrative machinery for handling EU business. Two main reasons account for its top ranking. The first is that the UK has, even after the devolution of powers in recent years to Scotland and Wales, a fairly centralized political system. This is so both in terms of the powers that are exercised in and from London (most of the devolved powers are in policy areas where the EU's involvement is limited) and in terms of the party political system, which almost invariably produces governments where one of the two main parties—Labour and Conservative—have a comfortable working majority in Parliament. In preparing itself for deliberations and negotiations in EU forums, the British government is thus not inconvenienced by having to accommodate the views of subnational levels of government or trying to find consensual positions among governing coalition parties.

The second reason for the high quality of the UK executive's EU arrangements is less political and more administrative. The key institutional adjustments that enable the UK executive to "deal with Europe" have been made within the framework of an already existing effective administrative machine. Whereas many other member-state governments have either had to build on less efficient civil services or have chosen to create new structures, the UK's executive arrangement for framing, coordinating, and conducting relations with the EU have been located very much within the proven Whitehall model.

The political level. At the political level relevant ministers are responsible for specific policy issues. They must, however, work within the framework of the government's overall strategy toward the EU, and this—as Burch and Holliday[2] and Bulmer and Burch[3] have shown—has increasingly been formulated from Downing Street. This centralization is partly a reflection of the style of the Blair government and partly a result of the increasing involvement of the heads of government of all member states in the making of EU strategic policies and decisions.

The prime minister is, of course, subject to some constraints in setting the broad guidelines for Britain's policies in the EU, but these are for the most part political rather than structural. Certainly the cabinet as a body is not too much of a problem since it has long ceased to be a forum where *real* policy discussions occur. The extent and nature of the political constraints vary between occupants of the office and over time. So, Thatcher held sway for most of her premiership, but as her internal party position weakened in the late 1980s she was increasingly forced to accommodate the rather more pro-European views of her foreign secretary and chancellor—to such an extent that she agreed to Britain joining the Exchange Rate Mechanism in 1990, even though she would have preferred not to do so. The maneuverability of Thatcher's successor, John Major, on EU policy was permanently restricted during his years as prime minister (1990–1997) by the growing tide of strong Euro-skepticism within his party. Tony Blair's major restraint has been his powerful chancellor of the exchequer, Gordon Brown, who has taken a much more cautious view than the prime minister on the question of whether or not Britain should adopt the euro.

The administrative level. There are four main mechanisms within the executive for dealing with EU affairs at the administrative level:

1. *The departmental level.* There is no single template setting down the arrangements that individual departments of state must have for managing their EU-related work loads. Nor could there reasonably be so given that EU policy penetrates deeply into the business of some departments but only at the margins of others. So, for example, the Department for Environment, Food, and Rural Affairs (DEFRA—incorporating the former Ministry of Agriculture and part of the Department of the Environment, Transport, and the Regions [DETR]) and the Department of Trade and Industry are much affected by the UK's EU membership, but the Department of Health and the Department for Education and Skills are much less so. Different departments accordingly and necessarily have different arrangements.

2. *The Foreign Office.* The Foreign Office deals with the detailed overall coordination of Britain's EU policies and also is the main depart-

ment in respect of the EU's external "political" policies—the Common Foreign and Security Policy (CFSP), the European Security and Defense Policy (ESDP), and enlargement policy. The work is undertaken in the European Union Directorate, which covers not just EU-level business but also bilateral relations with the other EU member states. Most of the work of the Directorate is parcelled into two subdirectorates: EUI (Internal) covers internal policies such as the operation of the market, justice, and home affairs and regional policy; and EUX (External) covers all external policies, either fully—as with the CFSP and enlargement—or in a coordinating role, as with trade and development.

3. *The European Secretariat.* Located within the Cabinet Office, the European Secretariat has a staff complement (in 2005) of 18 officers. The Secretariat's main responsibilities are to provide strategic advice to the government, and especially to the prime minister, on policy toward and within the EU, and to promote coordination between national ministries in their EU-related work. The central and high-level role of the European Secretariat is illustrated by the fact that under Tony Blair the head of the Secretariat has also carried the title of "Prime Minister's European Policy Adviser" and has been physically based in Downing Street rather than in the (admittedly close-by) Cabinet Office itself. Another indication of the importance of the Secretariat is seen in that the UK Permanent Representative returns from Brussels every week to attend a Friday meeting in the Secretariat where senior officials from relevant departments review and anticipate EU business.

4. *The UK Permanent Representation to the European Union (UKREP).* The "EU embassy" is physically perfectly positioned in Brussels for its liaising, intermediary, and lobbying tasks, being located directly opposite the Commission's main Berlaymont Building and being almost immediately adjacent to the Council's main Justis Lipsius Building. It has a total staff of around 80, which is comparable in size to that of most other large and medium-sized member states.[4] These staff are drawn from all of the government departments that are significantly affected by EU policies, though the largest "contingent" is from the Foreign Office—of which UKREP is part.

Parliament

Parliament undertakes a number of roles in respect of the UK's relations with the EU, the most important of which concerns the scrutiny of proposed EU legislation. This involves considering around 1,100–1,300 EU documents annually,[5] including Commission documents and drafts of EU legislation.

Legislation is considered by both Lords and Commons committees. The House of Commons European Scrutiny Committee meets about four times a month and divides documentation into issues for debate in one of its three standing committees for debate on the floor of the House (only a rare occurrence), for decision by the Committee, or for noting by the Committee. The House of Lords Select Committee, which is assisted by seven policy-based subcommittees, receives the same documents as the Commons' Committee, but concentrates more on major EU issues. It debates an average of 25 issues annually.

On the whole, the UK government has treated Parliament's scrutiny requirements seriously. For example, in 1998, Jack Straw, then home secretary, wrote to the European Scrutiny Committee, "responding positively" to the Committee's request for improved scrutiny over the EU's Pillar III. Straw offered Parliament the six-week scrutiny period provided in the Amsterdam Treaty's protocol even before it was ratified. This concession meant that there would be a six-week period between the receipt of co-decision and cooperation proposals by the EU Council of Ministers and Parliament and the point at which the Council considered the matter for decision. Straw also confirmed that he accepted the principle, set out subsequently in the UK's 1999 amended Scrutiny Reserve Resolution,[6] of withholding ministerial agreement to any such proposals until the completion of parliamentary scrutiny. However, he reserved the right to waive this requirement for matters considered to be routine, trivial, confidential, or urgent.

The European Scrutiny Committee has reported that the six-week period is usually sufficient to give time for the UK parliamentary scrutiny committees to examine proposals, although it has added that there are still cases of unacceptable delays in relation to information.[7] The Committee has also reported that there have been three unacceptable breaches of the Scrutiny Reserve Resolution, which had required the presence of a minister to explain.[8]

Regionalization

David Allen comments that the UK's institutions have been adjusted successfully to meet the demands of EU membership,[9] and indeed, most features of UK governance have been affected by the EU in some way, from the political parties to pressure groups and from the Bank of England[10] to local government. However, one of the more interesting features of adjustment, in a state regarded as one of the most centralized in the EU, has been regionalization.

Regional devolution, which properly began with John Major's

attempts in 1994 to improve the distribution of the EU's Structural Funds by providing more efficient and better-integrated government offices within the English regions to complement the Scottish, Welsh, and Northern Ireland offices,[11] was taken up with enthusiasm by Major's successor. It may be that Blair and his government were anxious to show that the UK, like the EU's other large states, had devolved power to its regions. By 2000, unelected regional boards and assemblies were active in England; London had its own elected mayor and assembly; and Scotland and Wales both had elected bodies—a parliament and an assembly respectively. Northern Ireland was a special case—a power-sharing executive with an elected assembly was provided for in 1998, but it had to be suspended in the light of events. However, the 2003 Northern Ireland Assembly Elections Act has set the process in motion again.

For Scottish and Welsh political actors, devolution has opened up opportunities to extend their EU operations. Both have an office in Brussels, which has enabled them to develop informal relationships with EU officials[12]; the two "regions" have developed links with other European regions; and Scottish and Welsh ministers sometimes attend meetings of the EU's Council of Ministers—although when they do, they represent the UK's interests, not those of their own areas.

England, however, still does not have elected regional assemblies. Following a single abortive referendum on the subject in the northeast of England, the elected assembly program was dropped.[13] This decision means that the English regions will only be Europeanized up to a point for the foreseeable future.

■ Complying with EU Policies and Legislation

The Transposition Record
So far as the government is concerned, the transposition of EU law (by incorporation into UK law) is rarely an issue because of the agenda within which EU laws are enacted and the forums in which they are molded. The UK government, like all EU governments, accepts the primacy of EU law over national law, and has agreed during treaty and policy negotiations to accept the extension of EU policy competences. As EU policies develop, UK representatives input into the appropriate decisionmaking processes. Hence, by the time a directive has received the approval of the Commission, Council, and European Parliament, the UK's representatives, along with those of fellow member states, have already played an extensive part in shaping it.

In light of this, it is not altogether surprising to find that the UK usually transposes EU laws promptly and is in the middle range of the EU-25 states in the transposition "league tables" that are issued annually by the Commission. That said, all of the EU's member states have a high level of compliance, with the range normally being somewhere between 95 and 99 percent.

Implementing EU Law

However, the policy process does not end with transposition. Once enacted, the way in which EU law is implemented is also of great significance in drawing an accurate picture of Europeanization in the UK. Implementation, unlike the somewhat apolitical transposition process described above, is set against a background of popular and media-induced Euro-skepticism.[14] Sometimes it also meets the inflexibility of established interests of groups that may see the EU as a means of serving their own purposes but only inasmuch as it requires limited adaptation on their part. Sometimes groups opposing a specific piece of EU legislation see implementation as the opportunity for a second bite of the cherry, and may lobby within the UK to ensure that it is applied as lightly as possible. Alternatively, relevant officials may be insufficiently aware of the need and extent for change.

The way in which the policy process is conducted in the UK has an impact on EU implementation. In the past, some interests have "captured" ministerial departments to the extent that in 2001 the government was forced to replace the long-standing Ministry of Agriculture, Fisheries, and Food, with its ultra-close links to the National Union of Farmers, by a new department. The new department, the Department for Environment, Food, and Rural Affairs, assumed environmental, community, and consumer responsibilities alongside those of agriculture.[15] This rearrangement, at least in theory, widened the policy community and required that policymaking within DEFRA ought now to include representatives of various different interests. As the case studies below suggest, its policy networks are not, however, all-inclusive.

Implementing Environmental Policy

Environmental policy is a highly Europeanized policy, developed partly by means of treaty amendments and partly by means of highly regulatory European Action Programmes. It is not without contention at the EU level, however. In the past, as Peterson has commented, it has been responsible for some degree of discontent between the EU's Industry and Environment Directorates-General.[16] More recently, there have been differences of views between EU treaty-makers and environmental groups, and between small "green" states and larger or newer member states.[17]

The UK has a reasonable record on environmental concerns, particularly in relation to pollution—for example, the 1957 Clean Air Act did not depend upon an EU directive. However, the UK's response to EU initiatives has been variable. For example, in 1980 the EU introduced its acid rain directive, designed to control acid rain by regulating emissions of sulfur dioxide,[18] but it was not until 1986, long after the other member states, that the UK issued enabling legislation.[19] The reason for inactivity was Margaret Thatcher's reluctance to accept that there was any relationship between the output of power stations and the geochemistry of an area. However, in the later 1980s, the Conservative government became more anxious about environmental issues, and Her Majesty's Inspectorate of Pollution, reporting to the Department of Environment, was instituted in 1987.[20] Thatcher herself began to express concerns about global warming and the need to protect the ozone layer[21] and in 1990 the Environmental Protection Act was passed.[22] Environmental policy became an even more significant issue on the UK's agenda during the 1990s under John Major.[23] For example, in 1995 an Environment Agency, empowered to assess levels of environmental pollution and to promote environmental interests, was established.[24]

The election of a Labour government in 1997 meant that environmental issues were consolidated into what become known as "the Third Way" approach of attempting to marry a social-democratic polity to liberal economic policy. By 2005, Labour was conceding the debt the country owed to the EU's environmental policies and was acknowledging that caring for the environment in the context of industrial production—known as "sustainable development"—was a prerequisite of economic effectiveness.[25]

A study conducted across the EU-15 by Matthieu Glachant for the Centre for Industrial Economics in 2000 showed that the UK had, in some cases, already been overcompliant.[26] The privatization program that was launched at the end of the 1980s under the Thatcher government meant, for example, that the transition to using gas instead of coal for the provision of energy had enabled the UK to reach the EU's CO_2 reduction target very quickly, despite its initial fierce opposition to it on the grounds of cost in the early 1980s. Glachant's conclusion was that there was no implementation deficit for EU environmental directives, although he based this conclusion partly on the fact that there were pre-

existing situations—some of them unrelated to environmental awareness—that assisted implementation in the member states (including the
UK) that he studied.

However, the level of compliance, even within environmental policy, may differ from sector to sector. The evidence that the UK has
become a model environmentally aware EU state is, despite Glachant's
findings, ambiguous. Moreover, the Commission's report on the implementation and enforcement of Community environmental law in 2003[27]
(published July 2004) showed that of the 95 directives that had not been
properly applied by the then EU-15 on a range of environmental issues,
the UK was guilty of failing to fully implement secondary obligations
contained in EU law in seven cases. Five of these were related to
improvement of water quality, one to the natural environment, and the
other to waste management. Nine of the EU-15 states had a better record
than the UK, while five had a worse one. The UK's approach toward
implementing EU environmental legislation can be illustrated by reference to two case studies on aspects of waste management.

A mountain of ozone-depleting refrigerators. The issue of waste
management became a topic of particular interest to the UK's citizens
between 2001 and 2003. During this period, the UK government found
itself embarrassed about its failure to implement EU Regulation
2037/2000 on the safe disposal of substances that damage the ozone
layer. The substance in question was hydrochlorofluorocarbons
(HCFCs) and, among other places, it is found in the foam used within
refrigerators manufactured before 1996. Article 5 of the regulation pro-
hibited the use of HCFCs as refrigerants, specifically naming domestic
refrigerators and freezers. Article 16 required HCFCs to be replaced (for
recycled items) or destroyed (if the item were to be disposed of) by
"environmentally acceptable technologies." A date of January 1, 2002,
was set as the deadline for implementation.[28]

Although the final version of the regulation was not adopted by the
Council of Ministers until June 2000, the DETR (DEFRA's predecessor
in terms of the environment) began a consultation process in relation to
the proposed regulation (itself a response to the Montreal Protocol[29]) in
September 1998.[30]

In November 2001, however, concern was expressed by industry
about the state of readiness of the UK to deal with its old refrigerators.
Before the regulation deadline, these items had been simply crunched in
giant metal cutters, or were disposed of in refuse sites (minus their
doors), or were repaired and recycled, sometimes by being exported to

developing countries.[31] Such methods would no longer be acceptable after the cutoff date. If fridges and freezers were to be destroyed, they would have to be compressed by a special processing plant with closed units that could capture HCFCs in liquid form.[32] Unfortunately, the UK had only two suitable plants, and had, at that stage, no plans for providing more.[33] Up to March 2002, only four permits had been granted to local authorities—who are at the sharp end of waste disposal—enabling them to export 100,000 fridges for disposal to Germany (one of the few states that already had the facilities). Eleven other local authorities, overloaded with redundant fridges and freezers, had applied for permits.[34] The UK government responded to the situation by announcing that it would provide £6 million to help local authorities with storage until the end of March 2002.[35]

The House of Commons' Select Committee on the Environment, Food, and Rural Affairs held an investigation into the affair and its report, published in June 2002, noted that a "fridge mountain" had appeared in the UK. The situation had deteriorated because, now that both the recycling and the disposal of fridges were so expensive and problematic, retailers would no longer collect old appliances when delivering new ones. The result was that waste disposal sites were piled high with old fridges, and a number of new (illegal) entrepreneurs were adding to the problem by collecting them at £10 per item from householders and then dumping them.[36] In July 2002 DEFRA issued a press release announcing that an additional £40 million would be made available to local authorities to assist them with storing and recycling old fridges.[37]

Michael Meacher, environment minister from 1997 to 2003,[38] initially claimed that the European Commission was to blame. Answering a question in the Commons in January 2003, he said that on a number of occasions from 1999 onward his officials had sought elucidation from the Commission as to whether the regulation referred specifically to foam, rather than just to coolant gases.[39] Meacher told the Commons that clarification had not been obtained until June 2001 and that his department had been thus "badly let down by the Commission."

The Select Committee on the Environment commented that this did not explain why the government had not passed on the clarification to local authorities when it was finally obtained. Neither did it explain why the government had not gone ahead in advance of clarification and instituted its own procedures, especially as, it transpired, legal advice on the matter had been given to departmental civil servants early in 2000.[40] Meacher explained, lamely, that the lack of action was because he was afraid that the government would resist forcing industry to initiate an expensive, and possibly unnecessary, program and that he would get labeled as a "trendy" for his pains. The Select Committee, unimpressed, pointed out that, by inaction, a business opportunity had been lost. It turned out also that the DETR had neglected to include the retail trade in fridge recycling and disposal in its policy network for the 1998 consultation process, and had no idea just how many surplus fridges—in fact, around 2.5–3 million per year—were likely to be left on local authorities' hands.

Meacher withdrew his denigration of the Commission on being presented with the Select Committee's evidence, and told the Committee that, "in cold blood," he would not repeat it. The Select Committee's report ended with a stringent criticism of the government, as epitomized by the DETR, its successor DEFRA, and the environment minister.

Since this episode, it appears that the fridge mountains have become molehills. Although in March 2004 there was still a backlog of old fridges, the Environmental Services Association (ESA), which represents the UK's waste management industry, thought there was now sufficient capacity to deal with them.[41] It is less certain, however, that the underlying problem has disappeared.

Mountains of waste mismanagement. On October 16, 2003, the UK government was the subject of a case[42] brought against it by the Commission for failing to fulfill its obligations in relation to Council Directive 1999/31/EC on the landfill of waste.[43] The Commission told the European Court of Justice (ECJ) that the UK had failed to put in place the measures needed to comply with the directive by the deadline of July 16, 2001. The Court found for the Commission, and ordered the UK to pay costs to the Commission.[44]

In December 2002, the government had set up the Hazardous Waste Forum to monitor the disposal of dangerous materials. Shortly after the ECJ judgement, at the end of December 2003 the forum issued a report[45] that criticized the government for failing to respond also to a 2000–2001 EU decision on waste management.[46] The decision, which builds on Council Directive 1999/31/EC on the landfill of waste, bans the mixing of toxic waste with nontoxic waste material, and extends the list of hazardous substances to items such as television sets, mobile phones, old cars, and garden pesticides.[47] It should have come into operation in July 2004.

The implications of the directive and of the decision are extensive. The directive requires the closure of landfill sites that do not meet the required specifications for treatment of waste; the decision increases both the type and volume of dangerous waste requiring special treatment. However, because of the UK's failure to implement the 1999 landfill directive satisfactorily, the new system could not be put into operation until July 2005. To compound the problem, the government did not update its own list of Hazardous Waste Regulations in accordance with EC decisions,[48] with the result that waste disposal companies were again unable to prepare for implementation.[49] The ESA complained that this was another lost business opportunity, and that the environmental impact of unregulated operators dumping toxic waste was potentially serious.[50]

The UK and Noncompliance:
Evidence from the Case Studies

Gerda Falkner and colleagues have studied the issue of noncompliance with EU legislation.[51] Their findings, which are based on research in the field of labor law, suggest that noncompliance may be related to opposition, although they note it may be the opposition of those who implement rather than those who take part in enacting EU law. Interestingly, Falkner and colleagues also found that noncompliance is not always linked to opposition at all, but may result from administrative shortcomings or from interpretation problems where it is unclear to administrators what an EU law requires.[52]

In the case of Regulation EC 2037/2000 (the "fridge mountain"), we have shown that administrative shortcomings definitely played a part in its poor implementation, although it is not so clear whether these shortcomings resulted from inefficiency, from lack of coordination (a departmental reshuffle took place in the middle of the process), or from unexpressed opposition (either to the law, to the government, or to the government minister). Interpretation problems do seem to have afflicted the minister, at least. It is possible that the misconception belonged initially to Meacher's civil servants, but it would be harder to argue that they were still unsure after receiving legal advice in early 2000.[53]

The notion of opposition to Regulation EC 2037/2000 is a more difficult issue to determine. There is no evidence of overt hostility on anyone's part to an environmental regulation that was intended to implement the Montreal Protocol that had been readily signed by the UK government. Within the context of the UK's recent environmentally friendly agenda, such opposition seems particularly unlikely. However, a reluctance to act until it was made clear that action was necessary does suggest that the UK may not have changed its spots regarding implementation of environmental regulation as much as it claims.

This theory gains validity in the case of management of waste within landfill sites. Misinterpretation is ruled out as a possible factor—the UK admitted to the ECJ, for example, that it had not fully transposed the directive by the agreed deadline[54]—and therefore the delay on implementation must be due to either concealed opposition or, of course, to inefficiency. Both the ESA and Friends of the Earth[55] appear to concur with the notion of inefficiency.

Whatever the reasons for its failure to implement the two EU laws, the study of both cases suggests that while the UK's record is not obstructionist, it finds some degree of difficulty in complying with EU law that requires a change of direction or of vision. As Glachant found, overcompliance tends to result when a piece of EU legislation dovetails into an existing political framework. It may be, as the case studies suggest, that ineffective or inefficient compliance is the outcome when EU laws do not dovetail.

■ **How and in What Ways
Does the UK Influence the EU?**

*Inputting into the EU:
Core Policy Interests and Issues for the UK*

In terms of uploading, the UK's "awkwardness" has not prevented both Conservative and Labour governments involving themselves actively in EU policy deliberations and negotiations. Some of this involvement has been aimed, it is true, at slowing policy advance at the EU level, but by no means has all of it been so. Indeed, in a few policy areas, most notably ones associated with the completion and operation of the internal market, the UK has been a strong champion of the advancement of integration.

Much has been made of how the UK's input into the EU changed when Labour replaced the Conservatives in government in May 1997. From having been a strongly Euro-skeptic party in the 1980s, Labour came to accept the EU much more in the 1990s, while the Conservatives appeared to travel in the opposite direction during their years in government between 1979 and 1997. However, the reality shows a different picture—the change has been as much about mood and style as about substance. So, for example, almost immediately after being elected, Labour agreed at the June 1997 European Council meeting that the

Community Charter of the Fundamental Social Rights of Workers should be incorporated into the Treaty Establishing the European Community. Nevertheless, this has had little practical effect in the UK. Indeed, Labour has given a much higher priority to establishing a flexible labor market than to entrenching strong worker's rights—as illustrated in 2005 when it led a coalition of states in the Council to veto Commission proposals to tighten up on permissible opt-outs to the 48-hour weekly working limit under the Working Time Directive.

Mood and style are important, however. Under Labour the UK has sought to engage more positively with its partners: to be, and to be seen to be, less negative. But this change in "atmospherics" should not disguise the fact that on most of the core issues that have dominated the EU over the last 20 years or so, Labour's positions have not been fundamentally different from those of its Conservative predecessors. This is because both parties, or at least party leaderships, have shared a broadly similar vision of the sort of EU they want to see: one that provides for a properly regulated Internal Market in which the four freedoms (of goods, services, capital, and labor) prevail and beyond which states cooperate—but do not, for the most part, integrate—on matters of mutual interest and potential benefit. The core issues, and the UK's position in regard to them, are as follows.

Treaty Revisions

In all of the intergovernmental conferences that have produced treaty revisions over the years, UK governments have consistently been in "the slow integration stream." That is, they have adopted broadly intergovernmental positions and on most issues—be they concerned with institutional or policy reform—have usually been in the vanguard of resistance to "supranationalist advance." Tony Blair acted little differently from earlier Conservative governments during the three years (2002–2004) that the Constitutional Treaty was being negotiated. He continually emphasized the importance of Britain needing to retain its sovereignty in key areas of policy. He was also similar to his predecessors by agreeing to considerable extensions to Qualified Majority Voting in areas where this was deemed to be necessary in the interests of EU efficiency.

The Internal Market

When she was prime minister, Margaret Thatcher was one of the foremost champions of the opening-up of the Internal Market and of the Commission-driven Single European Market program. Tony Blair's government has very much followed in Thatcher's steps in this regard, influenced by Britain's heavy dependence on trade and by its strengths in sectoral areas that have not been fully liberalized—such as financial services. Labour has constantly pressed the case for the need to continue an opening-up and liberalizing momentum if the European economy is to be able to compete in world markets. Indeed, Blair's government sought to make liberalizing and "modernizing" economic reform within the framework of the Lisbon Process the main focus of its EU presidency in the second half of 2005.

In adopting this position, Labour has found friends across much of the EU, not least among new member states. It has, however, met with some resistance from "old" EU states, notably France and Germany, which have been concerned that too much liberalization might endanger their long-established, and electorally popular, "social market" economic foundations.

Economic and Monetary Union

Since it joined the European Community in 1973, the UK has consistently been wary of the many proposals that have been made and the various actions that have been taken to forge European Economic and Monetary Union (EMU). The case made by EMU's proponents that the Internal Market necessarily requires a single currency, common monetary policies, and tightly coordinated macroeconomic policies has either not been accepted or has been regarded as involving "too much, too soon" for the UK.

In broad terms, four main arguments are made in the UK against joining the single currency:

- The EMU system is too rigid. "One size fits all" is not appropriate for such a large and diverse economic area as Europe, where very different economic circumstances apply in different areas and where asymmetries cannot be much assisted by spending policies from the center (because of the EU's small budget) or by labor market mobility (Europe has a much more rigid labor market than the United States).
- The UK is especially different. This is so particularly since its economic cycle is not in alignment with most of the rest of the EU.
- The sovereignty price is too high. The prospect of the transfer of more powers to the EU level, especially in such a key and sensitive policy area as macroeconomic and monetary policy, is a step much too far in loss-of-sovereignty terms.
- The euro "is not working." Since the launch of the single currency

in 1999 the UK has outperformed "euro-land" in most respects, especially in terms of having higher growth rates and lower unemployment.

The position of the Labour government has not been to rule out possible EMU membership for the UK at some point in the future—which the opposition Conservatives virtually have done—but rather to say that when five specified (and very general) economic tests have been met, the government will consider whether to recommend membership to the British people in a referendum. There is little likelihood in the foreseeable future that the tests will be deemed to have been passed, or even if they were, that the government would risk the referendum given the level of Euro-skepticism in the UK.

Enlargement

Given their visions for the EU, British governments naturally have been strong supporters of its enlargement. Quite simply, a larger EU means a larger Internal Market. As long as applicant states have met the formal criteria for opening accession negotiations—the so-called Copenhagen conditions—and as long as they meet the EU's terms in the negotiations, then they have received the UK's backing.

The UK has not been much influenced by the concerns expressed in several member states that have more integrationist visions of the future of the EU. In such states the increasing diversity of the EU—especially if it involves Turkish membership—is a worry, with greater diversity being seen to threaten the coherence of the EU and the prospects of integrationist advance. For the UK such "threats" are a further attraction of enlargement.

Agricultural Reform

The UK has long supported reform of the Common Agricultural Policy (CAP). But the sort of reform it has wanted to see has been more than just the movement that has taken place since the mid-1990s from price support to income support. Rather, the UK has advocated a much more radical reform in which EU spending on agriculture—which has hovered at just under 45 percent of the total EU budget in recent years—is greatly reduced.

This position has brought the UK into conflict with some of its neighbors, especially France—which receives just over one-quarter of total CAP spending. The conflict became particularly sharp following a deal between French president Jacques Chirac and German chancellor Gerhard Schröder in late 2002. Under the agreement, which Chirac and

Schröder managed to "impose" on other member states, CAP spending was to be protected at existing levels until at least 2013. Blair subsequently attempted to have the basis of that deal reopened in the context of negotiations on the 2006–2013 financial perspective (medium-term financial planning instrument)—a maneuver that found support in a few other member states but resulted in Blair being sharply attacked by Chirac and Schröder.

The EU's Budget

The budget has featured prominently in Britain's relations with the EU: more prominently, perhaps, than is warranted by the sums involved since the total budget amounts to only just over 1 percent of total EU gross national income (GNI) and less than 3 percent of total public expenditure. There are two reasons for this prominence. First, as a believer in a limited, if not a minimalist, EU, the UK has wanted to see EU spending kept at low levels, whereas some states have wanted to see it increased. Second, Britain is a major contributor to the EU budget. This is mainly because of Britain's relatively small agricultural sector, but the high proportion of its trade outside the EU is also a contributory factor. In 1984, Thatcher negotiated a rebate—or, technically, an "abatement"—amounting to two-thirds of the net contribution, but even allowing for this rebate Britain has remained the EU budget's largest net contributor after Germany.

This situation has meant that Britain has taken a tight budgetary line within the EU. More specifically, it has argued and pressed for restraint when the multiannual financial perspectives—within which annual budgets have been framed since 1988—have been negotiated.

The negotiations on the 2007–2013 financial perspective illustrate the UK's budgetary stance, show how it can find allies on aspects of its stance, but demonstrate also how budgetary issues can create major problems for the UK. Regarding the stance, the UK rejected the Commission's initial proposal for level funding with the 1999–2006 perspective, which involved setting a cap of 1.24 percent of EU GNI for committed expenditure. The UK wanted the cap to be 1.0 percent. Regarding finding allies, the other major net contributors—Germany, France, the Netherlands, Sweden, and Austria—also initially backed the 1.0 percent cap. Regarding the creation of problems, France and Germany edged away from the 1.0 percent when the Luxembourg presidency in June 2005 suggested a compromise limit of 1.06 percent. Paralleling this action, France led calls from several EU states for the abolition of the UK's rebate, which led to a stiff British response. Senior ministers declared that the rebate could only be reconsidered if it was within the context of a wider debate on the budget as a whole: a debate in which CAP spending, and what UK politicians sometimes privately describe as "the French rebate," would be featured.

Foreign Policy

Given its history, its extensive interests and special relationships overseas, its large military forces, and the fact that it is one of only two European nuclear powers (France is the other), the UK has inevitably been centrally involved in the development of EU foreign and defense policies. The involvement has been such, indeed, that it frequently has been a lead player. This was, for example, the case with the initiative launched by Tony Blair and Jacques Chirac at their 1998 St. Malo summit, which led to what has become the fledgling European Security and Defence Policy (ESDP). It was the case also with the Franco-British-German-led initiative of 2005, designed to persuade Iran not to build a military nuclear capability.

But though the UK has been active within the EU's CFSP and ESDP, it has been so on the basis of two "conditions" that have sometimes brought it into conflict with other member states. The first has been an insistence that the policy area remains primarily intergovernmental in form, with all major decisions to be taken by unanimity. The UK government has not been the only member government inclined in this direction, but it has been the principal "outrider," which has resulted in it attracting much of the criticism from these member states that—dissatisfied with the EU's weak foreign-policy "performance" in the Balkans, Afghanistan, Iraq, and elsewhere—have wished to see foreign policy being given a more supranational base. The second "condition" has been an insistence that EU foreign and defense policy should be firmly based on the maintenance of a strong transatlantic partnership. No EU member state wishes for poor transatlantic relations, but some—especially France—are more inclined than the UK to emphasize that in some respects and on some policy issues the EU must take its distance from the United States. This difference of emphasis within the EU on the nature of relations with the United States was accentuated in respect of the 2003 US-led invasion of Iraq and its consequences, when the EU was completely unable to find common positions. Some states—most notably the UK, Italy, Spain, and most of the soon-to-be new EU member states from central and eastern Europe—supported the invasion, while other states, notably France and Germany, opposed it.[56]

■ Conclusions: Trends and Prospects

As this chapter has shown, the UK's position in and relationship to the EU is not as straightforward as it is often portrayed. That is to say, the picture is not accurately captured simply by describing the UK as a somewhat distanced and Euro-skeptic state.

In terms of being distanced, it is true that in some respects the UK is less Europeanized than other EU-15 (pre–May 2004) states. This is seen most notably in the party political debate (where fundamental questions about the status and nature of Britain's membership are still raised) and among public opinion—where polls show much lower levels of EU consciousness and knowledge than is the case in other member states. But in important respects the UK has been at least partly Europeanized. This is especially the case at senior levels of government, where mechanisms have been established and operating procedures have been developed to produce a highly efficient executive machinery for conducting relations with the EU. In addition, the UK's record of transposing EU law equals and sometimes exceeds that of most other member states.

However, our case studies suggest that efficiency does not always extend to implementation, especially where less senior officials are involved, and where implementation is related to introducing secondary legislation or complex arrangements needed to put an EU law into practice. Europeanization has its limitations in these situations.

As for being Euro-skeptic, it is inarguable that Euro-skepticism does run more deeply in the UK than in any other member state, reflected and promoted as it is by a largely Euro-skeptic press and by many politicians (especially in the Conservative Party and the UK Independence Party) who press for either a highly minimalist EU or for UK withdrawal from the EU. But this Euro-skepticism should not mask the fact that the UK in important ways has also been a positive and active member state. It has not hesitated to engage fully in debates at the EU level on such key issues as the Constitutional Treaty, EMU, the Lisbon Process, and the CFSP. If the nature of its contribution to these debates has been seen to be less "pro-European" than the contributions of, say, France and Germany, events in the mid-2000s suggest that the UK has not necessarily been misguided in terms of the EU's interests. The UK may fairly be described as a "critical friend" as well as a sometimes "awkward partner."

▩ Notes

1. On this, see, for example Börzel, "Pace-Setting, Foot-Dragging, and Fence-Sitting."

2. Burch and Holliday, "The Blair Government and the Core Executive."

3. Bulmer and Burch, "The Europeanisation of Core Executives—the UK."

4. For the staffing sizes of all EU-25 Permanent Representations see Hayes-Renshaw and Wallace, *The Council of Ministers.*

5. Baines, "Parliamentary Scrutiny of Policy and Legislation," p. 78. She notes that this represents an increase from the 800–1,000 documents of the mid-1990s.

6. House of Commons Modernisation Select Committee, second report, Annex 1. Most EU member states do not have any equivalent.

7. House of Commons, Select Committee on European Scrutiny, "European Scrutiny: Thirtieth Report" (London: Stationery Office Ltd., 2002).

8. Baines, "Parliamentary Scrutiny of Policy and Legislation," p. 73.

9. Allen, "The United Kingdom," p. 131.

10. When Labour made the Bank of England independent in 1997, it fulfilled one of the Maastricht criteria.

11. Mather, *The European Union and British Democracy*, p. 157.

12. Allen, "The United Kingdom," p. 143.

13. Prescott, "Elected Regional Assembly Referendum in the North East."

14. Allen, "The United Kingdom," pp. 119, 129–130. Allen's chapter subtitle—"A Europeanized Government in a Non-Europeanized Polity"—captures the essence of the ambiguities within the UK's political system.

15. See the mission statement of DEFRA: http://www.defra.gov.uk/corporate/aims/aimobjs.pdf. The mid-1990s BSE crisis and the 2001 outbreak of foot-and-mouth disease, and the limitations of MAFF in responding to them, acted as catalysts. Both crises, of course, led to uneasy relations with the European Commission (Allen, "The United Kingdom," p. 135).

16. Peterson, "Playing the Transparency Game."

17. Geddes, *The European Union and British Politics,* p. 136.

18. Commission of the European Communities (1980): *Directive on Acid Rain*, 80/779/EEC (Brussels).

19. Just in time to catch the 1988 Acid Rain Directive.

20. Smith, "Policy Networks and Policy Change in United Kingdom Industrial Pollution Policy 1970–1990," p. 6.

21. Thatcher, "Speech to the Royal Society on Environmental Issues."

22. Smith, "Policy Networks and Policy Change in United Kingdom Industrial Pollution Policy 1970–1990," p. 6.

23. Geddes, *The European Union and British Politics,* p. 136.

24. House of Commons, *Environment Act* (1995), clauses 2–10.

25. UK Government White Paper: *Prospects for the EU in 2005* (Cmnd 6450, London: Stationery Office Ltd., 2005). The document commented that during the forthcoming UK presidency the government would prioritize meeting the Kyoto Protocol targets and reviewing the EU's Sustainable Development Strategy.

26. Glachant, "Lessons from Implementation Studies," p. 6. Much of the information in this paragraph is taken from Glachant's article.

27. Commission of the European Communities, *Fifth Annual Survey on the Implementation and Enforcement of Community Environmental Law*, p 40.

28. Council of the European Communities, *Regulation (EC) No 2037/2000 of the European Parliament and of the Council on Substances That Deplete the Ozone Layer*.

29. "The Montreal Protocol on Substances That Deplete the Ozone Layer," signed by the UK, and implemented in the EC by EC regulation 2093/94, 1987.

30. House of Commons, Environment, Food, and Rural Affairs Committee, "Disposal of Refrigerators," p. 6.

31. Ibid.

32. Brown, "EU Law Causes Unwanted Fridge Mountains: New Regulation Forbids CFC Foam Being Dumped in Landfill Sites." *The Guardian*, Janaury 14, 2002.

33. House of Commons, "Disposal of Refrigerators."

34. Brown, "EU Law Causes Unwanted Fridge Mountains. "

35. The Select Committee noted that no payments were actually made until April 2002.

36. House of Commons, "Disposal of Refrigerators,"p. 7; Brown "EU Law Causes Unwanted Fridge Mountains. "

37. Department for Environment, Food and Rural Affairs, "Extra £40 Million to Help Local Authorities Dispose of Fridges" (DEFRA News Release 292/02, 2002).

38. Meacher was removed from his ministerial post in 2003; it has been suggested that this was because of his outspoken views about genetically modified foods, not because of his inefficient disposal of old fridges.

39. House of Commons, *Hansard Debates 29539: col 413*.

40. House of Commons, "Disposal of Refrigerators." The EFRA Committee report is the source of information about ensuing events.

41. Environmental Services Association, "EC Regulation No 2037/2000 on Substances That Deplete the Ozone Level."

42. European Court of Justice, *Judgment of the Court (Third Chamber) of 16 October 2003*.

43. Council of the European Communities, "Council Directive 1999/31/EC of 26 April 1999 on the Landfill of Waste."

44. Under Article 69(2) of the ECJ's Rules of Procedure.

45. Hazardous Waste Forum, "Hazardous Waste—An Action Plan for Its Reduction and Environmentally Sound Management."

46. Council Decision 2000/532/EC as amended by Decisions 2001/118/EC, 2001/119/EC, and 2001/573/EC amend former decisions based on Article 1(a) of Council Directive 75/442/EEC on waste and Council Decision 94/904/EC, which establishes a list of hazardous waste following Article 1(4) of Council Directive 91/689/EEC.

47. Commission of the European Communities, *Commission Decision of 16 January 2001 Amending Decision 2000/532/EC as Regards the List of Wastes*.

48. Commission of the European Communities, "Commission Decision 2001/532/EC, May 2000."

49. Environmental Services Association, "Government Inflicts Unnecessary Risk on Environment: So What's the Point of DEFRA?"

50. Ibid.

51. Falkner, Hartlapp, Leiber, and Treib, "Non-Compliance with EU Directives in the Member States." Falkner et al. looked at directives, rather than regulations, but there is a case for making the assumption that the same findings apply, given that the way in which directives are enacted in the UK almost entirely excludes all but governmental actors in any case.

52. Ibid., pp. 456–465.

53. Meacher may have wanted to discuss further with his civil servants the lack of information provided to him by his Department after the issue of the Select Committee Report, although his opportunity to do so would have been limited since its publication coincided with his removal from government.

54. European Court of Justice, *Judgment of the Court (Third Chamber) of 16 October 2003.*

55. Claire Wilton commented: "The Government has been too slow in encouraging industry to take action, despite the fact that it has known about this change in the law for the past five years." (In Friends of the Earth, "Industry Unprepared for New EU Law on Toxic Waste.")

56. Since the invasion, the EU-25 states have adopted a profusion of positions regarding whether they have been prepared to actively support peacekeeping and humanitarian operations in Iraq, and if so on what terms.

8

Ireland:
Brussels and the Celtic Tiger

Richard B. Finnegan

TO STATE THAT THE place of Ireland in world politics is modest is not to engage in irresponsible hyperbole. Nor is Ireland's place in the European Union one that should be exaggerated. The Republic of Ireland's 4 million people are on an island the size of the state of Maine, set apart geographically from the center of Europe. We should begin with the recognition that the importance of the European Union (EU) to Ireland is considerably greater than the importance of Ireland to the Union. A senior member of the European Union, Ireland has been, and is, as pro-Europe as any state in the EU, and has benefited as much or more than any member state. Yet Ireland's posture has been altered by its economic growth and in the future Ireland will position itself differently in terms of the EU budget, social issues, and voting presence.

■ How and in What Ways Does the EU Influence Ireland?

For Ireland, the primary impact of the EU has been in the economic realm, especially the Single Market, the Common Agricultural Policy, and the Structural Funds in fostering Ireland's dramatic economic growth. Ireland's entry into the Union played an important part in its relationship to Great Britain and, to a limited degree, developments in Northern Ireland. Women's rights in the area of social policy, and Irish neutrality in the security domain, have also been distinctive policy issues for Ireland.

The Relationship with Britain

On January 1, 1973, Ireland's entry into the European Union not only fastened the Irish economy to those of the states of the EU, but also forged a relationship that symbolically diminished the primacy of the link to Britain. That psychological break should not be underestimated given the long and antagonistic colonial relationship between the two countries. Ireland becoming among the most "European" of the member states is not unrelated to departing the British orbit. In fact, Ireland's close relationship with Britain made entry into the European Community (EC) more difficult as the linkage to Britain's economy was so extensive that the Irish government could not risk being outside the EC external tariff barrier were Britain within it. Ireland's application to the EC was thus paired with London's and, thus, was put on hold for a decade due to the rejection of the British application.

Entry into the EU shifted Ireland's balance of trade from the almost exclusive focus on the United Kingdom to a more balanced distribution. In 1960, 75 percent of Irish exported goods went to Britain, while 50 percent of imported goods came from Britain. By 2004 the figures had dropped to 18 percent of Irish exports and 30 percent of Irish imports. The volume of Irish exports to the European Union, however, had increased sharply from 7 percent to 49 percent during the same period, while imports to Ireland from the EU had increased 40 percent by 2004.

Some years ago in 1978, the European Court of Human Rights ruled against the United Kingdom in a case that the Republic of Ireland had brought to it over the treatment of prisoners in Northern Ireland, which reflected the long antagonism over the issue of the partition of Ireland in 1922. The judgment of the court was that the UK authorities in Ulster had engaged in "inhumane and degrading treatment" of Irish Republican Army detainees, an embarrassment to the British who had argued that what was done to the prisoners was not torture but was necessary—a position that was not persuasive to the republic.

Finally, in 1979, Ireland opted to join the European Monetary System (EMS). Britain chose not to enter, reflecting Margaret Thatcher's arm's-length policy with respect to Europe. The Irish punt was severed from the pound for the first time since 1826, and that decision was much debated within the government. Ireland ran the risk of substantially altering its balance of payments, as much of Ireland's trade in 1979 was still with the United Kingdom. Ireland, after 1992, then opted to join the euro, introduced in 2002, and fixed its currency to that rate in 1998, while the UK chose not to join the euro zone. The euro was another in a series of important policy choices that moved Ireland closer to Europe and more distant from Great Britain.

Ireland's Rapid Economic Growth

The surge of growth in the Irish economy is seen as directly related to Ireland's membership in the EU. The Irish rate of growth from 1987 to 2000 was 140 percent, while the United States in this period grew 40 percent and the EU 35 percent. Ireland's growth earned the country the sobriquet "Celtic Tiger."

In 30 years, Ireland transitioned from a relatively closed and backward economy to an open globalized economy.[1] Rejecting protectionism and adopting incentive planning after 1959, Ireland began shifting the basis of the economy from agriculture to industry and service, and shifted industrial development from reliance on a paucity of domestic capital to attracting foreign direct investment.[2] After 1973, the Irish negotiated dispensations from the EU tax policies to continue to generate industrial development through tax breaks to foreign firms. A surge of agricultural economic growth after entry into the European Community came from the benefits of the Common Agricultural Policy (CAP) to the farmers of Ireland and their access to new markets. Estimates put the growth of the Irish GNP, due to the CAP, at between 5 and 10 percent.[3]

The European Monetary System stabilized Irish currency and trade as the punt was based upon the German mark rather than the volatile British pound. Currency stability in Ireland was compounded by the United Kingdom's choice not to participate in the EMS (except for 1990–1992) and the extensive trade with the UK. Despite the narrow band of fluctuation allowed, and the currency fluctuations of 1992 and 1993, the Irish defended the punt. Following the demands of the Maastricht Treaty in 1992, Ireland labored to bring the value of their currency into accord with the conditions for entering the euro zone and did so by 1999. Thus the EMS encouraged greater, though not perfect, discipline in Ireland's public finance and guidance for fiscal policy for nearly a decade in accord with the EU conditions set down to meet the goal of adopting the euro.

The grants from the EU's Social and the Regional Funds assisted the development of the west of Ireland and the infrastructure within the country. When Ireland entered the EU it was among the poorest states in the EU, and the entire country qualified for the Cohesion Funds. The European Regional Development Fund (ERDF) allowed the Irish

Industrial Development Authority to offer generous grant packages based on the funds. From its entry in 1973, Ireland has received more of the EU Structural Funds per capita than any other state, at one point in the 1970s getting 13 percent of the EC funds with only 1 percent of the EC population.[4] The Social Funds directed at vocational training and employment for youth were about 13 percent higher for Ireland than for the other EU countries in the 1980s. The Irish received from the second EU Community Support Framework (CSF), for example, about 1,800 punts per capita between 1994 and 1999, a significant amount by any measure. The funds have been important for Ireland's medium-term financial planning and have been considered to be very successful in public infrastructure development such as improving freight handling at Dublin Airport, building roads, dredging Waterford Port, treating wastewater, and protecting coastal areas. In fact, the border and western region counties of Ireland still qualified for some ERDF Regional Cohesion Funds up to 2004, as that area earned only 72 percent of the EU average GNP. Earning these EU funds looked a bit contrived, however, as the government divided Ireland into two regions, leaving the poorer border, midland, and western regions separate from the more prosperous east, and thus it appeared to some EU members that Ireland was "subsidy shopping" by economically gerrymandering the country.

By 2000, some EU members, notably Germany, France, and the Netherlands, viewed Ireland's economic growth as caused by EU subsidies and thought that it was no longer reasonable for Ireland to be receiving them. The Germans, given their own high costs for reunification, were reluctant to pour more money into the Structural Funds for more well-off areas, and suggested criteria such as participation in the euro, or high annual rates of growth, as disqualifications for getting funds. Bolstering this argument is the fact that the CSF provided by the EU to Ireland from 1989 to 2000 did amount to about 2.6 percent of GNP as Ireland was the beneficiary of the doubling of funding designed to aid countries' adjustment to the Single Market. Irish economists, however, argue that Structural Funds have actually accounted for about 2 percent of the Irish GNP growth while the remaining 6 to 8 percent or more rate of GNP growth has been spurred by foreign and domestic investment in computers, software, and pharmaceuticals. Moreover, GNP figures alone overstate Irish growth as it counts earnings from foreign firms that are repatriated.[5] In a relatively rare occurrence, Ireland and the EU Commission got into an open controversy over the 2001 Irish budget that was seen by the Commission as outside the boundaries of the Stability and Growth Pact and so "exuberant" in fiscal policy as to earn a rebuke from Commissioner Pedro Sobles. The Irish minister for finance, Charles McCreevey, responded openly and the subtler elements of the Irish situation, and the constraints of the EMU, were lost in the shouting.[6]

Ireland still has, for example, a very high rate of poverty among industrialized nations. Despite Ireland's stellar economic growth of recent years, almost a quarter of the country's population is still on the verge of poverty. A European Union "Survey on Income and Living Conditions" report noted that just fewer than 23 percent of the country's people were at risk of poverty in 2003, the latest year for which figures were compiled. Additionally, defining poverty as having an income under 60 percent of the median, more than 9 percent of people were "consistently poor," the report found. The average weekly gross income of households in the lowest income group, making up 10 percent of the population, was only around 120 euros, of which 94 percent was social-welfare payments. Single-parent households are the most deprived, with almost a third unable to afford new clothes and almost a quarter going without heat at times. Social Welfare Minister Seamus Brennan said the report showed how many people still "struggle on the margins of society."[7]

Ireland's eligibility as an "Objective I" region has obviously expired. However, in light of the poor regions of the new members of the EU, and Ireland's growth, the shift was inevitable and from 2007 to 2013, Ireland will be a net contributor to the EU budget. Dublin is fortunate to be able to adjust to the loss of funds over time from its current position of prosperity. Ireland's low rate of corporate taxation also was a point of contention with France and Germany in the 1990s. The number of new industries locating in Ireland was clearly disproportionate to its small size especially when compared to the size of the industrial economies of France and Germany. The difference in taxation between Ireland and the major industrial economies led to a call for harmonization of corporate tax policy in the EU as a whole. The Irish government, not surprisingly, resisted this pressure and was successful at the time of the Nice negotiations in keeping their 12.5 percent low rate. There were significant criticisms of Ireland by the EU for its excessively expansionist budget in 2000, for not implementing some environmental policies, and for subsidies to Aer Lingus. All of these issues contributed to the slow buildup of negative images of the EU in the Irish public that led to the negative vote on the Nice treaty.

The regeneration of the EU in the mid-1980s, through the elimination of nontariff barriers and the fairly quick transition to the Single

Market, provided the environment for very rapid Irish growth after 1987. The convergence of the Irish economy reaching a critical takeoff point with the emergence of a wider and deeper EU market synergistically fueled the Irish growth. The possibility of entering the Single Market encouraged the investment by Japanese and US firms in Ireland, providing an increased source of foreign direct investment. In addition, the growth of indigenous industry in Ireland had been spurred by a change in Irish policy after 1984. Between 1990 and 1998, Irish-owned manufacturing companies increased their employment by 20 percent and their exports by 50 percent. Improvements in Irish management and workplace innovation practices put the Irish economy in a particularly advantageous position. Irish companies were prepared in the late 1980s, as they were not upon entry in 1973, to take advantage of the EU market, evaluating their strengths and weaknesses and their potential expansion into sectors heretofore closed to them.[8] Greater entrepreneurial scope, especially in services such as banking and aviation, ensured that the Irish economy was poised to exploit the Single Market as well or better than most.

The adoption of a series of national plans that set targets in the realm of taxation, inflation, interest rates, and employment became the hallmark of the government's management of the economy from the mid-1980s to the present. The government adhered to the discipline of controlling inflation, reducing national debt and government spending in order to meet the criteria for entry into the euro zone and the Single Market. In a neocorporatist process of bargaining, the social partners, labor, business, and farmers entered into these agreements with government. In the late 1980s, the process was seen as necessary to fend off financial crisis, but it morphed into a continuing process of negotiation and agreement on macro goals, which allowed for stability and predictability in every peak group's expectations. Political scientist Brigid Laffan called this development "a process of learning how to manage internationalization and the emergence of international governance" through the use of the social partnership.[9] The Irish national planning documents had the major sectors agreeing to constraints on wage increases, on tax policy, and on social services. All sectors recognized that a small economy must maximize domestic policy consensus in order to be internationally competitive.[10]

Ireland's economy grew at just over 5 percent in 2005, a healthy level but well down from the double-digit rates seen during the "Celtic Tiger" years. Yet the evidence is clear that membership in the EU has benefited Ireland's economy in numerous tangible and intangible ways, from drawing in foreign investment funds, providing fiscal discipline, and reforming Irish firms to facilitating the highest rate of economic growth of any EU country over the last 15 years.

Women's Rights and Abortion

As a traditional Catholic society, women in Ireland had been excluded from the corridors of power and the halls of commerce, yet at the same time they held an especially venerated place in the society as the center of the family and as the conservators of religious and social values. Coupled with an emerging women's movement in Ireland, the EU directives in the 1970s on equality of pay and equality of opportunity, social benefits, employment, and retirement had the effect of significantly changing the rights of women. Changes in legislation in the 1970s guaranteed the equal treatment of women in the workplace and prompted the creation of the Employment Equality Agency to monitor and foster equality of opportunity for women. In 1990, for example, the EU Court of Human Rights forced the Irish government to pay Irish women social-welfare entitlements retroactively. Ultimately, a 1998 Equality Act that eliminated all forms of discrimination in Ireland superseded the equality legislation of the 1970s, engendered by the EU.

The issue of abortion was particularly important for Ireland and came to involve decisions of the European Court of Justice (ECJ) shaping the Irish Constitution. A case in Ireland that was appealed to the ECJ in 1991 decided that abortion services available in one community member could be advertised in another, that is, Ireland. On another Irish case, the European Court of Human Rights also decided that people in EU countries were free to travel to another member country, whatever their purpose, under Article 10 of the European Convention on Human Rights.[11] The European court decisions led to referenda passed in 1992 guaranteeing advertising in Ireland and unfettered travel throughout the EU. Thus, the constitution of Ireland was amended in accord with the decisions of EU courts on a matter that the Irish government felt needed special exclusion from EU decisions in the Maastricht Treaty in 1992.

Irish Neutrality

The pathbreaking 1996 white paper on Irish foreign policy, *Challenges and Opportunities Abroad,* notes "the extent to which Ireland . . . has come to express its foreign policy through the medium of the European Union." Membership in the EU has definitely enhanced the diplomatic status of Ireland. A small state on the perimeter of Europe, Ireland has direct and regular access to the policy elites of all the major countries of

Europe. The rotating presidency of the EU Council of Ministers gives Ireland high-profile visibility as Dublin focuses on the issues that it has elected to emphasize during its term. Participation in the EU brings Ireland into development and trade policy issues in the global arena that would be beyond the country's scope as an individual state.[12] The Permanent Representation to the EU in Brussels is the largest of all Irish diplomatic missions.[13]

Irish neutrality had emerged as a pragmatic response to political conditions in the 1930s, as Ireland could not, and would not, ally with Germany before and during the Second World War, but would not ally with Britain either as long as the island was partitioned. Neutrality became enshrined in Irish policy after the Second World War, somewhere between a practical policy choice and an enduring principle of Irish foreign policy. Originally anti-British in origin, the Irish came to sanctify the policy of neutrality, which then acquired additional resonance through opposition to nuclear deterrence, Cold War confrontation, and colonialism. Joining the European Union raised the question of Irish neutrality. The long-term objective of the EU was political and Article 224 of the Treaty of Rome specifies that the European Community could take common action during war, implying actions that could ultimately be inconsistent with Irish neutrality. When entry was put before the Irish people in a referendum, the economic pragmatists, such as Prime Minister Sean Lemass, argued that there was no threat to Irish neutrality in joining the Community. He demoted neutrality to a policy that was temporal and conditional and believed that EU political integration would come at the end of a long process of economic integration and, in the meantime, Irish neutrality would be maintained. The opponents of EU membership, on the other hand, elevated neutrality to an eternal principle guiding the Irish state. The Irish public, to the degree that neutrality entered their consideration at all, overwhelmingly opted for economic pragmatism when Ireland entered the Community in 1973.

In practice since 1970, European Political Cooperation (EPC) had evolved pragmatically into common declarations and support for members' actions, but the result was hardly a common EU foreign policy. The 1986 Single European Act (SEA) and the Maastricht Treaty of 1992 established the Common Foreign and Security Policy (CFSP) formally as part of the new EU structure. CFSP set broad EU foreign-policy objectives and required member states to pursue these goals (though the sharply different conceptions of the obligations of Pillar II among the member states has remained and the opt-outs make the CFSP cooperation less "e pluribus unum" and more "e pluribus pluribus"). At that, however symbolic, pressure on Ireland's declared neutrality has been institutionally increasing.

In 1982, the European Community imposed economic sanctions on Argentina in support of Great Britain after Argentina invaded the Falkland Islands (if one supports London) or recovered the Malvinas Islands (if one supports Argentina). The Irish went along with the sanctions until the British were prepared to invade the island. The Irish opted out at that point, saying that continuation of Irish sanctions was inconsistent with their policy of neutrality in the context of an armed conflict. Though creating much friction with London, other European Community members did not challenge the Irish action.

In 1986, the Irish government adopted the SEA through legislative approval rather than using a referendum on an amendment to the constitution. A private citizen, William Crotty, who argued that the Irish government could not legislatively approve a treaty that contained potentially unconstitutional provisions, and thus approval required a referendum, challenged that process. The Irish High Court did issue an injunction to postpone the SEA's ratification but, rejecting Crotty's argument, held that legislative approval was sufficient. The Irish Supreme Court then addressed the case on appeal and in the 1987 case *Crotty v. An Taoiseach* held that the section of SEA codifying European political cooperation did require an amendment to the constitution for ratification. Five judges thought that the SEA was fundamentally changing the future of the European Union from an economic union to a political union. Two judges, however, saw the EPC process as essentially consultative and not a concession of sovereignty and, thus, not abandoning neutrality. When Ireland approved the SEA through a constitutional amendment in 1987, it lodged a statement with the EU on neutrality, declaring that the act "does not affect Ireland's right to act or refrain from acting in a way which might affect Ireland's international status of military neutrality."[14] The issue was again raised in the 1992 referendum on the Maastricht Treaty, which took the western European Union and made it the putative defense arm of the EU, but the Irish people approved that treaty 69 percent to 31 percent.

The end of the Cold War allowed the Irish government more latitude to reformulate neutrality, as the EU sought more intergovernmental cohesion, but during this period neutrality became an issue in Irish political debate. Ireland, for example, failed to join NATO's Partnership for Peace, as an assertion of "neutrality," though Austria, Finland, and Sweden, and other European and EU neutral states, did join. The general public's perception of the Irish government's position on neutrality lacks clarity. In 2003, 58 percent of the Irish public favored joining an EU common defense strategy, but with the proviso that Ireland could opt out on a case-by-case basis. The 10 percent of the Irish public committed to EU common defense were counterbalanced by 19 percent wholly opposed to it. Thus, neutrality was seen as something threatened by a complete commitment to an EU common defense strategy (and helped contribute to the rejection of the Nice treaty in 2001).[15]

The 1996 foreign-policy white paper, *Challenges and Opportunities Abroad,* was clear enough. It noted that neutrality "has taken on a significance for Irish people over and above the essentially practical considerations on which it was originally based. Many have come to regard neutrality as a touchstone for our entire approach to international relations, even though in reality, much of our policy is not dependent on our nonmembership in a military alliance." Having said that, the white paper goes on to state that since 1973 "successive governments have indicated that they would be prepared to enter into discussion with other member states on the development of common arrangements in relation to security and defense matters." Finally, the white paper indicates that the ratification of the Maastricht Treaty bound Ireland to a "Common Foreign and Security Policy." [16]

The government made clear its position on the Amsterdam treaty in 1998 that it was willing to participate in an EU "common defense policy" and that the Irish public (62 percent to 38 percent) approved the treaty. In 1999, at the Helsinki Summit, the EU members agreed to the creation of a European rapid-reaction force (ERRF) of 60,000 troops. The Irish government indicated that the contribution of Irish forces did not violate Irish neutrality and pledged up to 850 troops and 80 police to the ERRF.[17] The Irish government has assigned officers to the EU Interim Military Committee and the European Council Secretariat and a representative from the Department of Foreign Affairs to an interim political and security committee. Critics argued that these actions required a referendum as it was rejecting the policy of Irish neutrality by stealth. The Irish government indicated that the rapid-reaction force is not a standing army but a contribution of forces from the EU states; moreover, the conditions for making a decision require unanimity among the members, are subject to a veto, and have an opt-out provision. Additionally, the mission of the ERRF was defined by the 1992 "Petersburg Tasks," which allow only humanitarian and peacekeeping responsibilities. Within the EU there are clear indications of a growth in security cooperation and Ireland's participation is probably inevitable, yet political scientist Nicholas Rees notes that "what is still missing in the Irish case is a thorough discussion of how Ireland develops its capabilities in ways that allow the state to make a positive contribution to European security inside ESDP [European Security and Defence Policy]."[18]

■ How and in What Ways Does Ireland Influence the EU?

The simple answer to this question is . . . not very much. The Irish delegation to the EU, while the largest of the Irish Foreign Affairs Department, is half the size of those of Denmark, Finland, Greece, and Sweden, and is always operating with scarce resources. The Irish style in the EU is reactive and focused. Irish bureaucrats are very comfortable with the EU style of policymaking as it replicates that of Ireland, with a relatively small elite from government and peak organizations in discussion and negotiation, as policy issues wind their way through the EU bureaucratic process. The Irish bureaucrats network very well and have a long relationship with the bureaucrats of the Commission, as Ireland was so long a recipient of Structural and Cohesion Funds. Ireland is not a mover of policy proposals and tends to work at shaping the proposals of others, nor does Ireland try to initiate policy or make proposals for institutional reform of the EU structure and procedures. The Irish bureaucrats tend to focus their resources on a few critical areas of policy that are highly important to Ireland such as agriculture, food, or financial services.

Specific individuals have had an impact beyond the size of the polity they represent, and as political scientist Laffan puts it: "Garrett FitzGerald, Brian Lenihan, Dick Spring or Rurai Quinn, displayed an aptitude for the Union's style of policy making, were clearly at ease in the Council chamber and reveled in the multinational and multicultural environment of the EU."[19] Pat Cox of the Fine Gael Party was elected president of the EU Parliament in 2002. Ireland has held the presidency of the Council on six occasions and the last, from January to June of 2004, under the presidency of Prime Minister Bertie Aherne, saw the new constitution of the EU approved, a formidable task (notwithstanding the ultimate fate of the constitution in 2005), and the accession of 10 new states to the EU.

Perhaps the most dramatic impact of Ireland on the chain of developments in the EU from the SEA to Nice was the Irish rejection of the Nice treaty in 2001. The Irish had been seen as firmly committed to Europe from the time of entry up to the adoption of the euro. More than

60 percent of Irish voters had approved the referenda on various EU treaties from 1972 up to 1998. Public opinion polls and the Eurobarometer polls regularly indicated that the Irish people believed EU membership was a good thing for Ireland and that Ireland had benefited from the EU.[20] Thus the defeat of the referendum on the Nice treaty held in June 2001 came as a shock to both the Irish government and the other EU members when Irish voters turned down the treaty by 53 percent to 46 percent on a very low voter turnout of 35 percent.

The shock was amplified by the fact that the government, the major parties, business associations, labor, farm organizations, and media all favored Nice and did not foresee the outcome at all. The opponents of Nice were mobilized by a variety of issues, some specifically Irish, such as the "No to Nice" group, which saw Nice as an EU threat to Irish family values through the potential availability of abortion. Others, such as the Green Party, saw Nice as an erosion of Irish sovereignty. The Progressive Democratic Party (PD) saw the closer integration of the EU as leading to the dominance of "social Europe" over "liberal Europe." The PD feared the curtailment of the free market and the provision of extensive social benefits rather than their preference for a more market-oriented economic system to foster competition and economic growth, and a more limited government role in the economy and society.

The confounding of the Charter of Fundamental Rights with the Nice treaty referendum did not add to the clarity of the public debate. The charter, which had been drafted and then adopted by various EU institutions in 2000, was an attempt to coherently integrate numerous documents stating human rights that were part of the EU corpus, including the European Convention on Human Rights. To incorporate them into the treaties would have made them subject to interpretation by the EU courts and applied to Ireland. The Irish government opposed this process as it represented a threat to the sovereignty of the Irish Constitution as interpreted by the Irish courts. The issue of abortion also lurked behind the opposition to the charter, as did same-sex marriage. One Irish member of the European Parliament stated: "That Charter can be used to bring abortion into Ireland through the European Court of Justice and we will be helpless." And the attorney general of Ireland stated that "it was at least possible" that the charter could legitimize or mandate same-sex marriage.[21] Of course the declaratory adoptions of the charter by the EU institutions in 2000 did not mean that it would become part of the treaties if Nice were adopted, and it did not mean that, if it were adopted at the EU Intergovernmental Conference in 2004, the result would be an assault on Irish moral values, but that was one message the Irish voters were getting. (Eventually, as it turned out, the Irish government agreed to the incorporation of the charter into the EU constitution at the convention in 2003 by specifying a number of amendments to the charter, but this was after the impact on the Nice debate.)

Observers offered reasons for the rejection by the Irish voters and the perspective of the observer, not surprisingly, framed the reasons so that each took away from the vote the confirmation they preferred. The Euro-skeptics saw the vote as a rejection of the increasing pooling of sovereignty and the creation of an EU state; the social conservatives saw the vote as an affirmation of Irish social and moral values. Journalists saw it as a chance for the voter to give a "bloody nose" to the Irish political establishment, which had taken the public support of Europe for granted. Foreign journalists brought up Ireland's economic growth and their self-satisfaction now that they were among the "haves" and thus were opposed to expansion to include poorer members. Ironically the low voter turnout actually meant fewer people had voted "No" for Nice, though a majority of the voters, than had voted "No" for Amsterdam in 1998, though a minority of the voters. But so few had voted "Yes," and so many had stayed home, that it meant a very large number of Irish people were unwilling to unhesitatingly vote for another EU treaty. Upon closer analysis, it turned out that the reason most voters either did not vote or voted "No" was that they had a lack of understanding and a lack of information about the treaty.[22]

The government was stung by the vote in June 2001 and, after being reelected in May 2002, responded quickly. At the Seville Summit, Ireland secured the agreement of EU members to two declarations that sought to make clear the Irish position on neutrality. On the first, the Irish government declared that it was not committed to any mutual defense agreement, nor to a European army, and would not commit forces to an EU response unless the action were approved at three levels: the United Nations, the government, and the Irish parliament, the Dail. In the second declaration, the European Council indicated that Ireland's policy of neutrality was in conformity with the EU treaties, including Nice, and EU treaty obligations could not force Ireland to depart from its policy. Armed with these declarations the government put the Nice treaty to the public again in October 2002. They created the National Forum on Europe and undertook a significant information campaign to inform the Irish voters as to what the EU meant to Ireland and what the Nice treaty contained. The National Forum published papers and held public forums and explored the issue of EU expansion and the EU impact on the future of Ireland. The exercise could be seen as a cynical manipulation of public opinion, but the forum came to be viewed by both the public and the politicians as beneficial in informing voters, in bridging the gap between the pro- and anti-Nice factions, and in fact providing a model for other EU members to bring EU issues closer to the public.[23] The referendum outcome in October was quite different from June of the previous year. With 49.5 percent of the voters turning out, 63 percent approved and 37 percent voted "No." Polls in Ireland showed that the voters' grasp of the issues in the Nice treaty went from 37 percent before June 2001 to 64 percent before October 2002.

Some observers see the votes on Nice as marking a break in the unqualified Irish enthusiasm for the EU and surfacing a degree of skepticism about some of the developments in the EU and the place of Ireland within it. The expansion of the EU will shift Ireland to becoming a net contributor to the EU budget and will dilute the voice and representation of Ireland in the EU as a whole. Some fear that the secular values of other European states potentially might be imposed upon Ireland through the instrument of the EU.

Were the Irish voters displaying domestic political discontent? As the French and Dutch rejection of the proposed constitution indicates, certainly public opinion in other member states appears to be using the status of the EU as a way to register the concerns of domestic politics. Did the EU democratic deficit create a sense of marginalization in the ordinary Irish citizen? Was the Irish public experiencing a form of Euro-fatigue based on the extensive changes in the EU from the SEA to the euro, the new EU constitution, the Charter of Fundamental Rights, and adding 10 new member states? The answer appears to be quite the contrary. The Irish public records the highest level of support for the EU among the member states both before the rejection of the Nice treaty in 2001 and continues to register the highest levels of support up to 2002, when the vote was reversed, and in 2003 and after. The Irish public, rather than fearing diminished influence in an expanded EU, registers the highest levels of public support among EU member states for enlargement, exceeding the publics of other states by 10–15 percent.[24]

■ How Does Ireland Implement and Comply with EU Policies?

The Irish policymaking process was relatively unprepared for entry into Europe, and the pragmatic approach to policymaking that prevailed in

Ireland from 1973 to 2001 led to three deficiencies in the Irish-EU interface. First, the departmental autonomy in the Irish civil service caused poor management of issues crosscutting through departments that should have been addressed by interdepartmental committees. Second, the Irish government mobilized bureaucratic resources to address issues in the short term, but there was little medium- or long-term coordination and cooperation in the Irish bureaucracy to achieve Irish goals in the EU. Finally, Ireland, since 1987, has fallen behind most member states in its rate of timely implementation of the laws and regulations establishing the European Single Market. The sheer weight of the EU legislation and the absence of legal specialists and bureaucratic support have prompted the Commission to institute proceedings against Ireland on implementation at a rate disproportionate to its size and population.

The responsibilities for EU matters are divided in the Irish government between the core group of the Departments of Foreign Affairs (the lead department) and Finance, and the office of the Taoiseach (an inner core that includes the Departments of Enterprise and Employment, Agriculture, Justice and Law Reform, and Environment). An outer group of departments become involved only as EU matters touch their mandates. The variety and complexity of EU regulation and issues, as Laffan points out, has created "a 'Europeanization' of government in the Republic."[25] The government officials regularly in Brussels become woven into the EU-Ireland interface at meetings of the Council of Ministers and the Commission's functionally divided 23 directorates and 250 working parties and committees. The ministers of the member governments and the bureaucrats of the EU interact in a series of policy circles. The directors of the European departments are at once policymakers, legislative negotiators, and policy implementers. At the European level, for example, there is the Committee of Professional Agricultural Organizations, the Union of Industries, the European Trade Union Confederation, and a host of sectoral organizations (banking, chemicals, textiles, etc.). The actual process, in fact, much more closely resembles neocorporatist policymaking involving developing positions, bargaining, reshaping, and further bargaining in an extended negotiation up to the point of approval.

Centralization and neocorporatism are features of Irish government that contribute to a democratic deficit in the Irish political process. While acknowledging the clear benefits of the social partnership in terms of macroeconomic policy, it is clear that bargaining over major directions in public policy without the press or members of the Dail involved represents a democratic deficit. The position papers are prepared by the various partners—business, labor, and farmers—and by key government figures and bureaucrats. These papers are then negotiated into major two- to five-year comprehensive plans and announced as a package to the Dail. In the Irish case, as a small country, the number of people who represent peak interests in Dublin is small, as is the number of ministers and civil servants. Thus their connection with a small group of Brussels technocratic specialists in policy means that a state-level neocorporatist model is replicated in two ways in the European policy process: the EU overall policymaking is neocorporatist and, for the microcosm of Ireland-in-Europe, the Irish circle of policymakers and policy-shapers is small and close-knit and needs to refer policy positions back no further than their respective clienteles. The decisionmakers in the Irish government have moved smoothly into the EU policymaking style and skillfully negotiate their way through the committees, advancing the interests of Ireland. Some interest groups, such as large farmers and industrial organizations, have also thrived in the Brussels environment. As political scientist Laffan states, "Groups in Ireland can play nested games at the national level and connected games in the Brussels arena."[26]

Until 2002 the Irish parties and the Dail have had relatively little influence on Ireland-EU matters. The absence of a committee system in the Dail, the orientation of the Irish members of the Dail Eireann to their constituencies, and the centralization of policymaking in the cabinet have made the Dail traditionally weak. The absence of a committee system eliminated a continual accounting on the part of the executive on European matters. The Joint Committee on Secondary Legislation was appointed in 1973 to monitor the implementation of the European directives. Given the weak role of the Dail in Irish government, and a lack of expertise, the committee did not engage in a critical oversight role. The appointment of a Joint Committee on Foreign Affairs in 1993 appeared to be a step in the right direction, but the committee had inadequate time and resources to consider the plethora of European matters affecting Ireland because its remit was also to cover all of Ireland's foreign relations. Another joint committee was established in 1995 to focus on European affairs, but as Laffan notes: "The record of both committees is mixed. Lacking resources and attendance, the committees are dependent on the Department of Foreign Affairs for information and positions," which is, of course, the point.[27] Neill Nugent bluntly stated: "The fact is that in Ireland EU policy tends to be in the hands of a small, government-dominated network of politicians and officials who listen to Parliament only as they see fit."[28]

The defeat of the Nice referendum in 2001 triggered changes in the policy process. Laffan notes that "changes in the core executive consisted in large measure of a deepening and formalization of the existing system rather than a radical reform."[29] A new position of minister of state for European affairs evolved. Since July 2002, that minister chairs an Interdepartmental Co-coordinating Committee on European Affairs that is host to senior civil servants. This committee serves as a distant early warning system for problematic issues that could arise from EU matters and meets with a cabinet subcommittee on European affairs every two weeks in order to discuss EU policy. In addition other interdepartmental committees have been created to address the previous absence of long-term policy coordination and policy planning. Within the Dail, a new Select Committee on European Affairs drawn only from the Dail was set up and has the task of sifting through EU policy documents and, if any issue is deemed significant, requesting a note on the policy from the relevant government department. The committees of the Oireachtas (the legislative and executive branches of the Irish government) consider the matters and make recommendations to the government. The cabinet is not bound to accept the opinion of the committee but the new structures and process bring EU policies under much greater scrutiny, eliciting more communication and cooperation between legislators, cabinet officials, and bureaucrats than heretofore in Ireland. The creation of the National Forum on Europe in 2002 not only served to educate the public, but also served to educate the representatives from the political parties, who were appointed in proportion to their seats in the Dail. The participation of legislators in the discussions and reviews of the papers created for the National Forum brought the level of sophistication of Dail members to a higher degree than had been done by the earlier committees.

The line between domestic law and European law in Ireland and all the members is increasingly blurred, and European law expands into domestic law to a greater and greater degree. The ECJ resolves conflicts between domestic law and EU law and, as seen below, decides on breaches in domestic observance of EU regulations and declares domestic law void if it conflicts with EU obligations. In Ireland, ECJ decisions have impacted such issues as gay rights, women's rights to equal pay, equal opportunity, pensions, and access to services in another member state. A British judge has said that EU law is "like an incoming tide. It flows into the estuaries and rivers. It can not be held back."[30]

Despite the benefits the Irish farmers have received from the EU's CAP, they were not pleased with two EU environmental regulations, one on birds in 1979 and another on protection of habitats in 1992. As the regulations controlled the actions on private land, they were unpopular with farmers and, as they required special efforts to protect species and their habitats, they were seen as burdensome. The farmers were resisting the regulations; Irish politicians dragged their feet, as they did not want to impose regulations on their constituents, so the government delayed implementation. This triggered the responses of environmental groups in Ireland such as Birdwatch Ireland, which wanted to use the EU regulations as a way to compel the Irish government to act on preserving the environment. Even though the EU Commission provided almost 9 million euros to facilitate implementation, the delays and conflicts prompted the EU Commission to bring Ireland to the ECJ twice for nonimplementation of the regulations. Eventually the government put the directive in place.[31]

These cases demonstrate the impact that EU regulations or standards have on Ireland and illuminate that the values and political culture of each member state have to adjust and accommodate to the EU directives in realms less dramatic than macroeconomic policy. The status of women in Irish law was challenged by the EU directive on social-welfare payments; the discriminatory elements of religious and moral values incorporated into Irish law were challenged by the claim of individual human rights; and finally the power of a juggernaut pressure group, Irish farmers, was balanced by the ability of environmental groups to add the weight of EU regulations to their position.

■ Future Trends and Prospects: Ireland and the Future of the EU

The choice of the convention model for deliberation on the future of Europe, and thus Ireland's place in it, ran against the traditional operational style of the Irish in the EU. Flying under the radar in the EU political process for decades, the Irish often quietly negotiated changes in EU directives to the advantage of Irish interests such as farmers. The EU bureaucratic process mapped well onto the Irish style, as noted above, and in the intergovernmental negotiations the Irish, as a small state, would work for the most part at the margins to achieve their goals. The Convention on the Future of Europe, called for by the EU Council in Laeken in December 2001, met from March 2002 to July 2003 and negotiated a draft constitution for the European Union. The convention was constructed to have a wide level of participation in the membership of the convention itself, the leadership in the Praesidium, and the 10 working groups. The Irish had to adapt to the open and fluid nature of the negotiation style of the convention as they preferred the insider style of the Intergovernmental Conferences.

Though the convention had taken the Irish vote on Nice as a message to respond to the issue of democratic deficits, the Irish delegation was slow off the mark and had little cohesion in the delegation. Moreover, the Irish government took a conservative position on the convention, fearing it would go beyond what the Irish government was willing to accept, and preferred to wait until the "real" negotiations took place at the Intergovernmental Conference. The Irish government's conservatism on issues of expanding EU competence and governance, and its hard line on Irish interests and threat of a veto of certain words and provisions, resulted in the Irish beginning to be seen as Euro-skeptics. On taxation policy, for example, the Irish would not accept Qualified Majority Voting, only unanimity reflecting their protection of their low corporate tax rate. This posture risked leaving the Irish out of shaping the decisions in the convention that was establishing a consensus on a number of EU issues. The Irish did join with the "seven dwarfs" that had certain common positions on the new constitution, but their unity was often more a function of opposing the institutional proposals of the large states. The smaller states preferred a rotating presidency and a strong Commission, as did Ireland.[32] In fact, the convention was very influential in developing the positions of the member states and delegates as they were shaping the documents, despite the outcome in the votes in France and the Netherlands, and will frame the discussion on EU development for decades to come.

The specific issues that Ireland will face in the future retain some that have been central to Irish concerns, such as the CAP and others, which will be a function of the development of the EU vertically and horizontally. The pressure on the CAP, from the World Trade Organization and the General Agreement on Tariffs and Trade, has disconnected the funding of the CAP from agricultural production but has not reduced the subsidies. Increasing pressure to adjust and renationalize the CAP payments will be a major agenda item for Ireland, which will resist changes in the CAP. The same is true for the equalization of corporate taxes across all the member states, for it will directly undermine one of the most powerful engines of Ireland's growth. Despite protocols to the EU treaties designed to preserve Irish religious and moral values, some in Ireland will always fear that a secularized EU will seek to change Ireland's laws with respect to abortion or same-sex marriage through the adoption, clearly sometime in the future, of the Charter of Fundamental Rights, or through interpretation of existing EU rights or directives. Though the Seville Declarations would seem to settle the status of Ireland on neutrality and European security and defense, there are those who see that posture as potentially problematic in a changing global system.

Finally, the expansion of the EU has shifted Ireland's small representation, 15 seats in a 626-member European Parliament, to the even smaller representation of 13 seats out of 732. The expansion of the EU will mean an inevitable shift in the duration and sequence of the presidency of the European Council and the opportunity for Ireland to hold such a leading role in Europe, and for that matter the world, for six months within each six years, will diminish. The adoption of Qualified Majority Voting within the EU on certain issues will inevitably expand and make Ireland's 7 votes out of 345 relatively inconsequential. Despite the defeat of the constitution in France and the Netherlands in 2005, the issues of the balance of power between the EU and the member states, the Charter of Fundamental Rights, the consolidation of the treaties into a constitution, and the role of the national parliaments versus the EU will remain on the agendas of the member states and will force Ireland to recalculate where it fits in the EU of the twenty-first century. Rising Euro-skepticism among some Irish political parties and elites, coexisting with public support for the EU equal to or greater than other EU members, is the fissure that will shape Ireland's future in the EU.

■ Notes

1. Reid, *The United States of Europe*, p. 248. Citing the "globalization index" of *Foreign Policy* magazine, Reid notes that Ireland ranks number one in globalization.

2. See Wiles and Finnegan. *Aspirations and Realities*, and Finnegan and Wiles, "The Invisible Hand or Hands Across the Water?" especially pp. 50–55.

3. O'Donnell, *Ireland in Europe, the Economic Dimension*, p. 5.

4. FitzGerald, *Reflections on the Irish State*, p. 158.

5. O'Donnell, *Ireland in Europe, the Economic Dimension,* p. 16.

6. Ibid., p. 20; Clinch, Convery, and Walsh, *After the Celtic Tiger*, p. 59.

7. EU Business, "Almost a Quarter of Irish Face Risk of Poverty: EU Survey."

8. The government at the time created Adaptation Councils for various sectors of the economy in order to prepare the firms for competition in a nonprotectionist economy. By and large it did not work as Irish firms were hit hard

by foreign competition after 1973. See Wiles and Finnegan. *Aspirations and Realities.*

9. Corporatism has many meanings, but in this instance it meant the movement away from laissez-faire arrangements in the setting of wages and even prices. Governments in Europe had moved in this direction in the 1970s with national wage agreements, and it signaled the explicit partnership of labor, government, and industry. Varieties of corporatism had emerged in Europe after the Second World War as governments sought stability, labor sought security, and industry sought profits. The implicit or explicit bargain was that each would cooperate to the degree necessary to achieve their ends: social-welfare programs for the workers, subsidies and tax benefits for industry, and political parties in government that would maintain the bargain. Laffan and O'Donnell, "Ireland and the Growth of International Governance," pp. 157–158.

10. Ibid., p. 165.

11. The cases in Ireland were *Attorney General v. Open Door Counseling* in 1988 and the *SPUC v. Grogan and Others* in 1989. The European case was *Open Door Counseling, Well Women's Center and Others v. Ireland,* 1992.

12. IGC 96 Task Force—European Commission, Department of Foreign Affairs, *Ireland: Challenges and Opportunities Abroad,* p. 52.

13. Ireland is underrepresented abroad. All the smaller states of Europe maintain twice the number of overseas missions and have twice the number of diplomats as Ireland; Laffan and O'Donnell, "Ireland and the Growth of International Governance," p. 172.

14. Keating, "Security Policy," p. 161.

15. Keatinge and Laffan, "Ireland: A Small Open Polity," p. 347. (The authors note that a study of Irish neutrality by Trevor Salmon concludes that it is nonbelligerence at best and self-delusion at worst.) Rees, "Europe and Ireland's Changing Security Policy," p. 69.

16. IGC 96 Task Force—European Commission, Department of Foreign Affairs, *Ireland: Challenges and Opportunities Abroad,* pp. 51–52.

17. Keeping in mind that the Irish military forces total 10,500 and their contribution to European and UN security missions is a total of 781. While the principle of neutrality is important, the number of Irish soldiers involved is quite small. Rees, "Europe and Ireland's Changing Security Policy," pp. 65–66.

18. Ibid., p. 71.

19. Laffan and O'Donnell, "Ireland and the Growth of International Governance," p. 171.

20. Keatinge and Laffan, "Ireland: A Small Open Polity," p. 341.

21. Regan, *The Charter of Fundamental Rights,* pp. 11–12.

22. O'Mahoney, "Ireland and the European Union," p. 27.

23. O'Brennan, "Ireland's European Discourse and the National Forum on Europe," p.125. The forum put out nearly 20 reports on a variety of aspects of the Ireland-EU relationship written by specialists and scholars that were clearly sound and valuable explorations and not restatements of the government's positions in pamphlet form.

24. Coakley, "Irish Public Opinion and the New Europe," pp. 100–110.

25. Laffan, "Managing Europe," p. 53.

26. Laffan and O'Donnell, "Ireland and the Growth of International Governance," p. 169.

27. Ibid., p. 168.

28. Nugent, *The Government and Politics of the European Union*, p. 418.

29. Laffan, "Ireland's Management of EU Business," p. 184.

30. Lord Justice Denning quoted in Chubb, *The Government and Politics of Ireland*, p. 51.

31. Laffan and Tonra, "Europe and the International Dimension," p. 452.

32. The dwarfs were Austria, Belgium, Finland, Ireland, Luxembourg, the Netherlands, and Portugal. Bausili, "Ireland and the Convention on the Future of Europe," p. 139.

9

Denmark: Euro-Pragmatism in Practice

Eric S. Einhorn and Jessica Erfer

SUMMER 2005 WILL BE noted as the start of one of the European Union's periodic crises as the Constitutional Treaty signed by the 10 leaders of the newly expanded EU the previous year derailed. Voters in France and the Netherlands, core EU states, voted to reject the treaty. There quickly ensued a series of confrontations over the new multi-year EU budget and over whether to proceed with negotiations with Turkey over future EU membership. The growth of "Euro-skepticism," even in the Union's "heartland," showed that despite its many successes, the EU is very much a work in progress. As a consistent hotbed of Euro-skepticism, Denmark emerged as a model of how democratic politics can cope with difficult issues of European integration.

Although Denmark joined the European Union (then the European Community [EC]) in 1973, after three decades it remains a pragmatic skeptic. Ever since the question of Denmark's relationship with European integration arose in the early 1950s, there have been recurring themes and interests at play. The economic dimension has always been primary; as a small, open economy with trade accounting for about one-third of the national economy, access to key European markets was a paramount concern. Historically Denmark had often been forced to choose between its two main markets: Great Britain and Germany.[1] Membership in the EC (along with Great Britain) in 1973 ended this issue, as did the creation of an ever-larger single European market in the following years.

Politically, Denmark had been buffered by European great-power

173

competition and had faced recurring security threats. Membership in NATO in 1949 (itself a contested issue) had given Denmark its first credible security guarantee in a century. European integration increasingly stabilized European foreign policies and indirectly promoted reduced European tensions and then the unexpected end of the Cold War. These developments further solidified Denmark's European security situation. On "softer" issues of pragmatic policy cooperation, Denmark's traditional support for regional and global cooperation was channeled into the EU enterprise, restrained only by Danish skepticism about EU ambitions to move toward an "ever closer union." By the 1990s Danish foreign policy was unambiguously internationalist, but with competing geographic and policy priorities. The EU is, however, a very dynamic organization, and each member state needs to reassess frequently its interests and position within the Union. Denmark's pragmatic, sober, and at times skeptical approach has generally served the country well.

EU issues have fully mobilized the institutions and processes of Danish democracy. From the start the Danish parliament (Folketing) has been actively and independently engaged in assessing "European" economic and political issues with merely accepting governmental proposals. Six national referenda have allowed the public to have its say directly, and twice (1992 and 2000) the public has vetoed EU proposals approved by both the government and parliament. Ironically as "consensus" on Denmark's pragmatic EU approach has strengthened in the past few years, skepticism has grown in many of the previously enthusiastic EU founding states (e.g., France and the Netherlands in 2005). Whether Denmark's experience in "Euro-pragmatism" will be a model for others remains an interesting question.

Denmark's modern economy was built on expanding trade. Starting with the modernization of agriculture in the nineteenth century, Denmark found markets for high-quality "value-added" products in a widening sphere of international trade. Until the post-1945 era, Denmark's international niche was agriculture, but particularly processed foods that could be profitably shipped to foreign markets. In the twenty-first century, Danish butter, bacon, beer, and cheeses have retained their global reputation. Denmark's dilemma was that free trade rarely prevailed unconditionally, especially in the agricultural sector. Foreign mercantilism protected colonial markets and enterprises, and agricultural interest groups in many large markets limited imports. Great Britain, Europe's most open trader, became Denmark's single largest market by the end of the nineteenth century. Despite greater protectionism, Germany, Sweden, Norway, and other foreign markets also expanded. Foreign trade provided Denmark with the raw materials, chemicals, and industrial products that sustained its economic growth and product enrichment.[2] After the World War I, economic dislocations increasingly restricted Danish access to its traditional European markets. When the economic crisis of the 1930s hit, Denmark found its expanding industrial production severely restricted by protectionism and neomercantilist policies and even its agricultural exports faced new barriers. The results were plunging commodity prices, soaring unemployment, and, in common with most other industrial countries, the worst economic crisis of the modern era.[3]

After the war Denmark demonstrated its commitment to fewer barriers to free trade by being one of the founding members of the General Agreement on Tariffs and Trade, the unsuccessful pursuit of a Scandinavian customs union in the 1950s, and finally membership in the British-sponsored European Free Trade Area in 1960. Danish attempts to join the EC began in 1961, after the British request for membership. The main logic behind the Danish application for membership was that they could not afford to remain outside of the Community for economic reasons, especially if Britain joined. Membership would bring with it major economic benefit, including joining the Common Agricultural Policy and the customs union, and also because Denmark relied heavily on other countries for certain goods. When France rejected British membership in 1963, however, Denmark quickly pulled its own application, perhaps in order to not alienate one of its largest trading partners.

The contentious debate preempting the 1972 referendum illustrates how the issue divided Danish society, yet the binding referendum passed overwhelmingly, with over 90 percent of eligible Danes turning out to vote on the issue.[4] The core of the pro-EC campaign had been economic advantage. Opponents of membership comprised a substantial portion of the Danish population, who were skeptical of the benefits of membership for economic, political, and even social reasons. Those leading the "Nej" ("No") campaign were mainly on the political left and feared that membership would weaken the welfare state and reduce national sovereignty. The skeptics and opponents remain, and their strength has tended to rise and fall with the performance of the Danish economy. Although EU issues have been prominent in Danish politics over the past three decades, Danes have also separated or at least "compartmentalized" the EU debate from many other political issues. The recurring national referendums on important EU decisions, and the periodic direct elections to the European Parliament (EP) since 1979, have helped focus attention on specific issues. Hence, EU issues rarely decide national elections, and national politics play a smaller role in EU elections than is the case in many other EU member states.[5]

A growing problem in Denmark is the cumulative effect of surrendered sovereignty. Since 1973, the European Union has become increasingly less about purely economic matters, and the six referendums Denmark has held since 1972 illustrate the increase in Danish skepticism toward the EU's sphere of influence. Aside from the referendum outcomes, the most recent of which was the rejection of the euro in 2000, Denmark has shown its reluctance to fully join European integration by using opt-outs as agreed on in 1992 in the Edinburgh compromise. Opt-outs allow Denmark to participate at a comfortable level, yet retain more sovereignty on important domestic issues. The problem with these opt-outs, however, is the harsh reality that Denmark *needs* the European Union, and not the other way around. Brussels may not allow Denmark to use opt-outs when the EU becomes a more politically powerful superstructure. Therefore, Denmark's exceptional history within the EU must be taken into account when considering the future, while at the same time this history challenges the perception that the EU is an all-or-nothing game. Will Denmark's constitutionally binding referendum and fickle population curtail further integration efforts? Will opt-outs force Denmark to be a European outlier, like Norway, and drastically reduce the Danish influence in European policymaking?

Balancing the perceived erosion of sovereignty has been the growing complexity and heterogeneity of the EU itself. During the past decade Denmark's position within the EU has generally been strengthened by both domestic and European developments. The "widening" of the EU in 1995 (Sweden, Finland, and Austria) was easily accommodated. The large expansion of the EU in 2004 to include 10 central and eastern European states raised some concerns, but fell in with the overall Danish view that "widening" the scope of European cooperation was a higher priority than "deepening" the Union into some form of federation. The two strategies are not mutually exclusive, but in practice "digesting" new and increasingly diverse member states significantly extends the horizon for Euro-federalist ambitions.

An important aspect of Denmark's relations with the EU has been its domestic political dimension. For more than 30 years the main political parties have generally agreed on the goals and terms of Danish membership. In the late 1960s through to the early 1980s, radical socialist parties gained electoral strength and their renewed faith in a socialist alternative penetrated deeply into the reformist Social Democrats, which had guided Denmark into the EC in 1973. The dramatic parliamentary election of December 1973 saw a disastrous fall in Social Democratic support, the rise of a new radical-right party (the Progress Party), as well as the return of the Communist Party into parliament. The pro-EC parties were severely weakened, but regained ground in the following elections. The pattern was thus established that opposition to the EC/EU has been concentrated from the left and right wings of Denmark's multi-party politics. Consensus in recent years has gradually incorporated some previous skeptics such as the Socialist People's Party and the small Christian Democratic Party. The only significant party opposed to Danish EU policies (and perhaps even membership) is the populist right-wing Danish People's Party.[6] The mainstream Social Democrats (since 2001 the main opposition party) remains integrationist.[7] Complicating the political balance in favor of EU pragmatism has been the reliance of mainstream governing coalitions (usually consisting of only a parliamentary minority) on the more Euro-skeptical or opposi-tional parties for ongoing parliamentary support. This requires careful compartmentalization of EU policy from domestic and other foreign-policy issues.

Despite this consensus "at the top," Danish public opinion has been more evenly split. This is reflected in continuing Danish and EU polls (e.g., Eurobarometer) and more significantly in periodic referendums on EU issues. A recurring tension in the Danish-EU debate has been the contradiction between the view that the EU is primarily an "intergovern-mental organization" rather like the United Nations, NATO, etc., and the concern about the "democratic deficit" of the European Union, that is, the minimal role of the public in choosing EU leadership and influenc-ing day-to-day policy decisions.

Finally the "European question" intrudes into many other political controversies including the issue of immigration and multiculturalism, economic performance and structural changes, and the sustainability of Denmark's generous welfare state (social policies). During the past 15 years the scope of EU policy concerns has expanded from a narrow eco-nomic/commercial focus to include almost every significant public poli-cy domain. Although Denmark has enjoyed increased economic prosper-ity and political stability during this period (and even before), EU issues remain controversial.

■ How and in What Ways Does the EU Influence Denmark?

Although EU affairs have consistently been high on the Danish political agenda over the past 35 years, two events give it special prominence.

First are the periodic elections for the European Parliament (last in 2004), which produce the usual flurry of electoral campaign activity. Second are those changes in the EU treaties that require a Danish referendum. Under terms of the 1953 Danish Constitution, sovereignty may be ceded to international organizations either by an overwhelming parliamentary majority (five-sixths of the members of parliament) or by a parliamentary majority backed by a national referendum. Six times since 1972, the Danish public has been asked to vote on EU issues (see Table 9.1).

Moreover, the campaigns every fifth year for elections to the European Parliament usually stimulate a broader debate about the country's relationship to the EU. In addition to candidate slates for each of the national political parties,[8] two special lists participate regularly in European parliamentary elections: the Popular Movement Against the EU *(Folkebevægelsen mod EU)*, which has strongly opposed Danish membership in the EU and dates back to the original campaign on EU membership in 1972, and the "June Movement" (Junibevægelsen*)*, which is strongly Euro-skeptic but accepting of minimal Danish participation in the EU. Thus the EU issue is frequently presented to the Danish public not only for debates about specific policies but also for more fundamental discussion. Danes have focused on EU issues during the referendums and EP elections rather than recycling mainly domestic political issues. This focus plus ample press and media coverage has kept the EU high in the consciousness of most citizens.

Recent Developments in Danish EU Policies

Thorough reviews of Denmark's complex relationship with the EU are

Table 9.1   Danish National Referendums on European Union Issues (in percentages)

Date	Issue	Yes	No	Turnout
1972	Membership in the EU	63.4	36.6	90.1
1986	Single European Act	56.2	43.8	75.4
1992	Maastricht Treaty (TEU)	49.3	50.7	83.1
1993	Maastricht Treaty with Edinburgh Declaration (revisions)	56.7	43.3	86.5
1998	Amsterdam Treaty	55.1	44.9	76.2
2000	Adoption of the euro	46.8	53.2	87.6

Source: Denmark. Folketinget. 2002. EU-Oplysningen. "Danske Folkeafstemninger om EU."

available elsewhere, but here we will focus on issues of continuing prominence.[9] Given the negative referendums on EU issues in 1992 (the Maastricht Treaty on European Union) and again in September 2000 (on adopting the euro currency), Danish politicians have tread warily. Recurring public opinion polls show a tendency for Danes initially to support EU development in the abstract, but to become far more skeptical during the heated referendum campaigns. As demonstrated by the 2000 euro currency case, this support can evaporate quickly.[10] Most Danish Euro-skeptics are opposed to EU ambitions in theory but not in practice. Denmark has therefore continued to participate broadly in the growing range of EU policy initiatives while remaining aware of the "limits." In turn, the EU has been flexible in recognizing the Danish opt-outs. Denmark continues to have a strong record in implementing EU directives. Danish personnel are broadly represented in various EU institutions (except on the board of the European Central Bank, which requires "full participation").

Following the September 2000 Danish referendum rejecting adoption of the euro as their national currency, Danish EU policy focused on the enlargement of the European Union, the four Danish opt-outs of 1992, and the proposed EU Constitutional Treaty that would finish the institutional reforms initiated with the 2000 Nice treaty. There would also be ample attention paid to ongoing developments in the Single Market, the freer movement of persons across internal EU borders (the Schengen Agreement), and other EU policy matters. Because the scope of the EU has penetrated so many public policy areas, there is often a European element to even traditional domestic political debates.

In the November 2001 parliamentary elections, nearly nine years of Social Democratic government under Poul Nyrup Rasmussen ended with a severe defeat for the party. It was replaced by a minority liberal-conservative coalition headed by Anders Fogh Rasmussen with conservative Per Stig Møller as foreign minister. This government would generally seek parliamentary support from the rightist Danish People's Party (DPP) headed by Pia Kjærsgaard, a harsh critic of the EU. Following Danish practice, however, the government would also seek support from the moderate opposition parties, including the pro-EU Social Liberals and Social Democrats. So while the government's EU policy could rest on the broad pro-EU parliamentary base, it would have to avoid provoking the DPP lest it lose its parliamentary basis for government. This would be especially important during the second half of 2002, when Denmark would again hold the rotating EU presidency. Danish voters tend to "compartmentalize" EU issues in the periodic referendum and European parliamentary elections, and rarely do these issues loom large in national elections. A study of the 2001 election indicates that foreign relations, including relations with the EU, were a minor concern of the electorate, who instead focused on social policy and immigration.[11]

Fortunately for the new government, the Danish economy performed well above the European norm despite the rejection of the euro in 2000.[12] Table 9.2 summarizes recent economic performance in Denmark and the 12 euro-zone nations. Although Danish growth lagged behind the "Euro 12" at the beginning of the decade, it has since been significantly higher. Danish unemployment and public finance figures are also better. Indeed Denmark meets handily all of the so-called Economic and Monetary Union (EMU) criteria, including having reduced its public debt from 47.3 percent of GDP in 2000 to an estimated 39.8 percent in 2005. France's debt increased from 57.1 to 65.8 percent of GDP and Germany's from 60.2 to 65.8 percent in the same period.[13] This economic performance is due to various far-reaching internal economic reforms that different Danish governments have pursued since the mid-1980s. Danes remain willing to pay high taxes to maintain generous public programs, which nevertheless remain under considerable financial stress. Structural economic changes, that is, allowing declining industries to shrink while encouraging newer industries and services, have paved the way to steady if modest economic growth. Energy self-sufficiency and modest oil and gas exports have helped too in recent years.

Table 9.2 Relative Economic Performance

	2000	2001	2002	2003	2004	2005[a]
Real Growth of Gross Domestic Product						
Denmark	2.8	1.3	0.5	0.7	2.4	3.0
Euro-12	3.7	1.7	0.9	0.6	1.8	1.4
Unemployment						
Denmark	4.4	4.3	4.6	5.6	5.7	4.9
Euro-12	8.4	8.0	8.4	8.9	8.9	8.7
General Government Financial Balance (percentage of GDP)						
Denmark	2.5	2.8	1.6	1.0	2.3	2.8
Euro-12	0.1	−1.8	−2.5	−2.8	−2.7	−2.9

Source: OECD, 2005, *Economic Outlook,* no. 78 (December), annex tables.
Note: a. 2005 figures are estimates. "Euro-12": Austria, Belgium, Finland, France, Germany, Greece, Ireland, Italy, Luxembourg, Netherlands, Portugal, and Spain.

■ How and in What Ways Does Denmark Influence the EU?

The 2002 Presidency

Denmark most recently held the rotating EU presidency from July to December 2002. The main task of the Danish presidency was to shore up the EU's planned eastern and central European expansion, with Denmark going down in the history books as the facilitator of such a historical event. The previous Danish presidency in 1993 had established the so-called Copenhagen Criteria for the entrance of new members into the European Union. The main principles established then were "that the candidate country must have achieved":

- stability of institutions guaranteeing democracy, the rule of law, human rights, and respect for and protection of minorities;
- the existence of a functioning market economy as well as the capacity to cope with competitive pressure and market forces within the Union; and
- the ability to take on the obligations of membership including adherence to the aims of political, economic, and monetary union.[14]

While expansion was not the only issue on the table during the Danish presidency, it was certainly the issue that received the most worldwide attention, thus thrusting Denmark into the public eye. Prime Minster Fogh Rasmussen even went so far as to call his country's presidency "the greatest foreign policy challenge Denmark has faced in modern history."[15] As successful as the Danish presidency was with presiding over successful accession of 10 new member states, the bone of contention that must now be taken on by succeeding presidencies is the issue of Turkey's accession.

Additional issues on the table during Denmark's presidency included the growing threat of international terror, illegal immigration, and further market liberalization, such as deregulation of EU utilities. The real challenge of the presidency, however, was to see just how much muscle Denmark could flex considering its history of opt-outs and treaty rejections. Denmark's relatively weak status within the EU stems from more than opt-outs—with few votes in the European Parliament, and indeed a small population, Denmark has traditionally stuck with a few pet issues, such as institutional transparency and environmentalism.[16]

Danish political leaders used the presidency to prove their proactive European policy. Long thought of as a European outsider, setting the stage for expansion allowed the Danish government to demonstrate otherwise. Additionally, this proactively set the stage for Danish leaders to initiate the referendum necessary to abolish the opt-outs. Therefore, an established goal of the conservative Danish government was to springboard off of a successful presidency into full EU membership (removal of opt-outs). This policy had one major problem: during the Danish presidency much attention was paid to European policy *after* the adoption of a constitution. The Danish government did not foresee the sudden anticonstitution reaction in other EU countries leading to the dramatic rejection of the European Constitutional Treaty by the French and Dutch voters in May–June 2005. The five largest parties in the Folketing even agreed to support the treaty due to "certain overall goals" they shared with regard to the EU. Within the Five Party Agreement of November 2004, it was agreed that the EU would remain an important agenda item for the Danish parliament and that increased parliamentary supervision would "afford the Folketing better opportunities to influence Denmark's EU policies at an early state."[17] While the outcome of the Danish presidency was seen as a success, there remains a tension between an ever-skeptical and volatile public opinion and the goals of the Danish government, especially after the postponement of the EU constitution decision.

■ How Does Denmark Implement and Comply with EU Policies?

Danes are among the most consistently "polled" people in the world, and the EU is a perennial issue. In assessing attitudes toward the EU, it is important to distinguish between these frequent public opinion polls, attitudes of political activists and parliamentarians, and the formal programs of Denmark's numerous political parties. While there has been notable stability in opinion and programs, there is also periodic change. It is important, if at times difficult, to separate attitudes toward the EU from overall political sentiment.[18] Nor should one expect full consistency from the public. The *Eurobarometer Survey* issued in spring 2005 gave a comprehensive view of Danish public attitudes. It found that only 17 percent of the public is totally opposed to Danish EU membership, with 59 percent generally favorable. As in earlier surveys, most of the opposition is found on the political left wing (18 percent opposed), but ironically right-wing respondents have a more negative view of the EU (24 percent, twice that of the left-of-center). The survey also found strong support for a common EU foreign policy (60 percent) and EU security and defense cooperation (66 percent), even though Denmark has a special opt-out in the latter area. About half those surveyed support adopting the euro currency, but a slightly smaller number still reject it. Likewise, 80 percent of Danes felt that their country had influence within the EU, but a slightly larger number recognize the decisive power of the larger EU states.[19]

The previous Eurobarometer poll (spring 2004) gives additional information on Danish attitudes toward EU issues. That poll, like earlier ones, showed that Danes as a whole are a fairly "contented" lot, which is not surprising given the country's long social-democratic tradition and recent return to prosperity. Danish public attitudes are realistic; although they believe that the EU is good for their economic interests, Danes recognize that the larger EU states make the important decisions. Hence Danes want to hang on to their veto rights. Danes fear the "outsourcing" of jobs both within the larger EU and globally, while more conservative Danes worry about the interests of Danish farmers.[20]

Although comparative data come mainly from the biannual Eurobarometer polls, other Danish polls give additional insights. There has been a trend toward greater support for the EU over the past few years. Gallup polls have repeatedly asked Danes whether they support Danish membership in the European Union (earlier the European Community). In May 2005 support for membership was exceptionally strong: 69 percent in favor and 26 percent opposed (5 percent undecided).[21] On the issue of the European Constitutional Treaty on which a referendum had been announced for late September 2005, opinion was also strongly favorable, with 56 percent in favor, 32 percent opposed, and 11 percent undecided. As in earlier surveys, men tend to be more supportive of the EU than women, but the gap has narrowed in recent years. There is still much stronger support for the EU among higher-educated and higher-earning Danes. There are two strong political sources of EU opposition: supporters of the right-wing DPP and radical socialist "Unity List" are strongly skeptical of the EU in general and the Constitutional Treaty in particular.[22]

European Union issues have been a divisive issue in Danish politics for more than 30 years, but not as sharply so in recent years. Between 1972 and 1998 political divisions in the Folketing (parliament) fluctuated but frequently reinforced domestic political contention. For example in 1986 the opposition parties (Social Democrats, Social Liberals, Progressive, and others) recommended rejection of the Single European Act that was submitted to a national referendum. The public, however, approved the measure with a substantial majority (see Table 9.1).[23] Over time, the main political parties have accepted both memberships and the various conditions (especially the 1992 opt-outs) as a political fact. The most recent example of this growing consensus is the Five Party Agreement of November 2004 on support for the proposed European Constitutional Treaty signed by the two governing parties (liberals and conservatives) and the main opposition parties (Social Democrats, Social Liberals, and Socialist People's Party). Together these parties hold more than 80 percent of the seats in parliament. The agreement spells out the prevailing pragmatism on EU issues: "The EU is not an ideological project, but a common framework for political efforts."[24] The parties accept that the draft Constitutional Treaty was the result of negotiations among 25 states, and that it mainly updates and improves governance, openness, and democracy in the expanded EU. The Five Party Agreement goes on to discuss how the treaty affects various Danish positions on EU policies and procedures as well as a common Danish program for EU efforts in the near future.[25]

■ Future Trends and Prospects

EU Policy and Democracy

No sooner had the EU morphed from a "common market" (later called the Single Market) into a "union" than there emerged a protracted discussion about a democratic deficit in the EU and its various institutions. In a strictly intergovernmental organization such as NATO or even the UN, there is broad acceptance that sovereign governments (all democratic in the first case, many not in the second) make decisions on the basis of unanimity or substantial majorities. As the EU strengthened institutions that directly represented the people of the member states, preeminently the European Parliament, the democratic deficit issue arose.[26] There are fundamental questions about how representative democracy can function at the international level. Some might say that decisions made by sovereign but democratic states in international organizations are by definition as democratic as those made by parliaments and domestic democratic institutions. The EU has evolved into a rather unique organization that is no longer in practice a typical international organization but an evolving "confederal" entity that combines intergovernmental decisionmaking (primarily through the European Council of Ministers) and representative co-decisionmaking through the directly elected European Parliament. There are also advisory bodies such as the Economic and Social Council that represent economic interests in a gesture to Europe's democratic corporatist traditions.

Voting and participation in policymaking are certainly minimal requirements for a democratic European Union, but as the debate about the Constitutional Treaty demonstrates, there are vigorously contested perspectives. National parliamentary supremacy has been the fundamental principle of European democracy even if various national and European charters of civil rights temper such supremacy. Similarly there is a tension between the EU's explicit commitment to "subsidiarity" (maximizing decentralization of matters not essential to operation of the EU) and the expanding scope of measures implementing a free "internal (European) market." EU enlargement policies also imply broadening of citizen guarantees and pressures to harmonize policies among the EU states so that citizens and businesses are treated equally. So the issue arises whether national laws and regulations can diverge significantly from EU directives. Over the past 20 years there has been a significant expansion of the scope of EU regulations; while there are cases of excessive bureaucratic (or "Euro-cratic") zeal, most are essential or at least useful in making the key components of the EU function. For a small homogeneous state such as Denmark with a tradition of centralized government and administration, these pressures on occasion cause domestic tensions. Denmark's efficient and law-bound policy process explains an interesting anomaly. Although Danes remain "reluctant" Europeans and have secured opt-outs from EU commitments, Denmark has the best record of implementing EU directives. The EU refers to this process as "transponding" EU directives into national law and regulations. In mid-2004, about 2.3 percent of EU directives had not yet been implemented by the member states. Denmark had only 10 EU directives unimplemented, only 0.7 percent. Several of the "original" (pre-1973) EU states had much worse records, most notably France with fully 4.2 percent (62) directives outstanding.[27]

An important element of Danish EU policy has been the close oversight by the European Affairs Committee of the Danish parliament. Originally created as the Market Affairs Committee prior to Denmark's accession to the European Community in 1973, this committee has remained an active link between the EP and the Danish government. It has inspired similar committees in several other EU countries, most notably Sweden and Finland that joined two decades later. As EU decisionmaking has become more complex—for example through "co-decisionmaking" with the European Parliament and the Council of Ministers—the European Affairs Committee has endeavored to keep the

EP "in the loop." Most recently the committee has updated parliamentary procedures to coordinate its EU oversight with the other parliamentary policy committees. Hence when the EU is proposing policies in, for example, agricultural or transportation areas, the appropriate Folketing committees will assist the European Affairs Committee in assessing the impact on Denmark.[28]

Denmark has several instruments for balancing national democracy with EU governance. First, Denmark achieved in 1992 the four opt-outs previously discussed. Those affecting defense and the EMU are the most important; in the latter case Denmark more than fulfills the EMU economic criteria in regard to inflation, public finance, and interest rates. Moreover the Danish krone's firm attachment to the euro further reduces the significance of the EMU opt-out. In the first decade of the EMU process, Denmark's economy (like the other nonparticipants, Great Britain and Sweden) has performed better than the 12 full members of the EMU. This type of performance was foreseen in the debate prior to the September 2000 referendum when Danish voters rejected adoption of the euro as the national currency. Such public skepticism expressed democratically has not hurt the country's EU situation.[29]

The opt-out on defense has been more problematic. Denmark has become increasingly active in international security affairs. This was long true in United Nations peacekeeping operations, but since 1990 Denmark has been more active in NATO and other multilateral military operations. Until 1998, this reservation applied mainly to the revival of the Western European Union after the Cold War. Since then the EU moved rapidly forward in implementing the Common Security and Defense Policy (CSDP) arrangements to which Denmark could only be an observer. With the split in the EU over policies toward the US invasion of Iraq in 2003 and thereafter, the CSDP has lost momentum. Nevertheless, the opt-out required Denmark to withdraw some of its forces in the Balkan peacekeeping operations when responsibility was shifted from NATO to the EU. During the Danish presidency in 2002, Denmark also had to relinquish its position temporarily to Greece (the next presidency) when CSDP matters came up. This was an odd inconvenience, but not a major problem for either Denmark or the EU.[30]

The Danish opt-out on Justice and Home Affairs (including police, immigration, and related issues) has been eroded by later policies aimed at pragmatic collaboration in this area of growing priority. Denmark is a full member of the EU/European Economic Area "Schengen" passport union. Although Denmark reserves the right to select which police and internal policy coordination measures it will join, the issue is no longer especially controversial. Neither is the fourth opt-out on EU citizenship; there has been no EU effort to subsume national citizenship under EU citizenship.

Europe a la Carte?

With frequent referendums, four opt-outs, and recurring debates about the country's role in the European Union, Denmark might be seen as the perpetual squeaky wheel in European cooperation. In fact Denmark's position in the EU has become more predictable and stable over the past few years. Danish objectives have been freely debated, negotiated, and voted upon in the context of a democratic process. Public opinion has been more positive on issues like future adoption of the euro currency, expansion of the EU, and most recently the European Union Constitutional Treaty. Strongly anti-EU parties did not draw additional support in the June 2004 elections to the European Parliament and in the February 2005 national elections.[31] Following the Five Party Agreement of November 2004, the government laid the foundation for a national referendum on the EU constitution, originally scheduled for late September 2005, but postponed in June 2005 following the treaty's defeat in France and the Netherlands. Denmark was not a participant in the immediately following struggle over the EU's budget framework for the coming six-year period, which dominated the European Council meeting in Luxembourg in mid-June. In the weeks that followed, the Danish government declared a period of "rugged pragmatism" in which the EU would develop policies that could regain the confidence of the public in many EU member states. Five points framed the Danish government's EU agenda: (1) focus on economic growth and job creation, (2) completion of the EU "internal market" including resolution of provisions for trade in services, (3) fewer EU subsidies (especially in the agricultural sector), (4) more security for citizens, and (5) a strengthened and more coherent role for the EU on the global scene.[32]

This agenda suggests a country that is active and committed to the European Union, and which is increasingly agreed on the overall framework for European integration in the coming decade. As Foreign Minister Per Stig Møller declared unambiguously in 2003, most Danes want concrete EU results rather than an abstract "United States of Europe."[33] Likewise, the Danish government, in launching the public debate about the EU Constitutional Treaty, emphasized its pragmatic and constructive clarification and rationalization of EU governance rather than loftier goals.[34] In the wake of the French and Dutch referenda rejecting the draft Constitutional Treaty, the Danish debate has been put on hold. As Prime Minister Fogh Rasmussen noted when he opened the new parliamentary session in October 2005, EU leadership has proclaimed a "thinking-pause" that may last for two years. Danes want to see progress in concrete EU issues such as renewed European economic growth, control and accountability of the EU budget, integration of the "new 10" into the EU mainstream, and other issues.[35] Three out of four Danes expect the EU to play an ever-larger role in their lives, but they want to steer that development.[36] Idealism can be found among Europhiles, but in common with its Nordic neighbors, Denmark prefers flexible, efficient, and democratic European goals rather than the emotional or ideological goals of earlier EU advocates.[37] Denmark has demonstrated that the reverse side of Euro-skepticism can be "Euro-pragmatism." This may be a useful lesson for many of its European Union partners.

■ Notes

1. This was especially true of the protectionist/neomercantilist interwar period (1920–1945). Although trade liberalization helped industrial trade after 1950, agricultural products, a major Danish export, did not gain easier access until membership in the EC.

2. A concise economic history of modern Denmark (of few in English) can be gleaned from Jörberg, "The Industrial Revolution in the Nordic Countries," pp. 375–485, and Jörberg and Krantz, "Scandinavia 1914–1970," pp. 377–459. Between 1870 and 1914, Danish milk and butter production tripled, port quadrupled, and grain production was up by 40 percent (Jörberg, p. 396).

3. In the 1930s negotiated bilateral trade agreements were common with state-controlled economies (e.g., Nazi Germany), but Great Britain's "imperial preference" system also hit Danish agricultural exports hard. Such "clearing agreements" balanced trade bilaterally through complex bureaucratic restrictions.

4. Denmark's 1953 Constitution requires a referendum whenever sovereignty is ceded to an international organization unless five-sixths of the parliament (Folketing) approves. In practice, Danish governments have held binding referendums whenever major EC/EU treaties are signed: six times between 1972 and 2005. Note that a majority in parliament must still approve such treaties and that to be rejected in a referendum the negative vote must be a majority of the votes cast *and* constitute 30 percent of registered voters. See Einhorn and Logue, *Modern Welfare States,* pp. 22–23, 86.

5. Svensson, "Five Danish Referendums on the European Community and European Union," pp. 733–750.

6. The Danish People's Party split off from the Progress Party in the mid-1990s, primarily over personalities, but remained strongly Euro-skeptical.

7. An exception was in 1986 when the Social Democrats pursued an

oppositional policy toward the EU's Single Market program and also Danish NATO policy. Both policies weakened the Social Democrats and were removed from their agenda almost as quickly as they had appeared.

8. The leftist "Unity List" (Enhedslisten), with six members in the Danish parliament, is strongly opposed to the EU but does not contest European parliamentary elections; its members generally support one of the two anti-EU lists.

9. For detailed background see the excellent essay in the first edition of this volume by Eliason, "Denmark: Small State with a Big Voice." See also Ingebritsen, *The Nordic States and European Unity.*

10. Eliason, "Denmark: Small State with a Big Voice," p. 193.

11. The November 2001 exit poll of voters indicated that "welfare" (social policy) was the primary concern of 55 percent of voters, with immigration next at 23 percent. The EU and foreign affairs was the primary concern of only 6 percent, with half of those indicating that "terrorism" was their focus. Anderson, "Valgkampen 2001; Vælgernes politiske dagsorden," p. 3.

12. Some might be tempted to say "because" of the rejection of the euro, but Denmark maintained its fixed exchange rate to the euro that it had adopted when the euro came into existence as an accounting currency in 1999. This was an extension of Denmark's "fixed" exchange rate vis-à-vis the German mark that dated back to 1982.

13. Organisation for Economic Cooperation and Development, *Economic Outlook,* appendix. The Maastricht Treaty of European Union of 1992 and the EMU agreement called for a maximum of 60 percent of GDP for public debt (as defined by the agreements). Most of the "Euro-12" countries have had problems with one or more of the EMU criteria.

14. Defined by the European Commission online at: http://europa.eu.int/comm/enlargement/intro/criteria.htm (accessed July 2005). The third point emphasizes acceptance of the "Acquis Communautaire": the accumulated EU laws and directives.

15. Anders Fogh Rasmussen, speech made on the Danish presidency on January 8, 2003. Available online at: http://www.eu2002.dk.

16. Such environmentalism has attracted opposition from the European Commission, which sees it as a barrier to market liberalization. An example is the Danish bottling case, which involved restrictions on the import of beverage containers without return deposits. Denmark lost this fight, opening the way to foreign containers that are now part of a growing trash problem.

17. Denmark, Folketinget. *Political Agreement* (Five-Party Agreement), p. 3.

18. A definitive analysis of Danish attitudes toward the EU may be found in Buch and Hansen, "The Danes and Europe."

19. European Commission, Eurobarometer 62, "Public Opinion in the European Union National Report, Executive Summary, Denmark."

20. Ibid.

21. Gallup poll, May 2005, reproduced in Carlsen and Mouritzen, eds., *Danish Foreign Policy Yearbook 2005,* p. 176.

22. Gallup, Ugens, no. 6, 2005.

23. Damgaard and Nørrgaard, "The European Union and Danish Parliamentary Democracy," p. 39.

24. Denmark, Folketinget. *Political Agreement* (Five-Party Agreement).

25. Ibid.

26. Although an "assembly" dates back to the origins of the European Economic Community in the 1957 Treaty of Rome, it was elected by the several national parliaments and had mainly the power of inquiry and discussion. Since 1979, the European Parliament has been directly elected at five-year intervals and its powers have increased significantly under the Maastricht Treaty on European Union (1993) and subsequent adjustments. Co-decisionmaking with the Council has given the EP real powers, and with the dismissal of the European Commission in 1999 (over scandals), its powers became more visible. The literature on the EP is vast; see for example, Rittberger, *Building Europe's Parliament.*

27. European Commission, "Internal Market Scorecard," pp. 9–10.

28. Denmark, Folketinget. "Beretning om reform" (Report on Reform).

29. See Eliason, "Denmark: Small State with a Big Voice," pp. 211–212, and Marcussen, "Denmark and European Monetary Integration," pp. 43 ff.

30. Friis, "The 2002 Danish Presidency—A Two-Thirds Presidency?" pp. 52–54.

31. An exception is the rightist populist Danish People's Party upon whose support the Liberal-Conservative coalition of Prime Minster Fogh Rasmussen relies for parliamentary support. Polls show that DPP voters are less anti-EU (although genuinely Euro-skeptical) than the party leadership, and in fact the DPP has not made EU issues a barrier to political collaboration with the government.

32. *Politiken*, "Hvad er det, Europa skal bruges til?" [What Is It That Europe Shall Be Used For?].

33. Møller, "European Foreign Policy in the Making," pp. 63–72.

34. Denmark, Folketinget, "Political Agreement Regarding Denmark in the Enlarged EU." This was already stated at the start of the EU Convention by the Danish government's white paper on Denmark and Europe published in June 2001, "Denmark and Europe: Enlargement, Globalization, Legitimacy" (unofficial translation, August 2001 by the Danish Foreign Ministry).

35. Rasmussen, "Statsminister Anders Fogh Rasmussens tale ved Folketingets" [Opening Speech to the Danish Parliament].

36. European Commission, "Public Opinion in the European Union. National Report: Denmark," p. 16.

37. Overall Nordic attitudes and policies are assessed in Ingebritsen, *The Nordic States and European Unity,* and more recently in Matlary, "The Nordics and the EU."

PART 3

—

THE 1980s

10

Greece:
A Most Enthusiastic,
Reluctant European

Nikolaos Zahariadis

THE PROCESS OF EUROPEANIZATION, that is, the EU's acquired policy competence and effects on member states, has been the topic of much recent analytical attention. Nowhere is this process more evident than in the case of Greece. Greece was often described in the past as the obstructionist "black sheep" of the EU, but Greek politicians in recent years have embarked on a sustained effort to reverse this image. In the name of the national interest, Greece would no longer be the EU laggard that it was in the past. Rather, Greece would revitalize its economy and modernize society and institutions to finally become a model to be imitated by aspiring EU entrants. The so-called modernists, under the tutelage of former socialist prime minister Costas Simitis, embarked on a radical policy of reforming the state and society using EU institutions, policies, and values as guideposts for many of the painful and costly decisions they made. The same vision of Greek-EU relations has been espoused by the reigning conservatives and other parties, ushering in a new era of common aspirations among the Greek political elite.[1] It would appear that Greece has finally been able to match its enthusiasm for EU membership to actual deeds that transform words into practice. However, despite good intentions and effort, many of the old ways and institutional dysfunction remain intact. Reluctance to commit, and most important, to abide by EU commitments, is pervasive.

▪ How and in What Areas
Does the EU Influence Greece?

Despite the economic character of the EU in years past, the Greek reasons for joining the EU were largely political and security-related in nature. Greece viewed the EU in the 1970s, when its application was activated, more as a way of consolidating internal democracy and as a security counterweight to the difficulties with Turkey in the Aegean rather than as a way of acquiring economic benefits.[2] Consequently, until recently issues of a political nature have dominated Greek debates relative to the merits of EU membership. It was only when the "Mediterranean Integrated Programs" were introduced in the mid-1980s that the ruling socialists awoke to the distinct possibility of having access to voluminous external funds for institutional modernization and economic development. Nevertheless, the salience of political benefits was still the norm until the mid-1990s, when the prime minister, Simitis, explicitly made the country's modernization under EU tutelage his highest priority.[3] By then economic health became critical to the prime minister's goals, which essentially transformed priorities from overt reluctance, indifference, and occasional opposition to EU decisions to closer cooperation with an eye toward maximizing funding and economic benefits.

It is impossible to put a figure on the level of EU influence in Greece. The affected areas span the entire spectrum of Greek life. However imperfect and problematic a summary figure can be, the level of inflows from the EU is considerable. The European Community's structural assistance budget for Greece for the entire 2000–2006 period stood at €25 billion, an increase of 1.1 percent more each year than in the previous period (1994–1999).[4] However, this amount is supposed to shrink by at least 35 percent during the period 2007–2013 because aid disbursements will be diverted in large measure to the newly admitted central and eastern European members.[5] In 2003, Greece received €3.363 billion or 2.22 percent of its GDP in net inflows (inflows minus outflows) from EU sources, down from an astounding 5 percent in 1993.[6] In terms of rankings, Greece ended up second in 2003 behind Portugal, which received 2.66 percent of net inflows. Measured in terms of euros per capita, Greece came in third with €305.3 per capita behind Ireland (€391.7) and Portugal (€333.4). However, looking only at absolute levels of inflows, the amount is relatively low, €4.84 billion, as opposed to Spain's €15.8 billion, the country with the highest inflows.

Nonetheless, these numbers are misleading. They might lead to the conclusion that Greek development is benefiting dramatically from EU funds. This is true, but only to an extent. One also needs to take into account absorption figures. The amounts above indicate funds allocated, but not monies spent. Absorption rates provide an important qualification to the whole picture. A big portion of EU funds comes in the form of Community Support Framework (CSF) monies. According to M. Evert—the former leader of the New Democracy Party, the reigning conservatives—the absorption rate of funds disbursed under the third CSF, that is, the rate at which allocated funds are currently spent, is on average only 30 percent.[7] Stated differently, 70 percent of allocated funds have yet to be used, while the Greeks negotiate spending levels for the fourth CFS in the spring of 2005. The rate over the years has not changed substantially. For example, an implementation progress report on transport projects in mid-1999 shows that Greece completed only 28 percent of its targeted new roadways and 29 percent of its new rail lines. By comparison, Portugal achieved 100 percent and 68 percent, and Ireland 92 percent and 100 percent of its targets, respectively.[8] The implication is that while a good deal of funds come into the country every year, relatively few are spent. How can the country expend huge political capital to secure funds and then not use them? Part of the answer lies with the national system of coordinating Greece-EU relations, and part rests with domestic institutional deficiencies at the subnational level.

Coordination of Greece-EU relations takes place within a bi-institutional framework. Both the Ministry of Foreign Affairs (MFA) and the Ministry of Economy and Finance (MEF) share responsibility for the advocacy and implementation of relations with the EU. It is natural in a system with two competing poles of influence for friction to arise, but the two institutions seem to have found a precarious modus vivendi. The MFA is primarily concerned with coordinating advocacy positions and legal aspects of implementation, while the MEF is more closely involved in the actual implementation of CSFs, where a good portion of EU funds flows. There exist EU specialized units within other ministries as well, such as agriculture, labor, etc., but the lack of intersectoral coordination leaves them pretty much in the dark. To be sure, the MFA is supposed to have primacy over such coordination, particularly with respect to the Permanent Representation unit in Brussels, but the lack of skilled staff and the absence of ministerial interest dramatically reduce any effectiveness these other units may have.[9]

Largely, its directorate-general for EU affairs exercises the coordinating role of the MFA. Subdivided into various units dealing with the

Internal Market, external affairs, justice, and other competencies, the directorate coordinates policy goals and strategies between the various Greek ministries. In addition, a special legal service for EU matters (ENY-EK) was created in 1986 in response to concerns about noncompliance and the political turn toward the EU within the then ruling Socialist Party.[10] It is charged with ensuring "the timely transposition of community law into national legislation, its correct enforcement and the country's compliance with the judgements and case law of the European Court of Justice."[11] Transposition (incorporation) of community directives into national law takes place either through presidential decrees or through ministerial decisions initiated by the relevant ministry. ENY-EK has identified several areas of priority, which include the Internal Market, the environment, and taxation. Through consultations and meetings with other public services in Greece and the Commission, ENY-EK has been able to produce considerable results reducing the number of infringements over the years while pressing for speedier transposition proceedings.

The MEF plays an increasingly important role, particularly since Prime Minister Simitis identified the country's entry into the euro zone as a top national priority in the late 1990s. Attention has focused largely on achieving macroeconomic stability and convergence with EU averages by adopting a series of measures, including disinflation, currency stability, improved taxation techniques to boost revenues, and a general rein on government expenditures to reduce annual budget deficits and the public debt. In 1998, the Bank of Greece, according to its current governor, set entry into the Exchange Rate Mechanism as an intermediate goal to be achieved by 1999 and final entry into the euro zone by 2001.[12] Achievement of both goals was driven largely by tight fiscal and monetary policies. Ministers from both major parties, G. Papantoniou (socialist) and G. Alogoskoufis (conservative), agree that major structural changes—such as labor reforms and public-sector improvements in competitiveness, which are needed to sustain progress in macroeconomic indicators—have not yet been tackled.[13]

The MEF also coordinates the advocacy and implementation of EU Structural Funds, a priority in the Greek government's crucial stabilization plan of 1995–1999. For this reason, a special unit was created under the control of MEF but outside the ministry's civil service structure to support "the overall implementation and organization of the 3rd CSF."[14] Financed by a budget of €32.35 million from the third CSF, the Management Organization Unit (MOU) provides to its managing authorities, Greek organizations created in 2000 with the explicit task of implementing the third CSF, with management tools, human relations methodologies, and transfer of know-how to aid in the consistent implementation of CSF projects. Although the MOU has had some successes in providing expertise, equipment, and infrastructural facilities to managing authorities, overall success with CSF projects has been tempered by low absorption rates.

The organizational design of Greece's implementation system appears adequate or at least not dramatically different from that of more "successful" EU member states. What seem to be missing, however, are two key elements.[15] First is the absence of political will at the top level to clearly articulate a set of priorities. The system's overall steering capacity is especially weak and prone to information deficiencies and sudden policy reversals. Second is the general underdevelopment of planning and staffing functions in Greek administration. Coupled with a general climate of political polarization, which has only recently subsided, the two elements have led to a series of suboptimal results. While Greek politicians have talked up EU membership and have exhibited an interest in exploiting its benefits, they have been unwilling and/or unable to put in place an institutional framework, complete with adequate human and organizational elements, that will actually turn rhetoric into practice.

■ How and in What Areas Does Greece Influence EU Policies?

Greece has not traditionally tried hard to influence EU policies.[16] But this does not mean that Athens has not tried or succeeded in getting its way. Because successive governments have focused largely on gaining political and security benefits from EU membership, Athens has naturally concentrated its efforts of influence in these two areas.[17] A good example is the Greek attempt to block EU recognition of the Former Yugoslav Republic of Macedonia (FYROM) in the first half of the 1990s. Small, industrially less advanced states can actually get their way in the EU when they are prepared to incur high costs, if necessary, and exploit decisionmaking rules for their own benefit.

The contemporary bone of contention between FYROM and Greece was thrust onto the international scene during the annual meeting of the Conference (now Organization) for Security and Cooperation in Europe in 1990. At that meeting, the Yugoslav representative distributed a memorandum charging Greece with suppressing the rights of the Slav-speak-

ing minority in Greek Macedonia. Remaining largely reactive in its policy, the government of conservative prime minister C. Mitsotakis took 15
months to formulate a coherent policy vis-à-vis FYROM.[18] Faced with
FYROM's application for recognition by the EU, following its declaration of independence from the Yugoslav federation in 1991, the Greek
government issued a memorandum outlining its official position on
December 4, 1991. It argued that while Greece did not harbor territorial
demands on FYROM, it nevertheless objected to its formal recognition
under the name Macedonia because the name implied territorial aspirations rooted in the recent past.[19] Recognition would come only if
FYROM changed its name, signed a treaty with Greece on the inviola-
bility of current borders, and renounced any hostile propaganda against
Greece including the existence of the so-called Slavo-Macedonian ghost
minority in Greece.[20]

Armed with the cabinet's decision, the Greek foreign minister, A.
Samaras, negotiated in Brussels with his counterparts the official EU
stance related to Yugoslavia in general and FYROM in particular. In a
European Political Cooperation (EPC) communiqué dated December 16,
1991, the 12 ministers agreed to recognize all the Yugoslav republics
that so wished with expressed reservations against "a Yugoslav republic" that must cease all hostile propaganda "against a neighbouring
Community State, including the use of a denomination which implies
territorial claims."[21] Originally, Greece had actually opposed the dissolution of Yugoslavia in addition to the explicit reference to the name
Macedonia. The main reasons for a softening of the Greek position were
institutional norms and rules and two-level games. Tziampiris argues
that Greek policymakers in Brussels had to operate within EPC rules
that facilitated the adoption of compromise positions, which differed
substantially from the more "extremist" Greek cabinet decision taken
earlier that month.[22] Side payments and reciprocity within the EPC
made such compromise possible. For example, compensation for the
negative impact of the war and economic sanctions against Yugoslavia
meant that Greece had to go along with EU wishes. In addition, Foreign
Minister Samaras agreed to eventually recognize the independence of
various Yugoslav republics leading to the dissolution of Yugoslavia
despite Greek misgivings and official policy in order to achieve agreement on the Macedonian issue. Moreover, playing a classic two-level
game, the conservative government consciously linked the issues of
signing the Treaty on European Union and accession to the Western
European Union in return for not pressing its allies too hard on the

Macedonian issue, at least not to insist on fulfillment of the three criteria in the language that the Greek cabinet prescribed.[23]

But the Greek government hardened its position later. Having rejected the European proposals for resolving the issue, the so-called Pinheiro package, the Greek government got EU agreement in Lisbon (June 1992) to recognize FYROM "under an appellation that will not include the term Macedonia."[24] After a series of failed efforts to find a compromise solution, exasperated EU allies recognized FYROM under that name, in violation of the Lisbon Strategy, in December 1993.[25] As a response, Greece imposed an embargo on FYROM, effectively banning all trade between the two countries save for humanitarian relief. The Commission retaliated by taking Greece to court. Although the European Court never rendered a decision, because FYROM and Greece agreed to normalize relations in 1995 before the Court had a chance to decide, the case points to the low point of Greece-EU relations. Relations between FYROM and Greece have subsequently improved, helping to usher in a marked convergence of views within the Common Foreign and Security Policy (CFSP) and in relation to EU activities in former Yugoslavia.[26]

The case study illustrates two main points about Greek influence over EU matters. First, Greece and other small EU members are willing to expend considerable capital to get what they want from the EU. Even though Greek security concerns are regional, and one may argue less salient to many of Greece's allies, successive Greek governments felt it important to devote resources to specific issues and get what they wanted. The so-called Macedonian Question represents one example of sustained Greek influence, sometimes to the consternation of EU allies, but there are others. More recently, Greece steered the difficult accession talks between Cyprus and the EU to a successful conclusion, while it has also strongly advocated, to the surprise of some analysts, Turkey's entry into the EU. In other words, regardless of the cost, Greece is, on occasion, determined and able to get its way.

Second, current EU rules favor small members, particularly in the area of foreign policy. Although Greece has consistently been in favor of a more federal EU structure[27] the current decisionmaking rules in the CFSP (and its predecessor, the EPC) provide an environment that increases the political weight of small members disproportionately to their power. The power (or threat) to veto EU decisions on numerous occasions during the imbroglio over Macedonia, Turkey, and Cyprus, has helped Greece get agreement on issues it considered vital over the misgivings of other allies. Moreover, the exclusive ability of national governments to define their national security interests, an argument made by the advocate general during the trial of *Greece vs. the Commission*, gives small members disproportionate power to make deals and block decisions they could otherwise not influence. This power is of course not limitless. Greece had to compromise on other matters of importance to get its way during the 1991 meeting, which established the European criteria for recognition. The fact that some members rendered EU support and solidarity empty later on further tempers the "disproportionate weight" hypothesis. Nonetheless, the point remains that the EU currently provides the structural opportunity for determined small members to get what they want.

■ How Does Greece Implement and Comply with EU Policies?

Many of the monetary benefits that Greece receives from EU funds come in the form of structural assistance. As a result, an effective regional policy has become an area of great interest to Greek governments since the 1990s. However, implementation has been subsumed under the broader national strategy of macroeconomic convergence and the Economic and Monetary Union.[28] As a result, despite high levels of funding, progress has been slow and outcomes not particularly encouraging. All Greek regions continue to be eligible for Objective 1 funds, meaning that per capita incomes have not risen above 75 percent of the EU's average. There are two related reasons for the outcome: low absorption rates and political-administrative inefficiencies.

Low absorption rates are primarily due to a lack of institutional networks and technical expertise at the local level. The current MEF minister puts the historical absorption rate of Structural Funds at 50 percent.[29] This figure of course masks significant differences between eligible regions. For example, in an in-depth study of the differences in Structural Fund implementation performance (first CSF) between the northern Aegean and southern Aegean regions, one author finds the average local government program absorption rates in the islands of the northern Aegean to begin at slightly over 30 percent in 1989–1991 and peak at over 60 percent in 1994.[30] The corresponding figure for islands in the southern Aegean was slightly less than 30 percent in 1991, but the absorption rate peaked to 100 percent by 1994. The differences are attributed to the type of inherited institutional networks, the type of economy that these regions sought to emphasize—for example, the southern Aegean islands focused more heavily on tourist development whereas the northern islands emphasized the development of agriculture—and the ability of local networks to mobilize private and public actors to coordinate resources at the local level. To a varying degree, technical expertise and overall coordination continue to be provided by the central government, reflecting a "top-down" developmental model. Nevertheless, the decision by the Dodecanese Prefecture Council and private actors to open an office in Brussels to facilitate cooperation and broaden the region's understanding of EU opportunities and expectations reflects a positive step toward a more effective and more efficient implementation.

Despite the influx of EU funds and a greater push for accountability and transparency, the political-administrative system in Greece continues to be a partisan, client-list system. Major reforms designed to decentralize Greek administration have been marred by corruption and inefficiencies. In 1997, 13 regions were created on top of the preexisting prefectures and local governments with the purpose of better coordinating funds and implementing models of regional development, particularly since Structural Funds by the EU necessitated the existence of regional governments of sufficient scope and scale. Nevertheless, control over these layers of government has been kept with central state authorities, and by extension the party that controls the government at the time. For example, the regional general secretary, the position with most authority in the region who has taken over all government departments from the now-elected prefect, is directly appointed by the minister of the interior.[31] Through the power of the purse, the central government maintains political authority while diffusing responsibility to lower, but partisan, levels of government. For example, of the GRD754 billion transferred by the state to the prefecture, 95.6 percent went to national state programs, such as major transport works, hospitals, and local health organizations over which prefects have no control.[32] Of roughly 25,000 prefecture employees, only 1,000 were actually employed by the prefectures. The rest were central-government employees on loan.[33] Much of the technical expertise and managerial know-how of the regional governments is actually supplied by the MEF. All in all, while implementation of EU regional policies is supposed to be pursued by autonomous regional governments, the way these governments have been created in Greece and the institutional networks of learning and adaptation that have been consequently created reproduce to a large extent the old patronage system that has served Greek political parties so well and Greek administration so poorly.

■ Greece's Record of Compliance with EU Directives

Greece's record is inadequate though it has improved recently. In the 1980s, the slow and inadequate compliance record was "one of the thorniest issues affecting Greece's relations with the EC."[34] Unfortunately, the country continues to suffer from long transposition delays and infringement proceedings despite measures taken to ameliorate the situation. The reasons for long delays in compliance remain largely domestic, although one cannot discount the (anticipated) sanctions and other compliance strategies that the European Commission often employs in pursuit of its mission to be the "guardian of the treaties."[35]

The absolute levels of compliance don't paint a flattering picture of Greece, but progress has been made over time and relative to other members. According to the latest figures, "131 Directives (around 8.5 percent of Internal Market Directives) have still not been implemented into national law in every Member State, though the deadlines agreed by the Member States themselves when they adopted the Directives have passed."[36] Greece belongs to the group of worst offenders, along with France, Italy, Germany, and Luxembourg. On May 31, 2004, Greece's transposition deficit—the percent of total number of directives not yet implemented into national law by the deadline—rose from 3.1 percent on November 30, 2003, to 3.9 percent.[37] The number of directives nonimplemented rose from 48 to 59 during the same period. While inadequate, Greece is neither the only country with poor results nor the worst offender. For example, Greece had only one directive still not implemented after two years in May 2004, in line with four other member states, while seven states had two or more nonimplemented directives.[38]

Moreover, the numbers show improvement over years past. For example, the number of directives not yet implemented as of May 2004 was reduced to 59 from 73 in May 1999. Dramatic improvements have been made in the area of notification delays. For example, during the period 1986–1998, the delay in notifying the Commission of nonimplementation of Single Market directives was 17.9 months. The number was reduced to 14.9 months over the period 1995–1999 (a 3-month difference) and further decreased to 10 months by 2003. By comparison, the average delay in notification for the worst offender in the period 1986–1998, Belgium, was 20.6 months, with a reduction to 19.8 months (0.8-month difference) during the period 1995–1999. In terms of cases brought before the European Court of Justice, the overall number was not reduced—it stood at 13 cases in 2000 and 2001—although improvements have been noted in the outcomes.[39] For example, in 2001 Greece lost only four cases, while the Commission refrained from action against Greece in nine cases because the latter was found to be in compliance. By contrast, in 2000 Greece faced sanctions in seven cases in 2000 and "won" only six.

What are the reasons for noncompliance? There are two explanations. First, Greece does not yet have the institutional capacity to implement all the appropriate legislation in a timely manner. Part of the reason lies with political unwillingness to clearly identify this issue as a priority and part of it lies with inadequate infrastructure and lack of legal/technical expertise. Commissioner Frits Bolkenstein's comments regarding Ireland's strides in implementation ring absolutely true about Greece: "Ireland's halving of its implementation deficit in only eight months shows what can be done when there is political will and commitment."[40] The Greeks have not yet taken that advice to heart, although the establishment of ENY-EK has gone a long way toward improving Greece's record.

Second, many infringements are in areas relatively "new" to Greece, such as the environment. A coherent environmental policy has only recently been adopted in Greece.[41] Part of the delay in this area may be attributed to close links between political elites and specific business interests.[42] As a result, much of the infrastructure, expertise, government attention, and citizen interest have been absent. Moreover, the construction of public works on a grand scale in the last four years has significantly increased the need for a better understanding of the repercussions for the environment.[43] A better understanding of the issues and greater technical expertise should improve compliance over time. While the Commission can play a constructive role in this area, much depends on Greek political will to reduce corruption, improve the efficiency and effectiveness of the public sector (which will in turn vastly improve implementation), and set compliance with European law as a key political target for improvement.

■ Future Trends and Prospects

This chapter has argued that Greek policymakers have sought to transform Athens's relations with Brussels from obstructionism to cooperation. Driven primarily by domestic considerations, this effort has largely born fruit. The Greek economy has improved dramatically; the public sector has been modernized to an extent, while great strides have been made in the area of foreign policy to foster cooperation with Balkan countries via multilateral, and more specifically, EU, channels.

However, as the case of regional policy illustrates, old problems continue to persist. Many institutional innovations at the national and subnational government levels have been used mostly as pretexts to attract EU funding. Despite the allocation of generous funding, implementation has been problematic. The results are mixed. Progress has been made, but it has been much less than expected.

Two current issues exemplify this trend of enthusiastic rhetoric and reluctant practice. The first deals with the accuracy of macroeconomic indicators. The issue is not merely a row over how economic progress is measured, but rather how trustworthy are Greek reports of perceived economic progress partly financed by EU funds. To be sure, this is not a problem isolated to Greece; it is pervasive throughout Europe, as the investigation over Eurostat's corruption and mismanagement allegations or the investigations over Italian figures demonstrate. The way the EU deals with Greece in this area serves as a model of how to deal with other countries in the future.

The problem arose in fall 2004 when the conservative Greek government alerted the Commission over the inaccuracy of Greek budgetary figures from 1997 to 2004. At issue were the accounting procedures adopted to calculate the annual level of defense expenditures. Since 1995, Greece has embarked on a massive modernization program of the armed forces bringing annual expenditures in 2003 to an estimated 4.2 percent of GDP in constant prices, the highest figure among NATO allies.[44] Purchases made under this effort have been reported by the reigning socialist government at the time as expenditures recorded upon delivery of the military equipment rather than as expenses incurred upon purchase. The result makes a big difference. Revised figures show that Greece failed to maintain its deficit below the euro zone's mandated figure of 3 percent since at least 1999. According to figures released by Eurostat, the budget deficit for 2004 rose to a whopping 5.3 percent of GDP as opposed to a forecast figure by the socialists of 1.6 percent.[45] Greek failure to take the necessary corrective measures also prompted the Commission to begin legal proceedings "for failing to report data accurately, regularly, and in a timely fashion."[46] The Greek government was eventually able to escape fines by its EU partners, but only because it agreed to a tough two-year program under the Commission's supervision to bring its budget deficit to 2.9 percent of GDP by 2006.[47]

The whole affair highlights two major points regarding Greek politics and Greece-EU affairs. First, socialist politicians, who lost the national elections in March 2004, assert that the conservatives have engaged in a political vendetta to absolve themselves of any blame for the politically controversial budget cuts with which they are faced. G. Papantoniou, the former socialist finance, and later defense, minister, claims he used the correct accounting methods and that the conservatives are using this issue as a diversionary tactic to avoid carrying through with their campaign promises.[48] In order to attempt deep cuts, the conservatives are using the previous government as a scapegoat and the EU as the rationale for doing so. While this is not unique to Greece, the episode vividly demonstrates the new way that the EU has used to settle domestic political scores. Whereas previously governments accepted all the credit for gains and blamed the EU for ills, they are now spreading the blame to the EU *and* the domestic opposition while absolving themselves of any responsibility for the consequences.

Second, the problem is not simply technical, but also political. The European Central Bank is eager to focus on tough action against Greece in order to use it as an example to other countries, particularly the newly admitted states before they enter the euro zone. However, finance ministers are hesitant in fear of pressing the matter too far. Several members, including France, Germany, Italy, and Portugal, are themselves under pressure to clean up their act because of their own deficit breaches. Besides, the Commission's recommendations for structural changes, such as independence for national statistical services and enhanced Commission capabilities to audit national accounts, have been summarily rejected by the UK and Germany.[49] The need for greater accuracy and transparency in national accounts is of vital economic importance to the EU, but the political desire to cling to national sovereignty continues to reign supreme.

The second issue deals with the usefulness of the current intergovernmental model of EU foreign policy in a post-9/11 world. Again the issue is not unique to Greece, but Greece is among the first EU countries to face the consequences of an assertive, some may argue unilateral, US policy and an opposing, but fragmented, EU perspective. The transatlantic rift between the United States and some EU members will challenge the current intergovernmental nature of EU foreign policy and call into question the utility of even having one under present conditions. The end result may well be a small group of EU states, with Greece surprisingly at the forefront, demanding a more united and assertive EU policy not simply to supplement but to an extent to counterbalance US hegemony.

At issue is the Bush administration's decision to recognize FYROM as the Republic of Macedonia. The issue has caused a stir among the Greek public and a possible reassessment of policies. While the issue in and of itself will not create a rift between Greece and the United States, it shows in the clearest terms the willingness of the Bush administration to act unilaterally to pursue its own interests. In this particular case, it is difficult to discern the US interests, other than a vague reference to FYROM's stability and a possible compensation for FYROM's support for the US effort in Iraq.[50] While Secretary of State Colin Powell, according to a Reuters report, reassured the Greeks "that the decision is not a turn against Greece and is not linked to the U.S. elections," it does not escape notice that the announcement came one day after President Bush's reelection, making it the first postelection US foreign-policy decision. The EU's foreign-policy chief, Javier Solana, was reportedly uninformed and surprised.[51]

This issue has rekindled the debate about the value placed on the European dimension of Greek foreign policy. While it is highly unlikely that Greece will seek to reorient its foreign policy and security outside the parameters of US influence and the transatlantic alliance, it is quite possible to observe debates for a major reorientation of the country's security doctrine more closely aligned with visions of a strong European foreign policy. Events of the last 30 years have tested the limits of US support for Greek security, especially vis-à-vis Turkey. While Greeks have traditionally placed a high value on the US factor in safeguarding the country's security, they have also lamented Washington's perceived favoritism of Turkish interests at the expense of Greece.[52] The recent tilt toward FYROM against Greek sensitivities can only bolster analysts calling for a more assertive European policy, one in which the Greeks can have a greater say. Coupled with the general deterioration of EU relations with the United States in light of the war on terrorism (and beyond), it is not unreasonable to expect Greek support for French (and other) calls for a stronger, more independent European foreign and security policy. The effectiveness of European desire for such policy remains a debatable point.

Indeed, the lack of a clear European voice was exemplified in the June 2005 rejection of the EU constitution in France and Holland. While the Greek government had already ratified it, the consequences of the rejection and the subsequent "freezing" of the process have significant implications for Greece in three areas. The first concern is about

Turkey's invitation to begin accession talks. Greece has supported Turkey's entry to the EU since 1999, but fears the possibility of keeping Turkey outside the EU will alienate and destabilize its eastern neighbor. As Prime Minister C. Karamanlis said a few days after the European Council's meeting in Brussels, "We have absolutely no reason to abandon the policy that we have been following until today."[53] Fortunately, this fear did not materialize and on October 3, 2005, the EU extended a formal invitation.

The second concern deals with funds to be received from the EU. Heavy haggling over the EU budget on the eve of the European Council's meeting in June 2005 highlights the deep worries Greece faces over eastern enlargement. More specifically, Greece feared that funds from the fourth CSF (2007–2013) would be cut dramatically and redirected toward the new members. The failure to agree on a budget figure indicates that Prime Minister Karamanlis was probably right. The British presidency had been charged with relaunching the negotiations. In light of the fact that it was Tony Blair who, among others, rejected the final figure as too high, it appears likely that the amount of 20.9 billion that Greece was rumored to have gotten out of the fourth CSF will be lower in the new round of talks.[54]

The final concern is potentially more alarming. In light of heavy borrowing requirements due to recent large budget deficits and the high public debt ratio, Greek government officials expect to pay more in interest payments.[55] Europe's current malaise following the rejection of the constitution lowered the euro's value in world currency markets. Coupled with the rise in the price of oil, which is measured in US dollars, Greek officials are faced with the strong possibility of negative economic repercussions. At a time when the government is pressured by the European Commission to reduce its budget deficit, it faces the distinct possibility of an economic slowdown, a reduction in revenues, and an increase in the cost of borrowing. While the rejection of the EU constitution did not bring about those problems, it certainly increased the likelihood of this negative scenario.

Since the 1996 decision of former prime minister Simitis to modernize the country and bring it closer to its EU allies, Greece has started to realize that it has greater leverage to get its wishes within a stronger, more integrated EU. But a lot more enthusiasm and considerably less reluctance are needed to turn realization into reality. At present, deep divisions in Europe over the future of the EU have made this an even more difficult task. Whether the country is up to it remains to be seen.

▧ Notes

1. Currently, there exists a widespread consensus over Greece's EU orientation among political parties, in contrast to the first socialist government's (1981–1985) expressed reservations. Differences between the two major parties are attributed to tactical concerns focused on domestic political consumption rather than substantive divergences regarding Greece's role in the EU. Chryssochoou, Stavridis, and Moschonas, "Greece and the European Union After Amsterdam," p. 188. For information on fluctuations in Greek public opinion toward the EU, see Mavris, "The Evolution of Greek Public Attitudes Toward European Integration."

2. Markou, Nakos, and Zahariadis, "Greece: A European Paradox"; Greek Ministry of Foreign Affairs, "The Course of Greece in the European Union."

3. For more information on the Greek road to convergence and EMU from the deputy minister of finance, who later became minister, see Christodoulakis, "The Greek Economy Converging Toward EMU."

4. The latest data are available in European Commission, "The Structural Funds in Greece."

5. Hope, "Regional Progress Masks Uncertainty," p. 1.

6. Data regarding new inflows are taken from Stagkos, "In 2003, 3.3 Billion Euros Came into Greece from EU Funds." Data for 1993 were taken from Alogoskoufis, "The Greek Economy and the Euro," figure 5, p. 144.

7. If historical figures constitute reliable indicators, the absorption rate is expected to go up as the deadlines for completion draw nearer. "Evert Worries About the 3rd CSF," *Ta Nea* (Athens, in Greek), July 12, 2004, p. N53.

8. Figures for Portugal's rail lines involve upgrades, not new lines. Data are taken from Kalaitzidis, "Does Regionalism Undermine the State?" p. 63.

9. Spanou, "Greece," pp. 170–171.

10. Ibid., p. 168.

11. Greek Ministry of Foreign Affairs, "General Overview," p. 1.

12. Garganas, "Greece and EMU: Prospects and Challenges," p. 120.

13. Alogoskoufis, "The Greek Economy and the Euro"; G. Papantoniou, the socialist finance minister credited with ensuring Greece's entry into the EMU, said characteristically in an interview with I. K. Pretenteris: "After entry into EMU, PASOK [the socialists] did not manage to identify the next step, the modernization of institutions and the welfare state"—Pretenteris, "Fines Are Coming from Brussels."

14. More information about this unit is provided on the Ministry of Economy and Finance's website, http://www.mou.gr.

15. Spanou, "Greece."

16. It is argued in the Europeanization literature that more industrially developed EU member states will attempt to "upload" their national policies onto the EU level in order to reduce implementation costs. According to this logic, Greece is expected to have less influence because it is a poorer member state. Börzel, "Pace-Setting, Foot-Dragging, and Fence-Sitting."

17. Markou, Nakos, and Zahariadis, "Greece: A European Paradox."

18. Zahariadis, "Domestic Strategy and International Choice in Negotiations Between Non-Allies."

19. For an extensive treatment of differences between Serbs, Bulgarians, and Greeks over Macedonia in the first part of the twentieth century, including the use of the name Macedonia to dismember Greece during its civil war (1946–1949), see Kofos, *Nationalism and Communism in Macedonia*.

20. For more information, see Zahariadis, *Essence of Political Manipulation*.

21. The entire EPC text is reprinted in Valinakis and Dalis, *The Skopjean Issue*, p. 51.

22. Tziampiris, *Greece, European Political Cooperation, and the Macedonian Question*.

23. Zahariadis, *Essence of Political Manipulation*.

24. The relevant text under Appendix II is reprinted in Valinakis and Dalis, *The Skopjean Issue*, pp. 100–102. The quote is from p. 101.

25. Zahariadis, *Essence of Political Manipulation*.

26. For more information about Greece-FYROM relations since 1995, see Zahariadis, *Essence of Political Manipulation*, and Kofos and Vlassidis, *Athens-Skopje: The Seven-Year Symbiosis (1995–2002)*. For more information on the general course of Greek foreign policy within the European context, see Ioakeimidis, "The Europeanization of Greece's Foreign Policy."

27. According to the objectives of Greece in the Convention for the Future of Europe, the country supports "the evolution of the European Union into a Political Union maintaining a federal, democratic character"; see Greek Ministry of Foreign Affairs, "The Five Strategic Objectives."

28. Andrikopoulou and Kafkalas, "Greek Regional Policy and the Process of Europeanization, 1961–2000." There is of course no one model of implementation that is effective in all contexts. Rather, implementation effectiveness and efficiency vary by the level of policy ambiguity (objectives and technology) and programmatic complexity. Zahariadis, "Europeanization as Program Implementation."

29. Alogoskoufis, "The Greek Economy and the Euro," p. 151.

30. Data are taken from Paraskevopoulos, *Interpreting Convergence in the European Union*, pp. 169 and 197.

31. Kalaitzidis, "Does Regionalism Undermine the State?" p. 106.

32. Hlepas, *Local Government in Greece*, p. 368.

33. Ibid., p. 367.

34. Iankova and Katzenstein, "European Enlargement and Institutional Hypocrisy," p. 279.

35. For a clear exposition of the various compliance strategies that the Commission employs and their relative effectiveness, see Börzel, "Guarding the Treaty."

36. European Commission, DG Internal Market and Services, "Internal Market Scoreboard, Press Release," p. 1.

37. Data in this and the next paragraphs are taken from various years of "Internal Market Scoreboards."

38. France had an astounding nine directives overdue and Germany five over the same period. Similarly, the number of infringement cases brought against Greece for violating EU jurisprudence stood at 79 by May 1, 2004. While the number is high relative to the United Kingdom, best performer with

24 cases, it is far better than three other EU states, France, Spain, and Italy. In fact, Italy and France represent over a quarter of all infringement cases during the same period.

39. Greek Ministry of Foreign Affairs, "General Overview," pp. 1–2.

40. European Commission, DG Internal Market and Services, "Internal Market Scoreboard, Press Release" pp. 1–2.

41. Giannakourou, "The Implementation of EU Environmental Policy in Greece."

42. Frangakis, "Law Harmonization," p. 184; Pridham, "Environmental Policies and Problems of European Legislation in Southern Europe," p. 63.

43. Greek Ministry of Foreign Affairs, "General Overview," p. 1.

44. Contrast this figure with the European average of 1.9 percent of GDP and the total NATO average of 2.6 percent. Figures were taken from NATO, "Defense Spending, 2003," press release.

45. The revised figure is derived under new accounting rules that mandate defense expenses be recorded when ordering (not upon delivery), resulting in lower revenues from local governments and public sector companies and including the high cost overruns associated with staging the Olympics in August 2004. See Chrysodora, "An Astonishing Jump of the Deficit to 5.2 Percent," p. N54.

46. Atkins and Parker, "Greece Faces Court Action over False Deficit Figures," p. 3.

47. Hope, "Tough Measures Are Necessary to Restore Credibility," p. 2.

48. See his interview with I. K. Pretenteris, "Fines Are Coming from Brussels."

49. Atkins and Parker, "Greece Faces Court Action."

50. Zahariadis, *Essence of Political Manipulation*, p. 209; US Department of State, "Daily Press Briefing" for November 4, 2004.

51. Kasule, "Washington Overrules Greece," p. 4.

52. Papasotiriou, "Relations Between Greece and the United States."

53. *Kathimerini*, "Athens Examines Brussels Fallout."

54. Chiotis, "Greece's 21 Billion Euros Between a British Rock and a Hard Place."

55. Chrysodora, "The Economy's Euro-Hit," p. 102.

11

Portugal and Spain: Mission Accomplished?

Sebastián Royo

JANUARY 1, 2006, MARKED the twentieth anniversary of Portugal and Spain's accession to the European Community (EC)—since 1992, the European Union (EU). European integration followed the establishment of democracy in Portugal and Spain in the 1970s, a precondition for EU membership. By the 1970s, their relative isolation from Europe had spearheaded their desire to become part of the EU and most Portuguese and Spaniards supported the integration process. Indeed, in the second half of the past century, the European Community epitomized in the eyes of Iberian citizens the values of liberty, democracy, and progress absent in their country. In addition, although some economists expressed reservations about the impact of EU membership, most Iberian entrepreneurs knew that their only future lay in Europe and that the modernization of their countries was contingent on European integration. Hence, belonging to the European club was a mission to be pursued.[1]

Surprisingly, however, membership negotiations lasted seven years. The negotiation process was hindered by political instability in both countries, and in the case of Portugal it was also marred by some decisions (including the nationalization of important sectors of the economy) that were made during the revolutionary period that followed the 1974 coup. Slow progress in the talks was also attributed to contentious bargaining over sensitive issues such as migrant workers, agriculture, fisheries, and particularly textiles.[2] French opposition to enlargement (based particularly on concerns over the impact of Spanish agriculture) further delayed the final agreement. The final obstacles to accession (i.e., free movement of workers, fisheries, the budget contribution, the British budgetary question, and the Integrated Mediterranean Program) were removed in subsequent negotiations throughout 1984–1985. The treaties of accession were signed in 1985, and Portugal and Spain joined the EU on January 1 1986. This long-awaited development had profound consequences for the EU and for both countries as well.[3] This chapter examines the effect that EU membership has had on Portugal and Spain, as well as the impact that both Iberian countries have had on the EU and the process of European integration.

■ How and in What Areas Does the EU Influence Portugal and Spain?

Since their accession, Portugal and Spain have played an important role in the process of European integration and have become, again, important actors in the European arena. They have contributed decisively to the development of a European Union with an institutional design that has been largely beneficial to their interests, and they have participated successfully in the creation and implementation of the Single Market and the European Monetary Union (EMU). Indeed, membership in the EU has brought many benefits to both countries.[4]

Political Considerations

From a political standpoint, Portugal and Spain have undergone profound transformations. Accession was viewed as a means to consolidate political and economic reforms, and as a push for modernization. In both countries, the political and economic elites viewed integration as the best way to consolidate the fragile structures of Iberian democracies, and considered Europeanization and democratization as complementary processes. Indeed the EU played a significant role in the success of the democratization process. First, it had a demonstrative and symbolic influence because Iberian citizens associated the EU and its member countries with the values of democracy and freedom. In addition, the EU had important indirect levers such as the democratic precondition for entry. Finally, the repetitive refusals to consider the Iberian applications for membership during the Franco-Salazar/Caetano years strengthened the positions of opposition groups and economic actors supporting democracy, and European governments exerted considerable bilateral pressures to follow through with the democratization process.[5]

Consequently, the democratic regimes installed in the 1970s have lasted far longer and attained a greater degree of stability than earlier democratic episodes, and EU membership finally ended the relative political isolation of both countries. Indeed, EU membership paved the way for the complete incorporation of Portugal and Spain into the major international structures of Europe and the West, as well as the normalization of these countries' relations with their European partners. Hence, from a political standpoint EU integration has been an unmitigated success, as both countries have consolidated their democratic regime and institutions.

The process of European integration has also influenced sociological and cultural developments. Both countries attempted to come to terms with their own identities, while addressing issues such as culture, nationality, citizenship, ethnicity, and politics. At the dawn of the new millennium it would not be an exaggeration to say that the Spaniards and the Portuguese have become "mainstream Europeans," and that many of the cultural differences that separated these two countries from their European counterparts have dwindled as a consequence of the integration process. EU integration, however, has also brought significant costs in terms of economic adjustment, loss of sovereignty, and cultural homogenization, as well as fears that have been exacerbated by issues such as size, culture, and nationalism.

Economic Consequences

From an economic standpoint, entry into Europe has contributed to the modernization of the Iberian economies. Although EU membership has not been the only reason for this development (i.e., in both countries the economic liberalization and modernization processes started in the 1950s and 1960s), European integration has played a critical role. Indeed, it was the perspective of EU integration that gave a final push to the modernization and liberalization of the Iberian economies. The Preferential Trade Agreements between the EU and Portugal and Spain resulted in the further opening of European markets to both countries. In addition, the prospect of EU membership acted as an essential motivational factor that influenced the actions of policymakers and economic actors, thus acting as a catalyst for change, as Portugal and Spain took unilateral measures in preparation for EC accession, including increasing economic flexibility, industrial restructuring, the adoption of the value-added tax (VAT), and trade liberalization.

At the same time, the fact that most citizens supported integration facilitated the implementation of (in many cases quite painful) micro-

and macroeconomic reforms, which allowed the political and economic actors to adopt economic policies and business strategies consistent with membership and the *acquis communautaire* (which at the time of accession included the customs union, the VAT, the Common Agriculture and Fisheries Polices, and the external trade agreements, and later the Single Market, the Exchange Rate Mechanism [ERM], and the European Monetary Union).

Overall, EU membership has had a very significant impact on economic policies. In this area, it has constrained significantly the economic strategies of the Portuguese and Spanish governments. In both countries, with a strong history of state intervention in the economy, the Single Market, EMU, and the EU competition policies have diminished the state role in the economy and constrained policy options. They have forced these governments to deregulate their economies, privatize public companies, and eliminate subsidies that had been used to sustain noncompetitive industries. This process however, was sometimes contentious. In Portugal, the privatization of public companies required a constitutional change, which was finally approved in 1989, and in both countries the governments often fought the European Commission over government aid to state companies.[6]

As a result of EU accession, trade barriers to the EU have been eliminated; markets and prices have been deregulated and liberalized; the labor market has been the subject of limited deregulatory reforms; a privatization program was started in the early 1980s to roll back the presence of the government in the economy and to increase the overall efficiency of the system; and competition policy was adapted to EU regulations.[7] In the 1990s, the desire of both countries to participate in the EMU led to the implementation of policies that resulted in fiscal consolidation, and the independence of their central banks.

Static effects.   In terms of static effects, EU membership offered opportunities for both trade creation and trade diversion. Portugal and Spain's trade with the Community has expanded dramatically over the past two decades. In the Spanish agricultural sector, while there was a profound impact as a result of the implementation of the Common Agricultural Policy (CAP) (Portugal does not receive CAP funds), Spain's trade balance benefited substantially from membership. The coverage rate (exports over imports) has increased steadily since 1992, peaking at 120 percent in 1997. In addition, the process of market liberalization that followed the implementation of the Single European Act contributed significantly to the increasing internationalization and openness of the Portuguese and Spanish economies, which increased from less than 40 percent in Spain and 25 percent in Portugal in 1986 to 65 percent and 35 percent in 2003.[8]

Dynamic effects. Moreover, membership has also brought about important dynamics effects. Portugal and Spain, each with relatively good infrastructure, an educated and cheap labor force, and a market of millions of potential consumers, offer an attractive production base. Foreign direct investment (FDI) has also been fostered by factors such as the deeper economic integration with other European countries, larger potential growth, lower exchange rate risk, lower economic uncertainty, and institutional reforms.[9] As expected, one of the key outcomes of integration has been a dramatic increase in foreign direct investment in both countries, from less than 2 percent to more than 6 percent of GDP in the decade following their accession.

One of the main consequences of these developments has been a reduction in the economic differences that separate each country from the European average. Table 11.1 shows the evolution of the average per capita income, which is the indicator of real convergence.

Macroeconomic Credibility

An additional outcome of EU membership has been to give Portugal and Spain additional macroeconomic credibility. When both countries joined the European Exchange Mechanism (in 1992 and 1989, respectively) the escudo and the peseta became more respectable because they became effectively pegged to the deutschemark. Following the crises of the ERM and the devaluations of 1992 and 1993, credibility was reestablished when it became clear that both countries would qualify to join the EMU at the outset. The EMU effects were very important: both countries had to maintain their exchange-rate peg within the ERM, keep inflation low, reduce their budget deficits to less than 3 percent of GDP, and try to cut the pub-

Table 11.1   Divergence of GDP per Capita, 1980–2004

	1980	1985	1990	2000	2004[a]
EU Totals	100.0%	100.0%	100.0%	100.0%	100.0%
Spain	74.2	72.5	77.8	81.0	98.0
Portugal	55.0	52.0	55.7	74.0	73.0

Source: Eurostat.
Note: a. After enlargement to central and eastern Europe.

lic-sector debt to below 60 percent of GDP. Hence the Iberian governments were forced to tighten fiscal policy, use privatization revenues to pay down debt, and further liberalize their economies. The culmination of this process was the largely unexpected participation of both countries in the EMU. Indeed, Portugal and Spain fulfilled the conditions established by the Maastricht Treaty and on January 1, 1999, both became founding members of the EMU (see Table 11.2). This development confirmed the nominal convergence of both countries with the rest of the EU.

The Stability and Growth Pact has forced them to maintain these policies. Indeed the most important consequence of Portugal and Spain's accession to the EMU has been the transformation of their macroeconomic policies and economic doctrines, which are now anchored around the principles of economic openness and macroeconomic equilibrium and orthodoxy. Thus, EMU membership has provided an important monetary and macroeconomic anchor.[10] Consequently, since Portugal and Spain joined the EMU their economies have performed in line with other European countries and the short-term outlook is positive.

The EU contributed significantly to this success through the Structural and Cohesion Funds.[11] The Agenda 2000 action program approved by the European Council held in Berlin in 1999 approved a budget of €195 billion for the Structural Fund and €18 billion for the Cohesion Fund for the 2000–2006 period. These funds had an immediate impact in addressing the investment needs of Portugal and Spain following accession in 1986, and made an important contribution to growth in aggregate demand in both countries.

Portugal and Spain have received the lion's share of these funds. During the 1994–1999 period, Portugal received €16.332 billion, or the equivalent of 3.3 percent of GDP. Under the latest plan (Agenda 2000), Portugal has been allocated nearly €25.994 billion from European funds

Table 11.2   Compliance of the EMU Convergence Criteria, 1996–2004

	Spain			Portugal		
	1996	1997	2004	1996	1997	2004
Inflation, %	3.6	1.9	3.3	2.9	1.9	2.6
General government deficit, % GDP	4.6	2.6	0.3	3.2	2.5	6.7
General government gross debt, % GDP	70.1	68.8	62.6	65.0	61.4	58.6
Long-term interest rates, %	8.7	6.4	3.64	8.6	6.4	3.64

Source: Eurostat, various years.

(2.9 percent of GDP) for the 2000–2006 period. Spain, for its part, received €45.592 billion between 1994 and 1999 (1.5 percent of GDP) and has been allocated a €56.205 billion for the 2000–2006 period (or 1.3 percent of GDP).[12]

The EU Cohesion Policy has helped strengthen the factors that contribute to economic growth (e.g., industrial, urban, or agricultural restructuring), macroeconomic stability, and the reduction of disparities among regions, making them more attractive to investors and thus acting as a development engine.[13] Consequently, in Portugal and Spain between 1990 and 2001 mean economic growth was well above the EU average: 2.3 percent in Spain and 2.4 percent in Portugal.

A significant proportion of the Cohesion Funds were invested in two areas in which Portugal and Spain lagged far behind the other EU member states: transport and the environment. The main priority for both governments was infrastructure, in particular roads. Consequently, one of the most obvious effects of these funds has been on Portugal and Spain's physical infrastructure.[14]

They have also invested heavily in environment-related projects, including wastewater management, deforestation and erosion, solid waste, wind farms, and eco-tourism projects.[15] Furthermore, these funds have also been used to improve education and skills and to help companies with investment, particularly in new technologies, which has contributed to expanded productive capacity and demand in both countries, making them more attractive places to invest. Consequently, as we have seen, FDI has soared, and the stock of FDI more than doubled between 1985 and 1990, and doubled again by 2000.

At the same time, EU funding has allowed rates of public investment to remain relatively stable since the mid-1980s. In both countries the funds have been a factor for stability because they have allowed Portugal and Spain to maintain their investment efforts even in times of budget restrictions, and to develop projects with significant structural impact (e.g., in infrastructure). The percentage of public investment financed by EU funds has been rising since 1985, reaching average values of 42 percent for Portugal and 15 percent for Spain. Moreover, the European Commission has estimated that the impact of EU Structural Funds on GDP growth and employment has been significant: GDP rose in 1999 by 9.9 percent in Portugal and 3.1 percent in Spain.[16] These funds have also improved the competitiveness of Iberian regions through the development of infrastructure networks, enhancing access to remote regions and thus cooperation among them, and promoting public-private partnerships that have improved institutional capabilities.

Finally, the EU Cohesion Policy has contributed to improved policy design and implementation capabilities in these countries, while promoting the exchange of best practices—an "evaluation culture"—as well as more accountability and transparency.[17]

■ How Have Portugal and Spain Influenced the EU?

Spain and Portugal have also played an important role in Europe and have asserted influence in a number of policy areas. The Iberian enlargement strengthened Europe's strategic position in the Mediterranean and Latin America, and led to the further development of a European system of cohesion and solidarity. Indeed, Spain and Portugal offered a new geopolitical dimension to the Union, strengthening it southwards, and ensuring closer ties with other regions that have been peripheral to the EU. They have also been engaged in policy debates on agriculture, fisheries, immigration/asylum, the Schengen Provisions, and the concept of European citizenship. Moreover, both countries have participated actively in the creation of the Single Market, the development of the EMU, and the recent enlargement process. Finally, in more recent years the Iberian governments have sought to influence the European debate on economic policies and reforms, and have supported further liberalization of economic policies, privatization, tax cuts, and deregulation, all of which contributed to the approval at the March 2000 Lisbon Summit of economic-reform targets aimed at making Europe the world's most competitive economy by 2010.[18]

From a political standpoint, Portugal and Spain have been strong supporters of the process of European integration. They played a very active role in drafting the EU Constitutional Treaty, with relevant politicians, such as the former Portuguese president and prime minister Mario Soares and the former Spanish cabinet members Loyola de Palacio and Josep Borrell, assuming leading responsibilities in the European Parliament and the Constitutional Convention. Indeed, Spain was the first EU country to hold a referendum to ratify the EU constitution (on February 20, 2005). The leading political parties backed the constitution, which led to the overwhelming victory of the "Yes" vote (the final result was 76.73 percent in favor and 17.24 percent opposed), but with a disappointing turnout (42.32 percent), motivated in part by lack of interest among Spanish citizens who took the outcome for granted.[19]

Reaching out to Latin America

Given Portugal and Spain's historical links with Latin America, the leaders of both countries pushed from the very beginning to strengthen the cultural, political, and economic ties between the two regions. In the 1980s and 1990s, Spain and Portugal led EU efforts to support the integration and democratization of the Latin American region. After 1986, Portugal and Spain actively sought to expand the European Political Cooperation process (later superseded by the Common Foreign and Security Policy) to include Latin America. They pushed the EU to concentrate in four main areas: pacification of Central America; support for democratization; support for regional integration; and the institutionalization of interregional dialogue.[20] At the same time, following the French and British model toward their former colonies enshrined in the Lomé Convention, Portugal and Spain fought to obtain a special status for their former colonies in Latin America, which led to the EU's "Common Declaration Regarding the Development and Strengthening of the Relationship with Latin American Countries." The Spanish premier, Felipe González, successfully fought to include the Dominican Republic in the European Union's Lomé Convention when France maneuvered to include Haiti.

In addition, both Spain and Portugal have led efforts to increase financial assistance to Latin American countries (particularly through the European Investment Bank), which increased from €37 million in 1985 to €367 million in 1995. In the 1990s a significant flow of FDI from Spanish firms to Latin America increased the financial clout of Spain in the region. In some Latin American countries Spain became the leading foreign investor and one of the leading trade partners. This led to a new focus on economic issues and the objective to secure trade agreements between Latin American countries or regional blocs, and the EU to institutionally secure Spanish economic investment in the region.[21] Subsequently, largely as a result of the Spanish efforts, the European Union concluded trade association agreements with Mexico in 2000 and with Chile in 2002 (finalized during the third Spanish presidency of the EU), and it signed an Interregional Cooperation Agreement with Mercosur (composed of Argentina, Brazil, Paraguay, and Uruguay), approved during the second Spanish presidency of the EU in 1995.[22] The EU is currently negotiating a free-trade agreement with Mercosur. Moreover, Portugal and Spain have pushed to develop further economic relations with Latin America and to open European markets to Latin American products. These actions led to the extension of the

System of General Preferences to several crops from Latin American countries.

Finally, the efforts to intensify the political and economic relationship between both regions were enshrined in the decision to organize regular summits with the participation of the heads of state of EU and Latin American and Caribbean countries. The first EU and Latin America and Caribbean summit took place in June 1999 in Rio de Janeiro and the second one in Madrid in 2002.

The Mediterranean Emphasis

Spain has also pushed the EU to forge new links with countries in the Mediterranean basin (especially with Morocco) and has become a leading proponent of increasing cooperation with these countries. Indeed successive Spanish governments have been arguing that this area is a European problem and that it has to be addressed through financial support, trade, and improved relations with these countries, which has contributed to putting the Mediterranean at the top of the EU agenda. For instance, the two Spanish commissioners in Brussels played a central role in the implementation of the Renovated Mediterranean Policy in 1992, which changed the terms of the relationship with these countries from one based on trade concessions to a new one based on EU financial transfers. Indeed, Spain fought for financial aid for northern African countries and was instrumental in the 1995 decision to allocate to the Mediterranean the equivalent of 70 percent of the funds that had been allocated to eastern European countries as part of the Phare program. This agreement was the basis for the European Mediterranean Conference. Furthermore, given the strategic importance of Morocco for Spain on issues such as immigration, fisheries, and agriculture, successive Spanish governments have pushed the EU to forge special agreements with this country and to move toward a free-trade agreement.[23]

Spain has also become more assertive in the eastern Mediterranean and has become deeply involved in the Middle East conflict, pushing for EU involvement in Mediterranean security initiatives. Madrid hosted the 1991 conference on the Middle East peace process. Spain was also instrumental in the development of the so-called Barcelona Process based on an Italian-Spanish proposal to set up a Conference on Security and Cooperation in the Mediterranean to deal with security, economic, and human rights issues. This initiative led to the creation of the Euro-Mediterranean Partnership with 27 participants, which seeks to strengthen bilateral links through association agreements, build a free-trade area, and to develop a Euro-Mediterranean dialogue. The Barcelona

Process led to a significant increase in the resources allocated to the Mediterranean region (which increased 22 percent in 1995).[24]

Cohesion and Structural Funds

Portugal and Spain were also instrumental in the expansion of the existing EC/EU Structural Funds to support backward regions and in the creation of a new Cohesion Fund. As we have seen, the Cohesion Policy to reduce disparities between the rich and poor regions has been an important objective of the EU. Despite the inclusion of this goal in the Treaty of Rome, the EU regional policy remained quite rudimentary from the 1950s through the 1970s.

The Portuguese and Spanish membership applications had raised fears in Italy and Greece about the impact over the Integrated Mediterranean Programs. The new president of the Commission, Jacques Delors, assumed personal responsibility over this issue, which became a major stumbling block during the 1987 negotiations to establish a Single Market. Led unofficially by the Spanish prime minister, Felipe González, the poorer member states (Greece, Ireland, Portugal, and Spain) argued convincingly that failure to meet their demands would undermine the foundations of the EC, and asked to be compensated in exchange for market liberalization.[25] They pressed hard for the approval of the Delors I five-year budget package, which sought to double, in real terms, the social and regional resources to a total of 60 billion ECUs from 1989 to 1993, with a particular focus on regions with a per capita GDP lower than 75 percent of the EC average. Finally, the European leaders agreed to double the Structural Funds by 1992 at a special Brussels summit in February 1988, and later that year to reform the EC Cohesion Policy.

Plans to introduce the European Monetary Union led to new demands for additional assistance for disadvantaged regions. During the Intergovernmental Conference on political union that led to the Maastrict Treaty, Portugal and Spain (with Ireland) demanded a new framework to enhance cohesion in the context of the monetary union. Once again, Felipe González led the charge to win greater commitments to cohesion in the Treaty on European Union (TEU). As a result, the treaty included several references to cohesion (Articles 2–3 and 158–162), and Article 161 established that the Council would set up the Cohesion Fund by the end of December 1993 to contribute to environmental and infrastructure projects. In addition, Spain demanded and won the inclusion of a special protocol to supplement the TEU's Cohesion Provision, which stipulated the need to review the size of

Structural Funds and that the Cohesion Funds would be for the benefit of member states with a per capita GDP below 90 percent of the EU average, earmarking 80–90 percent of the budget's fund to support transport and environmental projects.[26]

These conditions led to the approval of the Delors II budget package for the 1993–1999 period. Structural and Cohesion Funds accounted for nearly a third of the EU budget (almost €100 billion, with the Cohesion Fund set at €14.5 billion). While there is significant dispute on the usefulness of the Cohesion Policy, as we have seen, Spain and Portugal have become major beneficiaries of these programs, which also benefit the richer donor countries. Studies show that as much as 40 percent of EU-financed projects flow back to the donor countries via procurement and service contracts,[27] and according to the Commission a considerable share of expenditure (between 20 and 40 percent) has fed back into the Union's richest regions. The proportion of EU investment for primary beneficiaries that was subsequently spent on imports from other member states has been 14.7 percent in Spain and 35.2 percent in Portugal.[28]

Portugal does not receive funds from the Common Agricultural Policy, but Spain has played a significant role in the reform of the CAP. While their agricultural sectors are not as important as they used to be, they are still significant and both countries have been deeply involved in the CAP reform process with a special focus on issues such as: health, safety, and environmental concerns; the cost of adjustment; modernization of farms; improvements in production and marketing; and the training of farmers. While, in general, they have been supportive of the process of opening up the agricultural sector to further competition, they have sought to safeguard their farmers and products. Hence, they have supported most of the Commission reform proposals of 1988, 1992, and 1999 and the Agenda 2000. Spain, however, has adopted a tougher negotiation stance on issues such as the ceiling of the CAP budget, price cuts, compensatory payments, and guaranteed production of certain Mediterranean products.[29]

In sum, the Iberian countries have consistently supported the new dynamics of European integration, the goal of greater solidarity among member states, a strong CAP, the concept of monetary union, and the creation of common standards to eliminate barriers to trade and strengthen consumer protection. They have not applied for opt-outs from the treaties and they have attempted to participate as founders in the main European integration initiatives (such as the Single European Market or the EMU). Finally, both Portugal and Spain have advanced European agenda issues quite successfully during their EU presidencies.

▣ How Do Spain and Portugal Implement and Comply with EU Policies?

Mechanisms and Institutions for Implementation

The Portuguese and Spanish Constitutions include articles that provide for the transfer of sovereignty to supranational institutions. During the accession negotiations and the early years of membership, the Portuguese and Spanish executives enjoyed a high degree of control in the formulation of European policies. The Portuguese and Spanish Constitutions give strong powers to their prime ministers. In addition, the generalized consensus among political and economic actors in both countries on the benefits of EC/EU membership, and the "presidential" styles of the Portuguese (Soares and Cavaco Silva) and Spanish (Suarez and González) prime ministers, reinforced this pattern. In Spain, however-er, the decentralization process that followed the development of the autonomous communities, and the subsequent emergence of new actors that demanded equity in the process, has changed the pattern and the prime ministers no longer dominate the formulation of European poli-cies. The main institutional actors are now as follows.[30]

The executive. The Portuguese and Spanish executives, and in particu-lar their prime ministers, have been leading actors. The prime minister of each has set the basic European policy guidelines and European poli-cy has often reflected the preferences of the prime minister. This pattern has been favored by the relative weakness of interest groups, the quite often (particularly in Spain) one-party dominance of the legislature, and the relative lack of expertise and consensus among Portuguese and Spanish legislators on European issues. In both countries, European pol-icy is coordinated by the Secretariat of State for the European Union, which is part of the Foreign Ministry, and the Permanent Representation in Brussels. In Spain, the Comisión Interministerial para la Unión Europea is in charge of coordinating the different departments within the central administration.

Parliament. The Portuguese and Spanish parliaments have the sole authority to ratify EU treaties, which gives them control over EU consti-tutional decisions such as enlargement and reform (but they lack the power to reject or alter EU legislation). In Spain the legislature (Cortes Generales) has established a joint Committee for EU Affairs composed of members from house and the senate to monitor European policies. In both countries, parliaments play an oversight role: The sessions to control the government often include questions related to European issues and the prime ministers address their respective parliaments after every European summit. In practice, however, the impact of parliament in the formulation of European policy has been limited because constitutionally both political systems were strongly biased in favor of the executive. This has been reinforced by the need to transfer legislative autonomy away from national parliaments to the European Council, and to a lesser extent to the European Parliament.

The constitutional courts. EU membership has generated a large number of cases that have drawn the Spanish and Portuguese constitutional courts into legal disputes. In Spain, it has been forced to resolve numerous conflicts between the central government and the governments of the autonomous communities (AC) about the implementation and enforcement of EU directives, and in a 1995 ruling it authorized AC activities in international (and EU) affairs as long as they do not compromise the unity of Spanish foreign policy and do not create obligations to foreign powers. The respective constitutional courts have also asserted that European Community law lacks constitutional standing and have recognized the supremacy of Community law over domestic law at the infra-constitutional level.

Portuguese and Spanish courts have been ready to apply EU law, and over time they have incorporated the principles of the primacy and direct applicability of EU law and directives.

The Spanish autonomous communities. While Spain's autonomous communities (e.g., the Basque country, Andalusia, and Catalonia) have varying degrees of power, in general they are empowered to deal with a broad range of issues and have different degrees of financial autonomy. They have played an increasing role in EU affairs, implementing Community policies (particularly the CAP and environmental ones) and managing EU transfers to regional budgets. The ACs also have regional offices in Brussels, where they engage in lobbying efforts, and participate in the Committee of the Regions.

Implementation of Specific EU Policy Areas

The Common Fisheries Policy. EU membership has had a very important impact on many public policy areas. For instance, in Portugal and Spain the implementation of the EC/EU Common Fisheries Policy (CFP) has resulted in significant policy changes. Indeed, the CFP was created to curb the impact of Spanish fisheries because Spain has the largest fishing industry in the EU (about 30 percent of the total tonnage in the EU fleet, one-third of the fishermen, and 50 percent of the total EC catch at the time of accession), and it has a long history of fishing all over the world with numerous conflicts with other countries over the predatory practices of Spanish fishermen. EU membership, however, brought significant new constraints to the Portuguese and Spanish fleets, motivated by the EU desire to preserve stocks of fish and to minimize conflicts among neighboring countries' fleets.

As a result of accession, Portugal and Spain had to accept the EU regulations limiting the number of fishing vessels, fishing grounds, and catches. Only vessels listed in the Accession Act are allowed to fish in EU waters, and the EU only granted 150 licenses (Spain requested 300), and each vessel was granted access to a predetermined fishing zone. One particular conflict lasted for several years in the 1990s over the right of Spanish fishermen to fish in an area between Britain and Ireland, the so-called Irish Box, and one of the most public cases of non-compliance with a decision of the European Court of Justice (ECJ) occurred in this realm.[31] The Commission's attempts to reduce the fleet and limit subsidies have raised strong opposition in Spain, and Spanish owners have sought to exploit EU regulations to create fishing ventures in other member states to circumvent the quota system. This practice, which is perfectly legitimate, has led to conflicts with other countries, notably Britain, who retaliated through the Merchant Shipping Act, which required that some of the capital and the crew members be British and that catches be landed in British ports.

Fortunately for Spanish owners, the ECJ in a preliminary ruling provided the grounds that forced the House of Lords to reject the act. Portugal and Spain took advantage of the negotiations that followed Norway's application to redress the situation and demanded immediate incorporation into the CFP (i.e., a shortening of the 17-year transition period). The Council agreed in 1994 to incorporate the Portuguese and Spanish fleets in the CFP, and after some resistance from some member states, Spain finally joined in 1996, seven years before the original transition period. The Iberians also achieved an increase in their quotas from the EU, the abolition of the list of vessels, and Spain finally gained access to the Irish Box.[32]

The Common Agricultural Policy. The implementation of the Common Agricultural Policy is another good example of the transformation of domestic institutions and mechanisms to adapt to an existing common European policy. The agricultural sector was dramatically impacted by EU accession, particularly in Spain (as mentioned before, Portugal does not receive funds from the CAP). Although the economic importance of agriculture has declined since the 1950s, in 1986 it still represented 5.6 percent of the Spanish GDP and 16.1 percent of those employed (the EU average was 7 percent). This downsizing, however, did not lead to the modernization and specialization of the agricultural sector, which was still characterized at the time of accession by small units, part-time working, an aging population, and low technology. Accession meant the convergence of prices and support payments. Since Spain did not have much leverage during the accession negotiations, it was compelled to accept the existing members' conditions and bear the full cost of adaptation. As a consequence, Spain was forced to lift all trade barriers against EU member states and open up to a liberalized market, but it did not gain free access to EU markets until 1996, and France even gained a trade freeze against Spain's most competitive products (fruits and vegetables) until 1990. This affected prices, had a negative impact on employment in certain sectors, and intensified the regionalization of the agricultural sector.

When the transition periods were over, Spanish farmers took advantage of membership and overall the agricultural trade balance benefited from accession as the coverage rate (exports over imports) increased steadily starting in 1992 and peaking at 120 percent in 1997. Accession also stimulated the modernization of the sector, led to the abolition of obsolete agricultural processes, and increased investment substantially (particularly to increase production). However, many Spanish products (particularly in the processed-food market and in high-value-added products) remain uncompetitive, as agricultural productivity is still 50 percent of the EU average because the sector has failed to address its traditional technological backwardness, aging population, small units, and rural depopulation.[33]

In terms of implementation, the CAP has been a permanent source of conflict between Spain and the EU authorities since accession. As we have seen, the accession conditions were very tough and adaptation has proved very difficult for Spain. The problem was aggravated by the fact that the profile of Spanish agricultural products does not match the EU's, which led to the perception that the EU discriminated against Mediterranean products. This has led to a "permanent renegotiation" to reduce the level of protection differential with northern European agriculture, and to get Mediterranean products included in the general CAP scheme. The 1992 McSharry reform led to a switch toward income support that favored Spanish farmers, and between 1986 and 1997 Spain passed from being the 10th-largest beneficiary of CAP funds to fourth-largest one. However, the shift from production to income support has led to production limits, hindering the modernization of the sector. In addition, the reform failed to protect sensitive Spanish products such as sugar, wine, and olive oil, leading to new acrimonious accusations over the EU preference for non-Spanish agricultural products. The outcome of the Agenda 2000 negotiations was also satisfactory for Spanish agriculture because the EU maintained expenditure levels in agriculture, and Spain achieved significant concessions in products such as milk, wine, cereals, sugar, and beef. The Spanish experience with the CAP illustrates how a member state can negotiate from within the EU to be compensated for inequalities derived from accession conditions.

Environmental policies.   Another area in which EU policies have profoundly reshaped Portuguese and Spanish public policies has been in the environmental policy realm. Portugal and Spain did not have strong environmental records before accession and had only taken limited measures to protect the environment. European Union membership forced both countries to incorporate all EU environmental legislation and comply with certain standards on environmental policy, and they did not have any transitional period. At the same time, however, the EU provided Cohesion Funds to facilitate this transition and a large proportion of these funds has been used in infrastructure projects that exert environmental controls over drinking water, wastewater, solid waste, and erosion and deforestation.[34] Portugal and Spain have now successfully developed wind farms and eco-tourism projects (e.g., in Lisbon and the Tagus Valley), and have created new technologies recognized as success stories in this field, such as the promotion of clean water and beaches (e.g., the water decontamination projects in Lisbon) and to fighting forest fires.

   As a result of these investments and the transposition of EU environmental legislation, environmental standards have improved markedly in both countries. In addition, they have led to significant institutional and policymaking changes. New ministries of the environment were created (Spain was the last EU country to create one in 1996) and the local and regional authorities have also established multiple agencies dealing with environmental issues. In Spain the autonomous regions have the responsibility to control the day-to-day environmental policy and the central government is responsible for the framework legislation. Furthermore, the European Directive on Environmental Impact

Assessment, which provides the right of information and consultation, has allowed for the participation of environmental groups on authorization procedures for major projects, which has contributed to the upgrading of environmental standards. Overall, EU membership has led to a significant enhancement of environmental protection.[35] One of the most remarkable views when one travels throughout Portugal and Spain today is the sight of hundreds of new windmills over the Iberian hills, which seem to have replaced the old windmills immortalized in *Don Quixote*.

■ Portugal and Spain's Records on Compliance with EU Directives

While the record of the 25 member states in implementing EU laws and regulations has been mixed, Spain and Portugal have been among the best performers. Member states often fail to meet the deadline for implementation by a few months or even years. This "transposition deficit" has been a constant source of tension between Brussels and the member states.[36] According to the latest report from the EU Commission, of the countries in the First Division, Spain (and Lithuania) are "to be commended for being the only member states to have met the 1.5 percent interim target [in the transposition deficit] set by the European Council."[37] As of 2004, Spain had only 21 untransposed directives. Portugal, on the contrary, is placed in the Second Division, has an interim transposition deficit of 3.2 percent, and had 51 untransposed directives.

In order to avoid delays in transposing Internal Market Directives, the European Council set a "zero tolerance" target for directives whose implementation is over two years past due. Of the EU-15 member states, only Sweden, Portugal, and the Netherlands met this target. The Spanish record has deteriorated, and it has one overdue directive whose implementation is over two years late. For instance, recently Spain (and Germany) were warned that they faced legal action at the ECJ for failing to implement EU laws to liberalize their gas and electricity markets, an issue that is vital to the Union's economic growth and competitiveness.[38] Spain receives around 10 percent of the EU letters of formal notice. However, it has the lowest rate of investigated cases that led to formal infringement procedures (31 percent), and one of the lowest rates of cases referred to the ECJ (4.74 percent). It seems that Spain needs to be prodded to comply but, when warned, it opts for implementation rather than face a procedure in the ECJ.[39] Portugal has currently met the "zero tolerance target." These data show that, despite the original misgivings about the capacity of Portugal and Spain to implement EU legislation, both countries have an impressive record on the implementation of EU directives.[40]

■ Future Trends, Prospects, and Problem Areas

The main challenge confronting the Spanish and Portuguese economies in the short run will be competition from the new member states of central and eastern Europe.[41] This concern is based on the fact that eastern European countries specialize in labor-intensive and low-to-medium technology products (such as machinery, electrical equipment, textile goods, and automobiles), sectors that make up a large proportion of Portuguese and Spanish trade (i.e., 7.4 percent, 7.3 percent, 4.5 percent, and 20 percent, respectively, of total Spanish exports to the EU-15), and in which competitiveness via prices is of particular importance. At the same time, in the central and eastern European countries labor costs are between 20 percent and 60 percent lower than those of the EU. Therefore, there is the possibility that enlargement could lead to a loss of market share for Iberian products in the countries of the EU (which is the market for most of their exports).

However, a detailed analysis suggests that a negative outcome is not warranted. First, the EU has signed bilateral agreements with each of these countries since the beginning of the 1990s to liberalize trade (except for agricultural goods). This development has resulted in a significant increase of exports to the EU from these countries (an average of 12 percent, between 1989 and 1999). Despite this increase of imports from central and eastern Europe, Spanish exports to Europe expanded at a robust 13.4 percent average annual rate over this period. Second, the composition of EU imports from the new candidate countries and from southern European countries are similar to the import structure from other developing countries. Third, these countries compete in market segments of different quality as reflected by differences in unit values (export prices). Therefore, the direct impact on Portuguese and Spanish exports to third markets resulting from EU enlargement is likely to be modest. Finally, Sebastián points out that "the competitiveness of Spanish products could be bolstered in the short run as a result of real exchange rate appreciation of the currencies of aspirant countries, caused by higher rates of inflation while nominal convergence consolidates, and in the medium term, because of the reduction of wage differentials as real convergence progresses."[42]

At the same time, an additional concern is the impact that enlargement will have on the funds that the Iberian countries receive from the EU. Since the new member states are significantly poorer, enlargement will reduce the EU's average GDP per capita by between 10 and 20 percent, and hence the per capita income of Spain and to a lesser extent Portugal will be closer to the EU average (this is the so-called statistical effect). Spain's per capita GDP is now 98 percent of the EU-25 average and Portugal's 73 percent. This means that Spain will lose access to the Cohesion Fund and that many Iberian regions will no longer be eligible for aid, as funds are switched to the new member states. The EU countries and the Commission are currently discussing mechanisms to allow for a progressive phasing out of these funds to prevent their sudden cancellation as a result of the "statistical effect."[43] In the end, it is very likely that in the near future both Iberian countries (particularly Spain) will become net contributors to the EU budget. Hence, the political, electoral, and budgetary implications of these developments are daunting and unprecedented. In the absence of these funds, public investment will be greatly affected. Portugal and Spain should prepare to soften the blow of the loss of EU funds and develop new strategies to tap funds and programs that are not allocated by country, such as research and development funds.

To face this challenge, Spain and Portugal will have to further speed up the reform of their productive and economic structures to increase the productivity of their labor force, which is still significantly lower than the EU average. As a result of the enlargement process, Portugal and Spain will face increasing competition for their main nonagricultural exports—such as clothing, textiles, and leather. Problems should be anticipated in labor-intensive industries given the relatively low level of wages in central and eastern European states. Central and eastern European countries with lower wages produce all these goods at cheaper costs. Therefore, these countries will attract foreign investment in sectors where traditionally Portugal and Spain have been favored. Moreover, since the 10 new members have lower labor costs, it is likely that manufacturing plants currently producing in Iberia will be tempted to move production to eastern Europe. In this context it will be important for the leaders of both Iberian countries to continue pushing for a shift toward more capital-intensive industries that will require greater skills in the labor force but relying on standard technology (e.g., chemicals, vehicles, steel, and metal manufacturers).

Enlargement, paradoxically, may help in this process because it will also bring significant opportunities to Iberian firms (and those of the other EU members). Indeed, Portuguese and Spanish products will now have access to new markets, which will provide access to cheaper labor, and may help improve competitiveness. For instance, EU-funded infrastructure projects offer important opportunities to Spanish construction firms (six of the world's top 12 construction groups are Spanish) and many of them are already positioning themselves to work on these projects.[44]

From an economic convergence standpoint, given the existing income and productivity differentials with the richer countries, regardless of enlargement, the Iberian states will have to continue increasing their living standards to bring them closer to the current EU average. For this to happen, it is necessary that their economies grow faster than the other rich European countries. This growth will require further liberalization of their labor structures (both internal and external), as well as increasing competition within their service markets, and developing a better utilization of their productive resources. In addition, convergence will also demand institutional reforms in R&D policies, education, improvement of civil infrastructures, as well as further innovation, an increase in business capabilities, more investment in information technology, and better and more efficient training systems. Finally, a successful convergence policy will also demand a debate about the role of public investment and welfare programs in both countries. In the Iberian countries, increases in public expenditures to develop their welfare state have caused imbalances in their national accounts. Yet, both countries still spend significantly less in this area than their European neighbors (i.e., Spain spends 6.3 percent less in welfare policies than the EMU average). Effective, real convergence would demand not only effective strategies and policies, but also a strong commitment on the part of Spanish and Portuguese citizens to this objective.[45]

Politically, the EU is at a crossroads. The 2005 budgetary crisis and the Dutch and French rejection of the EU constitution have derailed the integration process. In Spain the expectation was that the victory of the "Yes" vote in the referendum on the EU constitution would pave the way for the success of future referenda. The victory of the "No" vote in France and the Netherlands was a disappointment. Prime Minister Rodriguez Zapatero reacted by calling for a continuation of the approval process. In Portugal, which in fall 2005 was suffering one of the worst economic crises since the 1970s, there was an increasing concern that the prevalent pessimistic mood could fuel anti-EU feelings. To avoid a possible spillover effect, the government decided to postpone the proposed referendum to approve the constitution, originally scheduled for October 2005.[46] If the EU constitution is not approved, both countries would be likely to support a "plan B," under which the constitution is abandoned and a core of EU members, led by France and Germany, would agree to enhance their cooperation in political and economic issues.

■ Notes

I would like to thank my graduate research assistant at Suffolk University, María González Albuixec, who helped me with the research for this chapter.

1. Royo, "From Authoritarianism to the European Union," pp. 95–96.

2. Dinan, *Ever Closer Union,* pp. 104–109.

3. See Royo and Manuel, "Some Lessons from the Fifteenth Anniversary of the Accession of Portugal and Spain to the European Union," and Royo, "The 2004 Enlargement."

4. Parts of this section have been published in: Royo, "The 2004 Enlargement"; Royo, *Portugal, Espanha e a Integração Europeia: Um Balanço*; and Royo, "From Authoritarianism to the European Union."

5. Pridham, "European Integration and Democratic Consolidation in Southern Europe," pp. 188–189.

6. Several privatizations were preceded by capital injections that breached EU competition rules. In Spain, for instance, the privatization of the car manufacturer SEAT, and the state airline Iberia, led to fierce arguments between the Commission and the Spanish government. Over the last decade, however, patterns of state aid in Portugal and Spain have been moving into line with the EU mainstream, as state ownership has declined as a result of the drive toward privatization.

7. Royo, "The 2004 Enlargement," pp. 291–292.

8. Data from Eurostat, various years.

9. Royo, "The 2004 Enlargement," p. 292.

10. Alfredo Marvao Pereira has estimated that the increase in monetary policy credibility and the reduction in interest rates will boost the long-term growth rate in Portugal by 0.4 percent a year and that the cumulative effect will be to increase GDP by 10 percent, a larger impact than that provided by the Cohesion Funds. See *The Economist,* "In the Club."

11. The program includes three sets of objectives: Objective 1 (regions whose development is lagging behind), Objective 2 (regions undergoing conversion), and Objective 3 (education, training, and employment).

12. Between 1993 and 1999 Spain received between 52 percent and 58 percent of the Cohesion Funds and Portugal between 16 percent and 20 percent,

and of the €28.212 billion that the EU provides in Cohesion Funds for 2000–2006, Portugal will receive 3.388 billion and Spain €12.357 billion.

13. In Spain the ratio between the richest and poorest regions was 3.49 in 1995 and was reduced to 2.24 by 1999. In particular, two regions (Extremadura and Galicia) have improved substantially. Part of the reason is based in the fact that growth in the nine Objective 1 regions increased between 1989 and 1993 by an average of 0.25 percent annually, and half of this increase was a direct result of the Structural Funds, which made up an important share of the autonomous communities' budgets: 5 percent on average. These funds also promoted the development of national regional policies, which contributed to the diminishing of the differences between the poor and richer regions. Family incomes have also increased faster than per capita GDP in the poorer regions. See Closa and Heywood, *Spain and the European Union,* pp. 207–212.

14. For instance, by 1998 Portugal had 840 km of motorways as compared with 240 km in 1987, and Spain spent 33.8 percent of its Cohesion Fund grants on roads between 1993 and 1998.

15. In Spain 49.8 percent of the Cohesion Funds were used in these projects between 1993 and 1998.

16. The Commission has estimated that Structural Funds helped boost GDP by 4.7 percent in Portugal between 1994 and 1999.

17. European Commission, *The Future of Cohesion Policy.*

18. Granell, "Europe's Evolving Economic Identity," pp. 64–75; Granell, "La Contribución Española al Nacimiento del Euro," pp. 57–66.

19. Portugal planned a referendum to ratify the EU constitution in fall 2005, but it was postponed after the ratification defeats in France and the Netherlands.

20. Grugle, "Spain: Latin America as an Ambitious Topic," pp. 73–90.

21. Toral, *The Reconquest of the New World*; Guillén, *The Rise of Spanish Multinationals.*

22. Piper, *The Major Nation-States in the European Union,* p. 305.

23. Closa and Heywood, *Spain and the European Union*, pp. 220–223.

24. Ibid., pp. 223–225.

25. In a stirring speech in Brussels in 1988 González proclaimed that "if some countries go through a tough, but necessary, exercise in order to converge their economic policies . . . others should logically respond with a similar effort of solidarity by accepting decisions which imply a higher level of social and economic cohesion." At the Copenhagen Summit he threatened to veto the EC budget if his demands for a doubling of the budget for Structural Funds were not fulfilled. Later on during the Maastricht negotiations he threatened a parliamentary rejection of the TEU in Spain and to veto EU enlargement to Austria, Finland, and Sweden unless his demands were met. See Piper, *The Major Nation-States in the European Union*, pp. 307–308.

26. Dinan, *Ever Closer Union*, pp. 430–437.

27. See "Spain Will Accept Drop in Funds if UK Takes Cut," *Financial Times*, June 10, 2005, p. 2.

28. European Commission, *The Future of Cohesion Policy.*

29. Granell, "Europe's Evolving Economic Identity," pp. 71–72.

30. Closa and Heywood, *Spain and the European Union*, pp. 59–82; Piper, *The Major Nation-States in the European Union*, pp. 310–313. See also Closa,

"Spain: The Cortes and the EU"; Marks, *The Formation of European Policy in Post-Franco Spain*; and Jones, *Beyond the Spanish State*.

31. Piper, *The Major Nation-States*, p. 316.

32. Closa and Heywood, *Spain and the European Union*, pp. 151–153.

33. Sumpsi, "La Agricultura Española Actual," pp. 2–14; Closa and Heywood, *Spain and the European Union*, pp. 135–143.

34. Spain used 49.8 percent of the Cohesion Funds in these projects during the 1993–1998 period.

35. Piper, *The Major Nation-States*, p. 316; Börzel, "The Greening of a Polity?" pp. 65–92.

36. This deficit shows the percentage of Internal Market Directives not yet communicated as having been fully transposed in relation to the total number of directives that should have been transposed by the deadline.

37. European Commission, "Second Implementation," p. 5.

38. "Germany and Spain Face Action on Opening of Energy Markets," *Financial Times*, March 14, 2005.

39. Closa and Heywood, *Spain and the European Union*, pp. 71–72.

40. The record however is murkier if we examine the number of cases under examination by the Commission for presumed noncompliance. For instance, in 2001 Spain had the largest number of cases and most of these cases (66.5 percent) were complaints on environment-related issues. In addition, there have also been controversies over the control of EU funds. For instance, in May 2005 the Commission demanded the devolution of 134 million euros in aid for the production of linen. This scandal originated in 1998 when some Spanish producers (the so-called fortune hunters) decided to take advantage of the EU support of linen production and, in order to receive EU subsidies, falsified documents and claimed harvests that had never taken place. This led to the development of new stricter controls.

41. From Sebastián, "Spain in the EU: Fifteen Years May Not Be Enough," p. 22.

42. Ibid., p. 22.

43. Only three Spanish regions (Galicia, Extremadura, and Andalusia) will qualify as Objective 1 regions (as opposed to the 12 regions that currently qualify). Based on the latest proposal from Brussels (June 2005) Portugal would lose 25 percent of the funds that the country currently receives.

44. See "Spain Will Accept Drop in Funds if UK Takes Cut," *Financial Times*, June 10, 2005, p. 2.

45. From "La Convergencia Real a Paso Lento," *El País*, February 14, 2000.

46. Following the summer 2005 EU summit to discuss the consequences of the French and Dutch referendums, and the decision of EU leaders to freeze the ratification process, Portugal was the first EU country to postpone the scheduled referendum to ratify the constitution. When this decision was made, the polls indicated that 31.3 percent of the Portuguese would vote "No," 34,9 percent would vote "Yes," and the rest were undecided. See "Portugal el Primero en Aplazar el Referendum tras la Cumbre," *El País,* June 18, 2005.

PART 4

THE 1990S

12

Austria: Friction and Mixed Feelings

Lisa Hunt and Gerda Falkner

AUSTRIA'S MEMBERSHIP IN THE European Union has been controversial in several respects. Problems arose prior to and after Austria joined the EU in 1995, both within Austria and internationally. That said, with a few notable exceptions, Austria's adaptation to EU membership has been relatively successful. The Austrian example presents a useful and challenging case study in terms of both top-down analyses (i.e., how the EU impacts on formerly national policy fields and political structures) and bottom-up analyses (i.e., how Austria as a member state tries to influence the EU and how it organizes domestic EU-related policy processes).

The immense challenge of the task and the resulting changes, combined with efforts to protect parts of the Austrian system from the challenge of supranational controls and decisionmaking, raise interesting questions as to whether any national system can "withstand" Europeanization,[1] as well as whether a relatively small member state can have influence at the European level of decisionmaking. Further questions concern how member states comply with EU directives and adapt new policies, yet still manage to safeguard some previously protected national interests, exert influence at the supranational level, and further the process of policy adaptation within the country.

In this sense, top-down and bottom-up analyses are far from independent of each other and are often, in effect, different aspects of the same process, with the gap between them showing what it is possible for one member state to achieve at the EU level. For example, the pressure on Austria to adapt its policies and its political institutions could have been expected to lead to an implementation gap. Studies have shown that when the "degree of misfit" between domestic policies and supranational goals is high, domestic stalemate rather than change often results,[2] in particular where change would affect deeply embedded national patterns.[3] Resistance to pressure to adapt and change in symbolically charged issue areas such as neutrality, federalism, corporatism, Alpine road transit, and the like, would therefore not come as a surprise. Both Austrian public opinion and implementation performance might be expected to react negatively.

However, such reactions to intense pressure to adapt, in fact, only really concern the level of public opinion, which, in itself, is rather dangerous in terms both of the future of European integration and Austria's future experience with it. For example, the much-debated "sanctions" by the EU-14 in 2000 seemed to have provoked more antagonism in Austria than successful learning about the EU's concerns regarding Austria's political choices.

This chapter outlines the effect the accession to the EU has had on the Austrian political system, focuses on the impact these changes have had on how Austria organizes itself in its attempts to influence the EU at the supranational level, and deals with one of the more problematic examples of Austrian compliance with EU policies: the controversial issue of Austria's right to control Alpine transit traffic through its territory. Finally, Austria's record of compliance with EU directives will be discussed, as well as the domestic climate regarding support for or opposition to compliance with European institutions.

■ How and in What Areas Does the EU Influence Austria?

Membership in the European Union entailed significant adaptations of the traditional Austrian political system, a challenge to which it rose quite impressively. The very democratic principles of the Austrian Constitution were affected by the transfer of competences to produce binding law, which was henceforth to be shared between the Austrian parliament (the Nationalrat) and the EC's Council of Ministers and, to a more limited extent, with the European Parliament. Austria's principle of the division of political powers has changed because national executives dominate the legislative process at the EU level. EU membership has also influenced the rule-of-law principle because the Austrian constitutional court's monopoly on the interpretation of Austrian law was restricted to purely national affairs. In the EU, the European Court of Justice (ECJ) enjoys primacy in the interpretation of EU law. Finally, the federalist principle of Austrian constitutionality, although not abolished, was deeply affected because many competencies and duties of the regions were shifted to the EU institutions.

Membership in the EU, therefore, had consequences for the balance and division of powers within Austria's central government and administration, and also within parliament. It also initiated a period of further dilution of the powers of the nine provinces (Länder), whose powers in relation to the central authorities in the federal state had always been relatively limited. Finally, one of the most notable features of the Austrian political system, the so-called system of social partnership, was significantly affected by EU membership with the erosion over time of its central and influential position in decisionmaking. On the whole, it can therefore be argued that the influence of the EU on Austria has been extensive and, while relatively successful, it has not been entirely uncontested or unproblematic.

The negotiations prior to Austria's accession to the EU progressed smoothly, with the exception of a few key policy areas. Surprisingly, Austria's status of permanent neutrality was relatively unproblematic, and issues such as agriculture, real estate markets, and Alpine transit rights proved more complicated and controversial. Nevertheless, the negotiations were concluded within 13 months, with the process of accession significantly eased by the fact that the preceding European Economic Area (EEA) agreement had already transferred a significant amount of the European Community's economic *aquis* to the European Free Trade Association states. Nevertheless, Austria was still effectively required to implement the entire *acquis communautaire* at once, which accounts for quite a dramatic level of innovation in the space of just a few years. As the necessary changes affected the principles of the constitution so fundamentally, a general referendum was held in Austria to test citizen approval. During the final phase of the campaign, those supporting membership gained in momentum by relying on professional marketing campaigns and successful usage of popular newspapers and media. In the end, 66 percent of those who turned out to vote in Austria supported joining the EU. The reasons for this success included both expectations of enhanced economic growth and wealth, and the fear of suffering political and economic isolation if Austria remained outside the EU.[4] The influence of the EU on Austria both in its adaptation to and subsequent experience of EU membership can be characterized as a process involving significant reorganizations and shifts in the relevant balance of powers. Reforms helped to modernize public administration and provide personnel with the skills necessary to function on a more international level (e.g., language skills). The overall structure of the government departments remained the same, but a new system was developed whereby the ministry coordinating the domestic handling of EU decisionmaking and heading up Austria's delegation to the EU's Council of Ministers would be selected on the basis of an agreed list, which gave priority to the ministry responsible for most of the necessary public expenditure entailed by the relevant task.[5]

In the Nationalrat, the main problem centred on a much anticipated shift of power in favor of the government and the central administration and away from the parliament in general. The government would have its power increased through its privileged access to EU decisionmaking at the expense of the more removed but directly elected political representatives. To counteract this situation, the Austrian Constitution was amended in order to give the directly elected first chamber of the Nationalrat certain powers to exercise more control over government actions at the European level. Article 23e of the constitution specifically states that the relevant government minister is required to keep the parliament informed about all EU-related matters and projects. In addition, and significantly, the Austrian parliament may agree to a binding opinion that restricts government representatives in EU-level negotiations, and it may vote in cases where such actions are likely to lead to the creation of the kind of mandatory law that would have required national legislative scrutiny in pre-EU times.

A similar problem affected the nine constituent units of the Austrian federal system (the Länder), but even more seriously. The already relatively limited powers of the Länder were encroached upon significantly both by the shift in the level of decisionmaking from the subnational to the supranational level, and by the absence of any co-decision power for the Länder as subnational entities at the EU level. Certain steps have been taken to somewhat ameliorate this situation in a way similar to that used to protect the powers of the Nationalrat. Article 23d of the constitution and a special state-Länder agreement regulate the participation of the Länder in relevant EU-related decisionmaking, requiring that they be duly informed and providing for power to issue binding opinions.

The final significant aspect of the Austrian political system that has been highly influenced both by Austria's accession to the EU and its subsequent experience of membership is that of institutionalized corporatist cooperation of the centralized peak associations of labor and management with the government in the shaping and development of public policies. These participants in the so-called social partnership[6] work together on a constant basis in both an informal and formal capacity. It was not uncommon in Austria for the government and the social partners to negotiate draft legislation before it was approved by the Nationalrat.[7]

■ How and in What Areas Does Austria Influence the EU?

EU membership has impacted the traditional Austrian model of politics, and the basic institutions of the national political system have lost power under the conditions of Euro-politics. In order to counteract these changes the Nationalrat, the Länder, and the social partners were accorded special rights in EU-related decisionmaking. Both parliament and the Länder gained power to formulate bargaining mandates for the Austrian minister in the EC Council, and the social partners were granted a privileged flow of information as well as more opportunities for participation at both the domestic and European levels of decisionmaking in economic and social matters.

Once Austria joined the EU, its national executives became its predominant decisionmakers at the EU level. These leaders have an interest in being flexible (i.e., not tightly controlled in Council negotiations). In fact, all the special provisions only allow for very limited counterbalancing of these national executives. The Austrian parliament's actual control over the government has been relatively limited as well, despite all the constitutional measures to protect it. Recently, the Nationalrat has given binding mandates to ministers only in a very few cases. Whereas in 1995, the Austrian parliament imposed 18 binding mandates, after five years of EU membership it only imposed one mandate, and, in 2004, there were no imposed mandates.[8] In general, confronted with manifold changes and often heavy time pressures when crafting a "national standpoint," the government's capacity to negotiate and, if necessary, change its view or make concessions is valued more than giving the directly elected representatives much of a say.[9] The low number of binding mandates imposed is not just because the Nationalrat has been unsuccessful in its attempts to effectively control the government in EU affairs; it has actually rarely tried to use this power.[10] The influence of the Länder is even less in practice, despite the fact that the Länder's interests in EU policies often diverge from those of the federal government according to their specific economic and legal situations.[11]

The condition of unanimity has meant that binding opinions in the Länder are very rare in practice. In 1995, there were eight binding opinions agreed on in the Länder; in 2000, there were four; and in 2005 there were seven accepted binding opinions.[12] In day-to-day practice, the Länder have even more difficulty in keeping up to date with EU negotiations than the parliament does. Often, the national position gets decided before representatives from the Länder can even adopt a common position.

After accession, the government stepped back from its concession that the social partners could participate in Austrian delegations to EU decisionmaking bodies on an equal footing. It argued that, according to EU rules, only government representatives are officially part of the national delegations. For special cases, the minister responsible, nevertheless, agreed to include social-partner representatives in the national delegation, although without the right to speak.[13] Therefore, the experience and influence of the social partners has changed, and generally declined, since Austria joined the EU, because of the conditions of EU membership. There are, however, variations between policy areas and some older, more established interest groups have actually grown in strength. In general, the Austrian social partnership has not fared so well in the years since Austria joined the European Union. The decline of this social model has not just been a direct consequence of EU membership but also has much to do with the prevalence of the less concertation-friendly center-right government.

In terms of how the adapted Austrian political system functions in practice, a primary source of bottom-up impact on the EU stems from the national government. It is notable, therefore, that in addition to the more contested policy areas where Austria came into conflict with the EU, the EU's attempt to intervene in the formation of the Austrian government in 2000 became probably the most prominent and controversial case of Austria having an impact on the EU, as well as the other way around.

In the parliamentary elections of October 1999, the previously dominant Social Democratic Party, the SPÖ, suffered a heavy defeat at the polls, leaving the formation of the next government somewhat up in the air. After a difficult period of negotiations between all parties, the center-right party, the ÖVP, eventually decided on forming a government in coalition with the controversial and extreme right-wing Freedom Party or FPÖ. The decision to include the FPÖ in the coalition government was very problematic from the beginning. However, the decision by the other 14 EU member states to sanction Austria for this move failed to bring about a change in the composition of the new government and may have ironically contributed to an erosion of support for the EU within Austria, even among those who would not identify themselves as what might be called FPÖ supporters or sympathizers.

While the subsequent "sanctions" had no basis in EU law, they were nonetheless issued when Portugal held the EU Council presidency. The Portuguese presidency claimed that the FPÖ's leader, Jorg Haider, had repeatedly questioned "the values and principles of humanism and democratic tolerance underlying the European project"[14] and the statement issued "on behalf of the 14 member states" set out three penalties to be imposed on Austria because it included the FPÖ in its government:

- The governments of the 14 member states will not promote or accept any official bilateral contacts at the political level with an Austrian government integrating the FPÖ.
- There will be no support for Austrian candidates seeking positions in international organizations.
- Austrian ambassadors in EU capitals will only be received at a technical level.

Before then, the only provisions discussing the suspension of membership rights in the Treaty on European Union (TEU) referred to the possibility of this action only in the case of "the existence of a serious and persistent breach" of basic principles (Article 7, TEU). Austria was at no stage accused of this kind of "serious breach," but the concern, nevertheless, existed that it could occur in the future under a government that included the FPÖ. The concern was also more for what could happen at the EU level of decisionmaking, rather than a desire to interfere in Austrian domestic politics. European leaders considered the domestic politics of a member state to be a legitimate concern because of the involvement of national governments in EU-level decisionmaking and their potential to affect policymaking at that level. However, the sanctions were not imposed by the EU per se, but rather introduced by the EU-14 for their bilateral relations with Austria.

Because Austria was not in violation of the criterion mentioned above, the action of the EU-14 against Austria was not actually in accordance with the EU treaties. The Union's basic rules not only set out clear procedures for potential sanctions, but also established provisions for respecting the national identities of the member states (Article E,

TEU), and for abstaining from any measure that could jeopardize the attainment of the objectives of the treaty (Article 10, Treaty Establishing the European Community [TEC]), and, very prominently, for non-discrimination against member states because of their nationality (Article 2, TEC).

Equally questionable was the problem that the EU-14 had rushed into issuing "sanctions" with little consideration for an exit-option other than the breakdown of the Austrian government. The use of the EU presidency to issue what was effectively a multinational and not an EU statement was also problematic.[15] To withhold support from Austrians seeking positions in international organizations seems to directly contradict the central EU policy of nondiscrimination on the grounds of nationality. In addition, this discrimination was not restricted to those who actually supported the FPÖ—or even the ÖVP's decision to go into government with them.

The EU-14 sanctions also proved ineffective in instigating the breakup of the coalition government. The government retaliated against them by threatening to hold a referendum against what it viewed as these unfair measures, rather than by initiating an alternative government formation. The Austrian government also threatened to use its veto power to block the introduction of EU legislation.[16] An ad hoc exit strategy was developed five months after the Portuguese presidency's initial statement, based on a report by the so-called three wise men (former Finnish president Martti Ahtisaari, German legal expert Jochen Frowein, and former Spanish foreign minister Marcelino Oreja). The three criticized the policies and activities of the FPÖ, but confirmed that the new coalition government had not acted against European values. On that basis, the sanctions were lifted immediately. Rather than causing its demise, the Austrian government emerged from this experience stronger than it had been at the outset.

■ How Does Austria Implement and Comply with EU Policies?

During the accession negotiations, the most discussed policy areas were those where EU policy, to a varying degree, clashed with long-standing, and often highly symbolic, Austrian practices and policies. These policy areas included some aspects of agriculture policy, markets for real estate, Alpine transit traffic and volume issues, and issues of Austria's neutrality policy. Surprisingly, as mentioned above, the neutrality issue proved to be less problematic than expected. Alpine transit issues, however, continue to be contested to this day and raise important questions regarding the ability of a small member state to protect its interests when its territory lies across one of the most important transport connections between northern and southern Europe, and specifically between Germany and Italy.[17]

Road transport and, in particular, transit traffic through the environmentally endangered Alpine province of Tyrol (Germany and Italy are connected by the Brenner Pass and extensively use the Austrian transit system) had already been an issue during the EEA negotiations when Austria gained only a few concessions to allow it to depart from the EU ideal of fully liberalized transport markets and free road transit. These concessions consisted of a general commitment aimed at shifting loads from road to rail, and the so-called transit agreement, to last for 12 years starting in December 1991. A system of "eco-points" made the number of transit units allowed dependent on the exhaust-fume level. Experts thought that the upper limit on the Austrian side would limit further increase in transit traffic (which it did not) and reduce pollution. In the membership negotiations, the earlier EEA agreement had to be renegotiated with a view to respecting the *acquis communautaire*. Studies suggested an increase in traffic of up to 100 percent until 2010 as a consequence of the EU Internal Market and Austrian membership.[18] The negotiations were extremely tough, and the Austrian goal of upholding the earlier transit agreement was not reached. Austria had to make concessions regarding both the length of the agreement's duration and the maximum weight of trucks. It also had to agree to liberalize all bilateral traffic (as opposed to transit) within two years after accession.

Facing increased transit traffic, Austria finally breached EU law by establishing transit fee increases and a Brenner Pass road toll. The case then went to the ECJ, which ruled against Austria in September 2000.[19] With the existing agreement due to expire at the end of 2003, there was pressure on all sides to resolve this issue. In December 2001, the Laeken European Council asked the Commission to present a new proposal for the extension of the ongoing system beyond the end of 2003. This new proposal, also opposed by Austria, covered a further three-year period (2004–2006) and aimed at extending the existing eco-point system into 2004, pending the introduction of a new Community pricing system for the use of such infrastructure.[20] The ECJ once again reprimanded Austria in September 2003 for having tried to limit traffic volumes by setting the level of tolls at approximately 60 percent above the EU norm (Case C-445/00). Accepted by the EU transport ministers but rejected in the first instance by the European Parliament, the amended regulation was finally accepted by a Conciliation Committee in November 2003. The regulation[21] set out the system for 2004–2006 based on the amended eco-point system, with exemptions included for vehicles from one member state (Greece) and those vehicles with sufficiently low emissions (as determined by a low eco-point rating). It did not however, set a quantitative limit on the volume of transit traffic through the region nor did it allow for such a limit in the future.

The issue remains unresolved and is a source of much controversy and opposition throughout all policy levels in Austria (elite, regional, public opinion). Traffic through the Brenner Pass increased by 15.2 percent in 2004[22] and post-enlargement, with even further increases on the horizon, there is much concern that the situation will only worsen over time, despite plans for the construction of the Brenner Pass Railway Tunnel. This unsettled situation has had significant repercussions in terms of public opinion, a potentially increasing problem with regard to Austria's future experience with European integration. It is also significant because it highlights the difficulty a smaller member state has in having its concerns addressed at the European level of decisionmaking and in the face of opposition from larger member states (most notably Germany and Italy in this regard).[23]

Austria's Record of Compliance/Implementation

The previous discussion makes it clear that Austria's EU membership has been characterized by a number of frictions. The EU's political structures and processes were not easily compatible with well-established customs (notably with the characteristic forms of Austria's corporatism and federalism). Not all specific Austrian interests and policy paradigms are shared by the other member states (for example, on transit). At the same time, recent domestic developments (notably the formation of governments including the Freedom Party) have led to protest and even sanctions at the European level. Two issues are of relevance here: first, the extent to which the adaptation requirements hampered (or did not hamper) the implementation record; and second, what effect the prevailing political climate has had on implementation, and for example on the reaction within Austria to the strong and multidimensional misfit between national and supranational goals.

Initially, Austria did not exactly improve the EU's implementation performance. In November 1997, Austria ranked last among the member states on implementing Internal Market rules. By November 1997, 10 percent of all relevant directives were officially not transposed. By May

1998, however, Austria had made a big leap forward on implementing EU directives and, despite only relatively moderate progress for a few years, it had improved substantially by 2003.

Naturally, there are implementation shortcomings beyond the mere failure to inform the Commission of having transposed/implemented a directive. Implementation may be incorrect or have no effect on everyday life in a member state (nonapplication). Such implementation failures are much more difficult to establish[24]; however, one can get an impression by comparing the various kinds of enforcement procedures imposed against nonconforming EU member states. By 2003,[25] Austria's performance was mixed. Among the cases in motion on the basis of having received a letter of formal notice, Austria ranked seventh among the member states (along with Ireland) with 99 cases. At the Commission's reasoned-opinion stage, Austria also came in a joint seventh (again with Ireland) with 38 cases. Finally, and most important, looking at the cases in motion before the European Court of Justice, Austria had slipped to the second-worst position (after Spain) with 22 cases of noted noncompliance.

In a recent large project directed by one of the authors,[26] the search for compliance patterns across all 15 EU member states revealed three clusters of countries, each showing a different typical pattern of reacting to EU-induced reform requirements. In the field of EU labor law directives (there are good reasons to expect that these findings can be generalized), the 15 EU member states studied surprisingly displayed quite a regular pattern of compliance or noncompliance, regardless of how the specific provisions actually fit with their relevant national policy legacy and governmental ideology. This study differentiated three different "worlds of compliance" within the EU-15: a world of law observance, a world of domestic politics, and a world of neglect. The three worlds do not indicate outcomes, but typical modes of treating implementation duties. The specific results of particular examples of compliance tend to depend on different factors within each of the various worlds: the traditional respect of the rule of law in the field can explain most cases in the world of law observance, while in the world of domestic politics the specific fit with political preferences in each case plays a much larger role, and in the world of neglect this fit is also true for administrative nonaction.

Austria clearly belongs to the world of domestic politics, where domestic concerns frequently prevail if there is a conflict of interests. In this group of countries, each single act of transposing/implementing an EU directive tends to happen on the basis of a fresh cost-benefit analysis. Implementation is likely to be timely and correct only where no domestic concerns dominate over the fragile aspiration to comply. In cases of a clash between EU requirements and domestic-interest politics, noncompliance is the likely outcome (at least for a rather long time). While in the countries belonging to the world of law observance (Denmark, Finland, and Sweden), breaking EU law would not be a socially acceptable state of affairs; noncompliance is much less of a problem in this second category. At times, their politicians or major interest groups even openly call for disobedience with European duties—an appeal not seriously denounced socially in these countries.

A second very important issue of public support indicates the extent to which such controversial debates as those over sanctions and Alpine transit rights lower enthusiasm for EU membership and raise criticism against specific aspects of European integration. According to the latest opinion polls, as of July 2005,[27] only 37 percent of Austrians consider membership in the EU to be a good thing, which is the second-lowest level of support after the traditionally Euro-skeptical United Kingdom. It is true that Austrians have been quite critical ever since they joined the EU, but in 1999 (i.e., before the sanctions) at least 42 percent had favored membership. In addition, in 2004 only 38 percent felt that Austria had benefited from membership but a remarkable 47 percent felt that, on balance, it had not benefited. As an example of support for the European institutions, 48 percent of the population would tend to trust the European Commission and 44 percent the European Parliament.

Significantly, on the issue of enlargement, Austria was a leading advocate of the 2004 enlargement but has been the main opponent of Turkish accession to the Union. Among the population, in 2004, 41 percent of Austrians felt that enlargement would decrease Austria's importance and influence in Europe and in 2001 a high 55 percent of the population were not in favor of Turkey becoming a member of the EU. In 2005 just 10 percent supported the Turkish bid for membership—in contrast to the 45 percent who supported Croatia's application. Therefore, the reaction to Turkey cannot be so easily explained as just increasing opposition to further enlargement, although this is certainly part of the problem. The strong opposition to Turkish membership in the Austrian population is the main driving force behind the government's policy on this issue and its solitary stance in the Council in September 2005, when it attempted to block agreement on the commencement of accession negotiations with Turkey. Rather than launching accession negotiations, Austria called for negotiations with an emphasis on increased "partnership" between the EU and Turkey instead of focusing on full membership.[28] It also called for opening formal negotiations with Croatia at the same time. It must also be noted that Austria was not the only member state whose populations were not supportive of the prospect of Turkish accession, with both France and Germany contending with complicated political situations and waning levels of popular support.[29] However, the issue in Austria is somewhat exacerbated by the internal political situation and the tendency of right-wing populist media and political parties and personalities to manipulate public disquiet. Austria's internal political situation makes the lack of public support a problem for EU integration, which the Austrian government can hardly ignore.

While the Austrian parliament ratified the draft Constitutional Treaty in May 2005, just 41 percent of the people supported this move, and 47 percent support the idea of a European constitution in general. Despite the successful ratification, the FPÖ-BZÖ, in pointing to the Dutch and French negative referenda, has declared that there should also be referenda on such matters in Austria. There have also been calls for referenda on the issue of Turkish accession to the EU, including that of Chancellor Wolfgang Schüssel.

This negative turn in public opinion against the EU and Austrian membership could have serious consequences for Austrian politics in the long run, depending of course on future events. The collapse of the FPÖ vote in regional elections in April 2005, and the subsequent split in the party that has led to the more "Haiderist" (that is, the faction supporting the controversial former FPÖ leader) members of the coalition government forming a new party (the Bündnis für die Zukunft Österreichs [BZÖ]), indicates that some changes are occurring already. While it is still far too early to draw even tentative conclusions from the decrease in support for the right wing in recent regional elections, the fact that the FPÖ-BZÖ tended to speak to parts of the population expressing Euroskeptical sentiments, but is now fractured, may have some significance for EU-Austrian relations. However, the resolution of issues concerning Alpine transit traffic and volume and the fact and success of further enlargements will likely be a decisive factor in improving public opinion.

■ Future Trends and Prospects

In the 11 years since it joined the European Union in 1995, the Austrian experience of EU membership has been mixed. Austria's political system coped remarkably well with extensive adaptation, and it has also performed relatively well in terms of implementation of EU directives and is likely to continue to do so in the future. When individual issues of domestic political salience are at stake, however, Austria often chooses to disregard certain aspects of EU law (and therefore has been classified as a country in the ideal-typical "world of domestic politics" in the field of compliance).[30]

The problem areas, and most notably the reaction to them within Austria, remain the same ones that have existed throughout 11 years of membership. The Alpine transit controversy is likely to persist, as confirmed by continued protests in 2005. Further accommodation with Switzerland, which can set high tolls unimpeded, may ameliorate the situation, as would a greater emphasis on rail transportation, which has already begun. However, these are all longer-term possibilities and even in the medium term the transport issue is likely to remain highly contentious in Austria. These problems, if left unresolved, could contribute to a buildup of bad feeling toward European integration in general. Further enlargements of the EU are also likely to prove problematic in terms of public opinion in Austria, most notably in relation to Turkey. The Austrian government confirmed the influence of anti-Turkish public opinion after it finally ended its blockade of the negotiations with Turkey in October 2005. Overall, the success of Austrian integration with the EU is a matter of the extent to which the negative feelings associated with this range of controversial issues converge or are exploited by populist elements manipulating public concerns about the lack of democratic accountability at both national and EU levels of decision-making. While support for such populistic parties in Austria may have fractured, if not decreased, by 2006, it is still true that public opinion on European issues remains a consideration for Austria's future with the European Union.

■ Notes

1. Europeanization is understood as an "incremental process reorienting the direction and shape of politics to the degree that EC political and economic dynamics become part of the organizational logic of national politics and policy-making" (Ladrech, "Europeanization of Domestic Politics and Institutions," p. 69).

2. Börzel, "Improving Compliance Through Domestic Mobilisation?"; Börzel, "Why There Is No 'Southern Problem'"; Duina, "Explaining Legal Implementation in the European Union"; Duina and Blithe, "Nation States and Common Markets"; Knill and Lenschow, *Implementing EU Environmental*

Policy; Risse, Cowles, and Caporaso, "Europeanization and Domestic Change: Introduction."

3. Knill and Lenschow, "Coping with Europe."

4. Wimmer and Mederer, *EG-Recht in Österreich.*

5. See Müller, "EU Co-ordination in Austria."

6. They include, in the Austrian case, both the structural (interest group setup) and the procedural dimensions (involvement in policymaking) of corporatism, which are extremely well developed. There are a number of quite hierarchically organized "chambers" (for business, labor, agriculture, etc.), that is, interest groups set up by Austrian law where membership is obligatory. The classic "social partner" institutions in Austria are thus the Chamber of Business (Wirtschaftskammer Österreich), the Chamber of Labour (Bundesarbeitskammer), the Conference of Presidents of the Chambers of Agriculture (PRÄKO), and the encompassing Austrian trade union confederation (ÖGB).

7. See Karlhofer and Talos, *Zukunft der Sozialpartnerschaft.*

8. Falkner, "Zur 'Europäisierung' des österreichischen politischen Systems," p. 57.

9. Falkner and Müller, *Österreich im europäischen Mehrebenensystem.*

10. Falkner, "How Pervasive Are Euro-Politics?"

11. Dachs, "EU-Beitritt und die Bundesländer," p. 203.

12. Falkner, "Zur 'Europäisierung' des österreichischen politischen Systems," p. 60.

13. Karlhofer and Tálos, *Sozialpartnerschaft und EU,* p. 141.

14. Quoted in Luif, "Austria: The Burdens of History," p. 106.

15. On legal aspects, see Pernthaler and Hilpold, "Sanktionen als Instrument der Politikkontrolle."

16. Luif, "Austria: The Burdens of History," p. 107.

17. Heinisch, "Austria: Confronting Controversy."

18. Wimmer and Mederer, *EG-Recht in Österreich,* p. 249.

19. Judgment of the Court of 26 September 2000. *Commission of the European Communities vs. Republic of Austria.* Failure of a member state to fulfill obligations, Directive 93/89/EEC, Tolls, Brenner Motorway, Prohibition of discrimination, Obligation to set toll rated by reference to the costs of the infrastructre network concerned. Case C-205/98. European Court reports, 2000, p. I-07367.

20. Luif, "Österreich in der Europäischen Union."

21. Regulation (EC) No 2327/2003 of the European Parliament and of the Council of 22 December 2003 establishing a transitional points system applicable to heavy goods vehicles traveling through Austria for 2004 within the framework of a sustainable transport policy. *Offical Journal* L 345, 31/12/2003, pp. 30–33.

22. "Austria Battles to Cut Down on Truck Traffic Through the Brenner Pass," April 2, 2005, available at http://www.eubusiness.com, accessed June 9, 2005.

23. Luif, "Österreich in der Europäischen Union."

24. See Falkner, et al., *Complying with Europe.*

25. Based on the latest available data (2003) from the European

Commission, *21st Annual Report on Monitoring the Application of Community Law*.

26. Falkner, et al., *Complying with Europe*.

27. *Eurobarometer*, July 2005; available at: http://europa.eu.int/comm/public_opinion/index_en-htm.

28. Daniel Dombey, " EU Seeks to Resolve Austrian Doubts over Turkey," *Financial Times,* September 27, 2005, p. 3.

29. Anton Pelinka, quoted in Stephen Mulvey, "Why Austria Was a Sticking Point," BBC News, available at http://news.bbc.co.uk/go/pr/fr/-/2/hi/europe/4304396.stm, accessed October 6, 2005.

30. Falkner, et al., *Complying with Europe*.

13

Sweden: Adaptation and Resistance

Johan Eliasson

IN 1962 SWEDISH PRIME Minister Erlander declared the European continent's Catholicism, conservatism, unbridled capitalism, and colonialism unappealing and undesirable to a Protestant, middle-way, anticolonial northern state.[1] Instead, Sweden chose to follow its own distinctive socioeconomic path grounded in social-democratic ideals of socioeconomic equality and conformity (not "standing out"), supported by continued military neutrality. Sweden cherished its *folkhem* ("people's home"—a well-established domestic metaphor for "the Swedish model" and Swedes themselves) referring to comfort, familiarity, security, and public service, but also perceived social superiority; this "exceptionalism"[2] meant Swedes saw few reasons for closer political and social ties to Europe.[3]

However, the decline in international appeal of third-way social democracy amidst stagflation in the 1980s,[4] as well as domestic economic problems, propelled a rethinking in the political and business establishment. By 1990 policymakers, business leaders, and industry groups espoused the economic benefits of EU membership, seemingly overriding longstanding fears of lower European environmental, labor, and consumer standards.[5] Notwithstanding overwhelming elite support, fierce debate ensued in the 1994 referenda campaign where ultimately, if barely, membership was approved by a slim margin (52 percent to 48 percent).

Today, as the country is undergoing rapid demographic and socioeconomic structural changes, the government has to continuously balance the desire for elite consensus on government EU policy with the more fluid domestic political scene crowded with one of the highest levels of EU skepticism in Europe. Opposition to integration is particularly strong among women, youths, and those ideologically to the left of center.[6] In the 1999 and 2004 EU parliamentary elections, anti-EU candidates secured 25 percent and 21 percent of Swedish seats, respectively; in the 2002 parliamentary elections, the left party and the Greens (both opposed to EU membership) garnered 14 percent of the votes. This continued lack of public enthusiasm for the EU and European integration permeates much of Swedish involvement in the EU even if, as is the case in older member states, a more nuanced assessment among Swedes of the value of EU membership in particular policy areas is discernible in polls and policy statements since 2002. Significantly lower food prices (by 20–25 percent) is one of the most appreciated consequences of EU membership, along with increased business opportunities, while the most negative opinions concern the European Monetary Union (EMU), social policies, and loss of national sovereignty.[7]

At the EU level, Swedish officials have had difficulties adjusting to being a "small state among others," frequently exhibiting old Swedish tendencies of exceptionalism, with a "large state" mentality, trying to exert influence above their means.[8] Swedish policymakers have also been criticized for frequent policy inconsistencies, and a lack of strategic goals for how it wants the EU to develop, that is, its *finalité*.[9] Swedes acknowledge they have been influenced by and learned from the way Finnish colleagues adjusted to membership, and how Finland handled its EU presidency. After holding the Swedish EU presidency in 2001, politicians and interest groups had "better learned how to operate [in the Union]."[10] In 2002 Sweden was excluded when the five largest member states met to discuss EU policies post-9/11, nor were they invited to a gathering of 11 small current and applicant states in the Netherlands to discuss a small-state alliance in the EU.[11]

This chapter aims to elaborate on the aforementioned, as well as other related issues, looking at institutional as well as policy developments. The most extensive and lasting effects of a decade of EU membership are found in economic, labor, and security policies. An in-depth analysis will focus on the vast changes in security and defense policies, including the wholesale surrender of a cornerstone of national identity, namely neutrality.

■ How and in What Areas Does the EU Influence Sweden?

A Closer Look at Security Policy: Goodbye to Swedish Neutrality

Having escaped wars since 1809, neutrality, while never part of domestic law or international agreements, assumed a central role in national identity as a constitutive part of the Swedish self-image, where "being Swedish is being neutral."[12] Following the Second World War, Swedish officials developed a mental correlation between domestic economic and social policies and neutrality,[13] with the latter seen as enabling a foreign policy dominated by the projection of Sweden as a neutral, impartial, moral custodian. The Swedish model was touted to other smaller, distant states, along with extensive economic assistance.[14] This international activism, defended with missionary enthusiasm domestically, became the external manifestation of national identity, cementing neutrality as the unquestioned security/political "supreme-ideology."[15] Universal conscription fostered national unity and ensured a mass-based army should an attack nevertheless occur. Public assurances that neutrality would remain unaffected by EU membership and that Sweden could opt-out of a future EU common defense policy perpetuated public expectations of a continuation of past practices.[16]

Yet the development of common EU positions and institutions, joint decisions, and actions in the realm of the Common Foreign and Security Policy (CFSP) and European Security and Defense Policy (ESDP), and numerous bi- and multilateral security and defense agreements (on armaments R&D and procurement, training, and troop structure), have been particularly profound for Swedish defense policy. There is new legislation on international service for enlisted personnel, more far-reaching agreements on international training and strategic development than ever before, and a new relationship with NATO, best summarized as "cooperation without formal membership"; all of these developments are predominantly the result of ESDP institutional developments and ties to the alliance.[17] Furthermore, the wholly state-owned armaments industry, the fifth largest in the world, has been relinquished.

Structural and Legal Changes

When the ESDP was first erected in 2000, Sweden pledged a limited range of assets and troops to the EU force catalogue. When it was revealed that Swedish contributions fell below those of smaller states such as Finland and Belgium, pressure mounted from other states, as well as Swedish opposition parties, resulting in an instantaneous increase in contributions to include offensive assets such as fighter aircraft.[18] To facilitate new commitments, legal restrictions prohibiting the deployment of certain units and assets for international operations (e.g., navy and air force combat planes) were also lifted.[19]

Armaments industry. As late as 1998 the wholly state-owned Swedish armaments industry, Europe's fifth largest, heavily protected and subsidized, remained "essential" to ensure self-sufficiency and bolster credibility in neutrality.[20] Despite economic problems due to skyrocketing costs and shorter production lines, political sensitivities (its ties to neutrality) and concerns for jobs hampered reforms. Swedish options were limited: either continue with subsidies through excess ordering (politically acceptable but economically disastrous, and direct subsidies are banned under EU regulations), join NATO (politically unfeasible), or try to ensure that production and technological skills remained in Sweden while securing required deliveries of new arms and other equipment. As the political will for EU defense cooperation intensified, a European armaments consolidation process with mergers and acquisitions took off, rendering possible new options for saving the industry. Policymakers began referencing the enhanced security inherent in EU membership and the political commitments made.[21]

To counter an electoral backlash, the government reached out to the opposition Conservative, Liberal, and Christian Democratic Parties. The latter, in their ideological preferences for fiscal responsibility and support for EU integration, insisted that excess state orders be cut, protectionist policies relaxed, direct subsidies abolished, and foreign bids invited for contracts and ownership. In 1999, parliament approved the first sale of former armaments giant, Bofors, in the face of vast public protests; yet by 2001 all Swedish defense industries had been acquired by foreign, mostly European, companies.[22] A 1999 invitation to join a European framework agreement on armaments letter of intent (LoI) turned out to be a salvation,[23] a welcome opportunity to engage in multilateral cooperation while seeking to retain domestic production and technical knowhow. The LoI essentially saved Swedish armaments production and competence, "locking in" the path of subsequent developments.[24] A high-ranking civilian official at the defense ministry acknowledged how "the ESDP significantly pushed the LoI, and to have said no to LoI would have been to resort to a kind of Albanian situation during the Cold War."[25] The development of the ESDP and the LoI also increased US confidence in Swedish security information policies, and the harmonization of Swedish policies with other LoI–NATO states meant Sweden, in 2001, received NATO member status for arms exports.[26]

New norms. Increased responsibilities and institutionalized committee work with EU and NATO peers, accompanied by a functional growth in staff stationed in committees in Brussels, also contributed to changes in officials' perspectives, resulting in a reorientation and reprioritization of the Swedish defense forces. By signing the 1999 Cologne EU Summit declaration on autonomous EU operations, Sweden surrendered its traditional, unequivocal, insistence on a UN mandate before engaging militarily.[27] Swedish foreign minister Lindh, a longtime skeptic of the ESDP, acknowledged "a remarkable shift in perspectives [in Swedish COREPER]," and that "we have taken notice in the government."[28] Several senior officials in Brussels expressed similarly altered perspectives over the course of repeat interviews from 2001 to 2003, shifts confirmed by third-party collaborations.[29] "With our presence in Brussels, . . . oversight and review mechanisms and daily interactions and planning . . . a *de facto* EU defense is emerging."[30] These developments fed back into Swedish security policy with repercussions on the fundamental basis of Swedish policy, its security doctrine.[31] While said to reflect "traditional Swedish values," the result of domestic debates was a lengthy doctrine (23 sentences, 140 words) adopted in February 2002, which "serves to better reflect our current situation [in light of] developments in Europe over the last few years, and political commitments."The doctrine conspicuously reflects the Europeanization of Swedish policies and increased responsibilities as a result of EU membership: "As a member in the EU Sweden participates in a common solidarity aimed at preventive war on the European continent."[32] At the same time, neutrality is said to "remain an option" and many continue their verbal commitments to the concept of neutrality.[33] Given the centrality of neutrality in Swedish politics and society, a certain continuation of old-style rhetoric to placate a skeptical domestic audience would be expected. However, there is agreement among scholars and international law experts that EU declarations, treaty clauses, commitments, and participation in a permanent military structure (the EU's security, political, and military committees), resulting in new norms and practices, are incompatible with neutrality, rendering Swedish neutrality a de facto thing of the past.[34]

In sum, opposition to EU defense cooperation, and perceived threats to neutrality and sovereignty, meant references to the CFSP and ESDP were slow to emerge as a regular part of Swedish policymakers' vocabulary, but by 2005 officials acknowledged the total revamping of the Swedish military structure and its interdependence with other member states. Active Swedish participation in ESDP has been necessary to counter the commonly perceived Swedish obstinancy vis-à-vis the ESDP among other Council members, and also to save its domestic defense industrial sector.[35] References to EU solidarity and interdependence now dominate government statements, where "vastly expanded international cooperation is a precondition for the survival of the Swedish defense industry and for the adaptability of the defense forces."[36] Numerous Swedish defense experts also agree that in order to meet obligations in the EU, including the new Swedish-led Nordic EU Battle Group, there remains no choice but to change to an all-voluntary army.[37]

Economic Policy

The years preceding EU membership saw negative economic growth in Sweden, and membership has undoubtedly contributed to its solid economic performance since the late 1990s. Joining the Internal Market exposed Swedish industry to increased competition and the government, with support from the conservative opposition bloc, embraced deregulation in accordance with the EU's Single European Act, while Swedish monetary targets followed EMU objectives as envisioned in the Maastricht Treaty. Reforms included central bank independence in 1999 (even before countries such as Britain), when price stability was proclaimed the primary objective of monetary policies, followed by tax cuts (particularly corporate tax rates, which are now among the lowest in the world), labor market reforms (flexible wages and work hours, investment in job training, abolishing centralized wage agreements), and the privatization of state monopolies—all deemed necessary for the export-dependent economy to grow. Economic experts credit EU membership and economic reforms (necessitated by EU regulations but also pushed by Swedish multinationals such as Volvo and IKEA, and information technology companies such as Ericsson and TeliaSonera, all with significant European market shares) with improving industrial competitiveness, increasing foreign direct investment, and raising growth.[38] Reforms, and dismal continental economic performance, led the Swedish economy to outperform the euro-zone average in 1999–2005.[39] The EU Commission praised Swedish reforms, declaring (in 2005) Sweden "the undoubted hero of the first five years of the [2000] Lisbon program."[40]

Unintended as it was, these otherwise positive developments actually made it more difficult for proponents to argue the case for joining the EMU. Besides diminishing currency fluctuations (historically hitting the krona) and abolishing exchange-rate fees, the most prevalent argument made by policymakers and business in the 2003 referendum campaign was that EMU membership would allow Swedish influence on policy decisions that invariably affect the highly interdependent Swedish economy.[41] Despite support from all the major parties, employer unions, industrial leaders, and several labor unions, these arguments failed to convince skeptical Swedes, who have largely assessed EU membership by way of economic benefits and personal financial gains vis-à-vis loss of sovereignty. The solid Swedish economic performance, Denmark's previous rejection of the euro, and strong nationalist arguments for retaining the krona by leading political and cultural figures boosted the "No" campaign, countering the overwhelming elite support for the euro. EMU membership was rejected by a 5-percent margin, and there is political consensus not to revisit the issue until 2010.

Declining corporatism. EU membership has dramatically altered the relationship between the state and interest groups, increasingly replacing the dominant corporatist structure with a more informal (domestically) and multi-institutional (in Europe) approach by interest groups.[42] While interest groups lack explicit legal entitlement to provide input on policy proposals, Articles 7(2) and 11(6) of the Swedish Constitution (a "desire to anchor decision in society") have traditionally been interpreted as requiring feedback from private-sector groups and unions before debating proposals in parliament, a Swedish process known as *remiss.*[43] This norm has been perpetuated by the fact that even in this centralized system many companies, associations, and foundations are charged with implementing, overseeing, and managing implementation of policy. Because of the way proposals work their way through the EU's institutions and committees, where the substance may change at any point in the process, once a proposal reaches the Committee of Permanent Representatives (COREPER) in Brussels there is often insufficient time to pursue the type of extensive domestic feedback and deliberation process common in Sweden. This has resulted in greater difficulties incorporating divergent views (the "societal anchoring") when framing Swedish EU policies, frequently generating antagonistic responses from labor unions. The latter, traditionally strong supporters of the Social Democratic Party, feel increasingly alienated. Much like their French peers, they regularly criticize government positions (e.g., EU enlargement and free movement of labor), making agreements on other domestic issues such as pension funds or education reform more difficult.

In response to the increasing number of issues debated and decided in the EU, leaving less time for domestic debates, many interest groups have joined with their European peers in utilizing EU institutional avenues to influence policy.[44] A few groups established offices in Brussels prior to accession, in response to growing Swedish exports to the EU and amidst fears the Single European Act would raise trade barriers, but transnational initiatives and participation in multinational union lobbying efforts rose significantly after 1995.[45] Industry associations and unions took their seats on the EU's Economic and Social Committee (ECOSOC), but after a period of "institutional learning" the Commission Comitology structure has proven more effective in promoting policy positions vis-à-vis the large and unwieldy ECOSOC. Many Swedish interest groups have also reformed decisionmaking structures, preferring to organize activities on functional rather than territorial bases, with some groups even establishing specific EU coordinators to oversee policy proposals that span several issue areas.[46] Studies also indicate that these new relations between interest groups and state agencies have taken hold.[47]

■ How and in What Ways Does Sweden Influence the EU?

Regional Cooperation

It is unquestionable that country size and capabilities matter in deliberations and decisionmaking in the EU's various institutions. Smaller states tend to make more use of EU institutions and to focus on particular areas where they can have the greatest impact in steering decisions in accordance with their own preferences. The Baltic Sea region, EU eastern enlargement, and transparency issues have been priorities for Sweden since 1995.

A Swedish "Baltic region offensive" was launched in 1996. This included massive economic aid (€1 billion up to 2003), social support (civil exchange programs and assistance in R&D), donations of military equipment and officer training, along with stepped-up advocacy of eastern enlargement. Working bilaterally and through regional organizations such as the Nordic Council, the Baltic Sea Council, and the Organization for Security and Cooperation in Europe, Sweden pushed the EU to pay greater attention to the region. The government presented a program to the EU Council for EU policies in the Baltic Sea region, including improved coordination of EU as well as individual member states' financial contributions to the Baltic states and Russia, along with specific proposals for integration of the social sector (e.g., exchange and visitor programs).[48] Describing developments since accession, Finance Minister Nuder explained that "cooperation around the Baltic Sea is now an everyday phenomenon, but it was not so back then [1994],"[49] resulting in greater convergence of Swedish, Nordic, and EU views on the Baltics and Russia. An EU-Russian scientific exchange program is one example of Swedish contributions in shaping EU policy in the region. Another is the Northern Dimension, launched by Finland in 1997 and subsequently backed by Sweden. Aimed at addressing nonmilitary security issues in northern Europe, including environment, health, telecommunications, and civil society, the two countries were instrumental in assuring official status for the Northern Dimension as an EU regional policy program.[50]

Enlargement

The 2001 Swedish EU presidency was devoted to enlargement and two other areas where Sweden has traditionally done well by European standards, resulting in a focus on the "three Es": enlargement, environment, and employment. The government, launching its largest information campaign ever, touted EU enlargement as "an obligation" and "necessary to end European divisions." The incessant Swedish focus on enlargement frustrated some officials from other member states, who complained that the three Es seemed to stand for enlargement, enlargement, and enlargement.[51] The Swedish focus on the Baltics and expansion should also be viewed in relation to the continuous debate on "deepening versus widening" the Union. As Swedes tend to oppose the former, enlargement is believed to prevent a rapid deepening. Notwithstanding less than expected enthusiasm from the Swedish public, the government's efforts contributed to speeding up enlargement, while also cementing a greater EU focus on the Baltic Sea region and Russia.

It is noteworthy that after enlargement was agreed, the Swedish government, nonetheless, sought to restrict labor mobility from new member states for fear of "social tourism," that is, new EU citizens flocking to Sweden to take advantage of its generous welfare policies. This proposal was handsomely rejected in parliament, where even the anti-EU parties, exhibiting typical Swedish adherence to rules and norms even when opposed to their content, argued that such restrictions would contradict the stated intention of the EU and its enlargement. Sweden thus joined a handful of states having no restrictions on labor migration. As it happened, one year post-enlargement the government acknowledged that it found no signs of flooded labor markets or "social tourism."[52]

Transparency and Crisis Management

Scandinavian citizens enjoy more access to documents through right-to-information laws, along with significant transparency in decisionmaking, than other EU states, exept the Netherlands. Most Swedes associate the EU's so-called democratic deficit with a perceived lack of transparency in EU decisionmaking, and Sweden has worked hard to increase both access and transparency in the EU. In 2000 several Swedish members of the European Parliament (MEPs), tacitly backed by the government, supported a Finnish MEP in the European Court of Justice (ECJ) challenging a Council decision classifying all Common Foreign and Security Policy documents.[53] The ECJ ruled under Article 255 of the Rome Treaty that the Council might impose partial disclosure on security-related issues without systematically limiting access to CFSP documents.[54] Lengthy negotiations ensued between the European Parliament and the COREPER before a compromise was reached on security information exchange.[55] Defense Minister von Sydow used numerous speeches and meetings during the Swedish EU presidency to promote greater openness and public disclosure of documents in the CFSP.[56] In 2002, the Swedish government published a proposal for "a right of access to EU documents" and was instrumental in the wording of Article 42 of the European Charter of Fundamental Rights (on access to EU documents).

Crisis management. Swedish experience has also been useful, and its influence discernible, as it pertains to civilian crisis management. Conflict management has been part of Swedish society and ways of thinking since the late nineteenth century, when unions rose and "peace agreements" were reached between labor and capital, followed by centralized wage negotiations—a system lasting until the early 1990s. Deeply rooted norms of egalitarianism have been transposed onto foreign policies through Sweden's international activism, solidarity with those less fortunate, and advocacy of international law and human rights. Swedes have long been leading actors in international organizations and mediations (including conflict prevention), and Swedish peacekeepers have also continuously figured prominently in UN operations.[57]

When the ESDP was first proposed, the government immediately opposed any militarization of the EU, including permanent military committees, saying: "We do not wish to proceed with separate institutions for military crisis management . . . oppose Solana's dual role . . . veto right and opt-out must both be kept . . . [and] strengthening civilian capabilities is the priority."[58] While the stabilizing and security-enhancing effects of strengthening civil society and the rule of law in developing countries is uncontested, challenges associated with crisis prevention include the difficulties of garnering the necessary political and public support for costly aid or policy programs; reactive crisis management, instead, tends to prevail. These challenges, combined with the historical emphasis on the more tangible military aspects of crisis management among particularly Continental members, helps explain the initially cautious response to Swedish preferences for heavy investments in civilian crisis management.[59] Yet inclusion of the civilian crisis management committee in the ESDP structure, as proposed by Sweden, won Swedish acceptance of the military aspects of ESDP.[60] The Swedish government vowed to make civilian crisis management its primary objective in the ESDP.[61] In 2001, the Council adopted a Swedish proposal for an "EU Program for Prevention of Violent Conflict," committing the EU to specific cooperative measures to prevent and mitigate conflicts, and the EU civilian crisis management committee has been instrumental in EU rule-of-law and police missions in such states as Albania and Macedonia.

■ How Does Sweden Implement and Comply with EU Policies?

Several Swedish reforms implemented since joining the EU have focused on facilitating consensual policymaking to better accommodate the rapidly growing number of actors involved in Swedish-EU policy, and to channel government input into the EU institutions. Both parliament (Riksdagen) and government structures have been altered to accommodate an increased diversification of sources of policy input (EU institutions, government, parliament, and interest groups) and the need for speedier decisions, making a "Europeanization" of governance discernible in new government and parliamentary committees, as well as iin new laws (e.g., changing the constitution to allow for EU Council decisions adopted through Qualified Majority Voting to apply domestically even when Sweden dissented). At the same time, and in line with the concept of subsidiarity, Swedish policymakers have worked to retain Swedish priorities in new laws when implementing EU directives and decisions.

Swedish parliamentarians monitor how ministers carry out their duties in the Council through an all-party parliamentary body, the EU Advisory Committee (EUAC), erected in 1995. Unlike regular Riksdag committees, the EUAC is not concerned with legislative bills, but the EUAC can call public hearings on any topic to be decided in the EU. The EUAC's regular Friday meeting is attended by the cabinet minister(s) due to participate in the following week's specific Council session(s), and to whom the EUAC issues recommendations. Refusal to follow the committee's recommendations (which has occurred) requires a written explanation from the government; even so, the government risks severe criticism and, ultimately, a parliamentary vote of "no confidence." Moreover, the government is required to keep the Riksdag as a whole continuously informed of its work in the EU. This is done through annual written reports of activities in the EU, and the twice-annual parliamentary EU debates, where all parliamentarians participate.

Yet there are signs of diminished parliamentary control and, along with it, a concentration of agenda setting and centralization of decision-making within the prime minister's office. On the anniversary of Sweden's first decade in the EU, Deputy Prime Minister Ringholm assumed a new title as minister for coordination of EU issues, explaining how "after ten years in the EU it is completely natural that EU questions are addressed as other domestic issues, thus moving [them] from the foreign ministry to the Cabinet Committee on Proposal Preparations (*Statsrådsberedningen*)."62 All EU questions affecting more than one department are now overseen by the Statsrådsberedningen, which in turn, based on the Finnish model, is now located in the prime minister's office. While some point to the centrality of the EUAC and the government's need for parliamentary support to stay in office, it is too early to tell whether this constellation will contribute to a more combative political climate with stronger party alignment on EU issues; increasing divides are already visible in regard to security policy.

A vast and experienced civil service, a tradition of administrative flexibility, and the capacity to mobilize resources efficiently and relatively quickly have also helped Swedes in adapting to EU laws and directives.63 Only the top positions in government ministries and agencies are elected or appointed, and full-time bureaucrats implement and oversee the day-to-day work of legislation and report to appropriate cabinet ministries. This vertical ladder of responsibility permeates regional and city authorities, easing nationwide uniform implementation. Regional associations and foundations that implement policy also report to regional government authorities.

Implementation and Compliance Records

Relative to other EU members, Sweden has made scant use of the ECJ in contesting and implementing EU decisions (with noticeable exceptions discussed above), seeking instead to affect decisions a priori or alter decisions through political bargaining;[64] neither do domestic courts play a significant role in implementing EU directives. Swedes' traditional respect for law and order—of abiding faithfully to agreements even if originally opposed—coupled with the extensive system of parliamentary involvement in policymaking and a strong civil service, have made implementation fairly smooth, if uneven, across most sectors.

Surprisingly, for a member traditionally touting its own environmental standards, the Swedish record of implementing environmental directives is the second-worst in the Union.[65] The latter is partly due to stricter Swedish rules and refusal to ease restrictions. Higher Swedish growth rates vis-à-vis the euro-zone countries (1999–2005) bolstered arguments that environmental protection, industrial competitiveness, and economic growth are not contradictory. Sweden presented a holistic plan to strengthen EU environmental regulations, especially maritime standards,[66] while showing willingness to compromise when needed; during a 2005 Council meeting the Swedes accepted a reduction of EU greenhouse-gas emissions by 15 percent, instead of its desired 30–40, percent by 2020.

■ Future Trends and Prospects

During the first half of its decade-long EU membership Sweden frequently sided with fellow Nordic states Denmark and Finland (as well as the Netherlands and Austria) on issues such as the EMU, defense, environment, and social policy, while the second half was characterized by increased divergence, particularly in regard to the EMU and defense, discrediting predictions of a "Nordic bloc" in the EU.[67] Swedish and Danish policies still exhibit many similarities, reflecting as they have their most Euro-skeptic populations.[68] However, similarities do not apply to immigration, where Swedish policies are among the most generous and least restrictive in Europe. With the highest percentage of first- and second-generation immigrants in the developed world[69] (currently one-fifth of Swedes are immigrants, a number expected to rise to one-third of the population by 2015), EU enlargement and European immigration flows are sure to cement new cultural roots and external country ties, likely changing the way Swedes view themselves and their place in Europe.[70] Swedish policymakers have supported a series of measures adopted by the Council related to asylum and immigration to the EU, and will likely continue to stress the need for even greater burden sharing.[71]

Sweden will likely continue its current path of adaptation, balancing staunch support for certain issues bound to be crucial over the coming decade, such as EU service-sector reform, asylum laws, transparency laws, and police cooperation, with continued resistance on others, including EU defense and alcohol policy. Swedish resistance to increasing the EU budget to above 1 percent of the average EU GDP is also likely to remain intact, and may have gained strength with the demise of the EU constitution.[72] The prospect of adopting the euro is also bleak, with no new debate on the issue likely before 2010.

■ Notes

1. In Cramér, *Neutralitet och europeisk integration*, p. 272.
2. Dörfer, "Sixty Years of Solitude," p. 605; compare Wahlbäck, *The Roots of Swedish Neutrality*. From 1989 to 1993 a budget surplus turned into a deficit of 12.3 percent of GDP. See also Ingebritsen, "Coming out of the Cold," p. 246, and Anderson, *Beslutsfatterna*.
3. On Sweden's value system, aloofness, perceived "exceptionalism," and relations with EFTA and the EC, see Cramér, Neutralitet och Europeisk," or *Neutralitet och europeisk integration*; Lawler, "Scandinavian Exceptionalism and European Union"; af Malmborg, *Neutrality and State-Building in Sweden*; Gustavsson, *The Politics of Foreign Policy Change*, p. 55.
4. The Swedish model was touted as "the expected and preferred path" for emerging east-central European democracies; for example, Cabinet Secretary Pierre Schori in *Dagens Nyheter*, January 13 and November 18, 1990. However, these states instead turned to neoliberal economic models and NATO. "Neither Swedish policy makers nor the public have realized how weak and geopolitically uninteresting the country has become," Östergård 1995, in Holmström, "Alliansfriheten-livboj eller kvarnsten?" p. 7; see Jakobson, "Sverige Övervärderar sin roll."
5. See, for example, Dahl, *Svenskarna och NATO*, p. 100.
6. Forskningsgruppen för Samhälls-och Informationsstudier, "Opionen kring EU, EMU och vissa militära allianser."
7. SOM Institute, "National Surveys," Bedömningar av förtroendet för tjugo samhällsinstitutioner 1986–2003, 2005.

8. Johnson-Theutenberg, "Bara Nato räddar Sverige"; personal interview, Brussels, 2003.

9. See, for example, *Dagens Nyheter*, January 5, 2005, although Prime Minister Persson laid out a limited view of his future vision of the EU in a speech at Humboldt University in 2000 (Persson "The Future of Europe Debate."

10. *Helsingin Sanomat*, June 11, 2002.

11. Tallberg, "Sverige ingen Stormakt" *Dagens Nyheter*, February 9, 2003.

12. Stutz, *Opinion 2001*; Bergendahl 1926, in Cramér, *Neutralitet och Europeisk Integration*; Anderson, *Beslutsfattarna*.

13. Foreign Minister Uden, 1947, in Möller, *Östen Uden*, pp. 298–299; compare af Malmborg, *Neutrality and State-Building in Sweden*.

14. See, for example, Lawler, "Scandinavian Exceptionalism and European Union." There were clandestine Swedish actions, particularly in the Second World War. See, for example, Tunander, "The Uneasy Imbrication of Nation-State and NATO"; Dahl, *Svenskarna och NATO*; Larsson, "Framtida Konfliktscenarier," p. 23.

15. Andren, *Säkerhetspolitik, Analyser och Tillämpningar,* pp. 84, 105.

16. Swedish Parliamentary Report, "Historiskt Vägval." On Swedish self-identity, see Elgström, "The Making of Swedish Neutrality"; Dahl, *Svenskarna och NATO*; af Malmborg, *Neutrality and State-Building in Sweden*; *The Economist*, "From Vikings to Peacemongers."

17. See, for example, Eliason, "Traditions, Identity, and Security."

18. *Göteborgs Posten,* September 8, 2000; *Svenska Dagbladet*, November 20, 2001.

19. Swedish deployments to Macedonia (FYROM) and Congo, under UN mandates but EU command, exemplify Swedish commitments to the UN and EU decisions and operations.

20. Bjurtoft, "Gamla sanningar omprövas när försvarsindustrin omprövas."

21. Persson, "Trygghet i en värld i förändring"; Lindh, "Swedish Foreign and Security Policy in a New Europe."

22. Including EADS, United Defense (USA), British Alvis, and Howaldtwerke-Deutsche Werft.

23. "Framework Agreement Between the French Republic, the Federal Republic of Germany, the Italian Republic, the Kingdom of Spain, the Kingdom of Sweden, United Kingdom of Great Britain and Ireland Concerning Measures to Facilitate the Restructuring and Operation of the European Defense Industry"; available at: http://www.forsvar.regeringen.se/pressinfo/pdf/loieng.pdf.

24. Compare von Sydow, "Reply in Parliament, 1999/2000: 1145," January 23, 2000.

25. Interview, Defense Ministry, June 2001.

26. See, for example, Schmitt, "European Armaments Cooperation," p. 62.

27. *Svenska Dagbladet*, June 18, 2000; von Sydow, Weekly Public Letters 26 and 34, 2001.

28. EU Advisory Committee, July 13, 2001.

29. Brussels, 2001, 2002, and 2003. Repeat interviews in Brussels confirmed new perspectives on how the ESDP should develop; in the words of one captain: "If the EU acts we will act regardless of UN mandate . . . and we see

things on a daily basis, of course we convey what is said, and what we think . . . even if policy is set in the capital."

30. Interviews, Brussels, 2001 and 2003.

31. Hederstedt, "Internationalisera Forsvaret!," *Dagens Nyheter*, February 7, 2002; Bratt, "Neutraliteten inte relevent"; *Svenska Dagbladet*, December 14, 2000; Wahlbäck, "Efter Neutraliteten."

32. *Dagens Nyheter*, February 11 and 13, 2002.

33. Lindh, "Swedish Foreign and Security Policy"; Schlaug and Nilsson-Hedström, "Folkomrösta om Alliansfriheten."

34. Wenger, "Von Köln bis Nizza," p. 120; *Financial Times*, October 5, 2001; Diedrichs and Wessels, "Die erweiterte EU als internationaler."

35. Johnson-Theutenberg, "Bara Nato räddar Sverige"; Madsen, "Fullfölj Tankarna"; Berg, "Neutraliteten har gjort sitt"; Interviews, Brussels, 2003; *Dagens Nyheter*, April 17, 2005; Bratt, "Sverige övervärderar sin Roll."

36. Foreign Affairs Committee summary of 2001/02:UU11 in *Krigsmaterielexporten* 2001, p. 2.

37. *Dagens Nyheter*, December 16, 2004, and April 17, 2005.

38. Nordea, "Markets," *Economic Outlook* (2005), pp. 19–22.

39. *Financial Times*, April 19, 2005.

40. "Report Exposes 'Heroes' and 'Villains' of Lisbon Process," March 17, 2005; available at: www.cer.org.uk.

41. Karl Kalthenthaler, Rhodes College, Speech at Syracuse University, April 4, 2005, citing interviews in a forthcoming book on EU central banks.

42. See for example Svensson and Öberg, "Labour Market Organizations' Participation in Swedish Public Policy-Making"; Bergman, "Sweden: Democratic Reforms."

43. Shively, *Power and Choice*, p. 235; Svensson and Öberg, "Labour Market Organizations' Participation in Swedish Public Policy-Making"; Hancock, "Sweden."

44. Social Democratic Party Congress, "Protocol."

45. Bergman, "Sweden: Democratic Reforms."

46. Landstingsorganizationen, "Hur arbetar LO I EU?" Sweden has 12 members in ECOSOC, two from each of LO (Swedish Confederation of Trade Unions), SACO (Swedish Confederation of Professional Associations), and TCO (Swedish Confederation of Professional Employees), all together representing 4 million Swedes.

47. Jacobsson, Laegreid, and Pedersen, *Europeanization and Transnational States.*

48. Swedish Government Bill 1997/98:70.

49. *Dagens Nyheter*, January 4, 2005.

50. The Northern Dimension is recognized as a regional program by the EU Commission; see: http://europa.eu.int/comm/external_relations/north_dim/.

51. *Svenska Dagbladet*, June 21, 2001; Östergård 1995, in Holmström, "Alliansfriheten-livboj eller kvarnsten?" p. 7; cf. Jakobson, "Sverige Övervärderar sin roll"; confirmed in interviews in Brussels, 2001. In Sweden's position paper for the 2000 IGC, enlargement, and all areas affecting the prospective enlargement, consumed more than half of the paper's content. "Enlargement is important, but . . . the Swedes tend at times to forget other

practical issues" (EU official quoted in *Svenska Dagbladet,* June 21, 2001).

52. *Dagens Nyheter,* April 26, 2005.

53. EU Council Decision 2000:527:EC, 2001:264.

54. See Judgment of the Court of Justice Court of First Instance, C-353:99. The Court of Justice held that Council Decision 93/731 neither requires nor prohibits the Council from considering granting partial access to documents.

55. *Interinstitutional Agreement of 20 November, 2002 between the European Parliament and the Council concerning access by the European Parliament to sensitive information of the Council in the field of security and defense policy.*

56. See, for example, Von Sydow, "Defense Minister Speech at the European Symposium on Public Opinion and European Security."

57. See, for example, Mjoset, "The Nordic Model Never Existed"; Cramér, *Neutralitet och Europeisk Integration*; Ingebritsen, "The Scandinavian Way and Its Legacy in Europe."

58. Foreign Minister Lindh in the EU Advisory Committee, November 12 and December 3, 1999. Previous decisions, declarations, and commitments (the Petersberg compromise and Cologne Declaration) made a revocation of EU declarations or a formal Swedish opt-out both politically and legally unfeasible; see Eliasson, "Traditions, Identity, and Security."

59. Personal interview, Brussels, 2003.

60. EU Advisory Committee, November 12, 1999.

61. Compare Parliamentary Defense Committee's public hearing, 2000/01:FoU6.

62. News Telegram in *Dagens Nyheter*, January 21, 2005.

63. See Ingebritsen, *The Nordic States and European Unity*, p. 233.

64. Compare Sverdrup, "Compliance and Conflict Management in the European Union."

65. For example, Ingebritsen, "The Scandinavian Way."

66. *Financial Times*, April 15, 2005; *Dagens Nyheter*, March 10, 2005.

67. Anderson, "Sweden: Retreat from Exceptionalism."

68. Einhorn, "Just Enough ('Lagom') Europeanization."

69. OECD 2000, in *The Economist*, "Mix and Match."

70. *The Economist*, "Krybbe to Grav."

71. For example, there are Council directives on minimum standards for the temporary protection of persons displaced by economic, political, or environmental disasters (2001), establishing minimum standards on asylum applications (2003) that require member states to provide health care, accommodation, schooling, and access to the labor market; and the incorporation of parts of the Dublin Convention into the EU legal *aquis* (2003).

72. Von Sydow, "New Swedish Policy." Sweden also promoted further trade liberalization, extended trade agreements with developing countries, and the expansion of the WTO.

14

Finland:
Consensual Politics,
Effective Implementation

Jussi Kinnunen and Tapio Raunio

WHEN ANALYZING FINLAND'S INTEGRATION policy, one is struck by the speed with which the political leadership turned its gaze from the east to the west. Within less than a decade Finland changed its status from a nonaligned country with close political relations with the Soviet Union to a fully committed member of the European Union. It was not enough that Finland just joined the EU: the successive Finnish governments have decided that Finland's place is in the inner core of the Union.

Indeed, Finnish European policy has been consistently pro-integrationist. In membership negotiations the center-right government led by Prime Minister Esko Aho of the Center Party, only 36 percent of whose supporters voted for membership in the referendum held in October 1994,[1] accepted the Maastricht Treaty without any major opt-out clauses or policy exemptions.[2] Since joining the Union, all main Finnish parties have pursued pro-integrationist policies, despite the fact that the electorate is less convinced about the benefits of integration than citizens across the EU as a whole.[3] In the three Intergovernmental Conferences (IGC) held since joining the EU, Finland has supported further transfers of competencies from the national level to the Union, together with the extension of majority voting in the Council and a stronger role for the Commission and the European Parliament (EP). Moreover, Finland joined the third stage of the Economic and Monetary Union (EMU) among the first countries—thus becoming the only Nordic country to so far adopt the single currency—and has played an active role in the further development of the Common Foreign and Security Policy (CFSP). Not even the new pace taken by the deepening defense dimension in the Convention and in the subsequent IGC made the Finnish leadership too hesitant.[4] The policy of nonalignment has been compromised, or even abandoned altogether, in the face of the advancement of the common EU defense policy. Finland can therefore with good reason be categorized as an "integrationist" member state.[5]

This chapter examines the adjustment of Finnish administration to EU membership from the perspective of implementation of European laws. The next section analyzes the impact of European integration in Finland, focusing on how EU membership has changed Finland's position in Europe and contributed to "parliamentarizing" the domestic political system. The third section maps out the basic features of the domestic coordination system for EU policies, emphasizing the way in which national positions are based on broad consensus between both the political parties and among the state institutions. Using the Habitats Directive as a case study, we then examine the implementation of EU legislation in Finland, arguing that the implementation of European legislation is a relatively noncontroversial issue in Finnish politics, with Finland possessing one of the best implementation records among the EU member states. The final section looks ahead to the future, arguing that Finland's EU policy is unlikely to experience any major changes.

■ How and in What Ways Does the EU Influence Finland's Policies?

Membership in the Union has obviously affected basically all policy sectors and political institutions in Finland, but arguably the most important change concerns Finland's role in Europe's political architecture.[6]

The significance of EU membership for Finland should not be underestimated, for it constituted a key element in the "process of wholesale re-identification on the international stage."[7] While the pro-EU camp argued, before the membership referendum held in 1994, that by joining the Union Finland would merely be maintaining or consolidating its place among Western European countries, there is little doubt that especially among foreign observers the "Western" identity of Finland was far less clear. After all, Finland shares a long border with Russia and had, during the Cold War, very close economic and political relations with the Soviet Union.

Indeed, Finland's integration policy cannot be explained without attention being paid to past experiences and the way they are interpreted.[8] The early history of Finland gave cause for a state-centric tradition in Finnish political culture. Nationalism, and the wars with the Soviet Union in 1939–1940 and 1941–1944, reinforced this tradition. State-centrism means in the Finnish case that values connected with the state, such as sovereignty and territoriality, have traditionally been strongly emphasized. This has led to a very limited position being given to alternative political communities, such as the one of a united Europe or the development of a strong regional level, in Finnish political thinking. Finnish political culture stems from Lutheran political concepts, which means that a connection to the cultural origins of European unification—to the Catholic political tradition—is very weak. Finland has, consequently, lacked any visible or politically influential federalist political movements or movements that would have worked strongly in favor of European political unification. In the Cold War era, this state-centric identity was furthermore emphasized due to the international situation and to two more attributes of Finnish identity achieving their legitimacy from it. These were a small-state tradition and the role of Finland as a borderland. Both of these traditions underlined Finland's position as an endangered territory. They have had far-reaching consequences for Finnish policy even after the Cold War era.

The role of Finland as a borderland became accentuated in the tense international situation of the Cold War, where the borderline between the two political blocs went along Finland's border with the Soviet Union. Finland was thus very concretely faced with the challenge of balancing between the two blocs in a difficult international situation, which, in the worst case, could have turned the Finnish territory into a battlefield. Another tenet that grew out of postwar political thinking in Finland was that of a small state. As a small actor—at least when assessed in terms of the qualities decisive in international politics—Finland was seen to be continuously in danger. By the early 1990s the Finns had thus become used to living, at least for five decades, in a world where state sovereignty and security formed the uncontested starting point for political life. When participation in European integration started to be discussed in Finland, the national political identity was very much that of a small state situated in the fringes of Europe and looking for protection for its territory and people.[9] A decade later, Finland is firmly anchored in the inner core of the Union. Geographically, Finland is obviously still in the periphery of Europe, but politically Finland's situation has changed dramatically since the Cold War ended.

The second major change concerns the domestic balance of power. Membership in the European Union has acted as an important exogenous factor in "parliamentarizing" decisionmaking in Finland. Constitutional amendments enacted since the early 1990s have strengthened the role of the government and the Eduskunta (parliament) in both domestic and foreign policy decisionmaking. EU matters belong almost exclusively to the jurisdiction of the cabinet. The government and particularly the prime minister are firmly in the driving seat, with the president (at least so far) intervening mainly when questions of utmost importance from the point of view of Finland's foreign policy are on the agenda.

The constitutional and political powers of the president have been reduced to such an extent that Finland fits rather uneasily into the category of semipresidential systems. The president directs foreign policy, but does so together with the government and through the government's ministerial committee. The president now focuses on promoting foreign trade and on what is left (and that is not much) of so-called traditional foreign policy matters, that is, Finland's relations with countries outside of the EU that are not handled via the Union. Nevertheless, the traditional authority enjoyed by the president in Finnish political culture should not be underestimated. The public seems to favor strong personalized leadership, and thereby the system of dual executive enshrined in the constitution may result in tensions between the government and the president, particularly under conditions of divided government when the president and the prime minister represent different parties.

■ How and in What Ways Does Finland Influence the EU?

When examining the system established for coordinating EU policies, two aspects are particularly noteworthy: the attempt for national consensus in domestically salient issues, and the relatively strong role accorded to the national parliament, the Eduskunta.

The priority of the national EU coordination system is to manufacture national unanimity or at least broad consensus, which can arguably be translated into additional influence in the Council.[10] While the overall aim "is to speak with one voice on all levels of decision shaping in Brussels," the importance attached to achieving such consistency varies between policy areas and individual legislative initiatives.[11] When a proposal is perceived as having significant national repercussions, the matter is debated at the highest political level in the Cabinet EU Committee, a ministerial committee for European matters where all the government parties are represented. Overall, the coordination system is based on wide consultation among both public and private actors, including the parliament and the relevant interest groups. Interviewed civil servants have emphasized that the manufacturing of national consensus combined with a constructive approach to negotiations at the EU level are the main strengths of the national EU coordination system.[12] The search for consensus prevails also in the other two Nordic EU countries, where the overriding goal of national EU policy coordination seems to be "to create decisions and policies reflecting national consensus or broad compromises. National unity in European affairs, including during the various stages of the decision-making process, is considered vital to the achievement of the best possible policy outcomes."[13]

While EU membership has necessitated the establishment of new interministerial coordinating structures, the overall organization of the state bureaucracy has remained intact. Table 14.1 shows the main stages and actors involved in the formulation of national EU policy. The Cabinet EU Committee was established in 1995.[14] It has become an important forum for formulating national policy in salient integration matters.[15]

The Foreign Ministry was initially given the overall responsibility for handling European matters. The ministry was in charge of coordinating ministerial EU policies and was the home of the EU Secretariat. However, this arrangement met a lot of criticism, especially from the individual ministries. Moving the responsibility for European issues from the Foreign Office to the Prime Minister's Office was argued to enhance the capacity of the whole state bureaucracy and the parliament to process EU issues. More important, this was seen to tie EU politics more closely to its proper context of domestic policymaking. The EU Secretariat was therefore transferred to the Prime Minister's Office in the summer of 2000. The Prime Minister's Office had meanwhile already carved out a prominent role for itself, in particular in relation to the EU summits.

The prime minister usually represents Finland in the European Council. The Eduskunta's Constitutional Law Committee decided prior to membership that the prime minister should represent Finland in the EU summits. However, President Martti Ahtisaari (Social Democrats) refused to accept this interpretation. In May 1995 Prime Minister Paavo Lipponen announced a statement, formulated jointly with the president's office, according to which the PM will always attend the summits and the president will attend them whenever she/he chooses. The current

Table 14.1   The Processing of EU Legislation in Finland

EU Level	Finland
1. Commission starts to draft a legislative proposal	1. The responsible ministry begins to process the matter
2. Commission enters into negotiations with interest groups and national ministries	2. The ministry negotiates with the Commission and formulates the initial national position
3. Commission publishes the initiative	3. The ministry decides the initial Finnish position. Eduskunta is informed of the matter
4. Commission sends the initiative to the Council	4. Interministerial negotiations determine possible changes to Finland's position
5. The European Parliament starts to process the matter	5. The Permanent Representation presents the Finnish position to Finnish MEPs
6. Council working groups debate the initiative	6. The responsible civil servant takes part in the Council working group and reports back to her/his superiors. The Grand Committee is informed of the matter and it can present its views on the proposal
7. COREPER processes the matter	7. The permanent representative, the minister, and the civil servant fine-tune the national position
8. The proposal is put on the agenda of the Council	8. Cabinet EU Committee decides on the negotiating mandate of the minister. The minister appears before the Grand Committee prior to the Council meeting

Source: Adapted from Mattila, "Valtioneuvosto," p. 139.

president, Tarja Halonen (Social Democrats), has continued the line of her predecessor through taking part in most of the European Council meetings. The dispute is important from the point of view of "parliamentarism" as the president is not accountable to the Eduskunta.[16]

The government is represented in the EU through Finland's Permanent Representation, which has performed a crucial role during the first decade of membership. The Permanent Representation not only participates in the work of the Committee of Permanent Representatives (COREPER), but is also an important source of information to Finnish civil servants, ministers, and members of the European Parliament (MEPs). The staffing levels of the Finnish Permanent Representation are relatively high for a small country and have increased as required. Staff levels have been 122 in 2000,[17] 94 in 2002, and during Finland's presidency of the EU (July–December 1999) there were some 130 staff attached to the representation. The staff includes national experts who represent Finland rather than the different branches of administration from which they come.

While it has been argued that European integration has contributed to the "deparliamentarization" of European politics, in Finland European integration has actually strengthened parliamentary government in two ways: through facilitating the move from a semipresidential system toward a more government-led polity, and by arguably improving the legislature's overall scrutiny of the executive, domestic legislation included.[18] While the Eduskunta cannot be categorized as a strong policy-influencing legislature, it has subjected the government to relatively tight scrutiny in EU matters. In fact, of the 25 member-state legislatures, the Eduskunta is probably the most effective in controlling its government in EU decisionmaking. The two main committees responsible for European questions are the Grand Committee and the Foreign Affairs Committee, the former handling first- (EC) and third-pillar (Justice and Home Affairs [JHA]) issues and the latter second-pillar (CFSP) matters.[19]

Particularly noteworthy has been the lack of conflict, or of even tension, between the government and the Eduskunta on the one hand, and between the government and the opposition on the other. The government is usually criticized by individual MPs from both opposition and government parties rather than by a united opposition or even by unitary party groups. Committee scrutiny of European matters in the Eduskunta differs in one important respect from the processing of domestic legislation: the government-opposition dimension does not play the only significant role in either the Grand Committee or in specialized committees. Granting the opposition a larger role in European matters facilitates broad backing for governmental action at the European level. As the opposition parties are involved in forming national policies, they also simultaneously share the responsibility for the outcome. This reduces on the one hand the likelihood of the main features of Finnish integration policy being altered after each parliamentary election, while on the other hand further lowers the probability of EU issues featured in domestic party competition.[20]

Having sketched the way in which national EU policy is formulated, the next section focuses on compliance with European laws through a case study of the Habitats Directive.

■ How Does Finland Implement and Comply with EU Policies?

The Habitats Directive

This section examines the implementation and adoption of Council Directive (92/43/EEC) on the conservation of natural habitats of wild flora and fauna in Finland.[21] Implementation literature often focuses on problems of implementation and therefore the picture is perhaps overly pessimistic. Political science also focuses on the use of power and conflicts, which further contributes to the bias. The main questions usually are (1) what happened, (2) why did it happen, (3) could there have been an alternative course of events, and (4) what can we learn from this.[22] Here the focus is on misfits in the creation of the Natura 2000 network of sites and, briefly, on the flying squirrels as a special case. Misfits refer to gaps in implementation of the Habitats Directive. These two cases are good examples not only of misfits but also of how solutions were found to these problems. The aim of the Habitats Directive is to protect certain animals and plants in addition to the election of habitat types. The directive required the creation of the so-called Natura 2000 network of sites by June 1998. Natura 2000 includes both Special Protected Areas (SPAs) below the Wild Bird Directive as well as sites proposed by the member states below the Habitats Directive. Finland has under the Birds Directive 452 sites covering 28,373 km² and 1,665 sites covering 47,932 km² under the Habitats Directive (Natura Barometer as of October 16, 2003). The selection of the areas and implementation of the program resulted in the worst environmental conflict in Finland's history.[23]

The member states have different strategies in both the creation and implementation of EU policies. Börzel divides member states' strategies into three categories (1) *pace-setting*, that is, pushing policies at the EU level according to the member state's policy preferences and taking into account the implementation costs; (2) *foot-dragging*, that is, blocking or delaying costly policies in order to prevent them or to receive compensation; and (3) *fence-sitting*, that is, forming tactical coalitions in negotiations with both previously mentioned groups in order to find the best outcome from the national point of view. In environmental matters, Finland is often regarded as a pacesetter, together with Austria, Sweden, Denmark, the Netherlands, and Germany.[24] The citizens' attitudes are strongly favorable to environmental protection and they also act accordingly. Moreover, in international comparisons Finland has had high rankings for sustainable environmental policy. In the 2002

Environmental Sustainability Index (ESI) of the World Economic Forum, Finland was at the top.[25] This was especially because Finland has succeeded in three key areas of environmental protection—minimizing air and water pollution, developing high institutional capacity to address environmental problems, and producing quite low levels of greenhouse gases.

Environmental concerns and civil activism are channeled both through the party system and interest groups. The Green League was established in the early 1980s. It has stabilized its position in the Finnish party system to the point that it was in government from 1995 to 2002. The Green League held the post of the minister of environment while in government, whereas the party with closest ties to the landowners, the Center Party, was in opposition. This is an important background factor for understanding the Natura 2000 conflict. It is also noteworthy that the citizens' pro-environment stance together with the establishment of the Green League has caused the other parties to "turn green." Moreover, all major international environmental organizations, such as Greenpeace, BirdWatch, and the World Wildlife Fund, have branches in Finland. In addition, there are domestic organizations such as Finland's Nature Association (SLL), with new ones created—sometimes more radical, as in the case of flying squirrels—if a need should arise.

Even if Finland in many respects qualifies as a pacesetter, interest groups have repeatedly criticized the Finnish government for fence-sitting in, for example, the creation of novel EU legislation on waste. Also, a glance at the Commission's nonconformity statistics (see Table 14.2 on p. 283) would suggest that Finland is rather a fence-sitter than a pacesetter. Indeed, there are more nonconformity cases to be found for Finland than for the other pacesetters. However, horizontally Finland has performed well and there has been only one bad application case. Pacesetters are economically sound industrial states that have strict and highly differentiated legal regulations as well as institutional means for both implementation and monitoring. Finland is a strongly regulative country like Germany and similarly demonstrates an opposite problem-solving philosophy to the reactive model of, say, Great Britain.[26] Moreover, the institutional capacity to handle environmental problems was developed at a relatively early stage. The Ministry of Environment was founded in 1983. Most environmental legislation also originates from the 1960s and 1970s. So, the Finnish government had in place both legislative means as well as administrative tools for addressing environmental concerns. However, in institutional games the Ministry of Environment has seldom held the strongest hand.

Figure 14.1   Finland's Environmental Administration

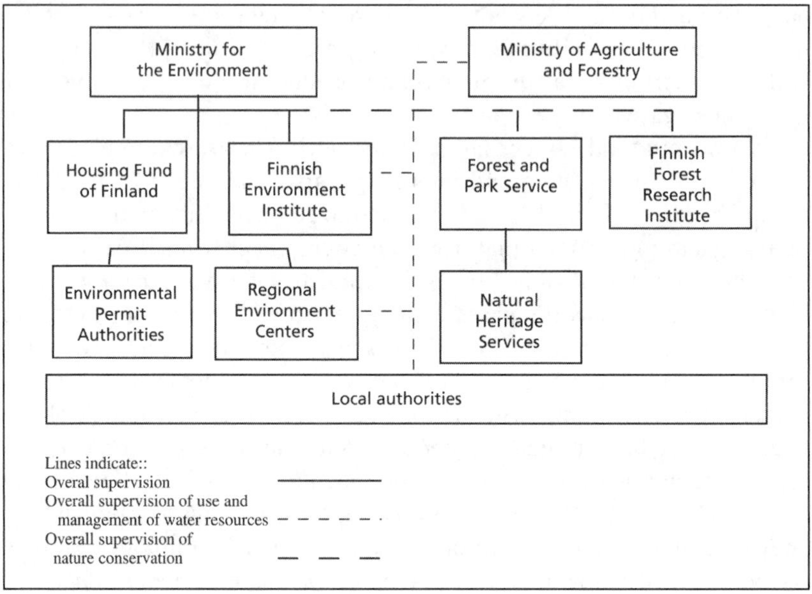

Source: http://www.vyh.fi/.

When Finland joined the EU in 1995, the country already had a strong legal background in environmental legislation.[27] In other words, the old environmental legislation was amended to meet the EU's demands. Finland's Nature Conservation Act (1096/1996, amended 492/1997 and 371/1999) does meet most conservation needs and matches the demands of the EU Bird and Habitat Directives. The act has a wide range of measures that can be used in nature conservation. It also includes the legislation necessary for the development of the Natura 2000 areas and their surroundings. Moreover, it contains regulations for public information and participation during preparation. The Nature Protection Decree (169/1997) lists protected species, threatened species, species in need of special protection, and species that need protection under the EU Habitats Directive.

Reflecting the unitary political system of the country, the role of central authorities is pivotal also in the environment sector (Figure 14.1). The administrative domain of the Ministry of Environment (MoE) is extremely horizontal. It is responsible for making sure that environmental aspects are given proper consideration in international cooperation as well as in the domestic arena at all levels of government and in Finnish society as a whole. It is responsible for policy preparation, strategic planning, leadership, and international cooperation for environment and housing policies. It is also responsible for relevant legislation and budgeting. Moreover, the Ministry of Agriculture and Forestry (MAF) is also involved in environmental administration. MAF supervises the use and management of water resources. It is also responsible (in part) to the Forest and Park Service.

The Regional Environment Centers' (RECs) (state's regional offices) main tasks include environmental protection and supervision of land use and construction. The centers gather and provide information on pollution and on the state of the environment. The Ministry of Agriculture and Forestry supervises work on the use and management of water resources. The Environmental Permit Authorities give permits for issues with major environmental impacts and also deal with most water pollution compensation claims. Environmental permits are required for actions that have major environmental impacts, take place under the Water Act, or which have been instigated or supported by the RECs. The Finnish Environment Institute, in turn, is the national center for environmental information, research, and development. Its main functions include collection and providing of data on the environment, environmental trends, and analysis of different phenomena. The Housing Fund of Finland is responsible for the financing of the state housing subsidies scheme (ARAVA) and other state-financed schemes including housing renovation grants, for example. The Forest and Park Service administers most state-owned nature conservation areas, other protected areas, wilderness areas, and outdoor recreational areas. It is responsible for administrative decisionmaking concerning these areas and the national monitoring and protection of many threatened species. The Finnish Forest Research Institute manages certain conservation areas that belong to its own network of research sites. The Finnish Oil Compensation Fund operates in connection with the Ministry of Environment and it is responsible for oil-combating equipment, maintenance of the capacity, and the costs for combating oil damages. Municipal local authorities in turn are responsible for implementation of the environmental policies at the local level.

Without doubt one can say that Natura 2000 has constituted the biggest environmental conflict in Finland during EU membership. Although the emphasis was on state-owned land, there were a lot of private land and water-area owners that were affected by the program. The extent of the program, poor dissemination of information, not hearing the landowners, and confusion about the compensation were the key points of the conflict, but there were also other underlying factors. Natura 2000 was the first project after the EU accession where people could express their feelings about the EU. In other words, Natura 2000 was a "lightning rod" for frustration with the EU. However, there was also real concern for the people in rural areas about Agenda 2000 and agricultural reform, eastern enlargement, and their impact on Finland. Natura 2000 could be seen as a key piece in a larger bundle of concerns.

The tight timetable and poor dissemination of information gave the landowners the impression that the whole process was unjust. Therefore, the hearing round in 1997 generated over 14,000 notifications and 1,000 statements. Some farmers even went to a hunger strike for awhile in protest against the Natura program. They felt the preparations were made in secret and that they were not heard. Nonetheless, the Ministry of Environment learned to improve their information strategy. At the same time, the Commission put pressure on Finland for compliance with the directive.[28]

There were three broad phases in the conflict. First, there was a *silent phase* of preparation (1994–1997). During this phase preparations took place in silence. Second, around the time of the publication of the Natura 2000 proposal, the conflict reached the *high-conflict phase* (1997–2002), which was highlighted by a storm of complaints from landowners. The handling of the complaints slowed down the implementation process. The misfits in implementation caused the Commission to send Finland a reasoned opinion in January 1998 (see Table 14.2). Action from the Commission resulted in more concrete action in Finland, with the government approving the Finnish proposal in August 1998.

But the real problem for the government was the court cases: how to inform the Commission? Should the disputed areas be included in information about the proposal—or excluded? Finland's final proposal could only be presented after all the complaints had been handled. Moreover, the court decisions created winner-loser situations that are hardly optimal ways to settle conflicts in the long run. About 1,600 cases reached the Finnish Supreme Administrative Court, but only some 2,300 hectares were taken off the Natura program. At the same time environmentalists got over 10 times more areas back into the protection program. After the court cases had ended, the number of SPAs rose rapidly (Table 14.2). Finland also got condemnation from the European Court of Justice (ECJ) in May 2003 regarding the Birds Directive. The misfit is caused by the same problem. The Finnish government informed the

Table 14.2   Progress in the Implementation of the Directives

Newsletter		SPAs Birds Directive			Habitats Directive		
Issue	Year	Sites	Area km²	% of land	Sites	Area km²	% of land
Dec.	1996	15	967		370	24,726	
Oct.	1997	15	967		370	24,726	
Sept.	1998	15	967		415	25,599	
Feb.	1999	439	27,500	8.1	1,380	47,500[a]	13.9
Nov.	1999	440	27,500	8.1	1,381	47,154	13.9
Dec.	2000	451	27,500	8.1	1,381	47,154	13.9
April	2001	451	27,500	8.1	1,381	47,154	13.9
May	2002	451	27,500	8.1	1,381	47,154	13.9
Dec.	2003	452	28,373	8.4	1,665	47,932	14.2

Source: EU Commission, Natura Newsletters, 1996–2004.
Note: a. Estimated.

Commission that the final proposal for the SPA could not be given before the court had given judgments on all the complaints. That was why Finland proposed only 15 sites at first. The Commission had little understanding for the Finnish justice system. From the Finnish point of view, being a strongly legalistic country matters, the complaints needed to be addressed in the proper legal manner in order to get legitimacy for the decisions.[29]

Third, during the *subsiding conflict phase,* the conflict slowly melted away (2002–present) as information flows were improved and many of the other stressful concerns, such as scares of the eastern enlargement, were lifted. Also, questions relating to compensation were solved: the Environmental Administration can offer compensation or purchase areas that need protection. However, the landowners are advised not to accept these offers—and for a good reason. If the property is taken without the consent of the landowner, the administration is forced to use independent outside evaluators. As a rule the compensations have been substantially better. Nonetheless, the last chapter of the conflict is pending. There are continuing legal battles over the use of Natura areas since the law allows use of the land unless species or nature is not harmed.

Another conflict in progress is that the Central Union of Agricultural Producers and Forest Owners (MTK) wrote the Commission (May 2004) of demands after losing its court battle in the Supreme Administrative Court in April 2004. They wanted to stop the Commission from handling the Finnish Natura 2000 program that deals with the Boreal Belt. The MTK suspected foul play in the way the areas for the national proposal were selected. The mistrust was based on the fact that neither the landowners nor MTK received, in electronic form, the documents the Finnish government provided to the Commission for decisionmaking about these areas. The Commission approved the Finnish proposal in January 2005, but the MTK and some landowners have asked the ECJ to overturn the Commission's decision.

Natura 2000 was also a large issue for the environmental groups and their legitimacy. Environmental interest groups supported the Ministry of Environment against other ministries but also confronted the MoE on occasion. Environmental organizations also kept the Commission up to date on events in Finland. Pressure provided by the Commission was pivotal for the timetable in which Natura advanced. On birds, the Commission took Finland to the ECJ and won. Moreover, the Commission also gave guidance to the national level. From interest groups' point of view, the Habitats forum was important on the EU level because all the significant groups were involved when areas were examined.

Domestically, the biggest controversies related to the Natura were solved within the government with little or no say from the opposition. Within the government, the Green League and the conservative National Coalition formed the opposite poles, with other parties divided between these two extremes. Decisive for the creation of the Natura 2000 network was the stance taken by the Social Democrats, the leading party in the government, and Prime Minister Lipponen especially. His viewpoint was that the Natura network is an EU matter that must be handled according to Finland's "pro-Europe" position. The EU also provided a good card in the domestic games. In other words, the EU defines action, and the Finnish government abides. Finally, the media probably had a significant role in the acceptance of the Natura program. The largest newspaper in Finland, *Helsingin Sanomat*, was clearly in favor of it. Opposition came mainly from regional newspapers such as *Lapin Kansa, Ilkka, Karjalainen,* and *Savon Sanomat*. The opposition got quite a lot of media coverage, but the outcome of Natura 2000 was pretty much according to the plans of the MoE and the environmentalists.

The Flying Squirrels

In addition to the Natura 2000 program, the protection of the flying squirrels has been one of the most controversial EU issues during membership. The flying squirrels are very strictly protected (Nature Directive Supplements II and 4a), which means that no stopping or rest-ing places of the squirrels can be destroyed. One aspect of the controversy is that no one knows the extent of the population of flying squirrels. There is a mapping project in progress that should be finished by 2006. If population is much larger than previously estimated, one can expect a rush in the offices of permits giving authority for derogations. Changing the Commission's stand on the protection of flying squirrels and moving it from the 4a list seems quite difficult, however. The controversy takes place at all available arenas from the local to European, and has continued for many years. Particularly, two areas have been problematic: construction of the E-18 road from Turku to Helsinki and the area of Konikallio in Forssa. However, similar problems have surfaced in other parts of Finland: the regional environment and forest centers have estimated that there are about 650 cases, of which approximately 95 percent have to do with forestry. In other words, cases like Konikallio and the E-18 are in the minority.

Apart from political conflicts, there are also legal battles. The EU has demanded changes to both Finnish environmental protection and forest law in regard to the flying squirrel in the form of a reasoned opinion. The reasoned opinion originated from the E-18 case. The misfit in this case arises from the fact that the administration on the national level perhaps did not originally realize how strict the EU legislation is. The protection law has since been reformed. At the preparation stage, the Ministry of Agriculture did not allow an environmental group (SLL) participation in preparation, except in the form of a statement, which is unusual. During summer 2004 changes to the law were debated in the Eduskunta. The final conflict dealt with compensations given to the landowners. Starting from July 1, 2004, the landowners got a right for compensation in cases where protecting the flying squirrels causes "significant nuisance."

The case of Konikallio is the oldest controversy concerning flying squirrels. It is a dispute over a mining and forestry project. The project generated wide local opposition and put local people in opposite camps. Environmentalists and landowners have taken the issue to court and both sides have interest groups in their support. The Regional Environment Center decided that 4.5 hectares is a sufficient protection area for the flying squirrel in that particular forest. Nonetheless, the 4.5 hectares was not sufficient for the local residents and the environmentalists. They brought in their own experts and complained about the calculations done by the authorities. This was a battle of experts, environmentalists against the environmental authorities. A forest company wanted to cut down the trees and there were also plans for mining. At one point, one of the environmental interest groups paid the forest-cutting contractor *not* to cut the trees. The MoE also made an offer to purchase the property, but at this point the conflict had become a matter of principle. The issue was taken to court. The administrative court decided that mining was against the law and the decision of the Regional Environment Center was overruled. Also, the Supreme Administrative Court ruled that cutting the trees must stop. In the case of the E-18 road, the Supreme Administrative Court ruled against the environmentalists: the road was built. However, many changes were made to the original plans and a good number of other issues were raised in the process—relating, for example, to hearings of the participants.

To summarize, Finland has had trouble in implementing the Habitats Directive. Both cases, the Natura 2000 and the protection of the flying squirrels, represent classic multilevel governance cases where issues concern the local, the regional, the national, and the EU levels. But it should be remembered that the case studies examined in this section are quite exceptional, particularly in terms of their level of conflict (and the ensuing media coverage). As will be argued in the next section, overall compliance with EU legislation is a noncontroversial issue in Finnish politics.

■ Complying with EU Policies and Legislation

There are three criteria that contribute to the ability to implement laws: (1) the technical quality of the laws, (2) the ability of the administration and dispute-settling organs to carry out their tasks, and (3) the willingness and capability of the Finnish subjects to obey the legislation. Concerning the first criterion, interviews with Finnish authorities testify that the technical quality of legislation has sometimes suffered from haste in preparation (in those cases that have space for national features) caused by the tight timetables on the EU level. Overall the quality of legislation seems to be good, however. Civil servants responsible for preparations are highly skilled and trained to deal with EU matters.

For the second criterion, as shown by the Commission's statistics, public authorities in Finland take implementation of EU legislation seriously. There are several explanations for this.

• The good implementation record reflects a legalistic political culture where compliance with norms and rules (and sticking to agreed timetables) is of the highest importance also in the context of purely domestic issues. To put it simply, pragmatic Finnish authorities are used to getting things done without additional fuss according to agreed timetables.

• During Finland's EU membership the government has invested a substantial amount of resources in training civil servants to better cope with EU issues. It is probable that this also contributes to the good implementation record.

• Finland is a unitary country with no directly elected or otherwise politically significant regional bodies. Hence there is very little formal need to involve subnational actors in the implementation process. There are areas such as waste administration, however, that form an exception to this pattern.

For the third criterion, implementation of EU legislation seems to be a relatively nonproblematic issue in Finnish politics. It is difficult to get horizontal information on overall implementation because most studies concern particular sectors. It also seems that instead of implementation studies, more is written nowadays on impacts, that is, evaluation studies. EU legislation is implemented according to the same procedures that are used for implementing domestic legislation. Sometimes it is said that Finns are more papal than the pope and follow legislation to the dot. To be sure, and as the case studies in the previous sections illustrated, occasionally conflicts do emerge both horizontally between ministries and interest groups at the national level and vertically between the national level and the municipalities. However, it is rare for the implementation of an EU law to attract attention in the media or to result in serious debates in the Eduskunta. Much obviously depends on the salience of the issues. But, even when the legislation is domestically important, the main debates—in the state administration and in the parliament—occur during the processing of the legislative initiative, not during the implementation phase.

Future Trends and Prospects

Looking forward, it is unlikely that the overall direction of Finnish integration policy will change. Finland has often been characterized as a "model student" of the EU that is willing to promote common goals and respects common rules and obligations. This is also evident in compliance with EU legislation. Pragmatism and adaptation have indeed been the leading qualities of Finnish integration policy. As a small country seeking economic stability and protection for its territory, Finland has consistently supported the building of a strong Union while simultaneously trying to ensure that the rules by which the EU operates facilitate equal treatment between large and small member states. Its status and history as a small state has also helped Finland to adapt itself to political integration, as Finland is used to conciliating its interests with those of other states.

National European policy can hence be characterized as flexible and constructive and has sought to consolidate Finland's position in the inner core of the Union. Successive governments have constantly underlined the importance of being present where decisions concerning Finland are taken. This argument was used extensively during the referendum campaign, in relation to joining the EMU, and in the readiness to support the further development of CFSP. Underlying this stance is a strong conviction that a strong and efficient Union can best protect the rights and interests of smaller member states, as intergovernmental processes tend to favor larger member states. The Finnish approach is thus in line with Soetendorp and Hanf, who argue that "small states in particular can reap advantages from membership of the EU. Here they can exert more influence and achieve more of what they seek than if they were forced to compete on their own in the 'international political market' with the larger powers. The formal institutions and procedures of the EU, in this view, provide both opportunities for being heard and protection against being overwhelmed by the larger members."[30]

■ Notes

1. The referendum on EU membership was held on October 16, 1994. A majority of 56.9 percent voted in favor and 43.1 percent against membership. Turnout was 74 percent.

2. By far the most difficult issue in the membership negotiations was making Finnish agriculture compatible with the requirements of the Common Agricultural Policy (CAP). The other policy sectors did not receive similar attention from the politicians or from the parties. Defense and foreign policy were important questions, but while they featured prominently in the domestic debate, they did not seem to cause problems in the negotiations, as Finland had agreed to all aspects of the CFSP (Arter, "The EU Referendum"). It is fair to claim that Finland was not a difficult negotiating partner. The government was not ready to jeopardize the positive outcome of the negotiations by being too ambitious or by tabling any specific demands (excluding agriculture) that could have been opposed by the other member states or the Commission.

3. The only Euro-skeptical party that has won seats in the national parlia-

ment is the center-right/populist True Finns. In the latest election, held in 2003, it captured 1.5 percent of the seats (Raunio, "Hesitant Voters, Committed Elite").

4. In the IGC in autumn 2003, Finland did express concerns about the wording of the mutual assistance clause, with the government being against an automatic obligation to provide military assistance. Similarly, the government aimed at preventing the emergence of a separate core in defense issues, arguing instead for a solution that would be acceptable to all member states. Despite such minor reservations, the government is committed to the further development of EU security policy.

5. See Raunio and Tiilikainen, *Finland in the European Union*, and Stubb, Kaila, and Ranta, "Finland: An Integrationist Member State."

6. This section draws on Raunio and Tiilikainen, *Finland in the European Union*, pp. 146–157.

7. Arter, "Small State Influence Within the EU," p. 691.

8. See Tiilikainen, *Europe and Finland.*

9. Ibid.

10. However, it is very difficult to examine whether such national unity does indeed lead to more bargaining power at the EU level. While there are anecdotal suggestions (see for example "Finland's Premier Gives Voice to the Fears of EU's Small States," *Financial Times*, September 9, 2003) that Finland has performed rather well in negotiations in Brussels, and while Finland has, under the right circumstances, been able to introduce its own items to the EU agenda (e.g., the Swedish-Finnish initiative on crisis management included in the Amsterdam Treaty and the Northern Dimension Initiative), this does not necessarily imply overall effectiveness in negotiations.

11. Stubb, Kaila, and Ranta, "Finland: An Integrationist Member State," p. 306.

12. See Kinnunen, "Finland: A Highly Institutionalized System," and Rehn, "Can a Neutralist Nordic Become a Core European?"

13. Damgaard, "Conclusion," p. 168.

14. Government work is coordinated through its statutory ministerial committees, all of which are chaired by the prime minister—the other three being the Cabinet Foreign and Security Policy Committee, the Cabinet Finance Committee, and the Cabinet Economic Policy Committee. They prepare decisions that are then given the final seal of approval by the plenary session of the whole cabinet.

15. See Kinnunen, "Finland: A Highly Institutionalized System," and Raunio and Tiilikainen, *Finland in the European Union*, pp. 96–112. Within the government a new portfolio of a minister of European affairs was created following the March 1995 elections. The minister was responsible for coordinating government's EU policy, but the experiment did not work as planned as individual ministries dominated decisionmaking within their jurisdictions. There has therefore been no actual minister of European affairs in the governments formed after the 1999 elections.

16. In parallel with the process of applying for EU membership, Finland was undergoing a period of rapid constitutional change that transformed it from a president-led polity to a parliamentary democracy. Under the old constitution,

EU matters would have been the prerogative of the president. Under the new constitution, in force since 2000, the president is directly elected and has the leadership in foreign affairs, but domestic and EU matters fall under the competence of the government (and the parliament). See Nousiainen, "From Semi-Presidentialism to Parliamentary Government"; Raunio and Tiilikainen, *Finland in the European Union*, pp. 96–112.

17. Mattila, "Valtioneuvosto."

18. See Raunio and Wiberg, "Building Elite Consensus" and "Parliamentarizing Foreign Policy Decision-Making."

19. See Raunio, "The Parliament of Finland."

20. See Raunio, "The Parliament of Finland" and Raunio and Tiilikainen, *Finland in the European Union,* pp. 72–95.

21. Based on Kinnunen, "14,000 Complaints," written as part of the EU Fifth Framework Programme, "Organising for the EU Enlargement 2003–2004."

22. Tala, "Lakien vaikutukset," p. 215.

23. See Oksanen, *Paikallisen ja kansainvälisen kohtaaminen luonnonsuojelussa.*

24. Börzel, "Pace-Setting, Foot-Dragging, and Fence-Sitting."

25. Yale and Columbia Universities carried out the study.

26. See Börzel, "Pace-Setting, Foot-Dragging, and Fence-Sitting," and Héretier, "The Accommodation of Diversity in European Policy-Making."

27. Currently, environmental protection has a constitutional status, with the environment mentioned specifically in Section 20 of the constitution (2000): "Nature and its biodiversity, the environment and the national heritage are the responsibility of everyone. The public authorities shall endeavor to guarantee for everyone the right to a healthy environment and for everyone the possibility to influence the decisions that concern their own living environment."

28. See Oksanen, *Paikallisen ja kansainvälisen kohtaaminen luonnonsuojelussa.*

29. From the point of view of institutional arrangements, there were only a few changes. In order to solve the problem of rising complaints from the regional level, the MoE created a working group for Natura that quickly handled complaints addressed to them. Complaints came straight to the ministers from the regional level and experts waited outside the meeting room in case someone had any questions.

30. Soetendorp and Hanf, "Conclusion," p. 193.

PART 5

THE 2004 ROUND

15

Poland: A Reluctant Member

Artur Gruszczak

FROM THE VERY BEGINNING of accession negotiations, Poland earned the reputation of a "difficult" or "obstinate" candidate. In the hot times of the Iraqi debacle and the US-led armed intervention, Poland was accused in the French and German press of being "America's Trojan horse" for supporting the use of force, sending 2,500 troops, and taking one of the occupation zones under its command. Doubts concerning Poland also stemmed from certain features of Poland's economic structures, social system, and political configurations, as well as from its international role, historically based aspirations, and sociocultural determinants.

Moreover, Poland sought to win over Brussels not only to its superiority of "being big in numbers" but also to its contribution to the demise of communism. Polish authorities wanted to convince the EU member states that any enlargement without Poland would be impossible. Heather Grabbe suggested that "only Poland has the luxury of being able to bargain hard, for Polish negotiators assume that factors like the country's size and geo-political importance would prevent the EU from excluding the country from the first group of accessions."[1] The firm stance adopted by Polish negotiators in the beginning of the accession talks caused growing irritation in the European Commission.

As a member of the European Union, Poland has convinced the other member states that it is interested in an active participation in the process of European integration, mapping out ambitious plans in the areas of Common Foreign Policy and Justice and Home Affairs.

Regime transition set forth in 1988 through a series of political pacts that brought about semirepresentative elections in June 1989, ending in the spectacular defeat of the ruling Communist Party along with its minor allies. As a result, in September 1989 the first non-Communist government in eastern Europe was established. One of the first priorities of the new government was an immediate rapprochement with the European Union under the battle cry of "return to Europe." On September 19, 1989, the trade and economic cooperation agreement between Poland and the European Economic Community (EEC) was signed. Seen at that time as an incentive to the democratic movement in the eastern bloc, it laid foundations for further development of economic relations between Poland and the then EEC.

The next step on the road toward the west was the association agreement, the so-called Europe Agreement, signed on December 16, 1991. It set out transitory measures for a period of up to 10 years with the aim of establishing free trade, and it provided for gradual implementation of the four freedoms of Internal Market, harmonization of national laws with *acquis communautaire*, institutional framework for the implementation and monitoring, and—last but not least—political dialogue. The commercial part of the Europe Agreement, an interim agreement on trade and economic cooperation, entered into force on March 1, 1992, and the whole association agreement came into effect on February 1, 1994. Two months later, on April 5, 1994, Polish prime minister Waldemar Pawlak submitted a formal application for membership in the European Union.

The structural dialogue, launched after the Essen European Council in December 1994, offered representatives of the Polish government an opportunity to participate regularly in EU activities. The dialogue proved to be an efficient tool for adjusting Polish institutions to the requirements of future membership in the EU. The white paper on adaptation to the Internal Market made the Polish government aware of its responsibility for the success of EU membership.[2] Dispersed decision-making bodies were reorganized and made subject to the Committee for European Integration (KIE), constituted by the parliament in August 1996. The Office of the Committee for European Integration (UKIE), established in October 1996, became a strategic center influencing the government and national parliament in their executive and legislative activities.

Poland formally opened accession negotiations on March 31, 1998. Poland assumed that the negotiations would be completed by the end of 2002 in order to make Poland's accession to the EU possible in 2004.[3]

The Buzek government (1997–2001), based on a center-right parliamentary coalition, began talks on the assumption that the most efficient tactics would be to close as many "easy" chapters as possible and then save difficult issues for the end of negotiations, hoping to be able to secure better terms for Poland. When the government changed following the parliamentary elections of September 2001, which led to the victory of a leftist coalition headed by the Alliance of Democratic Left (SLD), Poland provisionally closed 19 chapters while the remaining 10 chapters were subject to difficult and complex bargaining. The biggest obstacles and hardships were noted in such fields as agriculture, regional policy and Structural Funds, budget and finance, and justice and home affairs. Polish negotiators struggled with EU officials over such emotionally loaded issues as the movement of workers across state borders and unrestrained acquisition rights to real estate and property by EU individuals and legal entities. Voices were heard in Brussels as well as in the capitals of some candidate states that Poland was dragging its feet and was in fact not ready for full membership.

The Miller government (2001–2004) almost immediately lowered Poland's profile. Under pressure from the European Commission, the leftist government decided to concede and accepted the terms stipulated by Brussels for such issues as restrictions on the movement of Polish workers, limited subsidies for agricultural production, and a shorter transition period for property acquisition.

The accession negotiations were successfully concluded on December 13, 2002, and the Treaty of Accession was signed on April 16, 2003. In a referendum held on June 7–8, 2003, the clear majority of the voters (77.45 percent), with a convincing turnout of 58.85 percent, expressed their support for Poland's membership in the European Union.

■ How and in What Areas
Does the EU Influence Poland?

On balance, Polish membership in the EU is generally positive. In the political realm, Poland joined the EU as a strong member state with 27 votes in the Council (only two less than the "big four"), while the second-biggest new members (Hungary and the Czech Republic) had only 12. So, Poland expected to be an important player. The label of Poland as a pro-US, Euro-skeptical, agricultural country, attached by ill-disposed elites and the press in the "old" member states, initially restrained

Polish activities in the EU institutions and auxiliary bodies. The issue of the Constitutional Treaty also increased ill-will toward Poland. Defending the politically profitable Nice treaty, Poland was considered the biggest enemy of the constitution for Europe and changed its position only after the Spanish elections of March 2004. Considered to be something of an oddity regarding European integration, Poland as a "freshman" in the EU club initially had a hard time. It turned out, however, that Poland would not be a laggard and is evidently interested in further advancements of EU policies and projects, such as the Economic and Monetary Union (EMU), Schengen Agreeement, the Common Agricultural Policy (CAP) reform, and the Constitutional Treaty. The crisis provoked in mid-2005 by the French *"Non"* to the constitution for Europe and subsequent Dutch "No" in the constitutional referendum, improved Poland's position because public opinion polls showed unequivocally strong support for the constitution (one of the highest among the EU's 25 member states).

Public support for EU membership continued at a medium level.[4] The perception of accession was generally positive. According to an opinion poll conducted in May 2005 by the Center for Public Opinion Survey, 40 percent in Poland thought the accession was a breakthrough event, and the next 42 percent believed it was an important fact. Almost half of those surveyed claimed that the accession was good for Poland (see Table 15.1).

The main benefits for Poland were: free movement of persons, support for the agricultural sector, and more opportunities to work abroad. As far as disadvantages, the Poles saw only one clear factor widely: a rise in prices, especially of food. It was obvious that certain fears about the negative impacts of membership on Polish culture, religion, and social life, as expressed before accession, had been exaggerated. A May 2005 poll by the Center for Public Opinion Survey showed a significant decline in negative perceptions of EU influence in such areas as religiousness, tolerance, morality, and patriotism. In practical terms, it turned out that the round feared effects of membership, such as a decline in the agricultural sector as a result of growing competition from the other member states or buyouts of Polish properties, simply did not occur. On the contrary, Polish agriculture and farming were doing quite well, thanks to CAP subsidies and export opportunities. As for land and property acquisition, there was no "run for Polish soil." On the contrary, the Poles were buying land and properties abroad, especially in neighboring Germany.[5] Although the majority of EU member states (except for the United Kingdom, Ireland, and Sweden) applied for transition

Table 15.1   Changes in Attitudes Toward Polish Membership in the EU Before and After the Accession

Question:	Integration with the EU will/does bring Poland:			
	More benefits than losses	Benefits will equal losses	More losses than benefits	Hard to say
February 2004	39%	15%	38%	8%
May 2005	46%	21%	22%	11%

Question:	Integration with the EU will/does bring you personally:			
	More benefits than losses	Benefits will/do equal losses	More losses than benefits	Hard to say
February 2004	29%	22%	34%	15%
May 2005	27%	32%	23%	18%

Question:	Poland's accession to the EU will be/is:			
	More profitable for Poland than the EU	Poland's benefits equal the EU's benefits	More profitable for the EU than for Poland	Hard to say
February 2004	22%	17%	50%	11%
May 2005	26%	18%	36%	20%

Source: Center for Public Opinion, "Ocena pierwszego roku czlonkostwa Polski w Unii Europejskiej. Komunikat z badan, BS/115/2005," Warsaw, June 2005.

periods in opening their labor markets, anticipating wrongly an invasion of cheap Polish workers, economic migration was rather limited. While in 2003, approximately 400,000 to 450,000 Polish employees worked legally in the EU member states, an additional 100,000 to 120,000 worked illegally. Most of the latter worked as seasonal workers in construction, farming, and housekeeping. In 2005, the total number of Polish economic migrants rose to 670,000.

Accession has generally had a positive impact on Poland's economy. The economy successfully merged into EU structures and made a smooth transition into the Internal Market, despite unfavorable external economic factors, including the constant rise in oil and raw energy prices, jumps in production costs and prices, as well as the decline in EU economic development. Thanks to financial inflows from the EC budget, dynamic growth in Polish exports and a "preaccession consumption boom," the national economy was given a boost contributing to a 5.9 percent GDP growth rate in 2004. According to the Office of the Committee for European Integration, membership in the EU contributed to approximately 1.5 percent of the 5.3 percent rate.[6] The Polish zloty was strengthened against other currencies and this was widely cited as evidence of growing faith in the Polish economy since accession.

It was also expected and feared that accession would produce a strong inflationary leap because price differences between Poland and other EU countries were quite significant, especially for basic goods and services. Therefore, the price convergence between Poland and the EU was inevitable and led as expected to higher prices for dozens of Polish goods and services. Indeed, the inflation rate rose from 2.2 percent annually in April 2004 to 4.5 percent in April 2004 and 4 percent in October 2004. But from the beginning of 2005, the rate of inflation started to decline slowly and reached 3 percent in March 2005 and 1.5 percent in July 2005.[7]

Poland is one of the biggest beneficiaries of the EU's budget. Although the future of New Financial Perspective for 2007–2013 is unclear and the forecasts are perhaps too optimistic (2004 and projections for 2005), net transfers to Poland were higher than earlier estimates (see Table 15.2).

Net advantages for Poland should increase substantially in the next financial perspective. Estimated net financial transfers to Poland should reach €3.2 billion in 2006 and jump up to €6.9 billion in 2007 and €8.9 billion in 2008. The share of net payments in Poland's GDP

Table 15.2   Balance of the Financial Flows Between Poland and the EU, 2004–2005 (in million €)

		2004	2005 (projected)
Inflows	Total EU flows	2,793	5,791
	Pre-accession aid (Cohesion Fund inclusive)	1,010	1,925
	CAP	297	1,070
	Budget liquidity improvement	541	612
	Schengen Financial Instrument	103	104
Outflows	Transition facility fund	–	–22
	National contribution to the EC budget	–1,239	–2,099
	GNI	–853	n.a.
	VAT	–280	n.a.
	Traditional own resources	–105	n.a.
Balance		1,554	3,692

Source: UKIE, "Polska w Unii Europejskiej—doswiadczenia pierwszego roku czlonkostwa," Warsaw 2005, p. 305.

should rise from 1.2 percent in 2005 to 2.5 percent in 2007 and 3 percent in 2008.[8]

Until 2006, Poland will be able to take advantage of EU assistance programs. The oldest and best-known is the Phare program. It was created in December 1989 under Council Regulation (EEC) 3906/89 to assist the transformation of Poland and Hungary following the regime changes in these countries. Although initially designed as a stand-alone external assistance program following the 1993 Copenhagen European Council conclusions, the Phare program was reoriented toward supporting the "new democracies" in adapting to the requirements for European integration. Through a major reform in 1998, Phare was reoriented toward assisting the applicant countries of central and eastern Europe in their preparations for joining the EU. Between 1989 and 2000 a total of €2.584 billion was allocated to Poland. In the perspective for 2000–2006, Poland was expected to receive approximately €2.786 billion. In 1999, two other preaccession funds were established: ISPA (Instrument for Structural Policies for Pre-Accession) for infrastructural projects in the environmental and transport fields, and SAPARD (Special Accession Program for Agriculture and Rural Development). It is estimated that the total financial allocation for Poland in the period 2000–2006 would be approximately €1.183 billion from SAPARD and €2.184 to €2.694 billion from ISPA. Summing up, the total financial aid to be made available for Poland from 2000 to 2006 in the framework of the three assistance programs was estimated to be from €6.153 to €6.663 billion.[9]

■ How and in What Areas Does Poland Influence the EU?

Numerous problems of EU membership, particularly in the economic and social fields, significantly reduced Poland's room for maneuver. It was mainly political, even strategic, issues where Poland sought to outshine the rest of the EU members. It is worth mentioning that despite an institutional cooperation between Poland, Germany, and France (in the framework of the so-called Weimar Triangle established in 1991), the mutual relationship between Poland and the "core" of the EU worsened beginning in 2000. Therefore, Poland's bargaining position was significantly limited although it did not preclude undertaking numerous efforts, some of which were crowned with success.

In the economic realm, Poland sought to take advantage of the EU

Internal Market as a source of incentives and opportunities for a dynamically growing national economy. In this context, the EU's New Financial Perspective for 2007–2013 was of utmost importance.[10] Poland expected to benefit significantly and was looking forward to getting at least €60 billion or, in the most optimistic scenario, even up to €82 billion. From the beginning of the negotiations, Poland intended to take an active part promoting its major priority: maintaining a high profile for Cohesion Policy and securing adequate support for the least-developed regions. Poland launched a diplomatic action seeking to form a coalition of countries with common interests, including members of the Visegrad Group (Poland, Hungary, the Czech Republic, and Slovakia) and those who participated actively in the works of a much wider group of "friends of Cohesion Policy." The lack of consent at the June 2005 European Council on the New Financial Perspective should not be, however, regarded as Poland's failure. Polish prime minister Marek Belka had presented a flexible approach and was willing to compromise at the cost of lower benefits. Up to this point, the old Berlin financial agenda was still favorable to Poland.

Another question of prestige for Poland was the location of the European Agency for the Management of Operational Cooperation at the External Borders of the Member States (FRONTEX), which began its work on May 1, 2005. From the very beginning Poland lobbied intensively for locating that new EU body in Warsaw. Polish representatives stressed the fact that Poland had the longest external border, conducted an active policy toward the eastern neighbors, and was well prepared to challenge the issues of securing borders, combating transnational organized crime, and illegal immigration. In April 2005, the Justice and Home Affairs Council reached an agreement that the headquarters of FRONTEX would be situated in Warsaw. Polish officials did not disguise their satisfaction with that decision since they had had to compete fiercely with Hungary. As a result, Poland became the first new member state to host one of the EU agencies.[11]

Poland's Role in the "Orange Revolution"

The most spectacular examples of Poland's influence over EU politics were efforts to commit the EU to develop its relations with Ukraine. After the Copenhagen European Council in December 2002, the new European Neighborhood Policy (ENP) and the eastern dimension of EU policy moved up on the agenda. Poland, particularly interested in strengthening cooperation and partnership with Russia, Ukraine, and Belarus, became a strong advocate of the ENP. According to one of

Poland's Foreign Ministry officials, "Poland has a duty to take an active role in the creation of the Eastern Dimension of EU policy. This duty springs both from our national and European interests, our prospective EU membership, and from the shape and traditions of the relations with our eastern neighbors, whereas opportunities of actions are based on the historical and geographical proximity, the previous contacts and good understanding of our partners."[12]

Ukraine played a special role in Poland's eastern policy, considered to be a counterweight to Russia's influence. Good personal relations between the presidents of both states (Kwasniewski and Kuchma), close trade relations, a Ukrainian workforce in Poland of half a million, and cross-border contacts had contributed to continuous development of mutual relations since the mid-1990s. An international team of experts on Ukranian politics pointed out that after May 1, 2004, Poland had been actively involved in shaping EU policy toward its eastern neighbors in the framework of the ENP. Poland launched, in cooperation with Germany—despite differences over Iraq, transatlantic relations, and some bilateral issues—an initiative on EU policy toward Ukraine. The Foreign Office prepared a working document titled "Draft Elements Regarding a European Policy for Ukraine," presented in October 2004. They proposed "a proactive EU policy towards Ukraine, including a new agreement between the EU and Ukraine, flexibility in the existing visa regime, granting Ukraine the market economy status and a start of preparations for negotiations for the Free Trade Area."[13] There was, however, a crucial element of discord: Germany ruled out any perspective for Ukraine's EU membership while Poland advocated at least discussion on that issue.

There was no surprise that in times of deep political and social crisis in Ukraine, provoked in November 2004 by the ruling class,[14] Poland made strong efforts to involve the European Union in the process of peaceful transformation through mediation efforts and support for fair elections and political reforms in Ukraine. The European Union reacted immediately to the developments in Ukraine. It rejected the falsified results of the second round of the presidential elections and an official statement prepared by the Dutch presidency was issued very early on. However, strong declarations were not followed by decisive diplomatic moves.

Facing dramatically escalating conflict on its eastern border, Poland no longer hesitated to take rapid political and diplomatic action. President Aleksander Kwasniewski and Foreign Minister Wlodzimierz Cimoszewicz went to Kiev to take part in negotiations aimed at settling the political crisis. The official Polish position on the crisis was clear: the best solution for Ukraine would be to rerun the second round of the presidential election as soon as possible. Kwasniewski applied a two-track strategy. On the one hand, he intended to take advantage of his close, almost friendly, personal relations with outgoing president Kuchma. Therefore, he wanted to mediate between the two opposing camps and work out a compromise solution. At the same time, he urged the EU to take immediate diplomatic action to prevent open confrontation in Ukraine. He called on Javier Solana, another Kwasniewski acquaintance, to be more active in presenting the EU position.

There were also crowds of Polish politicians and political activists visiting Kiev's Independence Square. The appearance of Lech Walesa, former leader of the Solidarity movement, former president of Poland (1990–1995), and Nobel Peace Prize winner, had a symbolic meaning. Walesa's two-day presence in Kiev highlighted the link between the so-called Orange Revolution and Solidarity's own traditions of peaceful, negotiated transition; demand for freedom and dignity; and an anti-Soviet, emancipatory movement.

In two rounds of dramatic talks a special EU "troika" consisting of Polish president Kwasniewski supported by Foreign Minister Cimoszewicz, Lithuanian president Valdas Adamkus, and Javier Solana—the EU high representative for the Common Foreign and Security Policy, assisted by special envoy Nicolas Biegman—managed to draw three big Ukrainian players in the crisis—President Leonid Kuchma, Prime Minister Yanukovych, and opposition candidate Yushchenko—to the negotiating table.[15] On December 8, 2004, following a political pact concluded with the Ukrainian authorities and the opposition, the Ukrainian parliament amended laws to allow for a new round of elections. Yushchenko won this new election and was declared the official winner on December 28, 2004. The victorious Orange Revolution was over.

Numerous observers and commentators pointed out the positive involvement of Polish politicians and activists in appeasing the Ukrainian crisis. Taras Kuzio, an analyst of Ukrainian affairs, ascertained that "Poland and Lithuania dragged a reluctant EU into holding three round-table negotiations that paved the way for the December 8 compromise between the Ukrainian authorities and opposition."[16] In an enthusiastic mood, a Polish commentator claimed that "the Ukrainian revolution has catapulted Poland into the leadership of the European Union and released a new political dynamic across the region."[17]

In the heat of the moment, Poland tried to strengthen western influence on the new Ukrainian government as well as pro-Ukraine attitudes in the EU. Thanks to Poland's efforts, the European Council adopted a special declaration on Ukraine in December 2004, stressing its strategic significance as a key neighbor and partner of the Union. Polish members of the European Parliament (MEPs) were also active in settling the Ukrainian crisis. Strong support for the resolution on "The Results of the Ukraine Elections," adopted on January 13, 2005, was to a certain extent a result of Polish MEPs' activism.

■ How Does Poland Implement and Comply with EU Policies?

Annual Regular Reports issued by the European Commission in the years 1999–2003 acknowledged constant progress in Poland's adjustment to the conditions and requirements of EU membership. There were, however, a number of policy areas that the Commission criticized. These areas included: state administration, the judicial system, development of effective anticorruption measures, fiscal policy, environmental protection, and restructuring of large state-controlled enterprises.

There were also serious misgivings concerning Polish agriculture. From the very beginning of association talks, agriculture was treated as a "hot potato" issue. Its structure, share in the national economy, and low level of modernization and investment contributed to a common opinion of its being the most underdeveloped and outdated sector. Unfortunately for Poland's negotiating position, agriculture became a predominantly political issue. Poland lacked a coherent long-term strategy that would treat comprehensively market and price policy, rural development, the social consequences of restructuring, environmental issues, and the agro-food industry. The proposals for the amounts of production quotas and other supply-managing instruments included in the Polish negotiating position were—for products other than milk—rather moderate. They only made it possible for some subsectors of Polish agriculture and the agro-food industry to return to the levels of production reached at the end of the 1980s. The problem of direct subsidies was one of the most important issues discussed during the 2002 Copenhagen European Council. At the closure of the negotiations, it was decided that, for 2004, 2005, and 2006, Polish farmers should receive direct payments in the amounts of 36 percent, 39 percent, and 42 percent of full EC payments, respectively. In order to alleviate Polish farmers' confusion and disappointment, Poland was allowed to offer extra payments from its national budget up to 55 percent in 2004, 60 percent in 2005, and 65 percent in 2006 of the EU level. As one Polish expert observed, "the result of final agreements on direct payments is that Polish farmers shall not, as of the day of membership, be covered by all CAP regulations. This will happen only in 2013. By that time they shall operate in different, i.e., worse, economic conditions than farmers of the current EU member states, which means also worse competition conditions."[18]

EU institutions and some of the member states feared the operation of the Integrated Administration and Control System would become indispensable to the introduction of a standard system of direct payments. Some observers in the older member states doubted whether Polish peasants (the majority of whom were older people with lower education levels) would be capable of taking advantage of the subsidies and filling out the necessary application forms. It turned out, however, that the Polish authorities managed to introduce the necessary legal and technical measures and instruments. There was also a common interest in the Community's subsidies. By the end of March 2005, the Agency for Restructuring and Modernization of Agriculture made disbursements of approximately €1.5 billion to about 1.3 million applicants, that is, 88 percent of those entitled to the aid.

Restructuring the Steel Industry

Just as in the agricultural sector, the case of the metallurgical industry deserves particular attention. The Polish steel industry exemplifies the problems and dilemmas of the postsocialist economies of eastern Europe. In the Cold War era, Poland was among the major European steel producers. The steel industry, along with coal and copper mining, was a cornerstone of the Soviet-type economy predetermined by ideological and geopolitical factors. Huge steel mills built in the 1950s near Krakow and in the 1970s near Katowice, in the Silesian region—enormous investments devouring a large part of national income—were feeding not only local arms factories and heavy-industry plants, but in the majority of the cases sent steel back to the Soviet Union. Along with the costs of imports of iron ore and supplying the local industry with steel, Poland had to carry the burden of investing in the construction of steelworks, transport and communication infrastructure, and social policy with respect to the workers. Moreover, most of the Polish steelworks featured low productivity, low quality, and poor working conditions, as well as very high pollution levels.

The difficult political and economic transformation in the early 1990s came as a shock to the gargantuan metallurgical sector.

Liberalization in foreign trade, new rules of payments with Russia, and the "peace dividend" of downsizing military industry in Poland and the former USSR strongly affected the metallurgical industry.[19] Still, in the course of negotiations on the accession agreement between Poland and the EC, the issue of the steel industry became one of the most controversial points. Under these circumstances in 1991, the Bielecki government drew up a restructuring program to modernize the steel infrastructure, improve management, and increase productivity. Aware of the scale and depth of the heavy-industry restructuring problem, the European Commission consented to pressure from the Polish delegation and allowed some exceptions regarding steel products. It turned out, however, that the initial attempts at restructuring the whole metallurgical sector effectively ceased, because it meant shutting down ineffective and outdated plants, sharply reducing employment, and trying to overcome workers' resistance. Moreover, the financial and economic costs of restructuring were much higher than expected.[20]

Under pressure from Brussels, the Polish government adopted a restructuring program, in 1998, for the iron and steel industry, prepared in full cooperation with the European Commission. The program, however, did not produce significant progress in restructuring because it lacked a consistent and common approach on the part of major steel mills. The Polish government continued paying supports to the plants, utilizing more public aid, which meant exposing itself to Brussels's displeasure by acting in contradiction to Poland's obligations under the Europe Agreement. In spite of adopting a revised steel restructuring program in March 2002, the government could not expect substantive progress toward the privatization of the largest steel mills.

During the accession negotiations, the Polish delegation consequently defended the government's position and achieved partial success. Before closure of the negotiations in 2002, Poland managed to win another extension of the transition period, until the end of 2006, and confirmed exceptional measures for the steel sector in the Accession Treaty. These exceptions were possible because of state-led branch consolidation. In June 2002, four of the biggest steel companies formed a holding company, Polskie Huty Stali ([PHS] Polish Steel Mills), which was transformed at the end of the year into a unitary company having 70 percent of the shares in the national steel output.

In Protocol no. 8 to the Accession Treaty[21] new provisions on the restructuring of the Polish steel industry were set, allowing for prolonged state aid for steelworks. Until the end of the restructuring period, set for December 31, 2006, Poland will be able to provide approximately €800 million, mainly for financial restructuring, and will reduce the net productive capacity of finished steel products, by closing inefficient and nonviable plants. Poland was also granted a transition period for the implementation of EU environmental legislation for the steel mills.

In April 2003, according to Protocol no. 8, Poland submitted to the Commission a new restructuring program for the steel industry that met with the approval of the Council.[22] Furthermore, in October 2003, the Polish Treasury Ministry signed a shares purchase agreement with the second-biggest world steel company, the LNM Group, concerning the privatization of PHS. After the finalization of the transaction in March 2004, 95 percent of the sector had become privatized.

The European Commission, in the first monitoring report on steel restructuring,[23] stated in positive terms that in 2003 state aids granted to the steel companies were below the maximum ceiling, and that the capacity reductions were also respected. It stressed, however, that the restructuring of the steel sector was progressing at a slow pace and with significant delays. The beneficiary companies did not take full advantage of the opportunities arising from an improved steel market situation to seek maximum profit in order to finance the necessary investments and implement other restructuring measures. After PHS privatization, the second monitoring report,[24] published by the Commission in early August 2005, was much more optimistic. The Commission acknowledged a significant improvement in the performance of Polish steel companies, but it highlighted the temporary advantages of operating in an exceptionally good market with high demands and prices. Moreover, the Commission noted that some companies were still underperforming and might fail to become viable by the end of the restructuring period. The restructuring of the Polish steel industry faced delays, sometimes significant, especially in relation to investments, which, in the case of some companies, could affect their future viability.

Poland's Record of Compliance

The preaccession period was a demanding time for the political and social institutions of Poland. The requirement of implementing EU law in order to accommodate EU legal standards was a challenging issue in terms of institutional coordination and social consultation.[25] They had to develop an efficient internal system of coordination and cooperation between the government (relevant ministries and central offices), the parliament (two chambers, the Sejm and the Senat), and social partners. Fast-track procedures established in the parliament for "European legislation," good cooperation between European Commissions in both houses of the Polish parliament, and the intense work of government institutions allowed for a relatively rapid implementation of EU laws. The leading role was performed by the parliamentary European Legislation Committee, taking advantage of the European fast track and supported actively by the governmental Office of the Committee for European Integration. Constructive cooperation contributed to development of a synergistic model between the Sejm and the Council of Ministers. However, as Laskowska points out, an "effect of the functioning of this special procedure of the Sejm is the enhanced role of the C[ouncil] of M[inisters] in the legislative procedure."[26]

Since May 1, 2004, the Sejm and the Senat have been incorporated into the process of preparing and presenting Poland's positions regarding draft EU legal acts. As a result, the government delivered to the parliament over 20,000 documents sent by the General Secretariat of the Council. Among them there were 250 draft EU legal acts reviewed by the government, awaiting parliamentary approval to become official positions. The president, who is in charge of signing laws before their publication in the Official Journal (*Dziennik Ustaw*), also adopted a constructive approach. President Kwasniewski presented himself as a strong advocate of European integration and actively supported Polish accession to the EU. However, in certain cases it was presidential negligence that caused delays in transposition of EU laws. Such was the case of three laws regulating capital markets and financial transfers. In early August 2005, the lack of a presidential signature stopped their implementation and made the European Commission initiate infringement procedures in the field of financial services.

Nevertheless, Poland, like other new member states, performed quite well in implementing the *acquis communautaire*. Poland did not manage to improve its transposition record enough to reach the benchmark of the 1.5 percent deficit set by the European Council, but according to the latest available Internal Market "scoreboard" of July 2005, it was close to that target, showing a 1.7 percent rate (27 directives not notified) and thus making moderate progress of 33 percent compared with the July 2004 scoreboard.[27] In the sector of financial laws, Poland did significantly better, transposing all but one of the directives. Poland's performance regarding proper application of directives was worse. Although getting better results than the EU-15 member states, Poland had the highest number of infringements of Internal Market rules among the 10 new member states. The poorest record Poland noted in transposition of European and harmonization of standards was having the second-worst record among all the 25 member states.

Concerning the infringements, most of them were in the areas of the Internal Market, the environment, employment and social affairs, taxation, and the customs union.[28] Among particular cases mentioned were the restructuring aid for Gdynia, Gdansk, and Szczecin shipyards; state aid to the coal sector; and restructuring aid to steel producers Huta Czestochowa Co. and Mittal Steel Poland Co. Also, financial services were subject to criticism from the European Commission.

Although compliance and implementation were generally not political issues and did not give rise to emotional demonstrations, there was however a debate on the principal matter of the supremacy of EU law over national legal order. In two cases, the matter was referred to Poland's Constitutional Tribunal. The first case was a truly political/ideological case. A group of right-wing deputies from the Sejm complained that Poland's accession to the EU failed to conform to Poland's constitutional principles of sovereignty and the supremacy of the constitution in the established Polish legal system. In challenging the conditions of accession, the applicants focused their criticism of numerous provisions of the treaties. The Constitutional Tribunal, in its judgment of May 11, 2005, declared that the Accession Treaty was not inconsistent with the Polish Constitution.[29] Much more important and controversial was an earlier judgment of the Constitutional Tribunal regarding the European Arrest Warrant.

European Arrest Warrant—constitutional dilemma. As one of the new legal measures launched by the European Union after the tragic events of 9/11 in the United States, the Council adopted, on June 13, 2002, the framework decision on the European Arrest Warrant (EAW) and the surrender procedures between the member states. It was intended to replace traditional extradition mechanisms, especially those established in the two EU conventions of 1995 and 1996 that had not actually entered into force due to the lack of necessary national ratifications. As an EU legal tool, a framework decision is binding as to the end result to be achieved, though the choice of form and methods is left to national authorities. It does not require ratification and, in practice, national parliaments have little real choice other than to approve the necessary changes to their domestic laws for implementation.[30] The Polish legislature duly transposed the framework decision on the EAW, adopting, in March 2004, an amendment to the Criminal Procedure Code of 1997.

In the course of accession negotiations, however, the issue of the EAW appeared on the agenda as slightly troublesome. Divisions arose between Polish legal experts as to whether the EAW infringed on the

Polish Constitution or not. An opinion given by lawyers close to the presidential office prevailed, stating that no amendment to the constitution was necessary because the surrender procedure, regarding Polish citizens, to any of the EU member states on the grounds of the EAW is a judicial administrative measure and not an extradition mechanism forbidden by the constitution.

In January 2005, the regional court for Gdansk, considering the issuance of a procedural decision on surrendering a Polish citizen for the purpose of conducting a criminal prosecution in the Netherlands, questioned the admissibility of surrendering a Polish citizen to another EU member state on the basis of the European Arrest Warrant (Article 607t § 1 of the Criminal Procedure Code). The Constitutional Tribunal was asked to review the conformity of the above-mentioned normative act with the constitution. In its judgment of April 27, 2005, the tribunal declared that "Article 607t § 1 of the Criminal Procedure Code, insofar as it permits the surrendering of a Polish citizen to another member state of the European Union on the basis of the European Arrest Warrant, does not conform to Article 55(1) of the Constitution." However, the tribunal ruled that the loss of the binding force of the challenged provision should be delayed for 18 months following the day of official publication of that judgment. Explaining the reasons for the ruling, the tribunal underlined that "the fact that a domestic statute was enacted for the purpose of implementing secondary EU law does not per se guarantee the substantive conformity of this statute with the norms of the constitution. The obligation to interpret domestic law in a manner sympathetic to EU law (so as to comply with EU law) has its limits."[31]

Apparently the Solomonic judgment of the Polish Constitutional Tribunal rescued the EAW application in Poland. Although the transition period of 18 months was sharply criticized by some legal experts as devoid of reasonable and legal grounds, the ruling showed the strong will of the "guardians of the constitution" to adopt a European normative approach.

■ Trends and Prospects:
More Challenges in the Future

Poland's first year of membership in the EU was spent seeking its own way in the tangled structure of European Union politics. Given that those undertakings coincided with the crises in the EU over such issues as the Constitutional Treaty, the Lisbon Strategy, the Stability and Growth Pact, the European Security and Defense Policy (ESDP), and internal security mechanisms, the potential influence on the institutions and policies of the Union is hardly predictable. There are, nonetheless, certain features of Polish membership that allowed Poland to develop a provisional balance of views and structure future priorities and challenges.

In the realm of politics, Poland would assume a cautious attitude to the future of the EU. In the preaccession period, major political forces in Poland, including the ruling leftist coalition, displayed a rather Euro-skeptical stance toward integration. In the final stage of the negotiations, Polish authorities did not mask disappointment at being pressed hard by Brussels to accept what they considered poor conditions of membership. The parliamentary and presidential elections of September–October 2005 strengthened this tendency. The parliamentary elections were won by two right-wing parties: the conservative Law and Justice Party (PiS) and the liberal Civic Platform (PO). The presidential race ended with the rather unexpected victory of Lech Kaczynski, supported by the conservative Law and Justice Party (headed by his twin brother Jaroslaw). The new executive, as well as the majority in the parliament, consists of Euro-skeptics, that is, those politicians who had defended the Nice treaty, criticized certain provisions of the Constitution for Europe, preferred NATO over the ESDP, and denounced EU restrictions against new member states in such areas as free movement of persons and services, the CAP, and tax policy.

It seems that the new Polish executive and legislature would clearly prefer an "intergovernmental" and not a "supranational" Union. Given that the new ruling elite has been clearly hesitant about the EU Constitutional Treaty and fully satisfied with the Nice treaty, prospects for ratifying the Constitutional Treaty are bleak. The president-elect declared immediately that his presidency should contribute to a more active policy regarding European integration. However, that will probably mean an active participation in loose intergovernmental projects seeking to protect Warsaw's interests. Taking into account PiS's economic program pushing for better welfare policies, it would be hardly possible to reach the EMU criteria by 2007 (as assumed by the former government) and catch up with the Lisbon Strategy requirements.

Regarding the economy, Poland is optimistic, expecting continuous annual GDP growth of 4–5 percent, a progressive decline in unemployment (which currently is the highest in the EU at 19 percent), and further improvement of budgetary and financial conditions. The new Financial Perspective for 2007–2013 enables Poland to benefit greatly from EU structural programs.

Among the numerous challenges and problems, several are distinct. First, the absorption of Community funds flowing into the Polish economy and its infrastructure has much to do with the efficiency of central government, and the effectiveness of local administration and small and medium enterprises must be improved. Likewise, the Polish judicial system, challenged by the impact of EU law on its domestic legal system, must work more efficiently. The Polish agricultural sector must undergo further restructuring. Its anachronistic composition of very small, high-cost, low-efficiency individual farms has to be changed in order to compete with the biggest farming industries in the EU. Similarly, Polish mining and heavy industries, those anchors of development and modernization, should be adjusted to the requirements of a "knowledge-based economy." Although the achievements of the Lisbon Strategy do not augur well, Poland must adopt modernization, including investment in education, research, and development.

This last challenge goes to Poland's role as a "Western bulwark." Having the longest external border with the east, Poland has to prepare itself to enter the Schengen area of free movement of persons in a special way. On the grounds of the Accession Treaty, Poland got additional funds, a so-called Schengen facility instrument, for the years 2004–2006 to reinforce and modernize its border infrastructure on the eastern frontiers as well as to adequately prepare for membership in the Schengen Information System. This will not be an easy task and thus far the scoreboard is rather pessimistic, questioning Poland's readiness to meet the deadline of October 2007.

Poland has proven to be an ambitious member state. It has managed to develop pro-European policies, prepared adequately for membership, and, as a member state of the EU, has been searching for its own unique path in EU politics. What may be disquieting is that Polish achievements in the EU confirm Poland's peripheral orientation. Stress on the eastern dimension, involvement in Ukraine and Belarus, and efforts at strengthening the eastern border make Poland an "Eastern" member state. On the other hand, France's Mediterranean orientation or Spain's Latin American inclination show that such a regional specialization may prove a valuable asset.

■ Notes

1. Grabbe, "How Does Europeanization Affect CEE Governance?" p. 1015.

2. See Friis and Murphy, "The European Union and Central and Eastern Europe."

3. On cooperation between Poland and the EU in the prenegotiation period, see: Mayhew, *Recreating Europe*; Henderson, *Back to Europe*; Cordell and Antoszewski, *Poland and the European Union*.

4. Support for Poland's membership in the EU (Eurobarometer no. 62 and OBOP polls: Q.: "In general terms, do you think Polish membership in the EU is a good thing?") since the beginning of the present decade oscillated around 50 percent. At the time of the EU referendum it rose to 58 percent and just before the accession, in spring 2004, declined to 42 percent. Latest polls conducted in July 2005 showed 54 percent support. However, asked about the future of the EU (Eurobarometer no. 62, Q.: "If you were tomorrow told that the European Union had been scrapped, would you be . . ."), up to 61 percent of the Poles showed indifference and only 26 percent would be "very sorry."

5. "Unexpectedly, there is a growing interest among Polish citizens and businesses in purchasing real estate and enterprises west of Polish border, mainly in Eastern länders of the Federal Republic of Germany, since the real estate there turns out to be cheaper than Polish properties," quoted from: UKIE, *Poland in the European Union*, p. 8.

6. *Newsweek Polska*, May 8, 2004, p. 27.

7. Eurostat, *Euro-Indicators*, various releases; available at: http://epp. eurostat.cec.eu.int/portal/page?_pageid=0,1136173,0_45570698&_dad= portal&_schema=PORTAL.

8. Samecki, "Financial Flows Between the EU and Poland in 2004–2013," p. 47.

9. *Przeglad Rzadowy*, no. 9, 1999; available at: http://www.kprm.gov. pl/7810_7973.htm.

10. On the New Financial Perspective, see Mayhew, "The Financial Framework of the European Union, 2007–13."

11. See Adamczyk, "Europejska Agencja Zarzadzania Wspólpraca Operacyjna na Granicach Zewnetrznych Panstw Czlonkowskich Unii Europejskiej."

12. Kazana, "The Role of Poland in Creation of the Eastern Dimension," p. 61.

13. Stefan Batory Foundation, *Will the Orange Revolution Bear Fruit?* p. 14.

14. Ukraine's "Orange Revolution" was a series of country-wide civic protests and political actions following the presidential runoff election held on November 21, 2004. The two candidates in the second round of the electoral contest claimed victory. Independent opinion polls gave an 11 percent lead to opposition candidate Victor Yushchenko, while official results proclaimed a 3-point victory by Victor Yanukovych, incumbent prime minister supported by President Leonid Kuchma and Russia's Putin. Several hundred thousand of Yushchenko's supporters, decorated with orange ribbons, wearing orange, or carrying orange flags, demonstrated in the capital city of Kiev. At the same time, in the strongholds of Viktor Yanukovych, in eastern and southern Ukraine, there were actions that alluded to the possibility of the breakup of Ukraine or an unconstitutional federalization of the country should their candidate's claimed

victory not be recognized. See: "Orange Revolution," in *Wikipedia, the free encyclopedia*; available at: http://en.wikipedia.org/wiki/Orange_Revolution.

15. *Ukrainian News*, December 6, 2004.

16. Kuzio, "Poland Plays Strategic Role in Ukraine's Orange Revolution."

17. Matraszek, *Ukraine, Poland, and a Free World.*

18. Rowinski, "Agriculture—Costs and Benefits of Poland's Membership in the EU," p. 110.

19. Crude steel production declined from 14 million tons in 1990 to 11.1 million in 1994, 9.9 million in 1998, and 8.3 million in 2002. Employment in the steel sector fell from 147,000 persons in 1990 to 106,000 in 1992, then declining slowly to 91,000 in 1995, 87,000 in 1997, 55,200 in 1999, 31,600 in 2001, and 23,800 in 2004. See: IIIS, *Steel Statistical Yearbook 2004*, table 4, p. 10; Ministry of Economy of the Republic of Poland, "The Restructuring Programme for Polish Steel Industry. Update of 2002," figure 2, p. 15.

20. See Pawlas and Tendera-Wlaszczuk, *Poland's Economy Competitiveness with Respect to the Integration with the European Union.*

21. *Official Journal of the European Union* L 236, 9/23/2003, p. 948.

22. *Official Journal of the European Union* L 199, 8/7/2003, p. 17.

23. European Commission, COM 2004(443) final, 7/7/2004.

24. European Commission, COM 2005(359) final, 8/3/2005.

25. See Lippert, Umbach, and Wessels, "Europeanization of CEE Executives."

26. Laskowska, "The Parliamentary European Legislation Committee in the Approximation of Laws Procedure," p. 80.

27. European Commission, DG Internal Market and Services, "Internal Market Scoreboard," no. 14, July 2005.

28. See precise data in: European Commission, Secretariat General, "Situation of the Notification of National Measures of Implementing the Directives," July 11, 2005.

29. "Poland's Membership in the European Union (The Accession Treaty)"; available at: http://www.trybunal.gov.pl/eng/summaries/documents/K_18_04_GB.pdf

30. Alegre and Leaf, "Mutual Recognition in European Judicial Cooperation," p. 202.

31. "Application of the European Arrest Warrant to Polish Citizens"; available at: http://www.trybunal.gov.pl/eng/summaries/documents/P_1_05_GB.pdf.

16

Hungary:
From "Policy Taker"
to Policymaker

David Ellison

AS A NEW MEMBER of the European Union—Hungary joined on May 1, 2004—Hungary has been more of a "policy taker" than "policymaker." Though this role is slowly changing, one should not ignore the difficulties smaller, newer, and less developed states are likely to experience in attempting to influence EU policy outcomes in their favor. Nonetheless, Hungary avidly pursued EU membership and some 83 percent of voters came out in favor on April 12, 2003, in Hungary's referendum on EU membership (though voter participation at 46 percent was quite low).[1] Hungary likewise was the second country to ratify the Constitutional Treaty with a majority vote in parliament on December 20, 2004.[2] Despite problems with the ratification of the treaty in France and the Netherlands, Hungary remains firmly committed to pursuing further European integration.[3]

As a policy taker, like many other central and east European countries, Hungary was required to adopt the existing body of EU legislation before completing the accession process. Often pointed to as one of the more successful central and east European countries—both in terms of adopting EU legislation and in terms of attracting foreign direct investment (FDI)—Hungary takes a position of prominence in the New Europe. It is respected as an able and willing partner in the EU and it joined the EU with relatively few transitional arrangements in major policy areas.

EU membership clearly has an impact on decisionmaking structures and policymaking outcomes. This chapter will focus on the impact of

EU environmental policy and regulation on the Hungarian environment. As this chapter will argue, while EU membership clearly impacts environmental policy in Hungary, it is often difficult to distinguish the "European-ness" of this impact from other factors, such as globalization, democratization, privatization, FDI, and the demands of local interests and actors. As such, the term *Europeanization* is fuzzy. Moreover, the term appears to suggest—however unintentionally—that the impact of Europeanization is inherently beneficial. However, as a close look at the case of environmental politics reveals, this may not always be true. In some instances, EU membership may represent a step backward rather than a step forward or may raise as many new problems as it helps to resolve.

This chapter first discusses the concept of Europeanization and the principal factors affecting environmental policy and politics in Hungary. Second, it discusses the effect of EU membership and environmental policy on Hungary. Third, it considers the impact of Hungarian environmental interests on the EU policy framework. The fourth section discusses the methods and record of implementation of EU environmental policy in Hungary.

■ How and in What Areas Does the EU Influence Hungary?

Hungary is affected by a wide range of EU policies. This chapter focuses exclusively on the development of environmental politics in the context of Europeanization. Separating out the effects on Hungary of the EU environmental and market regulatory framework—that is, Europeanization—from the more general effects of globalization, democratization, privatization, FDI, economic rationalization, and the demands of local interests and actors presents significant difficulties. All of the central and east European countries—among them Hungary—have clearly been influenced by the demands of market integration, economic competition, and the emergence of increasingly international or global economic processes. While the impact of these factors has primarily come through their association with the European marketplace, most of the more market-driven impact would likely have occurred even without EU membership.

Distinguishing the impact of Europeanization from the broader range of phenomena noted above is potentially impossible. The force of market competition, industrial restructuring, privatization, and FDI in

Hungary has brought with it entirely new environmental problems. Thus, while EU membership has led to an increase in the level of environmental protection in some areas, the opposite has occurred in others; the phenomenon of free-market competition and the removal of restrictions on trade has likewise brought new challenges. In this sense, the concept of Europeanization is fuzzy. Marketization and globalization are equally compelling forces affecting the Hungarian environment. While they are to some degree synonymous with EU membership, they are also to some degree independent of it.

All of these forces together—Europeanization, democratization, marketization, and globalization—have both positive and negative impacts on the Hungarian environment. The imposition of the EU regulatory framework renders the effective regulation of environmental problems in Hungary both more likely and more problematic. In some respects, Hungarian environmental legislation was stricter than EU environmental legislation.[4] Where the EU environmental framework was stricter, some of the EU regulations have been welcomed by Hungarian environmental organizations such as the Clean Air Action Group (CAAG). But where the EU regulatory framework was not as strict, EU membership initially aroused considerable suspicion and concern (the Central and East European Working Group for the Enhancement of Biodiversity [CEEWEB] initially responded with considerable hesitation toward the EU Bird and Habitat Directives).

National environmental protection initiatives and improvements in the quality of environmental legislation (or for that matter even democratization itself) bear more than just the mark of Europeanization. While the communist past strongly discouraged the involvement of civil society or the independent initiative of environmentally minded experts, the transition to democracy in central and eastern Europe has radically altered the level of commitment of governments and the nature, quality, and strength of social environmental demands. Thus while one important force of environmental change is potentially the EU, a second and potentially even more important element of environmental change is the gradual evolution of civil society, nongovernmental organizations, and even political parties in central and eastern Europe.

Most theorists predict positive impacts on the Hungarian environment stemming from EU membership.[5] Despite such high expectations, EU legislation represents an average or generalized framework that is distinct from the practices of individual states. Many EU member states have far more extensive environmental regulations (in particular the Nordic states, the Netherlands, and Germany). EU environmental regulation thus represents a commonly agreed minimum level of European environmental regulation.[6] Where EU environmental regulation replaces stronger domestic-level regulation, the result is potentially a net loss in overall environmental quality. During the 1990s transition, Hungarian authorities were often inclined to drop stricter regulation in the hopes of promoting more economic growth. Thus in some respects, the overwriting of Hungarian environmental legislation may represent a loss.[7]

There are of course positive environmental aspects to EU membership. Hungary's 1999 EU Screening Report on the environmental chapter indicates a number of areas where Hungarian legislation failed to adequately comply with European requirements.[8] The original bargaining position of the Hungarian government pushed for "existing" plants built prior to 1998 to be excluded from EU emission regulations. The comparable clause in the EU's Large Combustion Plant (LCP) Directive, for example, was July 1987. No such transitional period was ultimately accepted in the final Accession Treaty. Many of the large polluters were older firms—in particular, Hungarian power plants, but also older industrial plants that would have remained exempt from EU limit values on SO_2 and other emissions. In the same vein, the European Commission repeatedly rejected demands for transition periods related to the discharge of "dangerous substances into the aquatic environment." On both of these counts, the Hungarian government relented, receiving only one brief derogation for emissions from large combustion plants. Compliance was promised by December 31, 2004.[9]

The regulation of limit values for some air- and water-borne substances was originally weak in Hungary and the monitoring of some substances was either inadequate or nonexistent. According to the Screening Report, Hungary did not previously monitor the rate of particulate matter (PM_{10}) or the presence of lead in the air. With respect to waste incineration, limit values for heavy-metal pollution previously did not exist. The EU likewise had stricter limit values on the discharge of arsenic, ammonium, iron, manganese, nitrite, boron, and fluoride into the water.[10] With respect to batteries and accumulators, there were previously no limit values for cadmium and heavy metals. The EU directive on asbestos likewise had a strong impact on Hungarian legislation. EU landfill regulations were much stricter than the older Hungarian variety. These were weakly regulated, if at all, and exhibited none of the modern features of landfills in western Europe.[11] According to Gille, as of about 2003, only 15 percent of the 665 registered municipal landfills met current EU technological standards. Moreover, another 620 smaller waste dumps remained unregistered and presumably did not meet the EU regulatory standard.[12]

Pressure from the European Commission to comply with EU regulation is frequently explained by EU insistence on the primary importance
of the Internal Market and the potential distortions due to weaker environmental regulations in central and eastern Europe.[13] This is true, for
example, of the EU position on emissions in the energy sector. Despite
the public-service character of the energy sector in Hungary, the
impending liberalization of the European energy market played a significant role in EU–Central and East European (CEE) negotiations.[14] The
European Commission pointed to the potential for market distortions
and repeatedly required Hungary to justify its position. The longest
derogation for Hungary is ultimately in an area having no real impact
upon competitive Single Market relations—that is, urban wastewater
treatment. In this case—despite its obvious importance for clean
water—Hungary and many other central and east European countries
received derogations until 2015. Many of these investments will be both
costly and time-consuming.[15] Two remaining derogations in the areas of
packaging and packaging-waste and the incineration of hazardous waste
likewise have few implications for the smooth functioning of market
competition.[16]

Data on the reduction of emissions in Hungary present a remarkable
image of success. As illustrated in Figure 16.1, remarkable achievements in emissions reductions and other pollution sources were made
over the period 1989–2002. Hungary has seen remarkable reductions in
the levels of major pollutants. Hungary's per capita emissions surpass
EU levels only in the case of sulfur oxides (SO_x). On all other major
emission types, Hungary is below average levels in the EU. Even with
regard to SO_x, Hungary has witnessed quite dramatic drops over the
period 1989–2000 that either equal or far surpass the rate of decline in
the EU. Finally, Hungary has continued to make considerable
progress—in particular in the reduction of SO_x emissions. The use of
fertilizers has increased since their initial dramatic decline before 1992,
and CO emissions have also recently risen slightly.

EU membership and the role of other factors in explaining these
changes require serious consideration. The strongest competing factors
are democratization, the decline of heavy industry and agriculture, privatization, and FDI. Separating out the exact role of market factors—in
particular the decline of heavy industry (above all, the steel and coal
sectors)[17] and agriculture—and the role of democracy from that of EU
environmental regulation is virtually impossible. All in all, however, a
relatively small share of the progress made is presumably a direct result
of the gradual adoption of the EU regulatory framework. The emergence

Figure 16.1   Per Capita Emission Levels and Fertilizer Use in Hungary and the EU-15

SOx

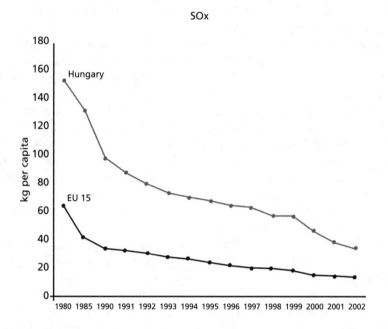

CO2

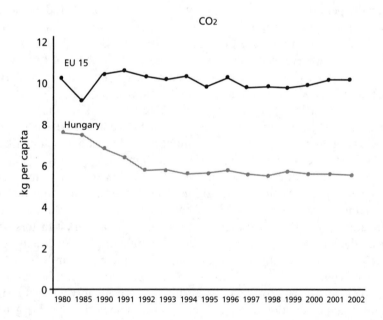

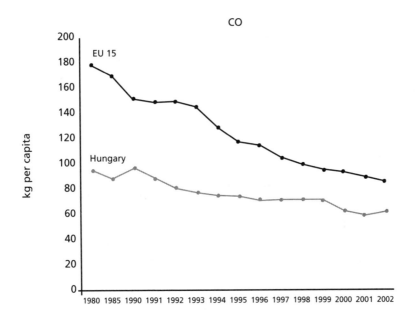

CO

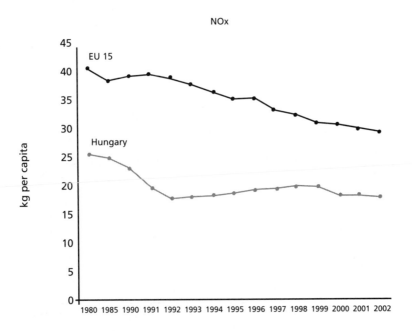

NOx

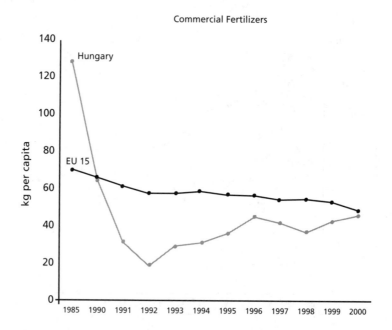

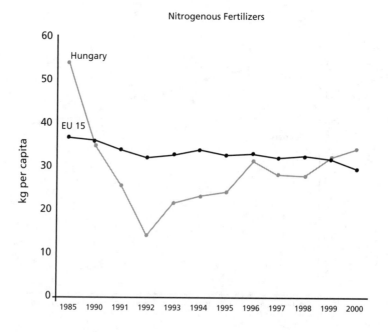

of democracy in 1989, initial changes in environmental policy, and the decline in heavy industry occurred quite early, long before EU membership negotiations—begun in March 1998—had a serious impact on the actions of national governments in central and eastern Europe.[18]

This is not to say the drive for EU membership played no role. The full adoption of the *acquis communautaire* (the existing body of EU legislation) was a clear requirement of EU membership. Yet the rise of environmental concerns in Hungary clearly predates the transition to democracy. Organizations such as the Hungarian Bird Life Association, DunaKör (the Danube Circle), and others were founded in the 1970s and 1980s. While social movements lost their momentum during the transition in the 1990s, many of their leaders became active in political parties and/or the Hungarian Ministry of the Environment and Water Management. Some 100 members of the DunaKör were able to win seats in the first Hungarian parliament in 1990.[19] Powerful forces thus began to shape the Hungarian environment before Hungary began pursuing the goal of EU membership.[20]

Both privatization and FDI had a significantly positive impact on the environmental performance of industry. For one, "separating the regulated from the regulators" presumably strengthens the role of the state as the enforcer of environmental regulation.[21] As at least one interviewee pointed out, old socialist-era firms were able—almost at will—to dump industrial waste into rivers and streams.[22] With privatization and as FDI flowed into Hungary, new environmental permits both required connections to the industrial sewage system and placed important restrictions on the discharge of emissions and other pollutants—frequently in line with existing EU guidelines.[23] In addition, some west European firms brought newer environmental technology with them from the West, thereby introducing cleaner production methods and contributing to improvements in the Hungarian environment.

From an environmental perspective, all reductions in emissions are a positive improvement. However economic and financial pressures may occasionally present either significant barriers to the successful realization of these goals, or encourage shortsighted solutions that trigger new environmental problems. Moreover, the requirement of fulfilling EU priorities may simply divert both attention and resources from other more pressing environmental concerns. Thus the current emphasis on economic growth in conjunction with the low level of civil-society development in Hungary may result in configurations of economic and political interest not well suited to the defense and resolution of environmental concerns. This particular configuration of economic and political interests may ultimately facilitate the relative dominance of EU-level policy priorities at the expense of national and local-level environmental concerns.[24]

Prioritizing Growth: Motorway Construction and the Intensification of Agriculture

As many in the environmental movement repeatedly protest, although the EU claims an interest in sustainable-development priorities,[25] the EU is first and foremost an economic union.[26] The onslaught of European integration is perhaps best represented by the elimination of barriers to trade within the Single Market and through the adoption of a common currency. Thus economic growth priorities frequently appear to outweigh environmental concerns.

Two specific areas provide good examples of ways in which EU membership and the emphasis on economic priorities create important challenges to the regulation of environment problems. For one, the impact of EU membership on Hungary and the remaining central and east European countries in the area of the environment is much broader than merely the impact of adopting EU environmental regulation. As the engine of globalization, the EU's Single Market legislation defends the basic logic of the market and generally prohibits attempts to soften its impact where these obstruct the free movement of goods, capital, and labor.[27] EU membership thus opens up CEE markets to EU products, economic activities, and infrastructure developments, all of which may have significant impacts on the environment and are increasingly difficult to mitigate via national-level legislation.

The opening of markets and integration into the EU marketplace has thus had a distinctly Europeanizing impact on the Hungarian environment. EU environmental regulations are not always up to the task of mitigating the impact of the market. Western environmental approaches typically have little impact on the upward spiral of production and consumption. One outcome of the introduction of market society and western market integration is a dramatic expansion of consumer society and the inevitable rise in the production of waste.

The impact of economic over environmental priorities is likewise felt in the considerable emphasis given to infrastructure projects in Hungary—in particular the construction of motorways. Objections from environmental groups range from the view that motorways are being prioritized without considering the more environmentally friendly advantages of rail and water transport,[28] to the claim that environmental and social concerns are neglected in the pursuit of construction projects and in related environmental impact assessments. The "M0" project to complete a ring highway around Budapest, for example, remains mired in controversy. Concerns were raised regarding potential threats to the Budapest water supply, possible disruptions of an important "wind channel," and the chemical and noise pollution levels the highway would generate for nearby inhabitants.[29]

Despite objections from CAAG that the decision to prioritize motorways is primarily a national-level decision, considerable pressure comes from the EU-driven Trans-European Networks (TENS) and the related Transport Infrastructure Needs Assessment (TINA) programs focusing on central and east European transport infrastructure development.[30] Although railway development is part of the TENS program, the TENS system likewise depends on highway networks. The Hungarian government has clearly locked onto the TENS program as an opportunity to upgrade and modernize its highway network.

EU membership is also likely to have a considerable impact on the intensification of agricultural production in Hungary and thus ultimately the increasing use of commercial fertilizers. Other concerns relate to EU plans to turn the Danube waterway into a major transport corridor with a minimum depth of 2.5 meters. While some NGOs (e.g., CAAG) tend to favor this project due to the potential shifting of traffic from road to waterways, other organizations remain strongly opposed to elements of the project due to their desire to rehabilitate many of the Danube side-arms (created by the meandering river paths).[31] Moreover, some groups argue that trends toward ever-bigger ships should be reversed and newer ships should instead be adapted to fit the Danube.[32]

The current emphasis on growth thus favors infrastructure development and the intensification of agriculture in Hungary. The result is likely to have an overall negative impact on the current state of the environment. While pollution intensity may be reduced as a result of some EU legislation, the overall amounts of pollution created and the impact of these different infrastructure projects on the existing environment are likely to be significant.

The following two examples illustrate the ambiguous impact of market integration and EU environmental policy on the ability of Hungary to pursue stricter environmental goals.

The Tetra Pak Generation and the Europeanization of Waste Production

The opening up of markets and EU membership has allowed the free movement of both goods and producers across borders. Thus, for example, the Swedish-Swiss firm Tetra Pak has set up shop in Hungary and produces carton packaging—for fruit juices and milk—and exports approximately 80 percent of its production.[33] The EU packaging and packaging waste directive originally required a 50 percent rate of packaging waste recycling by 2005, though figures for individual items were only required to meet the more modest goal of 15 percent recovery and recycling. Hungarian compliance with the packaging and packaging waste directive has now been postponed until 2012.[34] Estimated figures for Tetra Pak recycling in Hungary lie much below this figure (1–2 percent in 1999, 0.5 percent in 2003, and 3 percent in 2004).[35] While the Hungarian government introduced product fees in 1995 intended to motivate producers to ensure higher packaging material recovery rates (12.5 percent in 1996, 27 percent in 1999, and 50 percent in 2000),[36] little success has been achieved with respect to Tetra Pak–style cartons. Moreover, while the introduction of selective recycling systems in 2004 made it possible for citizens to recycle paper, plastic, and bottles, allowances have not been made for drink-carton packaging.

The recycling of Tetra Pak–type drink cartons is complicated since the containers themselves are made up of several layers of plastic, paper, and aluminum foil.[37] Alcoa aluminum has only recently developed a recycling system permitting the complete separation and recycling of all the constituent elements of Tetra Pak containers.[38] Since there is so far only one plant in Brazil experimenting with this new technology, more conventional recycling practices are likely to dominate in Europe for now. These involve either the separation of the paperboard material from the plastic and aluminum (the latter is then discarded and the paperboard pulped and recycled), or the thermal compression of the packaging material into chipboard (melting the plastic polyethylene solidifies the mass), or finally the burning of drink cartons in waste-to-energy incinerators producing small amounts of electricity.[39]

The above examples reflect the rosier west European scenario. In Hungary—with no selective collection system in place to deal with drink cartons and no recycling plants that handle this type of material—most of these drink cartons will end up in landfills or waste incineration plants. Although the drink-carton industry hoped to be able to collect and ultimately recycle 8 percent of their production in Hungary in 2005,[40] such figures remained well shy of the EU requirement of 15 percent by December 31, 2005. The three largest Hungarian drink-carton producers (Tetra Pak, SIG Combibloc, and Elopak) recently formed an association. Although this association reportedly has multiple goals—to raise "environmental awareness" and "inspire selective collection,"[41] it was intended primarily to help the industry achieve the EU's 15 percent target recycling and recovery rate for individual materials by December 31, 2005. This association has announced the seemingly unattainable goal—given the current selective recycling system—of 25 percent by 2008.

The Hungarian government reintroduced a product charge on nonrecyclable packaging materials that the drink-carton industry and other nonrecyclable packaging industry producers will have to pay if they are unable to meet the criteria established by the packaging and packaging waste directive—thereby placing the burden of inadequate selective waste collection systems on producers.[42] However, such practices inspire resistance on the part of producers, who presumably feel the national government should play a stronger role in promoting the selective collection of recyclable packaging materials. The Hungarian Mineral Water Association and Product Council filed a suit with the Hungarian constitutional court urging the tax be declared unconstitutional.[43] This law may also be subject to EU Article 177 proceedings for infringements on the free movement of goods.[44] Beverage Can Makers Europe requested the European Commission look into the matter, arguing that Hungarian authorities failed to consult with EU officials before introducing the law, and other European packaging organizations are likewise opposed to this policy.[45]

The Tetra Pak example remains a symbol of the problems inherent in the marketization of Hungarian society and the almost meteoric rise in consumption patterns.[46] It is likewise representative of the problems that emerged in the recycling sector in Hungary. While previously Hungary had a reasonably well-organized deposit and return system for beer and wine bottles, much of the recycling industry has since collapsed. With the rapid introduction of different types of plastic bottling (used, for example, for bottled water and many types of soft drinks) and Tetra Pak–type drink cartons, the traditional source of raw material for this sector has radically declined. The free export of recyclable waste products has likewise had an impact. Recycling rates faltered from about 1991 on. While beer and wine bottles remain subject to deposit-refund systems, the massive inflow of alternative packaging materials has placed an immense burden on existing recycling capacities.[47]

Finally, product charges are unlikely to have an impact on consumer behavior without a significant supply of substitutable products available on the Hungarian market. The low visibility of product fees on individual products sold in stores further weakens their potential impact.

Energy, Emissions-Trading, and the
Not-So-Renewable Biomass Generation

The effect of EU membership on Hungary has been more positive in some cases. Despite the respectable decline in SO_x emission levels, EU membership has led to the further reduction of SO_2 emissions in some power plants. Per capita SO_x emission levels dropped almost 64 percent between 1989 and 2002. Between 1995 and 2002, the SO_2 emission levels of power plants alone dropped approximately 47 percent. SO_2 emissions from power plants constitute the largest share of SO_x emissions (some 73.2 percent in 2000). Similar trends affect other power plant emissions. The most dramatic reductions have been in CO (82.1 percent), while somewhat less dramatic reductions have also been achieved for particulate matter (49.2 percent) and nitrogen oxides (36.3 percent).[48]

Two basic factors have driven emissions' improving investments in Hungary. First, as part of the Kyoto Protocol agreements, the EU has established a Joint Implementation (JI) emissions-trading system. Firms can invest in emissions-saving technologies in other countries and gain "carbon credits" to be used against local emissions. Second, the EU's LCP Directive required several of Hungary's coal-burning power plants to comply with tougher emissions standards by December 31, 2004. The Hungarian Energy Office's 2003 Annual Report identifies five coal-burning power plants whose emissions risked breaching this EU regulation.[49]

The combination of the EU LCP Directive and the potential for emissions trading led several power plant companies in Hungary to make emissions-reducing investments in biomass fuels.[50] Controversial, biomass-based energy production is problematic because biomass power plants burn wood (turned into wood chips) as their principal raw-material source. The Pannonpower plant in Pecs, for example, burns some 380,000 tons of wood per year.[51] The ownership structure of the Hungarian forests complicates the compatible regulation of environmental and profit-oriented interests. State "companies" control some 60 percent of Hungarian forests, but are also responsible for turning a profit.[52] Two such state companies consolidated their economic position by signing 10-year delivery contracts with Pannonpower.[53] Private owners equally interested in turning a profit control the remaining 40 percent of Hungarian forests.[54] Some reports even suggest a share of the wood is imported from Slovakia, Ukraine, and Romania.[55]

Several key questions regarding biomass energy production have since emerged. The first concerns the burden this will place on

Hungarian and neighboring forests and the second concerns why the Hungarian government has decided to support biomass energy production—apparently over other forms of renewable energy such as wind and solar. Despite support for the construction of biomass plants from the Hungarian national government, no government-funded background studies have been completed to analyze the potential burden on Hungarian forests.[56] According to a World Wildlife Federation (WWF) report, usage amounted to 70–80 percent of the "annual increment" (the amount of growth above existing stocks) in 2002. However, the four biomass plants were all completed after 2002 and raised overall demand. In 2002, Hungary's use of its annual increment was only below Finland's (at 84 percent).[57]

Complaints have already been raised about whether or not the Hungarian forests can supply the amount of wood needed for these plants and the WWF report points to claims of illegal clear-cutting. Other wood-using industries in Hungary have likewise raised concerns.[58] While plans exist to build newer biomass plants capable of burning "energy grass" and other types of vegetal matter (e.g., Pannonpower is investing in a new 30-megawatt burner), the technology has apparently not been fully tested. To date, all Hungarian biomass power plants burn wood logged from forests. Since figures for total logging are expressed in cubic meters, while estimates of biomass power plant needs are expressed in tons of wood burned (currently 1,082 tons or approximately 1.2 million cubic meters of wood per year), estimating the precise amounts currently required is complicated.[59]

Why the Hungarian government has decided to support biomass energy production over other forms of renewable energy production is more complicated. The Hungarian government appears to have decided to promote biomass production despite the great potential for wind energy in Hungary—some 700 megawatts of production have so far received environmental permits in Hungary.[60] The choice for biomass is presumably a function of the presence of power plants requiring conversion in order to be able to meet EU emission requirements, the lack of available capital for other conversion methods, and the advantages offered by JI (both for the international investor and for the domestic framework). In this way, Hungary could keep existing power plants open, meet the EU requirements for LCP emissions, and raise the share of renewable energy sources in Hungary.[61]

Thus, while on the surface the increasing share of renewables in Hungarian energy production may sound like a positive development, the future impact on Hungarian and surrounding forests remains a perplexing problem. Moreover, given current world concerns about global warming, the loss of forests that act as "carbon sinks" by absorbing excess CO_2 in the atmosphere introduces further complications.

■ How and in What Areas Does Hungary Influence the EU?

The ability of central and east European states to influence EU policy remains underdeveloped. This is in part true because until very recently, the central and east European states were primarily policy-takers rather than policymakers. The EU accession process permitted no opt-outs of any kind from the existing EU environmental policy framework, making it exceptionally difficult for the central and east European states—to date—to have a significant impact on the EU environmental policy framework.

With the advent of EU membership, one can expect the central and east European countries to rapidly become policymakers or contributors rather than policy-takers.[62] Within the European decisionmaking framework, environmental policy is typically subject to the co-decision procedure in the European Parliament and Qualified Majority Voting in the Council of Ministers. While Hungary is not a very powerful political partner in either of these bodies, given the relative importance of environmental issues in central and eastern Europe and given their relative budgetary cost, one can expect these countries to watch the evolution of EU environmental policy with great attention and attempt to influence it where possible. There are in fact already examples of Hungary working with other EU states.

Hungary and the UK, for example, issued a joint proposal in 2004 for the REACH Directive currently being debated in the EU. The "one substance, one registration" approach would help to simplify the registration of industrial chemicals and would require the registration of all hazardous chemicals (not only those used on animals).[63] A second example is offered by the activities of CEEWEB, which has mobilized to protect the biodiversity regions in central and eastern Europe from the type of fragmentation they have experienced in western Europe. In this respect, their cooperation with western organizations and their potential policy impact on the EU is expected to be positive.

The current emphasis on economic development over concern for the environment does not augur well for local efforts in promoting environmental policy. On the other hand, Hungary and most of the central and east European countries may likewise offer new potential for environmental action.

■ How Does Hungary Implement and Comply with EU Policies?

A few of the existing EU environmental regulations have not yet been implemented in Hungary and will only be implemented in the years to come. The incineration of hazardous waste and the packaging and packaging waste directives should be fully implemented and operational by 2006 and 2012, while Hungary has agreed to full compliance with the waste water directive only by 2015. The only other derogation Hungary received concerned the LCP Directive, but Hungary managed to achieve compliance with this directive by 2005.

On all other accounts, Hungary has either fully implemented existing EU environmental regulations or is in the process of doing so. In the context of the accession process, Hungary has adopted an extensive array of EU legislation dealing with the environment and other matters and has approximated the EU's existing environmental guidelines. In addition, Hungary has received derogations in a relatively small number of areas (four).[64] In this respect at least, Hungary's record of implementation compares quite favorably to that of other central and east European countries.

Since nonimplementation was not an option during the accession process, the real implementation issues for Hungary concern either its ability to monitor and enforce newly adopted EU environmental regulations, or the continued successful implementation of legislation required after 2004. For example, although Hungary has developed a National Waste Management Plan for 2003–2008, elements of this plan are still debated, such as the plan to double Hungary's waste incineration capacity with the construction of six new incinerators.[65]

With respect to the Hungarian record of compliance, many of the environmental NGOs in Hungary actively object that while the EU may have brought new and sometimes improved environmental legislation, the biggest problem with communist-era governments was the enforcement of existing legislation. EU membership, according to many of these organizations, has not so far brought substantial change. While EU environmental legislation has been faithfully transcribed into the domestic legal framework, monitoring and enforcement mechanisms have not been as effectively introduced.

The relative strength of environmental NGOs and green parties in Hungary—as in most of central and eastern Europe—is problematic. Hungary boasts a considerable number of environmental NGOs. But their relative independence from governmental bodies such as the Environmental Ministry is occasionally suspect due to their dependence on financing from the Environmental Ministry or other European organizations. The repeated failure of green parties to successfully contest elections in Hungary is indicative of the problems inherent in promoting a more "green"-oriented agenda. The current Green Party in Hungary enjoys virtually no support from the major national-level environmental organizations and is challenged for control of the environmental ticket by Védegylet (Protect the Future), whose leader, Sólyom László, became president of Hungary in June 2005. While the new president may give some renewed weight to environmental issues, the government focuses primarily on the priority of economic development.

Significant changes have occurred with respect to the overall degree of transparency of environmental issues. These may ultimately have a significant impact on levels of monitoring and enforcement in Hungary. While far from perfect, the dramatically heightened degree of scrutiny the EU membership and EU reporting requirements have introduced will presumably have a significant impact on both the public availability of data[66] and the likelihood that individuals or organizations will be able to hold firms or government to account.

More serious problems emerge regarding the ability of Hungarian environmental NGOs to actively participate in the decisionmaking process in Hungary. Despite the generally favorable NGO review of their relationship to the Environmental Ministry, NGOs strongly criticize their ability to access important environmental information and the degree of their involvement in decisionmaking—in particular in ministries other than the Environmental Ministry.[67] These documents draw particular attention to the so-called Highway Act, which effectively limits the ability of NGOs to have a significant impact on the planning of motorways in Hungary.[68]

The degree to which monitoring systems are managed and run by truly independent bodies represents a potential concern. While most air emissions are measured by the Hungarian National Meteorological Association, the air-monitoring system at the Dorog hazardous waste incineration plant (the largest such facility in Hungary) is currently managed by the French group Onyx. While outside observers may request data, no online independent and public monitoring system exists and there are occasionally problems with the availability of data. The local environmental organization has no funds with which to set up its own independent monitoring station and appears to lack the technical expertise as well. At the same time, the hazardous waste incineration capacity at Dorog has been doubled in recent years.[69]

There are a number of successes regarding both the implementation of and compliance with EU environmental regulations. The reduction of emissions and other pollutants noted above represents one important success. The connection of industry and households to sewage treatment plants will represent a second.[70] On the other hand, some elements of the existing enforcement mechanism are quite weak. According to the Hungarian Environmental Management and Law Association (EMLA), fines for infractions of environmental regulations in Hungary range from a minimum of 4 euros to a maximum of 600 euros—a surprisingly small sum. Collection rates are likewise relatively low (nationally, 33.1 percent of fines go unpaid). In Budapest, the share of unpaid fines is extraordinarily high (82 percent).[71]

Measures of increasing infringements on environmental law should, however, be seen in context. Approximately one-third of all policy implementation infringements in the EU involve environmental policy.[72] While some of the biggest offenders with respect to poor implementation of EU environmental policy are the less developed economies (Spain, Italy, Ireland, Greece, and Portugal), other frequent offenders are France, Germany, the UK, Belgium, and to a lesser extent the Netherlands and Austria.[73] Thus far, the central and east European countries have not achieved any notoriety on implementation infringements.[74]

Far more important potentially than Hungary's record of implementation and compliance is the question of the suitability of EU environmental policy to, and thus the consequences of, Europeanization for Hungary. The answer to this fundamental question remains shrouded in the haze of demands for economic development first, environmental protection second, the relative dominance of EU over local environmental policy orientations, and the relative weakness of civil society. There are clear benefits from EU membership, in particular with respect to the degree of transparency and the increasing potential for citizen action on the environment. But the emphasis on infrastructure spending, economic development, and EU environmental policy introduces new environmental problems and issues into the Hungarian environment.

■ Future Trends and Prospects

Many of the above examples suggest that EU environmental regulation is a relatively loosely structured tool for protecting the environment. Just as many new environmental problems have been unleashed by the problems of EU market integration and/or globalization. Moreover, it remains unclear how many of the changes in the Hungarian legislative framework might have occurred even without the pressures of EU membership. The transition to democracy has resulted in significant changes facilitating the active participation of opposition groups and civil nongovernmental organizations.

As many in the environmental movement in central and eastern Europe claim, the fact that the EU emphasizes economic over environmental factors and thus pays only lip-service to its stated goals of "sustainable development" is difficult to ignore. In this regard, the Europeanization of the Hungarian environment is a complex and multifaceted problem to which EU environmental regulation is not fully equipped to respond. And in some cases, EU regulation may ultimately constrain national-level environmental initiatives and enforce the supremacy of the EU's Internal Market. Further, other EU policy goals are frequently at odds with or raise concerns about environmental sustainability.

The dominance of the EU environmental regulatory framework in Hungary is occasionally a matter of some concern. Hungarian civil society is still weakly organized and environmental concerns typically do not top the social agenda. Moreover, environmental NGOs in Hungary are remarkably weak at the base, with almost no membership upon which to depend for revenues and protest actions. Thus policy initiatives, such as the example of biomass energy production, receive insufficient public attention. While environmental NGOs attempt to fill the gap, the power of industrial and political lobbies in Hungary is typically perceived as far greater.

Thus this chapter ends with a mixed picture of the impact of Europeanization on the Hungarian environment. There are clearly some positive aspects to the adoption of European environmental regulation. But there are likewise costs both in terms of the loss of some stronger pieces of Hungarian legislation and in terms of the increasing marketization and globalization of the Hungarian economy. While some in Hungary argue for a consistent emphasis on the foundation of sustainable development—suggesting this can be achieved with a radical shift of the structure of taxation from income to natural-resource use[75]—such argumentation risks the label of utopianism in a country now savoring the luxuries of modern consumer societies.

While Hungary's membership in the EU is likely to experience growing pains in coming years, Hungarians nonetheless seem committed to the idea of belonging to the European "Club." The greater mobility membership offers individuals who long endured significant restrictions on their ability to travel and experience other nations presumably motivates many to favor membership over other alternatives. The perception of economic gain was likewise a strong incentive. Finally, the credibility of commitments to the environment created by the level of EU scrutiny, monitoring, and enforcement—despite inherent costs—may ultimately prove to be one of the more important rewards of membership.

■ Notes

This chapter is based in part on a series of 30 interviews of leaders of environmental organizations conducted in Hungary in spring 2005. Their assistance and funding from the Associated Colleges of the Midwest Global Partners Project (supported by a grant from the Andrew W. Mellon Foundation) is gratefully acknowledged. I thank Viktória Szirmai for assistance in selecting organizations to interview, and Márton Rövid and Lukas Vrba for research assistance and data collection.

The subtitle to this chapter is a reference to an article published by the Swedish Institute for European Policy Studies (SIEPS), Stockholm, "From Policy Takers to Policy Makers: Adapting EU Cohesion Policy to the Needs of the New Member States," SIEPS 2005: 5.

1. See for example www.euractiv.com, "EU Accession: Sentiment Ranges Between Confidence and Uncertainty" (April 18, 2003).

2. See www.euractiv.com, "Referenda on EU Constitution: State of Play in the Member States" (August 4, 2005).

3. See for example the statements from Hungarian prime minister Gyürcsany Ferenc before the parliament on May 30, 2005 (www.meh.hu).

4. See for example Kerekes, "Economics, Technology, and Environment in Hungary," p. 146, and Gille, "Europeanizing Hungarian Waste Policies" and "Legacy of Waste or Wasted Legacy?" Pavlínek and Pickles provide an excellent overview of environmental legislation in some central and east European countries (including Hungary), both before and after 1989, in *Environmental Transitions,* chapter 8.

5. Lynch, "Closing the Deception Gap," suggests the greatest gain is likely to come from the closing of the "deception gap," that is, the increased degree of monitoring and the greater potential for enforcement of environmental policy that EU membership brings. Slocock, in "The Paradoxes of Environmental Policy in Eastern Europe" and "'Whatever Happened to the Environment?'" argues that the attraction of EU membership motivated many states to adopt EU environmental policies as rapidly as possible.

6. While some have argued that EU environmental legislation is more progressive than intergovernmentalist "least common denominator" predictions suggest, once adopted and implemented, EU-level environmental legislation becomes a commonly agreed minimum level of regulation.

7. See for example Kerekes, "Economics, Technology, and Environment in Hungary," and Gille, "Europeanizing Hungarian Waste Policies" and "Legacy of Waste or Wasted Legacy?" The latter, in particular, laments the elimination of Hungarian policies regulating the recycling of hazardous waste. Ellison, "Politics and the Environment in Central Europe," notes the diversion of attention from specifically Hungarian environmental problems and strategies.

8. See "Hungary Screening Results," Chapter 22: Environment (Directorate General for Enlargement MD 282/99).

9. Full liberalization of the European energy sector is planned for 2007. Partial liberalization began in 1999 and 2003. Hungary took its first steps toward liberalization of the energy sector in 2003. Large consumers were permitted to purchase electricity on the free market (www.BusinessHungary.com, "Power to the People! Edging Closer to a Fully Liberalized Electricity Market").

10. See the *Journal of the Hungarian Hydrological Society*, 2001.

11. While the practice of depositing waste in landfills previously did not involve any preparation of the terrain or separating out of recyclable materials, landfills now have to fulfill a number of EU criteria. For example, the land on which waste will be deposited is first sealed with a layer of plastic and drainage pipes collect seepage in a leaching pond at the bottom of the landfill. Methane gas is likewise vented out into the atmosphere and will eventually be collected and used as a biogas. More modern landfills engage in far more extensive selective separation of recyclables and the composting and reuse of organic waste.

12. Gille, "Europeanizing Hungarian Waste Policies," p. 123.

13. West European sectoral-level producer organizations frequently intervened in the accession process and insisted upon the creation of a "level playing field," that is, a regulatory framework that would reduce any competitive advantage by raising standards to a minimum level in central and eastern Europe (see Ellison, "Entangling Fortunes," chapter 4).

14. See the series of negotiating documents exchanged between Hungary and the European Union on the details of Hungary's request for transitional periods.

15. Hungary, for example, will build a wastewater treatment plant for Budapest on Csepel Island. This will require building a sewage-pipe system along the edge of the Danube that will transport minimally treated wastewater—currently flushed directly into the Danube from the west side of Budapest—all the way down to Csepel Island on the south side of Budapest. This project will require several years of planning and construction. The contract was signed in December 2004, and will cost between 500 and 537 million euros. Completion is currently scheduled for 2009 (see www.kvvm.hu, "Szennyvíztisztítási beruházás a fővárosban," December 2, 2004; and www.Aquamedia.at, "The First Sod Has Been Cut: Middle Europe's Biggest Waste Treatment Plant Has Been Agreed").

16. Inglis ("Enlargement and the Environment Acquis," pp. 143–144) suggests the EU ranks market priorities over environmental concerns. A safeguard

clause in the Act of Accession (Article 38) allows the European Commission to bar products from entry to the Internal Market or to withdraw community funds as a result of failure to uphold measures assuring the smooth functioning of the Internal Market.

17. Some of the survivors of the transition to market economies—power plants; oil refining; district heating; pharmaceuticals; and chemical, cement, sugar, and some remaining steel production—remain significant emitters.

18. Hungary's history of environmental regulation exhibits improvements even over the period 1980–1990. For example, between 1980 and 1993, Hungary was able to reduce its SO_2 emissions by some 54 percent, far surpassing its Helsinki Protocol commitment of 30 percent. However, the gradual bringing online of the four separate blocks of the PAKS nuclear power plant explains some of this decline (Kaderják and Lehoczki, "The Cost of Alternative Policies to Reduce SO_2 Emission in Hungary," p. 111). As Szirmai notes, Hungary, like many of the central and east European countries, began introducing environmental legislation in the 1960s and 1970s (Szirmai, "Protection of the Environment," p. 25; see also Pavlínek and Pickles, *Environmental Transitions,* chapter 8).

19. See the brief history of the Hungarian Green Democrats (www.zd.hu).

20. The history of green social movements in central and eastern Europe and Hungary is well documented. For a brief overview of the literature and the major steps in green activism in Hungary and central and eastern Europe, see Ellison, "Politics and the Environment in Central Europe," pp. 17–24.

21. Initially the prices of privatized firms were kept low in exchange for commitments to reduce emissions and the Hungarian government likewise set up a so-called environmental clean-up guarantee fund. Over the early years of transition, Hungarian privatization law was gradually strengthened—in particular in 1992—to make environmental audits obligatory for new investors. This was paralleled with liability commitments to cover the costs of environmental problems to emerge after the privatization had taken place (Páczi and Kaderják, "Environmental Impacts of Industrial Privatization in Hungary," pp. 54, 57, 62–63).

22. Many of these sites are now the target of clean-up programs organized by local NGOs and national and local governments.

23. See also Reiniger, "Hungarian Environmental Protection Licensing and Enforcement Procedures."

24. Ellison, "Politics and the Environment in Central Europe."

25. Sustainable development is mentioned six times in the Draft Constitutional Treaty approved in June 2004. This represents an attempt to integrate this concept more firmly into the core of the EU's environmental policy-making framework. Article 6 of the previous Treaty Establishing the European Community expressed a commitment to the goal of sustainable development.

26. See the common position of the green movement on EU membership in *Turning Green: Hungarian Greens on the EU.*

27. In Article 177 cases, the European Court of Justice has frequently sided against national environmental regulations based on EU directives that obstruct the free movement of goods (Cichowski, "Integrating the Environment").

28. CAAG published several critiques of this policy approach. See for

example Lukács, "Are Motorways Good for the Hungarian Economy?" and Kiss, "EU Accession, Transport and the Environment."

29. See for example Pato, "Hungary," p. 50.

30. The TINA project was originally designed in 1995 to deal with transport infrastructure development in central and eastern Europe. See Fleischer, *Considerations on Road Transport Networks Crossing Hungary*, pp. 5–6.

31. Many of these "side-arms" were lost when the overall level of the Danube in Hungary was lowered as a result of building the Gabcsikovo Dam in Slovakia.

32. Organizations such as the World Wildlife Federation (the Austrian branch), the Hungarian Greens, and the Danube Settlement Alliance have been organizing conferences and lobbying the Hungarian government. These organizations support the rehabilitation of existing side-arms and the protection of some bottleneck areas that likewise tend to be ecological hot spots. They likewise oppose the deepening of the riverbed and favor the use of smaller and more modern forms of river transport.

33. There are several producers of drink cartons in Hungary. Tetra Pak is currently the largest Hungarian producer of drink cartons with a 64 percent share of the market. Two of the remaining producers are SIG Combibloc (with a 27 percent share) and Elopak (with a 10 percent share) (*MTI EcoNews* [April 6, 2005, "Recycling Association Aims to Collect 8pc of All Used Drink Boxes"]).

34. The original packaging and packaging waste directive was amended by Directive 2004/12/EC. This new directive provided longer temporary derogations from the original directive for all of the new member states.

35. *REC Bulletin* (summer 1999), "Local Producer Boxed-in by Government," and *MTI EcoNews* (April 6, 2005, "Recycling Association Aims to Collect 8pc of All Used Drink Boxes").

36. Ibid.

37. Cartons not intended for long life do not always contain an aluminum layer (Oláh, "Waste Management of Tetra Pak Products in Hungary and Sweden," p. 15).

38. See www.azom.com, "World's First Carton Packaging Recycling Plant Using Innovative Plasma Technology" (May 16, 2005).

39. Oláh, "Waste Management of Tetra Pak Products in Hungary and Sweden," pp. 21–24.

40. *MTI EcoNews* (April 6, 2005, "Recycling Association Aims to Collect 8pc of All Used Drink Boxes"). According to the EU packaging and waste directive, producers had to ensure 15 percent recovery and recycling of individual packaging materials by December 31, 2005. The goal of 8 percent for the drink-carton industry falls short of this level.

41. *Pepper 21* (November 4, 2004), "The Alliance of Beverage Can Producers Start with Ambitious Aims."

42. Companies that successfully recollect 50 percent of their packaging will be exempted from these product charges (*Transitions Online*, "Uncorking a Debate Over Bottles," October 11, 2004).

43. See *Business and Environment* (July 2005, "Plastic Bottlers Challenge Hungarian Levy," p. 12).

44. Both the Danish and German models of product charges have met with

difficulties before the ECJ. While the ECJ appears to favor deposit-return systems, it has rejected product charge models that impose barriers to the free movement of goods (see Van Calster, "Something for Everyone in the Judgment of the European Court of Justice in the German Bottles Saga").

45. See *Business and Environment* (May 2005, "EU Countries Upset Packaging Industry," pp. 11–12). Article 95 of the Treaty Establishing the European Community in principle allows states to retain stricter regulations where these are necessary to protect the environment. Hungary's tax on nonrecyclable packaging materials is expected to have an impact on imported beer sold in cans and similar goods but is rationalized based on the fact that consumers otherwise bear the costs of their disposal in landfills (www.BusinessHungary.com, "The Costs of Going Green"). Europen, the European Organization for Packaging and the Environment, has likewise raised objections to this new law (see *European Bulletin* 29 [February–March 2005]).

46. See also Harper, "Encounters with Wild Capitalism."

47. See for example *REC* (1999, pp. 69–70). While selective recycling exists for PET-type plastic bottles (commonly used for mineral water), once collected, most of these bottles are shipped to China for recycling.

48. All data from the Web pages of the Hungarian Energy Office (www.eh.gov.hu) and Ellison, "Weighting the Politics of the Environment in the New Europe."

49. Hungarian Energy Office, "A Magyar Energia Hivatal 2003," p. 30.

50. Other power plants in Hungary invested in desulfurization filters (the Matra power plant), switched from coal to oil (Dunamenti power plant), or improved their incinerator technology to reduce their NO_x emissions (Dunamenti, Tisza II, and EMA power plants) (Hungarian Energy Office, "A Magyar Energia Hivatal 2003," p. 30).

51. Prime minister's office estimate based on data from the Hungarian Energy Office and published in a recent PowerPoint presentation (Gögös, "Javaslat a megújuló energiaforrasók elterjesztésére," p. 11).

52. Máthé and Pollard, "Ecological and Environmental Concerns of the Forest Biomass Use for Energy Production," pp. 9, 16; Benedek and Gálhidy, "Forest Degradation."

53. See www.nol.hu, "Biomassza-premier: fával vagy favel?" (August 24, 2004). The two forest companies mentioned are Mecseki Erdészeti (Mefa) Rt. and Somogyi Erdészeti és Faipari (Sefag) Rt.

54. The record of illegal logging activities—inasmuch as these are accurately recorded—is three times greater for privately owned forests in Hungary. However, this comprises a very small share of logging activities overall (UNECE/FAO, "Country Report: Hungary," p. 2).

55. Interview with a representative of the Hungarian branch of the World Wildlife Federation.

56. Despite a strong push for more biomass production coming from a recent EU report on renewable energy sources, even this report emphasizes the need for more sustainability studies (European Commission, "The Share of Renewable Energy in the EU," p. 37). Austria, which produces some 70 percent of its energy needs from renewable resources, produces only a very small amount of power from biomass (some 50 megawatts, an amount smaller than

Hungary's current 100+ megawatts from its larger biomass power plants). Finland is the only other country in western Europe to use a significant amount of biomass energy production.

57. According to Máthé and Pollard, Hungary used somewhat less of its annual increment in 2000. This number rose significantly already by 2002 ("Ecological and Environmental Concerns of the Forest Biomass Use for Energy Production," pp. 8, 14) and is presumably higher with the inclusion of wood now used for biomass production.

58. Máthé and Pollard, "Ecological and Environmental Concerns of the Forest Biomass Use for Energy Production," p. 16. See www.nol.hu, "Biomassza-premier: fával vagy füvel?" (August 24, 2004).

59. Máthé and Pollard provide the estimate in cubic meters ("Ecological and Environmental Concerns of the Forest Biomass Use for Energy Production," p. 14). The estimate of total tonnage is based on data collected on all Hungarian biomass facilities (including heating and power production).

60. Kazai, "Renewable Energy Sources."

61. As part of the EU's participation in the Kyoto Protocol, the EU adopted the "Renewables Directive" in 2001, setting minimum targets for the national share of renewable energy production by 2010. Hungary's commitment to this directive would raise its share of renewables from 0.5 percent in 2001 to 3.6 percent in 2010, the lowest among the new member states. Originally, Hungary was expected to achieve a target of 11.5 percent by 2010. But this target was reduced to 3.6 percent during the accession negotiations (WWF, *The Eastern Promise*, "Profile Report: Hungary," p. 1).

62. This transition is already evident in some areas. For example, with respect to the 2007–2013 framework perspective on the Structural and Cohesion Funds, there are already positive examples of attempts to become policy-shapers. See for example the recent SIEPS 2005 publication with the appropriate title, "From Policy Takers to Policy Makers: Adapting EU Cohesion Policy to the Needs of the New Member States."

63. See Warhurst, "REACH, a New Approach to Chemicals Regulation in Europe," p. 171.

64. See Ellison, "Politics and the Environment in Central Europe," p. 14.

65. Gille, "Europeanizing Hungarian Waste Policies," p. 127.

66. Perhaps the most important EU initiative in this regard is the European Pollutant Emission Register (EPER), which provides publicly available online information on the emissions of all factories in Europe (www.eper.cec.eu.int).

67. See the Civil Report, titled *Civil Report About the Implementation of Aarhus Convention in Hungary* (2005), submitted to the UNECE secretariat of the Aarhus Convention by members of green NGOs in Hungary.

68. Ibid.; Clean Air Action Group, "Communication to the Aarhus Compliance Committee."

69. Interview with representative of the local Dorog environmental organization.

70. Many objections are raised regarding the degree of technological overkill and the failure to adopt more locally based and environmentally friendly solutions. But the general concept of the need for wastewater treatment remains uncontested.

71. Environmental Management and Law Association, "Study on Respect for Community Environmental Law," p. 27.

72. See "Take Environmental Law into Your Own Hands," *Environment for Europeans 20,* June 2005, pp. 10–11. In recent history, this has been the case in previous European Commission studies of implementation (Inglis, "Enlargement and the Environment Acquis," p. 149).

73. See Commission of the European Communities, "Sixth Annual Survey on the Implementation and Enforcement of Community Environmental Law 2004" (SEC [2005] 1055).

74. While Hungarians exhibit concern for environmental issues—82 percent to 91 percent of Hungarians think the environment has an impact on the quality of life, should be considered in policymaking, and ranks equally with economic and social concerns—25 percent of Hungarians say they rarely or never attempt to protect the environment. In this regard, Hungary is second only to Poland (Eurobarometer, 2005, pp. 28, 31, 33, 41–42).

75. See in particular the work of Iván Gyulai, director of the Ecological Institute for Sustainable Development in Miskolc.

17

The Czech Republic: Waning Enthusiasm

Sharon Fisher

THE CZECH REPUBLIC BEGAN its postcommunist transition like other states in central and eastern Europe, with the "return to Europe" being one of the key themes of the November 1989 "velvet revolution." The country finally joined the European Union (EU) almost 15 years later, acceding on May 1, 2004, along with nine other new members. Although initial indicators signal that EU membership has brought overwhelming benefits to the Czech Republic, eagerness to support the European project now appears to be waning, both among the political elite and the population. Even the 2002–2006 ruling parties, which saw EU membership very favorably, were hesitant about adopting certain demands from Brussels that would potentially harm their popular support, particularly in the economic realm. Moreover, there is a danger that if the pre-election opposition comes to power after the June 2–3, 2006, parliamentary elections, the next government could adopt an even more rebellious attitude toward the EU.

Perhaps part of the reason for the Czechs' lack of enthusiasm for the EU in recent years relates to the chaotic domestic political situation, which focuses attention on petty party politics rather than on issues such as the country's international role. Following the June 2002 parliamentary elections, the country was ruled by a coalition consisting of the Social Democrats (CSSD), together with two center-right junior partners: the Christian Democrats (KDU-CSL) and the Freedom Union (US-DEU), all three of which are considered "Euro-enthusiasts." With little in common otherwise, the goal of EU membership served as one of the main factors in holding the fragile government together in the run-up to the Czech Republic's accession in May 2004. The three ruling parties had the narrowest possible majority in the lower house of the parliament, with the support of 101 out of 200 deputies, making governance very difficult and the approval of legislation a continual struggle. The situation was especially complicated in light of the general hostility of the two opposition parties: the Civic Democratic Party (ODS) and the Communists, which are classified as "Euro-skeptics" and "Euro-rejects," respectively.[1]

Given the tense political situation, the cabinet experienced several serious shake-ups after the Czech Republic's EU accession. From the 2002 elections through July 2004, the country was led by Prime Minister Vladimir Spidla, who was forced to resign based on the CSSD's poor results in the June 2004 elections to the European Parliament. After Spidla's departure, a new Czech government, led by Stanislav Gross, won a vote of confidence in the parliament in August 2004. However, that government started to crumble in early 2005, because of a scandal related to property held by Prime Minister Gross and his wife. Only after the approval of a third CSSD-led cabinet in May 2005, this time under Prime Minister Jiri Paroubek, did the political situation finally begin to stabilize. A virtual political unknown prior to his appointment, Paroubek demonstrated surprising agility in political maneuvering; having convinced his party's junior coalition partners to remain in the government, he forged agreement on a new policy statement, and persuaded the left-wing CSSD rebels to vote in favor of the revamped cabinet. After losing substantial support from 2002 through early 2005, the popularity of the CSSD finally started to recover under Paroubek.

Recent governments have tried, although not always successfully, to meet EU demands in a timely fashion. Nonetheless, legislation has often been blocked or at least delayed by the opposition. That is particularly true since former ODS leader Vaclav Klaus was elected to the presidency in early 2003 and the ODS won a near majority in the senate in November 2004. While Klaus has been the loudest Euro-skeptical voice on the Czech political scene, certain ODS representatives have been outspoken as well, complaining about such issues as the social benefits systems in western Europe and the size of the Brussels bureaucracy. Both Klaus and the ODS have been especially critical about the EU's infringements on the powers of the nation-state, ignoring the fact that it is globalization rather than the EU that has limited the space for maneuvering in the economic sphere, particularly for small countries such as the Czech Republic.

It must be noted that Klaus's position on the EU has evolved considerably since the early 1990s. During his term as Czech prime minister in 1992–1997, Klaus was largely pro-European, and it was his government that actually submitted the Czech Republic's application for EU membership in 1996. Even then, however, Klaus took a different approach from other central and east European candidates, as he emphasized the Czech Republic's "superiority," both toward the country's eastern neighbors and toward the occasionally protectionist west.[2] Klaus frequently presented his country as a "tiger," claiming as early as October 1993 that the economic transition was complete and describing the Czech Republic in May 1994 as "a nonleftist island" in central Europe.[3] Many people in the Czech Republic and abroad believed Klaus's rhetoric about the supremacy of the Czech model of reform, and the country became the darling of the west.

Klaus's fairytale story slowly begun to unravel, however, as the inconsistencies between his Thatcherite discourse and concrete policies gradually became apparent.[4] While Klaus continued to present his approach as right-wing, the Czech economy remained largely unrestructured, as his government delayed key reforms in an effort to maintain social peace. By 1997, the Czech "economic miracle" had disintegrated as confidence in the economy declined and the currency plummeted.[5] Coupon privatization, which was aimed at increasing popular support for reforms by making ordinary citizens into shareholders, was eventually seen as a negative phenomenon since the lack of sufficient regulation led to a situation where many Czechs put their shares in investment funds that were controlled by state-owned banks. As a result, corporate governance was absent, unemployment remained unnaturally low, and the banking system ended up in shambles. Klaus's cabinet fell in late 1997 due to a corruption scandal.

New parliamentary elections were held in the Czech Republic in June 1998, followed by the appointment of a minority cabinet led by Prime Minister Milos Zeman of the CSSD, with tacit support from Klaus's ODS. The Zeman government was not very ambitious in terms of fiscal reforms, but it did make considerable strides in privatization and restructuring. Although the Czechs were initially reluctant to sell off their "family silver" to foreigners, majority shares in all major banks were eventually sold to west Europeans. Zeman chose to go into retirement after his term ended in 2002, and he handed over the reins to Spidla.

Klaus's fall from power in 1997, combined with the demonstrated lack of success of his reform model, proved to be instrumental in shifting ODS attitudes toward the EU. The party could no longer talk about Czech "superiority," and it focused instead on spreading fear about the infringements that EU membership would have on Czech national sovereignty. In 2002, the ODS used an openly Euro-skeptical approach in the parliamentary election campaign for the first time, along the lines of the British Conservative Party. However, despite a relatively low level of support among the Czech population for EU accession, the ODS achieved worse-than-expected results.[6] After the 2002 elections, the ODS went into opposition.

■ How and in What Areas Does the EU Influence the Czech Republic?

Prior to EU accession, many Czechs were concerned about the possible negative effects of membership, including higher unemployment, a jump in consumer prices, and rising bankruptcies. Analysts warned that some Czech firms would be unable to compete in the Common Market and would be forced to fold, while others would be unable to meet the EU's stringent criteria. The effects of enterprise closings would be compounded by the fact that Czechs would be unable to seek employment abroad since most of the EU-15 countries demanded a transition period on the free movement of labor, a stipulation that was especially unpopular among Czechs since it made them feel like second-class citizens within the EU.

During the first year of membership, none of the projections of gloom and doom actually occurred, however. In fact, preliminary economic data demonstrated that the Czech Republic benefited substantially from EU accession, with most key indicators for 2004 showing the best results since the mid-1990s. As shown in Table 17.1, GDP growth accelerated to 4.7 percent in 2004, the fastest rate since 1995. Exports jumped 25.7 percent in local currency terms in 2004, also the highest growth rate since 1995. Meanwhile, the foreign trade deficit narrowed to its lowest level since 1994, before shifting to a surplus in 2005. Gross fixed investment was up by 5.3 percent in 2004, the fastest rate since 2001. Industrial output surged 9.5 percent in 2004, the best result since 2001. Those figures indicate that Czech industry gained significantly from EU membership. It must be noted, however, that foreign investors were responsible for much of the growth in industrial production, exports, and investment, as domestically owned industries were much less successful in competing on the international market. The Czech

Table 17.1   Economic Indicators in the Czech Republic (in percentages unless otherwise indicated)

	2000	2001	2002	2003	2004	2005 (prelim.)
Annual growth in:						
–GDP	3.9	2.6	1.5	3.2	4.7	6.0
–Industrial output	1.5	10.6	4.8	5.8	9.5	5.7
–Exports	23.4	13.2	–1.2	9.3	25.7	8.9
–Investment	4.9	5.4	3.4	4.7	5.3	3.7
–Inflation	4.0	4.7	1.8	0.1	2.8	1.9
Share of GDP:						
–Trade balance	–5.6	–5.1	–3.0	–2.8	–1.0	1.4
–Current account balance	–4.9	–5.4	–5.6	–6.4	–6.1	–2.0
–Public finance balance	–3.7	–5.9	–6.8	–12.5	–3.0	–2.6
Unemployment rate (ILO standards)	8.8	8.1	7.3	7.8	8.3	8.0
Net FDI inflows (in billions of euros)	€5.37	€6.11	€8.77	€1.60	€3.17	€8.17

Source: Global Insight, http://www.globalinsight.com/.

Republic is clearly benefiting from the surge in foreign direct investment (FDI) that was recorded in the period after accession negotiations began, with net annual FDI inflows reaching US$6.3 billion in 1999–2002.

Czech fears regarding higher prices and unemployment also proved to be unfounded. Although jobless rates reached all-time highs in early 2004, they started to gradually fall back during the second half of the year and continued to decline into 2005. Consumer prices did rise in 2004; however, that increase was based more on higher global energy costs than on the impact of EU accession. In any case, average annual inflation was still relatively low in 2004, at 2.8 percent, before dropping in 2005. One indication of the Czech Republic's economic stability during the first year of membership came when the Czech National Bank cut interest rates to a historic low of 1.75 percent in April 2005, 25 basis points below those of the European Central Bank (ECB). Czech interest rates remained below the ECB rate until October of that same year, when they were raised back to 2.0 percent.

The relative ease with which the Czech economy coped with the impact of EU membership was based on the fact that the Czech Republic was already well integrated with western Europe at the time of accession. In terms of foreign trade, there were only a few remaining barriers in place by the time the Czech Republic joined the EU, mostly in terms of agricultural products. One area in which Czech industry was negatively affected related to cigarette production, as the country's 55 percent customs duty on imports had to be scrapped after EU entry, making it cheaper to import cigarettes than to produce them domestically. Domestic cigarette production declined in the first year of membership, and several cigarette-manufacturing plants were closed.[7] Due to the EU's stricter veterinary standards, the Czech food industry was also adversely affected by membership, particularly in regard to meat products. The State Veterinary Administration (SVS) shut down 586 out of the country's more than 4,000 food plants in the run-up to EU accession, while only one-quarter of the firms processing animal products were deemed ready to supply the Common Market by late March 2004.[8]

In regard to policy, the EU has had a wide impact in a broad range of areas, from energy and the environment to agriculture and public procurement. The EU also encouraged the establishment of an independent civil service in the Czech Republic as well as the introduction of measures to strengthen rule of law.[9] Brussels has had an especially strong influence on the Czech energy sector, through directives on the gradual liberalization of the electricity and natural gas markets and requirements that energy companies separate regulated and unregulated operations such as distribution and trade. As a result, the Czech electricity utility, CEZ, was forced to spin off the regional distributors from its core operations, ostensibly contributing to a more competitive market. The EU has had considerably less influence over nuclear power, despite Austria's threats to veto the Czech Republic's EU accession if the Temelin plant remained in operation. In November 2001, Austria agreed to refrain from blocking the Czech Republic's completion of the energy chapter of the *acquis communautaire* after Czech leaders promised to implement more safety measures. The plant has continued to operate since the country's accession, despite frequent technical problems.

Another key change that occurred after EU accession was that the Czech Republic was forced to cut back substantially on industrial subsidies as well as incentives for foreign investors, in line with the requirements of the competition chapter of the *acquis*. The country had an especially difficult time closing that chapter due to a long-running conflict with the European Commission over government subsidies to assist in the restructuring of the ailing steel sector. In the end it was agreed that state support could only be granted with the aim of restructuring steel companies to make them competitive in the EU market. The lack of transparency of state assistance to the banking sector was another area of serious concern for the Commission. Although the sector was sold off almost completely to foreign investors under the Zeman government, the state took over the administration of many of the bad loans that were accumulated in the 1990s and continued to pay off that debt during the first years of EU membership.

The impact of the EU on such areas as decentralization is more ambiguous. While the EU does demand some form of regionalization for the distribution of Structural Funds, one study argues that the Czech Republic would have implemented regional self-government regardless of EU influence, as the country's constitution envisages the establishment of self-administrative units. The study also shows that the Czech Republic actually went considerably further in the area of decentralization than the EU had demanded.[10]

One area in which the EU has been largely unsuccessful in influencing Czech policy—despite efforts on the part of Germany and Austria—relates to the post–Second World War Benes decrees, which applied collective guilt to the Sudeten German minority in Czechoslovakia and led to the expulsion of some 2.5 million ethnic Germans from the country after the war. Since the fall of communism, the Benes decrees have continued to crop up as a source of seemingly never-ending conflict in the Czech Republic's relations with Germany and Austria, as conservatives in those two neighboring states threatened to block the Czech Republic's accession to the EU if the decrees were not abolished. Nonetheless, Germany and Austria failed to win over other EU member states to their side. When the European Parliament voted on enlargement in April 2003, the Czech Republic received the backing of 489 out of 565 deputies, while 39 were against and 37 abstained. Although that was the smallest number of votes in favor of any candidate country, the Czech Republic still won an overwhelming majority. For its part, Prague has on various occasions taken a conciliatory tone, with the Spidla cabinet issuing a statement in mid-2003 in which it distanced itself from the Benes decrees but said they could not be undone. In summer 2005, the Paroubek government went one step further by offering a gesture of appreciation to those members of the Sudeten German minority who were anti-Fascists, thus dismissing the principle of collective guilt. Even that act of reconciliation caused considerable commotion on the Czech political scene, as Klaus strongly criticized Paroubek's gesture and likened it to the opening of Pandora's box.

Table 17.2 shows that during the Czech Republic's first year of membership, from May 2004 to April 2005, the country was a net recipient of EU budget funds, with a gain of €240 million. That accounted for less than 0.3 percent of Czech GDP and was far smaller than the transfers going to certain older member states such as Greece. Part of

**Table 17.2   EU Budgetary Funds and the Czech Republic
(in millions of euros)**

	May–Dec. 2004	Jan.–Apr. 2005	May 2004– Apr. 2005
Accession funds	126.5	5.7	132.1
–Phare	79.7	2.4	82.1
–Ispa	13.3		13.3
–Sapard	33.5	3.3	36.8
Agriculture	90.8	208.6	299.4
Structural and Cohesion Funds	193.4	93.3	286.8
Entitlements	332.3	100.0	432.3
Total budget revenues from the EU	752.3	407.6	1,159.9
Total payments to the EU budget	554.2	365.6	919.9
Net position toward the EU	198.0	42.0	240.0

Source: Czech Finance Ministry, "Prvni rok v Evropske unii."

the reason for the low levels of transfers to the Czech Republic related to the relative unimportance of agriculture in the Czech economy and the comparatively even development of the country's various regions. Eurostat data have indicated that with the exception of Prague (which is much more advanced), all Czech regions reached a GDP per capita level that was 52–61 percent of the EU-25 average in 2002, much higher than the level of certain regions in other new member states.[11] In fact, the Czech Republic would have been a net contributor to the EU budget if not for extra compensation that the country received. In the first year, the Czech Republic received a total of €1.16 billion from the EU budget and paid out €919.9 million. Of the total funds received from the EU, €132 million were linked to the Phare, Sapard, and Ispa preaccession programs; €299 million went to agriculture; €287 million went to Structural and Cohesion Funds; and €432 million was for extra entitlements.[12] The Czech Republic's net benefits were somewhat greater if programs related to youth and educational exchanges had been included in those figures.

■ **How and in What Areas Does
the Czech Republic Influence EU Policies?**

The Czech Republic's weak position as a medium-sized state in a union of 25 countries is a source of frustration for many citizens, and the country will be influential only if it forms alliances with other member states having similar interests. One commentator wrote that the Czech Republic influenced EU policies only twice during its first year of membership: through Czech European Parliament deputy Jana Hybaskova's efforts to stop the genocide in Darfur and Foreign Minister Cyril Svoboda's success in pushing through his stance on Cuba despite pressure from Spain and France.[13] With regard to the latter case, a dispute broke out in January 2005 after Cuban leader Fidel Castro criticized EU countries for inviting dissidents to their embassy receptions in Havana. Spain encouraged others to put an end to those invitations in a gesture of goodwill toward Castro, and the country soon managed to win over a majority of the member states. Seeing that stance as a clear demonstration of EU weakness and a lack of solidarity with dissidents, Svoboda strongly opposed Spain's position and managed to push through a proposal giving each member state the right to invite whomever it wanted to its embassy. The Czech position was based largely on recent experiences with communism, and the country was backed by Poland in its efforts. Like Svoboda, former Czech president Vaclav Havel—himself a dissident during the communist regime—was also strongly critical of the EU stance, and he published an article slamming the position of Brussels in the French daily *Le Figaro* around the time of the dispute.[14]

Unlike many of the ex-communist countries that joined the EU in May 2004, the Czech Republic did not push for economic reform within the EU during the 2002–2006 term and did not protest when France and Germany violated the Stability and Growth Pact by overstepping budget limits. While the center-right government that ruled in neighboring Slovakia in 2002–2006 was eager to use the economic reforms that it implemented as a blueprint for change in the rest of Europe, in line with the EU's 2000 Lisbon Strategy,[15] the CSSD-led cabinet was a reluctant reformer that saw the "European social model" as one of the key advantages of EU membership. In fact, when German and French leaders accused the new member states of "tax dumping" and called for harmonization of taxation rates within the EU, then–prime minister Spidla was the only top representative from a new member state to support Germany's then-chancellor Gerhard Schröder in that stance.[16]

One potential explanation for the Czech Republic's limited impact on EU policies stems from the mixed messages that are being sent by the ruling elite. When Havel was president, he was largely in sync with the various governments on key foreign policy issues. However, Klaus's term has been marked by intense disharmony between the president and the Euro-enthusiast government, giving the impression of chaos. In fact,

Klaus stands out not only in the Czech Republic but also in Europe as a whole for his outspoken and increasingly radical criticism of Brussels.[17] He frequently uses foreign visits to attack both the Economic and Monetary Union (EMU) and the European constitution. Moreover, Klaus has made a number of outlandish statements, comparing the EU to the communist-era Council for Mutual Economic Assistance; calling for enlargement not just to Turkey, but also to countries such as Kazakhstan and Morocco;[18] and proposing that the EU be transformed into a looser alliance, which he referred to as the Organization of European States.[19] Many west European politicians find Klaus's radical criticism of the EU offensive, and he would most certainly be more effective in building alliances that could influence EU policies if he softened his approach. While Klaus's verbal outbursts have led to frequent clashes with Foreign Minister Svoboda, Spidla and Gross generally ignored them. It was not until Paroubek took over as prime minister that efforts were made to silence Klaus and to encourage the promotion of a more coherent and unified approach to foreign policy between the president and government.

The Czech Republic's position vis-à-vis the EU is further complicated by the fact that the country sent a relatively weak figure to represent it on the European Commission in Brussels. After failing at the position of prime minister, Spidla was nominated by the Gross cabinet for the post of commissioner, thereby offering him a polite exit from domestic politics and signaling that the country did not see its representation in Brussels as being of key importance. As the commissioner for employment and social affairs, Spidla has been largely supportive of maintaining the status quo,[20] while many of his counterparts from other new member states are using their positions to encourage change within the EU.

■ How Does the Czech Republic Implement and Comply with EU Policies?

As noted above, the recent CSSD-led governments have usually tried to meet EU demands in a timely fashion, but the opposition has often blocked or delayed such efforts. Political pressures and instability meant that the Czech government was not especially well prepared for EU accession and was forced to do some last-minute scrambling to push forward necessary legislation, giving the passage of certain laws an almost tragicomic dimension. For example, in late March 2004

President Klaus vetoed a bill on the value-added tax (VAT) that was supposed to take effect at the time of accession on May 1, criticizing the government for adding its own tax increases that overstepped EU requirements. The absence of the legislation would have caused considerable upheaval in Czech foreign trade, offering the possibility that certain transactions would be taxed twice. Overriding a presidential veto requires an absolute parliamentary majority of 101 out of 200 deputies, exactly the number of seats held by the ruling coalition. Nonetheless, two ruling coalition deputies, including Foreign Minister Svoboda, were hospitalized at the time the revote was expected to take place and were therefore unable to attend. Government overtures to the parliamentary opposition failed to gain any supporters, although one independent deputy did promise to back the bill. The coalition was forced to delay the revote until April 22, and it was approved only after Svoboda was flown in by helicopter from a hospital in Brno, were he was recovering from a serious car accident.[21]

Another example of last-minute fumbling related to a law on public procurement. As a precondition for receiving EU funds, the Czech Republic was required to approve legislation on public procurement to increase transparency. A few months before accession, the Commission complained that Czech procurement legislation was incompatible with EU law and expressed concern that the country would be unable to amend its law by the May 1, 2004, deadline. The country was forced to revise the legislation at the 11th hour.[22]

One case that is a clear demonstration of the Czech Republic's approach toward EU authority relates to fiscal reform. Like all new member states, the country will eventually be required to join the EMU, and it must first meet the criteria set out in the Maastricht Treaty relating to inflation, public finances, exchange rates, and interest rates.[23] Similar to the situation elsewhere in central Europe, fiscal reform represents by far the biggest challenge for the Czech Republic, partly because of the lingering costs of bailing out the banking sector prior to its privatization but also due to rising mandatory spending in connection with the aging population. While Slovakia pushed forward with major changes of its taxation, pension, health-care, and social-welfare systems in 2003–2005, the successive CSSD-led governments that held office after the 2002 elections used their narrow parliamentary majority and falling public support as an excuse to stall on reform.

Before going into the details of the debate on fiscal reform, it is important to understand the position of the key political actors. The five parliamentary parties cover the whole spectrum: from the opposition

ODS, which favors radical fiscal reforms (although not for the purpose of joining the euro zone) to the opposition Communists, who are strongly against any measures that would harm the poorer segments of society. The three ruling parties fall somewhere between those two extremes. The CSSD includes a mix of "modern" versus leftist social democrats, with the former group modeled on the centrist approach of the British Labour Party. While the two center-right junior partners pushed for more rapid fiscal reform in an effort to join the euro zone as quickly as possible, the CSSD was more cautious, for fear of splitting the party and pushing voters toward the Communists. Of the three CSSD prime ministers who held office after the 2002 elections, only Gross was in the "modern" CSSD camp, while both Spidla and Paroubek encouraged slower reforms, even at the cost of conflict with the EU and delays in EMU membership. As an example of the CSSD approach, during his term as prime minister, Spidla pointed out that reforms were unavoidable and added that they would be even more severe if the opposition ODS took over. He also stressed, however, that there was no rush in joining the euro zone, mentioning 2009–2011 as a possible timeframe. Although lukewarm, Spidla's backing of fiscal reforms apparently took voters by surprise, and one commentator speculated that the CSSD's falling support was based on the party's failure to reveal "the true state of public finances" prior to the 2002 parliamentary elections.[24]

In its initial program statement in summer 2002, the Spidla cabinet targeted a public finance deficit of 4.9–5.4 percent of GDP by the end of its term in 2006, a figure that aroused serious contention from the junior partners, who considered it an unambitious goal. In December 2002, Czech finance minister Bohuslav Sobotka—a representative of the CSSD's "modern" wing—drew up two alternative versions of public finance reform: one that would reduce the deficit to 4.9 percent of GDP by 2006 and a second, more radical scenario that would cut the gap to 3.7 percent of GDP. In a May 2003 meeting, ruling-coalition representatives agreed to a compromise, with a deficit target of 4.0 percent of GDP in 2006 and a further cut to 3.0 percent of GDP by 2008, leaving the final changes to the next government. Thus, the Czech Republic would meet the Maastricht criteria by 2008 and would be ineligible to join the EMU before 2010, after most of the other new member states.

Even with accession to the euro zone as a relatively far-off prospect, the government still needed to take certain steps to reduce state spending and bring budget deficits and public spending in line with levels that were agreed upon with the EU in the country's EMU Convergence Program. A first phase of fiscal reforms was approved by the parliament in late 2003 and included changes in VAT rates and excise duties to meet EU standards, as well as a gradual decline in the corporate income tax, falling to 24 percent by 2006. It should be noted that the corporate tax cuts were proposed only after the Slovak government had put forward its own tax reform plan, which spurred warnings in the local press that many Czech-based firms would soon relocate to Slovakia.[25] The reforms were approved fairly smoothly, despite considerable nervousness that the government's slim majority as well as opposition from within the CSSD would complicate the Czech cabinet's ability to push them through the parliament. Still, the Czech approach was criticized as piecemeal and haphazard, mainly because it failed to address the bigger problems that the country was facing, such as the need to reform the pension and health-care systems.

Although the Spidla cabinet had planned for more waves of fiscal reforms before the 2006 elections, they were delayed, as increased political instability and growing discord within the CSSD set the ruling coalition off-track. By 2005, a spate of favorable economic news decreased pressure on the government for further reforms, at least temporarily. After surging to 12.5 percent of GDP in 2003, the highest level of all the EU members and candidate states, the Czech Republic's public finance deficit dropped to an unexpectedly low 3.0 percent of GDP in 2004.[26] Thus, while Sobotka had previously talked about cutting 30 billion koruna from the 2006 state budget, he later admitted that such a large reduction would be unnecessary. In the first nine months of 2005, the Czech state budget was actually in surplus, another pleasant surprise for the government. Still, the positive fiscal results of 2004–2005 were not expected to last, as mandatory expenditures would continue to rise in the medium to long term, putting further strain on deficits. Many experts agreed that it was better for the Czech Republic to implement fiscal reforms before joining the EMU rather than afterward, as the authorities would have flexibility in terms of monetary policy and exchange-rate adjustments.

The need for fiscal reform put the CSSD in an awkward position vis-à-vis the EU. The party was a strong supporter of the EU as a guarantor of the continuation of social-welfare programs. Being forced to cut back on social spending as a way of pleasing the EU thus seemed contradictory, especially as countries such as Germany and France were overshooting their deficit targets. Inevitably, as the 2006 elections approached, the successive governments came up instead with measures that would actually cost the state more money, such as a proposal to implement tax cuts for low- and middle-income citizens. Paroubek also supported lowering the corporate income tax to 19 percent, in line with the rates in neighboring Poland and Slovakia. In addition, the cabinet was considering putting caps on payroll taxes from 2007 onward, a move that would put further strain on the budget, although those effects would only be felt by the postelection government.

What Is the Czech Republic's Compliance Record?

Given its recent political problems, it is hardly surprising that the Czech Republic has emerged as one of the laggards in regard to adopting necessary EU legislation. According to the European Commission's Internal Market Scoreboard that was issued in July 2005, the country achieved the worst results of the 10 new member states and was fourth from last overall. Still, the Czech Republic had committed fewer serious transgressions than certain other new member states such as Poland. Although the Commission may start proceedings against individual member states in cases of serious delay or faulty legislation, only five such procedures had been launched against the Czech Republic by June 2005.[27]

The Czech Republic's Permanent Representation in Brussels criticized the Commission's report, arguing that it overlooked the fact that the country had made remarkable progress in the previous year.[28] As described above, the ruling coalition was facing serious limitations in approving legislation due to its slim majority in the lower house of the parliament, lack of majority in the senate, and often hostile opposition from the president. The length of the country's legislative procedures, including the debates in the cabinet and the parliament, further slowed the approval of necessary laws. From June 2004 through the appointment of Paroubek's government in May 2005, the passage of legislation was also hindered by political instability.

Sometimes EU rules were violated simply out of ignorance. For example, shortly after EU accession one Czech daily pointed out that many of the country's 35,000 haulers were failing to comply with EU rules since half of the transport regulations that applied to them had yet to be translated into Czech. In that case, the Transport Ministry was to blame, since it had failed in its pledge to translate all regulations by the time of entry.[29]

For better or worse, Czech government representatives often mention the EU when introducing certain pieces of legislation. In that regard, Darina Malova and Tim Haughton distinguish between "scapegoating," where the government blames the EU for the introduction of unpopular policies, and "smoke screening," where European demands are used as an excuse to "mask" the government's real motivations.[30] In the Czech Republic there have been examples of both approaches.

With regard to the former, Finance Minister Sobotka has repeatedly scapegoated the EU in urging more rapid fiscal reform, trying to frighten more reluctant CSSD representatives into action. For example, in January 2005, Sobotka referred to a European Commission proposal according to which only countries with public budget deficits lower than 3.0 percent of GDP would be allowed to draw money from the Cohesion Fund as of 2007. Even though that measure was unlikely to be approved and enforced, the Finance Ministry warned that the high budget gaps could cost the Czech Republic billions of koruna worth of European funds.[31] At other times, however, Sobotka sent a more mixed message. For example, his ministry's initial state budget drafts for both 2005 and 2006 planned on deficits that were somewhat higher than the limit set in the country's Convergence Agreement with the EU. Although the Finance Ministry was criticized for overshooting those limits, ministry officials stressed that the pledge to reduce the rate of growth in state debt was more important than short-term compliance with the spending frameworks.[32]

One clear example of smoke screening relates to the country's decentralization program. The Zeman government, which implemented the plan, conveyed in its discourse that its reforms would meet EU demands. In reality, however, it appeared that the EU requirements for some form of regional administration were really only an excuse, and it was domestic political actors who shaped the reforms, going far beyond EU demands.[33]

Given the Euro-skeptical stance of Klaus and the ODS, compliance with EU norms has become a political issue among ordinary citizens in the Czech Republic. Prior to the country's accession, Czech public support for EU membership was lower than in many of its regional peers and tended to fluctuate according to the issues of the day. The Czech Republic held its referendum on EU accession on June 13–14, 2003, and the government's campaign prior to that event was aimed at addressing public fears about the potential negative effects of membership.[34] The ODS, for its part, sent mixed messages, despite the fact that many of its supporters were businessmen who strongly supported the Czech Republic's EU membership. In February 2003, new ODS chairman Mirek Topolanek said that he would work to ensure that the "Yes" vote won in the referendum; however, at the party's May 2003 executive council session, the ODS argued that the government was unable to defend the country's interests with regard to accession and demanded an agreement that the Czech Republic could voluntarily leave the EU in the future, if necessary. While Klaus refused to tell voters whether to vote "Yes" or "No," the Communists advised supporters to vote "No." Despite such negative signals from the elite, 55.2 percent of eligible voters participated in the country's first-ever referendum, of whom 77.3 percent supported joining the Union. The turnout was higher in the Czech Republic than in several other central European countries; however, only 41.7 percent of the electorate actually voted in favor of accession, which was a relatively poor result.[35]

Since the country's accession to the EU, public support appears to be declining. Even though fears relating to EU accession did not materialize, just 41 percent of Czechs polled in February 2005 said that EU membership benefited them, while 42 percent thought the opposite. In a poll that asked citizens to define their stance on the EU, only about 25 percent said they were "Euro-optimists," compared with 54.5 percent who proclaimed themselves "Euro-realists" and 20.5 percent who were "Euroskeptics."[36] Another poll conducted in August 2005 indicated that only 36 percent of Czechs were content with EU membership and 20 percent were dissatisfied, while 37 percent were ambivalent. Satisfaction with EU membership was expressed more frequently by Czechs with higher living standards, youth and students, managers, and ODS supporters.[37]

The Czech Republic has yet to approve the European constitution, and the government was saved from potential embarrassment by the "No" votes in the French and Dutch referenda. Even before those votes, the Czech Republic was seen as one of the few new member states where the constitution's approval was up in the air. The 2002–2006 ruling parties would have found it impossible to gain a constitutional majority in the parliament, given the opposition of both the ODS and the Communists. Prospects for a successful referendum were also questionable and became even more unlikely after the developments in France and the Netherlands threw the document's approval off-track.

▪ Future Trends and Prospects

While the Czech Republic was relatively supportive of the EU under CSSD leadership, that could all change very rapidly if the ODS comes to power after the June 2006 parliamentary elections. Fiscal reform will continue to be one of the key issues for the Czech Republic in the coming years, and it remains to be seen whether the country will meet its goal of entry into the euro zone by 2010. In that sense, an ODS victory would in certain ways be positive, as it would ensure more coherent reforms, assuming that the ODS wins enough votes to form a government and that the party lives up to its preelection promises. The ODS has vowed to launch radical reforms of the Czech fiscal system, with a 15 percent flat tax on personal and corporate income and a unified rate of VAT, also at 15 percent. Claiming that lower budget revenues would be balanced by restricted tax evasion, more consistent economic growth, and larger inflows of FDI, the ODS projects that the public finance balance would be reduced to zero by 2010.[38]

Despite the party's enthusiasm for fiscal reform, there are several reasons for hesitation with regard to the impact of a potential ODS victory on the Czech Republic's relations with the EU. First of all, the party may try to delay the country's entry into the euro zone, even after the fiscal requirements of the Maastricht criteria are met. Furthermore, if it goes forward with its fiscal reforms, the ODS could spark a race to the bottom, as other EU countries would likely be forced to lower their tax rates as well. Already, Slovakia's implementation of a flat 19 percent corporate tax rate in 2004 triggered a reduction in Austria. However, an even lower tax rate in the Czech Republic would have a greater impact, particularly given its long borders with both Austria and Germany and the ease with which companies from those two countries could relocate to the Czech Republic. Finally, with the EU's constitutional impasse unresolved by the time of the 2006 elections, the ODS's negative position on further EU integration could transform the Czech Republic from a partner that ranges between ambivalent and enthusiastic to one that is increasingly obstructive.

▪ Notes

1. See Kopecky, "An Awkward Newcomer?" p. 236.

2. Vachudova, *Europe Undivided,* p. 196.

3. Czech Radio, May 11, 1994.

4. See Orenstein, "The Political Success of Neo-Liberalism in the Czech Republic"; Fisher, "Czech Economy Presents Mixed Picture," pp. 31–38.

5. Pehe, "Czechs Fall from Their Ivory Tower."

6 See Kopecky, "An Awkward Newcomer?" pp. 238–241; Kopecky and Van Holsteyn, "The Grass Is Always Greener."

7. Czech News Agency, July 14, 2005.

8. Czech News Agency, March 31, 2004.

9. Vachudova, *Europe Undivided,* pp. 194–198.

10. Brusis, "Regionalisation in the Czech and Slovak Republics," pp. 89–105.

11. Eurostat News Release, January 25, 2005.
12. Czech Finance Ministry, "Prvni rok v Evropske unii."
13. Zlamalova, "Kdo uspel v Evrope."
14. Havel, "L'indecent hommage à Fidel Castro."
15. Malova and Haughton, "Challenge for the Pace-Setting Periphery."
16. Machacek, "Spidla vystupuje jako exot."
17. See Komarek, "Klaus a Evropa."
18. *Mlada fronta Dnes*, March 19, 2005.
19. Klaus, "Vytvorme jinou Evropskou unii,"
20. See Czech News Agency, September 20 and 27, 2004.
21. See Czech News Agency, April 22, 2004.
22. Czech News Agency, March 2, 2004.
23. "Treaty on European Union," Eur-Lex Official Journal, http://europa. eu.int/eur-lex/en/ (July 29, 1992).
24. Machacek, "Sobotka a Slovaci."
25. Novakova and Patockova, "Ceske firmy utikaji na Slovensko za niszi dani."
26. Eurostat News Release, September 26, 2005.
27. European Commission, DG Internal Market and Services, "Internal Market Scorecard," no. 15 (July 2005).
28. Czech News Agency, July 20, 2005.
29. Kalab, "Dopravci hresi a nevedi o tom."
30. Malova and Haughton, "Challenge for the Pace-Setting Periphery."
31. Czech News Agency, January 20, 2005.
32. Czech News Agency, September 1, 2004.
33. Brusis, "Regionalisation in the Czech and Slovak Republics," pp. 89–105.
34. Kopecky and Van Holsteyn, "The Grass Is Always Greener."
35. Kopecky, "An Awkward Newcomer?" p. 242.
36. Czech News Agency, April 17, 2005.
37. CVVM poll, reported in Czech News Agency, August 23, 2005.
38. Czech News Agency, July 22, 2003.

18

Slovenia and Slovakia: Joining the Club

John Occhipinti and Peter Loedel

ASIDE FROM ALLITERATION, WHY include Slovakia and Slovenia in the same chapter in this book? It would certainly be convenient if any confusion about these similar-sounding central European countries would stem only from their commonalities and not just their alliterative names. The two countries also share very similar flags and are indeed alike in many ways, at least superficially. For example, both are relatively small countries that gained their independence after years of existing as constituent parts of multiethnic communist states. In addition, both countries belong to NATO and have opted to relinquish or at least "pool" their newly found sovereignty in some areas and join the EU.

Of course, Slovakia and Slovenia are also quite different, and a good case could be made for devoting separate chapters in this book to each of them. These countries enjoy unique and rich histories and have experienced different paths to economic and political development and eventual membership in the EU. For example, Slovakia's membership was initially in doubt, as it seemed to flirt with a return to authoritarian rule, while Slovenia made steady progress all along.

Despite such differences, looking at the Economic and Monetary Union (EMU) and Justice and Home Affairs (JHA) can allow for fruitful comparison of these countries. As new EU members, Slovakia and Slovenia are still trying to "join the club" concerning participation in the euro zone and inclusion in passport-free travel area of the Schengen zone. Exploring these countries regarding these and related policy areas offers a useful way to study and compare them.

Slovenia

Though it has existed as a formal political entity only since 1918, when it formed part of Yugoslavia, Slovenia, by the end of the Cold War, was better positioned to join the European Community (EC) than its central European neighbors. Slovenia was Yugoslavia's most prosperous republic during the era of Tito, and it took steps to liberalize politically and economically after his death in 1980. Slovenia's eventual declaration of independence on June 25, 1991, came after its freely elected parliament had declared its right to do so in 1989, and 88 percent of its citizens had chosen this path in a historic referendum in December 1990. Consequently, the largely Serbian Yugoslav national army intervened to stop the secession and engaged the overmatched but well-positioned Slovenian militia, resulting in about 100 deaths and a military stalemate after just 10 days of fighting. With few Serbs living in Slovenia, Belgrade soon agreed to a negotiated settlement brokered by the EC and withdrew its army units, sparing Slovenia the kind of violence later experienced by Croatia, Bosnia, and Kosovo. Led by Germany, the EC formerly recognized the independent Republic of Slovenia on January 15, 1992.[1]

Owing to its long-standing cultural and commercial ties to western Europe, Slovenia's inclination to join the EU was virtually assured. In fact, by the time the EU promulgated the Copenhagen criteria in 1993, Slovenia was already a strong candidate for membership. The resolution of a dispute with Italy over the right of foreigners to buy property in the country allowed Slovenia to sign a Europe Agreement with the EU in 1996. At the December 1997 Luxembourg European Council, Slovenia was invited to be among the first six applicant states to initiate formal accession talks.

Negotiations on the various chapters of Slovenia's Accession Treaty began in February 1998 and proceeded relatively smoothly and quickly compared to talks involving the other applicants. For example, Slovenia was the first state to close talks on the environment and was among the three leading countries regarding the number of accession chapters it had successfully negotiated by autumn 2001. As with the other applicant states, talks on accession chapters with financial implications were the most problematic for Slovenia. However, with only 4 percent of its work force employed in the agricultural sector, matters related to the Common Agricultural Policy (CAP) were resolved without much trouble. Slovenia's most fundamental concern in the accession talks was that it might end up as a net contributor into the EU budget upon accession. Owing to its economic prosperity, Slovenia was already receiving the lowest amount of preaccession financial assistance from the EU per capita compared to other recipients. Slovenia's status as a net receiver from the Community budget was guaranteed at least until the end of 2006 through the negotiation of support from the CAP, Structural and Cohesion Funds, as well as annual lump-sum payments. In the end, both the turnout (60.2 percent) and "Yes" vote (89.61 percent) were relatively high for Slovenia's referendum on joining the EU, held on March 23, 2003.[2]

Like most of its EU partners, Slovenia is a multiparty parliamentary democracy in which most political power is wielded by the prime minister as head of government, based on the confidence of a majority of the national assembly (lower house). Slovenia's president is its head of state, but enjoys little effective executive power aside from extraordinary situations of electoral crisis or in cases of national emergency that would prevent the national assembly from convening. Janez Drnovšek, former prime minister and leader of the Liberal Democrats (LDS), has served as president since his election in December 2000 for the first of two possible five-year terms. In the parliamentary elections of October 2004, the center-right Slovenian Democratic Party (SDS) shockingly won a plurality of seats and formed a coalition government led by Janez Jansa, with support from three smaller parties (conservatives, Christian democrats, and pensioners). The electorate's unexpected desire for "change" consequently put the Liberal Democrats in opposition for virtually the first time since Slovenia's independence, despite their achievement of NATO and EU membership.

Slovakia

Following its peaceful separation from the Czechoslovakian federation on January 1, 1993, the Slovak Republic experienced a rocky road to EU membership under the semiauthoritarian government of populist and nationalist Vladimír Mečiar and his Movement for a Democratic Slovakia party (HZDS). Slovakia's Europe Agreement with the EU was signed in October 1993 but did not enter into force until February 1995. Its formal application for EU membership came in June 1996 but was not well received in light of the corruption in Slovakia's privatization process and virtual censorship of its media, as well as Prime Minister Mečiar's pro-Russian orientation and skepticism of both NATO and the EU. Mečiar's hold on power started to unravel after he assumed presidential powers amid a constitutional crisis created when Michal Kovac resigned from that office without a designated successor. This power play prompted protests both at home and abroad, including criticism from the EU. Amid this political climate, the elections of September 1998 swung against Mečiar, allowing a broad coalition to form under the leadership of Mikulas Dzurinda and his center-right Slovak Democratic and Christian Union (SDKU), backed by a diverse mix of ex-communist, pro-business, and ethnic Hungarian parties.

Hoping to encourage the new government to enact reforms, the European Commission quickly gave an optimistic report on Slovakia's membership aspirations. The Dzurinda government worked quickly to implement a reform agenda, and the country was later included among the six states endorsed by the December 1999 Helsinki European Council to start formal accession negotiations. These talks began in February 2000, during which time Slovakia strove to avoid missing the "first wave" of the EU's next enlargement. Over the next nine months, the Dzurinda government accelerated economic reforms and helped Slovakia close talks ("provisionally") on 10 chapters of accession. By October 2001, negotiations on 20 chapters had been completed, signaling that Slovakia had caught up with the so-called first-wave countries.

However, several issues in the remaining accession chapters proved difficult to resolve. Slovakia eventually pushed for and won transitional time periods to meet the EU *acquis* in areas such as energy and taxation. Regarding competition policy, Slovakia wanted to ensure government support for its ailing national power company and, like other applicant states, it hoped for the highest possible level of CAP subsidies for its farmers. Meanwhile, the Commission pressed Slovakia on issues such as corruption and the proper management of EU financial assistance, agricultural reform, and better protecting the rights of ethnic Roma. In the end, all of these matters were sufficiently resolved before the Copenhagen European Council at the end of 2002, which capped Slovakia's impressive comeback with an invitation for membership.

At least initially, the Dzurinda government benefited politically by steering the country toward membership in both the EU and NATO, and was returned to power after the parliamentary elections of September 2002. However, it was not long before many Slovaks started to question some of his economic initiatives, including how much they would benefit average Slovakians. While Dzurinda's liberal economic policies helped promote economic growth and won praise from foreign investors and the EU, they also created some transitional problems, such as the country's stubbornly high unemployment rate.[3] Nevertheless, support for joining the EU remained high, as was evident in the May 2003 referendum that resulted in a 92.46 percent "Yes" vote, despite a low turnout of 52.15 percent.[4]

Politically, an important question was whether the Dzurinda government or its successor could stay the course regarding Slovakia's accession commitments, while enduring attacks from populists on both the right and left that tried to exploit citizens' misgivings about their country's economic direction. This issue was at least partly reflected in the presidential race of April 2004, when the government's foreign minister, Eduard Kukan, did not qualify for the second round of voting. Instead, the runoff was between Mečiar, hoping for a political comeback, and his former-ally-turned-enemy, Ivan Gasparovic, the eventual winner. In this race, Gasparovic had benefited from the support of Robert Fico's left-leaning and populist Direction Party (Smer), which had called for reversing some EU-inspired economic reforms.[5] Slovakia's president serves as its head of state in a largely ceremonial capacity. However, the president can veto legislation, a provision that can become significant when a government cannot muster the simple majority needed to override. Since early 2004, the Dzurinda government has faced this challenge following defections from his own party, which has forced the governing coalition to seek support from the Euro-skeptic parties of the opposition.[6]

■ How and in What Ways Does the EU Influence Slovenia and Slovakia?

The Effects of Economic and Monetary Union

On the level of monetary cooperation and macroeconomic coordination, Slovenia and Slovakia have deeply embedded their respective nation's economies into the framework of the euro zone's monetary and fiscal policy. They have done so through two integrated strategies. First, in terms of monetary policy and exchange-rate policy, each must align themselves with the provisions of the European Monetary Union (EMU). These activities include a strong price stability focus for the respective national central banks, independence for each respective national central bank (Slovenian legislation on this issue was, for example, slow in coming), exchange rate stability vis-à-vis the euro (facilitated in part through the Exchange Rate Mechanism II [ERM II]—the grooming phase prior to the introduction of the euro), and general planning for the eventual adoption of the euro. Second, each country must maintain fiscal control so as not to overstep the original Maastricht convergence criteria. These criteria include maintaining an annual budget deficit below 3 percent of domestic GDP, below 60 percent of total debt, and achieving an inflation rate equal to or lower than the top three best-performing members of the euro zone. The 1995 Stability and Growth Pact reinforces these convergence criteria. These two strategies are interrelated as budget discipline will add stability to prices and exchange rates and allow for the eventual adoption of the euro. Both countries are eager to join the euro "club" at the earliest possible date and have largely upheld these rigorous standards. As such, they have both made great strides in the areas of monetary and fiscal policy and are today considered relatively strong potential members for the EMU (see Table 18.1).

On a more technical level, Slovenia and Slovakia have maneuvered their monetary policy and exchange-rate policy generally within the confines of the ERM II, although Slovakia has not officially joined. The ERM II has kept the ±15 percent fluctuation margins of the post-1993 ERM of the European Monetary System (EMS) and its minimal reciprocal agreements.[7] The general aim of the ERM II agreement is to encourage all participants to orient their economic policies toward encouraging exchange-rate stability and monetary convergence. In the obviously asymmetric ERM II, the burden of adjustment, however, will still fall on the participating countries outside the euro zone.[8]

Prior to accession, Slovenia and Slovakia were also required to pursue sound fiscal policies to achieve price stability and to help maintain low inflation. Before joining in May 2004, both nations had to prepare Pre-Accession Economic Programmes (PEPs), consisting of reporting government deficit and debt figures calculated in accordance with the EU methodology to the European Commission. The PEPs helped lay a solid foundation for the pursuance of credible monetary and exchange-rate policies, which would provide a smooth transition to

Table 18.1   Government Goals for ERM II Participation and Later Adoption of the Euro

	Exchange Rate Regime at Time of Accession	Euro Target Date	ERM II Participation
Slovakia	Managed float with euro as reference	As early as possible after EU accession—likely January 2009	2006 (first half)
Slovenia	Managed float with euro as reference	As early as possible after EU accession—likely by the end of 2007	June 2004

the ERM II and eventually the euro. The PEPs also demanded that the fiscal policies of accession countries converge on the euro zone at macroeconomic levels.

Implementation of and
Compliance to Economic and Monetary Policy

Since accession, Slovenia and Slovakia have been under pressure to conform to the euro zone's Broad Economic Policy Guidelines (BEPG), aimed at the whole range of economic policies of the member states. These guidelines supplement an annual cycle of policy discussion that provides policy guidance for growth- and stability-oriented macroeconomic policies, particularly budgetary policies; structural reform of product, capital, and labor markets; and advice on moving to a knowledge-based economy and sustainable and environmentally friendly development. In addition, the Commission and the European Central Bank undertake multilateral surveillance on an ongoing basis, involving monitoring and assessing economic developments and policies related to the BEPG. The Stability Pact and the Excessive Deficit Procedure (EDP) also weigh heavily on the accession states' fiscal policies. These are essentially a set of rules concerning fiscal policy that were included as part of the final stage of EMU, marking the end of the third stage of monetary union as specified in the Maastricht Treaty.

What is impressive to note in both the cases of Slovenia and Slovakia is that they have successfully managed to transition toward the convergence criteria for joining the euro zone. Deficit and debt figures are detailed in Table 18.2, along with some general macroeconomic data on inflation, unemployment, and annual growth.

Moreover, Slovenia has already made the leap into the ERM II and will likely be adopting the euro sometime in 2007, perhaps as early as

Table 18.2   Macroeconomic Data for Slovakia and Slovenia (2005)

	Deficit/GDP (3%)	Debt/GDP (60%)	Inflation (on an annual basis)	Unemployment (ILO)	Growth Rate of GDP[a]
Slovakia	3.8	43.0	2.9	15.9	5.1
Slovenia	1.6	28.6	3.2	5.9	3.1

Source: Data from Eurostat, General Economic Statistics, July 2005.
Note: a. Percentage change on previous year.

January 1 of that year. Of further note, both countries post levels of economic growth exceeding that of many of the pre-2004 15 member states—including Germany and France. In fact, they have both become rather outspoken proponents of a strict adherence and implementation of the Stability Pact and the EDP. In an ironic twist, it is now the new member states that are imposing fiscal discipline on the old member states.

Slovenia. From the outset, the European Commission and many analysts considered Slovenia an easy addition to the European Union. For example, Slovenia was viewed as a nation that would most easily, at least in comparison to its other central and east European counterparts, adapt to the monetary policies and conditions necessary to join EMU and to adopt the euro. Even before accession in May 2004, over 60 percent of the Slovenian economy was due to trade and investment with the EU.

In addition, by most measures leading up to accession in May 2004—whether focused on macroeconomic measures such as economic growth, interest rates, price stability (although the weakest link among such measures), market liberalization, or government borrowing—Slovenia ranked in the top tier of the 10 member states set to join. Perhaps because of its closer historical and geographical ties to Austria and the west, its relatively small population, and being driven by a firm focus by successive governments on implementing the Copenhagen criteria and the Maastricht criteria, Slovenia's foundation for EU membership was quite firm. By the time Slovenia joined in May 2004, it was one of the least-indebted countries of the entire EU—in 2004, 29.9 percent of GDP. Slovenia stands out as a model of macroeconomic good practice with a solid and sustainable transition to prosperity. Sound policy implementation has helped it avoid the fiscal and current account imbalances experienced elsewhere in the region. By 2002–2003, Slovenia's budget deficit (2.7 percent) was below the Maastricht cutoff of 3 percent. Economic growth rates hovered at a relatively steady 3 percent range throughout the period 2001–2005, with a high mark of 5.2 percent in the second quarter of 2005.

Analyzing reports and statements coming from the Slovenian finance ministry in the years preceding and just following accession, the government was firmly committed to early adoption of the euro—perhaps by 2007—and a quick leap into the ERM II mechanism.[9] It thus pursued a "managed float" vis-à-vis the euro during the period prior to accession and officially joined the ERM II in June 2004, just one month after joining the EU. A European Commission report on the convergence of the Slovenian economy with the euro zone indicated an economy in good standing, except in the area of inflation. Prices are shown in some tourist areas in both tolars and euros and surveys indicate that four out of five Slovenes carry euros as cash.[10] With a stable tolar within the ERM II, the national central bank, headed by Mitja Gaspari, has maintained exchange-rate stability, intervening only once since joining the ERM II.

Despite the generally positive economic outlook, there are a few areas of concern. Slovenia's tax burden has actually gone up over the last few years (albeit slowly) to nearly 40.3 percent of GDP, not far short of Germany's, drawing some concern about the overall competitiveness of the economy vis-à-vis countries such as Slovakia that have dramatically lowered their tax burden. While the new government has initiated discussion on a flat tax, it remains to be seen if it will be implemented. Other areas of difficulty center on the inflation rate, which once stood at triple digits in the early 1990s. Inflation rates have been stuck at about 7 percent annually since early 2000. However, concentrated efforts to rein in inflation appear to be working as the annual year-end inflation rate for 2004 stood at only 3.2 percent. The primary problem has been some government accommodation to public-sector wage demands and an exchange-rate policy that raised import prices.

In terms of structural reforms, Slovenia has made steady progress, albeit not quite shock therapy, in privatizing state industries. The pace has not been too quick—witness the difficulty in selling off the state-owned telecoms monopoly and the steel industry. And 40 percent of the economy is still in state hands (compared to 8 percent in Hungary). Reform and privatization of the banking sector has also been slower and more complicated than other areas, but foreign direct investment in the banking industry and in other sectors of the economy (including the domestic pharmaceutical giant Lek) show that the direction is positive. A sluggish high rate of unemployment, although steadily falling, indicates that further work is necessary in stimulating job growth—especially in liberalizing the economy to foreign investment.[11]

Overall, the transition to the EU has been relatively easy for the Slovenes. Despite some initial economic problems, Slovenia has quickly become an integral, solid member of the EU. Since December 2002, the government has been on a steady path of further economic reforms, perhaps to be quickened under the more right-wing and pro-reform SDS government led by Prime Minister Jansa. Nevertheless, past reforms, however cautious, have already paid off in terms of the likely membership in the euro zone by early 2007.

Slovakia. Seen as the traditionally poorer half of Czechoslovakia, Slovakia had struggled with postcommunist corruption and cronyism; in the mid-1990s, its economy was by all measures a "basket case," with unemployment hovering near 20 percent into early 2002. This contributed to the view at the time that Slovakia was a "black hole in the heart of Europe," to use a phrase coined by then–US secretary of state Madeleine Albright. But now things have turned around rather dramatically. Prime Minister Dzurinda's government has pushed through a number of reforms—especially in the area of taxation. An across-the-board flat tax of 19 percent replaced a corporate tax of 25 percent, and a personal income tax rate that topped out at 38 percent, and the government fully eliminated the inheritance tax. Overall, Slovakian citizens' share of the tax burden as a percent of GDP fell by 10 percent over 1995–2004. As a result, it has become a beneficiary of foreign direct investment equal to US$3 billion in 2004 alone. With labor rates close to one-eighth that of some of the western members of the EU, some see Slovakia as the automobile-manufacturing center of Europe. Not surprisingly, the World Bank rated Slovakia the world's top performer in terms of improving its investment climate.

Others compare Slovakia to Ireland (both joined the EU as poorer, more agriculturally based economies, with small populations).[12] The "Tatra Tiger" (named after the mountain range) has brought free-market reforms to health care, partly privatized social security, eased policies on hiring and firing workers, and privatized state-owned industries.[13] It has become a bastion of free-market, neoliberal polices. For example, Slovakia reacted positively to the "Kok Report" (released in late 2004), which identified the need to ease labor market restrictions and boost spending on education and research within the EU member states, and has criticized France and Germany for violating the Stability and Growth Pact.

In terms of monetary policy, the National Bank of Slovakia (NBS) has targeted 2008–2009 as the realistic date for the euro replacing the koruna (a move confirmed by the government in late 2004). It will fix the koruna's exchange rate to the euro within the ERM II beginning in 2006. The NBS has stated that it will adhere tightly to the Maastricht criteria and will no longer be able to devalue the koruna.[14] Inflation still remains a persistent problem for the economy. Energy price supports and deregulation have placed some inflationary pressures on the bank. The bank's goal is to reduce the rate to 3.5 percent in 2005 and 2.8 percent in 2006. As a sign of progress, in early 2005, the NBS was able to further cut interest rates as year-on-year inflation dropped to 3.2 percent. Finally, as of January 1, 2004, the government allowed shops and restaurants to freely accept euros (four months before formal accession). Many Slovak citizens already calculate prices in both korunas and euros.

Committed to adhering to the Maastricht criteria on deficits,[15] the government has had to make difficult cuts in spending on a variety of programs. As a result, it has been able to reduce the deficit from 7.2 percent in 2003 to 4.97 percent in 2004. The 2005 data and commitments show this deficit reduced to 3.8 percent. Unresolved costs of pension reforms have not been included in the most recent budget debates, adding to speculation that Slovakia will not be able to go below the 3 percent cutoff until 2006–2007. As Prime Minister Dzurinda has stated, however, the introduction of the euro and the attainment of the Maastricht criteria are "good for the people of Slovakia" and will be the "best road to the health of our economy."

Still, problems loom—unemployment remains high overall and, by western standards, about 20 percent of the country could be considered "poor." In addition, the costs of basic supplies, such as energy, have increased notably, impacting other sectors of the economy throughout the country. At the same time, significant regional disparities have endured. For example, the so-called golden Bratislava phenomenon has brought about an economic boom and almost no unemployment in many urban areas but economic crisis in the countryside, especially eastern Slovakia. Meanwhile, regions in the center and east of the country that tried early on to convert "heavy" industry to nonmilitary production are still suffering from the high unemployment created when those efforts failed. In contrast, economic conversion in other parts of the country has faired much better.

Complicating matters further is that the Dzurinda government is under pressure to make cuts in spending, while hoping that tax revenues do not fall below expected levels. The lack of modern infrastructure that the government hopes to improve with EU Structural Funds makes it more difficult to sustain some development activities in the outlying regions beyond Bratislava. Strikes by more militant unions (for example, in January 2003 among the state railway company) also indicated the tensions between the government's plans for deficit reduction and the need for social stability.

Other difficulties associated with the transition have occurred, especially in the areas of agriculture and environmental standards. Over 3,000 people in the dairy industry lost their jobs in 2003–2004 as a result of the inability or lack of capital necessary to meet the EU standards of production on health and safety. Furthermore, Slovakians may feel like second-class citizens, as their workers will not immediately be able to seek employment in the west (given the five-year transition period the older member states could impose). Farmers will be subjected to rigorous competition from western farmers who will still receive up to four times the amount of subsidies compared to their counterparts in the east.

Despite these and other problems, Slovakia has turned its economy around and is speedily headed toward EMU. It has largely internalized all of the required policies, procedures, and processes for membership in the euro zone. One could argue that Slovakia has proven itself a minor miracle in the transitioning economies of east-central Europe.

Justice and Home Affairs

As with other new member states, meeting the JHA *acquis communautaire* has been challenging for Slovenia and Slovakia not only because the policy area impinges on sensitive areas of national sovereignty and civil liberties, but also because it has been developing quite rapidly since 1999. This has provided new and old member states alike with something of a moving target, particularly after the terrorist attacks of September 11, 2001, which contributed to an acceleration of EU legislation on JHA. Moreover, the demise of communist-era criminal justice systems, collapse of the Soviet Union, and the onset of poor economic conditions in many parts of the region contributed to an increase in transnational organized crime (TNOC) throughout central and eastern Europe since the early 1990s. This has made the task of implementing the JHA *acquis* in the new member states more than simply a matter of getting the new countries into synch with the EU. Instead, this has been perceived as way to improve the effectiveness of the new members' ability to manage their borders, fight TNOC on their own, and to cooperate with their new EU partners in these endeavors.

How JHA in Slovenia and Slovakia Influences the EU. The ability of Slovenia and Slovakia to manage their borders and fight TNOC successfully has serious implications for security elsewhere in the EU. Specifically, achieving these goals is viewed as vital to ensuring that the eventual participation of the new member states in the Schengen zone will not worsen the organized-crime problem elsewhere in the free travel area or make the challenges posed by asylum-seekers more difficult to manage. In fact, the issues of crime fighting and border control in the new member states took on greater significance after September 11, and this perception was only enhanced by more recent acts of terrorism in Madrid in 2004 and London in 2005. Slovenia and Slovakia are recipients of EU funding guaranteed by the Accession Treaty's Schengen Facility, which provides more than €900 million to the seven new member states that will have external land borders with non-EU countries. Both countries are also planning to be among the first five new member states to have their border control measures and plans vetted by the EU in early 2006, which will allow the Council of Ministers to decide which countries can join the passport-free zone following the implementation of the second generation of the Schengen Information System (SIS II), slated for March 2007.

Implementation and compliance to the EU's JHA requirements. Preparations to meet the JHA *acquis* and join the Schengen zone have been under way since the accession process began. Negotiations of the Accession Treaty chapters on JHA proved to be among the most difficult and last to be closed, aside from those with financial implications. The six states of the so-called Luxembourg group, including Slovenia, did not open negotiations on JHA until May 2000, more than two years after the start of its accession negotiations. Slovenia was among the first three applicant states to close talks on JHA in December 2001. In contrast, Slovakia was among the last applicant states to initiate talks on JHA, doing so only in June 2001. However, it succeeded in closing this chapter in just two months.

Similar to other member states, both new and old, Slovenia and Slovakia have found it challenging to implement some parts of the EU's *acquis* on JHA and participate fully in the EU's emerging legal and institutional infrastructure of crime fighting and border management. Although most member states have experienced delays in implementing at least some legislative items in the JHA's *acquis*, the new member states, including Slovenia and Slovakia, have all received an impressive amount of financial support from the EU in pre- and postaccession assistance to help ensure that legislation is properly transposed and utilized. This assistance includes "twinning" agreements that have brought interior and justice ministry bureaucrats from the older member states to work directly with their counterparts in the acceding states, as well as financial help to support training programs, the implementation of new technology, and infrastructural improvements at border crossings.[16]

Slovenia. While Slovenia's proximity to western Europe has brought commercial benefits, its location has also made it a prime gateway for transnational organized crime. Specifically, the Slovene-Croatian border remains an important access point into the EU for traffickers of drugs, human beings, and weapons. In 2004, the country reported 5,646 illegal crossings of the Slovene border, with the highest number of illegal immigrants coming from Kosovo (1,323), Albania (1,153), Turkey (734), Bosnia-Herzegovina (470), Macedonia (413), Moldova (269), Croatia (194), Romania (192), and Iraq (89).[17] Illegal immigration into the country was up 25 percent by mid-2005 over the previous year, led by economic migrants from Serbia-Montenegro, Albania, and Turkey.[18] However, the problem of illegal immigration is nowhere near as severe as in 2000 and 2001, when more than 20,000 illegal immigrants were arrested annually.

This change is partly explainable by the various measures that have been initiated to strengthen Slovenia's borders, particularly with Croatia. In fact, because Croatia is unlikely to join the EU until after 2007, and it will probably take several years longer for it to qualify for the passport-free travel zone, Slovenia's frontier with it will be one of the EU's Schengen borders for the foreseeable future. With this in mind, Slovenia has been allocated nearly €120 million from the Schengen Facility for 2004–2006 to help improve its border management infrastructure. The country's border patrol has also instituted joint patrols with authorities from Croatia, as well as with Italy and Austria, to manage the present Schengen border. This kind of cooperation has resulted in the arrest of several human traffickers, who continue to target Slovenia as a key transit state on the so-called Balkans route. Finally, the proper management of the Slovene-Croatian border also necessitates resolution of the dispute between the two countries over its common sea border in Piran Bay.

As with almost every other member state, Slovenia does not have a perfect record regarding the implementation of the EU's JHA *acquis.*[19] However, at least regarding the transposition of antiterrorist measures, Slovenia's record is among the best compared to the other new member states. In fact, its performance in this regard is superior to several older member states, notably Italy, Ireland, Luxembourg, and Greece. Since the terrorist attacks in Madrid in March 2004, the EU has made public a series of periodic reports prepared by its counterterrorism coordinator, Gijs de Vries, indicating measures that have been implemented or not at the national level.[20] Of the 12 items tracked by the EU, Slovenia had failed to implement only two by the end of May 2005, namely framework decisions on money laundering, which were supposed to be transposed by May 2002, and on the freezing of property and evidence, which had a deadline of August 2005 and had only been implemented by four member states.[21] By the end of 2004 Slovenia had already implemented all of the United Nations' counterterrorism measures that were required by the EU, an accomplishment that six member states had yet to achieve by the summer of 2005.

Despite this relatively good level of success with antiterrorist legislation in general, Slovenia has experienced some difficulty with the implementation of the European Arrest Warrant (EAW), the crown jewel in the EU's efforts to promote judicial cooperation in criminal matters. To its credit, Slovenia was one of the few member states to transpose the EAW on time, doing so via a fast-track procedure on March 26, 2004—well before the May 1, 2004, deadline set for the acceding countries.[22] Only four other new member states managed to achieve this by the time of their accession to the EU. However, in February 2005, Slovenia was one of nine EU members highlighted in a Commission report for not being in proper compliance with the framework decision establishing the EAW.

In Slovenia's case, the problems are related to the procedure it has established and limitations it has placed on the scope of the EAW's application to certain categories of offenses. In addition, Slovenia's legislation requires that it will accept extradition requests via the EAW only if they are translated into Slovenian by the requesting state, similar to four other EU members that require the EAW to be transmitted to them only in their own national languages, rather than allowing English as an alternative. The Slovene legislation correctly permits the extradition of its nationals and legal residents, but provides that sentences can subsequently be served in Slovenia.[23]

Slovakia. As with Slovenia, Slovakia's location on the periphery of the enlarged European Union presents several challenges regarding border management and the fight against TNOC. Slovakia's frontier with Ukraine is especially troublesome, serving as one of the most popular land borders in the EU for illegal immigration, including both human trafficking and people smuggling. In addition, Ukraine may never become a member of the EU and, even if it does, it may never be allowed to join the Schengen free-travel area. This means that Slovakia and the EU must prepare for this border to be a more or less permanent Schengen boundary. In contrast, the country's much longer borders with Poland, the Czech Republic, Austria, and Hungary may only be controlled until late 2007, when Slovakia and its neighbors hope to become part of the free-travel area. In expectation of this, Slovakia plans to have its border control systems vetted in early 2006.

Preparations for joining the Schengen zone have been under way in Slovakia since long before its accession to the EU, funded by the Phare program. In addition, Slovakia has been allotted more than €47 million from the Schengen Facility for 2004–2006, primarily to reinforce its border with Ukraine. Among other tasks, this money will help support the construction of three new custom control points on the Slovak-Ukrainian border by 2010, as well as the upgrading of four existing railway and roadway crossings (two each) by 2007. Slovakia has also taken advantage of twinning programs offered by the EU.

Slovakian border guard officials have taken credit for a recent decline in illegal immigration, having arrested 3,400 illegal immigrants on the border with Ukraine in 2004, among the 8,400 questioned across the country that year, compared to 5,000 arrested on that border and 12,500 people questioned in 2003. Related to this, Slovakia continues to be challenged by the problem of human trafficking, serving mainly as a transit state for women from Ukraine, Moldova, and the Balkans. Slovakia's Roma women are sometimes victims of this crime as well. In June 2005, a US State Department report noted that Slovakia had made significant efforts to address its shortcomings regarding human trafficking, but that it still has inadequate measures to control this crime and address the needs of victims.[24]

By 2005, pressure on Slovakia's borders was also declining in the area of asylum-seekers, reversing a problematic trend that had begun around the time the country joined the EU. By 2004, asylum claims had declined over 20 percent in the older members, but they had actually increased 4 percent in the new EU states, with Slovakia having the most applications of any new member.[25] However, in the first half of 2005, asylum claims were down sharply across all of central Europe, with Slovakia enjoying the most dramatic decline of 78 percent.[26] Some of this decline stems from Slovakia's growing reputation as one of the least-open countries regarding refugees, having one of the lowest acceptance rates of asylum applications in the EU. In responding to criticisms of human rights groups, Slovakian officials have argued that they are rejecting many applications because they are logged by economic migrants and not true political refugees.[27]

Compared to both new and old member states, Slovakia's record concerning the implementation of EU antiterrorist measures was quite good by the end of May 2005. According to the de Vries report mentioned above, the country had yet to transpose the convention and related protocol on mutual legal assistance in criminal matters between EU member states, but this legislation was already in preparation and was expected to be approved in a timely manner. The report mentions that Slovakia had transposed most parts of the framework decision on terrorism, with the remainder on the liability of legal persons set to be incorporated into the county's new criminal code. This code was actually approved on May 24, too late to be included in the report. At the time, the only remaining item to be transposed was the framework decision on the freezing of property or evidence, but it was finalized by October 2005.

Concerning the European Arrest Warrant, Slovakia was unable to meet the deadline of May 1, 2004, and was among the last five new member states to do this. However, the matter was not terribly controversial in Slovakia, especially compared to the contentious debate and longer delays experienced in the neighboring Czech Republic. In the end, the transposition of the EAW in Slovakia took place with parliamentary approval on June 24, 2004, supported in parliament by all political parties aside from Mečiar's Movement for a Democratic Slovakia (HZDS), which abstained.

Although its implementation of the EAW was late, Slovakia was not among the nine member states criticized by the Commission for having significant flaws in its transposition of the framework decision, as was the case with Slovenia. However, the same Commission report pointed out that Slovakia's version of the EAW did not place any time limits on its high court for hearing prisoners' appeals, as called for by the framework decision. Interestingly, Slovakia joins Ireland and the UK as the only three countries not to exercise a provision allowed in the framework decision that permits a country to extradite one of its nationals via the EAW but to require that any sentence be carried out on its own territory, rather than in the requesting state—provided that this is requested by the convict.

■ Future Trends and Prospects

By the end of 2005, both Slovenia and Slovakia had settled into EU membership and were looking to the future. At the time, both seemed on track to join the more exclusive clubs of the euro zone and Schengen free-travel area. However, as with the other member states, the future of EU treaty reform and the implications of this for Slovene and Slovakian national concerns remained in doubt.

In 2005, both countries had ratified the Constitutional Treaty through parliamentary votes, not referenda. Popular support for the constitution was at about 60 percent in both countries, but more than 25 percent of those polled in each country were still undecided.[28] On February 1, Slovenia became just the third EU member to ratify the constitution, with the relatively new Jansa government easily obtaining the required two-thirds majority in the national assembly. In fact, just 4 of 90 MPs voted against the treaty (7 were absent for the vote).

With 116 of 150 voting in favor on May 11, 2005, the initial decision on the constitution in Slovakia was nearly as convincing, but the matter was somewhat more controversial than in Slovenia, and eventually, legally uncertain. During parliamentary debate, one of the Dzurinda government's coalition partners, the Christian Democrats (KDH), spoke out against the treaty, calling for a referendum to be held. The Communist Party (KSS) also criticized the treaty and joined the KDH in voting against it, as did three independent MPs, with four others abstaining. Before President Gasparovic could finalize the ratification with his signature, a group of 13 activists appealed to Slovakia's constitutional court to block this, arguing that a referendum should be required. In July 2005, following the failed referenda in France and the Netherlands, the court agreed to rule on the matter, leaving Slovakia's ratification in limbo. Although the existing constitution may be dead in its present form, this ruling could ultimately determine how Slovakia manages EU treaty reform in the future.

■ Notes

For their helpful comments and suggestions, the authors are grateful to Andrea Laskava and Rok Zvelc.

1. For more on this and related topics, see John K. Cox, *Slovenia*.

2. Compare to Fink-Hafner, "Slovenia," pp. 1130–1137.

3. Compare to Harris, "Europeanization of Slovakia," pp. 185–211, and Meseznikov, "The Emergence of Slovakia," pp. 13–14.

4. For more on politics in Slovakia and its relationship to the EU see Henderson, *The Politics of Slovakia*.

5. To clarify, Gasparovic is more moderate than Mečiar and does not necessarily identify with Fico or his political ideas. It is nonetheless important to note how the reform debate in Slovakia was connected to the issue of the EU's influence on the country.

6. Compare to Ucen, "Slovakia," pp. 1121–1129.

7. Unlike the multilateral parity grid of the old ERM, the ERM II currencies are linked to the euro on a bilateral basis only.

8. Decisions on central rates and the standard bands are taken by mutual agreement of the ministers of the euro-area member states, the ECB, and the ministers and central bank governors of the non-euro-area member states, following a common procedure involving the European Commission. The sustainability of central rates is monitored continuously and all participating parties (except the Commission) have the right to trigger a confidential procedure of realignment. Intervention at the standard, wide margins is automatic and unlimited (unlike the old ERM) between the ECB and the "pre-in" national central banks (NCBs). However, the ECB or the "pre-in" NCB has the right to suspend intervention if its price stability objective is jeopardized.

9. See Loedel, "Is There Room at the Table?"

10. "Over 52 Percent of Slovenes Support EU Membership, Polls Show," *Global News Wire*, May 1, 2005.

11. "Change and Frustration," Special Report on Slovenia, *Financial Times*, May 10, 2005.

12. This kind of enthusiasm is found in such titles of articles as "Slovakia: The Hong Kong of Europe?" *Transitions Online*, August 8, 2003.

13. "Once a Backwater, Slovakia Surges," *New York Times*, December 28, 2004.

14. "Slovak Central Bank Says 2008 Realistic Date for Introduction of the Euro," *Global News Wire*, February 24, 2003.

15. "Slovak Coalition Determined to Meet Maastricht Criteria," *Global News Wire*, May 27, 2003.

16. See Occhipinti, "Justice and Home Affairs," pp. 199–212.

17. "Slovene Police Smash Human Trafficking Ring," *BBC Worldwide Monitoring*, April 13, 2005.

18. "Slovene Police Report Illegal Migration Up in First Six Months of 2005," *BBC Worldwide Monitoring*, July 17, 2005.

19. "Slovenia Late in Implementing EU Counter-Terrorism Measures," *BBC Monitoring International Reports*, December 3, 2004.

20. Council of the European Union, "EU Plan of Action on Combating Terrorism—Update." See also *European Report*, "Terrorism: Patchy Performance for Implementing Laws Exposed," June 22, 2005.

21. The "framework decisions" of Pillar III are akin to the "directives" of Pillar I. That is, they provide legislative blueprints that need to be "transposed in national law."

22. Italy became the last EU member state to implement the EAW, when it did so in April 2005, almost 14 months after the original deadline of January 2004 (set for older member states but met by only eight of them). Italy also missed the extended deadline of June 2004, which was established after the terrorist attack in Madrid as part of renewed EU efforts to implement its JHA *acquis* in a timely fashion, particularly its antiterrorist legislation.

23. "Slovene Parliament Passes European Arrest Warrant Bill," *BBC Monitoring International Reports,* March 26, 2004.

24. "Trafficking Can Turn Anyone's Child into a Commodity," *Slovak Spectator*, June 11, 2005.

25. Tamsin Smith, "Smugglers Target Slovakia Border," *BBC News*, available at: bbc.co.uk (May 11, 2005).

26. "Asylum Flow to Rich Countries Still Falling: UN Refugee Agency," Agence France Press, September 6, 2005. Compare to Holt, "The Vanishing," and Vermeersch, "EU Enlargement and Immigration Policy in Poland and Slovakia," pp. 71–88.

27. "Economic Migrants Should Be Taken into Account—Experts," *CTK National News Wire*, August 27, 2005.

28. In Slovenia, Eurobarmometer polling indicated 60 percent favorable, 9 percent opposed, and 31 percent "don't know." In Slovakia, the results were 61 percent favorable, 11 percent opposed, and 28 percent "don't know." EUObserver.com, "EU Constitution: Where Member States Stand," February 21, 2005.

19

Malta and Cyprus: The Mediterranean Island States

Roderick Pace

THE 2004 EUROPEAN UNION enlargement included the Mediterranean island-states of Cyprus and Malta, two former British colonies and members of the British Commonwealth. The islands share a number of similarities but they are also dissimilar in distinct ways. The membership applications of both states initially presented the EU with a number of political difficulties. With respect to Cyprus, many member states would have preferred to see the island join the Union after the "Cyprus Problem" had been settled. As for Malta, the island showed a very high degree of Euro-skepticism. It froze its application in 1996 but reactivated it in 1998. Apart from this skepticism, the island's neutral status, enshrined in the constitution, could present insurmountable problems.

Compared with the other applicant states from central and eastern Europe, the two Mediterranean isles are more economically and politically advanced. This, combined with their small size, presented the EU with fewer problems of absorbing them. Indeed, both states had experienced self-government and democracy since their independence from Britain in the 1960s and a market economy much before that time. Both had had a long-standing economic relationship with the Union predating similar relations between the EU and new member states from central and eastern Europe by at least two decades. Malta and the European Community signed an Association Agreement in 1970, while Cyprus followed suit in 1972. In 1987, Cyprus embarked on the last phase leading to a customs union with the EU, while in 1989 the much-postponed

EU-Malta customs union was shelved indefinitely on the insistence of the Maltese government.

While it is too early to make a thorough assessment of the effects of EU membership on Cyprus and Malta, the membership impact is already being felt in both states. This chapter focuses on the effect of EU membership on Cypriot and Maltese domestic politics, on the ongoing process of economic reform and the two islands' quest to adopt the euro by 2008, and on salient security concerns.

The two island states enjoy a strategic position in the Mediterranean region. Cyprus is situated in the eastern Mediterranean close to the Middle East, Turkey, and the important maritime gateways of the Bosporus Straits and the Suez Canal. Malta is located in the middle of the Mediterranean Sea close to the main maritime highways that crisscross the region. For more than two millennia and no doubt due to its strategic value, Malta was held by the major powers that dominated the Mediterranean region from the Carthaginians down to the British. The history of Cyprus shows a similar pattern of development.

Malta, Cyprus, and Gibraltar, together with Alexandria, the Suez Canal, and Aden, at the tip of the Arabian Peninsula, formed part of Britain's highway or supply chain to India in the heyday of the British Empire. However, the situation changed rapidly after the end of the Second World War. The independence movement in the British Commonwealth and Britain's gradual retreat from the Far East transformed the geostrategic importance of Cyprus and Malta without, however, diminishing their importance. Both islands acquired a new strategic status as a result of the Cold War. Cyprus's new strategic value was derived from its proximity to the Dardanelles, the Suez Canal, and the turbulent Middle East region, not to mention its proximity to the countries of the Baghdad Pact,[1] one of the many US-inspired alliances surrounding the USSR as part of Washington's containment policy. In the central Mediterranean, the geostrategic situation was also somewhat similar. However, when the UK military bases were closed down in Malta in 1979, their functions were transferred to NATO military bases in Sicily. UK military bases continue to operate in Cyprus within the confines of the Sovereign Military Base Area (SBA) established by the Treaty of Establishment signed between the UK, Greece, Turkey, and Cyprus on August 16, 1960. The EU-Cyprus Act of Accession also affected the SBA.[2]

The two islands' histories also differ in many respects. In ancient times Cyprus formed part of the Hellenic world, as it still does in contemporary times. Its predominant culture is Hellenic and its predominant religion is Greek Orthodox, with Greek being the main spoken language, while the Turkish Cypriot minority in the northern part of the island is Muslim and speaks Turkish. By contrast, there are no sizable ethnic minorities in Malta and the spoken language is Maltese, descended from Arabic, the only surviving relic from the Arab period (A.D. 800–1000), while the main religion is Roman Catholicism. Both countries' histories are connected with Turkey's but in distinctly different ways. Malta, led by the Knights of St. John of Jerusalem, resisted incorporation into the Ottoman Empire in the epic "Great Siege" of 1565, while Cyprus fell to the Ottomans six years later in 1571.[3]

Given the small size of their domestic economies, both island states are heavily dependent on trade, especially in the case of Malta.[4] Both have developed tourism as an important source of national income but to a markedly different extent, as measured by its contribution to GDP. The economic sectors contributing to the national wealth of the two isles have evolved differently with, for example, agriculture enjoying a more important role in the Cypriot than in the Maltese economy. The different role of agriculture in the islands' economies is also connected to the difference in the physical territorial size of both islands and their respective population densities. Cyprus is 30 times the size of Malta. The Cypriot population, at 730,400, is twice Malta's, at 399,900.[5] In the world's population-density league, Malta with 1,192 persons per square kilometer ranks ninth while Cyprus with 81.61 per square kilometer is in the 114th place. Cyprus is wealthier than Malta: its GDP per capita in Purchasing Power Standards (PPS) compared with the EU average is 82.9 percent, while Malta's is 73.2 percent (EU-25 = 100).[6]

■ How and in What Ways Has the EU Influenced Malta and Cyprus?

Achieving Membership

Cyprus and Malta applied to join the EU respectively on July 4 and 16, 1990, under the Italian presidency of the Union. The European Commission's "Opinions" on both applications were published in 1993.[7] Both island states had to overcome a number of serious obstacles on their respective roads to membership. In Cyprus, there was a quasi–cross-party consensus in the Greek part of the island on the membership application and the widely shared view among political elites and the public alike was that membership could help resolve the "Cyprus Problem," which had arisen following the forcible division of the island by Turkey in 1974. The largest Cypriot political party, the Cypriot Communist Party—actual name, the Progressive Party of the Working People (AKEL)—at first opposed EU membership. This would have constituted a serious obstacle to be overcome had this position been doggedly adhered to by AKEL. However, at its 18th Party Congress (1995) AKEL changed its policy. This decision was probably influenced by the changes that had occurred in Europe following the fall of communism and the need felt within AKEL's ranks of adapting the party's political program to the new realities, including that of aligning itself with the European democratic left, an issue of political survival within the new European political context.

At the same time, the Cyprus Problem was more than just a domestic political issue. Indeed, a broader discussion of Cyprus's EU application has to be contextualized within the special links that Greece, Turkey, and the UK have with the island: the three states were involved in protracted negotiations culminating in the London-Zurich Accords of February 1959, on the basis of which a number of treaties were concluded according Cyprus a "conditional independence."[8] On the basis of these treaties, the UK siphoned off for itself a "sovereign base area" (the SBA) with a total land area the size of the island of Malta (99 square miles). Greece and Turkey secured the right to special links with the respective ethnic communities on the island and to station some troops there. Cyprus, Greece, Turkey, and the UK signed a Treaty of Guarantee in Nicosia in August 1960 by which they assumed joint responsibility for safeguarding the independence, territorial integrity, and security of Cyprus.[9] When Turkey invaded and partitioned the island in 1974, it invoked violation of this Treaty of Guarantee as the main pretext for its intervention.

Thus, when Cyprus applied for EU membership, its application became immediately entangled within the nexus of EU-Turkey relations, the tense relationship between Greece and Turkey, and Britain's military/strategic interests in the island. Greece, already an EU member state, supported Cyprus's application, but Turkey, which has a longstanding Association Agreement with the EC signed in Ankara in 1963, opposed it. The Ankara Agreement, together with Turkey's membership in NATO and the Council of Europe, strengthened Turkey's leverage vis-à-vis the EU. In particular, the Ankara Agreement envisaged Turkey's eventual EC membership in the longer term (after 22 years). Turkey applied for membership in 1987, but its application was rejected two years later. The application was relaunched following the 1995 EU-Turkey Customs Union Agreement. At the end of 2004, the EU finally agreed on the conditions for starting membership negotiations with Turkey, after considering the European Commission's appraisal of the main implications for the EU of Turkey's membership.[10]

Turkey, which does not recognize the government of the Republic of Cyprus, is the only state that recognizes the Turkish Republic of Northern Cyprus (TRNC) established in 1985. Turkey also maintains a strong military force in Northern Cyprus estimated to consist of around 35,000 troops.

A majority of EU member states were reluctant to "internalize" the conflict in the Union by admitting Cyprus. They initially preferred that the problem be resolved before Cyprus was actually admitted, believing that their stance would coax Cyprus into seeking a lasting solution. In fact, in its "Opinion" on the Cypriot membership application, the European Commission drew attention to the problems posed by the "de facto division of the Island," and that the membership application had been contested by the authorities of the self-styled TRNC.[11] However, the Commission, "following the logic of its established position, which is consistent with that of the UN where the legitimacy of the government of the Republic of Cyprus and non-recognition of the 'Turkish Republic of Northern Cyprus' are concerned, felt that the application was admissible."[12] Indeed, in 1997, the EU offered the TRNC the possibility of participating in the membership negotiations without requiring mutual recognition with the government of Cyprus, but the TRNC declined. The Commission also proposed that should the intercommunal talks between the Greek and Turkish Cypriots fail to lead to a political settlement of the Cyprus Problem, the question of Cyprus's accession should be reconsidered in January 1995.[13] In fact, that is what happened, but also, during that year, the EU-Turkey Customs Union Agreement concluded and complicated matters further since it implied the eventual application of trade preferences to the whole of Cyprus, and hence by implication Ankara's eventual recognition of the Greek-Cypriot government. It was also argued that goods from the TRNC could not enter the EU customs union through Turkey unless they came from ports controlled by the government of Cyprus. At the time, speculation was rife that Brussels had facilitated the conclusion of the customs union agreement in return for Ankara's lifting its objections to membership negotiations commencing with Cyprus. Indeed, in June 1995, at Cannes, the EU Council had reaffirmed that membership negotiations with Cyprus and Malta would commence "six months after the conclusion of the 1996 Inter-governmental conference and taking the outcome of that conference into account."[14] This speculation received a cold shower following the Turkey-TRNC Joint Statement of December 29, 1995, in which the two sides opposed Cyprus's EU membership, underlining that membership would only be possible in conjunction with a solution to the Cyprus Problem, and adding further that Cyprus could join the EU only simultaneously with Turkey.[15]

The EU gradually overcame these difficulties, and the European Council meeting in Helsinki in December 1999 underlined "that a political settlement will facilitate the accession of Cyprus to the European Union. If no settlement has been reached by the completion of the accession negotiations, the Council's decision on accession will be made without the above [the solution of the problem] being a precondition. In this, the Council will take account of all the relevant factors."[16] While thus yielding to pressures started in the EU Council by Greece prior to the 1994 Corfu European Council, and sustained thereafter, that Cyprus should be allowed to join the Union whether or not a solution had been found to the Cyprus Problem, the EU made it clear to Turkey that its own membership ambitions depended a lot on progress on this problem. The EU was trying, as it was also doing with Cyprus, to give Ankara the incentive to work for a solution to the Cyprus Problem.[17]

Membership negotiations commenced with Cyprus and Malta in 1998 and went into full gear in February 2000 together with the other eight applicant countries. Malta had in the meantime reactivated its application in 1998. The negotiations concluded at the end of 2002. A last-ditch effort to achieve a solution to the Cyprus Problem before enlargement on the basis of a UN plan (the Annan Plan) failed.[18] The final phase in this last attempt to push through an agreement began in February 2004 with intensive negotiations between leaders of the two Cypriot communities under UN auspices. At the end of these talks, UN secretary-general Kofi Annan optimistically expressed that a solution was "within reach."[19] Further negotiations in Bürgenstock, Switzerland, in March achieved some progress but the two sides failed to agree on all outstanding issues. At this point, as had been previously agreed, Annan stepped in to "fill in the blanks," and the plan was then submitted for approval by the two Cypriot communities.[20] Greek and Turkish Cypriots voted on the plan in two separate but simultaneous referenda on April 24, 2004. The Greek Cypriots voted to reject the Annan Plan while the Turkish Cypriots voted in its favor (see Table 19.1). As a result, the EU admitted the whole of Cyprus, but the *acquis communautaire* was applicable only in those areas controlled by the Cyprus government. The northern Turkish Cypriot enclave thus remained isolated.

In Malta's case, EU membership proved to be equally turbulent

Table 19.1   Referenda Results in Cyprus on the Annan Plan, 2004

	Turnout	Yes	No
Greek Cypriot community	88%	24.2%	75.8%
Turkish Cypriot community	87%	64.9%	35.1%

albeit in contrast to Cyprus only domestic political issues were mostly involved.[21] The Maltese were split down the middle between those who favored membership and those who opposed it. The Nationalist Party (NP), in government since 1987 except for a brief 22-month spell between 1996 and 1998, favored membership while the opposition Malta Labor Party (MLP), enjoying just under half of the support of Maltese voters, opposed it, proposing instead a "special relationship" with the Union based on a free-trade area agreement. Elected to govern the island in 1996, the MLP suspended the membership application and pursued instead the free-trade agreement option under the slogan of a "Switzerland in the Mediterranean." However, following the return to government of the Nationalist Party in 1998, as a result of an unprecedented and unexpected early election provoked by a split in the Labor Party and leading to a defeat for the government in a crucial parliamentary vote, the membership application was reactivated. After the end of the negotiations, the Maltese voters finally decided the issue in a referendum held on March 8, 2003, and a general election held on April 12 of the same year. In the referendum, close to 54 percent voted in favor of membership (turnout was 91 percent of registered and eligible voters), while in the election, the PN was returned to govern with slightly less than 52 percent of the valid votes cast (with turnout of about 95 percent). The main issue in the election was the EU membership question.[22]

The Political Effects of EU Membership

Mindful of the fact that political developments rarely follow a positively linear course and that it is too early to make a thorough assessment of the full impact of EU membership, there are clear signs that membership has begun to change the national political landscape in both Cyprus and Malta. It is too early to assess the nature of these changes, but what is certain is that both Cyprus and Malta witnessed a spate of political events and developments that up to a few months before would have been unthinkable. The political institutions of both island states have begun to adjust to the new domestic and European context instigated by membership in many ways.

Malta. The main change following EU membership was manifested by the Malta Labor Party's policy shift in favor of accepting membership. In Cyprus, membership instigated a relaxation of the restrictive measures applied by both communities on the "border" dividing them, without, however, bringing them appreciably closer to a formal agreement on a lasting solution to the Cyprus Problem. In Northern Cyprus, the Turkish Cypriot community's reluctance to be left out of the EU's enlargement led to the first serious challenge since 1960 to the strong political hold exercised by the community's leader, Rauf Denktash.

The referendum and election results in Malta, with high electoral participation rates on both occasions, left no doubt that a majority favored membership. This majority would probably have been larger had the MLP allowed its supporters a free vote on the issue. Faced with this setback, the MLP had to take a pragmatic approach to membership and switch its policy. This was not an easy U-turn to perform, considering that the Campaign for National Independence (CNi), headed by a former MLP leader and prime minister, Karmenu Mifsud Bonnici, had played a vocal part in the antimembership "No" campaign and had strong roots in the MLP. In November 2003, the MLP made an early start to its policy shift when its general conference approved a motion proposed by the party's executive to accept EU membership. A countermotion by Mifsud Bonnici was withdrawn following acceptance, by both sides, of an additional phrase to the main motion calling upon the MLP to do its utmost to counter all the negative effects that could result from membership.[23] Having taken the first step, the MLP contested the elections to the European Parliament held on June 12, 2004. Surprisingly it won three seats, to the governing Nationalists' two, out of the five seats allotted to Malta. Labor's performance was helped by the fact that the candidate of Alternativa Demokratika (AD), the green party, took away enough votes from the Nationalist candidates to allow the MLP to beat the Nationalists at the post for the third seat.[24] Following this success, Labor began its internal debate on the stand it should adopt within the Maltese house of representatives on the new European Constitutional Treaty when it came up for ratification. After a lengthy and often acrimonious internal debate in which Mifsud Bonnici and his CNi acolytes called upon the party to vote against the European constitution, the party conference was asked to vote on two resolutions—one proposed by the national executive favoring ratification with some reservations, mainly on Malta's neutrality, and the other by Mifsud Bonnici proposing a rejection of the constitution. The motion by the national executive was approved by 85.6 percent, while Mifsud

Bonnici's motion obtained only 14.4 percent of the votes.[25] The Maltese house of representatives thus voted unanimously in favor of the EU constitution on July 6, 2005.[26] The vote within the house signaled the beginning of a new political era in Malta in which all three Maltese political parties—namely, the governing Nationalist Party and the opposition Malta Labor Party, represented in parliament, and the small Alternativa Demokratika, which is not represented in the house of representatives—favor membership in the EU. This internal Maltese political convergence on EU membership occurred after the rejection of the Constitutional Treaty in the referenda in France and the Netherlands.

Cyprus. The effect of EU membership on the domestic political scene in Cyprus has been dramatic. However, in contrast with Malta, the elections to the European Parliament and the ratification of the European constitution did not jolt the political establishment. Cyprus ratified the European constitution on June 30, 2005, following a special two-day parliamentary session. Thirty MPs voted in favor of the constitution, 19 members belonging to AKEL voted against it, and one member of the Green Party (KOP) abstained because a request he had made for a referendum on the issue had been rejected. According to Article 169 of the Cyprus Constitution, international treaties have to be approved by parliament, through a simple majority of members present and voting, with at least one-third of its members present. The parties voting in favor were the Rally for Democracy (DISY), the Democratic Party (DIKO), the Social Democratic Party (KISOS), New Horizons (NEO), United Democrats (EDI), and the Democratic Movement (ADIK). The elections to the European Parliament saw the six seats allotted to Cyprus go to DISY (2), AKEL (2), DIKO (1), and For Europe (1) with hardly any surprises, though turnout at 71.19 percent was appreciably high (see Table 19.2).[27]

The more dramatic political tremors caused by EU membership

Table 19.2 Cypriot Voting Results for the EU Constitution, 2005

Party	Votes	Percentage	EP Seats
Democratic Rally	94,355	28.23	2
AKEL + Left + New Powers	93,212	27.89	2
Democratic Party	57,121	17.09	1
For Europe	36,112	10.80	1

Source: Cyprus News Agency, June 14, 2004.

were felt in the relations between the Greek and Turkish Cypriot communities. The first EU-instigated change took place in the Turkish Cypriot community, where two factors combined to weaken the hold of Turkish Cypriot leader Rauf Denktash. The first was linked to Turkey's keenness to improve its relations with the EU in light of its membership ambitions. This led to pressure on Denktash to force him to be less intransigent on the Annan Plan negotiations. In time, this flexibility proved not to be sufficient to satisfy Greek Cypriot expectations. The second factor was the increasing support for Turkish Cypriot political parties favoring an agreement on the Annan Plan so that the northern enclave would not miss out on EU membership. This led to the election of Mehmet Ali Talat, leader of the Republican Turkish Party (Cumhuriyetçi Türk Partisi), as prime minister in 2004, and subsequently as president of the TRNC in April 2005.

In April 2003, a year before Cyprus joined the EU, the TRNC, while still firmly in the hands of Denktash, took the unilateral and surprising decision to open its borders to allow Turkish Cypriots to travel to the southern part of the island provided they returned back on the same day. This arose from an increasing sense of isolation felt in the Turkish enclave given that Cyprus was joining the EU but that part of the country would continue to be barred from the benefits of membership. Soon after the decision to relax the controls on travel to the south, the TRNC allowed Greek Cypriots to visit the North for up to three days, provided they made suitable travel arrangements through a tour operator or supplied evidence on exit from the TRNC of having stayed in hotels.[28] At the end of April 2003, the government of Cyprus announced measures to make it easier for Turkish Cypriots and other persons lawfully residing in Cyprus to move from the occupied to the government-controlled areas. The government announced the creation of more controlled crossing points, a relaxation on the restrictions in force regarding tourists, and facilitation of the circulation of vehicles. However, the more important change from the Turkish Cypriot standpoint was the announcement of measures to facilitate the employment of Turkish Cypriots who live in the occupied areas by employers in the government-controlled areas with the same terms of employment applicable to other Cypriot employees.[29] These measures announced by the government in Nicosia included the facilitation of employment of Turkish Cypriot professionals, even though they obtained their qualifications in educational institutions considered illegal by the government of Cyprus; participation of Turkish Cypriots in EU educational programs and in local and European Parliamentary elections; facilitation of access to medical care; the issuing of travel documents; and the de-mining of the buffer zone. Other less ambitious though important measures occurred in the military field and included troop reductions by the Greeks in sensitive areas, in addition to de-mining operations.

The main event in Cyprus, prior to enlargement, was the rejection by the Greek Cypriots of the Annan Plan. This decision disappointed many in the EU. However, it is also significant that, as Claire Palley has shown in her more detailed analysis of the issue, Greek Cypriot misgivings on substantive parts of the plan were not answered prior to the poll. These included such matters as financing the unification of the island, the rules governing the recovery and/or compensation of land and property lost by Greeks in the northern part of the island as a result of the 1974 Turkish invasion (property rights), the UK's attempt to extend the territorial waters of its SBA on the back of the agreement, the security of the island postunification, and the proper functioning of the proposed institutional framework of the new state proposed under the Annan Plan.[30] In July 2004, the Commission proposed a set of comprehensive measures aimed to help end the isolation of the Turkish Cypriots by facilitating exchanges across the so-called green line.[31] This led to a new Council regulation and a new regime governing the free movement of goods, services, and persons across the "green line" separating the two Cypriot communities, which came into effect as soon as Cyprus joined the EU.[32] The legal basis of this "green line" regulation is Protocol 10 of the Act of Accession.[33] The protocol specifies that the application of the *acquis* is suspended in areas of Cyprus that are not under the effective control of the government, but the Council, acting unanimously, can define the terms under which provisions of EU law shall apply to the boundaries separating the Turkish-occupied northern part of the island from the government-controlled area and from the SBA.

■ How and in What Ways Do Cyprus and Malta Influence the EU?

Because Cyprus and Malta are small states and because they are also new members (May 2004), they have not had time to exert much influence on the EU up to this time. Their position in the Mediterranean, however, makes them geostrategically important, and Cyprus, with its mixture of Greek and Turkish cultures and politics, has the potential to serve as a bridge nation between Turkey and the European Union. Both states enjoy increased prestige within the Mediterranean region and their own subregion, attributed to them by the non-EU states on the basis that, as EU member states, Cyprus and Malta can influence the Union's policies. Both states are also relatively strong economically, so their membership has not drained the EU's limited budget. They are on the border of being either beneficiaries or contributors, depending on various rulings at different times. Malta, for example, worked hard to change the distribution key for the allocation of funds in order to take account of population density and gain extra funds. Malta has the highest population density in the EU. In December, the European Council decided that high population density should be taken into account in the allocation of the Cohesion Funds.[34]

How Do Cyprus and Malta Implement EU Law?

The analysis now turns to other issues directly related to EU membership. The implementation of the *acquis communautaire* by Cyprus and Malta, which started prior to membership and continued after, has led to a process of modernization, restructuring, and consolidation in a number of fields on the two islands.

Many of the reforms that Cyprus and Malta confront are related to their quest of joining the single currency, the euro, in 2008 and in achieving the goals of the so-called Lisbon Strategy. The Lisbon agenda was launched in March 2000 with the aim of turning Europe into "the most dynamic and competitive knowledge-based economy in the world, capable of sustainable economic growth with more and better jobs and greater social cohesion, and respect for the environment" by 2010.[35] Its aims were renewed by the European Council in the mid-term review of the policy carried out in spring 2005.[36] According to this strategy, the EU member states have to adopt a national plan for achieving the Lisbon goals. Accordingly, both Cyprus and Malta published their strategies, National Reform Programs (NRPs) as they are referred to by the Commission, in fall 2005. These strategies coordinate with the reform Convergence Plans, which the new member states are obliged to follow in the run-up to their joining the European Monetary Union (EMU), which for the time being involves those countries hoping to join the euro zone in the 2007–2009 period.[37]

The main initial difficulty with the reform process to adopt the EU *acquis* concerned whether Cyprus and Malta would be able to cope with the volume of EU laws that had to be transposed into national law, given the small size of their public administrations. The capacity to adopt the *acquis* is one of the main concerns that surfaces when discussing the role of small states in the EU. Constantin Stefanou expressed the issue rather succinctly: "The 80,000 pages of the *acquis* have to be transposed irrespective of whether the applicant country is Poland with a population of 38 million and a large civil service or Malta with a population of 400,000 and a civil service a fraction of the size of larger member states."[38] Limited capacity is a problem that the smaller states of the EU have to face even after joining the EU when additional pressures begin, such as those generated by the need to keep abreast with Commission and Council working groups and task forces.

Connected to this problem was another issue, namely whether the necessary legal changes could be approved by the respective parliaments as rapidly as required by the brisk pace of the membership negotiations. A "negotiating chapter" could not be temporarily closed before the EU had ascertained that the necessary adaptations to the *acquis* had been completed by the applicant states. Both Cyprus and Malta created parliamentary committees to scrutinize EU laws and to pilot their approval through their parliaments (see Table 19.3). These committees eventually proved their usefulness in the membership phase as well. They also permitted a stronger involvement of the two national parliaments in EU affairs. In Malta's case, parliament's role in the preaccession stage could have been problematic given the opposition's antimembership stance, but the government coped well by programing its parliamentary work and employing its parliamentary majority to approve the necessary bills. In the case of Cyprus, a simplified harmonization procedure was adopted after an uncertain start, which together with the European Affairs Committee within the house of representatives ensured the timely approval of legislation.[39]

Table 19.3　National Committees That Cooperate with the EU

	Name of Committee and Date of Establishment	Members
Cyprus	Committee on European Affairs February 25, 1999	15
Malta	Standing Committee on Foreign and European Affairs 1995/2003	9

Source: Third biannual report of COSAC, which takes account of developments up to April 4, 2005. COSAC stands for "cooperation between committees of the national parliaments dealing with European affairs and the European Parliament."

In addition, both Cyprus and Malta employed some of the preaccession funds to finance the farming-out of legal drafting and impact assessment reports of the introduction of EU measures to private firms and consultancies, thus reducing the pressures on the public administration.

In Malta's case, given that the membership issue would eventually have to be decided in a referendum, the government took the additional step of involving the organizations of civil society in the negotiating process by establishing an EU-Malta Action and Steering Committee, chaired by the minister of foreign affairs, that discussed the various negotiating positions prior to their adoption by the government. In addition, the government also set up a Malta-EU Information Centre to inform the public about the likely impacts of the more salient parts of the *acquis*.

The national civil services in Cyprus and Malta became involved at a very early stage in the negotiations, indeed during the "screening phase" when they met Commission officials to assess national legislation for its compatibility with the *acquis*. This hands-on approach led to the civil services in both states becoming deeply immersed in EU policies and issues. It was indeed a learning process in which civil servants were gradually socialized in the working methods of the European Commission. The implementation of the *acquis* also implied the modernization of a number of public services. For example, both Cyprus and Malta have had to overhaul their national statistics agencies to bring them up to the requirements and methods of the EU statistical agency, Eurostat. The improvements in the national statistical agencies of Cyprus and Malta led to the production of improved and useful statistical indicators about the two countries as well as to the identification of the relevant EU benchmarks against which to measure progress in such fields as education, competitiveness (Lisbon goals), the environment, and social conditions of the populace.

The broadening and deepening of the regulatory framework of the two states has necessitated the creation of many hitherto nonexistent regulatory authorities in both Cyprus and Malta. These independent bodies include the crucial competition authority, but also regulators in other sectors, mainly in the fields of telecommunications, resource management, environmental management, consumer affairs, and energy. The establishment of these authorities required the separation of the regulatory and supervisory role from that of providing goods or services. These new bodies are leading to a new political culture besides further strengthening the transformation of government's role more and more into that of a regulatory function.

In the economic sphere, Cyprus and Malta had to rein in their respective financial-services sectors, particularly the "off shore" activities, by strengthening their anti–money laundering regime and regulatory framework. Both Cyprus and Malta had to increase regulatory controls on their "open" shipping registers.[40] International and EU pressure to strengthen inspections by the Maltese and Cypriot maritime authorities of ships on their "open register" intensified following the December 12, 1999, *Erika* incident in which the single-hull tanker sank and spilled more than 10 million liters of oil into the ocean and on France's Atlantic coast. A related incident involving another tanker, the *Prestige,* which went down in November 19, 2002, causing another environmental disaster in Spain and France, intensified this pressure. Malta is ranked fourth and Cyprus fifth among those countries that maintain an open shipping register, though Malta and Cyprus registered a slight decline, respectively 3.5 percent and 1.2 percent, in registered tonnage during 2004.[41]

EU Budgetary Transfers

Cyprus and Malta are restructuring their economies. Malta has begun rolling back its intrusive state sector through privatization and, by 2008, it is scheduled to terminate all state subsidies that are incompatible with EU law to its shipbuilding and ship repair yards. Cyprus faces the challenge of modernizing its agricultural sector. But the application of the *acquis* has also led to a redistribution of advantages ("welfare" gains and losses) within the two islands: for example, freer trade with the rest of the EU has widened consumer choice and dampened inflationary pressures; but it has also increased competition for domestic producers. Consumer protection laws and environmental regulations have raised the costs of compliance to the producers of goods and services, and these can normally be passed on to consumers. However, such measures may lead to a gradual improvement of the quality of life, if properly implemented, and would have an impact on the two islands' competitiveness. The same can be said of health and safety regulations in factories and construction sites. It is therefore not easy, nor opportune, given the short time that has elapsed since Cyprus and Malta have joined the EU, to make many definite pronouncements on this "redistribution" effect.

Transfers from the EU budget are another important element of the membership package because they can help mitigate some of the negative effects of restructuring. However, these transfers are slightly more important in the case of Malta than of Cyprus. Malta is treated as a single Objective 1 region, meaning that the region is among the poorest of the EU with a GDP per capita in PPS below 75 percent of the EU average. Cyprus is eligible to aid under Objective 2 and Objective 3. Both Cyprus and Malta qualify for transfers under the Cohesion Fund since their GDP per capita in PPS is less than 90 percent of the EU average and both have embarked on a Convergence Program to join the euro zone.

The EU budgetary provisions for the period 2007–2013 approved by the European Council in December 2005 indicate that Malta will be a net beneficiary from the EU budget during the period indicated, and Cyprus will remain a net contributor. The Maltese prime minister claimed that Malta will receive €805 million at 2005 prices for the whole 2007–2013 period. Its contribution to the budget, including the UK rebate, is calculated at around €350 million, leaving Malta a net balance of €455 million.[42] The president of Cyprus indicated that Cyprus will receive around €580 million over the same period but that it would still remain a net overall contributor.[43] Other estimates indicate that Cyprus might be a net beneficiary.[44] What is significant in this case is that revised Commission-supplied GDP figures for 1997–1999 for Cyprus show that it should have been eligible for Objective 1 treatment for the period 2004–2006 but was not treated as such. For this reason, the December 2005 European Council allocated additional transfers to Cyprus and decided that the island's starting point in 2007 will be similar to that of those regions of the EU-15 that will have their regional aid gradually phased out in the period 2007–2013 because their GDP per capita has risen above 75 percent of the EU average as a result of the accession of poorer countries in the EU. These regions would have been classified under Objective 1 had enlargement not taken place.[45]

Transfers from the EU budget to Cyprus and Malta can help cushion some of the negative effects of the restructuring process. However, this does not preclude the importance of carrying out reforms. The operation of the Structural Funds requires the member states to submit sufficient projects that are eligible for such aid and projects have to be cofinanced by a smaller national contribution. These projects can strengthen the economic growth potential of the EU states. But setting aside these and similar issues, by far the most important economic challenge that Cyprus and Malta have to face as EU member states is to make progress on the "Maastricht Convergence Criteria," the macroeconomic indicators that will demonstrate their eligibility to join the EMU. For this reason both countries adopted an economic Convergence Program.

Joining the Euro Zone

The new member states are obliged to adopt the euro once they are ready to do so. It is up to each member state to indicate when it is ready to join the European Monetary Union. Preparations for EMU have essentially involved all the new member states, including Cyprus and Malta, in a three-stage process, the first of which started in the preaccession phase when they adopted certain preparatory measures by liberalizing capital movements and strengthening the independence of their central banks. The second stage commenced when the new member states joined the Exchange Rate Mechanism (ERM II) of the European Monetary System (EMS). The Maltese lira and the Cyprus pound entered ERM II on May 2, 2005. The Maltese lira joined at the central parity rate of Lm0.429300 to the euro while the Cyprus pound did so at the rate of £CY0.585274 to the euro within the standard fluctuation bands of ±15 percent.[46] Both Cyprus and Malta had missed joining ERM II in June 2004 with the "first wave" consisting of Slovenia, Estonia, and Lithuania, primarily because of their high fiscal deficits. Cyprus and Malta are planning to switch over to the euro on January 1, 2008, using a "big bang" approach. Malta has set up a National Euro Changeover Committee (NECC) under the direct responsibility of the cabinet (which has established an internal steering committee on the changeover). The NECC receives advice from the Central Bank of Malta and works in close collaboration with it. In the case of Cyprus, a Joint Coordinating Committee has been established between the Central Bank and the Ministry of Finance, chaired by the minister of finance.

Prior to, but particularly upon, membership, the new member states began to take the practical measures to introduce the euro and to follow monetary and fiscal policies dictated by the need to achieve the Maastricht convergence criteria as a condition for adopting the euro. These criteria are laid down in Article 121.1 of the Treaty on European Union.[47] Briefly, they comprise: (1) price stability: inflation rate must not exceed by more than 1.5 percentage points that of the three best-performing countries; (2) public finances: the government deficit has to be below the 3 percent of GDP and the level as well as the evolution of the government debt compared to the reference value of 60 percent of GDP; (3) exchange rate stability: observance of the normal margins of the exchange rate mechanism of the EMS without severe tensions of devaluation for at least two years; and (4) long-term interest rates: not exceeding by more than 2 percent that of the three best-performing countries in terms of price stability.

On the basis of the Stability and Growth Pact, member states are obliged to provide the Commission each year with detailed information on their economic policies and fiscal stances.[48] Those member states that have already adopted the euro follow what are called Stability Programs, while the new member states preparing to join EMU pursue Convergence Programs. It is only when they have satisfied the Maastricht criteria for two years that they are given the green light to join the euro "club."

The arguments surrounding EMU and its effect on new member states have been many, but they have turned mainly on whether the euro zone itself is an "optimal currency area"; the loss of monetary freedom it entails for its participants and how this may constrain their ability to cope with their respective economic developmental challenges and to deal with exogenous shocks considering that most of them, including Cyprus and Malta, still have a lot of "catching up" to do vis-à-vis the older member states; and lastly the timing of introducing the euro.[49] Underneath the surface of most of these critical perceptions lie some Keynesian "hangovers" based on the belief that governments can still influence the smooth running of their economies by adjusting demand.

Notwithstanding the many misgivings about the adoption of the euro, there are however some clear advantages. The public authorities in both island states are constrained to promote price stability and to restrict government spending by improving the efficiency of the public sector. Restrictive fiscal policies may also lead to a lower tax burden, which in turn affects consumption and the overall competitiveness of the economy. Low public debt and restricted government deficits strengthen the two islands' resilience to external economic shock. Furthermore, the two islands' economies are already strongly linked with the EU so that a substantive part of their goods and services trade takes place with the euro-zone countries, a trend that the changeover to the euro will help consolidate. However, the likely effects of the euro on both states are also different.

In Malta's case, around 33 percent of its merchandise exports, 58 percent of its imports, 41 percent of the earnings from tourism, and 49 percent of the spending of Maltese tourists overseas are connected with the euro zone. This indicates the share of the euro-denominated exchanges, which, *ceteris paribus*, will be taking place as soon as Malta joins the euro zone.[50] For Cyprus, the corresponding figures are 48 percent for imports, 41 percent for exports, and around 20 percent for tourist arrivals. The composition of tourist arrivals to both islands shows a marked UK-origin component: 41 percent of all arrivals in the case of Malta and 57 percent in the case of Cyprus. Hence the impact of joining the euro zone for the Cypriot and Maltese tourist sectors will continue to be influenced by the euro-sterling exchange rate as long as the UK remains out of the EMU. However, the Cypriot and Maltese tourist sectors depend on the importation of a number of goods and services, accounting for a substantive part of the two islands' high imports. The prices of these imports may stabilize as a result of the Cypriot and Maltese adoption of the euro much to the benefit of the tourist sector. The second observation is that Malta is more dependent on trade with the EU than Cyprus, and hence the impact of the euro in the trade sector is more significant in its case.[51]

Neither the statistical authority of Cyprus or Malta publishes the contribution of tourism to their respective country's national income but, in the case of Malta, tourism alone has been estimated to contribute around 24 percent of GNP[52] while, in the case of Cyprus, a report for the European Commission estimated tourism's contribution to be around 9.7 percent. However, in the latter case the writers of the report cautioned that "the actual importance of tourism for the Cypriot economy is far greater, because almost all other economic sectors support tourism. Only an in-depth analysis . . . would reveal the extent of Cyprus's dependence on tourism, but an initial estimate would indicate that tourism currently accounts for at least half of the island's economy."[53]

The Convergence Plans

The Convergence Plans adopted by Cyprus and Malta provide a snapshot of the way the two island states are confronting the EU membership challenge (see Table 19.4).[54] However, the changes they lead to, if successfully completed, go beyond the strict requirements of EU membership and help the two countries better confront the challenges posed by globalization. The state of their public finances illustrates this point. The two states started off with a huge deficit in their general government spending that in 2003 reached 9.6 percent of GDP for Malta and 6.3 percent of GDP for Cyprus. In Malta's case, the increase in the deficit was due to a one-time payment connected with the restructuring of the ship repair and shipbuilding yards. This payment was intended to free the yards from the burdens of existing debts and recurrent liabilities as part of the government's plan to restructure the sector and phase out all state aid that is incompatible with EU law by 2008.[55] Both Cyprus and Malta have meanwhile reduced their deficits, which in 2005 stood at 2.5 percent and 3.7 percent, respectively. Malta aims to achieve a deficit of 1.4 percent of GDP by 2007, while the corresponding target for Cyprus is 1.8 percent.[56]

Table 19.4   Aims of the Convergence Program and National Reform Program

Convergence Program		National Reform Program (2005–2008)	
Cyprus	Malta	Cyprus	Malta
1. Enhance competition and business climate 2. Increase the diversification of the economy 3. Promote R&D and ICT diffusion 4. Upgrade the basic infrastructure 5. Develop human capital	1. Privatization 2. Restructuring of public enterprises 3. Pension system reform 4. Health system reform 5. Industry: promotion of expansion in new sectors 6. Port reform 7. Public transport reform 8. Liberalization of the energy sector	1. Sustainability of public finances 2. Improve the quality of public finances by redirection of expenditure 3. Diversification of the economy toward higher value added 4. Promotion of R&D and ICT diffusion 5. Enhancement of competition and the business environment 6. Upgrading basic infrastructure 7. Human capital development 8. Enhancement of social cohesion 9. Ensuring environmental sustainability	1. Sustainability of public finances 2. Competitiveness 3. Employment 4. Education and training 5. Environment

On progress toward the attainment of the Lisbon Strategy goals, Malta did not fare well in the findings of a study prepared by the Centre for European Research (CER) in February 2005. This study showed that when the EU member states are ranked according to their achievement of the Lisbon goals, Malta occupies the 27th place in the league, below Romania and Bulgaria, which have not yet joined the EU.[57] The study was prepared for the Commission in time for the midterm review of the Lisbon Strategy. Malta was indicated as a "villain," that is, least willing to reform, while the more serious shortcomings were identified in the fields of education and training. Malta also performed badly in the case of the female participation rate in the labor force, which is the lowest in the Union. On the bright side, Malta was listed among the "e-ready" member states (strong in the area of becoming an information society) and as having the lowest tax burden for low-wage earners. The report stopped short of giving a definite judgment on Malta because it did not supply data for many of the key Lisbon indicators. Data released in 2006 by CER maintained Malta at the bottom of the league.[58]

By contrast Cyprus fared much better, placing 19th in the league. What the CER study picked up was that Cyprus "has the most expensive electricity prices for industrial users" in the EU-25, and it also ranks among the member states that pay the highest level of subsidies. Cyprus, along with Spain, was reported to have recorded the fastest growth in female employment and had the second-fastest growth rate in employment in the Union. When it comes to the transposition of the Lisbon directives into national law, by June of 2005 Malta placed second jointly with Finland in the EU-25, having transposed 95.2 percent of legislation, while Cyprus placed fifth, having transposed 92.1 percent of legislation.

Table 19.4 outlines the priorities that both states perceive in their national reform processes. The programs of the two island states bear a number of similarities that become more apparent following a more detailed assessment of the individual NRPs and CPs. Indeed, both Cyprus and Malta target fiscal consolidation, one of the main Lisbon targets, as their priority. This requires them to strive for a smaller public administration and redirection of public expenditure. Both states seek to buttress their international competitiveness through R&D and information and communication technology (ICT) diffusion, also to counter the negative effects of their loss of competitiveness in the manufacturing sector to emerging markets, particularly in Asia. They recognize the importance of education and training in their economic diversification strategies. In the energy sector, the challenge they perceive is to economize in order to lessen external dependence, and develop alternatives (Malta uses no alternative energy sources) and more liberalized national distribution systems. Both states plan to tackle the challenges of health expenditure and sustainable pension schemes, which arise mainly from the demographic changes that are occurring in both societies. Competitiveness requires them to provide a more congenial environment to small and medium-sized enterprises. The programs part company where the experiences of the two Mediterranean states differ considerably. For example, Malta inherited a very pervasive state sector that necessitated a more vigorous restructuring and a broader privatization program than in the case of Cyprus. The two states also favor the use of private-public partnerships in the case of key public-controlled economic sectors.

Implementation of the CPs and NRPs is the main challenge these countries have established for themselves, but as has been argued in this section the implementation of these programs has become a test or a measure of their modernization efforts. The decision by both Cyprus and Malta to be among the group of EU member states to join the EMU in 2008 has no doubt acted as a catalyst to their ongoing reform. This, combined with their small size, could see their economic dynamism increase in the next few years, provided that the international environment does not produce shocks large enough to unbalance their national efforts.

Security

One of the dividends the two Mediterranean island states desired from EU membership was an enhancement of their security. Cyprus saw membership as an instrument for resolving the Cyprus Problem, though of course there were no official or public illusions on the Cypriot side that this could happen quickly. The belief in the long-term prospects of a peaceful settlement of the Cyprus Problem finds resonance in a study by Nathalie Tocci, who wrote that while the short-term conclusions from the Cyprus case study may be dispiriting, the longer-term prospects may be brighter. Tocci agrees with Christopher Hill that in the longer term the EU can change the environments out of which conflicts spring and that this can also happen in the case of Cyprus.[59] Certainly, the situation in Cyprus outlined in this chapter has displayed a number of false dawns on a solution to the Cyprus Problem, but there have also been a number of developments that saw the relaxation of the de facto border that separates the two communities on the island. The thaw in relations between Greece and Turkey and the latter's own EU membership ambitions provide an added impetus to a solution, although the events of 2005, when Turkey made a unilateral declaration that by signing the customs union agreement with the EU it was not recognizing the government of Cyprus, did not help in this. Furthermore, Turkey's obstructionist attitude toward Cyprus and Malta within the so-called Berlin Plus arrangement is not conducive toward creating the right environment for a solution.

Both Cyprus and Malta have experienced initial moves toward Europeanizing their national foreign policy processes. Their small foreign ministries have immersed themselves in the EU's foreign policy and are oversupplied with an array of information on a number of world issues on the EU's agenda. Both states have to adopt national positions on these issues within the EU institutions. In addition, Cyprus and Malta are both situated on the edge of the EU's stability zone, and value the importance of a number of policy instruments such as the EU's Neighborhood Policy and the Euro-Mediterranean Partnership, whose aim is to stabilize the Union's neighborhood. Cyprus and Malta benefit from the international and intra-EU cooperation to combat international terrorism and illegal immigration. The two islands' security and welfare are improved by the EU's activities against the proliferation of weapons of mass destruction. Indeed, working through the EU institutions helps the two states better tackle the security challenges they face than if they had to work alone, given their limited human, military, and diplomatic resources. EU membership has also strengthened their prestige in the Mediterranean region.

However, when it comes to the development of the Common Foreign and Security Policy (CFSP), both Cyprus and Malta are only encountering minor setbacks so far. They are currently barred from participating in the European Security and Defense Policy (ESDP) initiatives in crisis management in which the use of NATO assets are involved, the so-called Berlin Plus arrangement, since they are not members of NATO or parties to the alliance's Partnership for Peace. The "Berlin Plus" arrangement between the EU and NATO had been reached in 2002. Turkey objected to the participation of both states and was about to exercise its veto in NATO to stop the whole process of cooperation. The Copenhagen European Council of December 2002, following a detailed agreement within NATO, decided that the arrangements and implementation of the "Berlin Plus" will apply only to those EU member states that are also members of NATO or parties to the Partnership for Peace.[60] Cyprus and Malta still retain the right to participate fully in the EU's CFSP and ESDP and to receive classified information, as long as the latter does not contain or refer to any classified NATO information. Turkey's objections may not be directly aimed at Malta but are more likely intended against Cyprus, whose government Ankara still does not recognize. Following the signing of the additional protocol to extend the EU-Turkey customs union to the new member states, Turkey issued a unilateral declaration saying that the signature of the protocol does not amount to recognition of Cyprus.

The main security threat for Malta comes from illegal immigration. It can only be eventually resolved within an EU context even though there are widespread expectations on the part of Malta that the EU could have done more. The phenomenon known as the "Mediterranean Boat People" affects all the southern EU member states, namely Spain, Portugal, France, Italy, Malta, Greece, and Cyprus, and through them the rest of the EU. In Malta's case, arrivals of such illegal immigrants have surpassed the natural birth rate. In a densely populated island such as Malta, illegal immigration has created a number of logistical problems, a financial burden, and the threat of the spread of communicable diseases. The EU has realized that it cannot resolve the problem on its own, while Spain has already called for a Euro-African summit to tackle it, which was endorsed by France in the Franco-Spanish summit.[61] Malta has repeatedly asked for EU solidarity to provide it with the financial means to mitigate the problem (housing the immigrants, resettling genuine refugees, and repatriating those who fail to obtain refugee status).

The majority of Malta's illegal immigrants originate in Libya, a country of destination for illegal immigrants mostly from sub-Saharan Africa, as well as a transit point for those wishing to go to Europe. An EU mission to Libya estimated that there were between 0.75 and 1.2 million illegal immigrants in Libya. Evidence shows that the transit route running through the country has gained in importance in the last three years. Libya shares 4,400 kilometers of border with six countries including three poor and unstable ones in sub-Saharan Africa, namely Sudan, Chad, and Niger. Its Mediterranean coast is 1,770 kilometers long, which adds to the difficulty of precluding clandestine boats from embarking on their journey to Europe.[62] Several proposals have been put forward by the EU on how to deal with the phenomenon, including a proposal to try to mitigate the migratory pressure by establishing a scheme for legal emigration to the EU, a logical solution in the light of Europe's aging population. A number of EU countries have begun helping Malta resettle some of the illegal immigrants. The United States has also begun taking in some immigrants, 90 people in the first quarter of 2006, following the meeting between President George W. Bush and Prime Minister Gonzi in Washington in October 2005. A resolution approved by the European Parliament on April 6, 2006, "recognised the difficulties encountered by Malta in managing the migration emergency of the last few years" and called on the EU to extend more aid to Malta.[63]

■ Trends and Prospects

The discussion in this chapter has stressed the similarities and dissimilarities between Cyprus and Malta, respectively the third-smallest and smallest of the EU member states. It is difficult, given that the two Mediterranean island states have only been in the EU for about two years, to attempt a comprehensive assessment of all the effects of EU membership on them. However, a number of conclusions have emerged from the above discussion: that so far both Cyprus and Malta are coping and the worst fears about their capacity to absorb the *acquis* or to play their role in the EU institutions are misplaced.

At the same time, membership has begun to affect their national politics. New avenues have opened up to subnational actors and organizations of civil society (NGOs) to influence the decisions of the Cypriot and Maltese governments through the EU institutions. NGOs are working in a more transparent and information-rich environment than they did before, and they can now align themselves with European transnational NGOs to influence decisions in their national domains. Environmental organizations have used such European connections to pressure the Maltese government to implement bird protection rules against hunters.

The process of economic reform in both states is moving ahead briskly. It has been argued here that besides permitting them to honor their EU commitments, these changes strengthen their resilience to exogenous shock and help them to better integrate into the global economy by strengthening the two islands' competitiveness. Integration in the EU has led to redistribution effects and helps strengthen economic efficiency. No discussion of the dynamic effects of membership was attempted here.

Some progress has still to be achieved on the security front and particularly the participation of Cyprus and Malta in the ESDP. By and large both Malta and Cyprus are more secure by participating in the CFSP and ESDP then they were before. They are in a better position to influence the EU's foreign policies in order to ensure that these work to their advantage. The problems they are encountering in the Berlin Plus arrangement do not obstruct participation in the rest of the CFSP/ESDP.

As to the particular security concerns of each, it is important to note that though a solution to the Cyprus Problem is not yet in sight, the EU has begun to positively influence relations between the two Cypriot communities. The relaxation of the de facto border separating the two communities and increased transactions between them may positively affect the Cypriot political context, making a future solution to the problem easier. Such a solution is unlikely to come before Turkey is admitted as an EU member state.

As for Malta's main security concern on illegal immigration, though a satisfactory solution has not been possible within the context of EU membership, the EU remains the only hope of finding one. Only the EU has the resources to meet the immediate threats that illegal immigration poses to all the EU member states of southern Europe and to the rest of the Union. It is only together with the EU that solutions to the problems in sub-Saharan Africa and other unstable regions, which are the root cause of the migratory flows, can be better resolved. The EU alone stands a chance of eventually securing through the necessary incentives the cooperation of transit states, such as those in North Africa, in helping to combat this phenomenon. And if a legal emigration system or a resettlement scheme for refugees has to be devised to try and lessen the pressure of illegal immigration, such policies can only be successfully conducted at an EU level.

▓ Notes

1. Signed in February 1955, it comprised the United Kingdom, Iraq, Iran, Turkey, and Pakistan.
2. "Act of Accession" as published in the *Official Journal of the European Union*, L 236, vol. 46, September 23, 2003 (http://europa.eu.int/eur-lex/en/archive/2003/l_23620030923en.html); henceforth referred to as the "Act of Accession."
3. Voltaire, "Rien n'est plus connu que la siege de Malte"—"Nothing is better known than the siege of Malta."
4. Malta's exports of goods and services to GDP ratio (provisional figure) stands at 75.8 percent (Central Bank of Malta, *Quarterly Review* 38, no. 1, 2005); latest available data for Cyprus pertaining to 1994 show exports of goods and services to GDP ratio to be 47.7 percent (World Bank, *Cyprus at a Glance*).
5. *Eurostat News Release*, 136/2005, October 25, 2005. All figures are for 2004 and those for Cyprus refer to the government-controlled area only.
6. Eurostat, *Regions: Statistical Year Book*—2005. The volume index of GDP per inhabitant quoted here in Purchasing Power Standards (PPS) is expressed in relation to the EU-25 average set to equal 100. If the index of a region is higher than 100, this region's level of GDP per inhabitant is higher than the EU average and vice versa. Figures are expressed in PPS, that is, a common currency that eliminates the differences in price levels between countries.
7. European Commission, "Commission Opinion on Malta's Application for Membership" and "Commission Opinion on the Application of the Republic of Cyprus"; both opinions were published in Brussels on June 30, 1993.

Henceforth referred to as the "Commission's Opinion on Malta" and the "Commission's Opinion on Cyprus" respectively.

8. Macris, Petranyi, and Macris, *The 1960 Treaties on Cyprus and Selected Subsequent Acts.*

9. Ibid., p. 127.

10. European Commission, "Communication from the Commission to the Council and the European Parliament: Recommendation of the European Commission on Turkey's Progress Towards Accession." Also, European Commission, "2004 Regular Report on Turkey's Progress Towards Accession."

11. "Commission Opinion on Cyprus," points 6 to 8.

12. Ibid., point 8.

13. Ibid., point 51.

14. Council of the European Union, "Conclusions of the Presidency, Cannes European Council," point 1.12, p. 13.

15. "Joint Statement by Turkish President Suleyman Demirel and TRNC President Rauf Denktash," December 29, 1995: available at: www.b-info.com/places/Turkey/news/95-12/dec29.tdn.

16. Council of the European Union, "Presidency Conclusions, December 10–11, 1999," point 9(b).

17. Pace, "The Domestic and International Politics of the Next Mediterranean Enlargement of the EU," pp. 77–101.

18. UN Plan on Cyprus, "The Comprehensive Settlement of the Cyprus Problem," as finalized in March 2004; available at: www.un.org/Depts/dpa/annanplan/annanplan.pdf (accessed December 20, 2005).

19. "Press Conference on Cyprus by Kofi Annan," UN Headquarters, New York, February 13, 2004; available at: www.un.org/News/ossg/hilites.htm (accessed on February 16, 2004).

20. UN Press Release SG/SM/9239, March 31, 2004; see also UN Press Release SC/8051 of April 2, 2004.

21. Pace, *Microstate Security in the Global System.*

22. Cini, "Malta Votes Twice for Europe," pp. 132–146.

23. Pace, "Malta's EU Membership," pp. 114–121.

24. Pace, "The Maltese Electorate Turns a New Leaf?" pp. 121–136.

25. In a press statement, the Malta Labor Party said that in the general conference, 825 votes were distributed of which 817 were valid. The motion of the national executive obtained 699 votes (85.6 percent) while that by Mifsud Bonnici obtained 118 votes (14.4 percent). Only five votes were invalid and three abstained. The statement can be accessed at: www.mlp.org.mt/stqarrijiet/print.asp?ContentID=STQ050702A (accessed December 30, 2005).

26. Motion 190 approved by the House of Representatives on the Ratification of the Treaty Establishing a Constitution for Europe; see also Department of Information, Government of Malta, "Press Release 1017," July 6, 2004.

27. Cyprus News Agency, "European Election Results—Final," Nicosia, June 14, 2004: Voting in the European Elections in Cyprus: Registered Voters: 483,311; Voted: 344,092 (71.19 percent); Valid: 334,268 (95.40 percent); Invalid: 8,747 (2.50 percent); Blank: 7,372 (2.10); available at: www.hri.org/news/cyprus/cna/2004/04-06-13_2.cna.html#02.

28. Decision No E-770-2003 dated April 29, 2003 amending Decision E-

762-2003 of the Council of Ministers (TRNC) dated April 21, 2003 regarding crossings from the Turkish Republic of Northern Cyprus to the South and from the South to the Turkish Republic of Northern Cyprus; available at: www.trnc-info.com/TANITMADAIRESI/2002/ENGLISH/D (accessed January 2, 2006).

29. See: www.moi.gov.cy/moi/pio/pio.nsf/All/745A5D6134331502C2256 D9F00338D9A?Open, Document.

30. I can hardly do full justice to this problem here and readers are referred to the very extensive analysis of the Annan Plan in Palley, *An International Relations Debacle.*

31. European Commission Press Release, IP/04/857, July 7, 2004.

32. European Council Regulation EC 866/2004 of April 29, 2004–OJ L 161, April 30, 2004—as subsequently amended; see consolidated text 2004R0866, August 7, 2005; Commission Regulation OJ L 259, October 15, 2005.

33. "Act of Accession," OJ L 236, September 23, 2003, p. 955.

34. Ibid., point 32(1).

35. Council of the European Union, "Conclusions of the Presidency, EU Council Lisbon, March 23–24, 2000.

36. Council of the European Union, "Conclusions of the Presidency, EU Council Brussels," March 23–24, 2005.

37. These are Estonia, Lithuania, and Slovenia (2007); Cyprus, Latvia, and Malta (2008); and Slovakia (2009).

38. Stefanou, *Cyprus and the EU*, p. 6.

39. Ibid., the "Foreword" by President G. Vassiliou, p. xv.

40. Open registers means briefly that shipping can be registered in those countries independent of the nationality of beneficial ownership so long as they satisfy the conditions of the host country.

41. UNCTAD, *Review of Maritime Transport 2004,* Geneva, 2005, pp. 32–38.

42. Malta-EU Information Centre, "Press Conference," reported in *Aggornat*, no. 312 (December 24, 2005).

43. Cypriot Press and Information Office, Nicosia, Press Release, "President Papadopoulos Returned from Brussels," December 19, 2005.

44. The writer in private interviews gathered this information with Cypriot officials who do not wish to be named.

45. Council of the European Union, "Financial Perspective 2007–2013," point 47.

46. The EU published two communiqués on the entry of Cyprus and Malta in ERM II on April 29, 2005. All details are included in the communiqués, which can be accessed at: http://europa.eu.int/comm/economy_finance/ publications/eurorelated_en.htm (accessed January 7, 2006).

47. Treaty on European Union and the Treaty Establishing the European Community, p. 85, and the Protocol on the Convergence Criteria, Treaty of Maastricht, Luxembourg, 1992, pp. 185–186.

48. The Stability and Growth Pact came into effect on January 1, 1999, when the euro was launched. It is based on Articles 99 and 104 of the Treaty of Maastricht, pp. 71–74.

49. For a summary of the main misgivings on EMU, see Patterson, *EMU and Enlargement: A Review of Policy Issues.*

50. The estimates here have been based on a Central Bank of Malta unpublished memo based on the Direction of Trade statistics published by the International Monetary Fund and estimates by the Central Bank on earnings from incoming tourists and expenditure by Maltese tourists overseas.

51. Figures supplied by the World Trade Organization (all figures in US$ millions unless otherwise stated): Cyprus exports 948, imports 5,502; Malta exports 2,492, imports 3,670. The share of trade with the EU-25 is: Cyprus exports 58.9 percent, imports 64.8 percent; Malta exports 47.2 percent, imports 72.3 percent. Figures available at: http://stat.wto.org/country Profiles/MT_e.htm and http://stat.wto.org/countryProfiles/CY_e.htm (accessed January 3, 2006).

52. A study by the Malta Tourism Authority (MTA), "Tourism and Development in Malta," estimated tourism to contribute 24.3 percent to GNP. In 2003 the MTA claimed that at the current level of tourism demand, pricing, and expenditure, Malta's tourism industry contributes to a maximum of 24 percent of the country's GNP; 22 percent of government income; 11 percent of imports and outflows; and 17 percent of full-time equivalent employment.

53. Siemon and Zwart, *Tourism on Cyprus.*

54. For Malta, see Malta, Ministry of Finance, *Convergence Program 2004–2007* and *Update of Convergence Program 2004–2007*; for Cyprus, see Cyprus, Ministry of Finance, *Convergence Program of the Republic of Cyprus 2005–2009.* The plans are all available at: http://europa.eu.int/comm/economy_ finance/about/activities/sgp/scplist_en.htm (accessed January 1, 2006).

55. Malta, Ministry of Finance. *Convergence Program 2004–2007*, p. 19.

56. Ibid.

57. Murray and Wanlin, *The Lisbon Scorecard V.*

58. Wanlin, *The Lisbon Scorecard VI.*

59. Tocci, *EU Accession Dynamics and Conflict Resolution*, p. 185.

60. Council of the European Union, "Conclusions of the Presidency, Copenhagen European Council."

61. "Immigration: initiative conjointe franco-espagnole auprès de l'Union européenne," *Fenêtre sur l'Europe.*

62. European Commission Report, *Technical Mission to Libya on Illegal Immigration 27 November to 6 December 2004*; available at: http://www.state-watch.org/news/2005/may/eu-report-libya-ill-imm.pdf (accessed December, 18, 2005).

63. European Parliament, Resolution P6 TA-PROV(2006)0136.

20

Latvia, Lithuania, and Estonia: Determined Euro-Atlanticists

Steven Stoltenberg

THE BALTIC STATES (LATVIA, Lithuania, and Estonia) expressed their intention to apply for membership in the European Union soon after regaining their independence from the Soviet Union in 1991. It may seem remarkable that three countries that had experienced 46 years of illegal occupation by the Soviet Union should so quickly decide to surrender a portion of their national sovereignty by seeking membership in a supranational institution such as the EU. However, they had at least three good reasons for doing so.[1]

First, the "Balts" were fully aware that, given their size and resources, they could not single-handedly secure their independence and sovereignty vis-à-vis their immensely larger and more powerful neighbor, Russia. A history of subjugation by Russia going back to the early modern period, combined with vulnerabilities such as large Russian-speaking minority populations (in the case of Latvia and Estonia) or geographic location (Lithuania blocks Russia's land access to its Kaliningrad "exclave"), gave the Balts an acute sense of vulnerability toward their eastern neighbor. Hence they quickly embraced a pro-Western foreign policy orientation, whose twin pillars were the goals of EU and NATO membership. The policy enjoyed broad support across the political spectrum (the only exception being parties representing the Russian-speaking minority or some populist forces), despite frequent alterations of government. NATO would provide the ultimate security guarantee, but EU membership would give the Balts leverage in dealing with the multitude of political, economic, and social issues that affected Baltic-Russian bilateral relations.

Second, there was the issue of identity. The Balts felt themselves to be genuinely part of European culture and civilization; therefore the EU was their "natural home."[2] In their early history, the Estonians and Latvians had been brought into the European orbit through subjugation by the Germanic knightly orders and later Sweden, Denmark, and Poland. The Lithuanians established their own medieval state but then joined in dynastic, and later political union with the Polish kingdom. In the modern era, each Baltic nation participated in decisive phases of European civilization: for example, they were actively involved in the Protestant Reformation, their educated classes embraced the nineteenth century's romanticist project of nation building, and for a short period between the twentieth century's world wars, they enjoyed the benefits of liberal democracy and prosperous market economies.[3] Thus, despite their geographical location on the periphery of Europe, and their role oftentimes as mediator between East and West, the Balts still felt themselves firmly anchored in the European community of nations. EU membership offered them confirmation of their "European-ness," moreover demonstrating that the post–World War II Soviet occupation was an "artificial" imposition that violated their true traditions, cultures, and identities.[4]

Third, there was the goal of achieving a level of material prosperity befitting peoples that considered themselves part of Europe. Fifty years of Soviet occupation, with its economy of shortages, gross mismanagement, and environmental degradation, only reinforced collective memories of better times when the Baltic States could boast levels of GDP equal to many other European nations. The early embrace of free-market economics, the rapid reorientation of trade away from the former Soviet republics to Europe, and the enviably high growth rates of the last half-decade, all testify to the Balts' determination to reestablish themselves as members of a sphere of European prosperity.

As the only former Soviet republics among the 10 candidate countries seeking EU membership in the 1990s, the Baltic States had to overcome a heavy historical legacy. First, there was the demographic and material devastation of the Second World War period and the forcible incorporation into the Soviet Union that followed. The period beginning in 1940 saw the combined horrors of the Holocaust, the deprivations of war, the "Red terror" that followed the Soviet takeovers in 1940 and 1945, mass deportations to Siberia, large-scale imprisonment in the "gulag," and a large loss of population due to emigration to the West. Estonia and Latvia were subjected to massive immigration of Russian-speaking settlers, a policy whose goal was clearly "russification" (under the guise of "sovietization"), that is, to reduce Latvians and Estonians to minorities in their own homelands and relegate their language and culture to a second-class status.[5] Nevertheless, sovietization ultimately failed to erase historical memories or undermine tenacious national cultures and identities. Mass independence movements emerged in all three Soviet republics in the late 1980s. Staring down Soviet power, the Balts succeeded in breaking free of the Soviet Union without provoking military intervention. This determination was then redirected to the process of reintegrating with the Euro-Atlantic community.

In their effort to join the EU, the Balts proved to be quick and eager learners. In fact, although Latvia and Lithuania opened their EU accession negotiations two years later than Estonia, they were able to conclude their negotiations at the same time in December 2003. The secret lay in the Balts' ability to turn adversity into opportunity. The severity of their experience as Soviet republics translated into an unhesitating embrace of rapid and thorough institutional reform. The wholesale rejection of the Soviet past was also reflected in the rapid overturn of elites and the relative youthfulness of governmental cadres, unencumbered by the mentalities of the Soviet era. Then there was the substantial assistance provided by various mentor states, evidence of the resurfacing of historical ties, and a cooperative/competitive relationship between the Balts themselves that served to accelerate the process. Baltic cooperation was embodied in the Baltic Assembly (an interparliamentary body) as well as the Baltic Council of Ministers, which coordinated the three countries' EU accession strategies. Baltic competition was evident in the way each country sought to outdo the other in the speed with which negotiation chapters were "closed." In sum, the Balts were able to create a synergy of advantages that enabled them not only to join the EU in 2004, but also establish themselves as leaders in the transition to market economies and democracy.

It would be inaccurate, however, to suggest that the Balts were willing to do whatever it took in order to comply with the conditions for accession laid down by the European Union's negotiators. The Balts often exhibited intransigence or resistance to the EU's directives. The Balts were not always convinced that their European counterparts fully understood their particular historical experience, or the post-Soviet context the Balts were facing. For example, did west Europeans fully appreciate the potential danger of a post-Soviet Russia, with its questionable adherence to democratic norms and its need to compensate for its traumatic loss of empire? And did the EU negotiators fully understand the difficulties of incorporating large Russian-speaking minorities into the body politic, minorities that had in large measure opposed Baltic independence and maintained some loyalty to the Russian motherland? The Balts were required, therefore, both to exhibit their willingness to meet EU conditions *and* to educate their European partners about specifically Baltic conditions.

The interplay between EU conditionality (I use the term *conditionality* comprehensively, to include the terms according to which new members could be admitted into the EU "club," as well as the mix of "carrot and stick" instruments available to the EU to encourage compliance) and the specific interests that the Balts saw fit to defend as vital to their viability as states, will constitute the remainder of this chapter.[6] I will focus on three case studies in order to show how EU conditionality shaped policy outcomes in key areas: in energy policy (Lithuania) and citizenship/social integration policy (Latvia and Estonia). Especially in the latter two cases, one can see a drawn-out cyclical process that involved negotiation, partial implementation of agreements or lack thereof, subsequent EU monitoring and pressure, further adaptation of EU recommendations into legislation, partial implementation, and so on, until a point where the EU ascertained that enough progress had been achieved to satisfy the primary accession criteria (the so-called Copenhagen criteria). In the end, the overarching goal of EU accession was decisive in getting the Balts to adopt certain policies, but within certain parameters that the Balts themselves defined and defended.

■ How and in What Ways Has the EU Influenced the Baltic States?

Lithuania: Nuclear Energy

Lithuania's Ignalina Nuclear Power Plant (NPP) contains two Chernobyl-type reactors (series RMBK-1500) that are in fact the largest reactors of their kind in the world. The decision to build the Ignalina NPP was made by Soviet authorities at the "All-Union" level without consulting local Lithuanian officials, and was part of an energy plan to supply the fuel-poor European part of the Soviet Union with electrical energy. Total capacity of the reactors was 2,600 megawatts, which exceeded Lithuania's domestic energy needs by at least three times. Toward the end of the Soviet period, the Lithuanian independence movement Sajudis focused on Ignalina as an example of the way in which Soviet rule had disregarded the interests and well-being of Lithuania's population. In September 1988, 20,000 persons linked hands in a chain around the plant, and antinuclear activists collected 750,000 signatures to protest plans to construct a third reactor at the site.

Over a period of 10 years following independence, assistance totaling €219 million was provided through the European Bank for Reconstruction and Development and others to upgrade Ignalina's safety, but the facility still failed to meet international standards in such areas as containment systems, design, fire safety, and operation certification. Because of safety concerns, and the EU's overall policy of energy diversification (Russia is the sole source of uranium for the plant), the European Commission's 1997 report on Lithuania states that Ignalina would have to be shut down "as soon as possible." But as accession negotiations started in 2000, it was clear that Lithuania's leadership, as well as significant portions of Lithuanian society, had changed their views regarding the importance of Ignalina to the country compared to the late 1980s during the Sajudis movement.

Lithuanian negotiators stressed that Ignalina supplies 80–85 percent of the country's electricity, and that decommissioning the plant would render Lithuania even more dependent on Russian oil and natural gas. They pointed to the costs of decommissioning, which they estimated would amount to €2.49 billion over a 30-year period. They argued that the EU's own estimates of between €683.9 and €854 million did not include costs such as renovating replacement power plants, connecting Lithuania to European electricity and natural gas grids, or paying compensation to the 4,500 displaced workers and surrounding communities. Lithuanian officials tried to present Ignalina in an economically positive light, since Lithuania earned significant income from its electricity exports. President Brazauskas was quoted as saying he thought Unit 2 was perfectly safe and there was no reason to shut it down, and if the EU insisted on doing so, Lithuania would not pay a single penny of the costs. The Lithuanian bargaining strategy was clearly to make the strongest case possible that decommissioning Ignalina would entail tremendous hardship to the Lithuanian economy and society. Therefore, Lithuania should be fully compensated by the EU.

EU negotiators held firm on their demand for decommissioning both reactor units, and the final agreement called for Unit 1 to go offline by the end of 2004, Unit 2 by the end of 2009. The EU did pledge €510.2 million through 2006 to support the decommissioning process, an inadequate figure even by its own estimates. It has pledged to provide further funds but argues the exact amount cannot be determined before adoption of the EU's 2007–2013 budget. The Lithuanians were unhappy that an exact figure could not be determined ahead of time and have given notice that Unit 2's final decommissioning will depend on adequate EU funding. Lithuania's National Energy Strategy stipulates that failure to secure financial assistance from the EU could lead to an extension of the plant's operations.

Unit 1 was in fact decommissioned at the end of 2004, and electricity output for 2005 was, as predicted, down by 28 percent, affecting mainly exports and export revenue. It is not clear, however, that Lithuania will adhere to its agreement to decommission Unit 2 at the end of 2009, despite the fact that EU funding is now secure due to the recent agreement on the EU's "financial perspective" for 2007–2013. First, nuclear industry experts claim that upgrades to Unit 2 have made it safer than originally perceived. Second, meeting Lithuania's domestic electricity needs by relying on other power sources, in particular the 40-year-old Elektrinai thermal power plant, will require expensive upgrades to the tune of €580 million by the year 2020. Third, the whole issue of Lithuania's energy dependency on Russia has become more paramount in policymakers' minds.[7] It is likely that the country's oil refinery complex, Maziekiu Nafta, will be sold to a Russian oil company with close ties to the Kremlin. The Russian-German agreement to construct the north European gas pipeline along the Baltic seabed, thereby bypassing any Baltic or central European transit state, is considered by the Lithuanians as a politically motivated effort to increase Russian leverage. To the Lithuanians, Russia's January 1, 2006, cutoff of gas shipments through the Ukraine's pipeline network demonstrated Moscow's willingness to wield energy as a weapon to exercise influence in its neighborhood. Finally, Lithuania's hope of connecting, via Poland, to the European electricity grid has come to naught with the collapse in late 2004 of negotiations with the Poles.

Lithuania's perception that energy dependency on Russia could return it de facto to Russia's sphere of influence will continue to shape elite policy choices in the years to come. However, Lithuania may not have much room for maneuver. It is doubtful the EU will allow Lithuania to renege on decommissioning Ignalina's Unit 2. And the costs involved in constructing an entirely new reactor, even if Lithuania's Baltic neighbors got involved, are prohibitive, while the electricity grid that would allow Lithuania to export electricity is not in place. Whether Lithuania deals successfully with the challenge of energy independence could in the end depend on whether the EU as a whole develops a coherent energy policy to address the vulnerabilities resulting from overdependency on Russian energy sources.

The Challenge of Social Integration: The Case of Latvia

Latvia's ability to achieve a consolidated democracy depends to a great extent on the integration of its large Russian-speaking minority (henceforth, for purposes of shorthand, I will refer to all Russian-speakers as the "Russian minority," even though this category includes ethnic non-Russians such as Ukrainians, Belarusians, and Poles). The decisive issue for social integration is the fact that approximately two-thirds of this minority, or 650,000 persons (28 percent of Latvia's population), did not receive Latvian citizenship after Latvia's independence from the Soviet Union. Instead, they received the status of "noncitizen residents" without the right to vote or hold public office. Needless to say, such a state of affairs has contributed to the alienation of this minority toward Latvia's fledgling democracy, and has exposed Latvia to constant criticism by Russia for its alleged violation of the minority's rights.

The EU, working in concert with the Council of Europe, the Organization for Security and Cooperation in Europe (OSCE), and individual EU member governments, has played a key role in getting Latvia to adopt policies toward its Russian minority that are in accordance with European and international standards, and that will most effectively facilitate the social integration process. Indeed, even when Latvia was adopting policies to comply with non-EU organizations' requirements, it was doing so with its eye on the main prize—eventual EU membership—knowing full well that compliance would enhance its candidacy.

Why did Latvia adopt this citizenship policy after independence rather than opting for the "zero option" of granting automatic citizenship to all persons resident on its territory? Contrary to a widely held misperception, Latvia's citizenship policy is not based on an ethnic concept of what constitutes the "nation," that is, citizenship was not reserved for ethnic Latvians only. The independent Latvian state established in 1991 sees itself as the legal continuation of the pre–Second World War Latvian state (the principle of "legal continuity").[8] The 1945–1991 Soviet occupation and annexation is considered illegal, as was the Latvian Soviet Socialist Republic that existed during this time. Therefore, after independence citizenship was given to those persons who had been citizens of the prewar Latvian state or their descendants. This included approximately 375,000 ethnically non-Latvians, of which 278,000 were Russians (38 percent of the total Russian minority). These were members or the descendants of the sizable pre–World War II Russian community, composed of orthodox Old Believers who had fled Tsarist persecution, and Russians who had fled Russia after the Bolshevik Revolution.

Mark Jubulis has argued persuasively that Latvia's citizenship policy is based on a "civic" conception of the nation, albeit "civic" in the broader sense of referring to a community of citizens who share a sense of solidarity, common historical experiences and memories, an adherence to a common set of political principles, and loyalty to a set of particular political institutions.[9] According to this sense of "civic," Jubulis argues, the Soviet Russian settler population did not constitute part of the Latvian "civic nation." Russian-speaking settlers viewed Latvia as an extension of the "Soviet cultural space" and inhabited an environment in which the Russian language and Russian culture were hegemonic. Latvians were expected to learn Russian and use it in most public situations, whereas Russian settlers made little if any effort to learn Latvian. Lack of knowledge of the Latvian language and culture undermined a sense of shared cultural identity. Also due to the Soviet distortion of history, Russian settlers lacked objective information regarding the pre–World War II Latvian state, the war era, or indeed the circumstances in which Latvia was "incorporated" into the Soviet Union. Opinion survey data show that the vast majority of Russian settlers opposed Latvian independence and were either hostile or indifferent toward the political institutions of the new Latvian state.

Membership in a "civic nation" is not ascriptive (i.e., assigned by birth) but can be acquired upon fulfilling certain criteria. Latvia's citizenship policy did not exclude possible extension of citizenship to Russian settlers provided they were willing to join the Latvian "civic nation" by acquiring a basic command of Latvian, the official state language, knowledge of Latvian history, as well as to declare loyalty to the Latvian state. This opened the door via naturalization (although practical implementation began only after passage of a citizenship law in 1994).

Latvia's citizenship policy has evolved within a force field defined by pressures issuing from multiple sources: first, from European institutions (Council of Europe, OSCE, EU), or Euro-Atlantic institutions (NATO) in which Latvia has sought membership; second, from domestic political forces, some of which advocated an ethnic conception of the "nation" (the nationalist right) or existed to defend the rights of the Russian minority; third, from Russia itself, which sought consistently to hamper Latvia's efforts to integrate with the West by highlighting the situation of the Russian minority; and fourth, from various Western governments in their bilateral relations with Latvia. The fact that Latvia has remained true to a civic conception of nationhood is thanks to the mutually reinforcing pressures coming from Western institutions and governments, combined with the firm commitment on the part of Latvia's mainstream political leadership. Russian pressure has played a role, but the disconnect between Russian political rhetoric and the reality on the ground in Latvia has reduced Russian leverage over time.

The first example of how this process unfolded was the drafting and passage of a new citizenship law by the first democratically elected Saeima, or parliament, in 1993. The first draft contained a quota system limiting the number of naturalizations allowed per year. The Council of Europe criticized the provision and stated that Latvia would not be eligible for membership unless the quotas were removed. The quotas remained during the second reading of the draft on June 21, 1994, but in response to the international pressure, President Ulmanis vetoed the law and sent it back to parliament, urging lawmakers to amend it in accordance with the OSCE's recommendation that quotas be replaced with a "windows" system favoring younger age groups. Despite opposition from nationalist right-wing parties, the amendments were adopted. Subsequently, the Council of Europe declared that Latvia's citizenship legislation met European standards and voiced its support for Latvia's membership. Latvia did in fact join in February 1995.

Latvia again came under scrutiny in the European Commission's 1997 report assessing Latvia's application for EU membership.[10] Although the Commission found that "Latvia presents the characteristics of a democracy, with stable institutions, guaranteeing the rule of law, human rights and respect for and protection of minorities," it nonetheless took issue with the "windows system" provision in the 1994 Citizenship Law (originally proposed by the OSCE), and urged Latvia to adopt policies that would accelerate the naturalization process. Consequently, the Latvian government proposed new legislation abolishing the windows system, granting citizenship at birth to the children of resident noncitizens, and simplifying the naturalization process for persons over 65 years of age. The amendments were approved by the Saeima, despite vigorous opposition from the nationalist right, and approved by 53 percent of Latvian voters in a national referendum held in October 1998.

Over the next several years, until Latvia concluded its EU accession negotiations in December 2004, the dialogue between EU and Latvian officials regarding social integration policy involved countless meetings, the drafting of expert studies, coordination between branches of the Latvian state bureaucracy, and a national debate conducted throughout Latvia's public sphere. Communication was also ongoing between the EU, the Council of Europe, the OSCE, and various individual governments. The EU Commission's yearly progress reports are a brief distillation of this complex process, but they do give an idea how recommendations by the EU and other institutions were followed by Latvian compliance and implementation.[11]

An important legislative milestone in the process of social integration was the Language Law adopted by the Saeima in July 1999. Its sponsors sought to provide legal guarantees for the status of Latvian as the sole state language. The law came under heavy criticism, however, from the EU and other Western legal experts for its vague language giving the government wide powers of interpretation and implementation, and specifically for language that infringed on the commercial rights of private business. President Vike-Freiberga, in office for only one week, vetoed the bill despite the fact it had passed parliament with an overwhelming majority, arguing the bill violated Latvia's international agreements. She demanded parliament amend the bill, taking into consideration seven specific OSCE recommendations. Despite opposition from left- and right-wing parties, the revised bill was adopted on December 9, 1999.

Latvia's Election Law, passed in 1995, stipulated that all candidates for national or local office had to demonstrate fluency in the Latvian language. In 1997 the Latvian Electoral Commission removed Antonina Ignatane from the list of candidates for local elections because she failed the required language examination. Ignatane took her case to the United Nations Human Rights Committee, which found on July 25, 2001, that Latvia's Election Law was contradictory to the International Covenant on Civil and Political Rights, to which Latvia was signatory. However, the findings of the UN Committee are recommendations only, and there was considerable opposition among Latvian lawmakers to amending the law. Pressure to do so continued to build as a second legal case was brought before the European Court of Human Rights in Strasbourg. The EU Commission's 2001 report noted the legal efforts to oppose the Election Law's language requirement, stating that "a liberal attitude will be especially important in the context of Latvia's admission to the EU." In February 2002, NATO secretary-general George Robertson addressed the Saeima and stressed that Latvia must adopt amendments to the law in order to meet NATO standards. This would be taken into account, he said, in making a decision regarding accession to NATO. The European Court of Human Rights decision of April 10, 2002, favorable to the plaintiff, included a declaration that Latvia must change its Election Law, leaving Latvian lawmakers no choice. On May 9 the parliament dropped the language requirement from the Election Law, but only after it had strengthened the status of the state language in the constitution.

The most recent "tipping point" in the process of social integration has been education. In 1998 the Saeima passed an education reform law, to be implemented starting in 2004, that mandated 100 percent instruction in Latvian in minority-language secondary schools starting in the 10th grade.[12] The purpose of the law was to dismantle the system of segregated instruction inherited from the Soviet period, encourage Latvian-language competency and social integration among minorities, and enhance language skills necessary for higher education and future employment. However, the education reform quickly became the cause célèbre of the Russian community, which viewed the reform as an attempt to undermine its culture and identity. In 1998 activists formed the Headquarters for the Protection of Russian Schools and staged numerous protest rallies. Russia also took up the cause, lambasting the reform as another attempt at "cultural genocide" by the Latvian authorities. In order to meet protesters halfway and reassure EU and OSCE officials of their commitment to social integration, Latvian lawmakers revised the bill to mandate 60 percent Latvian, 40 percent minority-language instruction (an 8 percent drop in the minority-language quotient compared to the status quo ante). The law went into effect September 1, 2004, but implementation has been gradual and schools are free to determine which core subjects will be taught in Latvian. Protests by the Russian minority community have not ceased, however.

One may conclude that the commitment of Latvia's leadership to Euro-Atlantic integration made it possible to maintain a policy of social integration that remained true to a civic-national vision of the nation, despite what was often vigorous opposition from the more nationalist political forces within Latvia. One measure of success was, of course, Latvia's admission to NATO and the EU, and the fact that for years European observers have assessed its human rights legislation as entirely meeting European and international standards, even if implementation was not always as vigorous as desired. Another measure of success, however, is the number of noncitizen residents who have naturalized; between 1995 and mid-2005, 96,646 persons, or approximately 20 percent of those eligible, have become Latvian citizens. The rate of naturalization has increased considerably since Latvia's accession to the EU.[13]

The Challenge of Social Integration: The Case of Estonia

After establishing its independence from the Soviet Union, Estonia faced challenges with regard to its citizenship and minority policies that were similar to those of its neighbor to the south, Latvia. Estonia too had been the victim of a forcible annexation by the Soviet Union in 1940 and a "reoccupation" following the expulsion of German armed forces in 1944. Most Estonians, as well as the Estonian diaspora and the international community, never recognized the Soviet "incorporation" as legal. Therefore, when Estonia declared its independence from Moscow in 1991, it asserted that its statehood was the legal continuation of the pre–World War II Estonian Republic. The international community quickly recognized the new Estonian state and accepted this premise of legal continuity, as it was consistent with its earlier policy of nonrecognition.

Before Estonia could hold its first postindependence elections, it needed to determine who were legal citizens of the newly independent Estonian state.[14] Would those Russian-speaking inhabitants who had settled in Estonia during the Soviet era be considered citizens on par with members of the "titular" (i.e., ethnically Estonian) majority population? Some in the Estonian independence movement accepted the "zero option" of automatically granting citizenship to all persons resident within Estonia's borders. But in the immediate postindependence atmosphere of patriotic fervor, a "bidding war" ensued between parties representing the ethnic Estonian population. The result was a Law on Citizenship (1992) that was far more restrictive. Invoking the principle of legal continuity, the law's advocates argued that only citizens of prewar Estonia or their descendants should be considered citizens. Soviet-era settlers were considered to have an ambiguous legal status, since they had come to Estonia as the result of an illegal occupation. However, the door was left open for them to naturalize after meeting certain conditions: two years' residency plus a one-year waiting period, competency in the Estonian language, and an oath of loyalty. These conditions were considered a minimal demonstration of the applicant's identification with and loyalty to the new Estonian state.

The nearly 40 percent of Estonia's population that now found itself deprived of citizenship rights was composed almost entirely of Russian-speakers (of whom approximately 80 percent were ethnically Russian) who had come to Estonia to work as a result of the Soviet Union's policy of industrialization. By and large, these were blue-collar workers and industrial managers who had mainly settled in the northeastern cities of Narva, Kohtla-Jarve, and Sillimae where industrial development was concentrated. The capital city Tallinn's large Russian-speaking population was composed mostly of political and administrative personnel. The magnitude of Russian-speaking in-migration is reflected by the following statistics: in 1934 Russian-speakers were only 8.2 percent of

Estonia's population, but by 1989 they had grown to 30.3 percent. Many had lived in Estonia for considerable time, had raised their families there, and considered Estonia their home. But there had been little integration or assimilation between the two ethnolinguistic communities: Russian-speakers remained geographically and culturally isolated. Estonians often felt that Russian-speakers barely concealed an attitude of cultural superiority when interacting with Estonians. Few Russian-speakers bothered to learn Estonian (only about 12 percent professed any knowledge of the language at the time of independence), and expected Estonians to learn Russian and use it in public situations.

Estonians' sense of mistreatment was compounded by feelings of demographic vulnerability. Estonians have always been conscious of their relatively small size as a nation, but in the twentieth century they faced unprecedented demographic contraction. Because of large-scale Soviet deportations in the 1940s and 1950s, the devastation wrought by World War II, emigration, and a low birth rate, the number of ethnic Estonians in 1989 was lower than the prewar figure. As a percentage of the total population, ethnic Estonians had fallen from 88.2 percent in 1934 to 60.3 percent in 1989.

A restrictive citizenship law was thus the result of a rising tide of national feeling that aimed at redressing historical injustice and the vulnerable position of the "titular" nation vis-à-vis the Russian-speaking community. To be sure, since the law foresaw the possibility of naturalization, Estonia was not, strictly speaking, an "ethnic democracy." As was the case in Latvia, the descendants of prewar, ethnically Russian citizens of Estonia were eligible for citizenship. So were approximately 40,000 Soviet-era settlers who had signed a register prior to 1989 attesting to their support for Estonia's independence. However, the vast majority of Russian-speakers did not support independence (only 25 percent voted "Yes" in a 1991 referendum on the issue) and their loyalty toward the Estonian state was deeply doubted by the Estonian majority. This suspicion was behind the residency requirement of "two plus one" years (counting from March 31, 1990), which effectively barred any newly naturalized Russian-speaking citizens from voting in the first important elections—the constitutional referendum of 1992, and the first parliamentary elections (also 1992). The latter elected a new parliament (Estonian: Riigikogu) that was composed entirely of ethnic Estonian deputies. It might also be argued that the conditions for naturalization (in particular the language requirement) were designed to discourage applicants and that the majority of Estonians secretly wished that Soviet-era settlers would repatriate to the Soviet Union or its successor, the Russian Federation. This was certainly the dominant perception of the Russian-speaking minority itself.

International observers, including fact-finding missions from various European and international organizations, concluded that Estonia's citizenship law did not, in fact, violate any international norms. Estonia was admitted to the Organization for Security and Cooperation in Europe in 1991 and the Council of Europe (CoE) in 1993.

However, with the breakup of Yugoslavia and the Soviet Union and the violent ethnic conflicts that ensued, Europe was committed to preventing the further spread of ethnic conflict in eastern Europe. It was feared that Estonia's citizenship law might create the potential for ethnic conflict, a situation potentially exacerbated by the fact that the Soviet Union (later the Russian Federation) continued to maintain over 500 military bases and 100,000 troops stationed on Estonian territory. Over the course of 1992, the Russian leadership became increasingly belligerent over what it perceived as gross violations of human rights and the construction of an "apartheid" system in Estonia. Russia now threatened to make an agreement on withdrawal of Russian forces contingent on resolving the human rights issue.

Tensions reached a peak in summer 1993. In June, the Riigikogu passed a Law on Aliens that sought to regulate the legal situation of noncitizens by transforming them into "aliens" who would be required to apply for Russian, Estonian, or other citizenship within two years' time. A Law on Education followed a week later that would eliminate secondary education in the Russian language starting in 2000. The Russophone community viewed these laws as the last straw. The Law on Aliens appeared as another attempt to forcibly expel the Russian-speaking population, while the Law on Education was seen as an attempt to eventually eradicate Russian language and culture. The city councils in the Russian-speaking–dominated cities of Narva and Sillimae threatened to hold regional autonomy referenda, a possible precursor to secession. The situation had all the ingredients for violent confrontation, with armed citizen groups threatening to take matters into their own hands.

The West realized that diplomatic intervention was required to defuse the crisis, but at this point the European Union had no means of playing that role and little "leverage" over the Estonian government. To be sure, in early 1992 Estonia's prime minister had declared that an Association Agreement with the EU was one of his government's top priorities, but it was too early to talk about the EU exercising "conditionality" in order to directly influence Estonian decisionmaking. Instead, the EU authorized the OSCE and its newly created position of high commissioner for national minorities (HCNM) to act on its behalf. Estonia readily agreed to the opening of an OSCE "permanent mission" and the mediation of HCNM Max van der Stoel since this was the best way to prevent Russian intervention in the crisis. In so doing, however, it now came under far more intense international scrutiny of its citizenship and minority policies.

Van der Stoel's vigorous shuttle diplomacy between the Estonia government and the Russophone community resulted in a compromise solution: President Lennart Meri would send the Law on Aliens back to parliament with amendments allowing for the issuance of five-year, renewable temporary residency permits to noncitizens on the basis of Soviet-era "permanent registration." The Russian-speaking community would be allowed to hold regional autonomy referenda (95 percent did in fact vote for autonomy) but would promise to abide by a supreme court decision afterwards on the constitutionality of the referenda (which were ruled to be unconstitutional). Van der Stoel's intervention had brought Estonia back from the brink of ethnic conflict. From this point on, interethnic relations began a slow but steady improvement.

It was just prior to the onset of the 1993 "summer crisis" when another international organization—the Council of Europe—was able to exercise leverage over Estonia's citizenship policy through "membership conditionality." The CoE required that Estonia promise to pass a law, giving noncitizens the right to vote in local elections, an important step toward full political enfranchisement. Estonia passed this law five days after its accession to the CoE, on May 19, 1993. The right to vote in local elections distinguishes Estonia from Latvia, which has never granted this right to its own noncitizen population.

Estonia's evolving relationship with the EU accelerated in the mid-1990s. To be sure, the prospect of Estonia's association with the EU was raised as early as 1991–1992 during the negotiations on the first Trade and Cooperation Agreement (concluded May 11, 1992). In December 1993, the European Council approved the so-called Copenhagen criteria for the admission of candidate countries, including for the first time in the history of its enlargement "respect for and protection of minorities." In 1994, two further milestones were reached: on July 18, the conclusion of a Free Trade Agreement between the EU and Estonia (entry into force: January 1, 1995), and on December 14, the beginning of negotiations on an Association Agreement (also referred to as the "Europe Agreement") that officially brought Estonia into the preaccession process (ratified by the Riigikogu on August 1, 1995). Estonia officially applied for EU membership in November 1995. The European

Commission, in examining Estonia's readiness to begin accession negotiations, published its "Opinion on Estonia's Application" as part of its
Agenda 2000 document. The Commission found that "Estonia needs to
take measures to accelerate naturalization procedures to enable the
Russian-speaking non-citizens to become better integrated into Estonian
society." The European Council at its December 17, 1997, summit in
Luxembourg decided that, on the basis of the Commission's "Opinion,"
the EU would open accession negotiations with Estonia the following
year (negotiations began March 31, 1998). The EU Commission was
also mandated to issue yearly *Regular Reports* that would monitor
Estonia's progress in fulfilling the Copenhagen criteria.

One may argue, therefore, that at least by the mid-1990s, EU conditionality became a prime factor in shaping Estonian leaders' decisions
with regard to minorities policy. The OSCE and the HCNM now became
more integrated into the process of Estonia's preparation for EU accession, with their effectiveness greatly enhanced by Estonia's eagerness to
fulfill the Copenhagen criteria. One should not assume, however, that
this process was entirely straightforward, that is, that the OSCE or EU
communicated its recommendations to Estonia, after which Estonian
lawmakers adopted these verbatim in the form of legislation or implementing regulations. In order to understand "legislative outcomes," one
needs to take several factors under consideration.

First, Estonian lawmakers responded to internal, domestic pressures
as well as the recommendations of external actors. Minority issues were
highly contentious, and elites had to contend with public opinion and
criticism, as well as competition, from opposition parties. Consequently,
amendments or revisions to citizenship and language legislation sometimes introduced new restrictions or higher barriers to naturalization.
When these new laws and regulations came under criticism from the EU
or OSCE, Estonian lawmakers often responded by meeting these criticisms only halfway (note that even such partial compliance was usually
credited as full compliance in the annual *Regular Reports*). Second,
Estonian lawmakers were able to take advantage of the ambiguities,
inconsistencies, or gaps in international or EU law, especially ambiguities as to the definition of terms such as immigrant, ethnic group, or
national minority. Many Estonians held that Soviet-era settlers were in
fact immigrants and not a national minority at all (Estonia could cite the
example of France or Greece as countries that similarly refused to recognize the existence of "national minorities"). It was difficult to expect
Estonia to adhere to norms not uniformly observed by all EU member
states themselves. Third, the OSCE and EU were not always consistent

in terms of their evaluations or recommendations. The Commission's *Regular Reports* were one of the most important instruments for assessing Estonia's progress in "respect for and protection of minorities." But there did not seem to be a clear methodology for ranking priorities or identifying issues that might carry sanctions for noncompliance. For example, in the Commission's very first "Opinion" on Estonia's candidacy, Estonia is criticized for the fact that noncitizens do not have the right to sit on the boards of some companies or join political parties. This is repeated in each and every *Regular Report* through 2002, but no short- or medium-term resolution is identified, nor is there any indication that noncompliance carries any risk (e.g., forfeiture of preaccession assistance funds). One has the impression that, at least with regard to the Copenhagen political criteria, the EU's "seal of approval" was as much a function of a political decision to keep the accession process moving forward as any adherence to objective measures.

One can see the interplay of these factors in specific cases. For example, in January 1995 Estonia's Law on Citizenship was revised. The residency requirement for applying for citizenship was *lengthened* to five years (at first it was not clear whether this would apply to Soviet-era settlers). Furthermore, in addition to the language exam, an exam on the Estonian Constitution was added. Both of these measures were popular among constituencies that wanted to tighten requirements for naturalization. The HCNM reviewed the amendments and recommended that the constitution and language exams be made easier, and that exemptions be made for elderly and handicapped applicants. The Estonian government responded by stating that the requirement of passing an exam on the constitution was common practice among EU member states, and challenged the HCNM to identify specific questions that he found too difficult. The HCNM identified three such questions. The Estonian government then (1) assured the HCNM that Soviet-era settlers would be exempt from the residence requirement, (2) removed the three difficult questions identified by the HCNM and a few others, (3) simplified the language exam but not according to the HCNM's recommendations (it consulted with other European linguistic experts), and (4) exempted only some elderly and handicapped persons (employing narrower age and category criteria). On the face of it, it would appear as if the Estonian government begrudgingly acquiesced to the HCNM's recommendations and applied measures as it saw fit, in some cases short of the original recommendation. These details were glossed over two years later in the Commission's "Opinion" on Estonia's membership application.

As the EU prepared its opinion on Estonia's readiness for accession with regard to "minority rights and the protection of minorities," it stated that it would rely on whether Estonia had implemented the HCNM's recommendations made in 1993–1997. The Estonian foreign ministry prepared a report that claimed Estonia had met all of the HCNM's recommendations except one—granting automatic citizenship to children born to noncitizen resident parents. The ministry argued Estonia was unable to meet that recommendation, because its citizenship law was based on the *jus sanguinus* principle (citizenship derived from parents) rather than the *jus soli* principle (citizenship due to birth within a state's territory). The HCNM largely concurred with the ministry's report but argued that Estonia's international treaty commitments obligated it to grant citizenship to children of noncitizen residents.

With the foreign ministry's and HCNM's reports in hand, the Commission drafted its positive assessment of Estonia's readiness to begin its accession negotiations, initiating a period of far greater EU involvement in Estonia's minority policy. First, there was the issue of who came under the definition of "minority." On June 1, 1997, Estonia had ratified the Council of Europe's Framework Convention for the Protection of National Minorities, but it had added a "declaration" stating that only citizens could be considered to be national minorities (the implication being that Soviet-era settlers were nothing more than "immigrants"). The Commission's 1997 "Opinion" accepted Estonia's right to add its own definition of "national minority" (other EU states had done likewise), but it did state explicitly that Estonia's definition was insufficient for the purposes of the "Opinion" (and therefore, for the EU):

> When it comes to assessing the situation of minorities in Estonia, a distinction should accordingly be made between rights and protection attendant on membership of an ethnic and cultural community irrespective of the nationality held, and differences in personal status deriving from the fact of not holding Estonian citizenship. In this respect, the definition of the concept of minority adopted by Estonia in its declaration when depositing the act of ratification of the Council of Europe's framework convention on minorities is not relevant and the situation of non-citizens also needs to be taken into consideration in this assessment.[15]

The "Opinion" is careful to cite several areas in which Estonia had recently made progress (making naturalization exams easier, exempting elderly persons from the exams, issuance of "alien passports" to ease travel for noncitizens, accelerating the issuance of permanent-residence permits, the right of noncitizens to vote in local elections, etc.). The "Opinion" also marks a shift in emphasis from *reactive* assessments of legislation already passed, to a *proactive* engagement on behalf of social integration. The major task here is identified as accelerating the rate of naturalization, primarily by increasing the opportunities for Estonian-language instruction. But the Commission does find areas where Estonia still needs to respond to HCNM recommendations, in particular granting citizenship to stateless children born in Estonia. Interestingly, there is a recommendation that Estonia's Law on Education (passed June 16, 1993) be revised, although reference to this law had been absent in earlier HCNM or OSCE documents. The law provided for the phasing out of state-funded Russian-language instruction at the high school level by the year 2000, and was viewed by the Russophone community as a hostile attempt to suppress Russian language and culture. The Commission's recommendation was that Russian instruction be continued indefinitely.

The issue of accelerating Estonia's naturalization process was no longer controversial; rather, it was a matter of developing a better national strategy for accomplishing this goal. The prospect of EU membership added significant impetus to a process that had languished since the early 1990s, despite repeated encouragement from the HCNM. Finally, in 1997 the government established a working group to begin drafting a national integration strategy. That same year, the government established a ministerial position for interethnic affairs. The first such minister, Andra Veidemann, was responsible for the establishment of an Integration Foundation and the drafting of a State Integration Program for the period 2000–2007. After submitting the draft for comment by NGOs, government bodies, academic experts, and the Russophone community, a revised draft was adopted by the government in March 2000. The program identified three areas of integration—linguistic, legal-political, and socioeconomic—but placed greatest emphasis on linguistic integration (increasing opportunities for Estonian-language acquisition). The document also stressed the importance for ethnic minorities of preserving their own language, culture, and traditions and marked an important watershed toward a "multicultural" model of social integration. Linguistic integration was also the primary focus of the section devoted to social integration in Estonia's National Programs for the Adoption of the Acquis (2000, 2001, 2002/2003).

The issue of automatic citizenship for stateless children was far more controversial. Despite the fact that the HCNM had recommended this as early as 1993, the issue had basically been off the table until the

Foreign Ministry's report to the OSCE Permanent Council in which Estonia justified its opposition to such a measure. This in turn elicited a response from the HCNM, in which he invoked a number of international conventions on the rights of children or the right of nationality. The Foreign Ministry responded that some of these conventions had not been signed by several EU member states (e.g., the Council of Europe's Convention on Nationality). But most important, the principle of *ius sanguinis* was the basis of Estonia's citizenship law (note, however, that the 1938 citizenship law, which served as the basis for the 1992 "reactivated" law, did in fact allow automatic citizenship for stateless children born in Estonia; this was removed in 1993). The HCNM suspected that what was really at issue for the Estonians was that children of nonnaturalized parents might not possess strong identification with, or loyalty to, the Estonian state. Nevertheless, after the publication of the Commission's 1997 "Opinion" it became clear that Estonia had little choice but to acquiesce. The government adopted a draft bill in December 1997 that granted citizenship to stateless children born in Estonia since February 26, 1997, upon application by their parents. Parliamentary debate dragged on for nearly a year until the final adoption of the law in December 1998. Originally it was estimated that the new law could affect as many as 6,500 children. Over the next seven months only 1,419 applications were filed, apparently reflecting the fact that most noncitizen parents preferred that their children naturalize at the same time as themselves, if at all. Thus, this may have been a policy driven more by the Western community's insistence that Estonia adhere to international norms rather than a grassroots demand from the Russophone community itself.

The battle over adoption of the Law on Stateless Children had been hard fought and lawmakers were eager to compensate for the liberalization of the citizenship law with more stringent language laws requiring candidates for parliament and local office to demonstrate an adequate level of competency in Estonian. Such new language requirements could have been problematic for Russian-speaking candidates in the country's northeastern cities (under Estonian law, it is permitted to use a language other than Estonian as an administrative language if non-Estonian speakers comprise more than 50 percent of the population in the municipality). The first laws stipulating language requirements for candidates had been passed in June 1996 as amendments to the Law on Language; however, no "control mechanism" for checking candidates' language knowledge was implemented. This was due to pressure from the HCNM, who argued that the law violated the UN's Convention on

Human and Political Rights and asked President Meri not to promulgate the regulation. But in November 1997 the Riigikogu passed new amendments that did enable the government to check candidates' language abilities. In order to comply with a ruling by the supreme court, these provisions were then introduced into the laws on parliamentary and local elections. The HCNM once again appealed to the president not to promulgate these laws, but he refused and the law came into force in March 1999, in time for the October local elections. The Estonian government was experiencing "monitor fatigue" and was now openly questioning the authority of the HCNM on the language issue. There was increasing pressure on the OSCE to close its mission in Tallinn, since the Estonians felt they had already met all of the OSCE/HCNM recommendations. It appeared as if the OSCE and the HCNM had exhausted their "political capital" and would be unable to pressure the Estonian government to remove the language requirements from the legislation.

However, the Estonians' room for maneuver was now considerably narrower, since the HCNM was reporting to the EU Commission and his opinions were entered into the *Regular Reports* on Estonia's progress toward accession. The 1999 *Report* states, "The current text [of the law on language] contradicts a number of international standards as regards freedom of expression, in particular those introduced by the European Convention on Human Rights, of which Estonia is a contracting party." This criticism was repeated in the 2000 *Report* and yet again in the 2001 *Report*: "although enforcement is weak in practice, these restrictions affect the right of non-Estonian speakers to choose their candidates, in particular at local level." To the stick of EU criticism was added a "carrot": the OSCE would close its mission once the language issue had been resolved. Finally, on November 21, 2001, the Riigikogu passed the necessary changes to the laws. It is doubtful whether at this point the OSCE would have had enough clout for a successful resolution without the additional pressure of the EU.

The 2002 *Regular Report* is the last report that contains a section on "respect for and protection of minorities." As a document, it reflects the considerable progress that Estonia had made in the period 1997–2001, the period in which EU conditionality, in concert with the activities of the OSCE and HCNM, was the most important factor affecting the shape of Estonia's minority policy. In addition to the legislative outcomes analyzed above, the report cites the following achievements:

• 117,000 non-Estonians had attained citizenship since 1995, although the annual rate of naturalization had slowed considerably (around 2 percent of the total number of resident noncitizens, or 3,000–4,000). The report is equivocal regarding the reasons for the slowing rate of naturalization, assigning probable cause to lack of motivation (costs outweigh benefits) or lack of proactive measures by the Estonian authorities (public information, resources to help prepare applicants for the exams).

• Uncertainties as to the status of noncitizens had been eased by granting permanent residence status to 216,000 persons and issuing 167,000 "alien passports" to facilitate foreign travel.

• Amendments to the Law on Aliens now ensured that cases of family reunification would not be affected by immigration quota restrictions.

• Following EU recommendations, implementation of provisions in the Law on Language concerning the use of the Estonian language in the public and private sectors would now ensure the principles of proportionality and justified public interest. The regulations were now explicit with regard to which professions were covered under the law, and what levels of language competency were required for each.

• Amendments to education laws provided for conversion to 60 percent Estonian-language instruction in high schools beginning in 2007 (earlier legislation had stipulated 100 percent as of 2000). Exceptions to the rule could be made and full-time Russian-language instruction could continue.

• The State Integration Program received on average approximately 3.5 million euros a year for its various language-training and social integration programs (50 percent EU, 50 percent Estonian funding).

The overall conclusion of the 2001 *Report* states that "In its 1997 Opinion, the Commission concluded that Estonia fulfilled the political criteria. Since that time, the country has made considerable progress in further consolidating and deepening the stability of its institutions guaranteeing democracy, the rule of law, human rights and respect for and protection of minorities."[16] The EU had declared, "mission accomplished."

In 1992 the leaders of a newly independent Estonia had faced the difficult question of how to define membership in the new polity. The inclusive "zero option" ran the risk of enfranchising large numbers of Russian-speakers disloyal to the Estonian state, with potentially destabilizing consequences. Instead, lawmakers chose a restrictive policy that disenfranchised 40 percent of the resident population while technically holding the door open to naturalization. This too had destabilizing potential given the Russophone community's opposition and Russia's threats, backed up by the presence of 100,000 troops still stationed on Estonia's soil. The skillful intervention of the OSCE's high commissioner in 1993 defused the potential for ethnic conflict and began a process of slow but steady rapprochement between the ethnic communities.

From that point on, it was clear that Estonia's basic minority policy would stay within the framework established in the first year of independence, but this did not exclude the possibility of liberalization. Due to the steady pressure applied by the Western community—at first through the OSCE and HCNM, but then increasingly by the EU—Estonia did in fact liberalize its laws regarding citizenship, language, and the status of noncitizens. This was not always done willingly, or in complete compliance with outside recommendations. But with the diminishment of ethnic tensions and the dawning realization that the large noncitizen population was there to stay, Estonian leaders began to understand that a successful policy of social integration required an easier process of naturalization and a proactive state policy, backed by money and resources, designed to assist individuals in meeting citizenship requirements. EU conditionality certainly played a role—leaders were aware that the benefits of eventual EU membership far outweighed the short-term political or financial costs of pursuing a policy of social integration.[17] But in the process, Estonia has been guided toward a model of democracy that will now guarantee a higher degree of political enfranchisement, civic integration, and respect for minority rights than might have been the case otherwise.[18]

■ How and in What Ways Do the Baltic States Influence the EU?

Given their small size (in terms of demographics, GDP, and territory), it would seem improbable that the Baltic States might wield enough influence within the EU to effect significant policy changes. Indeed, in order to do so, it is likely the Balts would have to form alliances with like-minded states, most likely states with whom Balts share a sense of cultural identity (semiperipheral societies wishing to reclaim their European identity), their historical experience of Soviet domination, their perception of security threats, or their (neo)liberal vision of the "good society." Natural alliances could thus emerge around issues of "mastering the past" (outstanding historical disputes), commonly perceived security threats from Russia or regional dictatorships (Belarus), support for concerted action against out-of-area repressive regimes (witness the Balts' forward-leaning support for the US-led war in Iraq), advancing the EU's Lisbon reform agenda, or in advancing the interests of the less-developed new EU member states (on EU budgetary issues, Structural and Cohesion Funds, etc.).

One can already see the clear outlines of an alliance in which the Balts may play an important role, and that is with regards to the EU's *Ostpolitik*, its policy toward Russia and the countries of the Commonwealth of Independent States. All three Baltic States are likely to join a central European configuration, perhaps led by Poland, in pushing for greater EU engagement in the area. Today the main issues are: consolidating the gains of the Orange Revolution in Ukraine and anchoring Ukraine in a Euro-Atlantic architecture; assisting democratization in Belarus; and developing an EU consensus on how to deal with a Russia that appears headed in an increasingly authoritarian direction. Lithuanian president Adamkus, together with Polish president Kwasniewski, played a key role in the Orange Revolution. Poland and Lithuania have lobbied the EU to ramp up its engagement on behalf of democratization in Belarus. The Balts also share central Europe's concerns about Russian attempts to dominate the region's energy markets. They have teamed up to lobby the EU against a Russian-German plan to build a gas pipeline on the Baltic seabed that would bypass their territories. In general, the Balts can be expected to oppose efforts by Russia to settle matters bilaterally with the EU "big three," particularly on matters directly affecting them (e.g., Kaliningrad), preferring instead to shape a general EU consensus that is less vulnerable to Russian pressures.

A recent example demonstrated how the Balts are able to shape European perceptions of Russia. In December 2004, Putin's government invited EU and other Allied nations' heads of state to the 60th anniversary celebrations of the Soviet Union's victory over Nazi Germany, held May 9, 2005, in Moscow. The invitation placed the three Baltic presidents in a quandary, since accepting the invitation could have been seen as acceptance of the Putin government's position that the postwar Soviet occupation was in fact a liberation followed by voluntary incorporation. In January Latvian president Vike-Freiberga broke ranks with her counterparts and announced she would attend, but then sent a letter to the other invited heads of state explaining Latvia's view of history. To the Russians, the most objectionable part of the letter was the president's equating the crimes of Stalin (mass executions, deportations, imprisonments, forced collectivization, etc.) with those of Hitler. Vike-Freiberga's letter might have been, in fact, more than a history lesson—

it was an attempt to alter European perceptions of the Putin government and its foreign policy vis-à-vis its neighbors. If Putin was unwilling to distance himself from the Soviet view of history, if he was unwilling to acknowledge the crimes of Stalin, then what did this say about the direction in which he was taking Russia?[19]

Vike-Freiberga's letter might have been disregarded as yet another example of the central Europeans' inability to overcome their "historical trauma," except for the fact that the controversy coincided with another issue that recently has strained relations with Russia, namely, the issue of border treaties with Estonia and Latvia. After six years of stalling on whether to sign and ratify the already-initialed treaties, the Russian government decided to offer this as an additional enticement to the Baltic presidents to attend the May 9 ceremonies. Vike-Freiberga was quick to announce she would not sign any treaty at that time for fear of sending the wrong signal about Latvia's view of history, but by the end of April it appeared as if the Latvians and Russians were close to deciding another date for the treaty signing. At the last minute, the Latvian government adopted a unilateral declaration that made explicit reference to the principle of the legal continuity of the prewar and current Latvian states (it did so after being advised by legal consultants that otherwise the treaty might raise constitutional issues). This was unacceptable to the Russians, who feared that this might call into question the current border, which includes a small section of Latvian territory ceded to the Soviet Union after World War II (presumably illegally, from a Latvian constitutional point of view). Negotiations were called off, and the border treaty continues to languish.

Estonian president Ruutel refused to attend the May 9 ceremonies, but negotiations as to when and where to sign the border treaty continued, and a signing ceremony did in fact take place in Moscow on May 18. The next step was for both countries' parliaments to ratify. Given the strained atmosphere of Estonian-Russian relations, the Estonian parliament voted to ratify the treaty, but included a legally nonbinding preamble to the ratification legislation with explicit language referring to the legal continuity of the Estonian state. As is the case with the Latvian treaty, "legal continuity" calls into question the legitimacy of the post–World War II Estonian-Russian border, which reflects Estonia's cession of approximately 5 percent of its prewar territory to the Soviet Union. For this reason, Russia now refuses to consider ratification.

Despite the fact that Estonia's and Latvia's borders with Russia are now the EU's eastern border as well, until recently the EU has been content to stay out of the border-dispute issue, preferring to encourage both sides to come to an agreement through bilateral negotiations. Perhaps due to the Balts' lobbying effort to present their view of history to the older EU member states, the EU's approach to the border-dispute issue appears to have shifted (a benchmark was the EU Parliament's resolution in May 2005 on Russia, which called on Russia to acknowledge and apologize for the occupation of the Baltic States). On July 19, 2005, the EU's General Affairs and External Relations Council adopted a resolution that supported the Estonian and Latvian positions in the border-dispute issue, and called on Russia to ratify the treaties.

It would be foolish to think that the Baltic States will always be able to persuade the EU to adopt their view on matters related to Russia. Europe's dependency on Russia's natural resources of gas and oil, as well as security issues such as organized crime and international terrorism, require the EU to take Russia's views seriously. But on matters where the unresolved issues of history impede, or where there is an opportunity to advance the agenda of democratization, the Balts' point of view may play an important role in developing an EU consensus.

■ Future Trends and Prospects

Only a couple of years after EU accession, the Baltic States find themselves in the rather strange position of appearing more committed to the project of European integration than the older member states themselves. The 2005 French and Dutch "No" votes in referenda on the EU Constitutional Treaty, followed by the EU's difficulty in reaching an agreement on its 2007–2013 budget, have caused profound concern over whether the "European project" has stalled or is in crisis. Have the Baltic States come on board a sinking ship? What will the consequences be for future economic development, not to mention their security vis-à-vis Russia?

The initial Baltic response to the French and Dutch referenda defeats was to downplay their significance. Lithuania had already ratified the constitution by parliamentary vote in November 2004, the first EU state to do so. Latvia did so in June 2005, also by parliamentary vote. Both votes took place with hardly any debate, a fact that elicited cynical comment in the press. Both states had consciously avoided the danger of submitting the constitution to national referenda. Polling had showed, for example, that in Estonia a third of all citizens had not even heard about the constitution, while only 4 percent said they were informed about its contents.[20] So at first Baltic leaders calmly predicted that despite the French and Dutch votes, the ratification process would continue. Estonia hedged its bets and delayed its ratification vote, stressing this was not a reaction to the French and Dutch votes, but rather an attempt to give legal experts more time to determine whether the Estonian Constitution would have to be amended first.

The failure of the Brussels summit in June 2005 to come up with a new EU budget brought home the fact that the EU now faces a more serious crisis indeed. Conflict over the budget revealed the fragility of the principle of solidarity in the face of member states' determination to defend national interests. "Old Europe" appeared willing to sacrifice Structural and Cohesion Funds for its poorer central European cousins in order to preserve its own subsidies and rebates. But the conflict seemed to go beyond the budget. National interests appear threatened by enlargement itself, that is, by newcomer states that some older members viewed as a threat to the European social model. The perception is that central European elites seem more eager to embrace the Anglo-Saxon or Nordic "social models," are committed to creating more competitive business environments, and offer lower labor costs to potential investors. The newcomers could tip the balance of power in the EU, forming alliances to liberalize services, reform the CAP, undermine collective-bargaining arrangements, and in general revitalize the Lisbon Strategy to make Europe more competitive in global markets. Some Baltic commentators argued that the referenda defeats were in fact expressions of dissatisfaction by average citizens that the enlargement process, conceived and implemented by elites, had not taken their social and economic concerns into account. The Baltic States had made colossal efforts to join the EU, only to find themselves less than welcome upon arrival.

Despite the current malaise concerning the future of the EU, there is plenty of evidence that EU accession has already benefited the Baltic States economically. Under the terms of the previous EU budget, in the period 2004–2006 Estonia is scheduled to receive €695.06 million, Latvia €1.164 billion, and Lithuania €1.538 billion in community aid, although the total amount actually spent will depend on each country's "absorptive capacity." Farmers have benefited significantly from direct payments (starting at 25 percent of the EU average and increasing 5 percent per year) and from the rise in agricultural prices. Economic growth rates, already the highest in Europe prior to accession, are now even higher. Estonia's GDP growth has gone from 7.8 percent in 2004 to 8.4 percent in 2005. Latvia's GDP growth went from 8.3 percent in 2004 to

9.1 percent in 2005. Lithuania has held steady at 7.0 percent for both years. Investment is up in all three countries. Estonia and Lithuania already meet all of the Maastricht criteria for joining the European Monetary Union and plan to adopt the euro by January 1, 2007. Latvia hopes to do so by January 1, 2008. Even if the Balts (and other newcomer states) are forced to accept a reduction in Structural and Cohesion Funds during 2007–2013 (one proposal is to cut these by 10 percent), they still stand to gain considerably from community aid. In fact, even under the budgetary terms offered by the UK, the Baltic States stand to gain more than any other EU state save Luxembourg if one divides member contributions by aid received, figured as a percentage of gross national income.[21] EU aid for infrastructural development should have a huge impact on modernizing transportation networks.[22]

The economic effect of enlargement on the Baltic States' labor markets has been more ambiguous. Fears of a massive influx of low-wage labor led all EU countries save three—the UK, Ireland, and Sweden—to impose two-year restrictions on labor immigration, renewable for up to seven years. Despite restrictions, and due to the fact that Baltic wages are among the lowest in the EU, thousands of Balts have left for work in the British Isles and Sweden, and thousands more work as seasonal laborers in other EU countries (where quotas apply). One commentator noted the irony in the fact that the Balts are now undertaking the same kind of migration that Slavic workers undertook during the Soviet period when they came to the Baltic States in search of jobs. The irony is even greater because Baltic out-migration is creating manpower shortages at home, which are likely to be filled by Slavic workers from Russia, Ukraine, and Belarus.

Two recent cases indicate that the free movement of relatively low-wage central European labor to western Europe may lead to conflict with domestic labor unions. In 2005, in Sweden, a construction trade union blockaded a construction site to prevent Latvian workers from entering, since their Latvian contracting company refused to pay its workers the equivalent of Swedish wages. The Latvian company was forced to withdraw and later went into bankruptcy. It has taken its case to the European Court of Justice.[23] Again in 2005, Ireland's largest trade union organized a protest against the hiring of Latvian workers at below-union wages by an Irish ferry company.[24] Growing west European resentment toward the competitive pressures exerted by less-expensive central European labor (both in domestic labor markets, as well as investments going to central Europe due to lower labor costs) may lead other EU countries to maintain their labor restrictions beyond the initial two-year limit. The issue is also forcing Europeans to confront another contradiction between an aspect of the cherished European social model—collective bargaining agreements—and European regulations on the free circulation of labor. The Nordic states are already on record as stating they will not support the services directive (liberalization of the service-sector economy) if the EU continues to support what they call "social dumping," or the influx of lower-cost labor from the new EU entrants.

Looking ahead, the atmosphere of uncertainty over the future of the European project that has gripped the EU since the French and Dutch referenda, compounded by weak economic growth and pressing social issues such as unemployment and immigration, is unlikely to abate. European enlargement has added new voices to the debate over the future of the European social model—with the new members largely sympathetic to the economically more liberal Anglo-Saxon and Nordic models. The Baltic States are likely to weigh in on the side of those who wish to revitalize the now-moribund Lisbon Process to make Europe more competitive in an increasingly globalized economy. But they are unlikely to wait for the rest of Europe to come onboard; instead, they will forge ahead in an attempt to close the gap between themselves and western Europe within a generation. If their performance to date is any indication, they stand a good chance of reaching that goal.[25]

▮ Notes

This contribution was written in the author's personal capacity and does not necessarily reflect the thinking of the US Department of State or the US government.

1. For a classic account of how the Baltic States secured their independence, see Lieven, *The Baltic Revolution.* The most comprehensive overview of developments in the Baltic States since independence, covering history, politics, economics, and social issues, is Smith et al., *The Baltic States.*

2. For a good general history of the Baltic States, see O'Connor, *The History of the Baltic States.*

3. An excellent history of the Baltic region in the modern era is Kirby, *The Baltic World 1772–1993.*

4. A recent anthology that examines issues of normative culture, historical identities, and regionalism is Smith, *The Baltic States and Their Region.*

5. Lithuania was spared large-scale immigration during the Soviet era primarily due to the absence of large-scale industrialization projects, which itself may be due to the skillful maneuvering of the Lithuanian Communist leadership, which hoped thereby to defend national interests. The Soviet leadership may have acquiesced in the knowledge this would establish greater legitimacy for the Lithuanian Communist Party.

6. Readers in search of a more academic discussion of the role of international organizations' conditionality in causing policy outcomes should see Kelley, "International Actors—Domestic Effects." She has recently expanded her argument in *Ethnic Politics in Europe*.

7. An excellent examination of the geopolitics of Russian energy as it affects the Baltics is the former US ambassador to Lithuania Keith Smith's *Russian Energy Politics in the Baltics, Poland, and Ukraine*.

8 See Ziemele, *State Continuity and Nationality*.

9. Jubulis, *Nationalism and Democratic Transition*.

10. To access the 1997 Commission's opinions on readiness of candidate countries, go to http://www.ena.lu/mce.cfm. Subsequent yearly *Regular Reports* on each candidate country's progress can be accessed at http://europa.eu.int/comm/enlargement/docs/index.htm.

11. After passage of major social integration legislation, EU recommendations focused on acceleration of the naturalization process and increased efforts to educate and inform the noncitizen resident population regarding the naturalization process. Latvian compliance involved: expansion of Latvian-language instruction programs; simplification of the citizenship examination; reduction of naturalization fees; creation of a National Social Integration program and four institutions responsible for its implementation; legislation to equalize the legal standing of citizens and noncitizens (e.g., in regard to access to accredited professions and unemployment benefits); waiving language examination requirement for graduates of Latvian secondary schools; and many other measures too numerous to cite here.

12. Latvia provides state-funded education in eight minority languages. There are 239 such schools serving the Russian-speaking minority population. Despite this fact, the Russian foreign minister, as recently as July 2005, decried Latvia's denial of the right to instruction in minority languages.

13. For exact data on naturalization figures, go to the website of Latvia's Naturalization Board: http://www.np.gov.lv/index.php? en=fakti_en&saite=residents.htm.

14. By far the most empirically detailed account of how Estonia's citizenship/naturalization/minorities policies took shape under the influence of international organizations and domestic politics is Sarv, "Integration by Reframing Legislation." Sarv's paper includes an indispensable bibliography of all government regulations and legislation, correspondence between the OSCE and the Estonian government, and other useful references.

15. See note 10 above.

16. See note 10 above.

17. For a contrary view that holds that EU conditionality was ineffective in influencing Estonia's or Latvia's minorities policy, see Hughes and Sasse, "Monitoring the Monitors."

18. For an examination of changes in the legal status of noncitizen residents now that Estonia and Latvia are EU members, see Van Elsuwege, "Russian-Speaking Minorities in Estonia and Latvia."

19. Russia has never fully repudiated the 1939 Molotov-Ribbentrop Pact and its secret protocols that relegated the three Baltic States to the Soviet Union's sphere of influence, leading to their forcible military occupation and

annexation in 1940. Prior to the breakup of the Soviet Union, in 1989 the Second Congress of People's Deputies declared the pact to have no legal basis, but stressed that responsibility lay with the then-Soviet leadership and not the Soviet people. Also, in 1991 the Russian Soviet Socialist Republic signed a treaty with Lithuania that recognized the events of 1940 to have been a violation of Lithuania's sovereignty, a treaty that was reaffirmed by the newly independent Russian Federation that same year. No subsequent Russian government has considered repudiating Molotov-Ribbentrop in full nor acknowledged the illegal occupation/annexation of the Baltic States. The Putin government has, in fact, turned back the wheels of time and has returned to the original Soviet position that the Baltic States voluntarily joined the Soviet Union of their own accord.

20. "Poll Suggests 36% of Estonians 'Never Heard' of EU Constitution," FBIS Report EUP2005031000085, March 15, 2005.

21. *Financial Times*, December 8, 2005, p. 2.

22. For more comprehensive data on the economic impact of accession, see Economic Intelligence Unit, "One Year On," and "Economic Forecasts Autumn 2005," available at: http://www.europa.eu.int/comm/economy_finance/publications/european_economy/2005/ee505en.pdf.

23. "EU to Criticize Sweden for Violating Free Circulation of Labor Regulations," FBIS Report EUP20051005102013, October 5, 2005.

24. "Latvian Workers Object of Protests, Anger in Irish Shipping Industry," FBIS Report EUP20051129341001, November 29, 2005.

25. For a more comprehensive look at the outlook for EU policymaking in 2006, see the Oxford Analytica report "Prospects 2006: Europe Will Move from Crisis to Stasis," December 12, 2005, available by subscription at their website, http://www.oxan.com.

PART 6

CONCLUSION

21

The EU and the Member States: A Comparative Analysis

Eleanor E. Zeff and Ellen B. Pirro

THE EUROPEAN UNION CONTINUES to enlarge as it develops into a one-of-a-kind phenomenon. More and more researchers are recognizing that the development of the EU is an interactive process that depends on strong and healthy ties between the EU institutions and the member states.

As the chapters in this book relate in detail, much progress toward integration has been made, especially in the economic area. The Single Market is a notable success, while the euro, after a shaky start, has been achieving its own niche among international currencies. Yet, even while EU leaders are congratulating themselves on their accomplishments, there are some disturbing signs, especially in the political arena.

The events of the past several years have highlighted the widening gap between the elites who created the EU and are moving it steadily toward integration and ordinary European citizens who object to some of the EU's planned moves. The chapters on France (Chapter 4) and the Netherlands (Chapter 6) comment on this growing chasm, which became obvious when both countries rejected the proposed new constitution in May 2005. The implications of the 2005 vote are considered throughout the book and raise a number of interesting issues. Can a constitution be created in small incremental steps, as some have suggested? Will the EU have to back away from further integration until it creates new mechanisms to lessen the democratic deficit? Will EU leaders recognize the need to take public opinion into account as they move forward?

It is also clear from many of the chapters that "Euro-skepticism" is on the rise. The United Kingdom and Denmark have been the most noted of the skeptics, but they are being joined by others including France, Sweden, and some of the newest members such as the Czech Republic, the Baltic States, and Poland. In the initial stages of the EU, Euro-skepticism was the refuge of those who feared loss of national identity. The newer form of Euro-skepticism, however, seems to be a reaction to loss of control by the national government and is prevalent not only in the mass population, but among some of the leadership as well. This Euro-skepticism can be seen in the reluctance of nations to implement EU directives and in resentment at having to defer social matters like environmental regulations (Hungary) and abortion (Ireland) to EU judgment. Discussions about national budgets and monetary systems likewise demonstrate this fear of loss of control. Two countries—Germany and Italy—have knowingly allowed deficits above the mandated levels and have not made any moves to amend the situation, which will probably precipitate further deficits. Greece may be following this example. If others do likewise, it bodes ill for continued EU development.

The issue of democratization throughout the EU is also significant. Establishing lasting democracies in the newest accession members and candidates is one of the motivations for EU expansion. To date, all of these countries have maintained a democracy, but it is noteworthy that a number of them are not without problems. Latvia, for example, has had nine governments in 10 years of independence. In Hungary, Slovakia, and Poland, there has been a persistence of Communist parties contesting the elections. And in many of the newest states, corruption and political scandals have become commonplace. The EU will need to develop strong measures to monitor and mentor the democratic process for some time to come.

For the older member states, one key concern continues to be implementation: Who does it? When and how is it accomplished? Who is affected? The chapters on France, Italy, and the Benelux nations detail carefully constructed routes for implementation of EU directives. For those members moving away from the status of recipients of EU development funds, implementation is becoming an increasingly important concern, and there are signs of problems as Ireland, Greece, Spain, and Portugal face losing the EU funds previously designated to help develop their infrastructures.

The EU's newest members also face implementation hurdles, as their weaker infrastructures and lesser-developed bureaucracies threaten to slow the integration process, especially as the enthusiasm of their citizens wanes and Euro-skepticism rises. Many of the newest members are working hard to become more active and gain a larger voice, as described in the chapters on Poland, Hungary, and Malta and Cyprus. However, some of the others, notably the Czech Republic, Poland, and the Baltic States, are more prone to slower, more reluctant implementation since accession. For most of these newest members, simply getting their compliance mechanisms in order has proven more of a challenge than they have been able to meet, but all are continuing their efforts.

■ Policy Analysis in the EU and Its Member States

This is an exciting time to be studying Europe. Not only are there major changes in the political landscape with the disintegration of the Soviet Union, the emergence of new states, and the growth of the European Union through accession, but scholars are utilizing new strategies and tools to examine these ongoing processes. And the European Union, with its unique character, provides a useful laboratory to examine theories of comparative politics in a new light. This book was designed to provide an introduction to the EU member states, new and old, and the ways they are incorporating EU governance into their domestic politics and daily lives, but it also fits within the growing field of European comparative politics and public policy, contributing in three significant ways.

The EU and Public Policy

First, we utilize a comparative policy approach to examine each member state. Each country chapter employs the same general heading structure and asks the same questions about member-state relations with the European Union. The country studies follow the tradition of comparative politics and comparative public policy research in asking why differing political systems choose similar policies and how member states deal with similar problems in their own individual contexts. The chapters in this book demonstrate how the political processes within the member states are linked with public policy processes.[1]

Stella Theodoulou states that "those who study policy comparatively are not just interested in the type of policy passed but how the policy is made, how it is delivered and what it achieves."[2] For example, in Chapter 16 on Hungary, David Ellison provides an in-depth examination of environmental policy and the complexities of implementing and complying with EU policy directives on the environment.[3] Ellison examines Hungary's environmental policy, beginning with domestic approval and implementation of EU directives and discusses the difficulties of compliance due to multiple influences on the policy process—including subnational governments, industry, and policy interest groups. Other chapters, such as those on France, Finland, and Italy, also discuss environmental policies and present further comparative illustrations of the multilevel dimensions of compliance with EU policy directives.

The EU and Europeanization

Second, the book contributes to the ongoing discussion of Europeanization. Europeanization can be defined as the meshing of domestic policy and implementation with the EU's policies and directives.[4] It is not simply a regional form of globalization—to the contrary, it is a much more substantive movement, changing the very nature of the governing structures within the member states.[5] Neither should Europeanization be equated with integration. The term *integration* echoes the goals of the 1960s, when scholars spoke of how the countries would unite, borders would evaporate, and there would be a United States of Europe.[6] The citizens of today's member states continue to think of themselves as "Poles" or "Italians." Nationalism still prevails, as witnessed in the recent debates over the EU's 2007–2013 budget, the so-called Common Asylum Policy, and the "No" votes on the EU Constitution. In many of the former Soviet states, nationalism is a new and major force behind policy choices.

As the preceding chapters show, Europeanization is a distinct process in a number of critical ways. For example, in Malta and Cyprus, accession to the EU has meant the creation of new government bureaucracies. France has created a special committee to facilitate more efficient and effective implementation of EU policies. While many Europeans want the economic benefits that EU membership brings, they also want to keep key elements and symbols of their nations and their nationalities. So, there is a constant struggle as Europeanization moves eastward and standards (especially economic ones) become increasingly uniform across the member states. As Thomas Risse has suggested, total Europeanization has not yet occurred because people do not characterize themselves as "European," but rather utilize national symbols and images for identity.[7] Until they begin to think of themselves as European, Karl Deutsch's "we-feeling" will be weak, and further integration difficult.[8]

The EU and Theories of Comparative Politics

Third, this book allows us to utilize the European Union to explore comparative political theory, and to look for some uniform explanations for the continuing development of the European Union.[9] Scholars have remarked on the growing gulf between the major "meta" theories and their derivative branches: rational choice, liberal-internationalist, and the newer constructivist approach.[10] We have taken no consistent theoretical approach in this book. However, there are a number of approaches in the field that have been used to further the understanding of the development of the European Union, including liberal intergovernmentalism, policy networks, and historical institutionalism, among others.[11] One of the newer methods, discourse analysis, has been successfully utilized by scholars such as Vivien Schmidt[12] and Claudio Raedelli[13] to explain EU policies. In sum, we view this book as a starting point for further exploration of the ongoing interaction between the member states and the evolving European Union. It is our hope that scholars and practitioners will take up the challenge.

■ Notes

1. Theodoulou, *Policy and Politics in Six Nations*; Adolino and Blake, *Comparing Public Policies*.
2. Ibid.
3. Multilevel governance is the "dispersion of authoritative decision-making across multiple territorial levels," Hooghe and Marks, *Multi-Level Governance and European Integration*. Both European integration and the phenomenon of greater regionalization across Europe have facilitated the development of multilevel governance. See also Laffan, "Ireland: A Region Without Regions"; Bukowski and Piattoni, *Between Europeanization and Local Societies*.
4. See Pirro and Zeff, "Europeanization, European Integration and Globalization" for definitions, citations, and the development of this issue.
5. Keohane and Nye, "Globalization: What's New?"
6. See Churchill, "The Tragedy of Europe," pp. 7–11; Haas, "The Uniting of Europe," pp. 145–149.
7. See Risse in Cowles, Caparoso, and Risse, 2001.
8. Deutsch et al., *Political Community and the North Atlantic Area*.
9. Nelsen and Stubb, *The European Union*; Wiener and Diez, *European Integration Theory*; Lichbach and Zuckerman, *Comparative Politics*; Hanf and Soetendorp, *Adapting to European Integration*.
10. Lichbach, "Social Theory and Comparative Politics"; World Politics, Symposium on "The Role of Theory in Comparative Politics."

11. Pollack, "The New Institutionalism and EU Governance; Peterson and Bomberg, *Decision-Making in the European Union*; Cowles, Caparoso, and Risse, *Transforming Europe*; Wiener and Diez, *European Integration*.

12. Schmidt, *The Futures of European Capitalism*.

13. Radaelli, "Technocracy in the European Union."

Acronyms

CAP	Common Agricultural Policy
CDU	Christian Democratic Union
CFSP	Common Foreign and Security Policy
CJD	Creutzfeld-Jakob brain disease
COREPER	Committee of Permanent Representatives
CSF	Community Support Framework (EU)
DG	directorate-general
DM	deutschemarks
EAW	European Arrest Warrant
EC	European Community
ECB	European Central Bank
ECOFIN	Council of Economic and Financial Ministers
ECOSOC	Economic and Social Committee
ECU	EC monetary unit prior to 1998
ECJ	European Court of Justice (the Court)
ECSC	European Coal and Steel Community
EDC	European Defense Community
EEC	European Economic Community (also, Common Market)
EFTA	European Free Trade Association
EIB	European Investment Bank
EMS	European Monetary System
EMU	Economic and Monetary Union
ERDF	European Regional Development Fund
ERDP	European Regional Development Policy
ERM (I & II)	Exchange Rate Mechanism

ESDP	European Security and Defence Policy
EUAC	EU Advisory Committee
EUROPOL	European Police Office
FDI	foreign direct investment
FNSEA	National Federation of Farmers' Unions
FF	French francs
FPÖ	Freedom Party (Austria)
GATT	General Agreement on Tariffs and Trade
GDP	gross domestic product
GNI	gross national income (EU)
GNP	gross national product
HCFC(s)	hydrochlorofluorocarbon(s)
IC	Instruction Committee
IGC	Intergovernmental Conference
IMPs	Integrated Mediterranean Programs
JHA	Justice and Home Affairs
MEPs	members of the European Parliament
NATO	North Atlantic Treaty Organization
NCP	New Commission Proposals
NO	nitric oxide
OECD	Organisation for Economic Cooperation and Development
ÖVP	People's Party (Austria)
PHARE	East European Countries Accession Program
PR	Permanent Representation
QMV	Qualified Majority Voting
R&D	research and development
SAP	Social Democratic Party
SEA	Single European Act
SGCI	General Secretariat of the Interministerial Committee
SGP	Stability and Growth Pact
SPÖ	Social Democrats (Austria)
SPD	Social Democrats
TEU	Treaty on European Union (aka, the Maastricht Treaty)
TRNC	Turkish Republic of Northern Cyprus
UKIE	Office of the Committee for European Integration
VAT	value-added tax
VER	Voluntary Export Restraints
WEU	Western European Union
WTO	World Trade Organization

Bibliography

"Act of Accession." *Official Journal of the European Communities* 46, no. 23.092003.

Adamczyk, Marek. "Europejska Agencja Zarządzania Wspólpracą Operacyjną na Granicach Zewnętrznych Panstw Czlonkowskich Unii Europejskiej." *Materialy Robocze*. Warsaw: Centrum Europejskie Natolin (January 2005).

Adolino, Jessica R., and Charles H. Blake. *Comparing Public Policies: Issues and Choices in Six Industrialized Countries*. Washington, DC: CQ Press, 2001.

af Malmborg, M. *Neutrality and State-Building in Sweden*. Stockholm: Utrikespolitiska Institutet, 2002.

Alegre, Susie, and Marisa Leaf. "Mutual Recognition in European Judicial Cooperation: A Step Too Far Too Soon? Case Study—the European Arrest Warrant." *European Law Journal* 10, no. 2 (2004): 200–217.

Allen, David. "The United Kingdom: A Europeanized Government in a Non-Europeanized Polity." In *The Member States of the European Union*, edited by Simon Bulmer and Christian Lequesne, pp. 119–141. New York: Oxford University Press, 2005.

Alogoskoufis, George. "The Greek Economy and the Euro." In *Contemporary Greece and Europe*, edited by Achilleas Mitsos and Elias Mossialos, pp. 131–155. Burlington, VT: Ashgate, 2000.

Amato, Giuliano, and Massimo L. Salvadori. *Europa conviene?* Roma: Laterza, 1990.

Andersen, Svein S., and Kjell A. Eliassen. "The EC as a New Political System." In *Making Policy in Europe: The Europeification of National Policy-Making*, edited by Svein S. Andersen and Kjell A. Eliassen. London: Sage Publications, 1993.

———. "Informal Processes: Lobbying, Actor Strategies, Coalitions and

Dependencies." In *Making Policy in Europe,* 2nd ed., edited by Svein S. Andersen and Kjell A. Eliassen. London: Sage Publications, 2001.

Anderson, Jeffrey J. *German Unification and the Union of Europe: The Domestic Politics of Integration Policy.* New York: Cambridge University Press, 1999.

Anderson, Jørgen Goul. "Valgkampen 2001: Vælgernes politiske dagsorden." *Working Paper* no. 12, The Danish Electoral Project, Aalborg University (2002). Available at: http://www.socsci.auc.dk/election/arbejdspapirer/val-garbpapirnr12.pdf (accessed November 18, 2005).

Anderson, Karen. "Sweden: Retreat from Exceptionalism." In *The European Union and the Member States: Cooperation, Coordination, and Compromise,* edited by Eleanor E. Zeff and Ellen B. Pirro, pp. 285–304. Boulder, CO: Lynne Rienner Publishers, 2001.

———. "Pension Politics in Belgium." In *The Handbook of Pension Reform in Western Europe,* edited by Karen M. Anderson, Elen M. Immergut, and Isabelle Schulze. Oxford: Oxford University Press, forthcoming.

Anderson, Karen M., Sanneke Kuipers, Isabelle Schulze, and Wendy van den Nouland. "Belgium: Linguistic Veto Players and Pension Reform." In *The Handbook of Pension Reform in Western Europe,* edited by Karen M. Anderson, Ellen M. Immergut, and Isabelle Schulze. Oxford: Oxford University Press, forthcoming.

Anderson, L. *Beslutsfatterna.* Stockholm: PM Bäckström Förlag, 1996.

Andren, N. *Säkerhetspolitik, Analyser och Tillämpningar [Security Politics, Analyses and Applications].* Stockholm: Norstedts Juridk, 1997.

Andrikopoulou, Eleni, and Grigoris Kafkalas. "Greek Regional Policy and the Process of Europeanization, 1961–2000." In *Greece in the European Union,* edited by Dionyssis G. Dimitrakopoulos and Argyris Passas, pp. 35–47. New York: Routledge, 2004.

Application of the European Arrest Warrant to Polish Citizens. Available at: http://www.trybunal.gov.pl/eng/summaries/documents/P_1_05_GB.pdf.

Arter, David. "Small State Influence Within the EU: The Case of Finland's 'Northern Dimension Initiative.'" *Journal of Common Market Studies* 38, no. 5 (2000): 677–697.

———. "The EU Referendum in Finland on 16 October 1994: A Vote for the West, not for Maastricht." *Journal of Common Market Studies* 33, no. 3 (1995): 361–387.

Atkins, Ralph, and George Parker. "Greece Faces Court Action over False Deficit Figures." *Financial Times,* December 1, 2004, p. 3.

Baines, P. "Parliamentary Scrutiny of Policy and Legislation: Procedures of the Lords and Commons." In *Britain in the European Union: Law, Policy, and Parliament,* edited by Philip James Giddings and Gavin Drewry. New York: Palgrave Macmillan, 2004.

Barca, F. "Il ruolo del Dipartimento per le Politiche di Sviluppo e Coesione." *Le Istituzioni del Federalismo* 22, no. 2 (2001): 419–445.

Bardach, Eugene. *The Implementation Game: What Happens After a Bill Becomes a Law.* Cambridge, MA: MIT Press, 1977.

Bausili, Anna Verges. "Ireland and the Convention on the Future of Europe." In

Ireland and the European Union: Nice, Enlargement and the Future of Europe, edited by Michael Holmes, pp. 133–150. Manchester, UK: Manchester University Press, 2005.

Belgian Minister of Finance. "The Belgian Stability Programme 2005–2008." Update. http://www.eu.int/comm/economy_finance/about/activities/sgp/country/countryfiles/be/be20042005_en.pdf.

———. "The Stability Programme of Belgium 1999–2002." http://www.eu.int/comm/economy_finance/about/activities/sgp/country/countryfiles/be/be19 981999_en.pdf.

Benedek, Jávor, and Lászlo Gálhidy, "Hungary: Forest Degradation with State Assistance," *FERN Briefing Note,* February 2005.

Berg, O. "Neutraliteten har gjort sitt." *Dagens Nyheter*, January 8, 1999.

Bergman, Torbjörn. "Sweden: Democratic Reforms and Partisan Decline in an Emerging Separation of Powers System." *Scandinavian Political Studies* 27, no. 2 (2004): 203–225.

Beunderman, Mark. "Berlin Signals End to Support for Lifting China Arms Ban." euobserver.com (accessed November 8, 2005).

Bindi, F., and M. Cisci. "Italy and Spain: A Tale of Contrasting Effectiveness in the EU." In *The Member States of the European Union*, edited by Simon Bulmer and Christian Lequesne, pp. 142–163. Oxford: Oxford University Press, 2005.

Bjurtoft, V. "Gamla sanningar omprövas när försvarsindustrin omprövas." *FOA* 6 (1998): 12–13.

Bocquet, Dominique. *La France et L'Allemagne*. Paris: Fondation Saint-Simon, 1996.

Börzel, Tanja A. "The Greening of a Policy? The Europeanization of Environmental Policy-Making in Spain." *South European Society and Politics* 3, no. 1 (summer 1998): 65–92.

———. "Guarding the Treaty: The Compliance Strategies of the European Commission." In *The State of the European Union*, edited by Tanja A. Börzel and Rachel A. Cichowski, pp, 197–220. Oxford: Oxford University Press, 2003.

———. "How the European Union Interacts with Its Member States." In *The Member States of the European Union*, edited by Simon Bulmer and Christian Lequesne, pp. 45–69. Oxford: Oxford University Press, 2005.

———. "Improving Compliance Through Domestic Mobilisation? New Instruments and Effectiveness of Implementation in Spain." In *Implementing EU Environmental Policy: New Direction and Old Problems*, edited by Christoph Knill and Andrea Lenschow, pp. 222–250. Manchester, UK: Manchester University Press, 2000.

———. "Non-compliance in the European Union: Pathology or Statistical Artifact." *Journal of European Public Policy* 8, no. 5 (2001): 803–824.

———. "Pace-Setting, Foot-Dragging, and Fence-Sitting: Member State Responses to Europeanization." *Journal of Common Market Studies* 40, no. 2 (June 2002): 193–214.

———. "Rediscovering Policy Networks as a Modern Form of Government." *Journal of European Public Policy* 5 (1998): 354–359.

———. "Why There Is No 'Southern Problem': On Environmental Leaders and

Laggards in the European Union." *Journal of European Public Policy* 7, no. 1 (March 2000): 141–162.

Börzel, Tanja A., and Thomas Risse-Kappen. "When Europe Hits Home: Europeanization and Domestic Change." *European Integration Online Papers* 4, no. 15 (2000). Available at: http://eiop.or.at/eiop/texte/2000-015a.htm.

———. "Conceptualizing the Domestic Impact of Europe." In *The Politics of Europeanization*, edited by Kevin Featherstone and Claudio M. Radaelli, pp. 57–80. Oxford: Oxford University Press, 2003.

Bossaert, Danielle. "Luxembourg: Flexible and Pragmatic Adaption." In *Fifteen into One? The European Union and Its Member States*, edited by Wolfgang Wessels, Andreas Maurer, and Jürgen Mittag, Manchester, UK: Manchester University Press, 2003.

Bratt, P. "Neutraliteten inte relevent [Neutrality not relevant]." *Dagens Nyheter* 2000, p. A10.

———. "Sverige övervärderar sin Roll." *Dagens Nyheter*, January 10, 1999.

Brown, Paul. "EU Law Causes Unwanted Fridge Mountain: New Regulation Forbids CFC Foam Being Dumped in Landfill Sites." *The Guardian* (London), 2002, p. 9.

Brunazzo, Marco, and Simona Piattoni. "Negotiating the Regulation of the Structural Funds: Italian Actors in EU Regional Policy-Making." *Modern Italy* 9, no. 2 (November 2004): 159–172.

Brusis, Martin. "Regionalization in the Czech and Slovak Republics: Comparing the Influence of the European Union." In *The Regional Challenge in Central and Eastern Europe, Territorial Restructuring and European Integration*, edited by Michael Keating and James Hughes. Paris: Presses Interuniversitaires Européennes, 2003.

Buch, Roger, and Kasper M. Hansen. "The Danes and Europe: From EC 1972 to Euro 2000—Elections, Referendums, and Attitudes." *Scandinavian Political Studies* 25, no. 1 (March 2002): 1–26.

Buck, Tobias. "EU Seeks to End Bias Among Investors: Commission Wants 'One Share, One Vote' Principle." *Financial Times* (London), October 17, 2005.

Bukowski, Jeanie J., Simona Piattoni, and Marc E. Smyrl, eds. *Between Europeanization and Local Societies: The Space for Territorial Governance, Governance in Europe*. Lanham, MD: Rowman & Littlefield Publishers, 2003.

Bulmer, Simon, and Martin Burch. "The Europeanization of UK Government: From Quiet Revolution to Explicit Step-Change?" *Public Administration* 83, no. 4 (December 2005): 861–890.

Bulmer, Simon, and Christian Lequesne, eds. *The Member States of the European Union*. Oxford: Oxford University Press, 2005.

Bulmer, Simon, and Wolfgang Wessels. *The European Council: Decision-Making in European Politics*. Basingstoke, UK: Sheridan House, 1987.

Burch, Martin, and Ian Holliday. "The Blair Government and the Core Executive." *Government & Opposition* 9, no. 1 (winter 2004): 1–21.

Cavatorto, S. "Attuare Maastricht e la politica delle 'rigidità flessibili'." In *L'Europa in Italia. Élite, opinione pubblica e decisioni*, edited by Maurizio

Cotta, Pierangelo Isernia, and Luca Verzichelli, pp. 333–368. Bologna: Il Mulino, 2005.

Censis. *Le pubbliche amministrazioni negli anni '90*. Milano: Franco Angeli, 1989.

Central Bank of Malta. *Quarterly Review* 38, no. 1 (2005).

Chiotis, V. "Greece's 21 Billion Euros Between a British Rock and a Hard Place." *Ta Nea*, June 15, 2005, p. N11.

Christodoulakis, Nicos. "The Greek Economy Converging Towards EMU." In *Contemporary Greece and Europe*, edited by Achilleas Mitsos and Elias Mossialos, pp. 93–114. Burlington, VT: Ashgate, 2000.

Chrysodora, Eirini. "The Economy's Euro-Hit." *Ta Nea*, June 6, 2005, p. I02.

———. "An Astonishing Jump of the Deficit to 5.2 Percent." *Ta Nea* (in Greek), September 1, 2004, p. N54.

Chryssochoou, Dimitris, Stelios Stavridis, and Andreas Moschonas. "Greece and the European Union After Amsterdam." In *Contemporary Greece and Europe*, edited by Achilleas Mitsos and Elias Mossialos, pp. 183–204. Burlington, VT: Ashgate, 2000.

Chubb, Basil. *The Government and Politics of Ireland*. London: Longman Publishing Group, 1992.

Churchill, Winston S. "The Tragedy of Europe." In *The European Union: Readings on the Theory and Practice of European Integration*, 3rd ed., edited by Brent Nelson and Alexander Stuff, pp. 7–11. Boulder, CO: Lynne Rienner Publishers, 2003.

Cichowski, Rachel A. "Integrating the Environment: The European Court and the Construction of Supranational Policy." *Journal of European Public Policy* 5, no. 3 (1998): 387–405.

Cini, Michelle. "Malta Votes Twice for Europe: The Accession Referendum and General Election, March/April 2003." *South European Society and Politics* 8, no. 3 (winter 2003): 132–146.

Civil Report. *Civil Report About the Implementation of Aarhus Convention in Hungary for the Second Conference of the Parties*. Almaty, Kazakhstan: May 25–27, 2005.

Clean Air Action Group. "Communication to the Aarhus Compliance Committee," unpublished document, Budapest, Clean Air Action Group, 2004.

Clinch, J. Peter, Frank J. Convery, and Brendan M. Walsh. *After the Celtic Tiger: Challenges Ahead*. Dublin: O'Brien Press, 2002.

Closa, Carlos. "Spain: The Cortes and the EU—A Growing Together." In *National Parliaments and the European Union*, edited by Philip Norton. London: Frank Cass, 1996.

Closa, Carlos, and Paul M. Heywood. *Spain and the European Union*. New York: Palgrave Macmillan, 2004.

Coakley, John. "Irish Public Opinion and the New Europe." In *Ireland and the European Union: Nice, Enlargement and the Future of Europe*, edited by Michael Holmes, pp. 94–113. Manchester, UK: Manchester University Press, 2005.

"Coalition Agreement Between the CDU/CSU and the SPD" (Koalitionsvertrag zwischen der CDU, CSU und SPD). Berlin, November 11, 2005. Available at: http://www.lvz-online.de/download/dokus/051112_koalitionsvertrg.pdf.

Collins, Ken, and David Earnshaw. "The Implementation and Enforcement of European Community Environmental Legislation." In *A Green Dimension for the European Community: Political Issues and Processes*, edited by David Judge, London: Frank Cass, 1993.

Commissariat général du Plan, ed. *Organiser la politique européenne et internationale de la France*. Paris: Rapport du groupe présidé par l'admiral Jacques Lanxade, rapporteur général Nicolas Tenzer, 2002.

Commission of the European Communities. "Commission Decision 2001/542/EC, May 2000, replacing Decision 94/3/EC establishing a list of wastes pursuant to Article 1(a) of Council Directive 75/442/EEC on waste and Council Decision 94/904/EC establishing a list of hazardous waste pursuant to Article 1(4) of Council Directive 91/689/EEC on hazardous waste (notified under document umber C(2000) 1147." (2000/532/EC)2000/532/EC; amended by 2001/537/EC2001).

———. *Commission Decision of 16 January 2001 Amending Decision 2000/532/EC as regards the list of wastes (notified under document number C(2001) 108*. Brussels: 2001/118/EC, 2001.

———. *Directive on Acid Rain*. 80/779/EEC. Brussels: European Communities, 1980.

———. Annual Survey on the Implementation and Enforcement of Community Environmental Law." Brussels, 27.7.2004 SEC (2004) 1025. Luxembourg: Office for Official Publications of the European Communities, 2004.

———. *First Report on Economic and Social Cohesion—1996*. Luxembourg: Office for Official Publications of the European Communities, 1999.

———. Report from the Commission to the Stockholm European Council: Improving and Simplifying the Regulatory Environment." Brussels, March 7, 2001: COM (2001) 130 final. Available from: http://europa.eu.int/eur-lex/en/com/cnc/2001/com2001_0130en01.pdf (accessed January 2, 2006).

———. "Sixth Annual Survey on the Implementation and Enforcement of Community Environmental Law." Brussels, August 17, 2005, SEC(2005) 1055. European Union.

Cordell, Karl, and Andrzej Antoszewski, eds. *Poland and the European Union*. New York: Routledge, 2000.

COSAC. "Third Bi-Annual Report: Developments in European Union Procedures and Practices Relevant to Parliamentary Scrutiny. May 17–18, 2005, Luxembourg.

Cotta, Maurizio. "Élite, politiche nazionali e costruzione della polity europea. Il caso italiano in prospettiva comparata." In *L'Europa in Italia. Élite, opinione pubblica e decisioni*, edited by Maurizio Cotta, Pierangelo Isernia, and Luca Verzichelli, pp. 17–59. Bologna: Il Mulino, 2005.

Cotta, Maurizio, Pierangelo Isernia, and Luca Verzichelli. *L'Europa in Italia: Élite, opinione pubblica e decisioni*. Bologna: Il Mulino, 2005.

Council of the European Communities. "Council Directive 1999/31/EC of 26 April 1999 on the Landfill of Waste." *Official Journal of the European Communities*. Brussels, no. L182/1-19 (1999).

———. "Regulation (EC) No. 2037/2000 of the European Parliament and of the

Council on Substances That Deplete the Ozone Layer." *Official Journal of the European Communities*, no. L244 (September 29, 2000).

———. *Fifth Annual Survey on the Implementation and Enforcement of Community Environmental Law.* Luxembourg: Office for Official Publications of the European Communities, 2004.

Council of the European Union. "Conclusions of the Presidency, Brussels European Counci, 23–24 March 2005." *Bulletin of the European Union*, no. 3 (2005).

———. "Conclusions of the Presidency, Cannes European Council, 26–27 June 1995." *Bulletin of the European Union*, no. 6 (June 26–27, 1995).

———. "Conclusions of the Presidency, Copenhagen European Council, 12–13 December 2002, Annex II." *Bulletin of the European Union*, no. 12 (2002).

———. "Conclusions of the Presidency, Lisbon European Council, 23–24 March 2000." *Bulletin of the European Union*, no. 3 (March 23–24, 2000).

———. "Financial Perspective 2007–2013." Report No. 15915/05 CADREFIN 268. December 19, 2005. Brussels: European Union; available at: http://ue.eu.int/ueDocs/cms_Data/docs/pressData/en/misc/87677.pdf.

———. "Presidency Conclusions. December 10–11, 1999. Helsinki European Council." Available from: http://ue.eu.int/ueDocs/cms_Data/docs/pressData/en/ec/ACFA4C.htm (accessed December 21, 2005).

———. "EU Plan of Action on Combating Terrorism—Update," 9809/1/05, Rev 1, Add 2, Brussels, June 10, 2005.

Cowles, Maria Green, James A. Caporaso, and Thomas Risse, eds. *Transforming Europe: Europeanization and Domestic Change.* Ithaca, NY: Cornell University Press, 2001.

Cram, Laura. "Integration Theory and the Study of the European Policy Process." In *European Union: Power and Policy-Making*, edited by Jeremy J. Richardson, 2nd ed. New York: Routledge, 2001.

Cramér, Per. *Neutralitet och europeisk integration.* Uppl. 1st ed. Stockholm: Norstedts Juridik, 1998.

Crawford, Leslie. "Spain Will Allow Drop if EU Funds if UK Takes Rebate Cut." *Financial Times* (London), June 10, 2005.

Cyprus, Ministry of Finance. "Convergence Program of the Republic of Cyprus 2005–2009." Available from: http://europa.eu.int/comm/economy_finance/about/activities/sgp/scplist_en.htm, December 2005.

Czech Finance Ministry. "Prvni rok v Evropske unii—ekonomicky rust a rovnovaha." May 2, 2005.

Dachs, H. "EU-Beitritt und die Bundesländer." In *EU-Beitritt als Herausforderung*, edited by P. Gerlich and H. Neisser. Wien: Signum, 1994.

Dahl, A-S. *Svenskarna och NATO.* Stockholm: Nordstedts, 1999.

Damgaard, Erik. "Conclusion: The Impact of European Integration on Nordic Parliamentary Democracies." In *Delegation and Accountability in European Integration: The Nordic Parliamentary Democracies and the European Union*, edited by Torbjörn Bergman and Erik Damgaard, pp. 151–169. London: Frank Cass, 2000.

Damgaard, Erik, and Asbjørn Sonne Nørgaard. "Delegation and Accountability in European Integration: The Nordic Parliamentary Democracies and the

European Union." In *Delegation and Accountability in European Integration*, edited by Torbjörn Bergman and Erik Damgaard, pp. 33–58. London: Frank Cass, 2000.

———. "The European Union and Danish Parliamentary Democracy." In *Delegation and Accountability in European Integration*, edited by Torbjörn Bergman and Erik Damgaard, pp. 33–58. London: Frank Cass, 2000.

Della Cananea, G. "Italy." In *The National Co-ordination of EU Policy: The European Level*, edited by Hussein Kassim, Anand Menon, Guy Peters, and Vincent Wright, pp. 129–146. Oxford: Oxford University Press, 2001.

———. "Italy." In *The National Co-ordination of EU Policy: The Domestic Level*, edited by Hussein Kassim, Guy Peters, and Vincent Wright, pp. 99–113. Oxford: Oxford University Press, 2000.

Demirel, Suleyman, and Rauf Denktash. "Joint Statement." December 29, 1995. Available at: www.b-info.com/places/Turkey/news/95-12/dec29.tdn.

Denmark, Folketinget. *Political Agreement Regarding Denmark in the Enlarged EU*. Copenhagen: Folketingets EU-Oplysningen; unofficial translation, November 2. Available at: http://www.eu-oplysningen.dk/upload/application/ pdf/408864ff/PoliticalAgreementregardingDenmarkintheEnlargedEU. pdf (2004; accessed November 18, 2005).

———. "Beretning om reform af Foketingets bhandling af EU-sager" (Report on Reform of the Parliament's Handling of EU Matters). Copenhagen: Beretning afgivet af Europaudvalget den 10. December 2004.

Department for Environment, Food and Rural Affairs, UK. "Extra 40 Million to Help Local Authorities Dispose of Fridges." *DEFRA News Release*, no. 292/02, July 18, 2002.

Department of Defense, Sweden. "Försvar för en ny tid," available at http://www.regeringen.se/sb/d/108/a/24528, 2004.

Deubner, Christian. "Food for Thought in 'Leftovers': France, Germany, and the Coming IGC on Institutional Reform." In *Franco-German Relations and European Integration: A Transatlantic Dialogue Challenges for German and American Foreign Policy. Conference Report*, edited by Johns Hopkins University American Institute for Contemporary German Studies, pp. 1–14. Washington, DC: The American Institute for Contemporary German Studies, 1999.

———. *The Future of the Franco-German Relationship, Discussion Paper No. 7/1*. London: Royal Institute of International Affairs, 1997.

Deutsch, Karl Wolfgang. *Political Community and the North Atlantic Area: International Organization in the Light of Historical Experience*. New York: Greenwood Press, 1969.

Diedrichs, U., and Wolfgang Wessels. "Die erweiterte EU als internationaler." *Akteur Internationale Politik* 58, no. 1 (2003): 11–18.

Dinan, Desmond. *Ever Closer Union: An Introduction to European Integration*. 3rd ed. Boulder, CO: Lynne Rienner Publishers, 2005.

Di Palma, Giuseppe, Sergio Fabbrini, and Giorgio Freddi. *Condannata al successo?: l'Italia nell'Europa integrata*. Bologna: Il Mulino, 2000.

Dörfer, I. "Sixty Years of Solitude: Sweden Returns to Europe." *Scandinavian Studies* 46, no. 4 (1992): 594–606.

Duina, F. G. "Explaining Legal Implementation in the European Union." *International Journal of the Sociology of Community Law* 25, no. 2 (1997): 155–179.

Duina, F. G., and F. Blithe. "Nation States and Common Markets: The Institutional Conditions for Acceptance." *Review of International Political Economy* 6, no. 4 (1999): 494–530.

Dyson, K., and Kevin Featherstone. "'Vincolo Esterno': Empowering the Technocrats, Transforming the State." *South European Society and Politics* 1, no. 2 (1996): 272–299.

Dyson, Kenneth H. F., and Kevin Featherstone. *The Road to Maastricht: Negotiating Economic and Monetary Union.* Oxford: Oxford University Press, 1999.

Economic Intelligence Unit. 2005. "One Year On: The Impact of EU Enlargement." *The Economist.* Available from: http://www.ey.com/global/download.nsf/Belgium_E/One_year_on_the_impact_of_EU_enlargement/$file/One%20Year%20On%20Report%2004.pdf.

Economist, The. "In the Club." *The Economist*, December 2, 2000.

———. "From Vikings to Peacemongers: The Nordics Work Hard at Being the World's Conscience." *The Economist (Special: The Nordic Region)*, June 12, 2003.

———. "Krybbe to Grav." *The Economist*, June 14, 2003, pp. 8–14.

———. "Mix and Match: Is a Large Flow of Migrants a Good or Bad Thing?" *The Economist (Special: The Nordic Region)*, June 12, 2003.

Eilstrup-Sangiovanni, Mette, and Daniel Verdier. "European Integration as a Solution to War." *European Journal of International Relations* 11, no. 1 (February 2005): 99–135.

Einhorn, E. "Just Enough ('Lagom') Europeanization: The Nordic States and Europe." *Scandinavian Studies* 74, no. 3 (2002): 265–279.

Einhorn, Eric S., and John Logue. *Modern Welfare States: Scandinavian Politics and Policy in the Global Age.* Westport, CT: Praeger, 2003.

Elgström, Ole. "The Making of Swedish Neutrality." *Cooperation and Conflict* 35, no. 3 (2003): 243–268.

Eliason, Leslie. "Denmark: Small State with a Big Voice." In *The European Union and the Member States: Cooperation, Coordination, and Compromise*, edited by Eleanor E. Zeff and Ellen B. Pirro, pp. 191–214. Boulder, CO: Lynne Rienner Publishers, 2001.

Eliasson, J. "Traditions, Identity, and Security: The Legacy of Neutrality in Finnish and Swedish Security Policies in Light of European Integration." *European Integration Online Papers* 8, no. 6 (2004).

Ellison, David. "Entangling Fortunes: The EU, Central and Eastern Europe, and the Eastern Enlargement." Ph.D. Dissertation, University of California, Los Angeles, 2001.

———. "Politics and the Environment in Central Europe." Paper presented at 62nd Annual Meeting of the Midwestern Political Science Association, April 15–18, 2004, Chicago, Illinois.

———. "Weighting the Politics of the Environment in the New Europe." Paper presented at 30th European Studies Conference, October 6–8, 2005, Omaha, Nebraska.

Environmental Management and Law Association (EMLA). "Study on Measures Other than Criminal Ones in Cases Where Environmental Community Law Has Not Been Respected in a Few Candidate Countries: National Report Hungary." Report commissioned by DG Environment, Budapest, EMLA, 2004.

Environmental Service Association. "EC Regulation No 2037/2000 on Substances That Deplete the Ozone Layer." *ESA Briefings* (2004). Available at: http://www.esauk.org/work/briefings/fridge.asp.

———. "Government Inflicts Unnecessary Risk on Environment: So What's the Point of DEFRA?" *ESA Press Statements* (March 25, 2004).

EU Business. "Almost a Quarter of Irish Face Risk of Poverty: EU Survey." 2005. Available from: http://www.eubusiness.com/Social/050124152031.4om0jho5 (accessed January 7, 2006).

European Centre for Parliamentary Research and Documentation (ECPRD). *European Affairs Committees: The Influence of National Parliaments on European Policies, an Overview.* Brussels: ECPRD, 2002.

European Commission. COM 2004(443) final. Brussels: European Union, 2004.

———. COM 2005(359). August 3. Brussels: European Union, 2005.

———. *21st Annual Report on Monitoring the Application of Community Law.* Brussels: European Union, 2003.

———. "Allocation of EU Expenditure by Member State 2004." Available at: www.europa.eu.int/comm/budget/agenda2000/reports_en.htm (accessed September 2005).

———. "Commission Opinion on the Application of the Republic of Cyprus." COM (93) 313 final 30.06.1993. Brussels: European Union, 1993.

———. "Commission's Opinion on Malta's Application for Membership." COM (93) 312 final 30.06.1993. Brussels: European Union, 1993.

———. "Communication from the Commission to the Council and the European Parliament: Recommendation of the European Commission on Turkey's Progress Towards Accession." COM 656 final. 6.10.2004. Brussels: European Union, 2004.

———. Copenhagen Criteria. In "Introduction"; available at: http://europa.eu.int/comm/enlargement/intro/criteria.htm (accessed July 2005).

———. *The Future of Cohesion Policy.* Brussels: European Union, 2003.

———. "Economic Forecasts, European Economy." Autumn, 2005. Brussels: European Union. Available from: http://www.europa.eu.int/comm/economy_finance/publications/european_economy/2005/ee505en.pdf.

———. Eurobarometer 62: "Public Opinion in the European Union National Report, Executive Summary Denmark." Autumn, 2004. European Union. Available from http://europa.eu.int/comm/public_opinion/archives/eb/eb62/eb62_dk_exec.pdf.

———. Eurobarometer 63.4: "Public Opinion in the European Union. National Report: Netherlands." Spring, 2005. Brussels: European Union. Available at: http://europa.eu.int/comm/public_opinion/archives/eb/eb63/eb63_nat_nl.pdf.

———. Eurobarometer 63.4: "Public Opinion in the European Union. National Report: Denmark." July 2005. Brussels: European Union.

———. Eurobarometer 64: "Public Opinion in the European Union." December 2005. Brussels: European Union. Available at: http://europa.eu.int/comm/public_opinion/archives/eb/eb64/eb64_first_en.pdf.

———. Eurobarometer 62: "Public Opinion in the European Union. Report No. 62." Brussels: European Union, 2004.

———. Eurobarometer 61: "Public Opinion in the European Union." July 2004.

———. Eurobarometer 54: "Public Opinion in the European Union." Report no. 54 (April 2001).

———. Eurobarometer, special issue: "The Attitudes of European Citizens Towards Environment," Brussels, April 2005.

———. Flash Eurobarometer. *The European Constitution: Post-Referendum Survey in the Netherlands* (June 2005). Available at: http://europa.eu.int/comm/public_opinion/flash/fl172_en.pdf.

———. "Fifteenth Annual Report on Monitoring the Application of Community Law–1997." *Official Journal of the European Communities* 41, no. C250 (August 10, 1998).

———. DG Internal Market and Services. "Internal Market Scoreboard," Commission Staff Working Paper, no. 13.

———. DG Internal Market and Services. "Internal Market Scoreboard." Press Release, January 12, 2004.

———. DG Internal Market and Services. "Internal Market Scoreboard." Staff Report no. 14. July 2005.

———. "Regular Report on Turkey's Progress Towards Accession." SEC (2004) 1201. Brussels: European Union, 2004.

———. "Second Implementation Report on the Internal Market Strategy, 2003–2006" (Brussels: European Commission, 2005).

———. "Structural Funds in Greece in 2000–2006." Available at http://Europa.eu.int/comm/regional_policy/country/overmap/gr/grec_en.htm.

———. "The Share of Renewable Energy in the EU." COM 366 final. Brussels: European Union, 2004.

———. "Technical Mission to Lybia on Illegal Immigration 27 November to 6 December 2004." Available from http://www.statewatch.org/news/2005/may/eu-report-libya-ill-imm.pdf.

———. Secretariat General. "Situation of the Notification of National Measures of Implementing the Directives." July 11, 2005.

European Court of Justice. *Judgment of the Court (Third Chamber) of 16 October 2003: Commission of the European Communities v United Kingdom of Great Britain and Northern Ireland. Failure of a Member State to Fulfill Its Obligation–Environment–Landfill of Waste–Directive 1999/31/EC.* Luxembourg: European Court reports, 2003, page I-12181, 2003.

European Environmental Agency. "Greenhouse Gas Emission Trends and Projection in Europe 2005." EEA-Report No. 8/2005. Luxembourg, Office for Official Publication of the European Communities, 2005.

Eurostat. various releases. "Euro-Indicators." Available at: http://epp.eurostat.cec.eu.int/portal/page?_pageid=0,1136173,0_45570698&_dad=portal&_schema=PORTAL.

————. *Regions: Statistical Year Book—2005*. Luxembourg: Eurostat, 2005.

Fabbrini, Sergio, ed. *L'europeizzazione dell'Italia: l'impatto dell'Unione Europea sulle istituzioni e le politiche italiane*. Rome: Laterza, 2003.

Fabbrini, Sergio, and Simona Piattoni. "Introduction: Italy in the EU—Pigmy or Giant?" *Modern Italy* 9, no. 2 (November 2004): 149–157.

Falkner, Gerda. "How Pervasive Are Euro-Politics? Effects of EU Membership on a New Member State." *Journal of Common Market Studies* 38, no. 2 (2000): 223–250.

————. "Zur 'Europäisierung' des österreichischen politischen Systems." In *Handbuch des politischen Systems Österreichs*, edited by P. Gerlich, H. Dachs, and F. H. Gottweis, pp. 51–63. Wien: Manzsche Verlags/Universitätsbuchhandlung, 2005.

Falkner, Gerda, Miriam Hartlapp, Simone Leiber, and Oliver Treib. "Non-Compliance with EU Directives in the Member States: Opposition Through the Backdoor?" *West European Politics* 27, no. 3 (May 2004): 452–473.

Falkner, Gerda, and Brigid Laffan. "The Europeanization of Austria and Ireland: Small Is Difficult?" In *Member States and the European Union*, edited by Simon Bulmer and Christian Lequesne, pp. 209–228. Oxford: Oxford University Press, 2005.

Falkner, Gerda, and W. C. Müller, eds. *Österreich im europäischen Mehrebenensystem: Konsequenzen der EU-Mitgliedschaft für Politiknetzwerke und Entscheidungsprozesse*. Wien: Signum, 1998.

Falkner, Gerda, Oliver Treib, Miriam Hartlapp, and Simone Leiber. *Complying with Europe: EU Harmonisation and Soft Law in the Member States*. Cambridge: Cambridge University Press, 2005.

Fargion, G., L. Morlino, and S. Profeti, eds. *Europeizzazione e rappresentanza territoriale*. Bologna: Il Mulino, 2005.

Ferrera, M. "Italia: aspirazioni e vincoli del 'quarto grande'." In *Le dodici Europe*, edited by M. Ferrera, pp. 73–93. Bologna: Il Mulino, 1991.

Ferrera, Maurizio, and Elisabetta Gualmini. *Rescued by Europe? Social and Labour Market Reforms in Italy from Maastricht to Berlusconi—Changing Welfare States*. Amsterdam: Amsterdam University Press, 2004.

Fink-Hafner, Danica. "Slovenia." *European Journal of Political Research* 43 (2004): 1130–1137.

Finnegan, Richard B., and James L. Wiles. "The Invisible Hand or Hands Across the Water? American Consultants and Irish Economic Policy." *Eire Ireland* 30, no. 2 (summer 1995).

Fisher, Sharon. "Czech Economy Presents Mixed Picture." *RFE/RL Research Report* 3, no. 29 (July 22, 1994).

FitzGerald, Garret. *Reflections on the Irish State*. Dublin and Portland, OR: Irish Academic Press, 2003.

Fleischer, Tamás. *Considerations on Road Transport Networks Crossing Hungary*. Budapest: Institute for World Economics, 2002.

Forskningsgruppen för Samhälls–och Informationsstudier. "Opionen kring EU, EMU och vissa militära allianser" (Opinions on EU, EMU and Certain Military Alliances). June 22, 2001.

Francioni, Francesco. *Italy and EC Membership Evaluated*. London: Pinter Publications, 1992.

Franck, Christian, Hervé Leclercq, and Claire Vandevievere. "Belgium: Europeanisation and Belgian Federalism." In *Fifteen into One? The European Union and Its Member States*, edited by Wolfgang Wessels, Andreas Maurer, and Jürgen Mittag. New York: Palgrave Macmillan, 2003.

Frangakis, Nicos. "Law Harmonization." In *Greece and EC Membership Evaluated*, edited by Panos V. Kazakos and P. C. Ioakimidis, pp. 181–186. New York: St. Martin's, 1994.

Friedman, Thomas L. *The World Is Flat: A Brief History of the Twenty-First Century*. 1st ed. New York: Farrar, Straus, and Giroux, 2005.

Friends of the Earth. "Industry Unprepared for New EU Law on Toxic Waste." Press Release, July 15, 2004.

Friis, Lykke. "The 2002 Danish Presidency—A Two-Thirds Presidency?" In *Danish Foreign Policy Yearbook 2002*, edited by Bertel Heurlin and Hans Mouritzen, pp. 46–64. Copenhagen: Danish Institute for International Studies, 2002.

Friis, Lykke, and Anna Murphy. "The European Union and Central and Eastern Europe: Governance and Boundaries." *Journal of Common Market Studies* 37, no. 2 (1999): 211–232.

Gallup, Ugens. Poll No. 6, 2005. Available from: http://www.gallup.dk/ugens_gallup/pdf_doc/ug_06_05.pdf (accessed July 6, 2005).

Garganas, Nikolas C. "Greece and EMU: Prospects and Challenges." In *Contemporary Greece and Europe,* edited by Achilleas Mitsos and Elias Mossialos, pp. 115–129, Burlington, VT: Ashgate, 2000.

Geddes, Andrew. *The European Union and British Politics*. Basingstoke, UK: Palgrave Macmillan, 2004.

George, Nicholas. "Finn Gives Voice to the Fears of EU's Small States." *Financial Times*, September 9, 2003, p. 8.

Giannakourou, Georgia. "The Implementation of EU Environmental Policy in Greece: Europeanization and the Mechanisms of Change." In *Greece in the European Union*, edited by Dionyssis G. Dimitrakopoulos and Argyris Passas, pp. 67–82. New York: Routledge, 2004.

Gille, Zsuzsa. "Europeanizing Hungarian Waste Policies: Progress or Regression?" *Environmental Politics* 13, no. 1 (2004): 114–134.

———. "Legacy of Waste or Wasted Legacy? The End of Industrial Ecology in Post-Socialist Hungary." *Environmental Politics* 9, no. 1 (2000): 203–230.

Giuliani, Marco. *La politica europea*. Bologna: Il Mulino, 2006.

Giuliani, Marco, and Simona Piattoni. "Italy: Both Leader and Laggard." In *The European Union and the Member States: Cooperation, Coordination, and Compromise*, edited by Eleanor E. Zeff and Ellen B. Pirro, pp. 115–142. Boulder, CO: Lynne Rienner Publishers, 2001.

Glachant, Matthieu. *Lessons from Implementation Studies: The Need for Adaptability in EU Environmental Policy Design and Implementation*. Paris: Centre for Industrial Economics at the Ecole des Mines de Paris [CERNA], 2000.

Goetz, Klaus H. "European Integration and National Executives: A Cause in Search of an Effect?" *West European Politics* 23, no. 4 (October 2000): 211–231.

Gögös, Zoltán. "Javaslat a megújuló energiaforrasók elterjesztésére." Unpublished presentation, 2005.

Government of Denmark. *Denmark and Europe: Enlargement, Globalization, Legitimacy.* White Paper, Danish Foreign Ministry, unofficial translation, August 2001.

Government of the United Kingdom. *Prospects for the EU in 2005.* White Paper. London: Stationery Office Ltd., 2005. Available from: http://www.fco.gov.uk/Files/kfile/White%20Paper%20Cmnd%206450.pdf (accessed January 3, 2006).

Grabbe, Heather. "How Does Europeanization Affect CEE Governance? Conditionality, Diffusion, and Diversity." *Journal of European Public Policy* 8, no. 6 (2001): 1013–1031.

Granell, Francisco. "Europe's Evolving Economic Identity: Spain's Role." In *Spain: The European and International Challenges*, edited by Richard Gillespie and Richard Youngs. London: Frank Cass, 2001.

———. "La Contribución Española al Nacimiento del Euro." In *Anales de los Cursos Académicos: Curso 2000–2001*, edited by Real Academia de Ciencias Económicas y Financieras. Barcelona, Spain: RACEF, 2004.

Graziano, Paolo. *Europeizzazione e politiche pubbliche italiane: coesione e lavoro a confronto.* Bologna: Il Mulino, 2004.

———. "La nuova politica regionale italiana: il ruolo dell'europeizzazione." In *L'europeizzazione dell'Italia: l'impatto dell'Unione Europea sulle istituzioni e le politiche italiane*, edited by Sergio Fabbrini, pp. 55–79. Rome: Laterza, 2003.

Greek Ministry of Foreign Affairs. "The Course of Greece in European Union." Available at: www.mfa.gr/english/foreign_policy/eu/eu_future/convention.html (accessed December 16, 2004).

———. "The Five Strategic Objectives of Greece in the Convention for the 'Future of Europe.'" Available at: www.mfa.gr/english/foreign_policy/eu/eu_future/convention.html (accessed December 16, 2004).

———. "General Overview." Available at: www.mfa.gr/english/foreign_policy/eu/greece/general.html (accessed December 16, 2004).

Grugle, Jean. "Spain: Latin America as an Ambitious Topic." In *Synergy at Work: Spain and Portugal in European Foreign Policy*, edited by Franco Algieri and Elfriede Regelsberger, pp. 73–90. Bonn: Europa Union Verlag, 1996.

Gualini, Enrico. *Multi-Level Governance and Institutional Change: The Europeanization of Regional Policy in Italy.* Aldershot, UK: Ashgate, 2004.

Guillén, Mauro F. *The Rise of Spanish Multinationals: European Business in the Global Economy.* New York: Cambridge University Press, 2005.

Gustavsson, J. *The Politics of Foreign Policy Change, Explaining the Swedish Reorientation on EC Membership.* Lund: Lund University Press, 1998.

Haas, Ernst. "The Uniting of Europe." In *The European Union Readings on the Theory and Practice of European Integration*, 3rd ed., edited by Brent Nelson and Alexander Stuff, pp. 145–149. Boulder, CO: Lynne Rienner Publishers, 2003.

Hancock, M. Donald. "Sweden." In *Politics in Europe: An Introduction to the Politics of the United Kingdom, France, Germany, Italy, Sweden, Russia, and the European Union*, 2nd ed., edited by M. Donald Hancock, pp. 347–401. New York: Chatham House Publishers, 2003.

Hanf, Kenneth, and Ben Soetendorp, eds. *Adapting to European Integration: Small States and the European Union.* New York: Longman, 1997.

Harper, Krista. 2001. "Encounters with Wild Capitalism: Post-Socialist Environmentalism in Hungary," summary of presentation at Woodrow Wilson Center, Washington, DC.

Harris, E. "Europeanization of Slovakia." *Comparative European Politics* 2 (2004): 185–211.

Havel, Vaclav. "L'indécent hommage à Fidel Castro." *Le Figaro*, January 28, 2005.

Haynes-Renshaw, Fiona, and Helen Wallace. *The Council of Ministers.* 2nd ed. New York: Palgrave Macmillan, 2005.

Hazardous Waste Forum. *Hazardous Waste—An Action Plan for Its Reduction and Environmentally Sound Management.* London: Stationery Office Ltd., 2004.

Hederstedt, J. 2000. "Internationalisera Forsvaret!" ISBN 91-973320-0-4. Defense Department Publication (Swedish Commander in Chief, writing in personal capacity).

Heilemann, Ullrich, and Hermann Rappen. "The Seven Year Itch? German Unity from a Fiscal Viewpoint." Economic Studies Program. Report No. 6, 1997. American Institute for Contemporary German Studies at the Johns Hopkins University. Available from: http://www.aicgs.org/Publications/PDF/sevenyearitch.pdf (accessed January 2, 2006).

Heinisch, Reinhard. "Austria: Confronting Controversy." In *The European Union and the Member States,* 1st ed., edited by Eleanor E. Zeff and Ellen B. Pirro, pp. 267–284. Boulder, CO: Lynne Rienner Publishers, 2001.

Hellermann, Gunther, Rainer Baumann, Monika Bösche, and Benjamin Herborth. "De-Europeanization by Default? Germany's EU Policy in Defense and Asylum." *Foreign Policy Analysis* 1, no. 1 (March 2005): 143–164.

Henderson, Karen, ed. *Back to Europe: Central and Eastern Europe and the European Union.* Philadelphia: UCL Press, 1999.

Héretier, A. "The Accommodation of Diversity in European Policy-Making and Its Outcomes: Regulatory Policy as a Patchwork." *Journal of European Public Policy* 3, no. 1 (1996): 149–176.

Hix, Simon. *The Political System of the European Union.* 2nd ed. Basingstoke, UK: Palgrave Macmillan, 2005.

Hlepas, Nicos. *Local Government in Greece.* Athens: Papazisis, 1999.

Holmstöm, Mikael. "Alliansfriheten-livboj eller kvarnsten? Centralförbundet Folk och Försvar." *Försvar i Nutid* 4 (2000).

Holt, Ed. "The Vanishing." *Times Educational Supplement*, April 30, 2004.

Holzinger, Katharina, and Christoph Knill. "Causes and Conditions of Cross-National Policy Convergence." *Journal of European Public Policy* 12, no. 5 (October 2005): 775–796.

Hooghe, Liesbet. "Belgium: Hollowing the Center." In *Federalism and Territorial Cleavages*, edited by Ugo M. Amoretti and Nancy Gina Bermeo. Baltimore: Johns Hopkins University Press, 2004.

Hooghe, Liesbet, and Gary Marks. *Multi-Level Governance and European Integration*. Lanham, MD: Rowman & Littlefield Publishers, 2001.

Hope, Kerin. "Regional Progress Masks Uncertainty." *Financial Times (Special Report: Greece)*, June 21, 2005, p. 2.

———. "Tough Measures Are Necessary to Restore Credibility." *Financial Times (Special Report: Greece)*, June 21, 2005, p. 2.

House of Commons. *Environment Act*. London: Stationery Office, Ltd., 1995.

———. *Hansard Debates 29539: Col 413*. London: Hansard Society, 2002.

House of Commons, Environment, Food, and Rural Affairs Committee. "Disposal of Refrigerators: The Governments Reply to the Committee's Fourth Report of Session 2001–02." Report No. 12, Special Report of Session 2001–2002. London: Stationery Office Ltd.

Hughes, James, and Gwendolyn Sasse. "Monitoring the Monitors: EU Enlargement Conditionality and Minority Protection in the CEECs." *Journal of Ethnopolitics and Minority Issues in Europe*, no. 1 (2003): 1–38. Available at: http://www.ecmi.de/jemie/download/Focus1-2003_Hughes_Sasse.pdf.

Hungarian Energy Office. "A Magyar Energia Hivatal 2003. évi tevékenységéröl." Hungarian Energy Office 2003 Activity Report. Budapest: Hungarian Engergy Office.

Iankova, Elena A., and Peter J. Katzenstein. "European Enlargement and Institutional Hypocracy." In *The State of the European Union*, edited by Tanja A. Börzel and Rachel A. Cichowski. Burlington, VT: Ashgate, 2003.

IGC 96 Task Force—European Commission. *Ireland: Challenges and Opportunities Abroad*. Irish white paper on foreign policy, March 26, 1996.

"Immigration: Initiative conjointe franco-espagnole auprès de l'Union européenne." *Fenêtre sur l'Europe*, October 18, 2005. Available at: http://www.fenetreeurope.com/php/page.php?section=actu&id=4717.

Ingebritsen, Christine. "Coming out of the Cold: Nordic Response to European Union." In *Europe's Ambiguous Unity: Conflict and Consensus in the Post-Maastricht Era*, edited by Alan Cafruny and Carl Lankowski, pp. 329–356. Boulder, CO: Lynne Rienner Publishers, 1997.

———. *The Nordic States and European Unity*. Cornell Studies in Political Economy. Ithaca, NY: Cornell University Press, 1998.

———. "The Scandinavian Way and Its Legacy in Europe." *Scandinavian Studies* 74, no. 3 (2002): 255–265.

Inglis, Kirstyn. "Enlargement and the Environment Acquis." *Review of Community and International Environmental Law* 13, no. 2 (2004): 135–151.

International Iron and Steel Institute (IIIS). *Steel Statistical Yearbook 2004*. Brussels: Committee on Economic Studies, 2004.

Ioakimidis, Panagiotis C. "The Europeanization of Greece's Foreign Policy: Progress and Problems." In *Mossialos*, edited by Achilleas Mitsos, pp. 359–373. Burlington, VT: Ashgate, 2000.

Ireland. Department of Foreign Affairs. *Challenges and Opportunities Abroad: White Paper on Foreign Policy*. Dublin: Government Stationery Office, 1996.

Jacobsson, B., Per Laegreid, and Ove K. Pedersen. *Europeanization and Transnational States: Comparing Nordic Central Governments.* London: Routledge, 2004.

Jakobson, Max. "Sverige Övervärderar sin roll." *Dagens Nyheter,* January 10, 1999.

Johnson-Theutenberg, B. "Bara Nato räddar Sverige." *Dagens Nyheter,* March 21, 2001.

Jones, Erik. "The Benelux Countries: Identity and Self-Interest." In *The Member States of the European Union,* edited by Simon Bulmer and Christian Lequesne. Oxford: Oxford University Press, 2005.

Jones, Rachel. *Beyond the Spanish State: Central Government, Domestic Actors and the EU.* New York: Palgrave, 2000.

Jörberg, Lennart. "The Industrial Revolution in the Nordic Countries." In *The Fontana Economic History of Europe: The Emergence of Industrial Societies,* Part II, edited by Carlo M. Cipola, pp. 375–485. Glasgow: Collins, 1973.

Jörberg, Lennart, and Olle Krantz. "Scandinavia 1914–1970." In *The Fontana Economic History of Europe: Contemporary Economies,* Part II, edited by Carlo M. Cipola, pp. 377–459. Glasgow: Collins, 1976.

Jubulis, Mark A. *Nationalism and Democratic Transition: The Politics of Citizenship and Language in Post-Soviet Latvia.* Lanham, MD: University Press of America, 2001.

Kaderják, Péter, and Zsuzsa Lehoczki. "The Cost of Alternative Policies to Reduce SO_2 Emission in Hungary: A Case for the Power Sector." In *Economics for Environmental Policy in Transition Economies: An Analysis of the Hungarian Experience,* edited by Péter Kaderják, pp. 110–130. Cheltenham: Edward Elgar, 1997.

Kalab, Vladimir. "Dopravci hresi a nevedi o tom." *Hospodarske Noviny,* July 1, 2004.

Kalaitzidis, Archimidis. "Does Regionalism Undermine the State? Lessons from Ireland and Greece." Ph.D. Dissertation, Temple University, 2004.

Karlhofer, F., and E. Tálos. *Sozialpartnerschaft und EU. Integrationsdynamik und Handlungsrahmen der österreichischen Sozialpartnerschaft.* Wien: Signum, 1996.

———, eds. *Zukunft der Sozialpartnerschaft: Veränderungsdynamik und Reformbedarf.* Wien: Signum, 1999.

Kassim, Hussein. "The European Administration: Between Europeanization and Domestication." In *Governing Europe,* edited by Jack Ernest Shalom Hayward and Anand Menon. Oxford: Oxford University Press, 2003.

Kasule, Kole. "Washington Overrules Greece, Recognizes FYROM as Macedonia." *Hellenic News of America,* November 2004, p. 4.

Kathimerini. "Athens Examines Brussels Fallout." *Kathimerini* (in English), June 21, 2005. Available at: www.kathimerini.com/4dcgi/news/content .asp?aid=57691,(accessed October 8, 2005).

Katztenstein, Peter J. "Sonderbare Sonderwege: Germany and 9/11." AICGS/German-American Dialogue Working Paper Series: A publication of the American Institute for Contemporary German Studies (Johns Hopkins University), Washington, DC, 2002. Available at: http://www.aicgs.org/documents/katzenstein.pdf.

Kazai, Zsolt. *Renewable Energy Sources: Achievements and Barriers in Hungary.* Budapest: EnergiaKlub, 2005.

Kazana, Mariusz. "The Role of Poland in Creation of the Eastern Dimension." In *Eastern Dimension of the European Union,* edited by Monika Zamarlik, pp. 61–66. Krakow: Instytut Studiów Strategicznych, 2004.

Keatinge, Patrick. "Security Policy." In *Ireland and EC Membership Evaluated,* edited by Patrick Keatinge, pp. 151–167. New York: St. Martin's Press, 1991.

Keatinge, Patrick, and Brigid Laffan. "Ireland: A Small Open Polity." In *Politics in the Republic of Ireland,* 3rd ed., pp. 320–349. New York: Routledge, 1999.

Kelley, Judith. "International Actors—Domestic Effects: Explaining Ethnic Politics in Europe." Terry Sanford Institute of Public Policy. Working Paper Series, no. SAN03-01 (2003). Available from: http://www-pps.aas.duke.edu/people/faculty/kelley/san03-01.pdf.

———. *Ethnic Politics in Europe: The Power of Norms and Incentives.* Princeton, NJ: Princeton University Press, 2004.

Keohane, Robert O., and Joseph S. Nye Jr. "Globalization: What's New? What's Not? (And So What?)." *Foreign Policy,* no. 118 (spring 2000): 104–119.

Kerekes, Sandor. "Economics, Technology, and Environment in Hungary." *Technology in Society* 15 (1993): 137–147.

Kinnunen, Jussi. "14,000 Complaints, Farmers on Hunger Strike and Flying Squirrels: Implementation of the Habitats Directive in Finland," 2004. Available at: http://www.oeue.net/.

———. "Finland: A Highly Institutionalized System," 2004. Available at: http://www.oeue.net/.

Kirby, D. G. *The Baltic World, 1772–1993: Europe's Northern Periphery in an Age of Change.* New York: Longman, 1995.

Kiss, Károly. "EU Accession, Transport and the Environment: Summary and Recommendations." Budapest, Hungary: Clear Air Action Group, 2002.

Klaus, Vaclav. "Vytvorme jinou Evropskou unii." *Lidove Noviny,* July 16, 2005.

Knill, Christoph, and Andrea Lenschow. "Coping with Europe: The Impact of British and German Administrations on the Implementation of EU Environmental Policy." *Journal of European Public Policy* 5, no. 4 (December 1998): 595–614.

———. *Implementing EU Environmental Policy: New Directions and Old Problems.* Issues in Environmental Politics. Manchester, UK and New York: Manchester University Press, 2000.

Kofos, Euangelos. *Nationalism and Communism in Macedonia: Civil Conflict, Politics of Mutation, National Identity,* vol. 12, *Hellenism—Ancient, Mediaeval, Modern.* New Rochelle, NY: A. D. Caratzas, 1993.

Kofos, Euangelos, and Vlasis Vlassidis, eds. *Athens-Skopje: The Seven-Year Symbiosis (1995–2002).* Athens, Greece: Papazisis, 2003.

Kohli, Atul, Peter Evans, Peter J. Katzenstein, Adam Przeworski, Susanne Hoeber Rudolph, James C. Scott, and Theda Skocpol. "The Role of Theory in Comparative Politics: A Symposium." *World Politics* 48, no. 1 (October 1995): 1–49.

Komarek, Martin. "Klaus a Evropa: proc tolik nenavisti?" *Mlada fronta Dnes*, March 19, 2005.

Kopecky, Petr. "An Awkward Newcomer? EU Enlargement and Euroskepticism in the Czech Republic." *European Studies* 20 (2004).

Kopecky, Petr, and Joop Van Holsteyn. "The Grass Is Always Greener . . . : Mass Attitudes Towards the European Union in the Czech and Slovak Republics." Paper presented at Public Opinion About the EU in East-Central Europe, April 2–3, 2003, at University of Indiana, Bloomington.

Kraamwinkel, Margriet. *Pensioen, emancipatie en gelijke behandeling*. Utrecht: Fed, 1995.

Kuzio, Taras. "Poland Plays Strategic Role in Ukraine's Orange Revolution." *Eurasia Daily Monitor* 1, no. 144 (2004).

Laar, Mart. "New Members Will Make the EU More Competitive." *European Affairs* 4, no. 3 (summer–fall 2003).

Labohm, Hans H. J. *Evaluation of the Netherlands EU Presidency*. Clingendael, The Hague: Working paper at the Institute of International Relations, 2004.

Ladrech, Robert. "Europeanization of Domestic Politics and Institutions: The Case of France." *Journal of Common Market Studies* 32, no. 1 (March 1994): 69–88.

Laffan, Brigid. "Ireland's Management of EU Business: The Impact of Nice." In *Ireland and the European Union: Nice, Enlargement and the Future of Europe*, edited by Michael Holmes, pp. 171–188. Manchester, UK: Manchester University Press, 2005.

———. "Ireland: A Region Without Regions—Odd Man Out." In *Cohesion Policy and European Integration: Building Multi-Level Governance*, edited by Liesbet Hooghe. Oxford: Oxford University Press, 1996.

———. "Ireland: Modernization via Europeanization." In *Fifteen into One? The European Union and Its Member States*, edited by Wolfgang Wessels, Andreas Maurer, and Jürgen Mittag. New York: Palgrave Macmillan, 2003.

———. "Managing Europe." In *Political Issues in Ireland Today*, edited by Neil Collins, pp. 46–57. Manchester, UK: Manchester University Press, 1994.

———. "The Politics of Identity and Political Order in Europe." *Journal of Common Market Studies* 34, no. 1 (March 1996): 81–102.

Laffan, Brigid, and Rory O'Donnell. "Ireland and the Growth of International Governance." In *Ireland and Politics of Change*, edited by William J. Crotty and David E. Schmitt, pp. 156–177. New York: Longman, 1998.

Laffan, Brigid, and Ben Tonra. "Europe and the International Dimension." In *Politics in the Republic of Ireland*, 4th ed., edited by John Coakley and Michael Gallagher, pp. 430–461. New York: Longman, 2005.

Laitner, Sarah. "Germany and Spain Face Action on Opening of Energy Markets." *Financial Times* (London), March 14, 2005.

Landstingsorganizationen. "Hur arbetar LO I EU? [How Does LO Work in the EU?]," 2004. Available at: http://www.lo.se/home/lo/home.nsf/unidView/6CCB7FAE92ECAF82C1256E4D0034EA56 (accessed April 23, 2005).

Lankowski, Carl. "Fraying at the Edge: Modell Deutschland Agonistes." Paper presented at the 9th Biennial Conference of the European Union Studies Association, March, 2005, Austin, Texas.

Larsson, T. "Framtida Konfliktscenarier." *Royal Swedish Academy of War Science* 1 (1999): 3–43.

Laskowska, Marzena. "The Parliamentary European Legislation Committee in the Approximation of Laws Procedure." In *Poland's Way to the European Union: Legal Aspects*, edited by Wladyslaw Czaplinski, pp. 69–81. Warsaw: SCOLAR Publishing House.

Lawler, Peter. "Scandinavian Exceptionalism and European Union." *Journal of Common Market Studies* 35, no. 4 (1997): 565–594.

Leibfried, Stephan." Der Einfluss Europas auf die Reformschienen in den Nationalen Wohifahrts—Welten." In *Politische Akademie der Friedrich–Ebert-Stiftung, Soziale Demokratie in Europa*, pp. 59–81. Berlin: Politische Akademie der Friedrich–Ebert-Stiftung, 2005.

Letter of Intent. 2000. "Framework Agreement Between the French Republic, the Federal Republic of Germany, the Italian Republic, the Kingdom of Spain, the Kingdom of Sweden and the United Kingdom of Great Britain and Northern Ireland Concerning Measures to Facilitate the Restructuring and Operation of the European Defence Industry." Available from: http://projects.sipri.se/expcon/loi/indrest02.htm.

Lichbach, Mark Irving. "Social Theory and Comparative Politics." In *Comparative Politics: Rationality, Culture, and Structure*, edited by Mark Irving Lichbach and Alan S. Zuckerman, pp. 239–276. Cambridge: Cambridge University Press, 1997.

Lichbach, Mark Irving, and Alan S. Zuckerman, eds. *Comparative Politics: Rationality, Culture, and Structure*. Cambridge: Cambridge University Press, 1997.

Lieven, Anatol. *The Baltic Revolution: Estonia, Latvia, Lithuania, and the Path to Independence*. New Haven, CT: Yale University Press, 1993.

Lindberg, Leon N. *The Political Dynamics of European Economic Integration*. Stanford, CA: Stanford University Press, 1963.

Lindberg, Leon N., and Stuart A. Scheingold. *Europe's Would-Be Polity: Patterns of Change in the European Community*. Englewood Cliffs, NJ: Prentice-Hall, 1970.

Lindblom, Charles. "The Science of 'Muddling Through'." *Public Administration Review* 19, no. 2 (1959): 79–88.

Lindh, A. (Foreign Minister). "Swedish Foreign and Security Policy in a New Europe." Speech at the National Conference of the Central Defense and Society Federation, January 24, 2001. Available at: www.cff.se/riks/2001/prog2001.html.

Lippert, Barbara. "European Politics of the Red-Green Government: Deepening and Widening Continued." In *Germany on the Road to "Normalcy": Policies and Politics of the Red-Green Federal Government (1998–2002)*, edited by Werner Reutter, pp. 234–252. New York: Palgrave MacMillan, 2004.

Lippert, Barbara, Gaby Umbach, and Wolfgang Wessels. "Europeanization of CEE Executives: EU Membership Negotiations as a Shaping Power." *Journal of European Public Policy* 8, no. 6 (2001): 980–1012.

Loedel, Peter. "Is There Room at the Table? The ECB, Enlargement, and the Stability Pact." Paper presented at Conference on European Union

Enlargement, 2003, at the Institute on Global Conflict and Cooperation, University of California, San Diego.

Luif, P. "Österreich in der Europäischen Union." In *Handbuch des politischen Systems Österreichs*, edited by P. Gerlich, H. Dachs, and F. H. Gottweis. Wien: Manzsche Verlags/ Universitätsbuchhandlung, 2005.

———. "Austria: The Burdens of History." In *Small States in World Politics: Explaining Foreign Policy Behavior*, edited by Jeanne A. K. Hey, pp. 95–115. Boulder, CO: Lynne Rienner Publishers, 2003.

Lukács, András. 2003. "Are Motorways Good for the Hungarian Economy?" Budapest: Clean Air Action Group.

Lynch, Diahanna. "Closing the Deception Gap: Accession to the European Union and Environmental Standards in East-Central Europe." *Journal of Environment and Development* 9, no. 4 (2000): 426–437.

Machacek, Jan. "Sobotka a Slovaci." *Mlada fronta Dnes*, September 23, 2003.

———. "Spidla vystupuje jako exot." *Hospodarske Noviny*, May 5, 2004.

Macris, Nicolas D., Andrea Petranyi, and Alexandros Macris, eds. *The 1960 Treaties on Cyprus and Selected Subsequent Acts*. Mannheim: Bibliopolis, 2003.

Madsen, Christian. "Fullfölj Tankarna," *Folk och Forsvar*, available at http://www.aff.s.se/vf91-08.htm.

Malova, Darina, and Tim Haughton. "Challenge for the Pace-Setting Periphery: The Causes and Consequences of Slovakia's Stance on Further European Integration." In *Après Enlargement: Taking Stock of the Immediate Legal and Political Responses to the Accession of Central and Eastern European States to the EU*, edited by Wojciech Sadurski et al. Florence: Robert Schuman Center, 2005.

Malta Labor Party. "Press Statement." 2005. Available from: www.mlp.org.mt/stqarrijiet/print.asp?ContentID=STQ050702A (accessed December 30, 2005).

Malta, Ministry of Finance. *Convergence Program 2004–2007*. May 2004. Available from: http://europa.eu.int/comm/economy_finance/about/activities/sgp/scplist_en.htm.

———. *Update of Convergence Program 2004–2007*. November 2004. Available from http://europa.eu.int/comm/economy_finance/about/activities/sgp/scplist_en.htm.

Malta Toursim Authority. "Tourism and Development in Malta." Available at: www.mta.com.mt/index.pl/tourism_development_in_malta?makePrintable =1 (accessed January 1, 2006).

Marcussen, Martin. "Denmark and European Monetary Integration: Out but Far from Over." *Journal of European Integration* 27, no. 1 (March 2005): 43–63.

Markou, Chris, George Nakos, and Nikolaos Zahariadis. "Greece: A European Paradox." In *The European Union and the Member States*, edited by Eleanor E. Zeff and Ellen B. Pirro, pp. 217–233. Boulder, CO: Lynne Rienner Publishers, 2001.

Marks, Michael P. *The Formation of European Policy in Post-Franco Spain: The Role of Ideas, Interests, and Knowledge*. Brookfield, VT: Avebury, 1997.

Mastenbroek, Ellen. "EU Compliance: Still a 'Black Hole'?" *Journal of European Public Policy* 12, no. 6 (December 2005): 1103–1120.

Máthé, László, and Duncan Pollard. "Ecological and Environmental Concerns of the Forest Biomass Use for Energy Production: A Critical Review of the Current Situation." WWF Report. Budapest, Hungary, 2005.

Mather, Janet. *The European Union and British Democracy: Towards Convergence.* Basingstoke, UK: Palgrave Macmillan, 2000.

Matlary, Janne Haaland. "The Nordics and the EU." In *Nordic Politics: Comparative Perspectives,* edited by Knut Heidar, pp. 247–261. Oslo, Norway: Universitetsforlaget, 2004.

Matraszek, Marek. *Ukraine, Poland, and a Free World,* 2004. Available at http://www.opendemocracy.net/content/articles/pdf/2251.pdf.

Mattila, Mikko. "Valtioneuvosto: Suomen EU-politiikan määrittelijä." In *EU ja Suomi: Unionijäsenyyden vaikutukset suomalaiseen yhteiskuntaan,* edited by Tapio Raunio and Matti Wiberg, pp. 135–150. Helsinki: Edita, 2000.

Mattila, Mikko, and Jan-Erik Lane. "Why Unanimity in the Council? A Roll Call Analysis of Council Voting." *European Union Politics* 2, no. 1 (February 2001): 31–52.

Mavris, Yiannis E. "The Evolution of Greek Public Attitudes Toward European Integration, 1981–2001." In *Greece in the European Union,* edited by Dionyssis G. Dimitrakopoulos and Argyris Passas, pp. 155–200. New York: Routledge, 2004.

Mayhew, Alan. "The Financial Framework of the European Union 2007–13: New Policies? New Money?" SEI Working Paper, no. 78 (2004). Available at: http://www.sussex.ac.uk/sei/documents/wp78_corrected.pdf.

———. *Recreating Europe: The European Union's Policy Towards Central and Eastern Europe.* Cambridge: Cambridge University Press, 1998.

Mazey, Sonia. "European Integration: Unfinished Journey or Journey Without End?" In *European Union: Power and Policy-Making,* edited by Jeremy J. Richardson. New York: Routledge, 2001.

Mazey, Sonia, and Jeremy J. Richardson. "The Commission and the Lobby." In *The European Community,* edited by Geoffrey Edwards and David Spence. London: John Harper, 1997.

McCormick, John. *Environmental Policy in the European Union.* Basingstoke, UK: Palgrave Macmillan, 2001.

Meseznikov, Grigorij. "The Emergence of Slovakia: From Ugly Duckling to Swan." *New Presence: The Prague Journal of Central European Affairs* (autumn 2004): 13–14.

Middlemas, Keith. *Orchestrating Europe: The Informal Politics of the European Union, 1973–95.* London: Fontana Press, 1995.

Miles, Lee. *Sweden and the European Union Evaluated.* London and New York: Continuum, 2000.

Mjoset, L. "The Nordic Model Never Existed, but Does It Have a Future?" *Scandinavian Studies* 64, no. 4 (1992): 652–671.

Møller, Per Stig. "European Foreign Policy in the Making." *The Brown Journal of World Affairs* 9, no. 2 (winter–spring 2003): 63–72.

Möller, Y. *Östen Uden: En biographi [Östen Uden: A Biography].* Stockholm: Norstedts, 1986.

Moravcsik, Andrew. *The Choice for Europe: Social Purpose and State Power from Messina to Maastricht.* Ithaca, NY: Cornell University Press, 1998.
Morris, Helen M. "EU Enlargement and Latvian Citizenship Policy." *Journal on Ethnopolitics and Minority Issues in Europe* 1 (2003; Brussels).
Müller, W. C. "EU Co-Ordination in Austria: Challenges and Responses." In *The National Co-Ordination of EU Policy: The Domestic Level,* edited by Hussein Kassim, Guy B. Peters, and Vincent Wright. London: Palgrave Macmillan, 2000.
Müller-Brandeck-Bocquet, Gisela. *Frankreichs Europapolitik.* 1 Aufl. ed. Wiesbaden: VS Verlag für Sozialwissenschaften, 2004.
Mulvey, Stephen. 2005. "Why Austria Was a Sticking Point." BBC News Online, at: http://news.bbc.co.uk/go/pr/fr/-/2/hi/europe/4304396.stm (accessed October 6, 2005).
Murray, Alasdair, and Aurore Wanlin. *The Lisbon Scorecard V: Can Europe Compete?* London: Centre for European Reform, 2005.
Nelsen, Brent F., and Alexander C. G. Stubb, eds. *The European Union: Readings on the Theory and Practice of European Integration,* 3rd ed. Boulder, CO: Lynne Rienner Publishers, 2003.
Newsweek Polska. May 8, 2004.
Niskanen, William A. *Bureaucracy—Servant or Master? Lessons from America.* London: Institute of Economic Affairs, 1973.
Nordea. "Markets." In *Economic Outlook,* available at: http://www.nordea. com/sitemod/upload/root/www.nordea.com%20-%20uk/ Productsservices/eMarkets/Economic_Outlook_UK_2005.pdf.
North Atlantic Treaty Organization (NATO). "Defense Spending, 2003," posted December 1. Available at: www.nato.int/docu/pr/2003/table3.pdf (accessed December 14, 2004).
Nousiainen, Jaakko. "From Semi-Presidentialism to Parliamentary Government: Political and Constitutional Developments in Finland." *Scandinavian Political Studies* 24, no. 2 (2001): 95–109.
Novakova, Pavla, and Martina Patockova. "Ceske firmy utikaji na Slovensko za niszi dani." *Mlada fronta Dnes,* April 24, 2003.
Nugent, Neill. *The Government and Politics of the European Union.* 3rd ed. Durham, NC: Duke University Press, 1994.
O'Brennan, John. "Ireland's European Discourse and the National Forum on Europe." In *Ireland and the European Union: Nice, Enlargement and the Future of Europe,* edited by Michael Holmes, pp. 114–132. Manchester, UK: Manchester University Press, 2005.
Occhipinti, John. "Justice and Home Affairs." In *European Union Enlargement,* edited by Neill Nugent. Basingstroke: Palgrave Macmillan, 2004.
O'Connor, Kevin. *The History of the Baltic States.* Westport, CT: Greenwood Press, 2003.
O'Donnell, Rory. *Ireland in Europe: The Economic Dimension.* Dublin: Institute of European Affairs, 2002.
Official Journal of the European Union. L 236 (September 23, 2003); available at: http://europa.eu.int/eur-lex/en/archive/2003.
———. L 199 (August 7, 2003); available at: http://europa.eu.int/ eur-lex/en/archive/2003.

Oksanen, Annukka. *Paikallisen ja kansainvälisen kohtaaminen luonnonsuojelussa. Tapaustutkimuksena Natura 2000–ympäristökonflikti Lounais–Suomessa.* Turku, Ann. Univ. Turkuensis C 192. Turku., 2003.

Oláh, Olivér. "Waste Management of Tetra Pak Products in Hungary and Sweden." Masters thesis, Industrial Ecology, Royal Institute of Technology, Stockholm, 2004.

Olsen, J. P. "European Challenges to the Nation State." In *Political Institutions and Public Policy: Perspectives on European Decision Making,* edited by Bernard Steunenberg and Frans van Vught, Dordrecht. Amsterdam: Kluwer Academic Publishers, 1997.

O'Mahoney, Jane. "Ireland and the European Union: A Less Certain Relationship." In *Political Issues in Ireland Today,* edited by Neil Collins and Terry Cradden, pp. 20–32. Manchester, UK: Manchester University Press, 2004.

Orenstein, Mitchell. "The Political Success of Neo-Liberalism in the Czech Republic." Preliminary draft, Institute for East-West Studies, 1994.

Organization for Economic Cooperation and Development (OECD). *Economic Outlook* 76 (December 2004).

Pace, Roderick. "The Domestic and International Politics of the Next Mediterranean Enlargement of the EU." *The European Union Review* 3, no. 1 (1998): 77–101.

———. "Malta's EU Membership: Chapter 1 Concluded, Chapter 2 Just Started." *Mediterranean Politics* 9, no. 1 (spring 2004): 114–121.

———. "The Maltese Electorate Turns a New Leaf? The First European Parliament Election in Malta." *South European Society and Politics* 10, no. 1 (April 2005): 121–136.

———. *Microstate Security in the Global System: EU-Malta Relations.* Valletta: Midsea Books, 2001.

Páczi, Erzsébet, and Péter Kaderják. "Environmental Impacts of Industrial Privatization in Hungary." In *Economics for Environmental Policy in Transition Economies: An Analysis of the Hungarian Experience,* edited by Péter Kaderják, pp. 39–68. Cheltenham, UK: Edward Elgar, 1997.

Padoa-Schioppa, Tommaso. "Italy and Europe: A Fruiful Interaction." *Daedalus* 130, no. 2 (spring 2001): 13–45.

Page, Edward C. "Europeanization and the Persistence of Administrative Systems." In *Governing Europe,* edited by Jack Ernest Shalom Hayward and Anand Menon. Oxford: Oxford University Press, 2003.

Palley, Claire. *An International Relations Debacle: The UN Secretary-General's Mission of Good Offices in Cyprus 1999–2004.* Oxford: Hart Publishing, 2005.

Papasotiriou, Charalambos. "Relations Between Greece and the United States." In *Contemporary Greek Foreign Policy,* edited by Panayiotis I. Tsakonas, pp. 606–616. Athens: Sideris, 2003.

Pappas, Spyros A. *National Administrative Procedures for the Preparation and Implementation of Community Decisions.* Maastricht: European Institute of Public Administration, 1995.

Paraskevopoulos, Christos J. *Interpreting Convergence in the European Union: Patterns of Collective Action, Social Learning, and Europeanization.* New York: Palgrave, 2001.

Parker, George. "Five of EU's Big Six Break Official Deficit Ceiling." *Financial Times*, September 27, 2005, p. 2.

Pato, Zsuzsanna. "Hungary." In *Billions for Sustainability? EU Regional Policy and Accession*, edited by Friends of the Earth. Bonn: Bund für Umwelt (FoE), 1999.

Patterson, Ben (ed.), Holger van Eden, Albert de Groot, Elisabeth Ledrut, Gerbert Romijn, Lucio Vinhas de Souza, and NEI Rotterdam. *EMU and Enlargement: A Review of Policy Issues Economic Affairs Series, ECON 117 EN 12/99*. Luxembourg: European Parliament, Directorate-General for Research, 1999.

Pavlínek, Petr, and J. Pickles. *Environmental Transitions: Transformation and Ecological Defense in Central and Eastern Europe*. London: Routledge, 2000.

Pawlas, Iwona, and Helena Tendera-Wlaszczuk. *Poland's Economy Competitiveness with Respect to the Integration with the European Union*. Warsaw: European Centre, Warsaw University, 1999.

Pehe, Jiri. "Czechs Fall from Their Ivory Tower." *Transitions Online* 4, no. 3 (August 1997).

Pernthaler, P., and P. Hilpold. "Sanktionen als Instrument der Politikkontrolle— der Fall Österreich." *Integration* 23, no. 2 (2000): 105–119.

Persson, G. (Swedish Prime Minister). "Trygghet i en värld i förändring." Speech at Utrikes Institutet/Central Förbundet Folk och Försvar (March 10, 1999). Available at: http://www.regeringen.se/galactica/service=irnews/owner=sys/action=obj_ show ?c_obj_id=28529.

———. "The Future of Europe Debate." Speech at Humboldt University Berlin, 2001. Available at http://europa.eu.int/constitution/futurum/documents/speech/sp181001_en.htm.

Peters, B. Guy. "Agenda-Setting in the European Union." In *European Union: Power and Policy-Making*, 2nd ed., edited by Jeremy J. Richardson, pp. 77–94. New York: Routledge, 2001.

———. "Bureaucratic Politics and the Institutions of the European Community." In *Euro-Politics: Institutions and Policymaking in the New European Community*, edited by Alberta M. Sbragia, pp. 9–26. Washington, DC: Brookings Institution, 1991.

Peterson, John. "Playing the Transparency Game: Consultation and Policy-Making in the European Commission." *Public Administration* 73, no. 3 (autumn 1995): 473–492.

Peterson, John, and Elizabeth E. Bomberg. *Decision-Making in the European Union*. New York: The European Union Series, St. Martin's Press, 1999.

Piattoni, Simona. "Regioni a statuto speciale e politica di coesione. Cambiamenti interistituzionali e risposte regionali." In *L'europeizzazione dell'Italia*, edited by Sergio Fabbrini, pp. 80–107. Rome: Laterza, 2003.

Pierson, Paul. *Dismantling the Welfare State? Reagan, Thatcher, and the Politics of Retrenchment*. Cambridge: Cambridge University Press, 1994.

Piper, J. Richard. *The Major Nation-States in the European Union*. New York: Pearson/Longman, 2005.

Pirro, Ellen B., and Eleanor E. Zeff. "Europeanization, European Integration and Globalization." *Whitehead Journal of International Relations and Diplomacy* 6, no. 1 (winter–spring 2005): 209–217.

Poland's Membership in the European Union (The Accession Treaty). Available at: http://www.trybunal.gov.pl/eng/summaries/documents/K_18_04_GB. pdf.

Politiken. "Hvad er det, Europa skal bruges til? [What Is It That Europe Shall Be Used For?]." June 22, 2005.

Pollack, Mark. "The New Institutionalism and EU Governance: The Promise and Limits of Institutionalist Analysis." *Governance* 9, no. 4 (1996): 429–458.

Posen, Adam Simon. "Overview: The Euro's Success Within Limits." In *The Euro at Five: Ready for a Global Role?* edited by Adam Simon Posen, pp. 1–22. Washington, DC: Institute for International Economics, 2005.

Prescott, John. "Elected Regional Assembly Referendum in the North East." Statement to the House of Commons, November 8, 2004. Available from: http://www.odpm.gov.uk/index.asp?id=1122739 (accessed January 2, 2006).

Pretenteris, I. K. "Fines Are Coming from Brussels: Interview with G. Papantoniou." *To Vima*, September 26, 2004. Available at: www.tovima.dol-net.gr/demo/owa/tobhma.print (accessed December 14, 2004).

Pridham, Geoffrey. "Environmental Policies and Problems of European Legislation in Southern Europe." *Southern European Society & Politics* 1, no. 1 (summer 1996): 47–73.

———. "European Integration and Democratic Consolidation in Southern Europe." In *Southern Europe and the Making of the European Union, 1945–1980s*, edited by António Costa Pinto and Nuno Severiano Teixeira, p. xiv. Boulder, CO: Social Science Monographs, 2002.

Przeglàd Rzàdowy. 1999. Available at: http://www.kprm.gov.pl/7810_7973.htm.

Putnam, Robert D. "Diplomacy and Domestic Politics: The Logic of Two-Level Games." *International Organization* 42, no. 2 (1988): 427–460.

Radaelli, Claudio M. "Europeismo tricolore." *Relazioni Internazionali*, no. 4 (1988): 92–98.

———. "The Italian State and Europe: Institutions, Discourse, and Policy Regimes." In *The European State and the Euro: Europeanization, Variation, and Convergence*, edited by K. Dyson, pp. 212–237. Oxford: Oxford University Press, 2002.

———. *Technocracy in the European Union.* New York: Longman, 1999.

Rasmussen, Anders Fogh. "Statsminister Anders Fogh Rasmussens tale ved Folketingets åbning tirsdag den 4. Oktober [Speech at the Opening of the Danish Parliament, Tuesday, 4 October]." Available at: http:// www.statsministeriet.dk/Index/dokumenter.asp?o=2&n=0&d= 2398&s=1 (accessed November 18, 2005).

Raunio, Tapio. "Hesitant Voters, Committed Elite: Explaining the Lack of Eurosceptical Parties in Finland." *Journal of European Integration* 27, no. 4 (2005): 381–395.

———. "The Parliament of Finland: A Model Case for Effective Scrutiny?" In *National Parliaments on Their Ways to Europe: Losers or Latecomers?* edited by Andreas Maurer and Wolfgang Wessels, pp. 173–198. Baden-Baden: Nomos, 2001.

Raunio, Tapio, and Teija Tiilikainen. *Finland in the European Union*. London: Frank Cass, 2003.

Raunio, Tapio, and Matti Wiberg. "Building Elite Consensus: Parliamentary Accountability in Finland." *Journal of Legislative Studies* 6, no. 1 (2000): 59–80.

———. "Parliamentarizing Foreign Policy Decision-Making: Finland in the European Union." *Cooperation and Conflict* 36, no. 1 (2001): 61–86.

REC. "Local Producer Boxed-in by Government." *REC Bulletin* (summer1999).

"Recycling Association Aims to Collect 8pc of Used Drink Boxes." *MTI EcoNews*, 2005.

Rees, Nicholas. "Europe and Ireland's Changing Security Policy." In *Ireland and the European Union: Nice, Enlargement and the Future of Europe*, edited by Michael Holmes, pp. 55–74. Manchester, UK: Manchester University Press, 2005.

Regan, Eugene. *The Charter of Fundamental Rights*. Dublin, Ireland: Institute of European Affairs, 2002.

Rehn, Olli. "Can a Neutralist Nordic Become a Core European?—Historical Trajectory and Political Culture in the Making of Finland's EU Policy." Paper presented at ECPR Joint Sessions of Workshops, March–April 2003.

Reid, T. R. *The United States of Europe: The New Superpower and the End of American Supremacy*. New York: Penguin Press, 2004.

Reiniger, Robert. "Hungarian Environmental Protection Licensing and Enforcement Procedures." Paper presented at Third International Conference on Environmental Enforcement, April 25–28, 1994, in Oaxaca, Mexico.

Republic of Cyprus. "The Policy of the Government vis-à-vis the Turkish Cypriots." April 30, 2003. Available at: www.moi.gov.cy/moi/pio/pio.nsf/All/745A5D6134331502C2256D9F00338D9A?Open.

Reynolds, Matthew. "Once a Backwater, Slovakia Surges." *New York Times*, December 28, 2004, p. W1.

Richardson, Jeremy J. "Policy-Making in the EU: Interests, Ideas, and Garbage Cans of Primeval Soup." In *European Union: Power and Policy-Making*, 2nd ed., edited by Jeremy J. Richardson. New York: Routledge, 2001.

———, ed. *European Union: Power and Policy-Making*. 2nd ed. New York: Routledge, 2001.

Risse, Thomas, Maria Green Cowles, and James A. Caporaso. "Europeanization and Domestic Change: Introduction." In *Transforming Europe: Europeanization and Domestic Change*, edited by Maria Green Cowles, James A. Caporaso, and Thomas Risse, pp. 1–20. Ithaca, NY: Cornell University Press, 2001.

Rittberger, Berthold. *Building Europe's Parliament: Democratic Pepresentation Beyond the Nation-State*. Oxford: Oxford University Press, 2005.

Rowinski, Janusz. "Agriculture—Costs and Benefits of Poland's Membership." In *Costs and Benefits of Poland's Membership in the European Union*, pp. 105–135. Warsaw: Centrum Europejskie Natolin, 2003.

Royo, Sebastián. "The 2004 Enlargement: Iberian Lessons for Post-Communist Europe." In *Spain and Portugal in the European Union: The First 15 Years*, edited by Sebastián Royo and Paul Christopher Manuel. Portland, OR: Frank Cass, 2003.

————. "From Authoritarianism to the European Union: The Europeanization of Portugal." *Mediteranian Quarterly* 15, no. 3 (summer 2004).

————. *Portugal, Espanha e a Integração Europeia: Um Balanço.* Lisbon: ICS, 2005.

Royo, Sebastián, and Paul Christopher Manuel. "Some Lessions from the Fifteenth Anniversary of the Accession of Portugal and Spain to the European Union." In *Spain and Portugal in the European Union: The First 15 Years,* edited by Sebastián Royo and Paul Christopher Manuel. Portland, OR: Frank Cass, 2003.

Samecki, Pawel. "Financial Flows Between the EU and Poland in 2004–2013." In *Costs and Benefits of Poland's Membership in the European Union,* pp. 30–58. Warsaw: Centrum Europejskie Natolin, 2003.

Sarv, Margit. "Integration by Reframing Legislation: Implementation of the Recommendations of the OSCE High Commissioner on National Minorities to Estonia, 1993–2001." Center for OSCE Research. Working Paper no. 7. Available from: http://www.core-hamburg.de/documents/35_CORE_Working_Paper_7.pdf.

Sauron, Jean-Luc. *L'administration Française et l'Union européenne* (English version). Paris: La documentation française, 2000.

Sbragia, Alberta M. "Italy Pays for Europe: Political Leadership, Political Choice, and Institutional Adaptation." In *Transforming Europe: Europeanization and Domestic Change,* edited by Maria Green Cowles, James A. Caporaso, and Thomas Risse-Kappen, pp. 79–96. Ithaca, NY: Cornell University Press, 2001.

Schlaug, B., and L. Nilsson-Hedström. "Folkomrösta om Alliansfriheten." *Dagens Nyheter,* December 9, 1999.

Schmidt, Vivien Ann. *The Futures of European Capitalism.* Oxford: Oxford University Press, 2002.

Schmitt, B. "European Armaments Cooperation: Core Documents." *Chaillot Papers,* no. 59, European Union Institute for Strategic Studies, Brussels, 2003.

Schmitter, Philippe C. "Some Alternative Futures for the European Polity and Their Implications for European Public Policy." In *Adjusting to Europe: The Impact of the European Union on National Institutions and Policies,* edited by Yves Mény, Pierre Muller, and Jean-Louis Quermonne. London: Routledge, 1996.

"Schröder warnt vor 'Überdehnung der europäischen Kompetenzen'." *Die Zeit,* no. 23, October 20, 2005.

Sebastián, Miguel. "Spain in the EU: Fifteen Years May Not Be Enough." Paper presented at the conference "From Isolation to Europe: 15 Years of Spanish and Portugese Membership in the European Union," Harvard University, November 2–3, 2001, Cambridge, Massachusetts.

Shively, W. Phillips. *Power and Choice: An Introduction to Political Science.* 4th ed. New York: McGraw-Hill, 1995.

Siemon, Smid, and Petra Zwart. *Tourism on Cyprus: Study on the Situation of Enterprises, the Industry and the Service Sectors in Turkey, Cyprus, and Malta*: IBM Global Services, Business Consulting Services for the European Commission, Annex II of the contract ETC/00/503332.

Skocpol, Theda. *States and Social Revolutions: A Comparative Analysis of France, Russia, and China.* New York: Cambridge University Press, 1979.

Slocock, Brian. "The Paradoxes of Environmental Policy in Eastern Europe: The Dynamics of Policy-Making in the Czech Republic." *Environmental Politics* 5, no. 3 (1996): 501–521.

———. "'Whatever Happened to the Environment?' Environmental Issues in the Eastern Enlargement of the European Union." In *Back to Europe: Central and Eastern Europe and the European Union,* edited by Karen Henderson, pp. 151–167. London: UCL Press, 1999.

Smith, Adrian. "Policy Networks and Policy Change in United Kingdom Industrial Pollution Policy, 1970–1990." Paper presented at the Political Studies Association Conference Proceedings, 1998.

Smith, David J., ed. *The Baltic States and Their Region: New Europe or Old?* Amsterdam: Rodopi B.V., 2005.

Smith, David J., Artis Pabriks, Aldis Purs, and Thomas Lane. *The Baltic States: Estonia, Latvia, and Lithuania.* London: Routledge, 2002.

Smith, Keith C. *Russian Energy Politics in the Baltics, Poland, and Ukraine: A New Stealth Imperialism?* Washington, DC: Center for Strategic and International Studies, 2004.

Smith, Tamsin. "Smugglers Target Slovakia Border." *BBC News Online,* May 11, 2005. Available at: bbc.co.uk.

Social Democratic Party Congress. 2003. "Protocol." Available at: http://wwwold.lo.se/demokratikongressen/protokoll/pdf/emu.PDF (accessed May 2, 2005).

Soetendorp, Ben, and Kenneth Hanf. "Conclusion: The Nature of National Adaptation to European Integration." In *Adapting to European Integration: Small States and the European Union,* edited by Kenneth Hanf and Ben Soetendorp, pp. 186–194. Harlow, UK: Longman, 1998.

Spanou, Calliope. "Greece." In *The National Co-Ordination of EU Policy,* edited by Hussein Kassim, B. Guy Peters, and Vincent Wright, pp. 161–181. Oxford: Oxford University Press, 2000.

Spence, David. "Structure, Functions and Procedures in the Commission." In *The European Commission,* 2nd ed., edited by Geoffrey Edwards and David Spence. London: Cartermill, 1997.

Staat van de Europese Unie. *Brief van de Minister van Buitenlandse Zaken en de Staatssecretaris voor Europese Zaken, 2005–2006.*

Stagkos, Filios. "In 2003 2.2 Billion Euros Came into Greece from EU Funds." *Ta Nea,* September 8, 2004, p. N54.

Stefan Batory Foundation. *Will the Orange Revolution Bear Fruit? EU-Ukraine Relations in 2005 and the Beginning of 2006.* Warsaw: Stefan Batory Foundation, 2005.

Stefanou, Constantin. *Cyprus and the EU: The Road to Accession.* Aldershot: Ashgate, 2005.

Stubb, Alexander, Heidi Kaila, and Timo Ranta. "Finland: An Integrationist Member State." In *The European Union and the Member States: Cooperation, Coordination, and Compromise,* edited by Eleanor E. Zeff and Ellen B. Pirro, pp. 305–316. Boulder, CO: Lynne Rienner Publishers, 2001.

Stubb, Alexander C. G., Helen Wallace, and John Peterson. "The Policy-Making Process." In *The European Union: How Does It Work?* edited by Elizabeth E. Bomberg and Alexander C. G. Stubb. Oxford: Oxford University Press, 2003.

Stutz, G. *Opinion 2001: Svenskarnas syn på samhället, säkerhetspolitiken och försvaret hösten 2001.* Styrelsen för Psykologiskt Försvar [Swedish Institute for Psychological Defense], 2001.

Sumpsi, J. M. "La Agricultura Española Actual. El Marco de Referencia." *Papeles de Economía Española* 60, no. 1 (1994): 2–14.

Svensson, Palle. "Five Danish Referendums on the European Community and European Union: A Critical Assessment of the Franklin Thesis." *European Journal of Political Research* 41, no. 6 (October 2002): 733–750.

Svensson, Torsten, and Per Ola Öberg. "Labour Market Organizations' Participation in Swedish Public-Policy-Making." *Scandinavian Political Studies* 25, no. 4 (December 2002): 295–315.

Sverdrup, Ulf. "Compliance and Conflict Management in the European Union: Nordic Exceptionalism." *Scandinavian Political Studies* 27, no. 1 (March 2004): 23–43.

Swedish Institute for European Policy Studies (SIEPS), *From Policy Takers to Policy Makers: Adapting EU Cohesion Policy to the Needs of the New Member States,* edited by Jonas Eriksson, Bengt O. Karlsson, and Daniel Tarschys. Stockholm: SIEPS. Available at http://www.sieps.se/publ/rapporter/bilagor/20055.pdf.

Swedish Parliamentary Report. *Historiskt Vägval: Följderna för Sverige I utrikes och säkerhetspolitiskt anseenede av att bli, respektive inte bli medlem i EU.* Stockholm: March 1994.

Szakacs, Judit. "Uncorking a Debate over Bottles." *Transitions Online* (October 11, 2004).

Szirmai, Victória. "Protection of the Environment and the Position of Green Movements in Hungary." In *Environmental and Housing Movements: Grassroots Experience in Hungary, Russia and Estonia,* edited by Katy Láng-Pickvance, Nick Manning, and Chris Pickvance, pp. 23–88. Aldershot, UK: Avebury Ashgate, 1997.

Tala, Jyrki. "Lakien vaikutukset. Lakiuudistusten tavoitteet ja niiden toteutuminen lainsäädäntöteoreettisessa tarkastelussa." Academic Dissertation, Oikeuspoliittinen tutkimuslaitosHakapaino, Helsinki. 2001.

Tallberg, Jonas. "Sveringe ingen Stormakt." *Dagens Nyheter,* February 9, 2003.

Tancerova, Barbora. "Slovakia: The Hong Kong of Central Europe?" *Transitions Online,* August 8, 2003.

Thatcher, Margaret. "Speech to the Royal Society." London, September 27, 1998. Available from: http://www.margaretthatcher.org/speeches/display-document.asp?docid=107346 (accessed January 3, 2006).

Theodoulou, Stella Z. *Policy and Politics in Six Nations: A Comparative Perspective on Policy Making.* Upper Saddle River, NJ: Prentice Hall, 2002.

Tiilikainen, Teija. *Europe and Finland: Defining the Political Identity of Finland in Western Europe.* Aldershot, UK: Ashgate, 1998.

Tocci, Nathalie. *EU Accession Dynamics and Conflict Resolution: Catalyzing Peace or Consolidating Partition in Cyprus?* Burlington, VT: Ashgate, 2004.

Toral, Pablo. *The Reconquest of the New World: Multinational Enterprises and Spain's Direct Investment in Latin America.* Burlington, VT: Ashgate, 2001.

Treaty on European Union and the Treaty Establishing the European Community. 2003. Brussels: European Communities.

Tsebelis, George. *Veto Players: How Political Institutions Work.* Princeton, NJ: Princeton University Press, 2002.

Tunander, O. "The Uneasy Imbrication of Nation-State and NATO: The Case of Sweden." *Cooperation and Conflict* 34, no. 2 (1999): 169–203.

Turning Green: Hungarian Greens on the EU. Budapest: ETO-Print Press, 2003.

Tziampiris, Aristotle. *Greece, European Political Cooperation, and the Macedonian Question.* Burlington, VT: Ashgate, 2000.

Ucen, Peter. "Slovakia." *European Journal of Political Research* 43, no. 7/8 (December 2004): 1121–1129.

UKIE. *Poland in the European Union—Experiences of the First Year of Membership.* Warsaw: UKIE, 2005.

Ukrainian News. December 6, 2004.

UNECE/FAO. "Country Report: Hungary." Joint UNECE/FAO Workshop on "Illegal Logging and Trade of Illegally Derived Forest Products in the UNECE Region: Causes and Extent." Geneva, September 16–17, 2004.

United Nations. "Press Release." *SG/SM/9239* (March 31, 2004).

———. "Press Release." *SC/8051* (April 2, 2004).

US Department of State. "Daily Press Briefing," November 4, 2004. Available at: www.state.gov/r/pa/prs/dpb/2004/37819.htm (accessed November 18, 2005).

Vachudova, Milada Anna. *Europe Undivided: Democracy, Leverage, and Integration After Communism.* Oxford: Oxford University Press, 2005.

Valinakis, Yiannis, and Sotiris Dalis, eds. *The Skopjean Issue.* Athens: Sideris, 1994.

van Calster, Geert. "Something for Everyone in the Judgment of the European Court of Justice in the German Bottles Saga." *RECIEL* 14, no. 1 (2005): 73–77.

van Elsuwege, Peter. "Russian-Speaking Minorities in Estonia and Latvia: Problems of Integration at the Threshold of the European Union." European Centre for Minority Issues. ECMI Working Paper, no. 20 (2004). Available from: http://www.ecmi.de/download/working_paper_20.pdf.

Vermeersch, Peter. "EU Enlargement and Immigration Policy in Poland and Slovakia." *Communist and Post-Communist Studies* 38, no. 1 (March 2005): 71–88.

Von Sydow, B. (Defense Minister). "Defense Minister Speech at the European Symposium on Public Opinion and European Security." Brussels (April 4, 2001).

Wahlbäck, Krister. "Efter Neutraliteten [After Neutrality]." *Internationell Säkerhet* 3 (2000): 36–45.

———. *The Roots of Swedish Neutrality.* Stockholm: Swedish Institute, 1986.

Wallace, Helen. "Politics and Policy in the EU: The Challenge of Governance." In *Policy-Making in the European Union*, 3rd ed., edited by Helen Wallace and William Wallace. Oxford: Oxford University Press, 1996.

Wallace, Helen, and William Wallace, eds. *Policy-Making in the European Union*, 4th ed. Oxford: Oxford University Press, 2000.

Wanlin, Aurore. *The Lisbon Scorecard VI: Will Europe's Economy Rise Again?* Centre for European Policy Reform, London. Available at: http://www.cer.org.uk/pdf/pr_661_lisbonvi.pdf.

Warhurst, A. Michael. "REACH, a New Approach to Chemicals Regulation in Europe: A Brief History, Key Features, and Expected Outcomes." *Journal for European Environment and Planning Law* 2, no. 3 (2005): 164–172.

Wenger, A. "Von Köln bis Nizza: Die Bedeutung der Gemeinsamen Europäischen Sicherheits–und Verteidigungspolitik für die Schweiz." *Swiss Security Bulletin, Zurich: FSK, ETHZ* (2001): 99–125.

Wessels, Wolfgang, Andreas Maurer, and Jürgen Mittag. *Fifteen into One? The European Union and Its Member States*. New York: Palgrave Macmillan, 2003.

Wiener, Antje, and Thomas Diez. *European Integration Theory*. Oxford and New York: Oxford University Press, 2004.

Wikipedia. "Orange Revolution." In *Wikipedia: The Free Encyclopedia*. Available at: http://en.wikipedia.org/wiki/Orange_Revolution.

Wiles, James L., and Richard B. Finnegan. *Aspirations and Realities: A Documentary History of Economic Development Policy in Ireland Since 1922*. Westport, CT: Greenwood Press, 1993.

Wimmer, N., and W. Mederer. *EG-Recht in Österreich*. Wien: Manz, 1990.

World Bank. "Cyprus at a Glance." August 25, 2005. Available from: http://www.worldbank.org/data/.

World Trade Organization. "Country Profile." Various years. Available at: http://stat.wto.org/CountryProfile/WSDBCountryPFHome.aspx? Language=E (accessed January 3, 2006).

———. "Statistics." 2005. Available at: http://www.wto.org/english/res_e/statis_e/its2005_e/section1_e/i05.xls (accessed January 1, 2006).

World Wildlife Federation (WWF). *The Eastern Promise: Progress Report on the EU Renewable Electricity Directive in Accession Countries*. 2004. Gland, Switzerland: World Wildlife Federation.

Wright, Vincent. "The National Co-Ordination of Europe Policy-Making: Negotiating the Quagmire." In *European Union: Power and Policy-Making*, edited by Jeremy J. Richardson. New York: Routledge, 1996.

Zahariadis, Nikolaos. "Domestic Strategy and International Choices in Negotiations Between Non-Allies." *Polity* 35 (July 2003): 573–594.

———. *Essence of Political Manipulation: Emotion, Institutions, and Greek Foreign Policy*. New York: P. Lang, 2005.

———. "Europeanization as Program Implementation: Effective, Efficient and Democratic?" Paper presented at the annual meeting of the American Political Science Association, September 1, 2005, Washington, DC.

Zeff, Eleanor E. "The Budget and the Spending Policies." In *European Union Enlargement*, edited by Neill Nugent. New York: Palgrave Macmillan, 2004.

Zeff, Eleanor E., and Ellen B. Pirro, eds. *The European Union and the Member States: Cooperation, Coordination, and Compromise*. 1st ed. Boulder, CO: Lynne Rienner Publishers, 2001.

Ziemele, Ineta. *State Continuity and Nationality*. Leiden, Netherlands: Martinus Nijhoff Publishers, 2005.
Zlamalova, Lenka. "Kdo uspel v Evrope." *Hospodarské Noviny*, April 29, 2005.

The Contributors

Karen M. Anderson is associate professor in the Department of Political Science at Nijmegen University in the Netherlands. Her research focuses on the comparative political economy of the welfare state, the impact of European integration on national welfare states, and the role of unions and social democratic parties in welfare state restructuring processes. Her research has appeared in *Comparative Political Studies, Zeitschrift für Sozialreform, Canadian Journal of Sociology,* and the *Journal of Public Policy.*

Christian Deubner is currently senior collaborator at the French Institute for International Economics, CEPII, in Paris, and is responsible for European policy issues. He has numerous publications on European politics, French-German relations, and foreign economic relations. He also worked at the German "Research Institute on International Politics and Security" at the German Institute for International and Security Affairs (SWP), and since 1998, headed its Research Group I, Integration and External Relations of Europe.

Eric S. Einhorn is professor of political science at the University of Massachusetts, Amherst, and is a specialist in Danish politics. He is coauthor of *Modern Welfare States: Social Democratic Politics and Policy in the Global Age.*

Johan Eliasson is assistant professor at East Stroudsburg University, Pennsylvania. He teaches international relations and comparative politics, is the faculty coordinator for the European Studies Organization, and has several publications addressing economic and political issues in transatlantic relations, international security, and European integration.

David Ellison is assistant professor of political science at Grinnell College. His work addresses the political economy of the Eastern enlargement. He conducts research and has published on the consequences of political and economic integration into the European marketplace.

Jessica Erfer recently received her MA in political science from the University of Massachusetts, Amherst. She has recently been working on Danish politics with Eric S. Einhorn.

Gerda Falkner is head of the Department of Political Science at the Institute for Advanced Studies (IHS) in Vienna, Austria, and associate professor of political science at the University of Vienna. Her most recent book is entitled *Complying with Europe* (coauthored).

Richard B. Finnegan is professor and chair of political science and director of Irish Studies at Stonehill College and also teaches Irish politics at Harvard University. He is the author or coauthor of six books on modern Ireland, most recently, *Women and Public Policy in Ireland: A Documentary History, 1922–1997.*

Sharon Fisher is senior economist with Global Insights' Country Intelligence Group. In this role, she conducts economic and political analysis, risk assessment, and forecasting on a number of European countries, including the Czech Republic. She is the author of the forthcoming book entitled *Political Change in Post-Communist Slovakia and Croatia: From Nationalist to Europeanist.*

Marco Giuliani is professor of comparative and European politics in the Department of Social and Political Studies of the University of Milan. He mainly works on the relationship between the European Union and the member states, focusing on Europeanization and compliance studies. His recent publications include *La Politica Europea* and "Europeanization in Comparative Perspective: Institutional Fit and National Adaptation," in Kevin Featherstone and Claudio M. Radaelli (eds.), *The Politics of Europeanization.*

Artur Gruzczak is assistant professor of political science at Jagiellonian University in Krakow, Poland. He also coordinates EU Justice and Home Affairs Forum at the European Center–Natolin in Warsaw, Poland. He has written on problems of governance in East-Central Europe, EU enlargement, and internal security of the EU.

Lisa Hunt is a researcher in the Department of Political Science at the Institute for Advanced Studies (IHS) in Vienna, Austria. Her work has focused, among other things, on the EU's foreign and security policy and relations with Southeast Europe as well as on Austria's relations with the EU.

Michael Kaeding is currently completing his PhD in the Department of Public Administration at Leiden University in the Netherlands. His research focuses on the transposition of EU directives into national law.

Jussi Kinnunen is a researcher in the Network for European Studies at the University of Helsinki. He is currently involved in a project that studies Europeanization in Finnish politics and governance.

Carl Lankowski is deputy director of area studies and coordinator for European area studies at the Foreign Service Institute, US Department of State. From 1995 to 2000, he was research director at the American Institute for Contemporary German Studies.

Peter Loedel is professor and chair of the Department of Political Science at West Chester University, West Chester, PA. He is the author of three books on European monetary and security cooperation as well as many other articles on the European Union and European monetary politics.

Janet Mather is senior lecturer in politics at Manchester Metropolitan University, UK. She is the author of *The EU and British Democracy: Towards Convergence* and of *Legitimating the EU: Aspirations, Inputs and Performance*.

John McCormick is professor and chair of the Department of Political Science at Indiana University–Purdue University, Indianapolis (IUPUI), and research fellow at the Sussex European Institute in Britain. His research interests focus on EU policy, transatlantic relations, and the global identity of the EU. Recent publications include *Understanding the European Union, Comparative Politics in Transition,* and *The European Superpower.*

Neill Nugent is professor of politics and Jean Monnet Professor of European Integration at Manchester Metropolitan University, United Kingdom. Recent publications include *European Union Enlargement* (editor) and the sixth edition of *The Government and Politics of the European Union.*

John D. Occhipinti is professor of political science and director of European Studies at Canisius College in Buffalo, New York. He is author of *The Politics of EU Police Cooperation: Toward a European FBI?* as well as several recent chapters and articles on Justice and Home Affairs (JHA) in the EU. He has also lectured on JHA for the US State Department and served as cochair of the European Union Studies Association interest section on teaching.

Roderick Pace is lecturer in international relations and European studies, director of the European Documentation and Research Centre of the University of Malta, and a member of the board of directors of the Institute for Islands and Small States Studies. He has published more than 60 articles in academic journals and books, including *Microstate Security in the Global System: EU-Malta Relations.*

Ellen B. Pirro is an adjunct associate professor of political science at Iowa State and Drake Universities. She is the author of several books and articles, including "Europeanization, European Integration and Globalization," with Eleanor E. Zeff in *The Whitehead Journal of Diplomacy,* and coeditor of the first edition of *The European Union and the Member States.* She is currently working on theories of international and comparative politics and the foreign policy of the European Union.

Simona Piattoni is associate professor of political science at the Department of Sociology and Social Research of the University of Trento, Italy, where she teaches comparative and European politics. She has written on clientelism (*Clientelism, Interests and Democratic Representation* and *Clientelismo, L'Italia in prospettiva comparata*) and on territorial governance (*Between Europeanization and Local Societies,* with J. Bukowski and M. Smyrl, and *Informal Governance in the European Union,* with Thomas Christiansen).

Tapio Raunio is professor of political science at the University of Turku. His current research focuses on the role of parties and parliaments in European politics and on the Finnish political system. He has published articles in journals including the *European Journal of Political Research, Journal of Common Market Studies, Party Politics,* and *Scandinavian Political Studies.*

Sebastián Royo is director of the Suffolk University Madrid Campus and associate professor in the Government Department at Suffolk University in Boston. His research interests include Southern European and Latin American economic policies and institutions. Royo is an affiliate of the Minda de Gunzburg Center for European Studies at Harvard University where he cochairs the Iberian Study Group. His articles have been published in *South European Society and Politics* and *West European Politics,* among other journals. He has also written several books, most recently *Spain and Portugal in the European Union: The First Fifteen Years* (with P. Manuel).

Steven Stoltenberg is foreign affairs analyst in the Office of Analysis for Europe at the US Department of State, responsible for the Poland and Baltic States. Prior to this he was chair for the Central Europe Advanced Area Studies programs at the Foreign Service Institute in Arlington, VA. He has also taught at the University of California-Berkeley and Warsaw University in Poland.

Nikolaos Zahariadis is director of international studies and associate professor of political science at the University of Alabama at Birmingham. He is a Michael Dukakis Chair Lecturer, a Ron B. Casey Fellow, and past president of the International Studies Association–South. He has published widely on comparative public policy and European political economy. His latest book is entitled *Essence of Political Manipulation: Emotion, Institutions and Greek Foreign Policy.*

Eleanor E. Zeff is associate professor of politics and international relations at Drake University in Des Moines, Iowa. She has written several books and articles on the European Union, including "The Budget and the Spending Policies" in Neill Nugent's *EU Enlargement,* and she was coeditor of the first edition of *The European Union and the Member States.* She is also the academic adviser for student Fulbright Scholarships at Drake, and she regularly accompanies students to European Union simulations.

Index

About the Book

THOROUGHLY UPDATED, THIS NEW edition of *The European Union and the Member States* explores the complex relationship between the EU and each of its now 25 members.

The country chapters follow a common format, considering: How and in what areas does EU policy affect, and how is it affected by, the member states? What mechanisms do the member states use to implement EU policy? What is each state's compliance record?

Covering the full range of issues—from economic, social, and environmental, to security, to home and justice affairs—the authors offer an insightful discussion of the interplay of EU initiatives with strong, existing national policies and traditions.

Eleanor E. Zeff is associate professor of political science at Drake University. **Ellen B. Pirro** is adjunct associate professor of political science at Iowa State and Drake Universities.